Understanding Regulation
Second Edition

Understanding Regulation

Theory, Strategy, and Practice

Second Edition

Robert Baldwin, Martin Cave, Martin Lodge

OXFORD
UNIVERSITY PRESS

*This book has been printed digitally and produced in a standard specification
in order to ensure its continuing availability*

OXFORD
UNIVERSITY PRESS

Great Clarendon Street, Oxford OX2 6DP

Oxford University Press is a department of the University of Oxford.
It furthers the University's objective of excellence in research, scholarship,
and education by publishing worldwide in

Oxford New York

Auckland   Cape Town Dar es Salaam   Hong Kong   Karachi
Kuala Lumpur Madrid Melbourne Mexico City   Nairobi
New Delhi Shanghai   Taipei Toronto
With offices in
Argentina Austria Brazil Chile Czech Republic France Greece
Guatemala Hungary Italy Japan South Korea Poland Portugal
Singapore Switzerland Thailand Turkey Ukraine Vietnam

Oxford is a registered trade mark of Oxford University Press
in the UK and in certain other countries

Published in the United States
by Oxford University Press Inc., New York

First edition published 1999
Second edition published 2012
Reprinted 2012

ISBN 978-0-19-957608-1

Cover illustration: Governor, or 'Fly-Ball Governor', invented by James Watt
to regulate the supply of steam in order to preserve a nearly fixed engine speed.
Circa 1785 © Mary Evans Picture Library

■ ACKNOWLEDGEMENTS

We are grateful to a number of individuals for their help with this book. For research assistance, textual comments, and work on manuscripts, we thank Vanessa Finch, Amanda Tinnams, and Emma Wilson.

We also express our appreciation to all of those colleagues at LSE who have assisted in a variety of ways in the production of this text—and, not least we thank colleagues with whom we have taught on the LSE's M.Sc. in Regulation and on the LSE's Short Course on Regulation. Martin Lodge would like particularly to acknowledge the support of the ESRC Centre for Analysis of Risk and Regulation. We are grateful also to the colleagues with whom we have co-authored or co-edited works on regulation and who have allowed us to draw on those publications in writing this book. We thank in particular Tony Ballance, Julia Black, Damian Chalmers, Veerle Heyvaert, Ian Marlee, Henry Rothstein, and Lindsay Stirton.

■ PREFACE TO THE SECOND EDITION

Since the first edition of *Understanding Regulation* was published in 1999, the practice and study of regulation has changed dramatically. Politically, there have been shifts from emphases on deregulation to 'better regulation' and back again. There have been calls for lowerings of regulatory burdens on businesses and for increasing resort to 'lighter-touch' regulatory systems and regimes that delegate controls to businesses. These calls fell silent after the start of the credit crisis of 2007–9, but they can be expected to re-emerge in coming years. The legacy of such movements and political fashions has, however, been a developed interest in non-traditional strategies of regulation—in methods of influence that constitute alternatives to 'command and control'. Newly popular devices—such as 'nudging'—have found their way on to politicians' agendas and there have been redoubled concerns to debate such issues as the legitimacy of different regulatory systems and approaches.

Regulatory studies and theories have also progressed significantly over the past dozen years. Regulation has become the subject of discrete courses and degree programmes around the world and new journals have emerged to deal with the subject. Most disciplines now provide numbers of scholars who see regulation as a primary area of research and teaching. As a result, a host of new theories and perspectives have been brought to bear on regulation and have enriched understandings.

This edition seeks to come to grips with all of the newer developments referred to. In doing so, it continues the broad approach of the first edition and sees regulation as a subject that is best understood from a multi-disciplinary perspective. The addition of Martin Lodge, a political scientist, as co-author is a happy furthering of this position.

Robert Baldwin, Martin Cave,
and Martin Lodge,
March 2011

◾ CONTENTS

▓ LIST OF FIGURES

■ LIST OF TABLES

ABBREVIATIONS

ALARA	As Low as Reasonably Achievable
ALARP	As Low as Reasonably Practicable
BATNEEC	Best Available Technology Not Entailing Excessive Costs
BAU	Business as Usual
BCC	British Chambers of Commerce
BRE	Better Regulation Executive
BRTF	Better Regulation Task Force
BT	British Telecom
C & C	Command and Control
CAA	Civil Aviation Authority
CBA	Cost-Benefit Analysis
CDM	Clean Development Mechanism
CRI	Centre for the Study of Regulated Industries
DAB	Digital Audio Broadcasting
DG	Director General
DGES	Director General of Electricity Supply
DTI	Department of Trade and Industry
ECJ	European Court of Justice
EMS	Environmental Management System
EPA	Environment Protection Agency (US)
ESRC	Economic and Social Research Council
ETS	Emission Trading Scheme
EU	European Union
EUI	European University Institute (at Florence)
FCCC	Framework Convention on Climate Change
GAAR	General Anti-avoidance Rules
HSE	Health and Safety Executive
IA	Impact Assessment
ILR	Independent Local Radio
ITA	Independent Television Authority
ITC	Independent Television Commission
JBL	*Journal of Business Law*

MLR	*Modern Law Review*
MMC	Monopolies and Mergers Commission
NAO	National Audit Office
NCC	National Consumer Council
NRA	National Regulatory Agency
OFFER	Office of Electricity Regulation
OFGAS	Office of Gas Supply
OFGEM	Office of the Gas and Electricity Markets
OFT	Office of Fair Trading
OFTEL	Office of Telecommunications
OFWAT	Office of Water Services
OJLS	*Oxford Journal of Legal Studies*
OMB	Office of Management and Budget
OMC	Open Method of Coordination
ONP	Open Network Provision
ORR	Office of the Rail Regulator
PBR	Principles-based Regulation
PCC	Press Complaints Commission
PIG	Public Interest Group
RA	Radio Authority
RAB	Regulatory Asset Base
RCBA	Risk Cost Benefit Analysis
REC	Regional Electricity Company
RIA	Regulatory Impact Analysis
ROSCO	Rolling Stock Leasing Company
RPI-X	Retail Price Index less efficiency factor X price cap
SFAIRP	So Far As Is Reasonably Practicable
SME	Small and Medium Enterprises
TOR	Tolerability of Risks
TUC	Trades Union Congress

1 Introduction

Our aim in writing this book is to introduce readers to those practical and theoretical issues that we see as central to the study of regulation. We set out to describe the nature of those issues, to indicate how regulatory practitioners and scholars have dealt with them and to offer arguments on potential responses to regulatory difficulties. The focus is not on providing 'how to' accounts of regulatory experience. Instead, our aim is to highlight the contested areas and issues that are produced by regulation. We hope that this volume will add to exchanges between different viewpoints. Many of the examples in this book draw on the British experience, but we aim to make the text relevant to a wider international audience interested in regulatory activities broadly defined.

Over the past decades, regulation has been a topic that has stimulated discussions in a host of disciplines—notably law, economics, political science and public policy, sociology, history, psychology, geography, anthropology, management, and social administration. Given this breadth of interest, regulation is a subject or field of study that calls for a multi-disciplinary approach. Economists, for instance, are likely to benefit from the insights of political scientists and sociologists on such matters as the practicalities of implementation and enforcement. Similarly, lawyers' messages concerning the limitations of different kinds of rules and enforcement processes might profitably be taken on board by economists and others. Analogous points could be made from the perspectives of other disciplines. This edition is written by a lawyer, an economist, and a political scientist, but will attempt both to draw from a wider range of disciplinary perspectives and to be accessible across disciplines. Highly technical approaches and terminology will be avoided where possible. It is hoped, therefore, that the analysis offered will prove useful to regulatory studies in a wide variety of areas.

Regulation has become a matter of topical debate in a way that it was not even a single decade ago. This global phenomenon was partly prompted by the activities of international organizations. Criticisms and concerns with regulatory orthodoxies became increasingly prominent during the financial crisis of 2007–9, when calls for deregulation and 'light-touch' regulation suddenly gave way to daily demands for more rigorous regulation of the financial markets. Elsewhere, too, regulation had attracted supporters and opponents alike. Supporters saw regulation as a technocratic device that had the potential to exert rational controls over important economic and social activities. Sceptics regarded regulation as little other than 'red tape' and a potential burden on economic activity.

It is, therefore, fair to say that by 2011, the claim that we are living in an age of the 'regulatory state' had become widely accepted as the R-word had penetrated ever more social domains across countries.[1] Over the past decade, regulation has risen in the academic agenda to become both a field of study in its own right and a fertile source of new perspectives on the agendas of longer-established disciplines. Substantial contributions to regulatory debates have been made by political scientists, economists, lawyers, sociologists, anthropologists, and others. Writings on regulation have become well-represented across scholarly publications, and a diversity of university courses and programmes, as well as research centres, have emerged to deal with various aspects of the theory and practice of regulation. Some of these have treated regulation as a generic subject taught in interdisciplinary programmes; others have specialized in specific areas, such as financial services, environmental protection, communications, or utilities.

As a consequence, regulation can be said now to have reached a state of maturity, both in an intellectual and in a practical sense.[2] Intellectually, theoretical perspectives have developed rapidly into an impressive body of scholarship and, in the world of practice, there has developed a distinct and expanding international and national 'regulatory community' that shares similar languages, concepts, and concerns. The language of regulation has penetrated diverse policy domains and talk of regulatory strategy has become part of administrative life. In this process, central regulatory issues such as those relating to standard-setting and enforcement have become matters of regular discussion in different policy and academic communities.

What is Regulation?

Regulation is often spoken of as if an identifiable and discrete mode of governmental activity,[3] yet the term 'regulation' has been defined in a number of ways.[4] Selznick's notion of regulation as sustained and focused control

---

[1] See M. Moran, *The British Regulatory State* (Oxford, 2003); 'Understanding the Regulatory State' (2002) 32 *British Journal of Political Science* 391–413; and contrast this with G. Majone, 'The Rise of the Regulatory State in Europe' (1994) 17(3) *West European Politics* 77–101.

[2] For comparison with the position a decade ago see R. Baldwin, C. Scott, and C. Hood, 'Introduction' in R. Baldwin, C. Scott, and C. Hood (eds), *A Reader on Regulation* (Oxford, 1998). See also R. Baldwin, M. Cave, and M. Lodge, 'Introduction' in R. Baldwin, M. Cave, and M. Lodge (eds.), *Oxford Handbook of Regulation* (Oxford, 2010).

[3] See Baldwin, Scott, and Hood, *Regulation*, ch. 1.

[4] See B. Mitnick, *The Political Economy of Regulation* (New York, 1980), ch. 1; A. Ogus, *Regulation: Legal Form and Economic Theory* (Oxford, 1994), ch. 1; G. Majone (ed.), *De-Regulation or Re-Regulation?* (London, 1989).

exercised by a public agency over activities that are valued by a community has been referred to as expressing a central meaning,[5] but it is perhaps useful to think of the word regulation being used in the following different senses:[6]

As a specific set of commands—where regulation involves the promulgation of a binding set of rules to be applied by a body devoted to this purpose. An example would be the health and safety at work legislation as applied by the Health and Safety Executive.

As deliberate state influence—where regulation has a more broad sense and covers all state actions that are designed to influence business or social behaviour. Thus, command-based regimes would come within this usage, but so also would a range of other modes of influence—for instance, those based on the use of economic incentives[7] (e.g. taxes or subsidies); contractual powers; deployment of resources; franchises; the supply of information, or other techniques.

As all forms of social or economic influence—where all mechanisms affecting behaviour—whether these be state-based or from other sources (e.g. markets)—are deemed regulatory. One of the great contributions of the theory of 'smart regulation' has been to point out that regulation may be carried out not merely by state institutions but by a host of other bodies, including corporations, self-regulators, professional or trade bodies, and voluntary organizations.[8] According to this third, broad usage of the term 'regulation', there is no requirement that the regulatory effects of a mechanism are deliberate or designed, rather than merely incidental to other objectives.

As a final comment on the concept of regulation, it should be noted that regulation is often thought of as an activity that restricts behaviour and prevents the occurrence of certain undesirable activities (a 'red light' concept[9]). The broader view is, however, that the influence of regulation may also be *enabling* or *facilitative* ('green light') as, for example, where the airwaves are regulated so as to allow broadcasting operations to be conducted in an ordered fashion, rather than left to the potential chaos of an uncontrolled market.

---

[5] P. Selznick, 'Focusing Organisational Research on Regulation', in R. Noll (ed.), *Regulatory Policy and the Social Sciences* (Berkeley, CA, 1985), 363, quoted Ogus, *Regulation*, 1.

[6] See Baldwin, Scott, and Hood, *Regulation*, ch. 1; J. Black, 'Critical Reflections on Regulation' (2002) 27 *Australian Journal of Legal Philosophy* 1–95.

[7] On the distinction between command-and incentive-based regimes, see S. Breyer, *Regulation and Its Reform* (Cambridge, MA, 1982); Ogus, *Regulation*, esp. ch. 11; and R. Baldwin, 'Regulation: After Command and Control', in K. Hawkins (ed.), *The Human Face of Law* (Oxford, 1997).

[8] See N. Gunningham and P. Grabosky, *Smart Regulation* (Oxford, 1998).

[9] On 'red light' and 'green light' rules and regulations, see C. Harlow and R. Rawlings, *Law and Administration* (3rd edn, Cambridge, 2009); Ogus, *Regulation*, 2.

Issues on the Regulatory Agenda

There is a tendency to associate regulation with the post-privatization control of the utilities. The language and practice of regulation, however, looks back on a much longer history. In Britain, regulation has been practised since at least the Tudor and Stuart periods.[10] In the nineteenth century, there was a burgeoning of regulation, with the emergence of specialist regulatory institutions[11] and a host of measures dealing with public health and employment conditions.[12] Developments in the supply of railway, water, gas, and electricity services led to the introduction of controls over prices, safety, and quality of service.[13] Elsewhere, too, regulation was practised widely and transferred from one domain to another. For example, initial railway regulation drew on provisions governing turnpikes.

During the twentieth century, a steady growth in regulation took place from the 1930s onwards. That decade saw the licensing of goods and passenger carryings by road as well as the advent, in the fishing industry, of marketing boards that fulfilled both operational and regulatory functions. The nationalization of core industries, such as the railways, were even framed as issues of regulation. For example, the 'godfather' of the UK public corporation model post-1945, Herbert Morrison, defined the ministerial function vis-à-vis public corporations as being 'regulatory and supervisory in character'.[14]

In the post-war period, marketing boards followed in the cotton, crofting, sugar, and iron and steel industries, and the first US-style independent regulatory agency was established in Britain in 1954 with the Independent Television Authority.[15] The ITA was innovatory in combining a degree of independence from government with the carrying out of adjudicatory and regulatory, as well as policy-developing, functions. In the United States, such independent regulatory bodies had been carrying out key functions of government since the Inter State Commerce Commission was established in 1887 to limit discriminatory pricing by railroads. In the ITA's wake followed a series of regulatory agencies that were created in the 1960s and

---

[10] Ogus, *Regulation*, 6–12; 'Regulatory Law: Some Lessons from the Past' (1992) 12 *Legal Studies* 1.

[11] O. MacDonagh, 'The Nineteenth-Century Revolution in Government: A Reappraisal' (1958) 1 *Historical Journal* 52.

[12] P. Craig, *Administrative Law* (5th edn, London, 2003), ch. 2.

[13] See J. Foreman-Peck and R. Millward, *Public and Private Ownership of British Industry 1820–1990* (Oxford, 1994), esp. chs 1–3; C. Foster, *Privatisation, Public Ownership and the Regulation of Natural Monopoly* (Oxford, 1992), chs. 1 and 2.

[14] H. Morrison, *Taking Stock*, PRO MT 47/15, S.I. (M) (47) (32), 18 July 1947. See also M. Lodge, *On Different Tracks* (Westport, CT, 2002).

[15] B. Sendall, *Independent Television in Britain: Origin and Foundation*, vol. 1: *1946–62* (London, 1982).

1970s to deal with issues in such areas as monopolies, gaming, industrial relations, civil aviation, discrimination, and workplace health and safety.

During the 1980s and 1990s, much stress was placed by governments and commentators on the problems and costs of regulation and the case for deregulating the economy.[16] The privatization drive of the same period, however, produced a new burst of regulation, carried out by a host of new regulatory bodies such as OFTEL (1984), OFGAS (1986), OFFER (1989), OFWAT (1990), and the Office of the Rail Regulator (1993). In addition, administrative changes produced a new Environment Agency in 1996 and from the creation of the National Lottery there emerged an Office of the National Lottery to oversee the providing private operator, Camelot.

By the mid-1990s, some 25 million customers were served by the main four regulated utilities industries alone. Their total annual turnover of £51 billion represented around 8 per cent of the annual gross domestic product of the UK, and not only the results of regulation but the processes used to regulate had prompted unprecedented concern. Regulation and deregulation had moved to positions high on the political agenda. Conservative administrations had sought, since 1985, to deregulate, cut red tape, and substitute competitive pressures for regulatory action. The Department of Trade and Industry's Enterprise and Deregulation Unit had been established in that year in order to review all new legislative instruments and assess the compliance costs they would impose on businesses. That body, later called the Deregulation Unit and housed in the Cabinet Office, had, by 1996, started to subject regulations to a newly taxing process of 'regulatory appraisal',[17] but the high point of deregulatory action had come with the passing of the Deregulation and Contracting Out Act 1994 which *inter alia* had given ministers the power to use secondary legislative to eliminate burdens and controls. No rigorous

---

[16] See J. Kay, C. Mayer, and D. Thompson (eds), *Privatisation and Regulation: The UK Experience* (Oxford, 1986); D. Swann, *The Retreat of the State: Deregulation and Privatisation in the UK and US* (Brighton, 1988); K. Button and D. Swann (eds), *The Age of Regulatory Reform* (Oxford, 1989); also see the White Papers: *Building Business, Not Barriers*, Cmnd. 9794 (London, 1986); *Lifting the Burden*, Cmnd. 9751 (London, 1985); *Releasing Enterprise*, Cmnd. 512 (London, 1988); Department of Trade and Industry, *Burdens on Business* (London, 1985); Cabinet Office, *Checking the Cost of Regulation* (London, 1996); *Regulation in the Balance* (London, 1996); M. Derthick and P. Quirk, *The Politics of Deregulation* (Washington, 1985); V. Wright, 'Public Administration, Regulation, Deregulation and Reregulation', in E. Eliassen and J. Kooiman (eds), *Managing Public Organisations: Lessons from Contemporary European Experience* (London, 1993).

[17] See *Regulation in the Balance* and Chapter 15 below. Under Labour, the Deregulation Unit was renamed the Better Regulation Unit in 1997. In 2006, these functions were split into two: the Better Regulation Executive (supporting government departments) and the Better Regulation Commission (tasked with overseeing the implementation of initiatives). In 2008, the Better Regulation Commission was replaced by the Risk and Regulation Advisory Council (which in itself ended its activities in 2009). The core of regulatory reform initiatives moved to the then Department of Business, Enterprise and Regulatory Reform (BERR). At the time of writing (2011), the Better Regulation Executive remained located within the (now called) Department of Business, Innovation and Skills.

review of the impact of such initiatives was, however, carried out by the Major government and promises of 'bonfires of red tape' were not fulfilled.

It was in the field of utilities regulation that the most urgent political debates took place towards the end of the last millennium.[18] Attention focused on the issues of efficiency, accountability, and fairness in the system of regulating by means of Directors General and their accompanying offices. A host of books and reports emerged from all parts of the political spectrum to put forward a large number of reform proposals.[19] These were accompanied by significant contributions, many of which originated to the practice of economic regulation of utilities, in industrial economics.[20]

In parallel to these developments in the regulation of economic and social activities, there was also the rise of regulation *inside* government. This included a growing prominence of formal auditing and financial controlling activities, the emergence of oversight mechanisms that sought to check on the quality or effectiveness of public services, such as prisons, schools, hospitals, and universities, as well as the growing codification of ethics provisions supposedly guiding public officials. All of these processes had been regulated in one way or another, but, despite considerable variations across domains, the 'regulation industry' inside UK government witnessed a considerable growth at a time of wider reductions in public service staff numbers elsewhere.[21]

By the turn of the millennium, the appropriateness of regulatory strategies and structures had become a significant public concern, and this led to a set of responses and debates over the first decade following 2000.[22]

---

[18] For a review of this debate see R. Baldwin, *Regulation in Question* (London, 1995).

[19] See e.g. C. Veljanovski, *The Future of Industry Regulation in the UK* (London, 1993); Adam Smith Institute, *Who Will Regulate the Regulators?* (London, 1992); P. Hain, *Regulating for the Common Good* (London, 1994); Centre for the Study of Regulated Industries, *Regulating the Utilities: Accountability and Processes* (London, 1994); National Consumer Council, *Paying the Price* (London, 1993); C. Graham, *Is There a Crisis in Regulatory Accountability?* (London, 1995 and reproduced in Baldwin, Scott, and Hood, *Regulation*); D. Helm, *British Utilities Regulation* (Oxford, 1995); M.E. Beesley (ed.), *Regulatory Utilities: A Time for Change?* (London, 1996); *Regulating Utilities: Broadening the Debate* (London, 1997); DTI Green Paper, *A Fair Deal for Consumers: Modernising the Framework for Utility Regulation*, Cmnd 3898 (March, 1998).

[20] J. Vickers and G. Yarrow, *Privatisation: An Economic Analysis* (Cambridge, MA, 1988); M. Armstrong, S. Cowan, and J. Vickers, *Regulatory Reform: Economic Analysis and British Experience* (Cambridge, MA, 1994); D. Newbery, *Privatization, Restructuring and Regulation of Network Utilities* (Cambridge, MA, 1999).

[21] C. Hood, C. Scott, O. James, G. Jones, and T. Travers (eds), *Regulation Inside Government* (Oxford, 1999); C. Hood, O. James, G.B. Peters, and C. Scott (eds), *Controlling Modern Government* (Cheltenham, 2004); M. Lodge and C. Hood, 'Regulation Inside Government: Retro-Theory Vindicated or Outdated?' in R. Baldwin, M. Cave, and M. Lodge (eds), *Oxford Handbook of Regulation* (Oxford, 2010).

[22] M. Lodge, 'Regulation, the Regulatory State and European Politics' (2008) 30 (1/2) *West European Politics* 280–301; T. Prosser, *The Regulatory Enterprise* (Oxford, 2010); D. Oliver, T. Prosser, and R. Rawlings (eds), *The Regulatory State: Constitutional Implications* (Oxford, 2010).

One prominent issue was the governance of regulatory bodies. In the British context, debates on this matter led not just to a merger of regulatory bodies in energy and communications, they also produced a change in the leadership structure, with the original, and initially much-fêted 'Director General'-model being replaced by collective decision-making boards. Indeed, the widely reported collapse of the privatized railway infrastructure provider, Railtrack, and its transfer into a 'non-dividend paying' public company, as well as the associated fall-out between ministers and the then regulator, confirmed arguements that the regulatory reforms of the 1980s and 1990s were far from achieving depoliticized stability: instead, the world of regulation continued to be one of high politics.[23]

A second concern related to the effects and biases of regulatory regimes. In particular, there was a growing worry about investments in infrastructures and the environmental effects of regulated industries, especially with regard to climate change.[24]

A third debate that grew in the new millennium was one driven by the emergence of new technologies and products. New products have come to market with increasing speed in recent times and consumers' preferences have shifted, especially as consumers have become increasingly critical of the food production chain in the light of a series of food safety scandals, starting with so-called 'Mad Cow Disease'. The arrival of genetically modified (GM) food and the new communications technologies, for instance, are two areas that have produced rafts of new control challenges and in another area—gambling via the internet—new technologies have changed the frontiers of existing regulatory regimes.[25]

With respect to regulatory strategy, the past decade has witnessed a growing appetite to explore the potential of 'non-traditional' methods of regulation. Commentators have, for instance, devoted new attention to the potential and limitations of market-based control strategies such as franchising and permit-trading regimes. There has been greater weight given to arguments for controlling not by state regulation but by 'meta-regulation' and regimes that focus on auditing the control regimes being operated within businesses and corporations themselves.[26] A further recent change that has emerged in

---

[23] M. Lodge, 'The Wrong Type of Regulation?' (2002) 22(3) *Journal of Public Policy* 271–97.

[24] D. Helm, *The New Regulatory Agenda* (London, 2004). For example, the UK government published proposals to reform energy regulation in late 2010 that was supposed to incentivize low-carbon forms of energy generation; see 'Nuclear option poised to test coalition further', *Financial Times*, 17 Dec. 2010.

[25] For a comparison between 'high' and 'low tech' policy domains and regulatory responses, see J. Black, M. Lodge, and M. Thatcher (eds), *Regulatory Innovation* (Cheltenham, 2005).

[26] J. Braithwaite, 'Meta Risk Management and Responsive Regulation for Tax System Integrity' (2003) 25 *Law and Policy* 1–16; C. Coglianese and D. Lazer, 'Management Based Regulation: Prescribing Private Management to Achieve Public Goals' (2003) 37 *Law and Society Review* 691–730; P. May, 'Performance-Based Regulation and Regulatory Regimes: the Saga of Leaky Buildings' (2003) 25 *Law*

parallel with such 'auditing' approaches has been the growth of a tendency to see regulatory issues in terms of risks and to see control issues as questions of risk management.[27] At the same time, governmental bodies have echoed these approaches, and bodies such as the UK's (then) Better Regulation Task Force have commended the use of 'more imaginative' thinking about regulation and have stressed the need to adopt minimalist or self-regulatory controls in the first instance.[28] Similar ideas have also come increasingly on to the agenda of international bodies, such as the OECD with its 'high-quality regulation' initiative and the European Union with its own extensive programme on (regulatory) impact assessments. As a result of this international and national concern, the 'better regulation' agenda diffused internationally, moving these discourses towards emerging economies such as Brazil.[29]

Such discussions of 'meta-regulation' and 'steering' raised questions about the bodies that should be given the task of regulating and the level of government at which regulation should be positioned. Just as calls for 'meta-regulation' indicated the interest of some commentators in placing the control function within the corporation, others grew more concerned about the degree to which regulation operated inside the government itself and still others saw the important shift to be towards regulation by supra-national bodies (state or private) within a framework of globalization.[30]

Another important focal concern has developed in influence over the last decade. A strand of scholarship has emphasized the degree to which regulatory regimes are fragmented, multi-sourced, and unfocused.[31] On this view, fragmented regulatory authority is frequently encountered within national systems, and public, private, and (increasingly) hybrid organizations often share regulatory authority. This perspective suggests that to study regulation

---

and Policy 381–401; C. Parker, 'Regulator-Required Corporate Compliance Program Audits' (2003) 25 *Law and Policy* 221–44; M. Power, *The Audit Society* (Oxford, 1997); M. Power, *Organized Uncertainty: Designing a World of Risk Management* (Oxford, 2007).

[27] J. Black, 'The Emergence of Risk-based Regulation and the New Public Risk Management in the UK', (2005) *Public Law* 512–48; C. Hood, H. Rothstein, and R. Baldwin, *The Government of Risk* (Oxford, 2001). See also H. Rothstein, M. Huber, and G. Gaskell, 'A Theory of Risk Colonization' (2006) 35 *Economy and Society* 91–112.

[28] Better Regulation Task Force, *More Imaginative Thinking About Regulation* (London, 2003).

[29] K. Wegrich, *Das Leitbild "Better Regulation": Ziele, Instrumente, Wirkungsweise* (Berlin, 2011); M. Lodge and K. Wegrich, 'High Quality Regulation: Its Popularity, Its Tools and Its Future' (2009) 29 (3) *Public Money and Management* 145–52.

[30] J. Braithwaite and P. Drahos, *Global Business Regulation* (Cambridge, 2000); D. Kerwer, 'Rules that Many Use: Standards and Global Regulation' (2005) 18 *Governance* 611–32; E. Meidinger, *Competitive Supra-Governmental Regulation: How Could it be Democratic?* Buffalo Legal Studies Research Paper Series 2007-007 available at http://ssrn.com/abstract=1001770; P. Pattberg, 'The Institutionalization of Private Governance: How Business and Nonprofit Organizations Agree on Transnational Rules' (2005) 18 *Governance* 589–610.

[31] J. Black, 'Decentring Regulation: Understanding the Role of Regulation and Self-regulation in a "Post-Regulatory" World' (2001) 54 *Current Legal Problems* 103–47.

by looking at single regulatory agencies is to adopt rather a limited viewpoint. Such 'decentred' interpretations of regulation have also highlighted the need to take on board the multi-level character of regulation, in which standards may be set or agreed at supranational or international levels and enforcement may take place in the locality.

When more specific regulatory questions have been explored, there have also been dramatic changes of treatment during the new millennium. A regulatory issue that has been particularly productive of fresh theories and approaches has been that of enforcement and compliance. Long gone are the days when one might comfortably profess to be an advocate of either 'compliance' or 'deterrence' approaches. In the wake of the well-established theories of 'responsive regulation'[32] and 'smart regulation',[33] newer theories of 'problem-centred'[34] regulation have moved compliance theory onwards, and have then been both exposed to criticism and refined. More attention has been paid to motivations and behaviours,[35] to interactions of control systems,[36] and to 'risk-based' and 'principles-based' approaches to regulatory enforcement.[37]

As regulation has come to the forefront of public debates in recent years, some particular issues have exerted an especially strong grasp on public and political attentions—on either a continuing or an ephemeral basis. There has, for instance, been a sustained concern about the 'evils' of regulation, such as 'red tape', overload, and the excessive bureaucratization of economic and social life. Critics have suggested that regulation creates major barriers to competitiveness and economic growth, and such worries have been fuelled by benchmarking exercises and league tables such as the World Bank's 'Doing Business' reports.

In some cases, particular items have shifted place on the regulation agenda—so that debates about the virtues and vices of deregulation and privatization have, as noted, given way to post-millennium discussions of regulatory improvement and 'better regulation'. In these newer conversations about regulation, it has become accepted, not only that regulation is necessary for the functioning of a market economy, but that regulatory oversight remains essential in the running of public services, especially those involving

---

[32] I. Ayres and J. Braithwaite, *Responsive Regulation* (Oxford, 1992).
[33] N. Gunningham and P. Grabosky, *Smart Regulation* (Oxford, 1998).
[34] M. Sparrow, *The Regulatory Craft* (Washington DC, 2000).
[35] C. Sunstein and R.Thaler, *Nudge* (New Haven, 2008); C. Jolls, C. Sunstein, and R. Thaler, 'A Behavioural Approach to Law and Economics' in C. Sunstein (ed.), *Behavioural Law and Economics* (Cambridge, 2008).
[36] R. Baldwin and J. Black, 'Really Responsive Regulation' (2008) 71(1) *Modern Law Review* 59–94; J. Black and R. Baldwin, 'Really Responsive Risk-Based Regulation' (2010) 32(2) *Law and Policy* 181–213.
[37] See Chapters 13 and 14 below.

naturally monopolistic elements, such as networks. An initial emphasis on economic regulation that was supposed to 'wither away' over time has been replaced by a realization that there is a continuing need for regulatory oversight and an imperative to add environmental and sustainability objectives to the earlier, primarily economic and social, objectives.

These freshly developing agendas of regulation have not, however, always gelled into highly coherent packages of policy or theory. The 'better regulation' group of initiatives can, for instance, be seen as rich in tensions and contradictions. Thus, calls have been made for more evidence-based regulation (and data-intensive, risk-based regulation) but, at the same time, governments have demanded that regulators make fewer informational and data supply demands on businesses. Similarly, the past decade or so has seen the spread of rationalistic and formal modes of evaluating regulatory proposals (notably 'Regulatory Impact Assessments') and, at the same time, many governments have urged regulators to move towards the kinds of regulatory styles that are least likely to score convincingly in RIA appraisals—such as more user-friendly and less formal modes of control (see, further, Chapter 15). In itself, the 'better regulation' agenda could be seen as an uneasy rhetorical package that combines a continuation of the 'anti-red tape' message and the belief in technocratic and 'rationalizing' tools for enhancing regulatory quality.[38]

By 2010, regulation had come to occupy a place at the forefront of public debate in more than one domain. The financial crisis that was initially to have led to a 'return of the state' pointed to the problems that could be caused by an over-reliance on the self-regulatory capacities of private organization.[39] It also highlighted a series of issues regarding enforcement styles and overall regulatory arrangements. By 2011, regulatory debates continued to be dominated by demands and warnings, on the one side, to impose 'more' regulation (in many variants: more rules, tougher sanctions, growing distinctiveness and 'professionalization' of regulators) and, on the other, cautioning that 'more' regulation would have considerable undesirable effects. The financial crisis also added to global regulation debates on such matters as how systemic risks could be coped with across jurisdictions, and how national regulators (through the Basel III agreement) could coordinate their 'macroprudential' actions and impose capital requirements to cope with overheated national economies.[40] Environmental disasters, such as the Louisiana oil-spill of 2010, brought their own regulatory disputes.[41]

---

[38] T.O. McGarity, *Reinventing Rationality: The Role of Regulatory Analysis in the Federal Bureaucracy* (Cambridge, 1991).

[39] M. Lodge and K. Wegrich, 'Letter to the Editor', *Public Administration Review* (2010).

[40] 'Bank Regulators Agree on Global Sweep to Tackle Credit Bubbles', *Financial Times*, 11 Jan. 2011.

[41] National Commission on the BP Deepwater Horizon Oil Spill and Offshore Drilling (2011), *Final Report* (www.oilspillcommission.gov/final-report, last accessed 14 January 2011). The 'National Commission on the BP spill' criticized the lack of resources allocated to the regulator and called for the

As a result of such developments and crises, regulation now occupies its place as a central organizing concern for the worlds of practice and research alike. At the same time, it has increasingly been asked whether regimes of regulation or self-regulation can satisfactorily solve complex problems—and not just in the context of the financial crisis. Advocacy of different regulatory strategies has, moreover, tended to proceed on a cautious basis and critiques of regulation have tended to emerge in a process of interaction between the study and the practice of regulation.

The Organization of the Book

Part I of the book reviews a series of general issues in regulation, namely: why regulate at all (Chapter 2); how 'good' regulation can be identified (Chapter 3); how the origins of regulation and regulatory changes can be explained (Chapter 4); and how regulatory failures can be understood (Chapter 5). It also considers, in Chapter 6, the challenges of regulating risks and the vision of regulation as a risk-centred activity.

Part II of the book then looks at strategic issues and how regulation can be carried out. Central concerns are: choices of regulatory strategy (Chapter 7); self-regulatory, 'meta-regulatory', and complex regimes (Chapter 8); franchising (Chapter 9); and emissions trading (Chapter 10). Part III examines enforcement and implementation matters. It starts with a general review of these issues in Chapter 11 before looking at the more particular approaches of responsive regulation (Chapter 12); and risk-based regulation (Chapter 13). The problems that are encountered in choosing types of regulatory standards are considered in Chapter 14, together with the case for principles-based regulation.

Part IV turns attention to questions of evaluation of the quality of regulation. Cost-benefit testing and Regulatory Impact Assessment are looked at in Chapter 15. Accountability and procedural fairness concerns are discussed in Chapter 16. Finally, the role and incidence of competition and coordination between regulators is addressed in Chapter 17.

Part V reviews a host of issues that relate to the governmental levels at which regulatory systems are located. Chapter 18 deals generally with regulation at different levels before Chapter 19 considers the European

creation of a new safety regulator. The Commission also criticized the prevalence of self-regulation in the sector, especially the role in which the 'American Petroleum Institute' which produced national and global technical standards, was predisposed to rely on 'industry autonomy'. It called for the creation of an industry-based safety standard-setting body and enforcing—a demand that was widely contested, with opponents noting in particular the financial implications of these proposals—see 'US "cannot walk away" from oil in deep water', *Financial Times*, 12 Jan. 2011.

dimension to regulation. Development and globalization issues are covered by Chapters 20 and 21, respectively. Part VI then looks at utility or network industry issues, and focuses on: price setting in natural monopolies (Chapter 22); using competition in network industries (Chapter 23); separation and contestability in network industries (Chapter 24); implementing price controls (Chapter 25); and efficiency and innovation in network industries (Chapter 26). Conclusions are offered in Chapter 27.

Part I
Fundamentals

2 Why Regulate?

Motives for regulating can be distinguished from technical justifications for regulating. Governments may regulate for a number of motives—for example, they may be influenced by the economically powerful and may act in the interests of the regulated industry or they may see a particular regulatory stance as a means to re-election. Different commentators may analyse such motives in different ways, and a variety of approaches to such analysis will be discussed in Chapter 3. To begin, though, we should consider the technical justifications for regulating that may be given by a government that is assumed to be acting in pursuit of the public interest.[1]

Many of the rationales for regulating can be described as instances of 'market failure'. Regulation in such cases is argued to be justified because the uncontrolled marketplace will, for some reason, fail to produce behaviour or results in accordance with the public interest.[2] In some sectors or circumstances, there may also be 'market absence'—there may be no effective market—because, for example, households cannot buy clean air or peace and quiet in their localities. In this chapter, we discuss the traditional 'market failure' rationales for regulating, but we also consider the argument that there may be other reasons to regulate and that these have a basis in human rights or social solidarity, rather than market, considerations.

Market Failure Rationales

MONOPOLIES AND NATURAL MONOPOLIES

Monopoly describes the position in which one seller produces for the entire industry or market. Monopoly pricing and output is likely to occur and be sustained where three factors obtain:[3]

---

[1] For detailed reviews of public interest reasons for regulating see S. Breyer, *Regulation and Its Reform* (Cambridge, MA, 1982), ch. 1; A. Ogus, *Regulation: Legal Form and Economic Theory* (Oxford, 1994), ch. 3; E. Gellhorn and R.J. Pierce, *Regulated Industries* (St Paul, MN, 1982), ch. 2; J. Kay and J. Vickers, 'Regulatory Reform: An Appraisal', in G. Majone (ed.), *De-Regulation or Re-Regulation?* (London, 1989); B. Mitnick, *The Political Economy of Regulation* (New York, 1980), ch. 5; C. Sunstein, *After the Rights Revolution* (Cambridge, MA, 1990), ch. 2; C. Hood, *Explaining Economic Policy Reversals* (Buckingham, 1995).

[2] See also J. Francis, *The Politics of Regulation* (Oxford, 1993), ch. 1.

[3] See Gellhorn and Pierce, *Regulated Industries*, 36–7 and Chapter 15 below. On regulating monopolies generally see C. Foster, *Privatisation, Public Ownership and the Regulation of Natural Monopoly* (Oxford, 1992), ch. 6; Ogus, *Regulation*, 30–3; Breyer, *Regulation and Its Reform*, 15–19;

- A single seller occupies the entire market.
- The product sold is unique in the sense that there is no substitute sufficiently close for consumers to turn to.
- Substantial barriers restrict entry by other firms into the industry, and exit is difficult.

Where monopoly occurs, the market 'fails' because competition is deficient. From the public interest perspective, the problem with a firm occupying a monopolistic position is that in maximizing profits it will restrict its output and set price above marginal cost. It will do this because if it charges a single price for its product, additional sales will only be achieved by lowering the price on the entire output. The monopolist will forgo sales to the extent that lost revenue from fewer sales will be compensated for by higher revenue derived from increased price on the units still sold. The effects of monopoly, as compared to perfect competition, are reduced output, higher prices, and transfer of income from consumers to producers.

One response to potential monopolies is to use competition (or antitrust) laws so as to create a business environment that is conducive to competition. Where a 'natural monopoly' exists, however, the use of competition law may be undesirable.[4] A natural monopoly occurs when economies of scale available in the production process are so large that the relevant market can be served at the least cost by a single firm. It is accordingly less costly to society to have production carried out by one firm than by many. Thus, rather than have three railway or electricity companies laying separate networks of rails or cables where one would do, it may be more efficient to give one firm a monopoly subject to regulation of such matters as prices and access to the network. Determining whether a natural monopoly exists requires a comparison of demand for the product with the extent of the economies of scale available in production. If a firm is in a position of natural monopoly then, like any monopoly, it will present problems of reduced output, higher prices, and transfers of wealth from consumers to the firm. Restoration of competition by use of competition law is not, however, an appropriate response, since competition may be socially costly and thus regulation of prices, quality, and output as well as access may be called for. The regulator will try to set price near incremental cost (the cost of producing an additional unit) in order to encourage the natural monopolist to expand its output to the level that competitive conditions would have induced.

Francis, *Politics of Regulation*, ch. 3; E. Gellhorn and W. Kovacic, *Antitrust Law and Economics* (St Paul, Minn., 1994), chs. 3 and 4.

[4] On natural monopolies see M. Waterson, *Regulation of the Firm and Natural Monopoly* (Oxford, 1988), ch. 2; Foster, *Privatisation*, ch. 6.2.

Not all aspects of a supply process may be naturally monopolistic. As Ogus points out,[5] the economies of scale phenomenon may affect only one part of a given process—for instance the *transmission* of, say, electricity, rather than its *generation*.[6] The task of many governments and regulators (at least those committed to minimalist regulation) is to identify those parts of a process that are naturally monopolistic so that these can be regulated while other aspects are left to the influence of competitive forces.[7]

WINDFALL PROFITS

A firm will earn a windfall profit (sometimes called an 'economic rent' or excess profit) where it finds a source of supply significantly cheaper than that available in the marketplace.[8] It may do so by, say, locating a rich seam of an easily extracted mineral; by coming upon a material efficiency in a production process; or by possessing an asset that suddenly escalates in value—for example, a boat in a desert town that has been flooded. Regulation may be called for when it is desired either to transfer profits to taxpayers or to allow consumers or the public to benefit from the windfall.

Where the windfall is the result of planned investments of money, effort, or research, or where society might want to create incentives to search for new efficiencies, products, or areas of demand, there is a case for allowing windfall profits to be retained. (If 'excess' profits are earned, it may be appropriate to limit these so that rewards and incentives are proportionate to the effort or investment that has produced the return.) In the desert town, it may be desirable to encourage some individuals to store boats in order to cope with periodic floods. If, however, the windfall is the result of good fortune rather than effort, exploration, or research, the case for taking the profits for public benefit may be stronger. Even in such cases, however, there will still be an argument for leaving windfall profits where they lie. If the state deprives a property owner of the windfalls that flow from such ownership, this may be seen by market actors as rendering property rights less secure, and this uncertainty may be bad for business generally. The balance between the public's gains from intervention and any negative effects on markets will have to be assessed in specific cases.

---

[5] Ogus, *Regulation*, 31.
[6] G. Yarrow, 'Regulation and Competition in the Electricity Supply Industry', in J. Kay, C. Mayer, and D. Thompson (eds), *Privatisation and Regulation* (Oxford, 1986).
[7] See Chapter 23 below, and the White Paper, *Privatising Electricity*, Cmnd. 322 (London, 1988).
[8] See Breyer, *Regulation and Its Reform*, 21.

EXTERNALITIES

The reason for regulating externalities (or 'spillovers') is that the price of a product does not reflect the true cost to society of producing that good, and excessive consumption accordingly results.[9] Thus, a manufacturer of car tyres might keep costs to consumers down by dumping pollutants arising from the manufacturing process into a river. The price of the tyres will not represent the true costs that production imposes on society if clean-up costs are left out of account. The resultant process is wasteful because too many resources are attracted into polluting activities (too many tyres are made and sold) and too few resources are devoted by the manufacturer to pollution avoidance or adopting pollution-free production methods. The rationale for regulation is to eliminate this waste—and to protect society or third parties suffering from externalities—by compelling the internalization of spillover costs—on 'polluter pays' principles.

INFORMATION INADEQUACIES

Competitive markets can only function properly if consumers are sufficiently well informed to evaluate competing products.[10] The market may, however, fail to produce adequate information and may fail for a number of reasons: information may cost money to produce (e.g. because researching the effects of a product, such as a drug, may prove expensive). The producer of information, however, may not be compensated by others who use that information (e.g. other manufacturers of the drug). The incentive to produce information may accordingly be low. There may also be incentives to falsify information—where, for example, consumers of the product are ill-positioned to challenge the falsification and seek remedies for damages suffered or where they face high costs in doing so. Areas in which consumers purchase a type of product very infrequently may give rise to this problem. The information produced may, in addition, not be of sufficient assistance to the consumer—for instance, because the consumer lacks the expertise required to render technical data useful. Finally, collusion in the marketplace, or insufficient competition, may reduce the flow of information below the levels consumers might want. Producers, as a group, may thus fail to warn consumers about the general hazards or deficiencies associated with a product. Breyer notes that until the US government required disclosure, accurate information was unavailable to most buyers in that country

---

[9] See Breyer, *Regulation and Its Reform*, 23–6; Ogus, *Regulation*, 35–8.
[10] See F. Hayek, 'The Use of Knowledge in Society' (1945) 35 *American Economic Review* 519; Breyer, *Regulation and Its Reform*, 26–8; Ogus, *Regulation*, 38–41.

concerning the durability of light bulbs, nicotine content of cigarettes, fuel economy for cars, or care requirements for textiles.[11]

Regulation, by making information more extensively accessible, accurate, and affordable, may protect consumers against information inadequacies and the consequences thereof, and may encourage the operation of healthy, competitive markets.

CONTINUITY AND AVAILABILITY OF SERVICE

In some circumstances, the market may not provide the socially desired levels of continuity and availability of service. Thus, where demand is cyclical (for example, as with passenger air transport to a holiday island) waste may occur as firms go through the processes of closing and reopening operations.[12] Regulation may be used to sustain services through troughs—for example, by setting minimum prices at levels allowing the covering of fixed costs through lean periods. This would be justified where the extra costs imposed on consumers by pricing rules are less than those caused by the processes of closing and opening services in response to the business cycle. The subsidizing of off-peak by peak travellers will, however, raise issues of equity to be considered alongside questions of social policy. In the case of some products or services—for example, water services—it may be considered, as a matter of social policy, that these should be generally available at least to a certain minimum standard. In the unregulated market, however, competition may lead to 'cream-skimming'—the process in which the producer chooses to supply only the most profitable customers—and services may be withdrawn from poorer or more geographically dispersed groupings of customers. Regulation may be justified in order to produce socially desirable results, even though the cross-subsidizations effected may be criticizable as inefficient and unfair.

ANTI-COMPETITIVE BEHAVIOUR AND PREDATORY PRICING

Markets may be deficient not merely because competition is lacking: they may produce undesirable effects because firms behave in a manner not conducive to healthy competition. A principal manifestation of such behaviour is predatory pricing. This occurs when a firm prices below costs, in the hope of driving competitors from the market, achieving a degree of domination, and then using its position to recover the costs of predation and increase profits at the expense of consumers. Preconditions for a rational firm to engage in predatory pricing are that: it must be able to outlast its competitors once prices are cut below variable costs; and it must be able to maintain prices well

---

[11] Breyer, *Regulation and Its Reform*, 28.   [12] Ogus, *Regulation*, 43–6.

above costs for long enough to recover its prior losses. The costs of entry to and exit from the market must, accordingly, allow it this period of comfort before new competition arises. The aim for regulators is to sustain competition and protect consumers from the ill-effects of market domination by outlawing predatory or other forms of anti-competitive behaviour.

PUBLIC GOODS AND MORAL HAZARD

Some commodities, e.g. security and defence services, may bring shared benefits and be generally desired. It may, however, be very costly for those paying for such services to prevent non-payers ('free-riders') from enjoying the benefits of those services. As a result, the market may fail to encourage the production of such commodities, and regulation may be required—often to overcome the free-rider problem by imposing taxes.

Similarly, where there is an instance of moral hazard—where someone other than the consumer pays for a service[13]—there may be excessive consumption without regard to the resource costs being imposed on society. If, for example, medical costs are not met by the patient, but by the state or an insurer, regulatory constraints may be required if excessive consumption of medical services is to be avoided.

UNEQUAL BARGAINING POWER

One precondition for the efficient or fair allocation of resources in a market is equal bargaining power. If bargaining power is unequal, regulation may be justified in order to protect certain interests. Thus, if unemployment is prevalent it cannot be assumed that workers will be able to negotiate effectively to protect their interests, and regulation may be required to safeguard such matters as the health and safety of those workers. Inequalities of bargaining power may thus be the products of relative positions in the marketplace, but they may also stem from asymmetries of information. Workers, for instance, may be poorly placed to secure health protections from their employers because they lack the information that would put them on an equal footing in negotiations.

SCARCITY AND RATIONING

Regulatory rather than market mechanisms may be justified in order to allocate certain commodities when these are in short supply. In a petrol

---

[13] See generally G. Calabresi, *The Cost of Accidents: A Legal and Economic Analysis* (New Haven, 1970).

shortage, for example, public interest objectives may take precedence over efficiency so that, instead of using pricing as an allocative instrument, the petrol is allocated with reference to democratically generated lists of priorities.

RATIONALIZATION AND COORDINATION

In many situations, it is extremely expensive for individuals to negotiate private contracts so as to organize behaviour or industries in an efficient manner—the transaction costs would be excessive.[14] The firms in an industry may be too small and geographically dispersed to bring themselves together to produce efficiently. (This might happen when small fishing concerns in a sparsely populated area fail to make collective marketing arrangements.) Enterprises may, moreover, have developed different and incompatible modes of production. In these circumstances, regulation may be justified as a means of rationalizing production processes (perhaps standardizing equipment in order to create effective networks) and in order to coordinate the market. Centralized regulation holds the advantage over individual private law arrangements, where information can be more efficiently communicated through public channels and economies of scale can be achieved by having one public agency responsible for upholding standards.[15]

It is noteworthy that this rationale for regulation is based more on the desire to *enable* effective action to take place than on the need to prohibit undesirable behaviour.

PLANNING

Markets may ensure reasonably well that individuals' consumer preferences are met, but they are less able to meet the demands of future generations or to satisfy altruistic concerns (e.g. the quality of an environment not personally enjoyed).[16] There is also, as far as altruism is concerned, a potential free-rider problem. Many people may be prepared to give up some of their assets for altruistic purposes only if they can be assured that a large number of others

---

[14] See Ogus, *Regulation*, 41–2; S. Breyer and P. MacAvoy, 'The Federal Power Commission and the Coordination Problem in the Electrical Power Industry' (1973) 46 *Southern California Law Review* 661.

[15] In the transportation sector, coordination and regulation by a central agency may be needed in order to organize a route network—see S. Glaister, *Deregulation and Privatisation: British Experience* (Washington, DC, 1998).

[16] See Ogus, *Regulation*, 54; R.B. Stewart, 'Regulation in a Liberal State: The Role of Non-Commodity Values' (1983) 92 *Yale Law Journal* 1537; Sunstein, *After the Rights Revolution*, 57–61.

will do the same. The problems and costs of coordination mean that regulation may be required in order to satisfy such desires.[17]

Rights-based and Social Rationales for Regulating

It has been argued, notably by Tony Prosser,[18] that the market failure rationale does not adequately justify the range of regulatory activities that are commonly undertaken. He suggests, moreover, that the market failure analysis treats regulation as second-best to market allocation and that this does not properly explain or justify current practice. Prosser, accordingly, points to the relevance of two further rationales for regulating—to protect human rights[19] and to further social solidarity.[20] In doing so, he takes issue with the assumptions that market solutions are always the best ways to deal with decisions on the allocation of goods and services, and that non-market failure rationales for regulating are essentially arbitrary. The idea that market allocations are 'technical' whereas social justice issues are 'political' is also questioned. What can be said as a matter of description, says Prosser, is that environmental and many other regulators can properly be seen as seeking to further social objectives, rather than as simply acting to correct market failures. Even where markets are involved, regulatory laws, on such a view, are not limited to merely correcting the market but often serve to constitute market relations, to provide the frameworks of rights and processes that allow markets to work, and to protect markets from fragmentation. In many contexts, accordingly, regulation can be seen as prior, not secondary, to the market and as a first-choice method of organizing social relations.[21]

---

[17] Ogus, *Regulation*, 54.

[18] T. Prosser, 'Regulation and Social Solidarity' (2006) 33 *Journal of Law and Society* 364–87; 'Public Service Law' (2000) 63 *Law and Contemporary Problems* 63–82. See also C. McCrudden, 'Social Policy and Economic Regulators' in C. McCrudden, *Regulation and Deregulation* (Oxford, 1999) and M. Feintuck, 'Regulatory Rationales Beyond the Economic' in R. Baldwin, M. Cave and M. Lodge (eds), *The Oxford Handbook of Regulation* (Oxford, 2010).

[19] See R. Brownsword, 'What the World Needs Now: Techno-Regulation, Human Rights and Human Dignity' in R. Brownsword (ed.), *Global Governance and the Quest for Justice* (Oxford, 2004).

[20] A developing of the argument is offered in T. Prosser, *The Regulatory Enterprise: Government Regulation and Legitimacy* (Oxford, 2010), 11–20, where four rationales for regulation are distinguished: (1) regulation for economic efficiency and consumer choice (market-centred regulation); (2) regulation to protect rights; (3) regulation for social solidarity; and (4) regulation as deliberation (the provision of processes to resolve problems). See also H. McVea, 'Financial Services Regulation Under the Financial Services Authority: A Reassertion of the Market Failure Thesis?' (2005) 64 *Cambridge Law Journal* 413–48; J. Black, 'Critical Reflections on Regulation', *LSE Centre for Analysis of Risk and Regulation (CARR), Discussion Paper 4* (2002).

[21] See C. Shearing, 'A Constitutive Conception of Regulation' in P. Grabosky and J. Braithwaite (eds), *Business Regulation and Australia's Future* (Canberra, 1994).

Consistent with such regulatory rationales are examples of regulating for reasons of distributional justice, rights protection, and citizenship—as, for example, where regulated utilities are obliged to apply geographically averaged tariffs or to meet universal service obligations. Governments, indeed, regulate on a host of matters simply in order to further social policies such as the prevention of discrimination based on race, sex, or age. Social objectives, moreover, are sometimes furthered by regulating even where this involves overruling the preferences of market players and acting paternalistically. Thus, society may, as a matter of policy, decide to act in the face of drivers' desires and demand that seat belts be worn in motor vehicles. In the strongest form of such paternalism, the decision is taken to regulate even where it is accepted that the citizens involved would not support regulation and that they are possessed of full information on the relevant issue.[22]

Conclusions: Choosing to Regulate

There are, as seen above (and in Table 2.1) a number of well-recognized reasons commonly given for regulating. It should be stressed, however, that in any one sector or industry the case for regulating may well be based not on a single but on a combination of rationales—be these market failure-, human rights-, or social solidarity-based. Health and safety regulation, for example, can be justified with reference to such matters as externalities, information defects, unequal bargaining, human rights, and paternalism.[23]

A second point to be borne in mind in considering whether to regulate, is that the market and all its failings should be compared with regulation and all its failings. Any analysis of the need to regulate will be skewed if it is assumed that regulatory techniques will operate perfectly. We will see during this book that all regulatory strategies have strengths and weaknesses in relation to their implementation, as well as their design. Regulatory and market solutions to problems should be considered in all their varieties and with all likely deficiencies and side-effects if true comparisons are to be effected.

---

[22] Ibid., 51–4.

[23] Breyer, *Regulation and Its Reform*, 34; Prosser, 'Regulation and Social Solidarity'.

Table 2.1. Rationales for regulating

Rationale	Main aims of regulation	Example
Monopolies and natural monpolies	Counter tendency to raise prices and lower output. Harness benefits of scale economies. Identify areas that are genuinely monopolistic.	Utilities.
Windfall profits	Transfer benefits of windfalls from firms to consumers or taxpayers.	Firm discovers unusually cheap source of supply.
Externalities	Compel producer or consumer to bear full costs of production, rather than pass on to third parties or society.	Pollution of river by factory.
Information inadequacies	Inform consumers to allow market to operate.	Pharmaceuticals. Food and drinks labelling.
Continuity and availability of service	Ensure socially desired (or protect minimal) level of 'essential' service.	Transport service to remote region.
Anti-competitive and predatory pricing behaviour	Prevent anti-competitive behaviour.	Below-cost pricing in transport.
Public goods and moral hazard	Share costs where benefits of activity are shared but free-rider problems exist.	Defence and security services. Health Services.
Unequal bargaining power	Protect vulnerable interests where market fails to do so.	Health and Safety at Work.
Scarcity and rationing	Public interest allocation of scarce commodities.	Petrol shortage.
Rationalization and coordination	Secure efficient production where transaction costs prevent market from obtaining network gains or efficiencies of scale. Standardization.	Disparate production in agriculture and fisheries.
Planning	Protect interests of future generations. Coordinate altruistic intentions.	Environment.
Human rights	Protection of weaker citizens.	Discrimination. Embryology.
Social protection	Social solidarity.	Broadcasting.

3 What is 'Good' Regulation?

To decide whether a system of regulation is good, acceptable, or in need of reform it is necessary to be clear about the benchmarks that are relevant in such an evaluation.[1]

A temptation for some economists may be to assert that regulation is good if it is efficient in the sense that it maximizes wealth.[2] It can be objected, however, that wealth maximization provides no ethical basis for action, that it cannot justify any particular distribution of rights within society, and that, as a result, it cannot be used to measure regulatory decisions affecting rights.[3]

This is because there is circularity in the assertion that one should distribute rights (e.g. to pollute or to be free from pollution) in a manner that maximizes wealth. For every particular, given, distribution of wealth, there is a specific allocation of further rights that will maximize wealth—thus, how best to allocate the new supply of petrol would be governed by who owns the machinery that burns petrol.[4] Deciding distributional issues on the basis of wealth maximization, accordingly, assumes a given distribution from the start. Similarly, it is circular to state that rights should be allocated to those who value them most—valuation itself depends on assumptions about

---

[1] See generally, R. Baldwin and C. McCrudden, *Regulation and Public Law* (London, 1987), ch. 3; R. Baldwin, *Rules and Government* (Oxford, 1995), ch. 3; J.O. Freedman, *Crisis and Legitimacy* (Cambridge, 1978); C. Radaelli and F. De Francesco, *Regulatory Quality in Europe* (Manchester, 2007); J. Stern, 'The Evaluation of Regulatory Agencies' in R. Baldwin, M. Cave, and M. Lodge (eds), *The Oxford Handbook of Regulation* (Oxford, 2010).

[2] See R.A. Posner, 'Utilitarianism, Economics and Legal Theory' (1979) 8 *Journal of. Legal Studies* 103; id., 'Wealth Maximisation Revisited' (1985) 2 *Notre Dame Journal of Law, Ethics and Public Policy* 85.

[3] See R. Dworkin, 'Is Wealth a Value?' (1980) 9 *Journal of Legal Studies* 191; id., 'Why Efficiency' (1980) 8 *Hofstra Law Review* 563; id., *A Matter of Principle* (Cambridge, MA, 1986), ch. 13; S. Kelman, 'Cost-Benefit Analysis: An Ethical Critique' (1981) 5(1) *Regulation* 33; A. Kronman, 'Wealth Maximisation as a Normative Principle' (1980) 9 *Journal of Legal Studies* 227; C.G. Veljanovski, 'Wealth Maximisation, Law and Ethics: On the Limits of Economic Efficiency' (1981) 1 *International Review of Law and Economics* 5; E.J. Weinrib, 'Utilitarianism, Economics and Legal Theory' (1980) 30 *University of Toronto LJ* 307; C. Fried, 'Difficulties in the Economic Analysis of Rights', in G. Dworkin, G. Bermont, and P. Brown (eds.), *Markets and Morals* (Washington, 1977). For a review of the literature see N. Duxbury, *Patterns of American Jurisprudence* (Oxford, 1995), 400–6.

[4] This statement assumes that there are transaction costs. If there are no transaction costs and parties can bargain in a friction-free manner then, as the Coase Theorem tells us, *any* distribution of rights will maximize wealth and the owners of petrol-burning machines will end up using the petrol even if it is not allocated to them in the first instance. This implies, again, that wealth maximization offers no help at all in deciding how to allocate rights. See R. Coase, 'The Problem of Social Cost' (1960) 3 *Journal of Law and Economics* 1; Veljanovski, 'Wealth Maximisation', 5; and L.A. Bebchuck, 'The Pursuit of a Bigger Pie: Can Everyone Expect a Bigger Slice?' (1980) 8 *Hofstra Law Review* 671.

the allocation of rights (one can only value if one has something to value with or else the valuation takes place in the realms of fantasy). Questions of justice, it follows, cannot be answered by economists' appeals to efficiency and distributional questions such as whether it is right to allow an extra unit of pollution (thus shifting the balance of rights from, say, river user A to polluting factory owner B) have to be made on the basis of grounds other than efficiency.[5]

This is not to say that efficiency may not be a factor to be taken into account in making regulatory judgements.[6] We may want to take on board the wealth implications of particular distributional choices when deciding, say, how to allocate rights between polluters and potential victims. What we should be wary of is using efficiency as a single measuring rod or justification for regulatory decisions. This will involve either circularity, as noted, or the assumption that the present distribution of wealth, together with a bias in favour of those with wealth, is acceptable.[7]

A further moral objection to wealth maximization relates to its implication that it is right to allow B to interfere with A's rights (e.g. by polluting their river or exposing them to a hazardous substance) if B generates enough wealth to compensate A for the harm done. Human beings, the objection runs, have certain basic rights that it would be morally objectionable to put up for sale. Certain risks, it might similarly be said, should not be imposed on individuals' lives no matter what the price, compensation, or wealth gain on offer.[8]

Five Criteria for Good Regulation

More plausible than wealth maximization is an approach to regulatory evaluation that involves looking at those arguments that have general currency when regulatory arrangements and performance are discussed in the public domain. Certain arguments have force in debating whether this or that

---

[5] For a statement of non-economic substantive goals that would justify regulation according to a 'civic republican' viewpoint see C. Sunstein, *After the Rights Revolution: Reconceiving the Regulatory State* (Cambridge MA, 1990).

[6] On economists' contributions see R. Cooter and T. Ulen, *Law and Economics* (Glenview, IL, 1988), ch. 1 and see Chapter 15, below, on the cost-benefit testing of regulation.

[7] Those possessing wealth will gain in efficiency-based decisions because they value rights more highly and are better placed than poorer persons to generate further wealth from the rights at issue: see C.E. Baker, 'The Ideology of the Economic Analysis of Law' (1975) 5 *Philosophy and Public Affairs* 3; G. Minda, 'Towards a More "Just" Economics of Justice—A Review Essay' (1989) 10 *Cardozo Law Review* 1855.

[8] For governmental acknowledgement of this point see HM Treasury, *The Setting of Safety Standards* (London, 1996), 9.

regulatory action or regime is worthy of support (is 'legitimate').[9] These arguments involve reference to one or more of five key tests:

- Is the action or regime supported by legislative authority?
- Is there an appropriate scheme of accountability?
- Are procedures fair, accessible, and open?
- Is the regulator acting with sufficient expertise?
- Is the action or regime efficient?

The five tests, or criteria, should be explained before their role in assessing regulation is discussed further.

THE LEGISLATIVE MANDATE

This criterion suggests that regulatory action deserves support when it is authorized by Parliament, the fountain of democratic authority. If the people, through Parliament, have instructed certain regulators to achieve result X, and those regulators can point to their having produced result X, then they are in a position to claim public support. They have fulfilled their mandate.[10]

It might be very proper to judge regulators according to their success in fulfilling their mandates. Unfortunately, however, it is seldom easy to state in precise terms what this should involve. Most regulatory statutes give regulators broad discretions and implementing the mandate thus involves interpretation.[11] A statute, for example, may order a regulator to protect the

---

[9] For governmental statements on the criteria for good regulation see Better Regulation Task Force (BRTF), *Principles of Good Regulation* (London, 2003). The principles are: Proportionality, Accountability, Consistency, Transparency, and Targeting; Department of the Taoiseach, *Regulating Better* (Dublin, 2004), www.betterregulation.ie (looking to necessity, effectiveness, proportionality, transparency, accountability, and consistency). See also the Australian government, *Department of Industry, Tourism and Resources: Regulatory Performance Indicators* (Canberra, 1999); S. Argy and M. Johnson, 'Mechanisms for Improving the Quality of Regulations: Australian Productivity Commission' (Staff Working Paper, July 2003). For Canada, see Treasury Board of Canada Secretariat, *Federal Regulatory Process Management Standards* (Ottawa, 1996). The World Bank view is set down in World Bank, *Doing Business in 2004: Understanding Regulation* (Washington, DC, and Oxford, 2004). See also OECD, *Guiding Principles for Regulatory Quality and Performance* (Paris, 2005). For other definitions of good or better regulation see Mandelkern Group on Better Regulation, *Final Report* (Brussels, 13 Nov. 2002) ('Mandelkern Report').

[10] If Parliament is yet to provide a mandate because no regulatory statute has been passed in an area— say, when a regulatory Bill is being debated—any discussion of 'good' regulation is more open-ended than usual. Reference, in such circumstances, is likely to be made to the four criteria other than the mandate that are discussed here and also to governmental claims to possess a mandate for a certain regulatory approach (based, for instance, on manifesto statements) and to more general arguments concerning social justice. See, for example, the Better Regulation Task Force's 2003 statement that good regulation should be: Proportionate, Accountable, Consistent, Transparent, and Targeted (Better Regulation Task Force, *Principles of Good Regulation* (London, 2003).

[11] See K.C. Davis, *Discretionary Justice* (Chicago, 1969), 39 and on British utilities see T. Prosser, *Law and the Regulators* (Oxford, 1997), 15–31. Lowi suggested that many US regulatory statutes were

interests of consumers, but it may be silent on the balance to be drawn between industrial and domestic or large and small consumers' interests.

Such statutes, moreover, often set out objectives that exist at mutual tension. Achieving certain objectives may necessarily involve trading off performance in relation to other stated objectives. Regulatory statutes, in addition, often give regulators scope for exercising judgement and devising solutions. (They do this because legislators generally have limited information and expertise in specialist areas and, though knowing that there is a problem, tend not to know how to solve it.) It is, in such cases, impossible to point to clear objectives. Legislators, furthermore, may deliberately avoid setting down precise objectives because they want regulators to have the freedom to cope with problems as they arise in the future—to meet the emergent challenges of new risks, innovative operations, novel technologies and so on. For all of these reasons, regulators are seldom, if ever, involved in the mechanical transmission of statutory objectives into results on the ground,[12] and the mandate benchmark, though of relevance, will rarely provide an easy answer to questions of legitimation.

ACCOUNTABILITY

Regulators with imprecise mandates may, nevertheless, claim that they deserve the support of the public because they are properly accountable to, and controlled by, democratic institutions. Thus, a regulatory agency might claim that it is accountable for its interpretation of its mandate to a representative body and that this oversight renders its exercise of powers acceptable.[13]

A difficulty with this criterion is that controversy will often attend the selection of the individuals and bodies that provide accountability. If Parliament itself or another elected institution is not the body holding the regulator to account, then the arrangement may be criticized as unrepresentative. Where control is exercised by certain institutions (e.g. courts), the competence of those institutions in specialist areas may also be called into question. Issues also arise as to the appropriate degree of accountability, the resources that should properly be devoted to accountability, and the acceptability of any trade-off between accountability and the effective pursuit of regulatory objectives.[14]

---

devoid of any meaningful guidelines—see T.J. Lowi, *The End of Liberalism* (1969 and 2nd edn, New York, 1979).

[12] On the 'transmission-belt' model of implementation and its inadequacies see R.B. Stewart, 'The Reformation of American Administrative Law' (1975) 88 *Harvard Law Review* 1667.

[13] See G.E. Frug, 'The Ideology of Bureaucracy in American Law' (1984) 97 *Harvard Law Review* 1277, 1355–61, 1334–9.

[14] On accountability generally, see Chapter 16 below and C. Graham, *Is There a Crisis in Regulatory Accountability?* (London, 1996).

DUE PROCESS

The basis of the due process claim is that public support is merited because the regulator uses procedures that are fair, accessible, and open. Thus, attention is paid to equality, fairness, and consistency of treatment, but also to the levels of participation that regulatory decisions and policy processes allow to the public, to consumers, and to other affected parties. The underlying rationale of such a claim is that proper democratic influence over regulation is ensured by due process being observed and that this influence has a legitimating effect.[15]

The criterion is, again, however, limited in so far as further guiding principles are required in order to explain, for example, who should be able to participate and in what manner. Trade-offs, once more, have to be made against the effective implementation of the mandate. Thus, more participation may lead to less effective decision-making and eventually to stagnation in the regulatory system. To expand participatory rights beyond a certain point may not, moreover, be consistent with the development and exercise of appropriate levels of expertise and judgement.

Disputes may also arise concerning the acceptable *mode* of participation. Lawyers, for instance, may see certain (perhaps formal or trial-type) methods of participation as appropriate in circumstances that those from other disciplines (e.g. political science or economics) might see as calling for quite different arrangements.

EXPERTISE

Certain regulatory functions may require the exercise of expert judgement. This is liable to be the case where the decision-maker has to consider a number of competing options or values and come to a balanced judgement on incomplete and shifting information. In these circumstances, the regulator may claim support on the basis of his or her expertise, and the nature of the task at hand, rather then offering to give reasons, or justifications. 'Trust to my expertise' is the essence of such a claim.[16] Experts thus assert that they will come to the most appropriate decision and achieve the best results most rapidly when freed from duties of explanation.

One problem with this test is that it may be difficult for the public to assess whether the decisions or policies arrived at have been produced by the application of expertise. Claims of expertise may also be questionable where

---

[15] See Stewart, 'Reformation', 1667.

[16] For a defence of expertise, see J.M. Landis, *The Administrative Process* (New Haven, 1938); for discussion see J. Mashaw, *Bureaucratic Justice* (New Haven, 1983), 26–9.

the expert fails to explain why *this* issue demands expert judgement (a communications failure that the expert may say flows from the lack of expertise of the lay public). A natural distrust by lay persons of those who lay claim to expertise also serves to undermine demands of support from specialists. This may be the case particularly where experts refuse to give full reasons for their actions, deny access to decision-making processes, or pursue narrow and arcane modes of analysis. Conflicts of opinion between experts again affect their credibility. Nor can it be assumed that experts are neutral—decisions involving judgements will inevitably have a political aspect as competing interests are affected by regulation and as tensions are resolved in a particular manner.

Within the 'risk society', it can be argued, the case for trusting to experts grows ever weaker. Commentators such as Beck and Giddens[17] argue that in risk society traditional securities can no longer be relied on, and that, increasingly, society is preoccupied with the future and 'manufactured risks'—those that are produced by mankind, not nature, and which stem from technological advances so as to create new risk environments for which history provides us with very little previous experience. The resultant uncertainties, it is argued, cannot be 'solved' by further scientific advances. Experience, accordingly, tells us more and more often that we cannot rely on experts to guide us in our choices, but must insist on a new political dialogue built on the death of deference to those claiming special expertise.

EFFICIENCY

A regulator may claim support on the basis of acting efficiently and, in doing so, may make two kinds of claim. The first of these urges support on the basis that the legislative mandate is being implemented at the least possible level of inputs or costs and there is productive efficiency.[18] This, of course, is a claim afflicted by all the problems discussed above in relation to the mandate—notably those arising from the imprecision of that mandate. It is particularly difficult to measure efficiency when the mandate fails to set down consistent or coherent objectives,[19] or where a regulator's functions intermesh with those

---

[17] For concise reviews of issues see U. Beck, 'The Politics of Risk Society' and A. Giddens, 'Risk Society: The Context of British Politics', both in J. Franklin (ed.), *The Politics of Risk Society* (Cambridge, 1998). See also U. Beck, *Risk Society* (London, 1992); id., *The Reinvention of Politics* (Cambridge, 1997); A. Giddens, *Beyond Left and Right* (Cambridge, 1994).

[18] One can distinguish effectiveness as addressing the issue of whether desired results are actually achieved (irrespective of costs).

[19] See C.G. Veljanovski, 'Cable Television: Agency Franchising and Economics', in Baldwin and McCrudden, *Regulation and Public Law*.

of other agencies and departments.[20] It is difficult, moreover, to assert that a particular method of regulating achieves 'better' results than alternative methods when the latter have not been put to the test in the relevant arena.

A second version of the efficiency claim urges support on the basis that the regulation at issue leads to results that are efficient—as judged by criteria set down with a degree of independence from the mandate. Reference might thus be made to the regulatory regime's allocative efficiency (whether it is impossible to redistribute goods to make at least one consumer better off without making another consumer worse off) and its dynamic efficiency (whether there is encouragement of desirable process and product innovation and whether the system produces flexible responses to changes in demand).[21]

Leaving aside the problem of showing that alternative systems would not offer superior performance, such claims present difficulties because, as noted, efficiency is not a value independent of distributional considerations and efficiency in itself provides no answers on distributional issues or in defining the regulatory mandate. The pursuit of efficiency may, indeed, conflict with legislative statements on distributional matters and, accordingly, the appropriateness of efficiency claims may be especially questionable in those spheres of regulation where distributive concerns are central.[22]

The extent of a conflict between efficiency and social or distributional objectives may itself be a matter of dispute. Thus, Prosser[23] has contested Foster's[24] view that the performance of British utilities regulators should be judged according to the benchmark of efficiency. The objection is that the main utilities statutes do not make maximizing economic efficiency an overriding regulatory goal and that a series of social obligations and non-economic ends (such as are implied in the concept of universal service) are legislative objectives of at least equal importance—that regulatory goals are 'mixed and include irretrievably varied rationales, economic and social'.[25]

---

[20] See J. Black, 'Decentring Regulation: The Role of Regulation and Self-Regulation in a "Post-Regulatory World"' (2001) *Current Legal Problems* 103–46.

[21] See Cooter and Ulen, *Law and Economics*, 17–18; R. Baldwin and M. Cave, *Franchising as a Tool of Government* (London, 1996), section 4.1.

[22] See R. Baldwin and C.C. Veljanovski, 'Regulation by Cost Benefit Analysis' (1984) 62 *Public Administration* 51.

[23] See Prosser, *Law and the Regulators*, 15–24; 'Regulation and Social Solidarity' (2006) 33 *Journal of Law and Society* 364–87.

[24] C. Foster, *Privatisation, Public Ownership and the Regulation of Natural Monopoly* (Oxford, 1992), ch. 9.

[25] Prosser, *Law and the Regulators*, 24. See also Chapter 2, above, on rationales for regulating and Chapter 15, below, on the application of cost-benefit testing to regulation.

The Role of the Five Criteria

The above five claims, it can be seen, are all fraught with difficulties but collectively they constitute a set of benchmarks for assessing regulatory regimes. These are the rationales that are employed and have currency in real-life debates on regulation and its reform.[26] Arguments in support of (or arguments criticizing) regulators that do not fall under these five headings will be deemed irrelevant by most members of the public. Thus, if I argue that the Director General of OFGEM should be supported in her work because she is kind to animals or gives to charity, this will be seen as missing the point. If I say that she deserves support since she is achieving her statutory objectives, acting in a fully accountable, open, and fair manner, bringing expertise to bear, and making good use of her resources, these are likely to be seen as relevant assertions.

Judging the extent to which regulation is legitimate is not to offer a sociological assessment of the actual support that a regulator enjoys (this might have been achieved by good public relations or even misrepresentation); it is, rather, to offer an assessment of the legitimacy that a regulator *deserves*.[27] What matters is the collective justificatory power of the arguments that can be made under the five headings. Strong claims across the board point to regulation that deserves support; generally, weak claims indicate a low capacity to justify.

How, though, can trade-offs between claims be dealt with? How can it be said whether a weakening of rights of participation in return for improvements in satisfying the statutory mandate is a good or a bad thing?[28] The answer is that, at the end of the day, the weight that individuals place on each legitimating argument will reflect their personal political philosophies and, in the absence of all universal agreement on the nature of an ideal world, persons will differ on matters of weighting. As for corporate bodies, these will vary in sizes, market positions, cultures, and so on and, accordingly, they may be expected to differ in the way that they weight different criteria when conceiving of good regulation. What different individuals and corporations may agree on more fully, however, is the set of relevant benchmarks themselves. Any perusal of debates on regulation will reveal their exclusive usage—though different labels may be used to designate those criteria.[29]

---

[26] See Baldwin, *Rules and Government*, 47.
[27] See R. Barker, *Political Legitimacy and the State* (Oxford, 1990), 20–7; D. Beetham, *The Legitimation of Power* (London, 1991), 13.
[28] See Baldwin, *Rules and Government*, ch. 3, for a more extended discussion, and for comment on such an approach see T. Prosser's book review of *Rules and Government* at (1996) 59 *MLR* 762–5.
[29] For examples see Baldwin, *Rules and Government*, 47.

This means that, short of those discussing regulation simply exposing their political differences, much can still be said in making assessments of regulatory performance. It can be asked, notably, whether performance on one of the five fronts can be improved significantly without material loss on another. (This kind of discussion is the meat and drink of most regulatory debates.)

Where policy choices involve trade-offs between furthering the different criteria, a determination of that choice will demand reference to a political philosophy or position. Designers or reformers of regulation should bear in mind, however, that performance under some headings (e.g. the legislative mandate) may be linked, under certain conditions, to performance under other headings (e.g. fairness and openness of processes). Thus, if a regulatory regime is perceived by the public or industry to be unfair, the regulator may enjoy low levels of co-operation, and this may impede performance in satisfying the mandate. This means that a reformer may not have the option of effecting an extreme trade-off between fairness or openness and more efficiency in achieving mandated ends—public reaction will stand in the way of achieving this efficiency. The implication is that, whatever the philosophy of the regulatory designer or reformer, that individual or institution should be wary of endorsing regulatory designs that score conspicuously badly on any of the five tests. Performance, as judged on the other criteria, may be affected detrimentally by such a course of action.

How, then, can legitimacy be improved in the real world? The answer is by taking steps to improve ratings according to the five tests. To give some brief examples, under the mandate, measures could be taken to improve the clarity of the mandate and to achieve agreement on its terms. A regulatory body could, thus, publish its vision of the mandate and hold discussions and consultations on this. Such steps will lend legitimacy to the regulator's vision of the mandate. Alternatively, regulators and ministers could, at periodic intervals, jointly produce statements of aims in explanation of the mandate and these could be put to Parliament for approval.[30] Regulators' claims to be properly accountable might be improved by such steps as the creation of a specialist parliamentary select committee (a Select Committee on Regulated Industries) or by strengthened (perhaps publicly funded) standing consumer bodies for specific industries or products. Due process claims could be improved by reforms to increase information flows and participation in regulatory decisions and policymaking and there might, for instance, be a role for statutory or court-mandated requirements that regulatory rules be disclosed whenever they are in operation. Expertise claims might be reinforced by legislative or administrative actions to designate those issues that are matters of judgement for the regulator and by improving levels of training

---

[30] For discussion of ministerial policy guidance systems, see R. Baldwin, *Regulating the Airlines* (Oxford, 1985), ch. 9, and below, Chapter 16.

and resources where these are inadequate. Efficiency claims might be strengthened by taking steps to clarify the mandate and by improving flows of information to the public. Whether cost-benefit testing of regulation has a role on this front is discussed in Chapter 15.

To summarize: regulatory regimes and actions can be assessed by making judgements about the merits of legitimating claims under the five headings set out. To assess in this manner is not to evaluate the moral correctness or legality of the regulatory action or regime, but to make a judgement as to its worthiness of public support. In making that judgement, personal visions have to be tempered by considering the responses of other parties. Assessing regulation thus involves areas of agreement (on benchmarks) but also of divergence (on the weighting of different desiderata). Debates on the merits of particular regulatory approaches and of potential reforms can, nevertheless, make fruitful use of the five benchmarks, and these criteria will be referred to throughout the course of this book.

Measuring Regulatory Quality

If 'good regulation' is to be pursued, it is essential that there is a capacity to measure not merely the quality of regulation but also the performance of regulatory improvement tools, institutions, and policies.[31] Many governments look to assess the quality of regulation, but the OECD has also conducted 'ex post evaluations of regulatory tools and institutions'.[32] Both kinds of measurement are required because policymakers will need to know both whether regulation is acceptable in quality and whether this is due to the regulatory improvement steps that they are taking—rather than due to other causes, such as the independent activities of regulators or the actions of self-regulatory bodies, regulated firms, or supra-governmental bodies.

---

[31] See also the discussion of the 'Better Regulation' movement in Chapter 15 below. For discussions of performance measurement in UK government see, e.g., Office of Government Commerce, *How to Manage Performance* (Stationery Office, 2002), www.ogc.gov.uk; Audit Commission, *Aiming to Improve: The Principles of Performance Measurement* (June 2000), www.audit-commission.gov.uk/reports/AC-REPORT; Audit Commission, *On Target: The Practice of Performance Indicators* (2000), www.audit-commission.gov.uk; HM Treasury, *Executive Agencies: A Guide to Setting Targets and Measuring Performance* (HMSO, 1992); NAO, *Good Practice in Performance Reporting in Executive Agencies and Non-Departmental Public Bodies* (2000), www.nao.gov.uk; Comptroller and Auditor General, *Measuring the Performance of Government Departments* (2000–01 HC 301, 22 March 2001), www.nao.gov.uk.

[32] OECD, *Regulatory Performance: Ex Post Evaluation of Regulatory Tools and Institutions*, Working Party on Regulatory Management and Reform, 60V/PGC/Reg (Paris, 2004).

The measurement of regulatory quality and regulatory improvement tool performance, however, is extremely challenging for a number of reasons.[33] A first of these is that measuring regulatory quality (and tool or policy or institutional performance) depends not merely on the benchmarks that are seen as relevant but also on the policy objectives at issue and the balance between different objectives or benchmarks that is seen as appropriate.[34] As has been seen in the discussion above, these are contentious issues, and conceptions of quality are likely to vary according to audience, constituency, market position, or even discipline—even where there is broad agreement on the criteria that are relevant to quality assessments. This will usually be due to divergent weightings of the various criteria. Professional economists may, for instance, stress the pursuit of efficiency, citizens and politicians may emphasize the importance of furthering accountability, transparency, and other process values, and certain firms may place special value on such matters as international competitiveness or potential for growth.

A second challenge is independent of issues about chosen benchmarks and can be summarized in the question: Which aspect of regulation is to be measured? Attention here might focus on the particular task that the regulator is carrying out.[35] Thus, one object of measurement might be the quality of the detection work done by the regulator, another might be the quality of policies and rules produced, and another might be the regulator's performance in implementing those policies and rules. Further targets of measurement might be the regulatory regime's dynamism and its capacity to adapt to change. Another way of breaking down the different aspects of regulation to be measured is to use a four-part division into inputs, processes, outputs, and outcomes.[36] Input-based assessment of performance is common and looks to such matters as numbers of inspectors and inspections, and the resources that are devoted to control. Process- or compliance-based assessment is also carried out frequently, and this measures adherence to procedural requirements and other laws, policies, or guidelines. What are

---

[33] Radaelli and De Francesco, *Regulatory Quality in Europe.*

[34] S. Weatherill, 'The Challenge of Better Regulation' in S. Weatherill, *Better Regulation* (Oxford, 2007), 4.

[35] See the DREAM framework of tasks discussed in Chapter 11 below.

[36] Performance evaluation is a key part of the better regulation agenda: see, e.g., NAO, *Measuring the Performance of Government Departments* (London, 2001); OECD, *Results-based Management in the Development Co-operation Agencies: A View of Experience* (OECD, 1999); OECD, Working Party on Regulatory Management and Reform, *Regulatory Performance: Ex Post Evaluation of Regulatory Tools and Institutions*, GOV/PGC/REG (2006)6 (OECD, 2004). On the difficulties of assessing performance see e.g. P. Hopkinson, P. James, and A. Sammut, 'Environmental Performance Evaluation in the Water Industry of England and Wales' (2000) 43(6) *Journal of Environmental Planning and Management* 873–96; on responses to performance evaluation see e.g. S. Modell, 'Performance Measurement and Institutional Processes: A Study of Managerial Responses to Public Sector Reform' (2001) (12) *Management Accounting Research* 437; G. Bevan and C. Hood, 'What's Measured is What Matters: Targets and Gaming in the English Healthcare System' (2006) 84(3) *Public Administration* 517.

less common are output-based assessments—which measure the extent to which the goals of the specific programme are achieved—and outcome-based assessments, which evaluate the impact of the regulatory system against the broad objectives of the agency (rather than the specific programme). In moving from input measurement to process, output, and outcome evaluation the value of any findings is likely to rise (as the link to regulatory objectives strengthens), but the difficulty and cost of the measurement process will escalate as the connection between regulatory action and effect on the ground becomes more difficult to establish.

Almost as much contention may arise regarding the targets of measurement as in relation to the balances of benchmark criteria to be used in measurement—or, indeed, the policy outcomes that are to be set up as the overall framework for any assessment. A look at the way that different governments measure regulatory quality shows the degree to which they can vary in targeting their assessments. As Radaelli and De Francesco point out, the Dutch and Belgian regimes, for instance, focus their evaluations on administrative burdens and regulatory complexity[37] and this stands in stark contrast with the systems encountered in the USA and Canada, which look more directly to regulatory outcomes and net benefits for citizens.[38]

A third challenge of measurement is encapsulated in the question: Whose regulatory performance is being assessed? As is made clear from numerous regulatory theories ranging from 'regulatory space' and 'smart' to 'network' and 'decentred' accounts,[39] much modern regulation is carried out within networks of controls that involve numbers of different kinds of regulators, control devices, and policies. In regimes that are 'decentred', 'polycentric', or 'networked', it cannot be presupposed that it is possible, unproblematically, to measure the discrete system of control that is operated by a target regulator, regulatory strategy, policy, or tool—regulatory processes and outputs may result from cumulations of regulatory systems that may vary from issue to issue regarding their constituting elements and the degrees of coordination or disharmony within the network. Efforts to measure regulatory quality have, accordingly, to come to grips with complex issues regarding ascriptions of responsibility for those aspects of performance that are focused upon for the purposes of measurement. Those issues will inevitably prove to be not only complicated but politically controversial.

---

[37] See also J. Torriti, 'The Standard Cost Model' in Weatherill, *Better Regulation.*
[38] Radaelli and De Francesco, *Regulatory Quality in Europe,* ch. 4.
[39] See L. Hancher and M. Moran, 'Organising Regulatory Space' in L. Hancher and M. Moran, (eds), *Capitalism, Culture and Economic Regulation* (Oxford, 1989); C. Scott, 'Analysing Regulatory Space' [2001] *Public Law* 329; N. Gunningham and P. Grabosky, *Smart Regulation* (Oxford, 1998); J. Black, J 'Decentring Regulation: Understanding the Role of Regulation and Self-regulation in a 'Post-regulatory' World' (2001) 54 *Current Legal Problems* 103–46.

A further difficulty flows from decentred regulatory regimes and affects efforts to legitimate and to measure performance within these. If it is the case that a regulatory regime involves numbers of regulators of different kinds— state and non-state, national and trans-national, public interest and private/ commercial—there are likely to be complex interactions of legitimation claims, numbers of competing conceptions of regulatory quality, and a variety of processes for furthering legitimation claims.[40] In addition, the jurisdictional boundaries between different regulators may be both overlapping and unclear, and the mandates being pursued by different bodies may diverge.

Such complexities pose huge challenges in assessing the legitimacy and performance of either individual regulators or the collectivity of controlling bodies that impacts on a given area. There is, indeed, no easy answer here, but an understanding of these challenges is, according to Black, furthered by taking on board three key features of legitimation within polycentric regimes: first, it involves organizations that are institutionally associated or 'embedded' and relationships within this institutional environment that shape the construction and contestation of legitimacy; second, communications about legitimacy are dialectical—the processes of explanation and justification are shaped by not only those making legitimation claims but also those to whom such claims are addressed, and, third, the communicative structures in which legitimacy claims are constituted and articulated will themselves mould the nature of those claims.[41] For regulators who seek to justify their actions within polycentric regimes, the most pressing problem that they may face is that they engage in a variety of discourses in an attempt to satisfy a variety of different regulatory communities, but that they find themselves unable to reconcile the conflicting demands made by those communities.[42]

Conclusions

What constitutes 'good regulation' is difficult to establish and is a matter that is inevitably subject to contention. Commentators and governments

---

[40] See J. Black, 'Constructing and Contesting Legitimacy and Accountability in Polycentric Regulatory Regimes' (2008) *Regulation and Governance* 137–64 and see Chapter 16 below on accountability. It is arguable that most regulatory regimes will possess some degree of polycentricity—see Black, 'Constructing', 157.

[41] Black, 'Constructing', 157 argues: 'Accountability tools are not neutral technical instruments but discursive technologies embodying their own logics and interpretive schemes, and can have constitutive and transformative effects.'

[42] Black, 'Constructing', 157–8.

alike have tended to avoid setting out precise, substantive blueprints and, instead, have tended to set down lists of qualities that are thought to be desirable in a good regulatory regime. This approach possesses the considerable advantage that cumulations of criteria allow parties with divergent interests and politics to engage in debates on regulatory quality by agreeing roughly on the relevant evaluatory benchmarks (Table 3.1)—even if they disagree on balances between these and on final substantive outcomes.

A disadvantage of cumulations of benchmarks is, as noted above, that divergent and inconsistent approaches to the pursuit of regulatory quality can be encountered not merely between different jurisdictions, but within individual governmental programmes. There is no 'single vision', and this can lead governments to spin out policies that undermine each other as one strand of policy piles on top of another.[43]

The way forward is not, perhaps, to abandon the use of multiple criteria in evaluating regulatory quality—numerous governments are wedded to these, and a single vision would both prove unacceptable to different states, interests, or individuals, and would be excessively restrictive. What is needed is an effort to deal more rigorously with trade-offs between objectives and values. As for measurement issues, it is clear that newly rigorous processes have to be instituted for assessing the performance of both regulatory regimes and regulatory improvement tools, policies, and institutions. Those evaluative processes have to be capable of dealing more openly than at present with the different conceptions of 'good' regulation that are spread across societies and markets, and also with differences of view on those aspects of regulation that it is appropriate to measure. Evaluations, moreover, have to come to grips with the 'ascription of responsibility' issues that were noted in discussing networked regulatory regimes.

---

[43] See C. Radaelli, *Memorandum to the Regulatory Reform Committee* (HC 2007–8, Fifth Report of Session Volume II: Evidence 190–2), p. 191—pointing to significant tensions between numbers of regulatory improvement initiatives within the UK and the EU—as between the espousal of Impact Assessment processes and desires for less intrusive regulatory styles, and between efforts to set enforcement on a data-rich risk basis and prescriptions on the reducing of informational burdens on business. On such tensions see also R. Baldwin, 'Better Regulation: Tensions Aboard the Enterprise' in Weatherill, *Better Regulation*.

Table 3.1. Benchmarks for regulation

Claim to legitimacy	Essence of claim	Problems
Legislative mandate	Authorization from elected legislature.	Parliament's intention may be vague.
		Stated objectives for regulation may exist in tension or conflict.
		Parliament may have delegated the power to flesh-out objectives.
		Large discretions may be given to regulators.
Accountability or control	Regulator is properly accountable and controlled and so is democratically responsive.	Is the body holding to account properly representative?
		Is the trade-off of accountability and efficiency acceptable?
Due process	Support is merited because procedures are sufficiently fair, accessible, and open, to expose to democratic influence.	Who should be allowed to participate?
		What is the acceptable trade-off between openness or accessibility and efficiency?
		Is the *mode* of participation appropriate?
Expertise	'Trust to my expertise' because a judgement has to be made on the basis of a number of factors and variables and specialized knowledge skills and experience have to be applied.	Public is poorly positioned to evaluate expertise.
		Difficult for expert to explain reasoning or judgement to lay persons.
		General distrust of experts and arcane language.
		Public desire for openness and accountability.
		Conflicts between experts undermine public confidence.
		Public may see experts as self-interested or captured.
		Public sceptical of neutrality of regulatory decisions where certain parties gain advantages.
Efficiency	Legislative mandate is being implemented efficiently.	See problems of legislative mandate claims.
	Efficient results are produced.	Conflicts with legislative mandate may arise.
		Distributional questions may be begged or left out of account.
		Measuring efficiency is difficult.

4 Explaining Regulation

In explaining how regulation arises, develops, and declines, a number of broad approaches can be adopted.[1] These approaches may set out merely to describe and account for regulatory developments, they may be prescriptive and offer a view on how regulation *should* be organized, or they may serve a combination of these functions. Similarly, accounts of regulation may constitute commentaries on regulatory developments that are delivered with detachment from the sidelines or, together with their proponents, they may participate on the field of play and, intentionally or otherwise, may themselves contribute to regulatory changes.

In looking at explanations of regulation, one can distinguish between those approaches that emphasize exogenous (external) factors that shape the evolution of regulation (such as the force of interest groups, dominant ideas, or the underlying nature of the economy) and those emphasizing endogenous factors such as institutional cultures.

This chapter's discussion progresses in four parts. First, we consider various 'interest'-based accounts (both 'public interest', and 'interest group' approaches). Then, we move to accounts that stress the importance of 'ideas' and of 'institutions'. Such an approach to classifying the literature allows us to consider not only the relative emphases that particular explanations place on the role of exogenous or internal factors, but also the political and practical influence of those explanations or schools of thought and the nature and origins of the forces that drive such explanations.

At the end of the chapter, we examine how (and whether) the different kinds of analysis can be combined to enhance understandings and explanations of regulatory actions and change.

Public Interest Theories

Public interest theories centre on the idea that those seeking to institute or develop regulation do so in pursuit of public interest-related objectives

---

[1] For early reviews of the myriad varieties of regulatory theory see B. Mitnick, *The Political Economy of Regulation* (New York, 1980), ch. 3 and R. Horwitz, *The Irony of Regulatory Reform: The Deregulation of the American Telecommunications Industry* (Oxford, 1989).

(rather than group, sector, or individual self-interests).[2] Proponents of regulation are thus seen as acting as benevolent agents for the public interest.[3] Regulation's purpose is to achieve certain publicly desired results in circumstances where, for instance, the market would fail to yield these. (The grounds given for such action are likely to involve reference to one or more of the reasons for regulating outlined in Chapter 2.)[4]

Consistent with such a vision is an emphasis on the trustworthiness and disinterestedness of expert regulators in whose public-spiritedness and efficiency the public can have confidence.[5] It is a vision that implies a highly benevolent view of political processes. It assumes some form of objective knowledge that can establish the presence of 'market failures' and that can respond with the appropriate instruments. The 'public interest' world is a world in which bureaucracies do not protect or expand their turf, in which politicians do not seek to enhance their electoral or other career prospects, in which decision-making rules do not determine decisions, and a world in which business and other interest groups do not seek special exemptions or privileges.[6] In short, this is a world of few transaction costs and institutional biases. Instead, regulation is based on some form of dispassionate expertise and objective standards. On such a view there can, for example, be a non-error-prone and unslanted statement on whether industry is investing in infrastructure in order to protect security of supply. The public interest approach also assumes the possibility of unproblematic enforcement and compliance.

Not surprisingly, a number of problems, theoretical, practical, and political, beset this public interest view of the regulatory process. A first difficulty is that an agreed conception of the public interest may be hard to identify.

[2] See M.E. Levine and J.L. Forrence, 'Regulatory Capture, Public Interest and the Public Agenda: Towards Synthesis' (1990) *Journal of Law, Economics, and Organization* 167; M. Hantke-Domas, 'The Public Interest Theory of Regulation: Non-Existence or Misinterpretation?' (2003) 15 *European Journal of Law and Economics* 165–94; B. Morgan and K. Yeung, *An Introduction to Law and Regulation* (Cambridge, 2007), ch. 2.

[3] See e.g. J.M. Landis, *The Administrative Process* (New Haven, 1938); R.E. Cushman, *The Independent Regulatory Commissions* (New York, 1941). For a British public interest account, see I. McLean and C. Foster, 'The Political Economy of Regulation: Interests, Ideology, Voters and the UK Regulation of Railways Act 1844' (1992) 70 *Public Administration* 313–31 at 329: 'Our test of seven hypotheses about the origins of regulation has shown that the best-supported is that both Gladstone and the MPs who voted on his bill were moved by their perceptions of the public interest.' I. McLean, 'The History of Regulation in the United Kingdom: Three Case Studies in Search of a Theory' in J. Jordana and D. Levi-Faur (eds), *The Politics of Regulation* (Cheltenham, 2004).

[4] Public interest visions of regulation may complement 'functionalist' accounts of regulatory origins and developments in so far as functionalism sees regulation as largely driven by the nature of the task at hand (as identified in terms of public needs and interests) rather than by private, individual, or self-interests.

[5] See Landis, *Administrative Process*.

[6] B. Barry, *Political Argument* (London, 1965), ch. 11.2; J.W. Roxbee Cox, 'The Appeal to the Public Interest' (1973) 3 *British Journal of Political Science* 229–41.

Instead, as many might contend, regulation generally takes place amidst a clashing of images of the public interest, as implied in the previous paragraph. Public interest theories are said to fail to take into account such clashes and to lack both a suitable understanding of politics and an appreciation of the inherently contested nature of knowledge.[7] Interest groups, the critics say, can be expected to clash over such matters as the distribution of benefits and costs of regulatory instruments.

A further problem stems from doubts concerning the disinterestedness, expertise, and efficiency that the public interest approach attributes to regulators.[8] Regulators may succumb to venality and be corrupted by opportunities for personal profit so that regulation is biased by the pursuit of personal interests, as will be explored below.[9] Regulators, in the alternative, may be accused of tendencies to act in pursuit of their own institutional ends by protecting and expanding their jurisdictional turf. Doubts may also be cast on the competence of regulators, which may not be sufficiently high to yield public interest ends—perhaps because rewards and career structures may lack the requisite attractiveness or because training needs and disciplinary emphases are poorly attended to.[10] Finally, capture theorists, discussed in more detail below, may suggest that public interest theory understates the degree to which economic and political power influences regulation. Thus, it is argued that regulatory polices and institutions often become (or, in some versions, begin life) subject to the influence of powerful regulated parties, or even politicians or sectors of consumers, so that regulation serves the interests of these parties or sectors, rather than those of the wider public.[11]

Even for those capture theorists who are prepared to concede that regulatory regimes are sometimes established in pursuit of public interest objectives, the public interest vision may only be persuasive in relation to the earliest stages of the life-cycle of regulatory affairs.[12]

Regarding results,[13] the public interest perspective is prone to attack on the basis that regulation often seems to fail to deliver public interest outcomes. Some observers see this as an indication that appropriate lessons must be

---

[7] See J.G. Francis, *The Politics of Regulation: A Comparative Perspective* (Oxford, 1993), 8. On the public interest as a balancing of different interests; as a compromising approach or a trade-off concept; or as national, social, or particularistic goals, see Mitnick, *Political Economy of Regulation*, 92–3.

[8] See G. Stigler, 'The Theory of Economic Regulation' (1971) 2 *Bell Journal of Economics* 3; G. Kolko, *Railroads and Regulation* (Princeton, 1965); Mitnick, *Political Economy of Regulation*, 111–20.

[9] Mitnick, *Political Economy of Regulation*, 94.

[10] See Landis, *Administrative Process*, 66.

[11] See E. S. Redford, *Administration of National Economic Control* (London, 1952), 251–2.

[12] See M.H. Bernstein, *Regulating Business by Independent Commission* (New York, 1955) (life-cycle theory is discussed below at p. 47).

[13] On which the most telling comment is perhaps that of newly appointed football manager John Bond, who said: 'I promise results, not promises'. Quoted, B. Fantoni, *Private Eye's Colemanballs* (London, 1982).

learned from failures so that better regulatory regimes can be designed.[14] The message for others is that regulation is doomed to failure and that policies of deregulation should be looked to.

Nevertheless, the public interest—or 'benevolent'—approach continues to be defended by some commentators, who argue for the development rather than abandonment of this vision.[15] Stephen Breyer, for example, suggests that it is useful to maintain a normative approach that considers 'what reasonable human goals a program might sensibly have, regardless of its historical origins. It assumes that regulators seek in good faith to attain such goals, regardless of the existence of other possible motives in fact.'[16]

Interest Group Theories

A second broad approach to regulation stresses the extent to which regulatory developments are driven not by the pursuit of public interest but by the particularistic concerns of interest groups. This approach (partly alluded to in the previous section) has most prominently been associated with the so-called 'economic theory of regulation' (often also linked to labels such as private interest, Chicago/Virginia school, public choice, special interest and 'capture' theory). We consider the 'economic theory' first before moving to other social science traditions that similarly stress the importance of interest groups in the regulatory process.

The *economic theory of regulation* builds on the assumption that actors are inherently self-regarding and orientated at maximizing their own (material) interest. It assumes that all parties involved in regulation seek to maximize their utility (self-interest) (politicians, for instance, seeking votes to maximize their cash incomes); it assumes that all parties are as well informed as possible and learn from experience; and it also assumes that regulation is costless (hence overall efficiency will not be affected by levels of regulation).[17]

Most prominent among these accounts is the capture argument. The idea of capture is primarily associated with George Stigler, who suggested that: 'as a rule regulation is acquired by the industry and is designed and operated primarily for its benefit'.[18] Accordingly, regulation is inherently

---

[14] See C.R. Sunstein, 'Paradoxes of the Regulatory State' (1990) 57 *University of Chicago Law Review* 407.

[15] See C. Sunstein, *After the Rights Revolution* (Cambridge, MA, 1990).

[16] Breyer, *Regulation*, 10.

[17] S. Peltzman, 'Towards a More General Theory of Regulation' (1976) 19 *Journal of Law and Economics* 211.

[18] Stigler, 'Theory of Economic Regulation', 3; see also G. Kolko, *The Triumph of Conservatism* (New York, 1977).

about (degrees of) 'capture'. According to the orthodox accounts of the economic theory of regulation,[19] where there is a failure of competition, or the existence of monopoly, there will be monopoly profit and the legislature will give the regulator the power to dispose of these economic monopoly rents. The regulated industry thus will have an incentive to influence the regulator so as to benefit from a 'regulatory rent', and there will be a market for regulation. This means that the regulator will be captured by the industry, since industry will have more to lose or gain than the regulator. Compact, organized interests (say, solicitors) will usually win at the expense of a diffused group (say, users of legal services). The commodity of regulation will go to those who value it most, and producers will thus tend to be better served by regulation than the (more diffused, less organized) masses of consumers.

In other words, the regulatory process is seen as characterized by a collective action problem—only concentrated interests with a high material stake will tend to succeed in instituting collective action. Diffuse interests (such as 'citizens at large') will rarely manage to mobilize. The regulator is, in turn, seen as a politician-regulator who is largely interested in re-election. When faced with the choice of courting electoral support from voters and increasing the potential campaign contributions of a powerful (concentrated) industry that seeks regulatory protections, this politician-regulator will err on the side of industry and will take comfort in the (at most) low number of votes that are likely to be lost from this decision. He or she, for example, would tend to choose to increase campaign donations by awarding a monopoly license for cement imports, rather than to protect potential house-purchasers from inflated costs by taking action to ensure competition in building supplies.

A number of modifications and variations in the economic theory of regulation have been put forward. For example, according to Peltzman, the regulatory process will to some extent reflect wider social interests—but will still be dominated by the regulated interest. Gary Becker, in contrast, has argued that once an industry has successfully captured the monopoly rents from any particular regulatory intervention, this will trigger countervailing interests to mobilize to contest the acquired rents. In the end, no 'monopoly rent' will survive.[20] Such a view of interests mobilizing and

---

[19] Stigler, 'Theory of Economic Regulation', 3; see also R. Posner, 'Natural Monopoly and Regulation' (1969) 21 *Stanford Law Review.* 548; id., 'Theories of Economic Regulation' (1974) 5 *Bell. Journal of Economics* 335; W.A. Jordan, 'Producer Protection, Prior Market Structure and the Effects of Government Regulation' (1992) 15 *Journal of Law and Economics* 151; E.D. Bó, 'Regulatory Capture: A Review' (2006) 22(2) *Oxford Review of Economic Policy* 203–25; J. Light, 'Public Choice: A Critical Reassessment' in E.J. Balleisen and D.A. Moss (eds), *Government and Markets* (Cambridge, 2010).

[20] G. Becker, 'A Theory of Competition among Pressure Groups for Political Influence' (1983) 98 *Quarterly Journal of Economics* 371.

counter-mobilizing, however, tends to assume an equal ability of interests to mobilize, and this has been regarded with considerable scepticism.[21]

Sam Peltzman further reassessed the economic approach by exploring regulatory developments that seemed, at first sight, to go against 'capture' orthodoxy, namely those developments witnessed in the period between the mid-1970s and mid-1980s.[22] He argued that regulation tends to produce incentives for firms to dissipate their wealth (e.g. when faced with controlled prices at a time when costs increase) and that regulatory rents can be eradicated by regulation itself. A point can thus arrive when a return to the position prior to regulation becomes more attractive to regulated parties than continued regulation. Therefore, according to Peltzman, the economic theory of regulation can tell a coherent story about most of the examples of deregulation (suggesting these are explicable due to the *disruption* of regulatory rents); it does, nevertheless, leave some important questions unanswered— for instance, about 'the design of institutions and their adaptability'.[23]

Other accounts highlight the problematic nature of focusing on a 'politician-regulator' and the assumption that such political actors will follow interests in a 'weathervane' fashion. For example, Barke and Riker focus on the importance of political interests, and argue that regulation has to be understood as a process through which political actors built coalitions.[24] Hirshleifer expands the notion of pursued self-interests by stressing the importance of taking the bureaucratic interests of regulators into account.[25]

As with the wider 'public choice' approach in social science, approaches inspired by the economic theory of regulation have been open to question on a number of fronts.[26] Thus, explaining the nature and origins of preferences in the posited 'markets' for regulation proves difficult. Parties may lack determinate (or consistent) preferences on political or regulatory issues and individuals may behave altruistically in certain important respects. They may, for instance, identify with legislative, group, agency, or bureaucratic objectives and may behave in different ways according to the roles they adopt as, say, consumers of services, career strategists, or professional designers of regulatory policies. Regulators or bureaucrats may, moreover, be prevented from acting in self-serving ways by lack of information, expertise, or commitment.

---

[21] See M. Olson, *Logic of Collective Action* (Cambridge, MA, 1974).

[22] S. Peltzman, 'The Economic Theory of Regulation after a Decade of Regulation' (1989) *Brookings Papers in Macroeconomics* 1.

[23] Peltzman, 'Economic Theory of Regulation', 40.

[24] R. Barke and W. Riker, 'Political Economy of Regulation with some Observations on Railway Abandonments' (1982) 39 *Public Choice* 73–106.

[25] J. Hirshleifer, 'A Comment' (1976) 19 *Journal of Law and Economics* 241–4.

[26] See C. Hood, *Explaining Economic Policy Reversals* (Buckingham, 1994), 24; B.-A. Wickstrom, 'Regulation of Natural Monopoly: A Public Choice Perspective' in A. Midttun and E. Svindland (eds), *Approaches and Dilemmas in Economic Regulation* (Basingstoke, 2001).

Interest groups' activities may affect regulation in a manner that interferes with the realization of private preferences and regulatory bureaucracies may have lives beyond the sums of their parts. Economic theory-based arguments, moreover, often ignore or underrate such important motives as ideologies, policy goals, emotional identifications, personality limits, prejudices, and moral stances.[27] Environmental regulators may actually be motivated by altruistic concerns about environmental quality!

The economic approach offers one view of regulatory capture, but the diversion of regulation away from public interest objectives may be explained quite differently from the perspectives encountered in other disciplines. Motives can be seen in less simple terms than mere wealth maximization—to include, for instance, ideological, bureaucratic, or social objectives. Stress, thus, can be placed on the propensity of bureaucrats to seek to maximize agency budgets,[28] or to engage in 'bureau-shaping' so as to create job satisfaction,[29] or to maximize the political influence and scope of competencies of the agency.[30]

Further contrasts have been drawn between the assumptions of the Chicago school of law and economics—that legislators and regulators seek to maximize their personal wealth—and the position of the 'Virginian' school of political economy, which sees legislators and regulators as pursuers of expected votes or ideological ends as well as cash, and which gives greater prominence to the interplay of pressure groups.[31] The problem of moving beyond wealth maximization and seeing utility maximization in broader terms is, however, that a loss of predictive power results and it is difficult to attribute relative weights to the various factors (money, votes, ideologies, and other preferences) that are all alleged to be being sought.[32] But what is more important in this context is the move among these schools towards the interest in, and analysis of, constitutional rules and institutional design—as we will note later.

In sum, these accounts see the process of politics as inherently about self-interested action. They have been highly influential in shaping wider literatures in regulation, whether they relate to self-regulation or to enforcement, to take just two examples (as will be noted in the following chapters).

---

[27] Self, *Government by the Market?*, 46.

[28] See W.A. Niskanen, *Bureaucracy and Representative Government* (Chicago, 1971).

[29] See P. Dunleavy, *Democracy, Bureaucracy and Public Choice* (Hemel Hempstead, 1991), 174–209.

[30] See G. Majone, *Regulating Europe* (London, 1996), 65; G. Majone, 'Cross-National Sources of Regulatory Policymaking in Europe and the United States' (1991) 11 *Journal of Public Policy* 79–106, esp. 94–7.

[31] See C.D. Foster, *Privatisation, Public Ownership and the Regulation of Natural Monopoly* (Oxford, 1992), 386–8; M.A. Crew (ed.), *Deregulation and Diversification of Utilities* (Dordrecht, 1989), 5–20.

[32] Foster, *Privatisation*, 387.

Other explanations of regulation have moved the theory in the direction of wider *interest-group politics*. This set of interest-group theorists sees regulatory developments as the products of relationships between different groups and between such groups and the state. Such theorists generally differ from proponents of public interest accounts in not seeing regulatory behaviour as imbued with public-spiritedness but as a competition for power. Versions of interest-group theories range from open-ended pluralism to corporatism.[33] Pluralists see competing groups as struggling for power and elections as won by coalitions of groups who use their power to shape regulatory regimes. In contrast, corporatists emphasize the extent to which successful groups are taken into partnership with the state and produce regulatory regimes that exclude non-participating interests.[34]

One classic interest-group-driven approach is the account by Marver Bernstein—often also associated with 'regulatory capture' (as noted earlier). Bernstein offers, in contrast to Stigler, a 'life cycle' version of regulatory processes. His 'life-cycle' theory points to a variety of forces (internal and external) in accounting for a regulatory trajectory that is characterized by an ageing process in which an initial 'public interest' regulatory regime gives way to capture by the regulated industry.[35] Regulation typically begins, on this view, as a policy response to a political call to protect the public from undesirable activity. In the first of four stages of life—termed *gestation*—concerns about a problem result in the creation of a regulatory body. Second, there follows *youth*, in which the inexperienced regulatory body is outmanœuvered by the regulatees but operates with a crusading zeal. As the first flush of political support for agency objectives dies away, *maturity* follows, and devitalization sets in. Regulation becomes more expert and settled, but as the agency moves out of the political mainstream it begins to pay increasing attention to the needs of industry. As vitality declines, the agency relies increasingly upon precedent when taking decisions, and adopts a reactive stance. Finally, *old age*, the fourth stage, arrives to be characterized by debility and decline, resort to ever more judicialized procedures, and the agency giving priority to industrial rather than public interests. In general, therefore, Bernstein points to the role of regulators in carrying out missions that legislators have negotiated between interest groups, consumers, businesses, and other affected parties—missions that effect compromises but are seen by participants, nevertheless, to be endeavours in pursuit of the public interest.[36]

---

[33] Francis, *Politics of Regulation*; G. Wilson, *Interest Groups* (Oxford, 1990); for a pluralist analysis of government see P. Self, *Political Theories of Modern Government* (London, 1985), 79–107.

[34] See O. Newman, *The Challenge of Corporatism* (London, 1980).

[35] Bernstein, *Regulating Business*. For criticism of the life-cycle theory, see, e.g., L.L. Jaffe, 'The Independent Agency—A New Scapegoat' (1956) 65 *Yale LJ* 1068; see also P. Quirk, *Industry Influence in Federal Regulatory Agencies* (Princeton, 1981).

[36] See Bernstein, *Regulating Business*, 76.

Somewhat less categorical about the inevitability of 'capture'—either at the point of origin (Stigler) or over time (Bernstein) was James Q. Wilson's account of regulatory politics in the US.[37] He concluded, after surveying diverse domains, that regulation could be understood as the outcome of interest-group constellations. Stigler's diagnosis of 'capture' was, according to Wilson, most appropriate to situations in which a concentrated interest-demanding regulation was not countered by a competing interest group. This, though, was only one of four potential constellations of interests, and in some domains such a constellation would not be encountered. For example, high transportation rates or electricity charges have immediate effects on down-stream industries—which are likely to lobby for rate-reductions—in this constellation (termed 'interest-group politics') it was unlikely that any one interest would dominate.

Equally, in those areas where there was no concentrated industry interest, 'capture' was not applicable (instead, Wilson diagnosed so-called majoritarian politics). Wilson also identified the possibility for entrepreneurial politics. In this world, regulation is adopted in the face of concentrated industry opposition and is advanced with only the support of diffused interests. In these cases, so-called policy entrepreneurs are said to have succeeded in building coalitions to challenge dominant interests. Examples here include Ralph Nader's long-standing activism against industry interests and the smoking ban for public (internal) spaces that spread across Europe in the early twenty-first century. A related account is also found in the area of environmental regulation. According to David Vogel, so-called 'baptist-boot-legger' coalitions between industry and 'green interests' were responsible for raising environmental standards.[38] Table 4.1 summarizes Wilson's argument.

Such refinements of the economic approach fail, nevertheless, to come to grips with one of the core problems mentioned by Peltzman—the lack of any account of the role played by institutional arrangements in the shaping of regulation. Examining this role is essential, say a number of commentators, as an antidote to the idea of parties as rational wealth and vote maximizers. Such institutional positions will be returned to shortly (pp. 53–63). Similarly,

Table 4.1. Variants in interest group politics

	Concentrated costs of regulation	Diffused costs of regulation
Concentrated benefits of regulation	Interest group politics	Client politics (capture)
Diffused benefits of regulation	Entrepreneurial politics	Majoritarian politics

Source: Adapted from Wilson, *Politics of Regulation*, 357–74; Hood, *Explaining Economic Policy Reversals*, 25.

---

[37] J.Q. Wilson, *The Politics of Regulation* (New York, 1980), 357–94. See also M. Olson, *The Logic of Collective Action* (Cambridge, MA, 1965) and Hood, *Explaining Economic Policy Reversals*, 24–6.

[38] D. Vogel, *Trading Up* (Cambridge, MA, 1995).

a pure interest-group-based approach misses out on the importance of ideas. Ideas may be used as a justification in regulatory argumentation, or ideas may reflect fundamental worldviews about the state of the world and inherent cause–effect relationships. It is to this literature we now turn.

'Power of Ideas' Explanations

In discussing the impact of ideas, ideologies, and beliefs, a number of different strains can be detected in the wider literature on public policy and regulation. One strain points to changing (party-) ideologies that shape approaches towards regulation and has been particularly prominent in discussions regarding 'deregulation' in the US and wider public sector reforms elsewhere. A second strain stresses the inherent plurality of rationalities or worldviews that characterize any debate regarding regulatory instruments. A third strain emphasizes the importance of deliberation and conversations. We discuss each of these strains in turn.

Turning, first, to those accounts that stress that 'ideas matter' for affecting policy change, it can be noted that the deregulatory programmes of the Reagan and Thatcher administrations prompted some commentators to argue that certain changes in regulation did not stem so much from the pressing of private interests as from the force of ideas.[39] (In such contexts, 'ideas' are taken to refer to intellectual conceptions 'which express how and why the government ought to control business'.[40]) Ideas might be distorted by political considerations when being applied but: 'they provide the essential basis of assumed social realities whereby political leaders explain and justify their policies to the public, backed by a media which keeps the range of "realistic" options within narrow limits'.[41]

For Derthick and Quirk, for example, regulatory reform in the US was one product of a change in intellectual climate that emerged from the spheres of economics, consumerism, and law. This intellectual climate could be summed up as hostility to existing regulatory regimes with their characteristics of capture, weak enforcement by agencies, red-tape, juridification, bureaucractization, high compliance costs, and ineffectiveness. Accordingly,

---

[39] Hood, *Explaining Economic Policy Reversals*, 29; see R.A. Harris and S.M. Milkis, *The Politics of Regulatory Change* (2nd edn, New York, 1996), esp. ch. 1; on the influence of public choice ideology see Self, *Government by the Market?*, ch. 3, esp. 65–7. See also E. Meidinger, 'Regulatory Culture: A Theoretical Outline' (1987) 9 *Law and Policy* 355.

[40] Harris and Milkis, *Politics of Regulatory Change*, 26.

[41] Self, *Government by the Market?*, p. xii; see also P.G. Hall (ed.), *The Political Power of Economic Ideas* (Princeton, 1989).

deregulation, as seen in the United States in the Reagan era, was driven not by interest-group pressures but by an intellectually guided process of economic rationalism that managed to benefit dispersed consumer groups at the expense of concentrated producer interests.[42] (Residential consumers, the evidence was said to indicate, benefited from the deregulation.[43]) For example, the widespread acceptance of regulation's vulnerability to 'capture' led to the conscious design of mechanisms to reduce the possibility of capture. In other ways, also, the diagnosis of capture changed the intellectual climate and resulted in changes in regulatory approaches. Hood notes, for instance, the adoption of automatic enforcement rules across some US policies to reduce the possibility of accommodation between agency and regulatee and the use of cross-domain regulatory agencies to reduce dependency on any one single industry.[44]

Although 'deregulation' is widely (and paradoxically) said to have resulted (across national contexts) in the growth and extension of explicit regulation across domains (utilities, social, and environmental regulation), the important contribution of the 'ideas matter' analysis is to suggest that the wider intellectual climate significantly shapes the type of regulatory instruments and institutions that are regarded as desirable. More broadly, Peter Hall has suggested that economic policy can be understood as a three-level system in which policy instruments and programmes follow broad economic policy paradigms.[45] In other words, the rise of the regulatory state (discussed in Chapter 20) and regulatory reform movements can be understood as responses of wider economic policy paradigm changes away from the 'welfare state'—or what has controversially been defined as shift from 'Keynesianism' to 'Monetarism'.

This first 'ideas matter' strain thus stresses the importance of the wider intellectual and political climate in shaping regulation. In contrast, the second strain concentrates more on the implicit theories inherent in particular regulatory approaches. Cultural theory points to four rival worldviews, with their contrasting and competing diagnoses and solutions to regulatory problems. These four worldviews emerge from distinctions made

---

[42] See M. Derthick and P. Quirk, *The Politics of Deregulation* (Washington, 1985) and Harris and Milkis, *Politics of Regulatory Change*, who argue: 'we must appreciate the history of the underlying ideas and institutions if we are to understand deregulatory outcomes of the Reagan revolution' (18). Harris and Milkis refer to 'the leadership role played by intellectual and political elites in establishing a new regulatory regime' (25).

[43] Peltzman, 'Economic Theory of Regulation'; T. Keeler, 'Theories of Regulation and the Deregulation Movement' (1984) 44 *Public Choice* 103–45. To some extent, the 'interests' literature (as illustrated above) has sought to account for these changes, for example by pointing to the depletion of rents or by pointing to successful coalition-building by political entrepreneurs.

[44] Hood, *Explaining Economic Policy Reversals*, 28.

[45] P. Hall, 'Policy Paradigms, Social Learning and the State: The Case of Economic Policy-Making in Britain' (1993) 25 *Comparative Politics* 275–96.

Table 4.2. Contrasting control styles according to cultural theory

Fatalism	Hierarchy
Control through unpredictable processes/inherent fallibility.	Anticipative solutions, forecasting, and management, response to enhanced authority and hierarchical ordering.
Individualism	Egalitarianism
Control through rivalry and choice, incentives to underpin market and individual choice processes.	Control through group processes, network style, participation.

on two dimensions. One dimension—called 'grid'—defines the extent to which individual behaviour is bound by rules; the second dimension—termed 'group'—defines the extent to which an individual regards herself as being embedded within group processes. Hierarchy is defined as 'high grid/high group'; egalitarianism as 'low grid/high group'; individualism as 'low grid/low group'; and fatalism as 'high grid, low group'.[46] Diagnosed problems and advocated solutions will reflect preferred worldviews. The four worldviews and their preferred regulatory strategy are summarized in Table 4.2.

To consider an example: if we regard prison directors as inherent gamers (i.e. always responding in creative ways to demands for compliance), then our preferred regulatory strategies will rely on surprise and unpredictability. If, in contrast, we regard prison directors as fellow professionals actively pursing shared goals, then regulatory strategies will reflect these values and emphasize peer-review and mutuality. In short, at the heart of any regulatory intervention is a particular 'core idea' about the nature of the world; and therefore they are advocated by those that share these ideas.[47] Such diversity of worldviews and consequent differences in regulatory approach will again appear throughout this volume, especially in relation to the enforcement literature.

Finally, the third 'power of ideas' strain emphasizes the importance of deliberation and conversation. This 'argumentative turn' follows Habermas and points to the importance of interpretative communities that are supposed to deliberate and come to shared understandings regarding the regulatory issues and processes.[48] In the wider literature, the idea of deliberation centrally concerns the advancing of citizenship through involvement, but also the

---

[46] M. Douglas, *Natural Symbols* (New York, 1982); C. Hood et al. *Regulation Inside Government* (Oxford, 1999); C. Hood, *The Art of the State* (Oxford, 1998).

[47] For different accounts, see G. Majone, *Evidence, Argument and Persuasion in the Policy Process* (New Haven, 1989); P.A. Sabatier and H.C. Jenkins-Smith, *Policy Change and Learning: An Advocacy Coalition Approach* (Boulder, CO, 1993); M. Lodge, K. Wegrich, and G. McElroy, 'Dodgy Kebabs Everywhere? Variety of Worldviews and Regulatory Change' (2010) 88 *Public Administration* 247–66. Ideas, in other words, do not exist on their own, but provide for 'hooks' that unite actors.

[48] For a more far-reaching discussion of this 'ideas matter' approach, see, for example, F. Fischer, *Reframing Public Policy* (Oxford, 2003).

increasing of intelligence in decision-making (especially in controversial areas, such as risk, for example regarding genetically modified foods). Deliberation is supposed to reduce, rather than enhance or reinforce, value conflicts (although empirical findings have been mixed).

In one important contribution to the deliberation discussion, Julia Black has advanced the idea of 'regulatory conversations'. This draws on ideas of deliberative democracy, on discourse analysis, and on ideas of self-referentiality, as noted below.[49] Black argues that, since regulation is inherently a communicative process, a better understanding of communication is critical for understanding (and arguably advancing) the regulatory process. A comprehension of communications within interpretative communities in the regulatory process facilitates understandings of rules and of conventions regarding the appropriate uses of discretion. Shared understandings are required to deal with the inherent uncertainty in the regulatory process in which the written-down never fully reflects reality (i.e. it allows for 'sense-making'); it provides for consensus on rules in the face of fragmentations of actors, and shared discourse triggers the dissemination of distinct knowledge production and thereby becomes a source of power in its own right. Ideas thus matter in facilitating a shared discourse between different parties which thereby create their own identities.[50]

In sum, the 'power of ideas' approach ranges from a focus on the underlying ideas that drive the designs of regulatory instruments, to a stressing of the importance of the broader intellectual climate that shapes regulatory instruments, to an emphasis on understanding the deliberations and discourses, the interactions and communication patterns that operate within regulatory domains and structure regulatory actions. It is a broad approach that might have difficulty in explaining why certain ideas take root, how ideas can be separated conceptually from interests, or in accounting for the patchiness of 'deregulation' (which has led observers to prefer the term 'regulatory reform').[51] In so far as it is conceded that ideas possess a force of their own, however, the 'power of ideas' accounts do qualify the economic theory of regulation's emphasis on the market as the key factor in understanding regulatory progressions. They emphasize the importance of plural

---

[49] J. Black, 'Regulatory Conversations' (2002) 29 *Journal of Law and Society* 163–96.

[50] As with other approaches, there is a linkage here between accounts stressing 'conversations' and 'proceduralization', namely that procedures are supposed to facilitate deliberative processes (see Black, who calls this 'thick proceduralization', J. Black, 'Proceduralising regulation: part II' (2001) 21 *Oxford Journal of Legal Studies* 33–58; 'Proceduralising regulation: part I' (2000) 20 *Oxford Journal of Legal Studies* 597–614.

[51] See Hood, *Explaining Economic Policy Reversals*, 29; P. Quirk, 'In Defence of the Politics of Ideas' (1988) 50 *Journal of Politics* 31; T.E. Keeler, 'Theories of Regulation and the Deregulation Movement' (1984) *Public Choice* 103–45.

rationalities in shaping regulation and they highlight also the prevalence of fads and fashions in regulatory politics (and possibly also in scholarship).[52]

Institutional Theories

Institutionalism has become such a broad church that it is hard to find anyone who would not claim to be an institutionalist. However, this universal agreement that 'institutions matter' does not extend much further. There are key differences across institutional approaches, ranging from those that emphasize the importance of formal rules in shaping behaviour, to those stressing the importance of political rules of the games in shaping diverse actors' behaviours, to those that regard all human action as embedded in their social context. Institutionalists, therefore, do not necessarily agree on where preferences come from, but they do agree on the notion that institutional structure and arrangements, as well as social processes, significantly shape regulation.[53] In other words, there is more driving regulatory developments than mere aggregations of individuals' preferences. Some commentators apply a number of well-worn distinctions between different approaches towards institutionalism (i.e. economic,[54] historical,[55] and sociological,[56]

---

[52] For alternative explanations of deregulation see Hood, *Explaining Economic Policy Reversals*, 29–33; Keeler, 'Theories of Regulation'; Peltzman, 'Economic Theory of Regulation'; L.W. Weiss and M.W. Klass (eds), *Regulatory Reform: What Actually Happened* (Boston, 1986).

[53] B. Morgan and K. Yeung, *An Introduction to Law and Regulation* (Cambridge, 2007), ch. 2.

[54] Classics include O. Williamson, *The Economic Institutions of Capitalism* (New York, 1985); D.C. North, 'Government and the Cost of Exchange in History' (1984) 44 *Journal of Economic History* 255; R. Matthews, 'The Economics of Institutions and the Services of Growth' (1986) 96 *Economic Journal* 903; M. Horn, *The Political Economy of Public Administration* (Cambridge, 1995). T. Moe, 'Political Institutions: The Neglected Side of the Story' (1990) 6 *Journal of Law, Economics, and Organization* 213; R.L. Calver, M.D. McCubbins, and B.R. Weingast, 'A Theory of Political Control and Agency Discretion' (1989) 33 *American Journal of Political Science* 588; W.H. Riker, 'Implications from the Disequilibrium of Majority Rule for the Study of Institutions' (1980) 74 *American Political Science Review* 432; K.A. Shepsle and B.R. Weingast, 'The Institutional Foundations of Committee Power' (1987) 81 *American Political Science Review* 85; B. Weingast and W. Marshall, 'The Industrial Organisation of Congress' (1988) 96 *Journal of Political Economics* 132; E. Ostrom, 'An Agenda for the Study of Institutions' (1986) 48 *Public Choice* 3; T. Moe, 'Interests, Institutions and Positive Theory: The Politics of the NLRB' (1987) 2 *Studies in American Political Development* 236.

[55] Classics include L. Hancher and M. Moran (eds), *Capitalism, Culture and Regulation* (Oxford, 1989), esp. their chapter 'Organising Regulatory Space'. C. Shearing, 'A Constitutive Conception of Regulation', in P. Grabosky and J. Braithwaite (eds), *Business Regulation and Australia's Future* (Canberra, 1993). C. Scott, 'Analysing Regulatory Space' (2001) *Public Law* 329–53.

[56] Classics include J. March and J. Olsen, 'The New Institutionalism: Organisational Factors in Political Life' (1984) 78 *American Political Science Review* 734; J. Meyer and B. Rowan, 'Institutionalised Organisations: Formal Structure as Myth and Ceremony' (1977) *American Journal of Sociology* 340; W. Scott, 'The Adolescence of Institutional Theory' (1987) 32 *Administrative Science Quarterly* 493; W. Powell and P. Di Maggio (eds), *The New Institutionalism in Organizational Analysis* (Chicago,

or the ill-defined suggestion that institutionalism is about 'ideas, interests, and institutions'). Here, however, we concentrate on three strains in the institutionalist literature: those that focus respectively on 'inter-institutional relations' (especially regarding institutional design questions); those primarily interested in 'intra-institutional forces' (especially the evolution of regulatory regimes over time); and those that emphasize the network and 'regulatory space' understandings of regulation.

INTER-INSTITUTIONAL RELATIONS

The unifying core of this literature lies in its interest in designing institutions and institutional relations to avoid particular problems widely associated with regulatory processes, for example, capture (as explored above). This literature represents the response to the argument that all regulation was about capture— instead, this literature asks how institutions can be designed to provide for benevolent outcomes and avoid widely diagnosed pathologies of regulation. More widely, this literature has also been influential in terms of focusing attention on 'rules of the game', in particular regulatory aspects, such as auctions.

One central concern of the institutional design literature is the question of 'Why delegate?'—should authority for regulatory activity be delegated to regulatory agencies (or other organizational forms), and if so, how? In addition, given the motive to drift or shirk, how can such behaviour be checked? More specifically, the 'Why delegate?' question relates to three key issues that have informed most of the literature on institutional design, namely the ideas of *information asymmetry, credible commitment,* and *blame avoidance*.

Turning to *information asymmetries* first, control over delegated actors is inherently limited, since not all possible states of the world can be foreseen, all contracts are inherently incomplete, and monitoring of actors is inherently costly and imperfect. This means that regulatory control is inherently limited, and this limitation applies in two ways. One relates to the political control of the regulatory agencies to whom politicians have delegated the oversight functions. The other dimension of limited control is that of the regulatory agency over the regulated industry (as would be identifiable as 'capture'). Such imperfections of control allow for discretionary activities or

1991); R.L. Jepperson, 'Institutions, Institutional Effects, and Institutionalism' in Powell and Di Maggio, *The New Institutionalism*. Also J. Black, 'An Economic Analysis of Regulation: One View of the Cathedral' (1997) *OJLS* 699; 'New Institutionalism and Naturalism in Socio-Legal Analysis: Institutional Approaches to Regulatory Decision-Making' (1997) 19 *Law and Policy* 53; P. Grabosky and J. Braithwaite, *Of Manners Gentle: Enforcement Strategies of Australian Business Regulatory Agencies* (Melbourne, 1986). Especially influential has been the idea of 'relational distance', see D. Black, *The Behavior of Law* (New York, 1976), 40–8.

'drift'.[57] Such drift can either be expressed by the regulatory agency's accommodation with the regulated industry, or with the agency focusing on the convenient and seemingly popular rather than on the difficult and potentially controversial.

Is drift, like capture, inevitable? Or rather, does this mean that regulatory activity is inherently 'out of control' and liable, therefore, to pervert initial preferences? The institutional design literature has provided for a range of tools to deny the universal applicability of the 'bureaucracy out of control' charge. Most prominently, McNollgast (Matthew McCubbins, Roger Noll, and Barry Weingast)[58] have pointed to three devices that have the potential to control agencies, and have emphasized, in particular, the importance of procedural devices. For them, control can be exercised firstly through so-called *police patrols*, specific institutional units that focus on controlling the agency. Examples of police patrols can include parliamentary committees, audit units, and other specific oversight bodies. As 'police patrol' implies, such a control is very costly: it requires constant monitoring (and hope that the 'crime' is conducted at the time of looking), and even where 'drift' is being detected, it is questionable (especially in the world of 'iron triangles') that sanctions will be applied. A second device is the so-called *fire alarm*. Here politicians rely on affected constituencies to ring the alarm bells where they think that the regulatory agency's activities are 'disagreeable'. Politicians then have the chance to assert their authority over the agency. This mechanism is clearly far less costly than police patrols, but it requires that interests mobilize and be heard—and it requires political willingness to act.[59] In other accounts, fire-alarms are activated through courts, with some suggesting that a preference for fire-alarm mechanisms in the US has created the impression of adversarial regulatory relationships in the US.

McNollgast favour a third device, namely procedural rules or *deck-stacking*.[60] In other words, they suggest that, through procedures, agencies can be placed on 'autopilot'—they will generate decisions within the scope

---

[57] This is a traditional bureaucracy question: Is it always out of control? Drift is defined here as the deviation of an actor's activities beyond the boundaries of behaviour as required by regulatory statute. The most famous (and influential) account was William Niskanen's analysis of *budget-maximizing* bureaucracies that successfully avoided political oversight to a particular point and were characterized by the ambition to expand power (defined as size of budget). See Niskanen, *Bureaucracy and Representative Government*.

[58] M. McCubbins, R. Noll, and B. Weingast, 'Administrative Procedures as Instruments of Political Control' (1987) 3 *Journal of Law, Economics and Organisation* 243–86.

[59] Such arrangements are not only limited to this particular literature. For example, Ayres and Braithwaite in their *Responsive Regulation*, suggest the empowerment of 'public interest groups' as a fire-alarm to counter the potential dominance of industry groups.

[60] The term 'deck-stacking' has been taken from the world of card-games. As in a card game, the 'deck of cards (procedures)' is stacked in favour of (or against) particular interests. This forces particular actors to 'play' the regulatory game in the light of given provisions and resources (i.e. 'cards').

of the legislative intent. Consultation periods, for example, are said to generate particular biases in decision-making by requiring the paying of particular attention to specific issues (such as the environment). Macey, in an extension of this argument, points to the importance of deck-stacking devices, contrasting procedural devices (in the US literature, the somewhat controversial example is the *Administrative Procedures Act* of 1946) with structural devices, the latter including rules governing appointment, budgets, and such like. In other words, while information asymmetry does generate particular problems of control, the literature does suggest the existence of devices to reduce the possibility that regulatory agencies are inherently 'out of control'.

The so-called time consistency problem relates to *credible commitment*.[61] The credible commitment problem refers to any human exchange in which a promise regarding behaviour in the future is potentially open for renegotiation. For example, if a country seeks to attract private investors, then it needs to signal a 'good' regulatory environment. As will be explored in Chapter 20's discussion of regulation and development, the problem of credible commitment emerges once a certain investment has been made. If such an investment has high asset specificity (i.e. high fixed assets), then it is costly to exit from the business if the government reneges on promises regarding the regulatory approach that it will adopt. In other words, if there is a threat that governments or regulators will turn interventionist or impose social or environmental standards, then private investors are said to reduce their willingness to invest. Thus, the credible commitment problem is about the likelihood that particular regulatory settlements will continue over time (especially in the light of changes in government); more formally, it is about the likelihood that the preferences of the 'enacting coalition' will be reversed over time.

The institutional design literature suggests that the more potential a political system provides for unchecked political behaviour, the greater the credible commitment problem, and therefore the more important it is to make particular regulatory devices 'irreversible' or prohibitively expensive to reverse. In contexts where legislation can lead to the rapid change in the jurisdiction of regulatory agencies, the literature advocates the use of licenses and contracts (thereby minimizing discretion on behalf of political/regulatory actors).[62]

A final key dimension that engages the literature on institutional design is that of legislative motives or *blame-avoidance*. Most famously, Fiorina put forward a so-called 'blame shift' hypothesis: political actors would delegate

---

[61] B. Levy and P. Spiller, 'The Institutional Foundations of Regulatory Commitment' (1994) 10 *Journal of Law, Economics and Organization* 201–46.

[62] See Levy and Spiller, 'Institutional Foundations'; A. Estache and L. Wren-Lewis, 'On the Theory and Evidence on Regulation of Network Industries in Developing Countries' in R. Baldwin, M. Cave, and M. Lodge (eds), *Oxford Handbook of Regulation* (Oxford, 2010).

tasks where these were politically embarrassing or damaging; but keep those tasks where the 'political opportunity cost' was positive (such as kissing babies and other supposedly electorally beneficial activities).[63] Whether such blame shift argument can be empirically supported is somewhat problematic, as voters seem not fully predictable as to whom they blame when things go wrong.[64] Indeed, heads of regulatory agencies seem not always willing to follow through on a political blame shift logic when they make sure that blame boomerangs back onto their political 'masters', rather than fall on their own swords. More broadly, these accounts shift emphasis towards explaining regulatory behaviour in terms of *reputation*. Thus, regulatory action can be explained by their audience and the nature of threats with agencies being particularly concerned to protect their autonomy and discretion (i.e. 'turf'). Thus utility regulators might concentrate on nominal rather than real price increases and pharmaceutical regulators' behaviour might be primarily concerned with public image.[65]

Bringing these different literatures together in a comprehensive treatment of the institutional design literature, Murray Horn points to four dimensions that direct (legislative) decision-makers in choosing institutional forms.[66] *Decision-making costs* are the opportunity costs incurred by those taking political decisions (in Horn's case, legislators). The higher these costs are, the more likely it is that delegation will occur. *Commitment costs* are the potential costs that a future generation of policymakers will be likely to incur in reversing an initial decision. *Agency costs* are the expenses involved in monitoring a regulatory authority. The higher these are, the less likely it is that a delegation will be made. Finally, *uncertainty costs* arise from the genuine uncertainties that programmes will occasion and which will impact on allocations of benefit flows among affected constituencies.

These factors apply to the key institutional design dimensions whether they relate to the degree of delegation to regulatory agencies, the choice of

---

[63] M. Fiorina, 'Legislative Choice of Regulatory Forms' (1982) 39 *Public Choice* 33–66. In a later refinement, Fiorina suggested that delegation to agencies would be pursued in areas of high uncertainty, whereas a reliance on statute and enforcement through courts would be pursued in case of certainty about the future (M. Fiorina, 'Legislator Uncertainty, Legislative Control, and the Delegation of Legislative Power' (1986) 2 *Journal of Law, Economics and Organization* 33–51. For a comprehensive discussion of blame in political life, see C. Hood, *The Blame Game* (Princeton, 2011).

[64] M. Horn, *The Political Economy of Public Administration* (Cambridge, 1995); C. Hood, 'The Risk Game and the Blame Game' (2002) 37 *Government and Opposition* 15–37.

[65] D. Carpenter, 'Protection without Capture' (2004) 98 *American Political Science Review* 613–31; *Reputation and Power* (Princeton, 2010); P. Joskow, 'Inflation and Environmental Concern' (1973) 17 *Journal of Law and Economics* 291–327; M. Maor, 'A Scientific Standard and an Agency's Legal Independence' (2007) 85 *Public Administration* 961–78; M. Maor, 'Organizational Reputation and Jurisdictional Claims' (2010) 23 *Governance* 133–59.

[66] M. Horn, *The Political Economy of Public Administration* (Cambridge, 1995).

ownership structures, or the choice of institutional oversight mechanisms.[67] In the area of regulatory agencies, for example, Horn notes the important effect of a 'revolving door' mechanism in preventing capture: given that regulators aspire a move (or return) to the regulated industry, they will not wish to appear as easily 'captured', but instead will seek to acquire a reputation for 'competence'. Given the relative short-term nature of careers as regulatory officials, however, the effects are a bias towards carrying out short-termist 'high impact' regulatory activities, rather than 'low level' difficult work that requires a long-term perspective. More broadly, the institutional design literature points to key aspects of both theoretical and empirical importance. It also emphasizes that there is no simple 'one size fits all'. Instead, institutional design is inherently a political choice that reflects the constellations of a particular context. This includes the specifics of the political system, especially in the light of the particular commitment issues associated with political institutions. This also includes the sectoral specificities, such as the ability to monitor the outputs and outcomes of regulatory activities. Furthermore, this perspective suggests that institutional design is capable of achieving desired outcomes—in other words, this is a theory that is not at all sceptical about regulation.

INTRA-INSTITUTIONAL FORCES

As suggested at the start of this chapter, one strand of the regulatory literature sees regulatory change as driven by forces that come from within organizations. What unites these diverse accounts is an emphasis on self-destructive processes that partly emerge from a process of filtered responses to changes in the wider environment of the regulatory system. Institutional design matters and the widely proclaimed importance of *path dependence* does matter to some extent[68]—but only in so far as to generate largely unpredictable responses and ongoing changes. Regulation is therefore limited, if not inherently about non-control. Four particular lines of enquiry that emphasize this particular strain of regulatory thinking can be distinguished: *institutional*

---

[67] As a result, this broad approach has triggered a small industry in studies of 'regulatory agencies' (often labelling these organizations 'IRA'—independent regulatory agency); see F. Gilardi, 'Policy Credibility and Delegation to Independent Regulatory Agencies: A Comparative Empirical Analysis' (2002) 9 *Journal of European Public Policy* 873–93; M. Thatcher, 'Delegation to Independent Regulatory Agencies: Pressures, Functions and Contextual Mediation' (2002) 25 *West European Politics* 125–47.

[68] T. Boas, 'Conceptualising Continuity and Change' (2007) 19 *Journal of Theoretical Politics* 33–54; P. Pierson, 'Increasing Returns, Path Dependence and the Study of Politics' (2000) 94 *American Political Science Review* 251–67; *Politics in Time* (Princeton, 2004); J. Mahoney, 'Path Dependence in Historical Sociology' (2000) 29 *Theory and Society* 507–48.

layering, perversity, self-referential, and *regulatory space/network* approaches. This section considers each one in turn.

Institutional layering accounts relate to a very traditional interest in the study of organizations, namely how organizations and rule-systems respond to changes in their environment.[69] In contrast to accounts that suggest immediate adaption, *layering* type accounts suggest that processes of initial resistance and partial accommodation will be commonplace.[70] For example, pressure for reform will initially be rejected, then partly accommodated and, if pressure is continuing, finally lead to overall transformation.[71] Therefore, the expectation is that regulation evolves over time, not by radical change or U-turns, but rather by incremental adaptation, leading to additions and extensions. These moderated processes of adaptation mostly reflect the biases of the organizations that are supposedly to enact demands for change. As a result, organizations filter out the difficult or controversial, or focus on the popular and convenient, rather than the problematic.[72] Over time, this leads to the emergence of regulatory systems characterized by competing logics and, thus, inherent tensions. These tensions, in themselves, are a source of regulatory activity and change.

Perversity accounts are related to ideas that focus on competing logics and incremental adaptation. These accounts follow an intellectual lineage that goes back to the seminal work by Robert Merton,[73] and they stress the limits of intentional action. Regulation, therefore, is at least as much about unintended consequences as about intended outcomes (we return to this discussion in the chapter on enforcement). Sam Sieber, for example, though not writing about regulation directly, pointed to seven reverse mechanisms that would pervert intended action—and all of them have direct implications for the study of regulation.[74] Sieber's seven mechanisms are:

---

[69] More broadly, historical institutionalist accounts have come up with four broad processes of gradual change that do not rely on 'exogenous shocks' or 'critical junctures'. Apart from 'layering', these include 'displacement' (the removal of existing rules and the introduction of new ones), 'drift' (the changing impact of rules due to changes in the broader environment or habitat), and 'conversion' (changing interpretation and application of rules); see J. Mahoney and K. Thelen, 'A Theory of Gradual Institutional Change' in J. Mahoney and K. Thelen, *Explaining Institutional Change* (Cambridge, 2010); A. Greif and D. Laitin, 'A Theory of Endogenous Institutional Change' (2004) 98 *American Political Science Review* 633–52; W. Streeck and K. Thelen, 'Introduction: Institutional Change in Advanced Political Economies' in W. Streeck and K. Thelen (eds), *Beyond Continuity* (Oxford, 2005); K. Thelen, *How Institutions Evolve* (Cambridge, 2004); K. Orren and S. Skowronek, The *Search for American Political Development* (Cambridge, 2004).

[70] R. Laughlin, 'Environmental Disturbance and Organizational Transitions and Transformations: Some Alternative Models' (1991) 12 *Organizational Studies* 209–32.

[71] Laughlin, 'Environmental Disturbance'.

[72] E. Clay and B. Schaffer (eds), *Room for Manoeuvre* (London, 1984).

[73] R. Merton, 'The Unintended Effects of Purposive Social Action' (1984) 1 *American Sociological Review* 894–904.

[74] S. Sieber, *Fatal Remedies* (New York, 1981). We will come across examples of all of these mechanisms throughout this volume. One example of such perversity is to be found in the literature

- *functional disruption*: where regulation frustrates the functioning of the system, thereby worsening the overall outcome;
- *exploitation*: where opponents succeed in achieving the opposite of the intended effects;
- *goal displacement*: where the process of regulating drives out the overall objective of regulating;
- *provocation*: where opposition and antagonism are mobilized, rather than compliance achieved;
- *classification*: where labelling effects have reverse effects, such as when attempts at stigmatizing behaviour become badges of honour;
- *over-commitment*: where the resource intensity of seeking to achieve unobtainable objectives reduces the resources to achieve obtainable objectives;
- *placation*: where the illusion of regulatory compliance distracts from danger signals.

In sum, these writings stress the importance of inherent paradoxes and potential 'surprises' that are generated by counter-learning environments.

A similar diagnosis of the inherent limitations of regulatory interventions is shared by those cultural theory accounts that were discussed earlier. As noted, the key interest has largely lain in the biases and worldviews that are incorporated into regulatory instruments and 'styles'. Cultural theory, however, also points to potential limitations of each approach which are largely generated through exploitation, counter-learning, and cognitive limitations: individuals and organizations seek to filter out information that seems to suggest a rejection of favoured instruments and underlying cause–effect relationships.[75] In brief, egalitarian regimes suffer due to high degrees of 'clubbiness'; 'individualist regimes' suffer from encouraging selfish individualism, namely gaming and cheating; a regime emphasizing unpredictability suffers from encouraging distrust and therefore reduced 'openness' and

on enforcement which points to phenomena such as counter-learning or stigmatization—see also C. Hood, *Limits of Administration* (London, 1974).

[75] C. Hood, 'Control over Bureaucracy: Cultural Theory and Institutional Variety' (1996) 15(3) *Journal of Public Policy* 207–30; *The Art of the State* (Oxford, 1998); C. Hood, C. Scott, O. James, G. Jones, and G. Travers, *Regulation Inside Government* (Oxford, 1999); C. Hood, O. James, G.B. Peters, and C. Scott (eds), *Controlling Modern Government* (Cheltenham, 2004); M. Lodge and K. Wegrich, 'Governing Multi-level Governance: Comparing Domain Dynamics in German Land–Local Relationships and Prisons' (2005) 83(2) *Public Administration* 417–42; M. Lodge and K. Wegrich, 'Control over Government: Institutional Isomorphism and Governance Dynamics in German Public Administration' (2005) 33(2) *Policy Studies Journal* 213–33; Lodge, Wegrich, and McElroy, 'Dodgy Kebabs Everywhere?'. More broadly, M. Thompson, R. Ellis, and A. Wildavsky, *Cultural Theory* (Boulder, 1990). It should be noted that there are overlaps between cultural theory and potential interest group politics accounts, especially the advocacy coalition framework (although representatives of that approach would reject the linkage). The linkage exists in the joint emphasis on clashes between worldviews (belief systems) and attempts by winning coalitions to institutionalize their preferred beliefs in regulatory instruments.

'collegiality'; whereas a hierarchist regulatory approach suffers from potential over-reliance on expertise. Therefore, an over-reliance on any single world-view invites side-effects and exploitation. In contrast, the careful 'hybridization' of regulatory strategies is said to provide for more stable solutions.[76] Whether such 'clumsy solutions' (as some cultural theorists call hybrids) do indeed offer such a stairway to a perversity-free and stable heaven of regulation is however still a matter of debate.[77]

Self-referential accounts of regulation have largely been influenced by the work of Niklas Luhmann, Gunther Teubner, and Helmut Willke.[78] The idea of self-referentiality involves an understanding of society that is increasingly differentiating into subsystems that are shaped by their own codes (hence the biological metaphor of 'autopoiesis'). Each subsystem (law, economy, politics, religion, etc.) is seen to have its own rationality, yet to be able to react with its environment so as to self-generate and reproduce.[79] Regulatory developments, accordingly, come to be analysed in terms of the nature, compatibilities, and interactions of autopoietic systems.[80]

Communication rather than any theory of action is at the centre of these accounts. As subsystems communicate in their own 'code', direct intervention becomes increasingly problematic, if not impossible. The instruments of law (speaking the language of 'law') do not directly translate into the language of the economy—therefore they require translation and 'arrive' in the economic subsystem not only in translated (distorted) form, but also with significant time delay. Thus, control is inherently limited, the consequence of this being

---

[76] Hood, *Art of the State*; Hood et al., *Regulation Inside Government*; 6 P, 'Institutional Viability: A Neo-Durkheimian Theory' (2003) 16(4) *Innovation* 395–415.

[77] M. Verweij, M. Douglas, R. Ellis, C. Engel, F. Hendricks, S. Lohmann, S. Ney, S. Rayner, and M. Thompson, 'The Case for Clumsiness' in M. Verweij and M. Thompson (eds), *Clumsy Solutions for a Complex World* (Basingstoke, 2006); Lodge and Wegrich, 'Governing Multi-level Governance'; Lodge, Wegrich, and McElroy, 'Dodgy Kebabs Everywhere?'.

[78] G. Teubner, *Dilemmas of Law in the Welfare State* (London, 1986); *Law as an Autopoietic System* (London, 1993); G. Teubner, R. Nobles, and D. Schiff, 'The Autonomy of Law: An Introduction to Legal Autopoiesis' in D. Schiff and R. Nobles (eds), *Jurisprudence* (London, 2003); N. Luhmann, 'Law as a Social System' (1989) 83 *NWULR* 136; H. Willke, *Systemtheorie III: Steuerungstheorie* (Stuttgart, 1995). Autopoiesis as a term was initially coined by Humberto Maturana. There are significant differences between these authors; space limitations prevent a discussion of the finer details of this particular debate.

[79] See G. Teubner (ed.), *Autopoietic Law: A New Approach to Law and Society* (Berlin, 1988); id., *Juridification of Social Spheres* (Berlin, 1987); id., *Law as an Autopoietic System* (Oxford, 1993); Luhmann, 'Law as a Social System', 136; M. King, 'The Truth about Autopoiesis' (1993) 20 *Journal of Law and Society* 218; W.H. Clune, 'Implementation as an Autopoietic Interaction of Autopoietic Organisations' in G. Teubner and A. Febbrajo (eds), *State, Law and Economy as Autopoietic Systems: Regulation and Autonomy in New Perspective* (Milan, 1992); J. Black, 'Constitutionalising Self-Regulation' (1996) 59(1) *MLR* 24.

[80] See Black, 'Constitutionalising Self-Regulation', 24; G. Teubner, 'After Legal Instrumentalism? Strategic Models of Post-Regulatory Law', in Teubner (ed.), *Dilemmas of Law in the Welfare State* (Berlin, 1985); M. Wilke, 'Societal Regulation through Law', in G. Teubner and A. Febbrajo, *State, Law and Economy* (Milan, 1992).

either completely ineffectual regulation (the attempt at intervention is being rejected) or overbearing regulation that destroys the viability of the respective subsystem. For Teubner, attempts at intervention and 'transplanting' regulation is at best about creating 'irritation effects'—with eventual outcomes being highly uncertain. Teubner calls this the 'regulatory trilemma': when law seeks to relate to other sub-systems, law may either be irrelevant to the other sub-system and therefore may have no effect whatsoever (termed 'mutual indifference'), or through creeping legalism law may inhibit the other sub-system, therefore constraining that other system's viability, or law's self-reproductive capacity itself may be harmed through being 'over-socialized' by the other sub-system.

Niklas Luhmann is widely linked with the argument that denies the possibility of control (and steering). In fact, he is associated with comparing attempts at economic policy interventions with the Hopi Indian's rain-dances or suggesting that the welfare state resembled an attempt to 'inflate cows in order to increase milk supply'.[81] In general, accounts stressing autopoiesis or self-referential systems suggest that hierarchy is dead and attempts at 'coupling' different systems are problematic and, therefore, regulation is most likely to be ineffectual. Communication, on this view, achieves irritation and structural coupling, but never purposeful communication.[82] Regulation is replaced by evolution.[83] Indeed, rather than simply stressing failure, the emphasis is on the non-instrumental character of knowledge and meaning.[84]

Somewhat less pessimistic are the accounts by Teubner and Willke in that both acknowledge the possibility of control. In both these cases, the limited solution to this regulation problem is two-fold—contextual steering through proceduralization and/or encouraging self-learning within social subsystems.[85] In the former, reliance is placed on the importance of indirect steering through procedural devices that encourage sub-systems to steer themselves to desired outcomes without the negative side-effects of direct

---

[81] N. Luhmann, 'Der Staat des politischen Systems' in U. Beck (ed.), *Perspektiven der Weltgesellschaft* (Frankfurt/Main, 1998), 369, trans. M. Lodge. For a debate in the German context, see R. Mayntz (1987), 'Politische Steuerung und gesellschaftliche Steuerungsprobleme' reprinted in R. Mayntz (ed.), *Soziale Dynamik und politische Steuerung* (Frankfurt/Main, 1997).

[82] R. Mayntz and F. Scharpf, 'Politische Steuerung—heute?' *MPIfG Working Paper 05/1*, January 2005. Available at http://www.mpifg.de/pu/workpap/wp05–1/wp05–1.html

[83] G. Teubner, 'Evolution of Autopoietic Law' in Teubner (ed.), *Autopoetic Law: A New Approach to Law and Society* (Berlin, 1988).

[84] G. Teubner, R. Nobles, and D. Schiff, 'The Autonomy of Law: An Introduction to Legal Autopoiesis' in D. Schiff and R. Nobles (eds), *Jurisprudence* (London, 2003); Luhmann, 'Law as a Social System'.

[85] For proceduralization, see J. Black ,'Proceduralizing Regulation: Part I' (2000) 20 *Oxford Journal of Legal Studies* 597–614; 'Proceduralizing Regulation: Part II' (2001) 21 *Oxford Journal of Legal Studies* 33–58.

intervention.[86] In the latter, the emphasis is on incentivizing self-learning capacity among differentiated sub-systems.

To summarize, 'intra-institutional' accounts lay special stress on endogenous processes that encourage regulatory change and adaptation. They also display a shared emphasis on the inherent tensions that emerge in the face of not only changing environmental requirements but also competing demands. They also share, to a degree, a certain scepticism regarding the effectiveness of intended regulatory intervention.

NETWORK THEORIES AND REGULATORY SPACE

Many theories of regulatory development are at their most comfortable when considering the effects of a single regime on a sector or issue—as when they seek to explain, say, the performance of the Environment Agency. A body of work on 'networked regulation', however, points out that, in reality, many risks and social or economic problems are controlled by networks of regulators. Regulation, on this view, can often best be seen as 'decentred', rather than simple and focused.[87]

This mixing of regulators and strategies may be necessary and desirable. Ideas regarding regulatory networks therefore are analytical, descriptive, and advocative. Governments frequently have to spread enforcement and policy-making powers across numbers of agencies.[88] The proponents of 'smart' regulation, moreover, argue that it will often be helpful to mix state controls with quasi-regulatory influences and constraints that operate within corporations.[89] Similarly, it may be useful to mix command and control methods with other regulatory instruments, such as incentives that operate through trading mechanisms or taxation laws. Control over a social issue by means of a typical network might, thus, involve a government department legislating in accordance with supra-national legal requirements, a number of regulatory agencies applying a variety of regulatory instruments, some standard-setting authorities, a professional self-regulator, a large number of local and police authorities, and a diversity of voluntary bodies, regulated corporations, and other organizations.

The 'network' approach to analysis usefully draws attention to a series of challenges that have to be risen to if the overall regime is to succeed—notably

---

[86] Again, the emphasis on procedural law as put forward by Teubner and Willke provides for an interesting overlap with those institutional design perspectives that emphasize the importance of hardwiring procedural and structural devices.

[87] See J. Black, 'Decentring Regulation: The Role of Regulation and Self-Regulation in a "Post-Regulatory World"' (2001) *Current Legal Problems* 103–46.

[88] See R. Baldwin and J. Black, *A Review of Enforcement Measures* (Defra, November 2005).

[89] N. Gunningham and P. Grabosky, *Smart Regulation: Designing Environmental Policy* (Oxford, 1998).

how coordination of efforts is to be achieved in the face of divergencies in such matters as: objectives, cultures, regulatory capacities, institutional environments, and control systems.[90] Network analysis also suggests that quite distinctive responses to coordination challenges can be identified, notably: resort to hierarchies and rules;[91] use of network management strategies;[92] reliance on collaboration through exchanges and markets; and procedural or institutional structuring.[93]

As a contribution to explaining regulatory developments, though, the network approach is especially valuable. It highlights the importance of appreciating the extent to which modern regulation is *decentred* and how many regulatory regimes are made up of numbers of institutions with characteristics that diverge across a host of dimensions. Analyses of regulatory change, on such a view, have to take on board the ways that different forces—whether internally or externally generated—may impact quite differently across the numerous organizations, cultures, and processes that, together, constitute the regulatory regime.[94]

These recent network accounts also relate to the well-established and long-standing 'regulatory space' account, initially put forward by Leigh Hancher and Michael Moran. The 'space' here is conceived of as a cluster of regulatory issues, decisions, or policies (a 'regulatory arena') that involves the interplay and competition between various interests.[95] Regulatory authority is widely shared between private and public actors (therefore making the distinction largely meaningless), and regulatory approaches are shaped by location, timing, and history. This 'space' account of diffused regulatory authority shares many characteristics of the long-standing 'liberal corporatism' discussion—one in which particular interests are involved in sharing authority with

[90] See below, pp. 159–63; E. Bardach, *Getting Agencies to Work Together* (Washington, DC, 1998).

[91] See, e.g., B.G. Peters, 'Managing Horizontal Government: The Politics of Co-ordination' (1998) 76 *Public Administration* 295; C. Hill and L. Lynn, 'Is Hierarchical Governance in Decline? Evidence from Empirical Research' (2005) 15 *Journal of Public Administration Research and Theory* 173–96.

[92] A. Esmack, 'The Functional Differentiation of Governance' (2009) 87 *Public Administration* 351–70; C. Heinrich, L. Lynn, and H. Milward, 'A State of Agents?' (2010) 20 *Journal of Public Administration Research and Theory* i.3–i19; C. Ansell and A. Gash, 'Collaborative Governance in Theory and Practice' (2009) 18 *Journal of Public Administration Theory and Research* 543–71; J. Kooiman and S. Jentoft, 'Meta-Governance' (2009) 87 *Public Administration* 818–36.

[93] See N. Machado and T. Burns, 'Complex Social Organization: Multiple Organizing Modes, Structural Incongruence and Mechanisms of Integration' (1998) 76 *Public Administration* 355, 370, 372; S. Goldsmith and W. Eggers, *Governing by Network* (Washington, DC, 2004), 69–75; Bardach, *Getting Agencies to Work Together*, 118–19.

[94] On the notion of 'regulatory regime' as: 'the complex of institutional geography, rules, practice, and animating ideas that are associated with the regulation of a particular risk' see C. Hood, H. Rothstein, and R. Baldwin, *The Government of Risk* (Oxford, 2001), 9.

[95] L. Hancher and M. Moran (eds), *Capitalism, Culture and Regulation* (Oxford, 1989); Scott, 'Analysing Regulatory Space'.

the state.[96] In the world of regulatory space, as in the world of regulatory networks, the idea of 'capture' makes only limited sense; regulatory authority is inherently shared, and private interests are driven to, or accept, playing legitimate roles in the regulation of themselves, of industry sectors (through associations), and of wider society. Attractive as the 'space' metaphor has been, though, it faces considerable problems in accounting for the boundaries of regulatory spaces and in explaining the different dimensions that characterize the 'topology' of the space—notably: the relative power of the different actors; the distribution of resource dependence relevant to the space; and the nature of the communication flows between actors. These criticisms have also been made with respect to network-based approaches.

Conclusions

Any review of major approaches to the explanation of regulation has to be selective, but the above discussion serves to outline the main tensions and differences of emphasis that are encountered in the regulatory literature. It would be rash to suggest that such theories can be synthesized so that reliable predictions can be made about all or most regulatory processes and developments.[97] Different theories exist at differing levels of generality and have varying applications and uses as explanatory tools. It therefore makes little sense to say whether one explanation or type of explanation carries more conviction than another without reference to a particular issue and context. Indeed, as the range of accounts has shown, differences between accounts do not just relate to the type of causal mechanisms they emphasize: differences go to the heart of disputes as to what constitutes or is understood as social science in general. What can be said is that, in seeking to explain particular regulatory developments, an awareness of the variety of available explanations does help the observer to evaluate the insights offered by different theories, to develop a sense of the limitations of, and assumptions underpinning, those theories, and to identify the kinds of information necessary for applying and testing them.

Is it possible to identify those situations in which one particular theory rather than another will have special explanatory force? The closest we may come to confidence here is where there is a 'smoking gun'—a piece of evidence that seems uncontroversially consistent with a particular theory.

---

[96] See G. Lehmbruch, 'Liberal Corporatism and Party Government' (1977) 10(1) *Comparative Political Studies* 91–126.

[97] See M. E. Levine and J.L. Forrence, 'Regulatory Capture, Public Interest and the Public Agenda: Towards Synthesis' (1990) *Journal of Law, Economics, and Organization* 167.

Thus, strong indications of regulator disinterestedness and benevolence may point towards the public interest account rather than the economic theory, and sometimes a regulatory decision may be revealed as a clear compromise between certain vying interests—and a vindication of the 'interest-group' account. More often, however, life will not be that simple, and different aspects of a regulatory development will resonate with different regulatory theories. Convincing accounts, like most constructions, will have to be assembled from different elements for different purposes and audiences, and the skill lies in contextualizing the composition.

What is clear from the above discussion is that there is an ever-emerging body of illuminating literature that helps us to improve our understandings of regulation. As the field of regulation has grown and matured, so has the discussion regarding theory (see Table 4.3).[98] To some extent, the different theories reflect different disciplinary preoccupations. It is possible, however, to identify also an emerging inter-disciplinarity, or at least a trans-disciplinarity of approaches in which there is an increased drawing on understandings of regulation that have emerged in different disciplines. Theories of regulation, it can now be said, have moved beyond 'learning from the US' literature on regulation, and European approaches to regulation easily stand side-by-side with the more US-influenced literature on institutional design. Regulation has never seemed more complex, but it has never been as well explored.

---

[98] M. Lodge, 'Regulation, the Regulatory State and European Politics' (2008) 30 *West European Politics* 289–301.

Table 4.3. Explaining regulation

Type of Theory	Main emphasis	Key problems
Public interest	Regulator acting in pursuit of public, rather than private, interests. Regulator disinterested and expert.	Difficult to agree a conception of public interest. Scepticism concerning disinterestedness, and public-spiritedness of regulators. Understates influence of economic power and prevalence of capture in regulation. Concern that public interest outcomes often fail to result. Understates competition for power amongst groups.
Interest group	Regulation as product of relationships between groups and with the state. Role of private economic interests in driving regulation. Incentives of firms to secure benefits and regulatory rents by capturing regulator.	Assumes that regulated parties are rational maximizers of own welfare. Difficulty of identifying preferences of parties. Possibility of altruism and public-spiritedness. Informational limitations may limit self-interestedness of actions. Role of groups and institutions may be underemphasized.
Ideas	Role of ideas in steering regulatory developments.	It may be hard to separate the force of ideas from the role of economic interests.
Institutional	Influence of organizational rule and social setting on regulation. Actors seen not purely as individuals but as shaped in action, knowledge, and preference by organizational rule and social environments.	How to balance institutional explanations with others in accounting for regulatory changes.
	Principal-agent issues and problems of democratic control of implementation. Institutional design as shaped by characteristics of political setting (or 'institutional endowment'). Institutional processes leading to self-destruction.	Regulatory authority not shaped in principal-agent relationship. To what extent do formal institutional settings require an additional understanding of informal norms and conventions? Over-determination of failure accounts.
	Regulatory authority diffused between and across public and private organizations.	Establishing boundaries of networks and spaces.

5 Regulatory Failure

One of the most well-established laws in social science is that policies and initiatives are usually born in hope and optimism, but eventually decline amid sadness and disappointment.[1] Such pessimism is often encountered in the field of regulation where it is not difficult to identify examples of 'regulatory failure'.[2] The media supply relentless copy on financial regulators who fail to spot dangerous systemic risks, or on safety regulators who fail to ensure the safety of oil-platform operations, or on other industry regulators who fail to collect fines, and so on.

What constitutes a regulatory failure is, however, more debatable than these initial, and apparently uncontroversial, examples might suggest. People will disagree as to what constitutes a 'failure' and its causes.[3] Failures can be foreseen, or they can come as 'rude surprises'.[4] Why regulators and regulatory regimes are seen to fail links to the visions of 'good' regulation that were explored in Chapter 3 and to the different ways of explaining regulatory developments that were discussed in Chapter 4. This chapter, accordingly, considers what regulatory failure involves before examining how we can understand the causes of regulatory deficiency and how remedies can be devised.

---

[1] H. Kaufman, *The Limits of Organizational Change* (Tuscaloosa, 1971), 105; P. Grabosky, 'Counterproductive Regulation' (1995) 23 *International Journal of the Sociology of Law* 347–69; C. Hood, 'Can We? Administrative Limits revisited' (2010) 70 *Public Administration Review* 527–34.

[2] See generally: Grabosky, 'Counterproductive Regulation'; W.P. Clune, 'Implementation as Autopoietic Interaction of Autopoietic Organizations' in G. Teubner and A. Febbrajo (eds), *State, Law and Economy as Autopoietic Systems Regulation and Autonomy in New Perspective* (Milan, 1992), 485–513; C. Sunstein, 'Paradoxes of the Regulatory State' (1990) 57 *University of Chicago Law Review* 407–41; M. Lodge, 'The Wrong Type of Regulation? Regulatory Failure and the Railways in Britain and Germany' (2002) 22 *Journal of Public Policy* 271–97; C. Hood and B. Peters, 'The Middle Aging of New Public Management: Into the Age of Paradox?' (2004) 14 *Journal of Public Administration Theory and Research* 267–82; R. Merton, 'The Unintended Effects of Purposive Social Action' (1936) 1 *American Sociological Review* 894–904; C. Hood, H. Rothstein, and R. Baldwin, 'Assessing the Dangerous Dogs Act: When Does a Regulatory Law Fail?' (2000) *Public Law* 282–305.

[3] P. Dunleavy, 'Policy Disasters: Explaining the UK's Record' (1995) 10 *Public Policy and Administration* 52–70; A. Boin and P. t'Hart, 'Institutional Crisis and Reforms in Policy Sectors' in H. Wagenaar (ed.), *Government Institutions* (Boston, 2000); A. Boin, A. McConnell, and P. t'Hart (eds.), *Governing after Crisis* (Cambridge, 2008); A. Boin, 'Preparing for Future Crises' in B.M. Hutter (ed.), *Anticipating Risks and Organising Risk Regulation* (Cambridge, 2010).

[4] T. Laporte, 'Anticipating Rude Surprises' in L. Jones (ed.), *Communicable Crises* (Amsterdam, 2007).

Identifying Regulatory Failure

The discussion of 'good' regulation in Chapter 3 suggests that regulators will 'fail' when they do not produce (at reasonable cost) the outcomes that are stipulated in their mandates or when they do not serve procedural or representative values properly. Thus, regulators may be criticized, *inter alia*, because they gain results inefficiently, or produce unwanted side-effects or because they lack transparency and accountability or exhibit bias and unfairness. Here it is worth considering the respective challenges of identifying outcome and procedural failures.

It is possible to identify a number of failings that have negative *outcome* implications.[5] These failings usually involve poor performance in discharging the core tasks of regulation: detecting undesirable behaviour; developing responses and intervention tools to deal with errant behaviour; enforcing those tools on the ground, and assessing and modifying regulatory performance.[6] A first difficulty in pinpointing an *outcome failure* is that, as noted in Chapter 3, most regulatory mandates are necessarily (and advisedly) flexible and open to interpretation. Debates about failure are, as a result, usually based on different understandings regarding objectives and problem-definition. Further difficulties relate to counterfactuals and trade-offs. When a regulatory system is accused of failure it is often relevant to ask: 'Failure compared to what?' This prompts comparisons between the outcomes produced by the given regulatory system and the hypothetical outcomes that would have been produced by doing nothing or by implementing some other regime of control. In both cases, it will be difficult to obtain reliable data with which to effect comparisons. Such exercises will be based on underlying assumptions and weightings and, as a result, what constitutes a failure and how much it matters when compared with other 'failures' will turn on tastes and political preferences. The matter of trade-offs constitutes a further evaluative difficulty, since real-life comparisons will often involve looking at regulatory interventions that produce a certain trade-off between numbers of risks against possible other interventions that produce other sets of risk trade-offs.[7]

Detection problems are often involved in charges of *under-regulation*—notably where this results from a lack of information-gathering on the risks and risk creators that impact on the achieving of objectives. Such

---

[5] Sunstein, C. 'Paradoxes of the Regulatory State'. Also note our discussion of 'better regulation' tools in Chapters 11, 13, and 14.

[6] On the DREAM framework of regulatory tasks, see Chapter 11 below.

[7] On risks and trade-offs see J.D. Graham and J. Baert Weiner (eds), *Risk vs. Risk* (Harvard, 1995). On identifying the 'intent' of the regulation, see O. James and M. Lodge, 'The Limitations of "Policy Transfer" and "Lesson Drawing" for Public Policy Research' (2003) 1(2) *Political Studies Research* 179–93.

under-regulation will do little to alleviate the continued occurrence of the problem in question. Deficiencies in regulatory detection often relate to the *inclusivity* of the rules and standards that regulators are applying. Under-inclusiveness will mean that the conduct that should be controlled is allowed to escape constraint, whereas over-inclusive rules will involve the excessive restriction of behaviour that should not be subjected to control.

Over-regulation is often associated with 'over-stringent' and 'over-prescriptive' regulation that reduces the possibilities for innovation and research. This kind of charge has commonly been made against 'best available technology'-standards in environmental regulation. Similarly, over-stringent regulation may also produce the perverse effect that it leads to 'under-regulation'. If prescription is over-precise, then it will be difficult to apply on the ground, since few complex events will be covered by the exact wording of the provisions at issue. Similarly, over-formalism and punitive enforcement styles may reduce the possibilities for cooperative relationships and healthy regulatory communications so that this can produce self-defeating outcomes (as where interventions in the banking field are designed to increase stability levels but, in fact, lead to destabilizing runs in the sector).[8] There has, indeed, been a diagnosed tendency for regulatory activities to have countervailing effects. This may happen when regulatees are induced to move activities to less-regulated areas (or, as in the example of transparency regulation, make their activities even less transparent), or when regulators move too quickly on 'new' risks (such as pharmaceuticals) and consumers are afflicted with fears and anxieties that lead them to stick to older, and more risky, goods (such as traditional medications).

Another 'response failing' may be associated with the choice of regulatory instruments. The meltdown of a financial system, for instance, may be regarded as a failure of regulatory instrument choice and design rather than enforcement. A price-control mechanism such as RPI-X may be seen to fail by incentivizing efficiency-seeking 'asset sweating', rather than infrastructure investment.[9]

Turning to enforcement failings, a common manifestation of these may be the prevalence of *creative compliance*—the practice of side-stepping rules, and negating regulations without breaking their formal terms.[10] Rules on safety may be 'complied with' by box-ticking, rather than substantive steps and, in processes of displacement, the regulations at issue may cause risks (of pollution, for example) to be shifted from a regulated to an unregulated

---

[8] M. Abolafia and M. Kilduff, 'Enacting Market Crisis: The Social Construction of a Speculative Bubble' (1988) 33(2) *Administrative Science Quarterly* 177–93.

[9] On price control mechanisms, see Chapter 22 below.

[10] See more generally Chapter 11.

operation.[11] Similarly, far-reaching transparency requirements may lead to an overall reduction of information in the regulatory process as risk-averse regulators and firms minimize the potential to be exposed at a later point. Another instance of displacement would be a gun-control law that leads regulatees to resort to other kinds of weapons, such as aggressive dogs.

At the heart of enforcement failings may be a more general problem: *failure to maintain reputation.* Reputation and credibility are critical in establishing and sustaining a regulator's ability to act autonomously.[12] If regulators are not perceived as having the capacity to act effectively against errant operators then regulatees, politicians, and other actors will no longer defer to them. More widely, without a reputation for competence, regulators will be blamed, even if they have no formal authority over a given field. For example, if the failings of one inspector in one region raises key issues about the capacity of food inspections in that area, it is not guaranteed that consumers will regard inspections in other regions as capable, regardless of evidence.

As for assessment and modification failings, these affect a regulator's ability to achieve desired outcomes because a regulator that cannot evaluate its own performance and adjust its strategies will not be able to cope with new challenges. Particular problems may arise here due to absences of data gathering and feedback systems. Another special difficulty may be that the regulator is unable to meet the challenges of change because it is hamstrung by excessively tight legislation and a political unwillingness to contemplate legal adjustments to powers.

In decentred regulatory regimes[13]—and networks in which numbers of regulators act collaboratively—the issue of regulatory failure is rendered more complex because responsibilities for failures, and successes, may not be clear. Outcomes may be collectively generated, or there may be doubt as to the locus of responsibility for dealing with a problem. Regulatory failure also needs to be separated from the organizational failures of regulated parties. A late train arrival does not necessarily indicate poor railway regulation, although it may offer an indication of a wider failing in the regulatory system. The DeepWater Horizon oil spillage between April and June 2010 threatened wildlife and the economic survival of large populations along the Louisiana coastline. It might be interpreted as the product of a large-scale regulatory failure (given the extensive failings of the then Minerals Management Service). It can, however,

---

[11] Similarly, it is suggested that one shared assumption among investment bankers is that 'income tax is voluntary' (see, however, http://docs.law.gwu.edu/facweb/jsiegel/Personal/taxes/IncomeTax .htm; last accessed 10 December 2010).

[12] M. Maor, 'Organizational Reputation and Jurisdictional Claims' (2010) 23(1) *Governance* 133–59; D. Carpenter, *The Forging of Bureaucratic Autonomy* (Princeton, 2001).

[13] See Chapter 3 and J. Black, 'Decentring Regulation: The Role of Regulation and Self-regulation in a "Post-Regulatory World"' (2001) *Current Legal Problems* 103–46.

be seen as an industry-organizational failure in so far as critical warning signs were ignored.

It may, indeed, be argued that the boundaries between regulatory and organizational performance blur increasingly as regulatory activities are pushed inside private organizations as part of systems of enforced self-regulation. Similarly problematic is any attempt to draw a clear line between political and regulatory responsibilities. If regulators are not provided with the adequate legal powers or economic resources, it can be contended that any 'failure' is not of their own making. The Brazilian air transport system is often taken as a site of regulatory failure, since constant under-capacity brings considerable delays. Some responsibility for this state of affairs can, however, be traced to important political choices that were taken decades ago (as part of democratic transition), and these initial choices have been further accentuated by a continued unwillingness to upgrade the infrastructure. In some circumstances, moreover, regulators might defend their positions by arguing that they have been asked by their political masters to do the impossible: there may be some problems that cannot be solved.

Turning to *process failures*, regulators tend to fail procedurally when they do not develop and follow procedures that satisfy stakeholders' appetites for openness and transparency—or where the regime does not provide for accountability of an acceptably representative nature. A special problem will often be that different stakeholders have different expectations regarding processes, and they may converse differently in making 'accountability demands' and in responding to these.[14] As Julia Black has pointed out, these issues will prove especially pressing in decentred regulatory regimes where numbers of regulators operate at different levels of government and where they employ quite different assumptions about the nature of appropriate procedures. Such matters are, however, discussed more fully in Chapter 18 and will not be covered further here.

Overall, it can be concluded that, with reference to procedural and substantive outcomes, identifying regulatory failure involves journeying into inherently contested terrain. That said, it is time to look to causes and to consider *why* regulation goes wrong.

Explaining Regulatory Failure

At the broadest level, regulatory failure can be explained by insufficient resources and by epistemological limitations ('failures of imagination').

---

[14] See Black, ibid.

In this section we explore explanations of failure at two levels, the rhetorical and the analytical. Diagnosing why regulation fails is inherently about perceptions and (often implicit) models of the world, and therefore any reference to a theory of regulatory failure is linked to our beliefs on why and how particular regulatory interventions work.

Looking first at the rhetorical level, one high-level approach draws on the work by the economist Albert Hirschman, who notes three rhetorical strategies that are commonly employed to resist (what he calls) progressive policy interventions.[15] Equally, these rhetorical devices are widely employed to resist proposals for new types of regulations or to dispute the effectiveness of existing provisions. They are 'futility', 'jeopardy', and 'perversity'. For Hirschman, the *futility* position urges that, regardless of regulatory effort, no change to the existing problem will occur. People, for example, will not change their behaviour, regardless of regulatory intervention. Similarly, demanding prerequisites might be required for any particular intervention to have an effect. As a result, it is suggested, adopting any one particular measure will not alter the complexity of the existing problem. *Jeopardy* arguments contend that, despite the worthwhile character of a particular regulatory instrument, its deployment would risk wider achievements and/ or lead to a chain of undesirable side-effects. The inherent benefits of the narrow proposal would thus tend to be outweighed by the costs of the wider loss of other achievements (a widely used variant is the so-called 'slippery slope' argument). For example, adopting particular safety standards might be a good thing in itself, but may produce wider costs by risking legal challenges, causing pressure for further restrictions or, indeed, causing a shift in 'deviance' to more dangerous kinds of activities. A further example of such an argument would hold that the adoption of a particular information requirement would open the door (the 'flood gates') to much wider and extensive requests and requirements.

Finally, arguments based on *perversity* are used to suggest that regulatory interventions achieve the exact opposite of their intended outcomes. For example, it might be argued that prohibiting particular medication on precautionary grounds will cause further deaths by denying treatment, or speed restrictions will cause more speeding because the intended stigma turns into a symbol of open rebellion against oppressive authority.[16]

---

[15] A. Hirschman, *The Rhetoric of Reaction* (Cambridge, 1991).

[16] Focusing on self-defeating regulatory activities, surprises, or paradoxes, the wider literature distinguishes between various terms. All of them seek to attribute particular qualities to types of failures that make them more than trivial or 'normal'. Various authors speak about 'disaster', crises and fiascos, as well as 'catastrophes'. See Dunleavy, 'Policy Disasters'; Boin and t'Hart, 'Institutional Crisis'; Boin et al. (eds), *Governing after Crisis*; Boin, 'Preparing for Future Crises'; M. Moran, 'Not Steering but Drowning' (2001) 72(4) *Political Quarterly* 414–27; M. Moran, 'Review Article: Understanding the

In Chapter 4 we noted a number of explanations that pointed to the inherent limitations of regulation. Those explanations were organized into accounts that emphasize respectively: the pursuit of the public interest; the contest between different interest groups; the power of ideas; and institutional factors. In considering the causes of regulatory failure, it follows that the four different kinds of account produce quite varying explanations of regulatory failure. Examining those types of explanation is helpful in seeking to understand how regulation might fail, or has failed, in a particular context.

In brief, *public interest accounts* centre on the idea that those seeking to institute, operate, or develop regulation do so in pursuit of some conception of the public interest. Interpretations of what the public interest might be and how it is to be achieved will, however, be contested. Different conceptions of the public interest may compete for the regulators' attentions and different elements within the regulatory organization may pursue conceptions of the public interest that compete with each other. Thus, the enforcement division of a regulatory agency may not share the same vision as the policy department and this may make for ineffective delivery of outcomes or confused procedures.[17]

A second difficulty—one that would be acknowledged by all analytical approaches under consideration here—links to the bounded rationality that affects individual and organizational decision-making. Information is costly, and the capacity of any one individual, organization, or system to process all available information within time and other constraints is inherently limited. As a result, our decision-making is inherently bounded. One reason why regulation can go wrong, therefore, is the inherent uncertainty and ambiguity of knowledge. There is ambiguity as to the cause–effect relationships of regulatory instruments. We may assume, but not fully understand, why particular regulatory interventions prove particularly effective at any one time and place. An instrument that may have proved successful in one context may not necessarily play out the same way in a different area, since legal systems differ, political systems vary, and different constituencies are mobilized.[18] Indeed, the interaction between different regulatory instruments and regimes is not necessarily one that can be predicted. Because knowledge is limited, the likelihood that regulatory strategies achieve their intended effect in all cases is very low. Significant challenges will be presented by ambiguities about cause–effect relationships, competing interpretations about the nature of the problem at issue, ways to fix that problem,

---

Regulatory State' (2002) 32(2) *British Journal of Political Science* 391–413; M. Moran, *The British Regulatory State* (Oxford, 2003).

[17] See, e.g., R. Baldwin, 'Why Rules Don't Work' (1990) 53 *Modern Law Review* 321.

[18] R. Merton, 'The Unintended Effects of Purposive Social Action' (1936) 1(6) *American Sociological Review* 894–904.

and potential counter-learning by the array of diverse parties that is affected by the intended regulatory intervention. The regulators, as a result, may not be able to calculate which steps they have to take in order best to serve the public interest, and this may impede their endeavours in spite of their good intentions. Given the limits of our knowledge and understanding, one key strategy therefore is not to rely on grand schemes, but rather to employ incremental 'trial-and-error' approaches towards regulatory change.[19]

Interest group theories stress the extent to which regulatory developments are driven by the particularistic concerns of interest groups. Unsurprisingly, much of the literature that has focused on regulatory failure has pointed to the self-interested behaviour of key actors engaged in the regulatory process.[20] Capture theories would highlight the attempts of organized interests to shape the regulatory process to their own ends.[21] The economic theory of regulation would point to the ability of the economically powerful and the concentrated interests to bend regulation to their will.[22] Those focusing on politicians' behaviour would point to the problem of governments changing their minds over time (the 'time inconsistency problem'), and others would note the blame- and risk-avoiding behaviour of regulatory agencies that focus on realizing popular and convenient outcomes, rather than those that are important, difficult, and potentially unpopular.[23] As a result, the literature, as noted across other chapters in this volume, has advocated addressing the limitations of central oversight by seeking some alignment of organizational self-interest with regulatory objectives.

Ideas-based approaches emphasize the ways in which ideas, beliefs, and worldviews shape regulatory approaches and delivery. As noted in Chapter 4, a particular strand of such theories stresses the inherent plurality of rationalities or worldviews that characterizes any debate regarding regulatory instruments. Failures of regulation, on such accounts, would be explained in a number of ways. First, it might be contended that failure has occurred because the underlying cause–effect assumptions are flawed and the regulatory regime is built on unsustainable ideas. It might, for instance, be argued that central assumptions regarding regulatees are misguided and that regulated firms may be more prone to non-compliance or creative compliance than the

---

[19] On the case for moving from *ex ante* regulatory design to review and adjustment, see R. Baldwin, 'Is Better Regulation Smarter Regulation?' (2005) *Public Law* 485 and Chapter 15 below.

[20] See Lodge, 'The Wrong Type of Regulation?'.

[21] C. Hood, *Explaining Economic Policy Reversals* (Buckingham, 1994), ch. 2.

[22] S. Peltzman, 'The Economic Theory of Regulation after a Decade of Regulation' (1989) *Brookings Papers in Macroeconomics.*

[23] M. Horn, *The Political Economy of Public Administration* (Cambridge, 1995); B. Levy and P. Spiller, 'The Institutional Foundations of Regulatory Commitment' (1994) 10(2) *Journal of Law, Economics and Organization* 201–46.

founding philosophy presupposes.[24] A second kind of account of regulatory failure might build on the 'plurality of worldviews' perspective to argue that failures tend to be the products of the confusions of approach that lead to high levels of friction in communications and to uncertainties within business sectors. A third kind of account might stress the difficulty that some sets of ideas ('mindsets') have in coping with the changing challenges that all regulators have to face.[25] The essence of such accounts is liable to be that ideological conservatism produces under-performance by failing to adapt ideas to new circumstances, or by rejecting information that challenges existing dominant understandings. Systems theories would argue that such insularity and lack of responsiveness is a product of the tendency of those who operate within systems to close themselves off from outside disturbance.[26]

Institutional theories (of different ilks) tend to agree that institutional structures and arrangements, as well as social processes, significantly shape regulation. They will suggest that there is more driving regulatory developments than mere aggregations of individuals' preferences. Failures, from such perspectives, can often be seen as the effects of inter- and intra-institutional pressures. A special problem, on this view, may be 'drift': the tendency of a regulatory system to lose focus and direction. Information asymmetries can thus be said to generate a number of kinds of drift: (i) coalitional drift (governments changing preferences over time); (ii) agency drift (agencies not following their statutory objectives); and (iii) industry drift (industry not following regulatory requirements).

Another possible cause of failure that different institutionalists might note is the overlapping of different organizational understandings and the frictions that this can cause. Institutional theories would highlight, in particular, the ways in which the modern tendency to spread regulation across layers of government and types of organization produces regulatory effects that are not consistent with the original regulatory intentions. The complexity of the regulatory space leads to uncertain effects, as do the diverse assumptions and resources associated with different actors. Cultural theory (discussed above) adds to institutional understandings by stressing the importance of appreciating the inherent side-effects of any one regulatory strategy. Interventions

---

[24] See e.g. Baldwin, 'Why Rules Don't Work'.

[25] This position might combine with the 'exogenous' account of regulatory failure, namely that changing 'habitats' or environments challenge regulatory strategies and undermine their earlier effectiveness. The rise of online gambling, for example, may be seen as a fundamental challenge to national betting regulation.

[26] R. Laughlin, 'Environmental Disturbance and Organizational Transitions and Transformations: Some Alternative Models' (1991) 12(2) *Organizational Studies* 209–32; G. Teubner, *Dilemmas of Law in the Welfare State* (London, 1986); G. Teubner, *Law as an Autopoietic System* (London, 1993); G. Teubner, R. Nobles and D. Schiff, 'The Autonomy of Law: An Introduction to Legal Autopoiesis' in D. Schiff and R. Nobles (eds), *Jurisprudence* (London, 2003).

based on predictable inspections, for instance, will encourage gaming; strategies based on surprise will reduce overall trust within the system; and interventions that are based on mutuality and peer review will lack outside scrutiny and will tend quickly to turn into closed (self-referential) systems. Similarly, systems relying on market-type processes of regulation are said to suffer from inherent lack of overall control and over-individualism. According to this account, any one strategy invites counter-effects as inherent weaknesses emerge as the products of social tensions and processes.

Table 5.1 provides for an overview of the distinct contribution that different approaches make.

Table 5.1. Regulatory failure

Broad approach	Theory	'Failure-mechanism'	'Remedy'
Interest-centred approaches	Public interest/ interest group/ economic theories	Collective action problem leads to regulation in favour of particular concentrated interests.	Enhance interest group participation and contestation.
Ideas-based approaches	Ideas and cultural theories	Inherent blackspots in any single or 'elegant' approach has side-effects and will be exploited by opposition.	Use 'clumsy' or 'hybrid' solutions.
Institutional approaches	Institutional design	Information asymmetries generate drift: (i) coalitional drift (governments changing preferences over time); (ii) agency drift (agencies not following their statutory objectives); and (iii) industry drift (industry not following regulatory requirements).	Need to accommodate particularities of political system to deal with 'commitment problem' through 'hardwiring' of institutional devices, such as (i) fire-alarms; (ii) deck-stacking; and (iii) police patrols (oversight).
	Layering	Side-effects of multiple regulatory regimes with different understandings and objectives operating side-by-side and overlapping.	Incremental regulatory adjustment to accommodate competing pressures and provision of conflict resolution space to accommodate competing interpretations; possibly also advocacy of comprehensive reform to bring different regimes into line.
	Unintended consequences	Intended actions cannot foresee inherent unintended consequences—because of bounded rationality, side-effects, counter-learning, and changes in the wider environment.	Reduce side-effects through incrementalism and attempts at enhancing 'rationality' in regulatory process.
	Self-referential systems	Systems close themselves off from outside disturbance.	Enhance self-reflexivity via proceduralization and self-learning.

Regulatory Remedies

What emerges from the above discussion is a differentiated picture of ways in which regulatory failure can be accounted for. It ranges from those cynical views that see regulatory failure as a mixture of sectoral lobbying, if not capture, and bureaucratic self-interest, to those views that see unintended consequences, whatever their origin, as an inherent aspect of social life. These explanations also suggest that we are faced with often contradictory advice on how to deal with regulatory failure. Space here does not allow us to offer an exhaustive review of remedies (which would restate much of the rest of this volume), but it is worth discussing three general recipes for regulatory improvement.[27]

Coordination. Problems of over- and under-regulation are often associated with failings in coordination.[28] Different regulators often focus on similar or the same activities, but do so using inconsistent methodologies and penalties, thereby imposing considerable and confusing compliance burdens on firms. In other areas, key problems remain outside any one regulator's attention as particular issues fall between the jurisdictional stools of different regulatory regimes and organizations. Indeed, when looking at the literature on failed control systems of a complex nature (such as space shuttle safety regimes), one of the most widely accepted suggestions is that such complex operations are vulnerable to the 'normalization of deviance'. In this process, small deviations from the norm prove to be acceptable at each individual stage of production but agglomerate over time and successive production stages so that they eventually lead to disastrous failure. Similarly, when fragmented regulatory regimes accept small deviations from the norm without seeing the proverbial 'whole picture', then overall regulatory failure is likely to ensue. As a result, the often-proposed remedy is that of 'more coordination' to centralize information, to maintain control, and to impose a more uniform regulatory process. Similarly, but from a very different intellectual tradition, Stephen Breyer argues for the need to bring in an 'oversight' panel to deal with problems associated with 'knee-jerk' political and regulatory responses to crises.[29]

Modes of seeking to ensure coordination are numerous and range from the merger of regulatory bodies to the imposition of common methodologies

---

[27] See also the discussion of the quest for better regulation in Chapter 15.

[28] See the discussion of network coordination in Chapter 8 below. Christopher Hood has called these failings in coordination 'multi-organizational sub-optimization'; C. Hood, *Limits of Administration* (London, 1974), 475.

[29] See S. Breyer, *Breaking the Vicious Circle: Towards Effective Risk Regulation* (Cambridge, MA, 1993).

(see the discussions in Chapters 8 and 18). There are, however, potential costs in attempting to advance coordination. Adjustments in terms of organizational change are linked to costs and can create uncertainties for businesses and consumers. Rationalizations can prompt the charge that over-centralized regimes do not allow for those differentiated treatments that allow responsiveness to specific contexts.[30] Any extensive attempt to coordinate, furthermore, is likely to accentuate problems with time-lags. In a world that refuses to stand still, delays are likely to make regulatory interventions ill-timed and poorly informed.

Coordination, in summary, is a notion that many parties welcome as a 'good thing'—but they may do so because it means very different things to different people. Whether 'coordination', in whatever form, will in itself avoid further regulatory failures is questionable—as discussions of 'polycentric' and decentred regulatory regimes reveal (see Chapters 8 and 18).

Organizational reform and learning. A second widely advocated—and utilized—remedy for regulatory failures is that of learning and evaluation. Much has been said about the largely symbolic nature of organizational change. Here, organizational change hardly ever follows functionally -required lines, but rather follows the so-called 'logic of appropriateness'. According to the 'logic of appropriateness', the inherent bounded rationality encountered in decision-making means that regulatory reform will not be conducted on the basis of exhaustive and comprehensive analysis that will reveal the optimal organizational and strategic arrangement for the particular issue in question. Instead, reform proposals will be based on limited searches.

Organizational learning is shaped by a number of factors. One factor is the limitations of decision-making that are inherent in any organization. Information processing, and the way in which organizations update their knowledge about their own processes and the world 'out there', is one of the crucial parts of any organization. These processes, though, are inherently biased. Dominant understandings within organizations 'filter' data, and any information that seems to contradict the dominant cause–effect understandings about regulation is likely to be filtered out of the system in order to avoid disturbing day-to-day functioning.[31] This filtering-out is dangerous for any organization, however: the processes of rejection expel not merely

---

[30] Some commentators, indeed, highlight the importance of redundancy, and the absence of coordination, as a means of minimizing the errors from any one strategy. See J.A. Rijpma, 'Complexity, Tight-Coupling and Reliability' (1997) 5(1) *Journal of Contingencies and Crisis Management* 15–23.

[31] If we had to question the utility and validity of all our actions all the time, we would not be able to function, but would rather spend all day and night procrastinating. Therefore, confirmation-seeking and the 'filtering-out' of information that seems to contradict our understandings is essential for our ability to make any form of decision.

information that deviates from the norm but also any potential signs of failure and keys to understanding this.[32]

A possible remedy for such narrowness is to introduce a 'challenge function' into organizational operations. This poses the question how the organization can ensure that this 'challenge function' plays a meaningful role, rather than meets rejection or produces such a fundamental questioning of approaches that any ongoing operation is gridlocked. As for the mode of setting up such a challenge function, some may bring in a special 'challenge committee', others will rely on 'peer reviews' among professionals, while another version is the so-called 'court jester' concept (an idea that was widespread in medieval courts and the Vatican).[33] Here the notion is that particular individuals are given the freedom to 'speak truth to power'. Overall, though, a process of organizational reform (often called 'root and branch' reform) that relies on organizational learning is an inherently demanding process that is very likely to reflect currently dominant worldviews and logics of appropriateness, rather than to offer genuine questioning of the challenges facing the regulatory organization or regime.

Clumsy solutions/hybrids. The case for reform is often accompanied with the charge that the existing regime constitutes the 'wrong type of regulation'. After matters have gone wrong, such arguments are often associated with demands for enhanced and intrusive systems of oversight. Some, however, may resist these proposals and argue that problems are associated with 'too much' oversight and that market-type processes should be utilized to decrease the incentives for gaming and cheating. As noted above (and in Chapter 3), a reliance on any single approach to 'solving' regulatory failure is inherently limited—it invites side-effects and exploitation by opposed interests. As a result, much emphasis has been placed, in a variety of literatures, on the importance of using redundancy and mixed strategies to deal with regulatory failure.[34] Overlap and contradictory tensions are said to offer one way to counter the inherent weaknesses of any one single regulatory approach (such as 'markets' or 'mutuality' or 'oversight') and it also introduces a certain amount of unpredictability, thereby reducing the possibilities for cheating. The general stress of cultural-theory-based approaches has therefore been to advocate so-called clumsy solutions—that is, approaches that mix elements from various 'pure' strategies in order to compensate against side-effects.[35]

---

[32] J.G. March, L.S. Sproull, and M. Tamuz, 'Learning from Samples of One or Fewer' (1991) 2(1) *Organization Science* 1–13; S.D. Sagan, *The Limits of Safety* (Princeton, 1993), ch. 5.

[33] C. Hood and M. Lodge, *Politics of Public Service Bargains* (Oxford, 2006), ch. 6.

[34] See, e.g., N. Gunningham and P. Grabosky, *Smart Regulation* (Oxford, 1998).

[35] M. Verweij, M. Douglas, R. Ellis, C. Engel, F. Hendricks, S. Lohmann, S. Ney, S. Rayner, and M. Thompson, 'The Case for Clumsiness' in M. Verweij and M. Thompson (eds), *Clumsy Solutions for a Complex World* (Basingstoke, 2006).

The related idea is that monocultures are more likely to suffer from disease than polycultures.

The extent to which such clumsy or hybrid solutions are able to maintain stability rather than self-destruct is a matter for debate. Similarly, it is difficult to see how clumsy solutions can easily be engineered, or whether they tend, in practice, to emerge in an accidental, 'layering' fashion. Although such an 'organic' growth of resilience through clumsiness might be regarded as bringing advantages over those approaches that believe in intelligent design, such arrangements will nevertheless be exposed to the kinds of regulatory failures that are associated with layering approaches—and which were noted above.

Conclusions

Looking across these three widely advocated 'solutions' to regulatory failure suggests that any remedy is associated with inherent trade-offs, side-effects, and limitations. It is unlikely that the adoption of any one remedy will safeguard against future regulatory failure. What do emerge, however, from the discussion offered by this and the previous sections are two key messages. One is that there may be importance in relying on redundancy in regulation—in avoiding resort to any one single instrument or organization to deliver desired regulatory outcomes and processes. The other message is that the importance of contestability should not be forgotten. If regulatory failure tends to flow, *inter alia*, from capture and 'closed' views as to the benevolence (or otherwise) of particular regulatory instruments, contestability offers a challenge to those restricted perspectives.

This chapter has cut across many of the themes of this volume. Regulatory failure occurs across all parts of regulatory activities and it raises key issues that we have noted in other chapters—notably Chapters 3 ('What is 'Good' Regulation?') and Chapter 15 ('Cost-Benefit Analysis and Regulatory Impact Assessment'). Any discussion of regulatory failure prompts consideration of the limits of intended social action. One of regulation's key attractions has been its suggestion that it offers a technocratic and 'safe' mode of control. The reality is that 'failure' is a contestable notion and that there are limits to human and organizational capacities—especially when collaborations are required in order to achieve results. As a result, it may be appropriate to regard the achieving of intended outcomes (and the acknowledgement of this) as the exception rather than the rule. Believing that 'regulation', on its own, will safeguard against failure, or accusations of this, is arguably the best recipe for further failure. We have noted, in this chapter, how different theories account for regulatory failure. Resisting charges of failure demands that the core varieties and mechanisms of failure are borne in mind, that regulators continue to consider how the likelihood of their occurrence can be minimized, and that the contestability of failure is addressed.

6 Regulating Risks

Regulation can be seen as being inherently about the control of risks, whether these relate to illnesses caused by the exposure to carcinogens, inadequate utility services, or losses caused by incompetent financial advice.[1] More formally, risk is usually defined as the probability of a particular event (or hazard) occurring and the consequent severity of the impact of that event. This notion of risk contrasts with the idea of uncertainty, a distinction provided by Frank Knight. The division drawn is between uncertainty—which is inherently impossible to measure—and risk, which is amenable to quantification.[2] To view regulation as concerned with the control of risk adds to our understanding of key regulatory debates across all dimensions of regulation, namely standard-setting, information-gathering, and behaviour-modification. At the same time, the regulation of risks (which needs to be separated from those discussions of 'risk-based regulation' that are dealt with in Chapter 13) points to a series of fundamental debates and worldviews. Risk regulation is centrally concerned with the highly contested management of Knightian risk and uncertainty, the challenges of dealing with uncertain popular responses to anticipated or realized risks, and the issues presented by communications about risks.[3]

Risk has been regarded as one of the key unifying themes that shape the contemporary social sciences. For the German sociologist Ulrich Beck, we are living in the age of the *risk society*.[4] Risks are no longer imposed by exogenous factors and regarded as a matter of fate. Instead, risks have taken on a different quality—they are no more just a matter of destiny or of change: rather, contemporary risks are increasingly manufactured in that they are the result of human decisions and actions. This state of, what he calls, 'advanced modernity', requires specific expertise to identify and recognize these, often global, risks. The increased use of the language of risk further

---

[1] See generally J. Black, 'The Role of Risk in Regulatory Processes', in R. Baldwin, M. Cave, and M. Lodge (eds), *The Oxford Handbook of Regulation* (Oxford, 2010). On the consequences of framing the objects of regulation as risks, see H. Rothstein, M. Huber, and G. Gaskell, 'A Theory of Risk Colonization' (2006) 35(1) *Economy and Society* 91–112.

[2] F. Knight, *Risk, Uncertainty, and Profit* (Boston, 1921).

[3] See also C. Hood, H. Rothstein, and R. Baldwin, *The Government of Risk* (Oxford, 2001); R. Kasperson and P. Stallen (eds), *Communicating Risks to the Public* (Dordrecht, 1991); B.M. Hutter (ed.), *Anticipating Risks and Organising Regulation* (Cambridge, 2010); B.M. Hutter and M. Power (eds), *Organizational Encounters with Risk* (Cambridge, 2005).

[4] U. Beck, *The Risk Society* (London, 1992); A. Giddens, 'Risk and Responsibility' (1999) 62(1) *Modern Law Review* 1–10.

raises complications in that a decision about consuming particular goods becomes one of risk and uncertainty, rather than categorical certainties (as in 'safe versus unsafe'). Modern societies might have unprecedented expertise in evaluating the presence of risks through scientific means, but such knowledge generates greater levels of insecurity. The tools for coping with modern risks, moreover, are, at best, limited, especially since their applications are likely to have transboundary, if not global, implications.[5] Indeed, implicit in these discussions is that contemporary risks differ in their quality to previous generations of risks in so far as the former may unintentionally generate greater (transboundary) unanticipated risks. This also implies that contemporary 'manufactured' risks also challenge class-understandings of politics,[6] in that the wealthy are unable to reduce their exposure to risks on the basis of wealth: it is access to knowledge and expertise that allows individuals, at least to some extent, to avert exposure to particular risks. More generally, though, Beck argues that contemporary societies' attempts to anticipate risks are inherently futile, as these risks cannot be calculated.[7] Indeed, according to this view, risk assessment exercises inherently underestimate real threats, as they rely on methodologies that legitimize individuals' exposures to incalculable risks.

Others also note that this age of required expertise goes hand in hand with an age that is increasingly distrustful of authority.[8] Indeed, for Mary Douglas and Aaron Wildavsky, the rise of egalitarian and individualist worldviews triggered a growing concern (if not obsession) with danger and risk and consequent interest in blame.[9] Others, too, have noted that the language of risk and attempts to verify 'safety' have reflected wider societal trends towards a greater distrustfulness towards expertise and authority—and these trends have at least to some extent motivated the move towards the 'regulatory state' (which is explored in more detail in Chapter 18).

Such a context points to a set of problems for regulation and regulators. Examples of debates about how to regulate risks are not difficult to find. They range from interests in acid rain, to concerns about the safety of large technical installations such as nuclear reactors, to the fears associated with mad cow disease (Bovine Spongiform Encephalopathy) and later worries about the safety of genetically modified foods. These debates also extend into

---

[5] A. Boin 'The New World of Crises and Crisis Management' (2009) 26(4) *Review of Policy Research* 367–77; U. Beck, *World at Risk* (Cambridge, 2009).

[6] See A. Giddens, *Beyond Left and Right* (Cambridge, 1994); M. Douglas and A.Wildavsky, *Divided We Stand* (Berkeley, 1982).

[7] U. Beck, 'Living in the World Risk Society' (2006) 35(3) *Economy and Society* 329–45.

[8] Also B. Wybbe, 'Scientific Knowledge and the Global Environment', in M. Redclift and T. Benton (eds), *Social Theory and the Global Environment* (London, 1994), 175–6.

[9] M. Douglas, *Risk and Blame* (London, 1992); M. Douglas and A. Wildavsky, *Risk and Culture* (Berkeley, 1982).

discussions of terrorism, critical infrastructures, and vanishing bee colonies or fish stocks. More broadly, conflicts about the extent to which the *precautionary principle* should be applied within countries, within the EU, and in global trade further points to the political significance of risk in the world of national and international regulation.[10]

The literature on the regulation of risk is thus interested in the causes of disaster and failure. Beck, for example, notes that 'Risk means the *anticipation* of catastrophe [...] Risks are always events that are threatening.'[11] Such scholarship seeks to distinguish between social, technological, and natural risks, but the boundaries between these different categories are fluid. Technologies, for example, are socially constructed and social choices have to be made in order to deal with natural risks. In relation to 'failures' to deal with risks, furthermore, a distinction needs to be drawn between those social sources of failure that involve intentional acts of obstruction and those that result from 'unintended' acts. For some, failure is inevitable, if only because of organizational processes that encourage 'deviance', and failure's consequences are—under particular constellations—unpredictable, due to the inherent complexity of organizational processes. Accordingly, this position requires a differentiated approach towards the risk regulation of different technologies.[12] Similarly, issues arise concerning the relative importance of addressing high-impact but low-probability risks as opposed to those that are of low impact but of high probability. How risks are perceived and responded to often has more to do with subjective matters than with any form of objective risk profiling. Inconsistencies between regulated domains suggest that fears and anxieties, moral panics, and such like have considerable mileage in explaining why particular risks are regulated in a 'heavy duty' manner and other risks are tolerated in a much more reactive way.[13]

A further focus of risk regulation debates is the organizational dimension of risk control. In particular, this relates to issues of procedures for decision-making, the increasing pushing of responsibility for risk management into private organizations (for example, in the HACCP (Hazard Analysis and Critical Control Points) approach),[14] the application of cost-benefit analysis,

---

[10] See, e.g., G. Majone, 'What Price Safety? The Precautionary Principle and its Policy Implications (2002) 40 *Journal of Common Market Studies* 89; V. Heyvaert, 'Guidance Without Constraint: Assessing the Impact of the Precautionary Principle on the European Community's Chemicals Policy' (2006) 6 *Yearbook of European Environmental Law* 27–60.

[11] Beck, 'Living in the World Risk Society', 332.

[12] C. Perrow, *Normal Accidents* (New York, 1999); D.Vaughan, 'Organizational Rituals of Risk and Error', in B.M. Hutter and M. Power (eds), *Organizational Encounters with Risk* (Oxford, 2005); M. Lodge, 'The Public Management of Risk' (2009) 26(4) *Review of Policy Research* 395–408.

[13] See generally Hood, Rothstein, and Baldwin, *Government of Risk.*

[14] This approach was formally endorsed by the World Health Organization in 1972, it was incorporated in the Codex Alimentarius in 1985, and became an international standard in 1994.

as well as how individuals and organizations operate within a context of bounded rationality and well-documented biases in decision-making.

This chapter concentrates on three central issues in the risk regulation debate, namely the problems of defining and assessing risks, the key regulatory challenges that are posed by risks, and four ways of organizing 'approaches' towards risk regulation. These approaches do not provide for 'one best way' to deal with the regulation of risks: rather, they emphasize that risk regulation is about choices that reflect fundamental assumptions about the vulnerability of particular social systems.

Defining and Assessing Risks

It seems uncontroversial to suggest that regulatory efforts should be devoted, as a first priority, to the reduction of the most severe risks that we face in society. A glance at the literature on risks reveals, however, that identifying and assessing risks is no simple matter.[15] Indeed, a first issue is 'what to look for', given the existence of threshold or sleeper effects, or major discontinuities and 'black swans'.[16] These different effects challenge assumptions of linearity or normal distribution-shaped risk probabilities.[17]

As noted, risk has been widely defined as the probability that a particular adverse event will occur during a stated period of time, or result from a particular challenge.[18] Important distinctions have, however, been drawn between different types of risk. Thus, probabilistic and unpredictable risks have been differentiated (thereby blurring the boundaries between uncertainty and risk).[19] In the case of the former, assessments of probability can be based on available statistics concerning past incidents. With unpredictable

---

It was also incorporated in European law under 2003/53/EC. See D. Demortain, 'Standardising through Concepts', *CARR discussion paper 45* (London, 2007).

[15] See Royal Society, *Risk: Analysis, Perception, Management* (London, 1992); S. Krimsky and D. Golding, *Social Theories of Risk* (Westport, 1992); B.M. Hutter, 'Risk, Regulation, and Management', in P. Taylor-Gooby and J. Zinn (eds), *Risk in Social Science* (Oxford, 2006); L. Sjöberg, 'Rational Risk Perception' (2006) 9(6) *Risk Research* 683–96.

[16] H. Brooks, 'The Typology of Surprises in Technology, Institutions and Development', in W.C. Clark and R.E. Munn (eds), *Sustainable Development of the Biosphere* (Cambridge, 1986); N. M. Taleb, *Black Swans* (London, 2007).

[17] 'Threshold effects' are defined as those where a particular tipping point leads to a cascading in the condition of a particular object; 'sleeper effects' refer to events where a previously dormant property emerges as a highly salient factor ('dormant vulnerability'), and 'black swans' refer to events with high impact that represent extreme outliers in terms of probability.

[18] See Royal Society, *Risk*, 2; B. Fischhoff, S. Watson, and C. Hope, 'Defining Risk', in T.S. Gluckman and M. Gough (eds), *Readings in Risk* (Washington, 1993); O. Renn, 'Concepts of Risk: A Classification', in Krimsky and Golding, *Social Theories of Risk*.

[19] See, e.g., P. Sprent, *Taking Risks* (London, 1988), ch. 2.

risks, evidence of a causal connection between events may be weak and unquantifiable. Some events may be 'one-off', non-repeating risks, where probabilities cannot be estimated and subjective assessments must be made. A related distinction lies between 'objective' and 'subjective' risks. The former are seen as scientifically assessable by experts and probabilistic, the latter as non-expert perceptions by the lay public.[20]

A further division can be drawn between *voluntarily undertaken* risks (e.g. from taking oral contraceptives or diet drinks) and *societally imposed* risks (e.g. from nuclear power stations), where citizens have little choice as to exposure. Again, *discrete* risks can be separated from *pervasive* risks, where the former are highly identifiable threats and events of a precise, bounded nature (e.g. earthquakes) and the latter are the risks borne as part of the 'normal' functioning of society—as, for example, presented by polluted air, water, and soil.[21] Further distinctions can, moreover, be drawn between risks that are reversible after actualizing and those that are not and between risks of different natures—be these natural, physical, biological, or social-communicative.

A core concern of risk studies has been to explain how risks are, or should be, perceived, assessed, quantified, and responded to.[22] Most of these approaches acknowledge that risk regulation is not merely about the 'real' consequences of a risk occurring and harm resulting, but also about the impact of mediating factors. A number of broad and varying approaches can be identified.[23]

---

[20] For a critique of this distinction, see, e.g., B. Wynne, 'Institutional Mythologies and Dual Societies in the Management of Risk', in C. Kunreuther and E.V. Lay (eds), *Risk Analysis Controversy* (Berlin, 1982). On the way that regulatory bodies assess risks in the USA, see C.F. Cranor, *Regulating Toxic Substances* (New York, 1993), esp. ch. 4.

[21] See M. Waterstone (ed), *Risk and Society: The Interaction of Science, Technology and Public Policy* (Dordrecht, 1991).

[22] See generally Royal Society, *Risk*, and B. Fischhoff, P. Slovic, S. Lichtenstein, S. Reid, and B. Combs, 'How Safe is Safe Enough?' (1978) 9 *Policy Sciences* 127. See also O. Renn, *Risk Governance* (London, 2008), esp. 12–45.

[23] We do not focus here on those studies that explore whether national styles 'matter' in risk regulation. Different views exist, ranging from those that suggest that national styles exist, others that point to 'flip-flop' patterns in stringency of risk regulation between US and European approaches, and those that see no clear patterns across countries and sectors whatsoever. See W. Gormley and B.G. Peters, 'National Styles of Regulation' (1992) 25(4) *Policy Sciences* 381–99; M. Howlett, 'Beyond Legalism? Policy Ideas, Implementation Styles and Emulation-based Convergence in Canadian and US Environmental Policy' (2000) 20 *Journal of Public Policy* 305–29; S. Kelman, *Regulating America, Regulating Sweden: A Comparative Study of Occupational Safety and Health Policy* (Cambridge, 1981); R. Löfstedt and D. Vogel, 'The Changing Character of Regulation' (2002) 21(3) *Risk Analysis* 399–416; D. Vogel, 'The Hare and Tortoise Revisited: The New Politics of Consumer and Environmental Regulation in Europe' (2003) 33 *British Journal of Political Science* 557–80; J.B. Wiener, 'Whose Precaution After All?' (2003) 13 *Duke Journal of Comparative and International Law* 207–62; J.B. Wiener and M.D. Rodgers, 'Comparing Precaution in the United States and Europe' (2002) 5 (4) *Journal of Risk Research* 317–49.

Technical perspectives, as seen in actuarial approaches, look to the relative frequencies of events that are amenable to 'objective' observation (e.g. numbers of deaths) and which assess probabilities by extrapolating from statistics on past events. Similarly, in epidemiological studies, populations exposed to a risk are compared to control populations and attempts are made to quantify relationships between risks and harms. Engineering approaches attempt to assess the probabilities of failures in complex systems even where there is insufficient data on the given system as a whole. Fault-tree or event-tree analyses are used and the failure probabilities for each component in the tree are evaluated before all such probabilities are sought to be synthesized.

Technical approaches, in general, seek to anticipate physical harms, average events over time and space, and use relative frequencies to specify probabilities. They are associated with the view that decisions on risks can be made on the basis of objective evidence that can be treated mathematically to produce a numerical result. This perspective has been used to assess not merely the quantum of risks but also their social acceptability. This latter application has, however, been much criticized by social scientists[24] on the grounds that what persons perceive as undesirable depends on their values and preferences and that technical strategies tend to undervalue objectives such as equity, fairness, public participation, and resilience.[25] Objectors have also contended that judgements are involved in selecting, defining, and structuring the 'risk problem' and that these influence subsequent conclusions.[26] Thus, these approaches are seen as potentially biased, requiring not just the existence of data, but also a belief in the possibility of technical analysis in dealing with risks. Such criticisms have eroded not only the idea of objectivity in risk assessment but also the presumed difference between expert and lay public views of risk—the critics of technical approaches hold that both technical and lay assessments of risks involve human interpretation, judgement, and subjectivity.[27] This, we will see below, has implications for those seeking to legitimate different regulatory approaches to risk. Nevertheless, it can be argued that technical assessments have a role to play, but their contribution has to be seen in the context of their inherent limitations.

[24] See, e.g., M. Douglas, *Risk: Acceptability According to the Social Sciences* (London, 1985); Renn, 'Concepts of Risk'; A. Mazur, 'Bias in Risk-Benefit Analysis' (1985) 7 *Technology in Society* 25; Beck, *Risk Society*; L. Clarke, *Acceptable Risk* (Berkeley, 1989).

[25] J.F. Short, 'The Social Fabric at Risk: Towards the Social Transformation of Risk Analysis' (1984) 49 *American Sociological Review* 711. For official acceptance that risk regulation 'cannot be reduced to a set of rules based on universal formulae for quantifying and valuing costs and benefits' but involves ethical and perceptual problems, see HM Treasury, *The Setting of Safety Standards* (London, 1996).

[26] See C.J.H. Vlek and P.J.M. Stollen, 'Rational and Personal Aspects of Risk' (1980) 45 *Acta Psychologica* 273; Cranor, *Regulating Toxic Substances*, 10.

[27] Royal Society, *Risk*, 97; B. Fischhoff, *Risk: A Guide to Controversy* (Washington, DC, 1989).

The *economic perspective* on risk transforms undesired effects into subjective utilities so that comparisons between different risks and benefits can be made using the currency of personal satisfaction. This provides a means of integrating risk analyses into decision processes in which various costs and benefits are assessed in pursuit of the allocation of resources in a way that maximizes their utility for society. This perspective has proven increasingly influential in court cases concerning compensation payments towards victims exposed to involuntary risks.[28]

Central difficulties for the economic approach[29] are how individuals' subjective utilities can be aggregated; how costs imposed on parties beyond the immediate transaction can be taken on board; how future risks are accounted for; how monetary units can be placed on risks of health losses or deaths; and how utilitarian, wealth-maximization, or contractarian ethics can be justified. The economic approach thus begs serious distributional questions (especially regarding third parties), and makes contestable assumptions both about the rationality of market decisions and concerning the freedom of choice and quality of information encountered in the marketplace. It is said to involve a range of judgements and modelling assumptions (such as the nature of utility maximization) and be highly prone to manipulation.[30] Moreover, it involves a bias towards the wealthy, since all methods of placing a monetary value on life (e.g. making reference to willingness to pay, insurance calculations, or court awards) are in some way based on the wealth of the victim and impliedly encourage saving the lives of the wealthy and imposing risks on the poor.[31]

The *psychological approach* to the definition and measurement of risk focuses upon individual cognition and such questions as how probabilities are perceived; how preferences relating to risks can be accounted for and how contexts shape individuals' risk estimations and evaluations. Individual risk perceptions are therefore placed in the foreground of analysis. Thus, several factors have been said to impinge on perceptions of seriousness of risks.[32] These include:

---

[28] See Renn, *Risk Governance*, 17–18.

[29] See, e.g., P. Slovic, B. Fischhoff, and S. Lichtenstein, 'Rating the Risks' (1979) *Environment* 4; M.S. Baram, 'Cost-Benefit Analysis: An Inadequate Basis for Health, Safety and Environmental Regulatory Decisionmaking' (1980) 8 *Ecology LQ* 463.

[30] See P. Self, *Econocrats and the Policy Process: The Politics and Philosophy of Cost-Benefit Analysis* (Basingstoke, 1975).

[31] See H. Otway, 'Public Wisdom, Expert Fallibility: Towards a Contextual Theory of Risk', in Krimsky and Golding, *Social Theories of Risk*.

[32] See Royal Society, *Risk*, ch. 5; Renn, 'Concepts of Risk'; P. Slovic, B. Fischhoff, and S. Lichtenstein, 'Perceived Risks, Psychological Factors and Social Implications' (1981) 376 *Proceedings of the Royal Society of London* 17; L. Gould et al., *Perceptions of Technological Risks and Benefits* (New York, 1988); C. Kam and E. Simas, 'Risk Orientation and Policy Frames' (2010) 72 *Journal of Politics* 381–96.

- catastrophic potential;
- degree of personal control over the size or probability of the risk;
- familiarity with the risk;
- degree of perceived equity in sharing risks and benefits;
- visibility of the benefits of risk-taking;
- potential to impose blame on risk creators;
- delay in the manifestation of harm;
- voluntariness with which the risk is undertaken.

These approaches suggest that individuals display biases in their behaviour when faced with different risks; for example, individuals display 'dread', have limited interest (or comprehension) in the language of probabilities, show both risk aversion and optimism-bias in their decisions, and rather place an emphasis on trust. Individuals, for instance, are more likely to purchase earthquake insurance in the immediate aftermath of an earthquake than during periods of 'build-up' (when the likelihood of the 'big one' striking is somewhat higher); or car drivers drive more cautiously in the immediate aftermath of viewing a car crash. In other words, risk perception studies are interested in seeking to understand better the individual biases that explain responses to risk.[33]

Risk, within such an approach, is seen as a multi-dimensional concept that cannot be reduced to a mere product of probability and consequences. Such a focus on the individual is, however, said to underplay the extent to which perceptions are affected by group, social, institutional, and cultural factors.[34]

Sociologists have addressed this under-emphasis by attending to social relations and institutions as influences on risk perception and by examining the ways that moral positions and valuations affect responses to risk. They have tended to stress the limitations of technical approaches and to argue that expert knowledge is not value-free, but conditioned by social contexts. They have empasized that public attitudes to risk are affected by a wide range of variables and that public tolerance of risk is a political issue in which the degree of public involvement in risk management processes may play an important role.[35] Students of organizations have pointed to the particular 'man-made' processes that accentuate risk within the setting of inter-organizational production processes. For example, Diane Vaughan has suggested that error is introduced through organizational processes that she terms 'the normalization of deviance', in that small deviations from the 'norm' that appear not to have any major consequences are tolerated and over time

---

[33] See also P. Slovic, M. Finucane, E. Peters, and D. MacGregor, 'Risk Analysis and Risk as Feelings' (2004) 24(2) *Risk Analysis* 311–22.

[34] See Royal Society, *Risk*, 11, 108; A. Plough and S. Krimsky, 'The Emergence of Risk Communication Studies: Social and Political Context' (1987) 12 *Science, Technology and Human Values* 4.

[35] See Krimsky and Golding, *Social Theories of Risk*, 356; Giddens, *Beyond Left and Right*.

become 'accepted'. Others have also noted that failure is inevitable, and that, therefore, risks associated with particular technologies are 'unmanageable'.[36] Indeed, students of security risks point to the problems identified in the 9/11 Commission report which cited organizational coordination problems and a 'failure of imagination' as among the causes for the failure to identify the potential terrorist threat.[37] The challenge is said to be that of developing political processes that will come to grips with these new risk-related issues.

Cultural theorists, in turn, have contended that attitudes to risk vary according to cultural biases—attitudes and beliefs shared by a group—and that risk is a plastic concept allowing the development of no single measure by which different cultural biases towards risk can be compared.[38] The four worldviews of cultural theory (as noted in Chapter 4) have different perspectives, and these produce their own explanations of variations in individual risk perceptions. Insightful initial work on risk perceptions has received mixed responses but, more recently, authors have sought to develop a 'cultural cognition' perspective regarding risk and have noted that individuals should be viewed as 'cultural evaluators'. Risk perceptions, on this approach, are a reflection of individuals' expressive appraisals of risky activities. Such differences, according to this view, should be recognized through deliberative fora, rather than be treated as ill-informed and requiring 'help' through the decision-making of experts.[39]

---

[36] B. Turner, *Man-Made Disasters* (London, 1978); D. Vaughan, 'Organizational Rituals of Risk and Error', in B.M. Hutter and M. Power (eds), *Organizational Encounters with Risk* (Cambridge, 2005); Perrow, *Normal Accidents*.

[37] 9/11 Commission, *Final Report of the National Commission on Terrorist Attacks Upon the United States* (2004), www.gpoaccess.gov/911/index.html

[38] The social construction of nature is therefore a partial representation of 'nature' with different worldviews seeing the vulnerability of nature in their particular perspective: for fatalists, nature is 'capricous' (requiring adaptation to unpredictable events), for hierarchists, nature is 'perverse and tolerant' (i.e. manageable within limits), for individualists, nature is 'benign' (always returning to equilibrium), and for egalitarians, nature is 'ephemeral' (highly vulnerable, causing egalitarians to be alarmed). See M. Thompson, R. Ellis, and A. Wildavsky, *Cultural Theory* (Boulder, 1990), 27; Douglas, *Risk and Blame*; Douglas and Wildavsky, *Risk and Culture*; M. Schwarz and M. Thompson, *Divided We Stand: Redefining Politics, Technology and Social Choice* (Hemel Hempstead, 1990); V. Mamadough, 'Grid-Group Cultural Theory: An Introduction' (1999) 47 *GeoJournal* 395–409; K. Dake, 'Orienting Dispositions in the Perception of Risk' (1991) 22 *Journal of Cross-Cultural Psychology* 61–82; C. Morris, I. Lanford, and T. O'Riordan, 'A Quantiative Test of the Cultural Theory of Risk Perceptions' (1998) 18(5) *Risk Analysis* 635–47. A more critical view is provided by S. Rayner, 'Culture Theory and Risk Analysis', in Krimsky and Golding, *Social Theories of Risk*. See also the collection of writings in A.Wildavsky, *Cultural Analysis* (New Brunswick, 2006).

[39] D. Kahan, 'Cultural Cognition as a Conception of the Cultural Theory of Risk' (2008) *Harvard Law School Program on Risk Regulation Research paper*, no. 08-20 (http://ssrn.com/abstract=1123807); D.M. Kahan, 'Two Conceptions of Emotion in Risk Regulation' (2008) 156 *University of Penslyvania Law Review* 740–66; H. Jenkins-Smith and K. Herron, 'Rock and Hard Place' (2009) 37(5) *Politics and Policy* 1095–129; L. Sjöberg, 'Worldviews, Political Attitudes and Risk Perception' (1998) 9 *Risk* 137–52.

Such cultural approaches to risk have been linked with psychological and sociological treatments in the work of 'social amplification theorists' who suggest that signals concerning risks are filtered through social amplification stations (e.g. groups of scientists; the media; pressure groups; and politicians) and that this filtering intensifies or minimizes certain aspects of risks.[40] In other words, the risk itself is attentuated or intensified through social interactions, which in themselves have further, secondary consequences. These consequences themselves lead to further amplification or attenuation effects. Thus, risk, according to these analyses, is an objective property, but it is also a social construction. These accounts also draw heavily on those findings that have focused on individual perceptions of risk, pointing to the different decision-making heuristics that characterize human decision-making (risk aversion, optimism bias, dread, and so on).[41] Similarly, the interaction between societal risk and the institutional risks organizations face when accepting to deal with societal risks has also pointed to the often unintended effects of organizational responses.[42] Other social scientists have focused on risk communication and have attended to the ways that messages about risks are conveyed; the politics of such message passing, and the institutional and cultural contexts under which risk messages are formulated and conveyed.[43]

To summarize, a host of different approaches to the definition and measurement of risks can be taken. These very differences raise issues about regulatory responses to risks and the ways in which risk regulation regimes can be justified or legitimated. Thus, high confidence in technical approaches to risk might be expected to lead to an emphasis on leaving risk regulation to experts and to establishing regulatory priorities with reference to technical evaluations. In contrast, a strong belief that risks are socially constructed might be taken to suggest that regulatory priorities and policies cannot be

[40] See, e.g., R. Kasperson, O. Renn, P. Slovic, H. Brown, J. Emel, R. Goble, J. Kasperson, and S. Ratick, 'The Social Amplification of Risk: A Conceptual Framework' (1988) 8 *Risk Analysis* 177–87; J. Kasperson, R. Kasperson, N. Pidgeon, and P. Slovic, 'The Social Amplification of Risk: Assessing Fifteen Years of Research and Theory', in N. Pidgeon, R. Kasperson, and P. Slovic (eds), *The Social Amplification of Risk* (Cambridge, 2003); P. Slovic, 'Trust, Emotion, Sex, Politics and Science' (1999) 19 (4) *Risk Analysis* 689–701; P. Slovic, *The Perception of Risk* (London, 2000).

[41] D. Kahneman and A. Tversky, 'Availability: A Heuristic for Judging Frequency and Probability', in D. Kahnemann, P. Slovic, and A. Tversky (eds), *Judging under Uncertainty* (Cambridge, 1982).

[42] H. Rothstein, M. Huber, and G. Gaskell, 'A Theory of Risk Colonization' (2006) 35(1) *Economy and Society* 91–112. See also C. Hood, 'What Happens when Transparency Meets Blame-Avoidance' (2007) 9(2) *Public Management Review* 191–210.

[43] See Royal Society, *Risk*, ch. 5; H.J. Otway and B. Wynne, 'Risk Communication: Paradigm and Paradox' (1989) 9 *Risk Analysis* 141; S. Krimsky and A. Plough, *Environmental Hazards: Communicating Risks as a Social Process* (Dover, MA, 1988). Evidence points to the limited effect of risk communication strategies in low trust environments, see R.F. Durant and J. Legge, 'Public Opinion, Risk Perceptions, and Genetically-Modified Food Regulatory Policy' (2005) 6(2) *European Union Politics* 181–200.

left to the 'objective' evaluations of experts, but have to emerge from demo-cratically legitimate processes of debate and consultation.

Risks: The Regulatory Challenges

A number of core challenges lie at the heart of any regulatory decision on the handling of risk.[44] The first challenge is the identification of risks and ques-tions about participation in decision-making. To some extent, such issues are of a technical nature and involve calculations regarding the probability of an event occurring and its impact. However, as numerous of the approaches considered above highlight, risk identification is also about public approval. Problems may arise from the tension between 'technical', 'rational', or 'expert' approaches and the perceptions of the public. The priorities that the public might establish will tend to appear irrational to experts, since citizens' perceptions of risk will be distorted by the range of factors noted above (e.g. the degree of personal control, familiarity, etc.) and will not correspond to figures based on products of probability and magnitude of harm. Not only will members of the public respond 'irrationally' to risks, but democratic processes may have limited potential to cope with information about risks.[45] Questions thus arise concerning the role of the public in decision-making on risks; on whether (and how) people should be informed of the risks they face; and the means by which decisions regarding risks can be legitimated in the eyes of the public.[46] One strand of the risk literature explores models of decision-making that aim to reduce conflicts about risk assessment and focuses on the potential of adversarial processes, administrative rules, and judicial review to legitimize risk regulation.[47] More general concerns are the extent and quality of information relating to risks; the reasons why there may be informational inadequacies when decisions on risks are taken; and the costs of risk-related information.[48] One view sees differences in public and expert perceptions of risk as a key element in the 'vicious circle' of factors that diminishes public trust in regulatory institutions, inhibits more rational regulation, and

---

[44] See J. Black and R. Baldwin, 'Really Responsive Risk-based Regulation' (2010), 32 *Law and Policy* 181–213; C. Hood and D. Jones (eds), *Accident and Design* (London, 1996).

[45] S.G. Hadden, *A Citizen's Right to Know: Risk Communication and Public Policy* (Boulder, 1989); D.J. Fiorino, 'Citizen Participation and Environmental Risk: A Survey of Institutional Mechanisms' (1990) 15 *Science Technology and Human Values* 226; J. Handman and E.C. Penning-Rowsell (eds), *Hazards and the Communication of Risks* (Aldershot, 1990).

[46] H. Margolis, *Dealing with Risk* (Chicago, 1996).

[47] See S. Jasanoff, 'The Misrule of Law at OSHA', in D. Nelkin (ed.), *The Language of Risk* (Beverly Hills, 1985).

[48] See K.R. MacCrimmon and D.A. Wehrung, *Taking Risks* (New York, 1982), 15–17.

contributes to random selection of regulatory priorities as well as inconsistencies of regulatory approach.[49]

A second regulatory challenge is whether an emphasis should be placed on *anticipation* or on *resilience*. The emphasis of anticipative approaches is therefore on identifying risks, and the minimization of the production of risks. A resilience-based strategy, in contrast, emphasizes the importance of mitigating the effects of hazards (such as informing citizens about risks and allowing them to make their informed choices), and ensuring that systems 'bounce back' from interruption. The stage at which intervention should take place is therefore a central issue. Risk management may involve the adoption of strategies to minimize the *production* of risks or it may be concerned with mitigating the adverse *effects* of hazards through implementing such measures as warning procedures, safety mechanisms, and contingency plans. Thus, a distinction is to be drawn between instruments that are active (which seek to modify the source of the risk—for example, by dynamiting the avalanche slope) and those which are passive and lessen undesirable effects (e.g. by evacuating populations within the potential avalanche path). This question of whether risk managers and regulators should anticipate and prevent, or should promote resilience and the capacity to withstand harms, is a recurring issue in the risk management literature.[50]

The debate about anticipative strategies links to the widely known *precautionary principle*. The basic idea of 'better safe than sorry' is potentially non-controversial. More formally, the precautionary principle suggests that in those cases in which there is a suspected, but not proven, risk of harm to the public or the environment, the burden of proof is on the producer of the risk to prove the lack of harmfulness. The German *Vorsorgeprinzip*, which later was incorporated within EU law, represented this approach, as did Principle 15 of the 1992 Rio Declaration, which suggested that states should apply the precautionary principle to apply 'cost-effective measures' to deal with potential threats of irreversible damage or the lack of scientific evidence.[51] Similarly, the European Commission defined its approach towards the precautionary principle in areas where 'scientific evidence is insufficient, inconclusive or uncertain' and where initial scientific evidence raised 'reasonable grounds for concern'.[52]

---

[49] See S. Breyer, *Breaking the Vicious Circle: Toward Effective Risk Regulation* (Cambridge, MA, 1993) (discussed further below).

[50] See e.g.Turner, *Man-Made Disasters*; H. D. Foster, *Disaster Planning* (New York, 1979); A. Wildavsky, *Trial without Error: Anticipation Versus Resilience as Strategies for Risk Reduction* (Sydney, 1985).

[51] United Nations 'Conference on Environment and Development', declaration; http://www.un.org/documents/ga/conf151/aconf15126-1annex1.htm (last accessed 29 November 2010).

[52] European Commission, *Communication on the Precautionary Principle* COM (2000)1. See also V. Heyvaert, 'Guidance Without Constraint: Assessing the Impact of the Precautionary Principle on the European Community's Chemicals Policy' (2006) 6 *Yearbook of European Environmental Law* 27–60.

Much discussion about the application of the precautionary principle centres around the potential irreversibility of particular innovations should they be adopted.

Opponents of the precautionary principle attack its potential to be exploited by political and economic interests.[53] In other words, the contestation of a supposed lack of 'scientific certainty' is utilized by powerful groups to shape regulation to their favour by exploiting popular fears and anxieties. Others, such as Wildavsky, point to the high opportunity costs that a strategy of anticipation involves: the search as well as the development of solutions to all risks is costly and consumes resources.[54] Similarly, the prohibition of progress by banning particular practices or products is seen by Wildavsky as overly restrictive—indeed, it might in fact encourage the acceptance of greater risks by restricting the consumption on products or substances that were adopted before the passing of precautionary principle-based safety rules. Critics therefore suggest that advocates of the precautionary principle wrongly believe that the default option (i.e 'doing nothing') is in itself 'risk-free'. In contrast, Wildavsky argues in favour of a resilience-based strategy that emphasizes the importance of systems being able to recover and rebound, therefore emphasizing processes such as trial-and-error processes. The key bone of contention in this debate is usually, however, one of degree, with opponents of the precautionary principle opposing the unsettled methodology and a 'strong' definition of the principle (which would be defined by automatic prohibitions). A 'weaker' definition would allow, rather than require, the application of the precautionary principle in cases of doubt.

A related, and fundamental, regulatory question is, therefore, whether regulators should err on the side of rejecting a true hypothesis, and thereby potentially under-regulate a risk, or whether regulation should be biased towards the accepting of false hypotheses and therefore to potentially 'over'-regulating. This means that decisions have to be taken as to the kinds of risks that should be treated as exceptional, if there is not to be more revision of the general principle that persons and products should be regarded as innocent, rather than as guilty until proven innocent.[55]

---

[53] G. Majone, 'What Price Safety? The Precautionary Principle and its Policy Implications' (2002) 40(1) *Journal of Common Market Studies* 89–109. A collection of criticisms is provided in J. Morris (ed.), *Rethinking Risk and the Precautionary Principle* (Oxford, 2000); J. Morris, 'The Relationship between Risk Analysis and the Precautionary Principle' (2002) 181(2) *Toxicology* 127–30; C. Sunstein, *Laws of Fear: Beyond the Precautionary Principle* (Cambridge, 2005).

[54] A. Wildavsky, *Searching for Safety* (New Brunswick, 1988).

[55] See also G. Brennan, 'Civil Disaster Management: An Economist's View' (1991) 64 *Canberra Bulletin of Public Administration* 30; H.G. Frederickson and T.R. LaPorte, 'Airport Security, High Reliability and the Problem of Rationality' (2002) 62 *Public Administration Review* 33–43.

A further key risk regulatory challenge involves the use of particular regulatory instruments as ways of addressing the issues covered in the above debates. For some, the practice of using cost-benefit analysis and other kinds of risk assessments has the potential to 'rationalize' debates by offering structures and additional information.[56] Others argue the case against an over-reliance on quantitive methods. They criticize the potential susceptibility of quantitative risk assessment instruments to problems of value assumption, qualitative data, administrative difficulties, equity, public acceptability, the lack of a single risk decision framework, and effectiveness. Such critics suggest that procedures for bringing different views together offer more potential to inform and advance debates about risk regulation.[57] Somewhere in the middle of such debates are those that argue the case for 'enlightened' assessments where instruments such as cost-benefit analyses are used to inform wider public debates about risk regulation.[58]

Another important concern is the design of institutions and techniques for managing risk. Involved here is the fundamental question of when risks should be seen as matters of public concern, rather than left for private handling.[59] Issues considered in the literature include the role of insurance mechanisms in shaping responses to risks and how insurance interacts with legal and regulatory structures relevant to risk-taking. Particular interests are the effects of insurance on the incentives created by liability rules and the problems of moral hazard and adverse selection within the insurance mechanism. When the regulation of risks is seen as primarily a matter for private organizations (as in a system of enforced self-regulation), this raises issues about the kind of obligations regulators impose on private organizations. Indeed, as the literature on *high reliability organizations* suggests, regulatory strategies are required that provide for organizational incentives to place resources into an error-intolerant and 'heedful' organizational culture that reduces the potential for man-made disasters.[60] Such organizations require the capacity and the

---

[56] K. Arrow, M. Cropper, G. Eads, R. Hahn, L. Lave, R. Noll, P. Portney, M. Russell, R. Schmalensee, V.K. Smith, and R. Stavins, 'Is there a Role for Benefit-Cost Analysis in Environmental, Health, and Safety Regulation?' (1996) 272 *Science* 221–2.

[57] J. Adams and M. Thompson, *Risk Review* (London, 1991) and A. Gorz, *Critique of Economic Reason* (London, 1989).

[58] C. Sunstein, *Risk and Reason* (Cambridge, 2002).

[59] See M.T. Katzman, 'Pollution Liability Insurance and Catastrophic Environmental Risk' (1988) *Journal of Risk and Insurance* 75.

[60] K. Weick, 'Organizational Culture as a Source of High Reliability' (1987) 29 *Californian Management Review* 1–27; K. Weick and K.H. Roberts, 'Collective Mind in Organizations' (1993) 38 *Administrative Science Quarterly* 57–81; T.R. LaPorte and P. Consolini, 'Working in Practice but Not in Theory: Theoretical Challenges of "High Reliabililiy Organizations"' (1991) 1 *Journal of Public Administration Research and Theory* 19–47; for a critical discussion of redundancy in this context, see J. Downer, 'Anatomy of a Disaster', *CARR discussion paper 61* (London, 2010).

resources to allow for back-up facilities, should the primary systems fail. However, studies of technologies and organizations suggest that redundancy can itself become a source of risk and failure, as it adds another layer of complexity to already highly complex organizational processes.[61]

A further issue of technique is whether risk management or regulation should be 'blame-oriented'—with precise allocation of liability and resultant incentives to take care—or whether a greater focus should be placed on collective or corporate design, rather than individual blame.[62] Indeed, it might be argued that a 'blame-free' institutional setup is likely to encourage learning and openness about problems in the handling of risky activities. This contrasts with the potential for risk-averse behaviour and gaming, if not manipulation in the case of systems that place a high emphasis on placing 'blame' and responsibility on any particular individual or organization.

A fourth question is whether a basis of knowledge can be generated that is adequate to found effective institutional designs for risk management. On the one hand, it is asserted that principles of good institutional design can be set down[63] but, on the other, sceptics point to current limitations in knowledge about the handling of risks in organizations. A fifth issue concerns the extent to which reductions in risks have to be traded off against other basic goals or alternative risk reductions. Some commentators, however, contest the view that trade-offs always have to be made and point to instances where actions designed to reduce risks have positive rather than negative effects on such matters as productivity and efficiency.[64]

The final issue to be noted returns to the theme of democratic acceptability and concerns the degree of participation in risk management decisions that is appropriate. One approach stresses the need for broad access to risk management processes and thereby accountability.[65] Further, it is argued that where scientific evidence about risks is inconclusive, there is a specially strong case for incorporating an 'extended peer community' of experts into risk management decisions.[66] The alternative view, however, doubts the benefits of broad participation, stresses the dangers of giving weight to 'unfounded public

[61] The most prominent exponent of this view is Perrow, *Normal Accidents*.

[62] Compare R.A. Posner, *Economic Analysis of Law* (Boston, 1986), 147–51 and B. Fisse and J. Braithwaite, 'Accountability and the Control of Corporate Crime' in M. Findlay and R. Hogg (eds), *Understanding Crime and Criminal Justice* (Sydney, 1988); E. Bardach and R. Kagan, *Going by the Book: The Problem of Regulatory Unreasonableness* (Philadelphia, 1982).

[63] See T. Horlick-Jones, *Acts of God?* (London, 1990).

[64] See E. Tait and L. Levidov, 'Proactive and Reactive Approaches to Risk Regulation' (1992) *Futures* 219.

[65] See S. Beder, 'The Fallible Engineer' (1991) *New Scientist* 38.

[66] Royal Society, *Risk*, 164.

fears', and argues for rational decisions by small groups of well-informed experts.[67]

In summary, seeing regulation in terms of risks highlights a series of challenges that confront regulators. Positions taken in relation to the issues discussed above will often link to the issue of confidence in forecasting and quantifying risks in an agreed manner. High confidence on these fronts will tend to favour anticipatory actions and the specification of outputs; low confidence will tend to favour emphasis on resilience, the specification of processes, and qualitative debates concerning uncertainties.

'Solutions' to Risk Regulation

Risk regulation, it is clear from the above, faces difficult problems in seeking legitimation, not least because of divergences in expert and lay perceptions of risk. What, then, can be done to improve the force of legitimating arguments? This section reviews four kinds of response. The first is based principally on an expertise rationale and the second on the accountability and due process rationales.

Stephen Breyer exemplifies the first approach in his book *Breaking the Vicious Circle: Towards Effective Risk Regulation*.[68] For Breyer, the regulation of small but significant health risks is plagued by three serious problems: *tunnel vision*—where there is over-regulation to the point that it brings about more harm than good; *random agenda selection*—where regulatory priorities are driven by issues coming to the public's attention rather than by rational appraisals of risks;[69] and *inconsistency*—where agencies use different methods to calculate the effects of regulation, and the values that regulators implicitly attach to the saving of a statistical life vary widely from one programme or agency to another.

The causes of these problems are said, again, to be threefold and to constitute a 'vicious circle' that diminishes trust in regulatory institutions and increasingly inhibits more rational regulation. The causes are: *public perceptions*—in which the public's evaluation of risk problems 'differs radically from any consensus of experts in the field' and does not reflect a 'rational' set of priorities;[70] *congressional action and reaction*—a tendency to respond to risks

---

[67] See R.S. Yalow, 'Radioactivity in the Service of Humanity' (1985) 60 *Thought* 517; Breyer, *Breaking the Vicious Circle*.

[68] Breyer, *Breaking the Vicious Circle*.

[69] N. Malhotra and A. Kuo, 'Attributing Blame: The Public's Response to Hurricane Katrina' (2008) 70(1) *Journal of Politics* 120–35.

[70] Breyer, *Breaking the Vicious Circle*, 33.

with detailed statutory directions that later experience shows to be inappropriate; and *uncertainties in the technical regulatory process*—the limitations of knowledge, data, and predictive power that afflict regulatory processes.

Breyer's solution involves institutional changes that reflect the view that a 'depoliticised regulatory process might produce better results'.[71] His suggestion has two parts: first, that a new career path be established to provide a group of civil servants with experience in working with health and environmental agencies, Congress, and the Office of Management and Budget; second, that a small, centralized administrative group be formed from such civil servants, one with a mission of producing a coherent risk programme and a set of rational priorities covering risk regulatory programmes.[72] The group would have jurisdiction over different agencies and would have a degree of political insulation to allow it to withstand various political pressures. It would have prestige, authority, and expertise, and would rationalize right across government. Its authority would flow from its outputs; 'insofar as a systematic solution produces technically better results, the decision will become somewhat more legitimate'.[73]

The difficulty with Breyer's proposal is that it involves heavy emphasis on legitimation through expertise at the expense of legitimation through emphasis on democratic policymaking, accountability, and due process in the form of participation. Breyer suggests that the group's proposals, plans, and findings would be openly available for comment and criticism, but at root what is proposed is a level of insulation from politics such as will allow the 'rational' decisions of experts to establish priorities for risk regulation, rather than public perceptions and desires. This presupposes to a considerable degree that risk-prioritizing can be dealt with technically as a mere product of probability and extent of harm. As already noted, however, a number of commentators might be expected to object strongly that experts are no more 'rational' than lay persons, that in 'risk society' scientists and experts create as many uncertainties as they dispel,[74] and that risk priorities are perceptual, distributional, and political matters that must be negotiated through exchanges of views, rather than laid down from on high by experts making hidden value judgements.[75] It can, furthermore, be objected that striving for greater rationality in the form of increased scientific accuracy

---

[71] Ibid., 56.   [72] Ibid.   [73] Ibid., 63.

[74] See J. Durant, 'Once the Men in White Coats Held the Promise of a Better Future', in J. Franklin (ed.), *Politics of Risk Society* (Cambridge, 1998).

[75] See, e.g., Giddens, *Beyond Left and Right* and Beck, *Risk Society*. For a review of Breyer's thesis, see V.B. Flatt, 'Should the Circle be Unbroken?' (1994) 24 (4) *Environmental Law* 1707. Flatt contends, *inter alia*: 'many of the "problems" with inconsistent risk values are not problems at all but actual policy choices that reflect societal values other than the explicit reduction of risk to human life' (p. 1713); 'some of our regulatory choices are not value judgements about *what* we should pay for regulation but rather *who* should pay' (p. 1718).

concerning risks may, beyond a certain stage, involve costs, delays, legal challenges, and the creation of new uncertainties that are socially undesirable—that this may produce a tendency both to under-regulate and to introduce mistakes into regulatory processes.[76] The value of more detailed risk analysis can, thus, be said to depend on normative judgements about the chosen uses to be made of such information.[77]

A contrasting approach to that of Breyer is offered by Shrader-Frechette, who points to certain strengths of risk-cost-benefit analyses (RCBA)—notably their systematic nature, clarity concerning social costs, and superiority to arbitrary, intuitive, and expert modes of decision-making.[78] Shrader-Frechette, nevertheless, seeks to remedy some of the weaknesses of RCBA by application of 'scientific proceduralism'. This process seeks to improve RCBA by three devices. The first of these is *ethical weighting*. This involves imposing a negative weight to the imposition of certain particularly undesirable risks, and it is envisaged that the public or its representatives could be involved in deciding which weighting scheme best represents its values. The central idea is that ethical considerations, rather than the RCBA itself, should govern priorities.[79] The second device is the use of *alternative risk analyses and evaluations*. Several risk analyses can be commissioned or allowed in relation to a single risk issue and this, it is suggested, will reveal information and assumptions more clearly than is possible with a single analysis. It will also allow citizens, as opposed to experts, to have a greater role in determining risk choices—it will lead policymakers to rely on procedural and democratic, rather than merely scientific, methods of evaluating and managing risks.[80] Finally, *weighted expert opinions* can be used to give emphasis in policymaking

---

[76] Indeed, in certain situations, it may be rational to 'economize' on rationality, see C. Hood and M. Lodge, 'Pavlovian Innovation, Pet Solutions and Economizing on Rationality' in J. Black, M. Lodge, and M. Thatcher (eds), *Regulatory Innovation* (Cheltenham, 2005).

[77] See Cranor, *Regulating Toxic Substances*, 120 and 130, who argues that the 'science-intensive' approach to regulation is slow because of its concern to develop 'perfect' regulations.

[78] See K.S. Shrader-Frechette, *Risk and Rationality* (Berkeley, 1991). For a wider contribution on the debate regarding deliberation, see J. Cohen and C. Sabel, 'Direct-Deliberative Polyarchy' (1997) 3(4) *European Law Journal* 313–42; S. Jasanoff 'Technology as Site and Object of Politics' in R.E. Goodin and C. Tilly (eds), *The Oxford Handbook of Contextual Political Analysis* (Oxford, 2006).

[79] See also the Tolerability of Risk (TOR) approach noted in Chapter 14 below, and discussed in HM Treasury, *Setting of Safety Standards*, 8–9, which allows risk-cost-benefit only within equitably established boundaries. Cranor suggests in *Regulating Toxic Substances* that, in relation to such problems as those posed by carcinogens, scientific knowledge and data for risk estimates is inadequate and that this presents a choice: to desist from regulating or to make decisions on the basis of available evidence and non-scientific policy considerations. Allowing the science-intensive perspective to dominate would thus lead to under-protection of the public, increased regulatory costs, and decreased policy accountability. The way forward, he states, is via the use of explicitly made policy guidelines and the *combination* of policy and scientific judgements. 'Once it is recognised that risk assessment (and regulation) is in part a function of policy considerations, public input, especially in a democratic form of government, becomes a relevant consideration to shape the process' (p. 134).

[80] Shrader-Frechette, *Risk and Rationality*, 187.

processes to the forecasts of experts whose risk estimates have been 'vindicated by past predictive success'—a process that comes to grips with the absence of any uncontroversially objective way to calculate risks in so far as it offers a checking system.

'Scientific proceduralism' thus rejects any assumption that risks can be estimated in a value-free way. It asserts the need to democratize RCBA and it stresses the value of open, pluralistic approaches in revealing realities. The technique, as set out by Shrader-Frechette, leaves open a number of unresolved issues—whether, for instance, weighting procedures oversimplify ethical considerations; whether democratic participation is better served by separating this from the RCBA than by weighting; how weighting processes can be combined with RCBA; whether policymaking in the real world allows the use of alternative and multiple RCBAs (and whether this will lead to confusion); and the extent to which expertise in one area of risk analysis can be transported to other areas. What is noteworthy for our purposes, however, is the proposed route to legitimation and the urging that risk analyses must be conducted within frameworks of greater participation and accountability—this contrasts quite starkly with Breyer's emphasis on expertise.

Other accounts stress a variety of aspects. For some, risk handling should be treated as an insurance problem. The key regulatory solution, therefore, is to reduce the price distortion in the market and therefore let individuals face the 'true' costs of their action. For example, consumers will think differently about purchasing houses in flood plains should they face the 'real' costs of insuring their property against flooding.[81] In other words, as in the case of crop failures, individuals should be exposed to the costs of their choices. In contrast to such individualist understandings of solutions to risk management, others would continue to emphasize the importance of enhancing the redundancy and resilience of private organizations, pointing to the literature on *high-reliability organizations*, as noted earlier. However, as noted, redundancy is costly and may be a cause of failure and risk in itself. Indeed, it may be true that the recipes for high reliability (redundancy, constant feedback, and a dedication to safety) are more applicable for some organizations and organizational fields than for others.[82]

---

[81] Of course, such insurance markets are also prone to perverse incentives; for a collection of essays on this theme, see R.K. Daniels, D. Kettle, and H. Kunreuther (eds), *Risk and Disaster* (Philadelphia, 2006); P. Freeman and H. Kunreuther, *Managing Environmental Risk Through Insurance* (Dordrecht, 1997); H. Kunreuther and E. Michel-Kerjan, 'Market and Government Failure in Insuring and Mitigating Natural Catastrophes', in J.R. Brown (ed.), *Public Insurance and Private Markets* (Washington, 2009).

[82] For a private organisation's system of 'near miss' reporting, see C. Macrae, 'Analyzing near-miss events' *CARR Discussion Paper 47* (London, 2007).

Conclusions

Focusing on the uncertainties involved in risk regulation serves to highlight a number of fundamental issues, ranging from the definition and identification of risks, critical debates about the principles inherent in any regulatory activity, to fundamental questions on the appropriate institutions for risk regulation. Issues arise relating to the perception of risk, the definition and classification of risks, and the construction of 'risk problems'. Particular concerns in the control of risks relate to divergences in lay and expert approaches; to the use of information in regulating uncertainties; and the susceptibility of risk control regimes to democratic and participatory mechanisms. As was seen in discussing the proposals of Breyer and Shrader-Frechette, very different approaches to 'rational' risk regulation can be taken, and the role of rationality in risk control is itself contentious. Inherent in any discussion about risk regulation is the dual nature of risk in regulation—on the one hand, regulating risks is about the 'objective' risk of things going wrong, often with tragic consequences. On the other hand, it is about dealing with the individual and social consequences and imaginations of risks. Indeed, how organizations seek to regulate risks also reflects on organizational cultures and levels of trust between different systems. As a result, how risk is perceived and what regulatory solutions are proposed is fundamentally shaped by underlying worldviews and understandings of cause–effect relationships. Risk regulation also raises the issue of whether some kinds of risks should be treated differently from others. Posner, for example, suggests that certain catastrophic risks need anticipative solutions because their impact would represent the eradication of humankind, despite the low probability of such events occurring.[83] He also calls for a fundamental transformation of (legal) education—with a much stronger emphasis on science and understandings of probabilities to advance the ability of legal and political systems to deal with risks.

Seeing regulation in terms of risks, and an awareness of the literature on risk control that is encountered in many disciplines, does add new dimensions to our understanding of regulation. It prompts new questions about perceptions of regulatory priorities, the construction and development of regulatory agendas, and the legitimation of both regulation and regulatory reviews. Reviewing the plurality of theoretical perspectives that offer models of risk regulation, how risks are being processed, and how risks should be regulated suggests that any attempt at regulating risks should involve the pluralization of analytical perspectives, rather than the reliance on any one analytical device alone.[84]

---

[83] R.E. Posner *Catastrophe: Risk and Response* (Oxford, 2004).
[84] D. Cohen and C. Lindblom, *Usable Knowledge* (New Haven, 1979); G. Majone, *Evidence, Argument and Persuasion in the Policy Process* (New Haven, 1989).

Part II
Strategies

7 Regulatory Strategies

If the state wants to control, say, the pollution of a river, it may approach the issue in a number of ways. It may decide to regulate the pollution directly by means of a government department or agency; it may rely on the polluting firms to self-regulate (perhaps under state oversight); or it might delegate the control function to third parties such as public interest groups and the commercial partners of the polluters.[1] Under these different arrangements, a number of instruments may be deployed. Thus, if the state regulates directly, the dumping of noxious substances may be made unlawful or, alternatively, the state may give rewards (e.g. tax deductions) to those existing polluters who reduce the levels of their discharges. Manufacturers might be compelled to tell the public how much pollution is caused in making each product or rights might be allocated so as to allow the victims of pollution to recover damages from polluters. In relation to many risks it may be appropriate to regulate by means of a mixture of instruments and to apply these through a variety of bodies—be these governmental, self-regulatory, corporate, commercial, or public interest group.[2]

This chapter looks at the main instruments that the state can use to regulate directly. Chapter 8 will then examine self-regulation and other modes of delegating the regulatory function to bodies beyond the state. In doing so, it will look at the case for relying on audits of corporate risk management systems (sometimes called 'meta-regulation') and the challenge of finding optimal mixes of regulatory instruments and institutions.

It is clear that choosing the right strategy for regulating matters. A regulatory system will be difficult to justify—no matter how well it seems to be performing—if critics can argue that a different strategy would more effectively achieve relevant objectives. How, though, can we map out the array of different regulatory techniques? A starting point, when focusing on direct state regulation, is to consider the basic capacities or resources that governments possess and which can be used to influence industrial, economic, or social activity. These have been described as follows:[3]

---

[1] See N. Gunningham and P. Grabosky, *Smart Regulation* (Oxford, 1998).

[2] Ibid., esp. ch. 6.

[3] See C.C. Hood, *The Tools of Government* (London, 1983), 5; T.C. Daintith, 'The Techniques of Government' in J. Jowell and D. Oliver (eds), *The Changing Constitution* (3rd edn, Oxford, 1994). Lawrence Lessig offers an alternative breakdown of 'modalities of regulation' into: law, markets, norms and architecture—see L. Lessig, *Code and Other Laws of Cyberspace* (New York, 1999).

To command—where legal authority and the command of law is used to pursue policy objectives.

To deploy wealth—where contracts, grants, loans, subsidies, or other incentives are used to influence conduct.

To harness markets—where governments channel competitive forces to particular ends (for example, by using franchise auctions to achieve benefits for consumers).

To inform—where information is deployed strategically (e.g. so as to empower consumers).

To act directly—where the state takes physical action itself (e.g. to contain a hazard or nuisance).

To confer protected rights—where rights and liability rules are structured and allocated so as to create desired incentives and constraints (e.g. rights to clean water are created in order to deter polluters).

A number of basic regulatory strategies are built on the use of the above capacities or resources and can be distinguished from each other as follows.[4]

Command and Control

The essence of command and control (C & C) regulation is the exercise of influence by imposing standards backed by criminal sanctions.[5] Thus, the Health and Safety Executive may bring criminal prosecutions against occupiers who breach health and safety regulations. The force of law is used to prohibit certain forms of conduct, to demand some positive actions, or to lay down conditions for entry into a sector.

Regulators who operate C & C techniques are sometimes equipped with rule-making powers (as is often the case in the USA). In the UK, however, it is common for regulatory standards to be set by government departments through primary or secondary legislation and then enforced by regulatory bureaucracies. C & C thus involves the setting of standards within a rule, it often entails some kind of licensing process to screen entry to an activity, and may set out to control not merely the quality of a service or the manner of

---

[4] On regulatory strategies in general use, see S. Breyer, *Regulation and Its Reform* (Cambridge, MA, 1982), esp. ch. 8; A. Ogus, *Regulation: Legal Form and Economic Theory* (Oxford, 1994), esp. pts. III and IV; Gunningham and Grabosky, *Smart Regulation*, ch. 2.

[5] On command and control and alternatives, see R. Baldwin, 'Regulation: After Command and Control' in K. Hawkins (ed.), *The Human Face of Law* (Oxford, 1997); N. Keohane, R. Revesz, and R. Stavins, 'The Choice of Regulatory Instruments in Environmental Policy' (1998) 22 *Harvard Environmental Law Review* 313–67.

production but also the allocation of resources, products, or commodities and the prices charged to consumers[6] or the profits made by enterprises.

The strengths of C & C regulation (as compared to techniques based, say, on the use of economic incentives such as taxes or subsidies) are that the force of law can be used to impose fixed standards with immediacy and to prohibit activity not conforming to such standards. In political terms, the regulator or government is seen to be acting forcefully and to be taking a clear stand: by designating some forms of behaviour as unacceptable; by excluding danger-ous parties from relevant areas; by protecting the public; and establishing penalties for those engaging in offensive conduct. Some forms of behaviour can thus be outlawed completely and the ill-qualified can be stopped from practising activities likely to produce harms. The public, as a result, can be assured that the might of the law is being used both practically and symboli-cally in their aid.

C & C regulation is not, however, problem-free and, during the 1980s in particular, a number of North American socio-legal scholars and econo-mists alleged a series of weaknesses.[7] Such concerns were echoed by many politicians on both sides of the Atlantic—particularly those predisposed to doubt the value of governmental rather than market-based modes of influence.

CAPTURE

A first worry was that in C & C regulation the relationships between the regulators and the regulated might tend to become too close and lead to capture—the pursuit of the regulated enterprises' interests, rather than those of the public at large.[8] A number of versions of capture theory have been put forward.[9] 'Life-cycle' accounts suggest that agencies progress through various stages until, lonely, frightened, and old, they become the protectors of the regulated industry, rather than of the public interest;[10] 'interest-group' explanations stress the extent to which regulators can be influenced by the claims and political influence of different groups; and 'private-interest' or

---

[6] For more detailed discussion of price control mechanisms see Chapter 17 below.

[7] See e.g. Breyer, *Regulation and Its Reform*; R.B. Stewart, 'Regulation and the Crisis of Legalisation in the United States' in T. Daintith (ed.), *Law as an Instrument of Economic Policy* (Berlin, 1998); id., 'The Discontents of Legalism: Interest Group Relations in Administrative Regulation' (1985) *Wisconsin Law Review* 685; E. Bardach and R. Kagan, *Going by the Book: The Problem of Regulatory Unreasonableness* (Philadelphia, 1982); Gunningham and Grabosky, *Smart Regulation*, 41–7.

[8] See C. Hood, *Explaining Economic Policy Reversals* (Buckingham, 1994), 21.

[9] For a review of these, see B. Mitnick, *The Political Economy of Regulation* (New York, 1980); also see P.J. Quirk, *Industry Influence in Federal Regulatory Agencies* (Princeton, 1981); G. Wilson, 'Social Regulation and Explanations of Regulatory Failure' (1984) 32 *Political Studies* 203.

[10] See M.H. Bernstein, *Regulating Business by Independent Commission* (New York, 1955).

economic analyses see regulation as a commodity liable to fall under (or to be established under) the sway of the economically powerful.[11]

The proximity of regulator to regulatee relationships that is associated with C & C techniques might be thought to be particularly conducive to capture in so far as agencies, when drawing up and enforcing rules, must rely to some extent on the cooperation of the regulated firms. Thus, the argument runs, regulators require a good deal of information in order to carry out their functions—say to fix appropriate standards on issues such as acceptable pollution levels or price increases. The primary, and best, source of such information will often be industry. The regulator, accordingly, requires some assistance from the regulated firms in order to make C & C regulation work. This gives the regulated firms a degree of leverage over regulatory procedures and objectives, a leverage that, over time, produces capture.

In response to allegations that C & C regulation is particularly prone to capture, it should be noted that many versions of capture theory would attribute capture to factors that operate in a manner unaffected by the particular regulatory technique employed. They might point, for instance, to broad political, institutional, or economic considerations.

LEGALISM

A second major concern with C & C regulation has been its alleged propensity to produce unnecessarily complex and inflexible rules, and indeed, a proliferation of rules that leads to over-regulation, legalism, delay intrusion on managerial freedoms, and the strangling of competition and enterprise.[12] Eugene Bardach and Robert Kagan have expressed concern at the extent to which US regulators have tended to over-regulate with over-inclusive rules (rules that apply to an unnecessarily wide array of instances or actions) and have given a number of reasons why such problems tend to occur. First, rule-makers find it very difficult to design precisely targeted rules (the informational demands are severe) and the tendency is to avoid such design and drafting difficulties by writing over-inclusive rules. Second, for political reasons, regulators tend to respond to particular problems or tragedies with general, or 'across-the board', rules and solutions. This gives the appearance of 'doing something about that sort of thing'. Third, pressures to reduce discretions in favour of the 'rule of law' (so as to make regulatory actions rule-governed) may come from politicians, those regulated, or consumers, and

---

[11] See R. Posner, 'Theories of Economic Regulation' (1974) 5 *Bell Journal of Economics* 335; G. Stigler, 'The Theory of Economic Regulation' (1971) 2 *Bell Journal of Economics* 3.

[12] See Stewart, 'Regulation and the Crisis of Legalisation'; Bardach and Kagan, *Going by the Book*; G. Teubner, *Juridification of Social Spheres* (Berlin, 1987); R. Harris and S. Milkis, *The Politics of Regulatory Change* (New York, 1989).

these pressures may induce the excessive production of rules. Fourth, regulators often wish to respond to a mischief before public concern dies down—while the memory of the disaster is still fresh. Working to the resultant short time-scales tends to produce rules that are broad-brush, rather than precisely targeted. Finally, there is what is dubbed the 'regulatory ratchet',[13] whereby regulatory rules tend to grow rather then recede because revisions of regulations are infrequent; work on new rules tends to drive out attention to old ones; and failure to carry out pruning leads the thickets of rules to grow ever more dense.[14]

In the context of British telecommunications, it has been argued that detailed, prescriptive rules can be a barrier to entry, can inhibit competition, and can discriminate between incumbent licensed operators and new entrants. When it was regulator, OFTEL urged a movement away from control by means of detailed rules contained in the licences of those given privileged access, towards 'open state' regulation that is based on general authorizations and which gives a stronger role to general competition and consumer protection laws, backed up by detailed guidance only where necessary.[15]

STANDARD-SETTING

Setting appropriate standards has been argued to pose major difficulties for regulators because the informational demands are so severe.[16] Thus, anti-competitive effects must be addressed; the appropriate *type* of standard must be selected—be this an output standard specifying a level of performance or an input standard calling for a particular design or specification of operation or machinery—and the level of exposure to judicial review may be high.[17] Setting the appropriate level of performance is, moreover, technically difficult and liable to be contentious. To give a simple instance, employing the example of pollution again, even if it is assumed that the regulator knows the beneficial values of particular levels of cleanliness in a river, and is clear on social objectives, setting the optimal level of allowable pollution (the level that minimizes the sum of abatement and damage costs) would require data on the differing abatement costs of all of the various polluters on the riverbank. The efficient level of pollution will, indeed, be specific to each enterprise, yet

---

[13] Bardach and Kagan, *Going by the Book*, ch. 7.

[14] On responses to these problems, see R. Baldwin, *Rules and Government* (Oxford, 1995), 183–5 and below, Chapter 14.

[15] See OFTEL, *Second Submission to the Culture, Media and Sport Select Committee: Beyond the Telephone, the Television and the PC—Regulation of the Electronic Communications Industry* (London, March 1998). Ofcom took over OFTEL's functions in December 2003.

[16] See Chapter 14 below for a general discussion of standard-setting, also Breyer, *Regulation and Its Reform*, 109–19; Ogus, *Regulation*, ch. 8.

[17] See Ogus, *Regulation*, ch. 8.

the regulator has usually to produce a generalized across-the-board rule. The result will be a broadly inefficient regime, with some enterprises finding it hugely expensive to meet the standard and others able to go better than standard at very little cost but given no incentive to do so.[18] A further worry, moreover, is that commands, and the standards they mandate, may prove unresponsive to changes in technologies, risks and other regulatory challenges so that, even if appropriate today, they may not deliver the right solutions tomorrow.

ENFORCEMENT

A final major difficulty said to be particularly associated with C & C regimes is that of enforcement. The complex rules attending such regimes have to be brought to bear on the ground by bodies of officials or inspectors, but enforcement is expensive, the techniques used give rise to contention, and the effects of enforcement are said to be uncertain.[19] On the latter point, for instance, the rules used in C & C systems may be too narrow or too broad in scope. They may, accordingly, fail to cover conduct that should be controlled, or else may constrain activity that should be unrestricted. In addition, there may be problems of 'creative compliance'—the practice of avoiding the intention of the law without breaking the terms of the law.[20] Command methods may also lack force when court sanctioning is weak and the rules, as a result, fail to pose a credible deterrent. Where, moreover, there is credibility of deterrence, there may be problems because adversarial industry to regulator relationships develop and this produces poor information flows to the regulator and a climate of defiance and resistance that produces poor compliance.[21]

Regulators employing C & C techniques thus face substantial difficulties of rule use. Not only must the rules employed be capable of enforcement and be accessible to regulated firms or individuals, but the appropriate types and levels of standards must be fixed, problems of scope (or inclusiveness) must be overcome, and issues of creative compliance dealt with. Such problems, moreover, must often be faced in political environments that are unlikely to produce the resources necessary for effective enforcement and are hostile to rules that impose compliance costs on industry or interfere with managers. In the light of such difficulties, some commentators have advocated a move

[18] See C. Sunstein, 'Paradoxes of the Regulatory State' (1990) 57 *University of Chicago Law Review* 407–41.
[19] For further discussion of enforcement, see Chapter 11 below and Baldwin, *Rules and Government*, ch. 6.
[20] See below, p. 232.
[21] Gunningham and Grabosky, *Smart Regulation*, 45; J. Braithwaite and T. Makkai, 'Trust and Compliance' (1994) 4 *Policy and Society* 1.

away from command-based strategies towards alternative, 'constitutive', 'less restrictive', or 'incentive-based' styles of control.[22] On the governmental stage also, numerous administrations and international bodies came to favour this kind of shift at around the end of the second millennium.[23] The strategies now to be described may be seen as the main alternatives to the C & C style of regulation—they are state-initiated but, as will be seen, may delegate regulatory functions in varying degrees to non-state actors.

Incentive-based Regimes

Regulating by means of economic incentives might be thought to offer an escape from highly restrictive, rule-bound, C & C regimes.[24] According to the incentives approach, the potential mischief causer, say a polluter, can be induced to behave in accordance with the public interest by the state or a regulator imposing negative or positive taxes or deploying grants and subsidies from the public purse. Thus, not only can taxes be used to penalize polluters, but rewards can be given for reductions in pollution, or financial assistance can be given to those who build pollution-reducing mechanisms into their production or operational processes. An example of such an incentive strategy at the broadest level was the differential tax on leaded and unleaded petrol that was introduced into Britain in 1987.[25]

The posited advantages of such schemes are numerous. They are, for instance, said to involve relatively low levels of regulatory discretion (as compared to C & C systems) because financial punishments or rewards operate in a mechanical manner once the regime is established. These low

---

[22] See Stewart, 'Regulation and the Crisis of Legalisation'; Breyer, *Regulation and Its Reform*. On incentive-based regulation see Ogus, *Regulation*, ch. 11. For a European view of the limits of command law, see G. Teubner, *After Legal Instrumentalism? Strategic Models of Post-Regulatory Law*, EUI Working Paper No. 100 (Florence, 1984).

[23] See, e.g., the UK Better Regulation Task Force, *Imaginative Thinking for Better Regulation* (London, 2003); OECD, Report on Regulatory Reform (Paris, 1997), vol. 2, pp. 193–202.

[24] See Ogus, *Regulation*, ch. 11; Daintith, 'Techniques of Government'; R. Breyer and R.B. Stewart, 'The Discontents of Legalism: Interest Group Relations in Administrative Regulation' (1985) *Wisconsin Law Review* 685. On the limitations of incentive-based regimes, see J. Braithwaite, 'The Limits of Economism in Controlling Harmful Corporate Conduct' (1982) 16 *Law and Society Review* 481.

[25] See generally: A. Ogus, 'Corrective Taxation as a Regulatory Instrument' in C. McCrudden (ed.), *Regulation and Deregulation* (Oxford, 1999); A. Ogus, 'Corrective Taxation and Financial Impositions as Regulatory Instruments' (1998) 61 *MLR* 767; S. Rose-Ackerman, 'Efficient Changes: A Critique' (1973) 6 *Canadian Journal of Economics* 572; W.J. Baumol, 'On Taxation and the Control of Externalities' (1972) 62 *American Economic Review* 307; P. Burrows, 'Pricing versus Regulation for Environmental Pollution' in A.J. Culyer (ed.), *Economic Policies and Social Goals* (London, 1974); D. Driesen, 'Alternatives to Regulation? Market Mechanisms and the Environment' in R. Baldwin, M. Cave, and M. Lodge (eds), *The Oxford Handbook of Regulation* (Oxford, 2010).

levels of discretion and structured modes of application reduce the dangers of regulatory capture in so far as regulators are not involved in constant negotiations, close relations, and information exchanges with regulatees as in the usual C & C scheme.

They are also said to leave managers free to manage. It is up to the regulated firm, not the bureaucrat or regulator, to balance the costs of polluting against those of abatement in a particular context and to devise means of reducing the mischief most efficiently. Managers are, accordingly, able to be more flexible concerning their modes of production than most C & C regimes allow.

Incentive-based regimes are, additionally, claimed to be cheaper to administer than commands[26] and to involve relatively light burdens of information collection and compliance costs. They, moreover, are said by proponents to encourage individual regulated firms to reduce harmful conduct as much as possible (to give an 'incentive to zero'), not merely down to the level that is demanded by the standard stipulated in a C & C regime—a standard liable, in any event, to be fairly lax because C & C regulators tend, for political reasons, to have to set a general standard soft enough to be met by poorer performers in the industry without causing financial crises or unacceptable unemployment.

The advantages of incentive regimes can, however, be exaggerated and a number of cautionary points should be borne in mind.[27] Such systems often have to be put into effect by means of highly complex systems of rules (the field of taxation, for instance, is not one renowned for simplicity).[28] Many of the problems associated with C & C regulation might thus be replicated in putting such systems into effect on the ground. Inspection and enforcement mechanisms might, moreover, have to be employed to prevent regulatees evading their liabilities (e.g. to taxes). The system might, thus, come to resemble C & C regulation and the distinction between incentives and penalty mechanisms might be less than first appeared.[29] As for overall costs, it cannot be assumed that these will be lower under a taxation as opposed to a command regime. In the former, the task of determining optimal abatement may be thrust on to regulated parties in circumstances where this involves higher costs than those that would have been incurred by a public regulator.[30]

Proponents of incentive systems tend to assume that those regulated operate, on the whole, in an economically rational manner. In practice,

---

[26] Baumol, 'On Taxation and the Control of Externalities', 307.

[27] For evaluation, see Ogus, *Regulation*, 250–6 and Breyer, *Regulation and Its Reform*, 278–80.

[28] See R.S. Markovits, 'Antitrust: Alternatives to Delegalisation' in G. Teubner (ed.), *Juridification of Social Spheres* (Berlin, 1987).

[29] See Bardach and Kagan, *Going by the Book*, chs. 8, 9, and 10; J. Braithwaite, 'The Limits of Economism in Controlling Harmful Corporate Conduct' (1982) 16 *Law and Society Review* 481.

[30] See Ogus, 'Corrective Taxation and Financial Impositions', 776–7.

however, many problems (e.g. hazards in the workplace) are the product of irrational, accidental, or negligent behaviour.[31] Incentive mechanisms may, accordingly, influence responsible parties more effectively than irresponsible, careless, or ill-informed individuals or firms—yet it is the latter group who are most in need of regulation. Regulatory lag may also prove a significant problem with incentive regimes because they operate indirectly. Thus, within a firm the effects of tax incentives may have to be transmitted from finance directors through operations managers to floor staff and this, even if successful, may take some time—the fish in the river may long be dead. Incentives may thus prove to be poor regulatory tools where periodic crises occur in the sectors involved, where such sectors are subject to rapid economic change, or where preventative measures need to be taken, rather than harmful effects penalized.

A core difficulty with incentive regimes may be predicting the effect on the ground of a given incentive. To continue the river pollution example, it will be very difficult to predict how much a certain level of taxation will clean up the river—or whether certain thresholds will be passed (e.g. pollution will rise to levels that the fish cannot survive). The effect on each firm sited on the river will differ and (assuming firm rationality) will depend, *inter alia*, on the profit derived within each production process from each unit of pollution. Fixing incentive levels in order to achieve acceptable outcomes may thus make informational demands at least as severe as those encountered within C & C regimes. It might be responded to this point that, in practice, the tax authorities could adopt a trial-and-error approach so that, in the river example, tax levels could be modified in response to water cleanliness readings and the desired purity could be arrived at over time.[32] The difficulty with such a solution, however, is that a process of incremental adjustment might work to control small risks but would not be acceptable if the regulated risks were potentially catastrophic. Thus, if the river contained the last breeding stock of a rare fish, it would be difficult to justify operating on a trial-and-error basis and running the risk of under-deterrence and fish kill through sub-optimal taxation.

The mechanical application of incentives may also bring disadvantages. Within C & C systems, enforcement can be used flexibly in an effort to achieve desired results and to limit the imposition of restrictions on particular firms or individuals where unduly onerous effects would result. In so far as incentive regimes operate mechanically, such tailoring to individual circumstances will not be possible. If a flexible and discretionary approach is adopted in relation to incentives (and there is no reason why this cannot be the case),

[31] See Braithwaite, 'Limits of Economism'.

[32] W. Baumol and W. Oates, 'On Taxation and the Control of Externalites' (1972) 62 *American Economic Review* 307.

another supposed difference from, and advantage over, C & C regulation falls away.

Presentationally and politically, a move from C & C towards incentive regimes may prove popular with firms regulated (especially where subsidies are offered), but public concern may arise on the grounds that socially harmful activity is not being stigmatized or condemned and that a licence is being given for undesirable behaviour.[33] Subsidies may be objected to as making payments from the public purse to those engaged in offensive conduct and negative incentives or taxes may be criticized not only for their failure to designate certain acts as unacceptable but also for taking away from industry the very resources that might have been committed to measures aimed at avoiding the undesirable consequences of their actions (e.g. to filtration systems).

As far as democratic accountability and access to the regulatory process are concerned, similar consultative and other procedures to those used in command and control regulation may be used. If it is hard to predict the effects of given incentives on the ground, however, it may be difficult to produce the results that such democratic inputs favour, and this can be seen as a weakening of accountability and access. Other accountability concerns may relate to the distributional effects of taxes (the question of who eventually pays[34]) and the degree to which complex tax rules tend to offer well-resourced regulated firms better access to rule-making processes than can be enjoyed by individual harm sufferers and small public interest groups.[35]

Market-harnessing Controls

COMPETITION LAWS

A direct method of regulating by channelling market forces is to influence competition within an area. Competition laws can thus be used instead of, or in conjunction with, regulation in order to sustain such levels of competition as will ensure that the market provides adequate services to consumers and the public.[36]

---

[33] See Ogus, *Regulation*, 225; also W. Beckerman, *Small is Stupid: Blowing the Whistle on the Greens* (London, 1995).
[34] See Ogus, 'Corrective Taxation and Financial Impositions', 775—who notes the regressive effects of some taxes and the difficult issue of how some corporations' tax costs are subsequently distributed between shareholders, employees, and consumers.
[35] Ibid., 786.
[36] On competition law generally, see R. Whish, *Competition Law* (6th edn. Oxford, 2008). On regulation versus competition, see below, Chapter 23.

Such laws can also be used to control market behaviour so as to prevent anti-competitive or unfair practices such as 'predatory pricing' by dominant operators (setting prices for one's products below cost in order to drive competitors from the market)[37] or effecting cross-subsidies from monopolistic to competitive sectors.

The telecommunications industry provides an example of competition law being used instead of classical C & C regulation. Thus, in contrast to the UK's use of a sectoral agency (OFTEL, later superseded by Ofcom) with sector-specific rules, the New Zealand government, on privatizing in the late 1980s, relied on general competition laws, applied in the courts, as a mechanism for influencing the telecommunications industry.

The broad advantages of reliance on competition laws are that they can be applied across the board to different sectors, the need for industry-specific regulation is avoided, and barriers to entry may be lower than in regimes incorporating large numbers of highly prescriptive rules. Consistent principles can also be developed across sectors and there are economies of scale in applying rules broadly.

Competition laws produce lower levels of intrusion into firms' internal decisions than are involved in C & C regimes, and flexibility in the industry tends to be greater under competition law regimes than in cases where behaviour is structured by an overseeing agency. Finally, enforcement involves relatively light burdens on the public purse because it depends on private actions in courts, rather than interventions by publicly funded regulatory agencies. Experience in New Zealand telecommunications suggests, however, that a number of drawbacks can be encountered when heavy reliance is placed on competition laws.[38] The broad principles established in competition laws may, for instance, not provide solutions to operational, technical, or commercial problems. Such issues are left to the parties to resolve in the courts and more effective solutions might, under certain conditions, be produced by a specialist overseeing agency. An agency, moreover, might develop and apply a greater level of expertise than the parties or the courts in dealing with such issues as the economics of interconnections. Guidelines established by a regulatory agency can reduce uncertainties and transaction costs for operators more efficiently than competition laws or the courts.

The courts system may, furthermore, be slow to develop guidelines on central industrial issues. Thus, following difficulties concerning the application of general competition rules to a dispute over interconnection by a new

[37] See J. Vickers, 'The Economics of Predatory Prices' (1985) 6 *Fiscal Studies* 24.
[38] For reviews of New Zealand experience, see: New Zealand Commerce Commission, *Telecommunications Industry Inquiry Report* (Wellington, June 1992); C. Blanchard, 'Telecommunications Regulation in New Zealand: How Effective is "Light-Handed" Regulation?' (1994) 18 *Telecommunications Policy* 154–64.

entrant (issues fought from New Zealand to the Privy Council in 1994[39]), the New Zealand government considered whether a new mix of institutions and rules would be appropriate.[40] One difficulty encountered in relying on judicially developed principles on such issues as interconnection is that rulings only emerge as cases happen to arise. Principles, accordingly, may develop sporadically, slowly, and may leave key issues untouched. Developing such principles, moreover, may involve asking the courts to stand in the shoes of business people and to make business decisions.[41] Evidential problems may also compound such reliance on the courts, thus, competition law may have a limited role in dealing with entry barriers where it is difficult to show these have been established on purpose by a dominant undertaking.

To point to some of the problems to be anticipated in using competition laws is not, of course, to say that such laws cannot play a very useful role in combination with other mechanisms of influence, such as C & C regulation in the classical style. Competition laws can thus substitute for excessively prescriptive C & C regulation on some issues and the latter can be used to impose structures and final solutions for industries in circumstances where competition law would be slow to provide answers on these fronts.

FRANCHISING

Franchising is a system of control that can be employed in naturally monopolistic sectors to replace competition *in* the market with competition *for* the market. It has been employed notably in the British independent television, radio, and rail industries. The underlying idea is that if applicants for franchises make competitive bids for an exclusive (or at least protected) right to serve a market for a given period and under conditions, they will bid on assumptions of efficient operation and, as a result, consumers will benefit—they will be served by operators who are not under immediate competitive pressure but who will behave in many ways as if they are. A fuller discussion of franchising is offered in Chapter 9.

REGULATION BY CONTRACT

Government departments or agencies can use the state's wealth and spending power to achieve desired objectives by specifying these in the contracts it agrees with enterprises. It can be stipulated, for example, that parties contracting to supply goods or services shall pay their own employees a

---

[39] See *Clear Communication* v. *New Zealand Telecommunications Corp.* [1994] 6 TCLR 138 (1995) 1 NZLR 385 (PC).

[40] See Baldwin, Scott, and Hood, *A Reader on Regulation*, ch. 1.

[41] See New Zealand Commerce Commission, *Telecommunications Regulation*, 83.

minimum wage.[42] The regulatory aspects of the contract may be incidental to the main purpose, which may be commercial, but the effect is to impose a regulatory standard across all firms contracting with the government. There is no need for a command base. A form of contracting out—Compulsory Competitive Tendering (CCT)—of local authority services has been used by government as a means of reducing service costs, and it brings with it local authority regulation of those who provide services under contractual terms. In some sectors, similarly, dependence on public funding has been used as a basis for encouraging both the development of self-regulation and the imposition of 'consensual forms of regulation'.[43]

TRADABLE PERMITS

A further technique that seeks to harness markets is the use of tradable permits to engage in an activity that has been deemed to require control (e.g. discharging pollutants into a water course).[44] Like franchising, the strategy can be used to control both entry into the market and subsequent behaviour within the market. Examples of the use and advocacy of tradable permits are to be found. Thus, since 1991 the US Environment Protection Agency (EPA) has sought to control sulphur dioxide emissions by allocating tradable emission permits to coal-burning electric power plants[45] and the EU launched its Emissions Trading Scheme in January 2005. By 2007, the Stern Review had advocated the broad use of trading mechanisms to combat climate change.[46]

Emissions trading is discussed in greater detail in Chapter 10 below, but a sketch of issues will be given here. In typical regimes, the public agency issues a given number of permits and each of these allows a specified course of behaviour (e.g. a polluting discharge of a fixed amount). Following the initial allocation, permits may be traded and this allows, say, a generating company to switch to cleaner fuels and sell its excess allowances to other firms. The initial distribution of permits may be carried out by auction or according to

---

[42] See T.C. Daintith, 'Regulation by Contract: The New Prerogative' (1979) *Current Legal Problems* 41. On governing through contracts, see I. Harden, *The Contracting State* (Buckingham, 1992) and N. Lewis and J. Goh, *The Private World of Government* (Sheffield, 1998).

[43] See Baldwin, Scott, and Hood, *A Reader on Regulation*, ch. 1; M. Cave, R. Dodsworth, and D. Thompson, 'Regulatory Reform in Higher Education in the UK: Incentives for Efficiency and Product Quality' in M. Bishop, J. Kay, and C. Mayer (eds), *The Regulatory Challenge* (Oxford, 1995).

[44] For a review of market-based instruments versus other regulatory tools, see: N. Keohane, R. Revesz, and R. Stavins, 'The Choice of Regulatory Instruments in Environmental Policy' (1998) 22 *Harvard Environmental Law Review* 313–67.

[45] D. Ellerman, R. Schmalensee, E. Bailey, P. Joskow, and J.-P. Montero, *Markets for Clean Air* (Cambridge, 2000).

[46] N. Stern, *The Economics of Climate Change* (Cambridge, 2007).

public interest criteria. The incentives within such systems are provided by the market in permits.

Advantages claimed for the strategy are, first, that permits can be allocated to those who will generate most wealth per unit of pollution. This is because those willing to pay most for the permits will be those who derive the most profit from polluting—in this sense, it can be argued, (at least on a set of not uncontentious assumptions), that the pollution is being put to the use that society values most. Second, the incentive to reduce harmful behaviour can, as in taxation regimes, operate down to zero, since the process of abatement will release permits for resale until the point where no harm is being done at all. Third, managers, again, are less restricted than in C & C regulation because they are free to decide whether and how to reduce harmful conduct in order to release permits. Fourth, regulatory discretions (and dangers of capture) are kept low because markets rather than bureaucrats are imposing restraints, and, finally, regulatory costs are low since, once established, the market in permits runs on its own accord.

The problems to be anticipated in relation to schemes with marketable permits are, however, numerous. Enforcement still has to be carried out to prevent non-permit holders from creating harms and to stop permit holders from exceeding the terms of their permits. Inspectorates, accordingly, require funding. Regulatory lag may also be a problem. If, for example, permits are used to control river pollution, it may be difficult to adjust pollution levels rapidly so as to cope with sudden drops in the river's capacity to absorb pollution (as might occur in a heatwave or drought). The difficulty is that permits are already issued, they are in the marketplace and bearing a given entitlement. (A response to the difficulty might be to give permits a floating entitlement that is adjustable by the regulator. This would give flexibility but might prejudice the operation of the market and would impose severe informational demands on the regulator.)

Permits, moreover, do not provide the resources needed to compensate the victims of harmful conduct and, politically, permits may create difficulties with electorates, since they may be seen as 'licences to pollute'. The system, in addition, demands that there be a healthy market in permits—which calls for such factors as a large number of potential buyers possessed of adequate information. If the market is deficient (perhaps because of uncertainties or lack of information), the value of permits may be low and the incentives to desist from harmful conduct may be weak. A further problem is that markets in permits may allow hoarding and the creation of barriers to enter into certain markets. This will be more likely where conditions favour collusion between certain large firms. The effects may be generally anti-competitive and may be unfair to less well-resourced firms. As for the areas where markets in permits can be used, some harms or pollutants may have to be prohibited absolutely and, accordingly, the tradable permit system will be inappropriate. Finally, it should be cautioned that democratic accountability and influence may be low once the system is up and running, since the market (and its degree of genuine competitiveness) will govern the price to be placed on pollution. Where markets are imperfect, it is also likely that information flowing into the public domain is below optimal levels.

Disclosure Regulation

Structuring the disclosure of information provides a mode of regulation that is not heavily interventionist. It does not regulate the production process, the level of output allowed, prices charged, or the allocation of products. Disclosure rules usually prohibit the supply of false or misleading information and may also require mandatory disclosure—perhaps obliging suppliers to provide information to consumers on price, composition, quantity, or quality (familiar demands in the food and drinks sectors).[47] Disclosure regulation may also involve the supply of information to the public directly by a scrutinizing regulator or governmental official. Thus, in October 1997, the then Agriculture Minister, Jack Cunningham, first put into action a policy of 'naming and shaming' food manufacturers who failed to comply with regulations on safety, product quality, and authenticity. Following a departmental survey, the Minister named sixteen pork and bacon brands as guilty of failing to declare the added water content of their products. These included suppliers of Tesco and J. Sainsbury.[48] More recently, the Environment Agency published details of the ten firms who had been fined the highest sums following its prosecutions in 2007.[49] 'Naming and shaming' is not, however, the only reason for state disclosure. Governments may also disclose information for exhortatory reasons (e.g. health campaigns), in order to raise standards by drawing attention to best practices in a field or to rank service providers in 'league tables' (as with schools).[50]

Disclosure regulation allows the consumers of products and services (or even voters more generally) to make decisions on the acceptability of the processes employed in producing those products or services. To rely on consumer or

[47] In the food sector there is a pressure group devoted to disclosure—the Food Labelling Agenda (FLAG). See generally K. Yeung, 'Government by Publicity Management: Sunlight or Spin?' (2005) *Public Law* 360–83. On voluntary disclosure by producers for 'ethical branding', marketing, and other reasons, see Yeung, loc. cit.

[48] See *Financial Times*, 29 Oct. 1997: '"Naming and Shaming" over Pork Product Labels'.

[49] Environment Agency, *Spotlight on Business* (Bristol, 2008), 22. The Health and Safety Executive also publishes details of convictions secured.

[50] The Major government instituted state-sponsored school league tables in the 1990s—see Yeung, 'Government by Publicity Management'.

voter preferences in this manner does, however, restrict the potential of disclosure as a regulatory instrument.

The main problems to be anticipated are, first, that users of the information disclosed, be they consumers or other citizens, may make mistakes; they may fail to use the information properly; fail to understand the implications of the data given; mis-assess risks; neglect to collect the full range of relevant information; lack the resources and expertise to research issues fully; and so may come to harm. Second, information users may not respond in anticipated ways to the flow of information. Considerations of economics rather than policy, politics, or social concern may shape their decisions. Thus, consumers, when purchasing products, may choose according to price, rather than other factors. They may, for instance, buy cheap products without responding to information suggesting that dangers are involved in consumption or that production of the goods involves a host of socially undesirable consequences (e.g. discharges of polluting effluents).

Third, the costs of producing the information may be excessive, as may the costs of processing it. Thus, if information disclosure rules were employed instead of C & C regulation in relation to food safety, a visit to the supermarket would involve a very lengthy process of scrutinizing labels. It might, in many circumstances, be far more efficient for consumers to rely on the expertise and protection of public regulators and inspectorates, rather than depend on their own individual assessments of risks.

Fourth, the risks associated with some products or activities may be so great that policymakers may feel that it is inappropriate merely to inform affected parties about these matters and C & C methods may be deemed necessary.[51] Fifth, where information regulation is employed there is always a danger that the information will be inaccurate and unjustifiable claims made. Policing of the quality of information will, accordingly, be necessary. This increases the costs of information-based regulatory regimes. Finally, standards may have to be applied to various items of information so that affected parties may make appropriate use of any data given. In the absence of such standards, information may be offered in a manner that does not assist, for example, consumers. Thus 'may cause cancer' is a phrase that discloses little concerning the size of any risk of cancer generated by using the product.

Given the above limitations of disclosure regulation, the case for the strategy is liable to be strongest where: the hazard involved is not potentially catastrophic or the difference between high- and low-quality products or processes is not likely to give rise to grave consequences; the relevant information can be processed at a reasonable cost; risks can be assessed accurately by affected parties; consumers of the products at issue, or other affected

---

[51] See I. Ramsey, *Consumer Protection* (London, 1989).

parties, can be relied upon to give proper consideration to the information given; and the accuracy and utility of information can be monitored and ensured through enforcement at acceptable cost. It can also be argued that, even where information strategies cannot be used as free-standing replacements for traditional command methods—as in environmental protection—the two approaches can be used as complementary instruments.[52] There is evidence that, at least where clear standards and credible penalty systems are found, public disclosures can create additional and strong incentives for compliance in such areas as pollution control.[53]

Direct Action and Design Solutions

Governments can use their resources to achieve desired results by taking direct action. Rather than set and enforce standards on, say, dust extraction levels in factories, central governments or local authorities can build properly ventilated premises and lease these to private manufacturers. Public ownership of infrastructure can, moreover, be combined with the franchising out of operations (leasing for fixed periods subject to conditions on use and renewal would produce similar results). Long-term investments can, by such methods, be rendered amenable to planning by government, and the replacement of unsatisfactory operators can be facilitated. Thus, in London the bus transport network is publicly owned, but routes are put out to competitive tendering or franchising.[54]

An advantage of direct action is that public money can be used to ensure furtherance of democratically established objectives in circumstances where firms, particularly small ones, might not invest in the required measures. A degree of subsidization may, by such means, be effected and public resources can be used to assist firms to reduce harms rather than to fund C & C enforcement regimes or to apply penalties that take money away from the enterprises that are asked to spend on avoiding undesired consequences.

Such subsidization, however, may give rise to distributional issues—concerning the fairness of access to subsidized premises, for instance—and subsidies may produce undesirable distortions of competition. An equally difficult problem may be that the public funding of a certain aspect of a production process may encourage firms to build operations around the

---

[52] See Gunningham and Grabosky, *Smart Regulation*, ch. 6 (by N. Gunninghan and D. Sinclair).
[53] See J. Foulon, P. Lanoie, and B. Laplante, 'Incentives for Pollution Control: Regulation or Information?' (2002) 44 *Journal of Environmental Economics and Management* 169–87.
[54] See S. Glaister, D. Kennedy, and T. Travers, *London Bus Tendering* (London, 1995) and S. Glaister, *Deregulation and Privatisation: British Experience* (Washington, DC, 1998).

funded element. As a result, innovation may not be driven by the market and the enterprises' responsiveness to markets and potential new technologies or processes may be blunted. Thus if the well-ventilated manufacturing premises are publicly owned and there are no other controls on dust levels in the air, there is little incentive for the private sector to devise new, more efficient ways to control dust. The manufacturers of dust extraction systems, for example, would be potentially selling their new designs to the procurement departments of public bodies, rather than to private firms. The incentive to innovate would, accordingly, be far weaker than under a regime of taxing dust exposures—which would lead companies to press extraction manufacturers for ever better ways of reducing dust and tax liabilities.

Finally, it should be noted that the 'direct action' approach tends to assume, perhaps unrealistically, that where the state provides a solution, this will remove the targeted mischief unproblematically. The reality, however, may be that the state may fall down on its ongoing obligations just as badly as the private sector. It cannot be assumed, for instance, that, in the above example, the state's dust extraction systems will be perfectly maintained and effective over time. Public bodies' failures to renew filters and maintain machinery may be as pronounced as those of private firms.

A different way that the state can use its resources to eliminate problems is through the use of design solutions. Thus, rather than regulate the mischief, the state can organize affairs so that the mischief cannot arise—or opportunities for the mischief to eventuate are minimized. It can 'design out' problems in a variety of ways. These include constructing the physical environment in a certain manner—as where parking is controlled by concrete bollards or road accidents are reduced by a road architecture that makes speeding impossible. The law can also be used for such design purposes—as where statutes set up markets in a configuration that ensures healthy competition and consumer satisfaction.[55] The labels of 'techno-regulation', 'architecture-based', and 'code' approaches are attached to such design strategies and some commentators make a case for dealing with some of the most daunting regulatory challenges in this way. Thus Lessig suggests that it is possible to regulate cyberspace through control of the software code that shapes the structure of cyberspace and dictates access to and participation in that space.[56] This could be done, he argues, by mandating software designers to build certain elements into software code in pursuit of public regulatory objectives.[57] The degree to which regulatory actors can escape such

---

[55] See R. Brownsword, 'Code, Control and Choice: Why East is East and West is West' (2005) 25 *Legal Studies* 1–21; D. Garland, *The Culture of Control* (Oxford, 2001); B. Morgan and K. Yeung, *An Introduction to Law and Regulation* (Cambridge, 2007), 102–5.

[56] See L. Lessig, *Code and Other Laws of Cyberspace* (New York, 1999).

[57] L. Lessig 'The Law of the Horse: What Cyberlaw Might Teach' (1999) 113 *Harvard Law Review* 501, 514–22.

architectural/code controls may, however, prove a point of contention—as may the extent to which such controls need to be combined with other types of regulatory instrument. These matters are explored in some detail in the extensive scholarly debates that relate to cyberspace and its control.[58]

NUDGE STRATEGIES

A regulatory strategy that purports to offer a user-friendly and a low-intervention alternative to more draconian controls is 'nudging'. This approach is highly influential in many government circles following the publication of Thaler and Sunstein's 2008 book *Nudge*.[59] Nudging involves structuring the architecture of decisions (so-called 'choice architectures') so that it is easier for consumers or others (such as regulatees) to act in ways that are beneficial. Studies in the fields of decision-making[60] and behavioural economics suggest that people tend to make poor choices for a number of reasons that Thaler and Sunstein identify (they process information in shorthand ways that are biased by immediate concerns and experiences, they tend to be too optimistic, and so on).[61] Nudging makes it easier to make the sensible decision but, according to a philosophy entitled 'libertarian paternalism', it purports to leave the target person or firm free to choose to take the non-sensible course of action. An example of nudging is establishing a presumption that all citizens consent to be organ donors unless they register their unwillingness to donate (which, Thaler and Sunstein stress, they should be able to do easily).

The nudging approach thus allows for decisions to be manipulated by public authorities, provided that it leaves decision-makers free to choose to behave as they, rather than the public authorities, see fit. In its ideal form, therefore, the approach cleverly combines an element of paternalism with the preserving of freedom of choice. It also offers the hope of using small changes in choice architectures to achieve considerable changes in outcomes.

Critics, however, might have two central worries about nudging. The first is that it is difficult, in real-life situations, to draw the line between manipulations that do not threaten freedoms of choice and those that do. Thaler and

---

[58] See A. Murray, *The Regulation of Cyberspace: Control in the Online Environment* (London, 2006); A. Murray and C. Scott, 'Controlling the New Media: Hybrid Responses to New Forms of Power' (2002) 65 *Modern Law Review* 491–516.

[59] R. Thaler and C. Sunstein, *Nudge: Improving Decisions about Health, Wealth and Happiness* (New Haven, 2008). Warning: the thesis of *Nudge* is expressed amidst a mass of personal anecdotes that some readers may find frustrating and exhausting. See also R.H. Thaler, C.R. Sunstein, and J.P. Balz, 'Choice Architecture' (2010). Available at SSRN: http://ssrn.com/abstract=1583509 (last accessed 7 December 2010).

[60] See, e.g., H. Simon, *Administrative Behaviour* (1947; 4th edn, New York, 1997).

[61] Thaler and Sunstein, *Nudge*, ch.1.

Sunstein give examples of easy cases in which consumers are confronted with helpful information on products but, in other circumstances, the rigging of the decision architecture may make 'non-sensible' choices (as seen by the nudger) quite difficult to take. Thaler and Sunstein, as noted, would respond that opt-outs must be easy but such assurances count for little if there is no reliable way to identify and protect the easy opt-out. They contend that it would be 'ridiculous' to have an inflexible rule on when opt-out costs are too high: 'the precise question of degree is not important. Let us simply say that we want these costs to be small'.[62] Critics, however, are liable to say that this is too easy a response. 'Ease of opt-out', they would stress, is a contentious issue that lies at the heart of nudging and the proponents' answer evidences the dangerousness of nudge: it treats the centrally important issue of opt-out feasibility as a small and relatively uncontentious matter. This approach, the objectors would say, sows the seeds of an illiberal system of control.

The second main worry is related and is that the processes of nudging are value-laden yet low in transparency. It might, thus, be contended that whether a nudged-for outcome is 'good' or 'beneficial' is not always obvious. The evaluation of an outcome's merits may reflect the nudger's conception of the good rather than the nudgee's or it may, simply, be an outcome whose merits are debatable and contested. Nudging, the objection goes, is not a device that is easily confinable to the pursuit of uncontentious benefits. In response, Thaler and Sunstein suggest that nudges are inevitable (all decisions are structured) and so they might as well be made benignly.[63] Nudge-sceptics would, however, say that this response misses a key point. Some manipulations of decisions, and control systems, are more open than others. If a government issues a law that prohibits citizens from smoking in public places, this is a mode of control that is open, discussed, and implemented after representative processes have been followed. If nudging is used, the process used to effect a nudge may be far more hidden from view—the nudge may flow from an administrator's decision on how to design a public building: a decision not subjected to advanced disclosure or debate. The danger of nudging is that, under the banner of neutrality, control regimes become less overt, less accountable, and more paternalistic.

Such concerns about the accountability and openness of nudging are not necessarily assuaged by Thaler and Sunstein's comments about the occasions *when* nudging will have the most potential for good. The authors suggest that nudging will be most useful where the nudgers or 'choice architects' have high levels of expertise and the nudgees face difficult decisions on which they have poor feedback and few opportunities for learning.[64] Sceptics would immediately voice worries that systems in which 'experts'

---

[62] Thaler and Sunstein, *Nudge*, 249.   [63] Thaler and Sunstein, *Nudge*, 235–7.
[64] Thaler and Sunstein, *Nudge*, 247.

manipulate the choices of less well-informed parties are exactly those scenarios which there are the greatest dangers that regulatees' and citizens' preferences will be overridden in the name of expert judgements of a spuriously neutral nature. There is, however, a Thaler and Sunstein response. They say that nudgers will be best able to make good guesses about what is best for the nudgees: 'when they have much more expertise at their disposal, and when the differences in individuals' tastes and preferences are either not very big (nearly everyone prefers chocolate ice cream to licorice) or when differences in tastes and preferences can be easily detected'.[65]

Whether this response will placate critics is doubtful. In the first place, it puts considerable faith in experts to identify those circumstances where divergencies of preference are small and to withstand the temptation to impose their own vision of the good. Second, it places nudging in the realm of expert judgement rather than that of open discussion. Third, the discussion of preferences fails to come to grips with the challenges posed by both distributions and strengths of preferences. Ice cream preferences are noted by Thaler and Sunstein, but their discussion only highlights the problem of allowing expert nudgers (or advocates of nudging) to judge preferences. If those parties who prefer liquorice ice cream consider that they are a group worthy of consideration, and if their preferences are very strong, they may object vehemently to nudges that favour chocolate ice cream and they may argue that a movement away from un-nudged choice of ice cream is an example of high-handed expertise at its most undemocratic. They might add that nudges that favour some groups within society rather than others are highly political in nature and should not be swept under the nudge carpet. If we are to have controls over choices that matter to us, and which affect social justice, they might say, let us do so after a proper process of open deliberation.

A third concern relates to the applicability of 'nudging' to the behaviour of corporations. Applying a nudge strategy to corporations presupposes much about the rationality and risk management capacity of such enterprises. Where potential harms may emerge from the cumulative actions of numbers of decision-makers, the nudging of particular decision-makers may not suffice to control the harm's emergence. This suggests that nudging has limited potential, especially in those industries where production chains are complex and extended.

A final worry about nudging is that, whether it is applied to individuals or corporations, its effectiveness may depend not only on the organizational capacity and rationality of the regulatees but also their dispositions. If regulatees are ill-disposed to comply with regulations or are committed to either

---

[65] Ibid.

creative compliance or an errant course of action, they are unlikely to respond well to nudges.[66] Nudging, accordingly, would not be a satisfactory way to regulate the movements of highly ill-disposed persons who present security risks. It might be added that, for similar reasons, nudging will often prove unsuitable as a means of controlling potentially catastrophic risks.

To conclude, in its ideal form and location, nudging offers a useful means of regulating social and corporate behaviour. This is not, however, a simple tool that carries with it no dangers. The most interesting issue with regard to nudging is not whether it can, in some situations, prove useful and uncontentious. Providing information on tobacco dangers is likely to meet general approval. The more acute questions are whether governments can identify and contain the potential for illiberality that this tool carries and whether its use can be targeted adequately at those areas where it will operate effectively and acceptably.

Rights and Liabilities

In the case of the factory that pollutes the river, the state might decide not to tax pollution or impose standards in a C & C regime, but to allocate rights (for example, to the enjoyment of clean water) so as to encourage socially desirable behaviour.[67] Thus, the argument goes, the prospective polluter will be deterred from such activity by his or her potential liability to pay damages when sued by the holder of the right to clean water (say, the angling club or the riparian owner downstream). The deterrent effect will be provided by the expected cost of polluting—which is the quantum of expected damages multiplied by the probability of those damages having to be paid out. In economic terms, the efficient level of deterrence is that which will ensure that the factory owner will spend money on avoiding pollution up to the point where the cost of avoidance exceeds the value of the harm caused by the pollution. (Beyond that point it is efficient to let the pollution occur and compensate the 'victims', rather than spend on abatement.)

If society desires this efficient level of deterrence, difficulties are encountered because the precise deterrent effects of liability rules are difficult to predict. Rights and mirroring liabilities may, moreover, fail to deter efficiently

---

[66] For an argument that the evidence is weak that nudging can be used effectively to increase population health, see T. Marteau, D. Ogilvie, M. Roland, M. Suhacke, and 'Judging Nudging' (2011) *BMJ* 342. Available at: http://www .bmj.com/content/342/bmj.d228.full (last accessed 26 January 2011).

[67] See generally Breyer, *Regulation and Its Reform*, 174–7; G. Calabresi and A. Melamed, 'Property Rules, Liability Rules and Inalienability: One View of the Cathedral' (1972) *Harvard Law Review* 1089.

for a number of reasons. Many undesirable events, for example, are the results of accidents, random events, and irrational behaviour. Deterrence, for this reason, does not operate in a mechanical and frictionless manner.[68] A further difficulty is that sub-optimal deterrence may occur where the wealth of the potential harm-causer is insufficient to allow them to fear a level of loss that correlates to the efficient level of deterrence. Thus a small oil tanker operator whose firm is worth $10 million cannot be adequately deterred, and induced to take appropriate precautions, by a potential liability of $60 million (which sum reflects the harm caused by potential spillage). That operator can only fear a potential loss of up to $10 million. This 'shallow pockets' issue would require a response beyond bare liability rules—and compulsory insurance to cover possible losses of $60 million or more might be appropriate.

Under-deterrence may also occur in liability regimes because enforcement costs for individuals may prove discouraging and lead many parties not to proceed to enforce their rights. Coordinating between victims may not always prove feasible, or it may involve high transaction costs. Evidential difficulties may reduce to a low level the probability of proving that the harm involved was caused by the actions of the defendant polluter. (If there is only a 50 per cent chance of proving causation, this halves deterrence. Uncertainties in the legal rules creating rights and liabilities will have a similar effect.) Many victims in the pool of victims may lack the resolve to proceed against the harm-causer and, to the extent that claims are not pursued, deterrent effects will be sub-optimal.

In reflection of such factors, the harm-causer will be likely to be able to settle out of court for negotiated sums that are lower than those that would create efficient levels of deterrence. Courts, of course, might attempt to correct for levels of deterrence that are too low—for example by granting damages that do not merely compensate for harms done but also include a punitive element that makes up for the under-deterrence liable to arise for the reasons cited. The courts will, however, face considerable informational hurdles if taking this course. The judiciary would find it extremely difficult to amass all relevant information about the array of potential actions for damages likely to follow, say, a pollution incident. If such actions are brought separately and serially, the court will not know at a given time in the process how many claims are to be aggregated in calculating total deterrence, nor will it be able to assess the gravity of claims to be brought at a future date.

One final problem is that insurance may limit the deterrent effect of liability rules and may generally make deterrence very difficult to assess. Under certain conditions, insurance may spread risks very widely and undermine deterrence. On the other hand, very high or even excessive levels of

---

[68] See D. Harris, M. Maclean, H. Genn, and S. Lloyd-Bostock, *Compensation and Support for Illness and Injury* (Oxford, 1984), 328 and on the deficiencies of liability rules in providing compensation see ch. 12.

deterrence (and for firms financial difficulties) may be caused if insurance is subject to restrictions, withdrawals, and crises, so that effective cover at affordable prices is not available. Thus, in the tort sector, what has been described as a crisis was experienced in the mid-1980s in the United States and Canada[69] and it has been the unpredictability of the liability insurance market that has urged a number of North American commentators to look to regulatory devices as alternatives to the tort system.[70]

Public Compensation/Social Insurance Schemes

Economic incentives to avoid undesirable behaviour can be created not merely by systems of taxation and subsidy but also by schemes of compensation or insurance that link premiums paid to performance records. One field in which a good deal of research into insurance-based incentives has been conducted is that of the working environment.[71] A review conducted in 1994[72] pointed to a number of insurance-based schemes dealing with workplace safety and health around the world. National schemes were encountered in several EU countries, the USA, Canada, Japan, and New Zealand, with strategies under development in Denmark, Poland, and elsewhere. These were all no-fault liability schemes and essentially compensatory, though some also provided means of funding improvements in conditions—as in the French, Swedish, and Albertan systems.

In the typical scheme, workers surrender their rights to sue employers for damages relating to health and safety failings, and, in return, are entitled to statutory compensation, often amounting to full payment of lost earnings plus costs. The employer's premiums depend on their organization's past claims experience.[73]

[69] See V. Finch, 'Personal Accountability and Corporate Control: The Role of Directors and Officers Insurance' (1994) 57 *MLR* 880, 915.

[70] See, e.g., G. Priest, 'The Current Insurance Crisis in Modern Tort Law' (1987) 96 *Yale LJ* 521; R.B.Stewart, 'Crisis in Tort Law? The Institutional Perspective' (1987) 54 *University of Chicago Law Review* 184; M. Trebilcock, 'The Social Insurance–Deterrence Dilemma of Modern North American Tort Law: A Canadian Perspective on the Liability Insurance Crisis?' (1987) 24 *San Diego Law Review* 929.

[71] See the work of the Eurofound: the European Foundation for the Improvement of Living and Working Conditions, a European Community institution, reported in: *Catalogue of Economic Incentive Systems for the Improvement of the Working Environment* (Dublin, 1994) (hereafter 'Eurofound Catalogue') and S. Bailey (ed.), *Economic Incentives to Improve the Working Environment* (Dublin, 1994).

[72] Eurofound Catalogue.

[73] See S. Bailey, 'Economic Incentives for Employers to Improve the Management of Workplace Risk'—paper to W.G. Hart Legal Workshop, 4 July 1995.

A central issue attending such schemes is whether state-administered or private insurance mechanisms should be employed. In relation to private provision, doubts exist concerning the extent to which private insurance companies can be relied upon to provide incentives to improve working conditions. The primary concern of private insurers is not to reduce hazards, but to generate profits for shareholders. Such insurers might not be prepared to spend money to isolate poor-risk, dangerous employers beyond profit-maximizing levels. It is true that competition in the insurance market will to some extent drive insurance companies to spend money on discriminating between risks, but there are limits to competitive pressures and, in any event, there is a tension between the basic function of insurance (to spread risks) and risk discrimination (isolating poor risks). This tension also imposes limits on the willingness of private insurers to identify poor risks and to apply localized economic incentives.

In such conditions, the tendency will be to confine risk discrimination to those sectors in which statistical guidance on the quantum of risks is readily available and affordable. Thus, in motor insurance, with a wealth of accidents, and, as a result, useful data available at reasonable cost, discrimination might be high, whereas in relation to workplace safety—where accidents are infrequent but often serious—weak statistics might be expected to lead to low levels of risk discrimination and the linking of cover and premiums to very broadly defined categories of risk.

For such reasons, Eurofound, the European Foundation for the Improvement of Living and Working Conditions, has proposed a publicly administered scheme linking premiums not to statistics on accident records—which were said 'not to make any sense' for firms with under 100 employees[74]—but to factors that could be measured properly such as the conditions of the working environment, the state of the factory's machinery, and so on. Such schemes, said Eurofound, would encourage the accurate reporting of accidents, whereas reliance on past accident records might be expected to encourage firms to massage their statistical returns—for example, by placing pressure on employees not to report accidents (e.g. by offering bonuses to accident-free teams of workers, and creating peer pressures not to report). Insurance-based schemes might also be combined with the use of incentives to improve conditions by allowing premium reductions to companies taking harm-reducing measures (e.g. moving to the use of low-emission materials or low-noise machines).

The further advantages pointed to by proponents of insurance-based schemes[75] are that they make employers conscious of the costs of their actions. Employers considering increasing pressures on workers to take risks

---

[74] Eurofound Catalogue, 19.   [75] Ibid., 24–5.

so as to escalate production levels will be aware that the potential extra profits derived from improved production will have to be weighed against the potential increases in insurance premiums that will follow an inspection by the insurance fund. Prevention will thus be given a higher priority by firms than would be the case under C & C regulation because harms will impinge more directly on their profits. Insurance-based schemes are said to offer incentives and financial motivations to *all* employers, in contrast with C & C strategies, which are so expensive to enforce that they are patchily and poorly applied on the ground.

A further strength claimed for incentive schemes is that they can achieve incentives to go better than fixed standards—indeed, incentives to zero can be instituted. This contrasts with C & C systems, which offer incentives to comply with designated standards but not to perform to higher standards. Employers, it is also said, will respond to the emergence of new hazards under incentive schemes without the need for new legislation.

To balance such sanguinity, however, some caveats do have to be entered. Compensation for workers may produce some undesirable incentives. Thus, if compensation is seen as generous or an easy option, this may encourage some individuals to accept injuries, dangers, or disabilities in return for cash. To work properly, moreover, such a scheme would have to involve the periodic inspection and rating of all employers and their premises. The resource implications are huge. Thus, inspection as envisaged would not be possible in the UK using the present staffing and resources of the Health and Safety Executive, whose current scheme of inspection involves, in the case of medium-sized firms, several years between visits. It might, indeed, be argued that the important difference between the proposed insurance scheme and the existing C & C system lies in the assumptions that are made concerning resources: that with a commensurate increase in resources, C & C could achieve as much.

The differences between an insurance-based scheme and C & C regulation may, thus, be liable to overstatement. In the former, inspectors would check compliance with rules designed to limit risks and would penalize non-compliance by imposing an adjusted premium. In C & C regimes, fines or administrative orders take the place of premiums as sanctioning devices. The insurance-based scheme, it could be contended, is merely a C & C regime with a variation in the sanction. Fines, after all, might be described as disincentives.

Conclusions: Choosing Regulatory Methods

In deciding whether to regulate or to leave matters to the market it is wise, as noted in the last chapter, to be realistic about the levels of performance that can be expected of regulatory regimes. To compare a friction-free vision of regulation with the imperfect operation of the market is to bias any analysis in favour of regulation. Similarly, in comparing different regulatory strategies, an effort must be made to take into account all the respective difficulties that will be encountered in their implementation. Thus, to compare C & C, with all its enforcement difficulties, to a series of 'less-restrictive' devices that are assumed to be enforceable in a problem-free manner is not to offer a balanced perspective.[76]

Enforcement, as has been noted, is not a difficulty confined to C & C regimes.[77] Nor, moreover, should the *positive* aspects of enforcement be ignored when reviewing C & C regulation. Enforcement procedures can be seen as the lifeblood of many regulatory systems. In Britain, for instance, enforcement practices tend to be more flexible, more administrative, and less prosecutorial than those encountered in the USA, where the most committed critics of C & C are to be found. C & C operates on the ground in a less restrictive and legalistic fashion on this side of the Atlantic, and it is the enforcement practices adopted that ameliorate many of the difficulties encountered in C & C regimes.[78] The objections to C & C, it could be said, often relate to a style of applying C & C regulation—one that is not the norm, say, in Britain.

The difference between C & C and other regimes may, indeed, be one prone to exaggeration since, as noted, many or most schemes require implementation through rules—be these command- or incentive-based. Proponents of C & C have to cope with difficulties of fixing the appropriate level of precision and inclusiveness in rules, of using rule formulations that cope with potential creative compliers, and of incorporating the right kinds of standards.[79] 'Alternative' regulatory methods often need rules, however, on matters such as: *when* incentives will apply; the *conditions* under which franchises will be held or marketable permits transferred; the *kind of information* to be disclosed; the *use* of publicly provided premises; the *extent and form* of liabilities; or the *nature* of premium variations in a social insurance system. Just as enforcement difficulties cannot be assumed away when moving to alternative or 'less restrictive' regulatory methods, neither, it should be repeated, can those problems that attend rule-making processes.[80]

[76] For an argument viewing C & C as a 'last resort', see Breyer, *Regulation and Its Reform*, ch. 9.

[77] See Ogus, *Regulation*, 250–6; Breyer, *Regulation and Its Reform*, 278–80; R. Smith, 'The Feasibility of an Injury Tax Approach to Occupational Safety' (1974) 38 *Law and Cont. Prob.* 730; P. Burrows, *The Economic Theory of Pollution Control* (Oxford, 1979), 33–5.

[78] See D. Vogel, *National Styles of Regulation: Environmental Policy in Great Britain and the United States* (Ithaca, NY, 1986).

[79] See Chapter 14 below and generally Baldwin, *Rules and Government*.

[80] See Markovits, 'Antitrust'.

It should also be cautioned that an historical association between certain regulatory methods and certain styles of implementation—for example, between C & C and the use of highly restrictive rules—should not be taken as a demonstration of inevitable or exclusive linkage. In North America in the 1980s, an enthusiasm for alternative methods of regulation was to a degree fuelled by concerns that C & C methods had led to a 'crisis of legalisation'.[81] Other possible causes of over-proliferation and complexity in rules can, however, be pointed to. Relevant factors may have been: the particular demands made of regulators by North American judges when seeking to control the rationality, fairness, and accessibility of rules and rule-making processes; the existence of certain conditions leading to litigiousness; the operation of certain statutory rule-making procedures; or the political contexts within which particular regulatory institutions operated.[82] Given the potential relevance of such factors, it is difficult to conclude with confidence that a move from C & C to alternative strategies constitutes even a start in combating excessive legalization. There may be a temptation when considering 'alternative' regulatory methods, to isolate their least attractive features and designate these as C & C intrusions—that, however, is, again, to rig the debate.

It should be remembered, at this point, that in most regulatory contexts combinations of regulatory methods tend to be employed. Thus, potential polluters may face some C & C regulations, but also may be subject to licensing or franchising conditions or sets of incentives operating though taxation and subsidy rules. They may have to supply information of various kinds, they are likely to be enmeshed in a network of liability rules, and may be able to avail themselves of publicly provided assets or services. In relation to a given regulatory issue it is, accordingly, necessary to look for the particular mixture of regulatory strategies that will best meet desired objectives—procedural and substantive.[83] It may, indeed, be necessary to consider mixes of regulatory strategies that may go beyond state-instituted regimes. The next chapter, accordingly, examines the potential of self-regulatory, corporate, and third-party controls.

Finally, it should be stressed that regulatory strategies will often have to change over time, either because they are under-performing or in order to meet the new challenges that are posed by such matters as new risks and risk creators or freshly imposed objectives. Such responsiveness will require that regulators are able to assess their own performance (a matter returned to in Chapter 12; see also Table 7.1) but also that they are able to institute the orders of change

---

[81] See Stewart, 'Regulation and the Crisis of Legalisation', 108–9.
[82] See, e.g., Bardach and Kagan, *Going by the Book*, and R.A. Kagan, 'Should Europe Worry about Adversarial Legalism?' (1997) 17 *OJLS* 165.
[83] See Gunningham and Grabosky, *Smart Regulation*, 14–19, ch. 6.

that are required for optimal regulation.[84] These may be 'first-order' changes such as adjustments of emissions standards. They may be more dramatic 'second-order' shifts in the types of control instrument used—say, from command and control rules to tax incentives, or they may be transformational 'third-order' changes that involve wholesale revisions of the regulatory landscape. These might involve, for instance, re-nationalizations or radical restructurings of industrial sectors or across-the-board replacements of state-operated regulation with market-driven trading regimes. Choices between these orders of change are at least as important as choices of control instruments and mixes of these. It is essential, accordingly, for regulators to operate systems that allow them to recognize the circumstances in which first- or second-order adjustments are insufficient or even counter-productive and when transformational shifts of strategy are required. What counts most is getting the broadest strategy right. As Russ Ackoff, the management thinker, said: 'The more efficient you are at doing the wrong thing, the wronger you become. It is much better to do the right thing wronger than the wrong thing righter. If you do the right thing wrong and correct it, you get better.'[85]

---

[84] On different orders of change, see J. Black, 'What is Regulatory Innovation?' in J. Black, M. Lodge, and M. Thatcher, *Regulatory Innovation* (Cheltenham, 2005), 8–11.
[85] S. Stern, 'A Fond Farewell to a Brilliant Thinker' *Financial Times*, 10 November 2009.

Table 7.1. Regulatory strategies: posited strengths and weaknesses

Strategy	Example	Strengths	Weaknesses
1. Command & Control	Health and Safety at Work	Force of law.	Intervenes in management.
		Fixed standards set minimum acceptable levels of behaviour.	Prone to capture.
		Screens entry.	Complex rules tend to multiply.
		Prohibits unacceptable behaviour immediately.	Inflexible.
		Seen as highly protective of public.	Informational requirements severe.
		Use of penalties indicates forceful stance by authorities.	Expensive to administer.
			Setting standards is difficult and costly.
			Anti-competitive effects.
			Incentive is to meet the standard, not go better.
			Enforcement costly.
			Compliance costs high.
			Inhibits desirable behaviour.
2. Incentives	Differential tax on leaded and unleaded petrol	Low regulator discretion.	Rules are required.
		Low-cost application.	Poor response to problems arising from irrational or careless behaviour.
		Low intervention in management.	
		Incentive to reduce harm to zero, not just to standard.	Predicting outcome from given incentive difficult.
		Economic pressure to behave acceptably.	Mechanical, so inflexible.
			Regulatory lag.
			Politically contentious as rewards wrongdoer and fails to prohibit offence.
3. Market-harnessing controls		Responses to market driven by firms, not bureaucrats.	No expert agency to solve technical or commercial problems in the industry.
(a) Competition laws	Airline industry	Can be applied across industries.	
		Economies of scale in use of general rules.	Uncertainties and transaction costs.
		Low level of intervention.	Courts slow to generate guidance.
		Flexibility for firms.	Principles develop sporadically.
(b) Franchising	Rail, television, radio	Enforcement is low cost to public.	Evidential difficulties.
		Low level of restriction.	Need to specify service.

		Respects managerial freedoms.	Tension of specification and responsiveness/innovation.
		Allows competition for market as substitute for competition in the market.	Uncertainties impose costs on consumers.
		Managers rather than bureaucrats respond to market preferences.	Requires competition for franchise but may be few bidders.
			Need to enforce terms of franchise.
(c) Contracting	Local authority refuse services	Combines control with service provision.	Potential confusion of regulatory and service roles.
		Sanctioning by economic incentive or non-renewal.	Poor transparency and accountability.
		Easier to operate than licensing system.	Judicial control weak.
(d) Tradable permits	Sulphur dioxide emissions (USA)	Pollution by greatest wealth producer.	Enforcement may require inspectorate.
		Incentive to reduce harm to zero.	Regulatory lag, lack of rapid response in crisis.
		Managerial freedom considerable.	No compensation for victims.
		Regulatory discretion low.	Requires healthy market for permits.
		Regulatory costs low.	Barriers to entry may be created.
			Some harms need to be prohibited absolutely.
4. Disclosure	Mandatory disclosure in food/drink sector	Low intervention.	Information users may make mistakes.
		Allows consumer to decide issues.	
		Lower danger of capture.	Economic incentives (e.g. price) may prevail over information (on, e.g., risk).
		Useful in low-risk sectors.	
			Cost of producing information may be high.
			Risks may be so severe as to call for prohibition.
			Policing of information quality and fraud may be required.
			Information may be in form undermining its utility.
5. Direct action and design solutions			
(a) Direct interventions	State-supplied work premises	Can separate infrastructure provision from operation.	Fairness of subsidies may be contentious.
			Funding costly.
		Assures acceptable level of provision.	Public sector involvement contentious.
		Useful where small firms in poor position to behave responsibly.	Innovations may not be market driven.

(*continued*)

Table 7.1. Continued

Strategy	Example	Strengths	Weaknesses
(b) 'Nudge' strategies	Consent to organ donation is assumed unless positive opt-out is exercised	Allows state to plan long-term investments. Low cost, combines influence with residual freedom of choice.	Freedoms may be undermined if opt-out is less than easy.
			Transparency and accountability of nudging may be low. May not work well where decision processes are complex. May impact poorly on regulated parties who are committed to errant conduct.
6. Rights and liabilities laws	Rules of tort law; right to, e.g., light or clean water	Self-help.	May not prevent undesired events that result from accidents and irrational behaviour.
		Low intervention. Low cost to state.	Individuals may not enforce due to costs. Evidential difficulties and legal uncertainties reduce enforcement. Victims may lack resolve and information to proceed, so deterrence sub-optimal. Difficult for courts to deter efficiently. Insurance may temper deterrent effects.
7. Public compensation / social insurance	Workplace safety schemes (USA, Canada, Japan, New Zealand)	Insurers provide economic incentives.	Incidence levels may be too low to allow risk discrimination.
		Low intervention in management.	Tension of loss-spreading and incentive to behave responsibly.
		Low danger of capture. Encourages accurate reporting of incidents. Makes employers aware of costs of activities. Good coverage, applied to all employers.	Inspection and scrutiny of performance expensive. May operate in very similar manner to command and control mechanism.
		No need to legislate for each individual harm.	

8 Self-regulation, Meta-regulation, and Regulatory Networks

Regulation, as noted in the last chapter, can be carried out by the state or by a variety of other organizations—notably by self-regulatory institutions, such as professional bodies, by trade associations, or by public interest groups, business partners, consumers, or corporations. Non-state organizations can be subjected to various degrees of oversight by the state and a host of different mechanisms can be used to effect such supervision. In this chapter, we look at the issues raised when control functions are exercised by self-regulators and by corporations acting under 'meta-regulation' arrangements. We then explore the challenges of using regulatory mixes and networks—of using combinations of instruments and regulatory organizations.

Self-regulation

Self-regulation can be seen as taking place when a group of firms or individuals exerts control over its own membership and their behaviour.[1] In Britain, it is encountered in a number of professions and sports and in sectors such as advertising, insurance, and the press.[2] A host of arrangements can be seen as self-regulatory and variations in the characteristics of self-regulatory regimes

---

[1] On self-regulation in general, see J. Black, 'Constitutionalising Self-Regulation' (1996) 59 *MLR* 24; A. Ogus, 'Rethinking Self-Regulation' (1995) 15 *OJLS* 97; National Consumer Council, *Self-Regulation* (London, 1986); A. Page, 'Self-Regulation: The Constitutional Dimension' (1986) 49 *MLR* 141; id., 'Self-Regulation and Codes of Practice' (1980) *JBL* 30; id., 'Financial Services: The Self-Regulatory Alternative', in R. Baldwin and C. McCrudden, *Regulation and Public Law* (London, 1987); R. Baggott and L. Harrison, 'The Politics of Self-Regulation' (1986) 14 *Policy and Politics* 143; Bardach and Kagan, *Going by the Book*, ch. 8; I. Ayres and J. Braithwaite, *Responsive Regulation* (Oxford, 1992), ch. 4; R. Baggott, 'Regulatory Reform in Britain: The Changing Face of Self-Regulation' (1989) 67 *Public Administration* 435; C. Graham, 'Self-Regulation', in G. Richardson and H. Genn (eds), *Administrative Law and Government Action* (Oxford, 1994).

[2] For a study of self-regulation and the American legal profession, see T. Rostain, 'Self-Regulatory Authority, Markets and the Ideology of Professionalism' in R. Baldwin, M. Cave, and M. Lodge (eds), *The Oxford Handbook of Regulation* (Oxford, 2010).

can be identified.[3] A first variable is the governmental nature of self-regulation. An association may self-regulate in a purely private sense—in pursuit of the private ends of its membership—or it may act governmentally in so far as public policy tasks are delegated to private actors or institutions.[4] Both forms of activity may, indeed, be combined. The process of self-regulation may, moreover, be constrained governmentally in a number of ways—for instance by statutory rules; oversight by a governmental agency; systems in which ministers approve or draft rules; procedures for the public enforcement of self-regulatory rules; or mechanisms of participation or accountability. Self-regulation may appear to lack any state involvement, but in reality it may constitute a response to threats by government that if nothing is done state action will follow.[5]

A second variable concerns the extent of the role played by self-regulators. A full role may involve the promulgation of rules, the enforcement of these on the ground, and the monitoring of the whole regulatory process. Self-regulation, however, may be restricted to one of these functions—where, for instance, rules are drafted by a self-regulatory organization but are enforced and monitored by a public agency. Self-regulation may merely operate as an element within a regulatory regime—a point to be returned to below.

---

[3] See Ogus, 'Rethinking Self-Regulation', 99–100.

[4] See Graham, 'Self-Regulation'; Baggott, 'Regulatory Reform in Britain', 435; and for studies of self-regulation in particular sectors see S. Dawson *Safety at Work: The Limits of Self-Regulation* (Cambridge, 1988); R. Baldwin, 'Health and Safety at Work: Consensus and Self-Regulation', in Baldwin and McCrudden, *Regulation and Public Law*; R. Ferguson, 'Self-Regulation at Lloyds' (1983) 46 *MLR* 56; M. Moran and B. Wood, *States, Regulation and the Medical Profession* (Buckingham, 1993); V. Finch, 'Corporate Governance and Cadbury: Self-Regulation and Alternatives' (1994) *JBL* 51; C. Scott and J. Black, *Cranston's Consumers and the Law* (3rd edn, Cambridge, 2000) ch. 2; I. Ramsay, *Consumer Protection* (London, 1989); A.G. Jordan, *Engineers and Professional Self-Regulation* (Oxford, 1992); Sir D. Calcutt, *Review of Press Self-Regulation*, Cmnd. 2135 (London, 1992–3); J.J. Boddewyn, *Global Perspectives on Advertising Self-Regulation* (Westport, CT, 1992); M. Moran, *The Politics of the Financial Services Revolution* (London, 1991); J. Black, *Rules and Regulators* (Oxford, 1997); Office of Fair Trading (OFT), *Voluntary Codes of Practice* (London, 1996); OFT, *Raising Standards of Consumer Care: Progressing Beyond Codes of Practice* (London, 1998). For a study of 'Responsible Care' in the Australian chemical industry see N. Gunningham and P. Grabosky, *Smart Regulation* (Oxford, 1998), ch. 4.

[5] See Black, 'Constitutionalising Self-Regulation', 27. The fear that such threats may induce was seen in the late nineties in relation to the accountancy profession. At the time, Roger Cowe noted in the *Guardian*'s City Column: 'Accountants have not been seized out of the blue with a desire for regulation. They are terrified of having it done for them by a Government that has already stripped them of the power to regulate on investment advice' (21 Feb. 1998). The Accountancy Foundation was set up in 2002 as an independent overseer of the accountancy profession. The Foundation's functions are now carried out by the Professional Oversight Board, a part of the Financial Reporting Council. In the legal arena, the Legal Services Act 2007 established the Legal Service Board in another movement towards independent supervision of a profession.

The degree of binding legal force that attaches to self-regulatory rules is a third variable to be noted. Self-regulation may operate in an informal, non-binding, voluntary manner, or it may involve rules of full legal force that are enforceable in the courts. Finally, self-regulatory regimes may vary in their coverage of an industrial sector—they may apply to all those who participate in an activity (perhaps because screening or licensing of entry is applied), or they may cover only those who join an association voluntarily.

WHY SELF-REGULATION?

The case for self-regulation, or incorporating elements of self-regulation into governmental regulation, rests principally on considerations of expertise and efficiency. Worries about self-regulation tend to centre on concerns relating to mandates, accountability, and the fairness of procedures.

EXPERTISE

A familiar claim in favour of self-regulation is that self-regulatory bodies can usually command higher levels of relevant expertise and technical knowledge than is possible with independent regulation—that, for instance, financial services practitioners know much more about their sector than a civil servant or bureaucrat ever could. It can be counter-claimed that such expertise and knowledge can be 'bought in' by bodies independent of the profession or membership, but proponents of self-regulation may respond that it is the ongoing proximity of links with the profession or membership that keeps expertise honed and information up to date—that such ongoing links are unlikely to be sustained where regulators are fully independent of the regulated group.

An aspect of expertise also relates to regulatory effectiveness.[6] It can be argued that self-regulators have a special knowledge of what regulated parties will see as reasonable in terms of regulatory obligations. This level of understanding, it may be claimed, allows self-regulators to make demands that are acceptable to affected firms or individuals, and this produces higher levels of voluntary compliance than is likely to be the case with externally imposed regimes of control. Misjudging levels of acceptability, the proponents of self-regulation argue, leads to low levels of voluntary compliance, high enforcement costs for taxpayers, and inefficient controls.

---

[6] On self-regulation and implementation, see W. Streek and P.C. Schmitter (eds), *Private Interest Government: Beyond Market and State* (London, 1985), 22–5.

EFFICIENCY

One set of arguments used by advocates of self-regulation emphasizes the potential of self-regulation to produce controls efficiently. Thus it is contended that self-regulators, with their easy access to those under control, experience low costs in acquiring the information that is necessary to formulate and set standards. They, furthermore, have low monitoring and enforcement costs and they are able to adapt their regimes to changes in industrial conditions in a flexible and smooth manner because they act relatively informally and tend to enjoy the trust of the regulated group.

The informality of voluntary self-regulatory systems can also be said to provide remedies where more formal systems would not. Thus, on 5 February 1998, Lord Wakeham, Chairman of the Press Complaints Commission (PCC), expressed fears in the House of Lords that if the Human Rights Bill were to graft a 'statutory superstructure' onto the voluntary press complaints system of self-regulation, negative consequences might flow. He argued that voluntary self-regulation allowed disputes to be resolved swiftly because of the commitment of newspaper editors and the amicable, informal way that the PCC conducted its work. It also, he maintained, allowed ordinary people to take up complaints against the press without having to find large sums of money. A move to place the scheme on a statutory footing, he feared, would place the courts in control, and would change the dispute resolution process into one characterized by legal defensiveness and lack of cooperation. Resolving differences and servicing apologies would be far more difficult within a legalistic system than in a cooperative regime, and the legal expenses involved would make remedies unavailable to ordinary citizens.[7]

As far as costs to the public purse are concerned, a further point in favour of self-regulation is that it tends to be paid for by those engaging in the regulated activity—this contrasts with the costs of external, or independent, regimes which are usually borne by the taxpayer.

Not all arguments under the efficiency heading do, however, favour self-regulation. The costs to the public purse of approving self-regulatory rules may be considerable, and the rules written by self-regulators cannot be assumed to be immune from the problems afflicting rules in C & C regimes—notably those difficulties associated with legalism, standard-setting, and enforcement. Where, moreover, self-regulation operates as a voluntary mechanism, not all of those who participate in a sector may subscribe to self-regulation. Much here depends on the incentives to participate that are

---

[7] See *The Times*, 6 Feb. 1998, p. 46. See also J. Black, *Rules and Regulators* (Oxford, 1997), 30–7 on 'interpretive communities' and the effect of shared interpretations in obviating the need for detailed specifications through rules.

provided by a self-regulatory system. These may include qualifications, certificates, or marks of quality (e.g. doctor, architect, British Standards); access to trading space (e.g. on exchanges); or avoidance of exclusions or boycotts of non-members (e.g. trade associations or cartels). Such incentives may often prove powerful, but where they are not fully effective, it is common for organizations to seek explicit recognition from the state and controls to make membership compulsory.[8] Self-regulation, in such circumstances, will then operate within a state-maintained framework. Where membership is not comprehensive, the public may prove to be ill-protected by a regime that controls the most responsible members of a trade or industry but leaves unregulated those individuals or firms who are the least inclined to serve the public or consumer interest.[9] In some sectors, indeed, the role of self-regulation has been severely limited because of difficulty in controlling mavericks to the extent necessary to assuage public concerns.[10]

MANDATES

The essence of a mandate claim is that the regulation at issue serves legitimate ends—as commonly identified with reference commonly to a set of legislative objectives. Apart from the usual problems of determining the content of the mandate, the special difficulty with some self-regulatory regimes is that the relevant objectives may be drawn up by bodies with no democratic legitimacy—for instance, by the members of a private association. It is then hard to justify actions that affect parties outside the association or to argue that the public interest is being served. On some issues, the public may demand that the government take responsibility for the regulatory function.

Such difficulties are less severe in self-regulatory regimes that are directed towards objectives that are set down in statutes or where individuals or groups with some democratic legitimacy have a role in drawing up objectives—for example, where a Secretary of State, a local authority, or

[8] See T. Daintith, 'Regulation' in International Association of Legal Science, *International Encyclopaedia of Comparative Law* (Tübingen, 1997), vol. 17, ch. 10, p. 20.

[9] See Scott and Black, *Cranston's Consumers and the Law*, 39. On the 'consensual paradox' and the tendency to regulate those who are least in need of regulating, see R. Baldwin, 'Health and Safety at Work', in Baldwin and McCrudden, *Regulation and Public Law*, 151–3. The National Consumer Council (Self-Regulation) has argued that those who have not agreed to follow the self-regulatory scheme tend to be the main source of consumer problems (noted, Graham, 'Self-Regulation', 195). The Director General of Fair Trading's report *Timeshare* (London, 1990) argued that limited membership of the controlling Timeshare Developers' Association meant that self-regulation was not working and that legislation was necessary in the timeshare sector. See also OFT, *Raising Standards of Consumer Care*, on the problem of the non-applicability of codes to non-members and the case for moving towards standards rather than codes.

[10] Graham, 'Self-Regulation', 196, cites the estate agencies sector as one in which voluntary self-regulation was encouraged by the Office of Fair Trading with little success, and legislative measures were subsequently taken.

other elected body fixes aims. Even in such cases, however, those sceptical of self-regulation may assert that special problems of capture arise—that such legitimate objectives or rules will tend to be subverted to private purposes where their pursuit and application is given over to a private body that is accountable to its private members and is in effective control of relevant information.[11] It can be said that this will be the case particularly where the self-regulator's functions include updating and formulating policies, interpreting rules, and adjudicating on applications of those rules. As far as enforcement is concerned, it has been alleged that self-regulatory bodies have an especially poor record in protecting the public interest through enforcing standards against errant members.[12] In numerous studies reference has also been made to the tendency of self-regulatory bodies to act anti-competitively on access requirements and prices, so that members' interests rather than those of the public are served.[13]

ACCOUNTABILITY

Critics of self-regulatory systems may see their existence as making manifest the capture of power by groups who are not accountable through normal democratic channels.[14] It would be a mistake, however, to think that all such systems are wholly unaccountable and free from controls other than those applied by members. As already indicated, self-regulators may be subject to non-member controls in a host of ways, notably to constraints deriving from the following:

- statutory prescriptions and objectives;
- rules that are drafted by or approved by other bodies or ministers;
- ministerial guidelines or criteria for consideration by the self-regulator;

---

[11] See Ogus, 'Rethinking Self-Regulation', 98–9.

[12] See R. Abel, *The Legal Profession in England and Wales* (Oxford, 1988), 250–8; Ogus, 'Rethinking Self-Regulation', 99. The OFT has noted that the large majority of trade associations have neither the powers nor the will to exercise effective control over those who breach codes of practice—see OFT, *Raising Standards of Consumer Care*, 16–17: 'trade associations, set up for the benefit of members, frequently are neither comfortable nor effective in the role of sectoral regulator'.

[13] See, e.g., S. Domberger and A. Sherr, 'The Impact of Competition on Pricing and Quality of Legal Services' (1989) 9 *International Review of Law and Economics* 41; A Shaked and J. Sutton, 'The Self-Regulating Profession' (1981) 47 *Review of Economic Studies* 217.

[14] See Ogus, 'Rethinking Self-Regulation', 98–9; N. Lewis, 'Corporatism and Accountability: The Democratic Dilemma', in C. Crouch and R. Dove (eds), *Corporatism and Accountability* (Oxford, 1990); I. Harden and N. Lewis, *The Noble Lie* (London, 1986). Graham, 'Self-Regulation', 203, makes the point that self-regulators operate outside the scope of the departmental select committees of the House of Commons and there is no equivalent to scrutiny by the National Audit Office, though the Office of Fair Trading does exercise some review in the financial services sector and areas where it has approved codes of practice.

- parliamentary oversight of the delegated legislation that guides the self-regulator;
- departmental purse strings and the influence that these provide.
- agency oversight;
- informal influences from government that are exerted in the shadow of threatened state regulation;[15]
- judicial review;[16]
- complaints and grievance-handling mechanisms (e.g. ombudsmen);[17]
- reporting and publication requirements laid down by government or Parliament.

Lack of accountability is thus not a necessary feature of self-regulation. The public are not liable to trust self-regulators, however, or see them as legitimate, if they are seen to be able to circumvent external controls, or to be more strongly accountable to their members than to the public or those affected by their activities. A field in which there was a dramatic evaporation of public trust in the accountability and transparency of self-regulation was that of legal services in the 1990s—where concerns about the management of complaints against solicitors eventually triggered wholesale reforms of regulation, new institutional structures, and a new regime of oversight.[18]

The key problem in identifying the proper level and form of accountability lies in deciding whether the self-regulation at issue is a matter of private control (a matter for resolution between members) or whether it is governmental (in so far as it affects the public interest) and merits democratic (or judicial) accountability accordingly. For their part, the courts have struggled to produce a clear line on the liability of self-regulatory bodies to judicial review.[19] The judiciary have, for technical and pragmatic reasons, proved

---

[15] Page, 'Self-Regulation', 149, cites the example of the Takeovers Panel. In 1968, the Government and Governor of the Bank of England threatened direct governmental regulation of takeovers unless the City Code was made more effective.

[16] On which see Black, 'Constitutionalising Self-Regulation' and Page, 'Self-Regulation'.

[17] See e.g. A. Mowbray, 'Newspaper Ombudsmen: The British Experience' (1991) *Media Law and Practice* 91.

[18] See R. Baldwin, M. Cave, and K. Malleson, 'Regulating Legal Services: Time for the Big Bang?' (2004) 67 *Modern Law Review* 787–817; D. Clementi, *Report of the Review of the Regulatory Framework for Legal Services in England and Wales* (London, 2004); Legal Services Act 2007. For a discussion of the US legal profession and the ideology of professionalism, see T. Rostain, 'Self-Regulatory Authority, Markets and the Ideology of Professionalism' in R. Baldwin, M. Cave, and M. Lodge (eds), *The Oxford Handbook of Regulation* (Oxford, 2010).

[19] See Black, 'Constitutionalising Self-Regulation', who cites as examples of 'current confusion', *R* v. *Lloyds ex p. Briggs* [1993] Lloyds LR 176 (Lloyds Council not liable to review) and *R* v. *Insurance Ombudsman ex p. Aegon Life Assurance Ltd, The Times,* 7 Jan. 1994 (Insurance Ombudsman Bureau not subject to review).

reluctant to review the sporting associations[20] but, in cases from *Datafin*[21] onwards,[22] have decided that bodies whose source of power derives from neither statute nor the prerogative may, nevertheless, be reviewed where they exercise public law functions, their power has a public element, or there is a 'governmental interest' in the decision-making power in question. Identifying when power is 'public' or governmental for the purposes of review has not, however, been made easy by the judges, who have applied a number of tests and stated, for instance, that where private power extends over substantial areas of economic activity, or affects the public interest and the livelihood of many individuals, this will not necessarily be subject to the rules of public law.[23]

How can the courts move towards a more coherent approach? Black has suggested that the courts, at least, should not look to the 'public' or other nature of the self-regulatory body when considering what systems of accountability are appropriate, but should look to the nature of the particular action or decision at issue; that a multifaceted approach to 'public' be taken (one recognizing the public nature of actions mediating different systems[24] within society, rather than simply state-to-individual relations); and that self-regulators be required to adopt processes that empower affected parties, rather than give expression to existing power relationships and parties of influence.[25] The value of such an approach lies in seeing each self-regulatory action or decision in its particular governmental context and in tailoring attendant calls for accountability accordingly. It recognizes that one body can have a number of different personae or functions—acting governmentally or in a regulatory manner on some issues but also being a corporate body, entering into contracts as a commercial enterprise or behaving as an employer in other contexts. It also urges that, as well as providing scrutiny through judicial review, the courts should seek to set the decisions or functions at issue in an institutional and procedural context that allows affected parties to participate appropriately. Such a flexible, or particularized, approach to accountability does, however, make it difficult to make general statements about acceptable arrangements.

---

[20] See, e.g., *Law* v. *National Greyhound Racing Club* [1983] 3 All ER 300; *R* v. *Disciplinary Committee of the Jockey Club ex p. Aga Khan* [1993] 2 All ER 853; *R* v. *Football Association ex p. Football League* [1993] 2 All ER 833. *R* v. *Jockey Club ex p. RAM Racecourses* [1993] 2 All ER 225.

[21] *R* v. *Panel on Take-overs and Mergers ex p. Datafin Plc and another* [1987] 1 All ER 564.

[22] See, for example, *R* v. *Chief Rabbi ex p. Wachmann* [1993] 2 All ER 249.

[23] See L.J. Hoffman in *R* v. *Disciplinary Committee of the Jockey Club ex p. Aga Khan* [1993] 2 All ER 853 at 875. Monopoly power does not ensure control at public law—see, e.g., *R* v. *Chief Rabbi ex p. Wachmann* [1993] 2 All ER 249; for criticism, see D. Pannick, 'Who is Subject to Judicial Review and in Respect of What?' (1992) *Public Law* 1.

[24] That is, different 'functional systems' such as the political, economic, and legal systems.

[25] See Black, 'Constitutionalising Self-Regulation', 54–6.

FAIRNESS OF PROCEDURES

As already indicated, schemes of self-regulation are liable to criticisms of unfairness in so far as non-members may be affected by regulatory decisions to which they have poor or no access. Past experience suggests that self-regulators have a sporadic, unstructured, and patchy record of consulting those with interests in the workings of their systems.[26] Third parties may also be excluded from the negotiations that establish self-regulatory regimes and their objectives, in the first place.[27]

The courts might act to demand proper access for affected parties on the lines noted above in discussing accountability but, as yet, self-regulators are free from general legal duties to consult non-members before taking decisions or devising policies. Nor are they subject to general duties to give reasons for the actions or decisions that they have taken.

The National Consumer Council (NCC)[28] has argued that self-regulatory regimes must be able to command public confidence, and has advocated that self-regulatory schemes should operate from within statutory frameworks and that each one should, *inter alia*, include the following basic features:

- strong external involvement in the design and operation of the scheme.
- as far as practicable, a separation of the operation and control of the scheme from the institutions of the industry;
- full representation of consumers and other outsiders on the governing body of the scheme;
- clear statements of principles and standards governing the scheme—normally published in a code;
- clear, accessible, and well-publicized complaints procedures to deal with code breaches;
- adequate sanctions for non-observance of codes;
- the maintenance and updating of the scheme;
- annual reporting.

To summarize on the case for self-regulation, the acceptability or otherwise of a self-regulatory regime falls to be judged, at the end of the day, by the five criteria discussed above, and for each rule or regime the relevant trade-offs have to be assessed. A key consideration may be whether the expertise and efficiency gains to be achieved by self-regulation do out-balance any

---

[26] See Graham, 'Self-Regulation', 198.

[27] See I. Ramsay, 'The Office of Fair Trading: Policing the Consumer Market Place', in Baldwin and McCrudden, *Regulation and Public Law*, 191.

[28] NCC, *Self-Regulation*, esp. p. 15. See Graham, 'Self-Regulation' and the reservations of Lord Wakeham concerning the placing of regimes on a statutory basis—discussed above.

weaknesses in mandate definition, accountability, and fairness that will re-main after appropriate steps have been taken to ward off criticisms on these fronts.

It was noted above that self-regulation may play a part as an element within a scheme of regulation. A mechanism allowing for self-assessment may, for example, be incorporated within a regulatory compliance system, or a role may be given to regulated firms (or organizations thereof) in drafting the rules that government officials will enforce. It may be that such a combination of self-regulation and regulation will offer a level of performance and accept-ability that is unobtainable by resorting to either strategy singly.

In order to throw more light on the potential of such 'partial' self-regulatory mechanisms and to move towards identifying the kinds of context in which use of such mechanisms will lead to results superior to externally imposed regulation, we now consider a well-known approach to self-regulation.

Enforced Self-regulation and Meta-regulation

Ayres and Braithwaite[29] distinguish enforced self-regulation from 'co-regulation'. Co-regulation they take to refer to industry-association self-regu-lation with some oversight and/or ratification by government.[30] Enforced self-regulation, in contrast, involves a subcontracting of regulatory functions to regulated firms.[31] Which functions should be delegated will vary by context, say Ayres and Braithwaite, but such delegations may include some or more of: the devising of their own regulatory rules, the monitoring of compliance, or the punishing and correcting of episodes of non-compliance. Thus, the primary function of government inspectors would be to audit the efficiency and rigour with which delegated functions are carried out. It is anticipated, however, that old-style direct government monitoring would still be necessary for firms too small to mount their own compliance-seeking operations. Violations of privately written and publicly ratified rules would, moreover, be punishable by law.

---

[29] I. Ayres and J. Braithwaite, *Responsive Regulation* (Oxford, 1992), ch. 4.

[30] See P. Grabosky and J. Braithwaite, *Of Manners Gentle: Enforcement Strategies of Australian Business Regulatory Agencies* (Melbourne, 1986).

[31] Ayres and Braithwaite, *Responsive Regulation*, 103; Julia Black argues that enforced self-regulation as conceived by Ayres and Braithwaite is not self-regulation proper, since self-regulation best describes the situation in which 'a collective group imposes regulation on its components'—see J. Black, 'An Economic Analysis of Regulation: One View of the Cathedral' (1997) 16 *OJLS* 699 at 706.

The term 'meta-regulation' similarly refers to processes in which the regulatory authority oversees a control or risk management system, rather than carries out regulation directly—it 'steers rather than rows'.[32] In the version put forward by Christine Parker and others, meta-regulation involves delegation of the risk control function to corporations.[33] The primary control responsibilities are thus carried out within the risk management systems of corporations and the regulator's role becomes the auditing, monitoring, and incentivizing of these systems. Thus, in the USA, the Environmental Protection Agency has for some time recognized and encouraged the use of Environmental Management Systems (EMSs)—intra-corporation policies and measures that are designed to control risks to the environment.[34] These systems create rules and management processes, and they structure resource allocations in pursuit of organizational goals. They can be subject to a variety of scrutiny mechanisms and involve degrees of oversight ranging from the voluntary/self-regulatory model to the strongly meta-regulated version. They may be certified to meet international EMS standards or standards set by trade associations,[35] and they may be independent of regulatory rules or linked to specific regulatory controls.

The potential advantages of delegating regulation down to the corporation are said to be numerous.[36] The expenses and strictures of command and control regimes can be replaced by systems that are cheaper and more effective because corporations are given the freedom and incentives to work out what, for their mode of operating, is the best way to avoid the given mischief. Under meta-regulation, each company will write a set of rules tailored to the specific context of the firm, and these rules will be scrutinized by a regulatory agency. This brings the further advantage, in, say, the environmental field, of better protections for the public because more stringent rules can be demanded of firms with lower compliance costs. Non-uniform standards can thus produce better results than across-the-board rules, which unduly restrict some firms yet are too lax in the case of others. Firm-specific

---

[32] On the general case for 'steering rather than rowing', see D. Osborne and T. Gaebler, *Reinventing Government* (Boston, 1992).

[33] See C. Parker, *The Open Corporation* (Cambridge, 2002); J. Braithwaite, 'Meta Risk Management and Responsive Regulation for Tax System Integrity' (2003) 25 *Law and Policy* 1–16; P. May, 'Performance-Based Regulation and Regulatory Regimes' (2003) 25 *Law and Policy* 381–401; M. Power, *The Audit Society* (Oxford, 1997), chs. 2 and 3; C. Parker, 'Regulator-Required Corporate Compliance Program Audits' (2003) 25 *Law and Policy* 221–44; C. Coglianese and E. Mendelson, 'Meta-Regulation and Self-Regulation' in R. Baldwin, M. Cave, and M. Lodge (eds), *The Oxford Handbook of Regulation* (Oxford, 2010).

[34] See C. Coglianese and J. Nash (eds), *Regulating from the Inside* (Washington, DC, 2001).

[35] Coglianese and Nash cite the examples of the Responsible Care program of the American Chemistry Council and the Sustainable Forestry Initiative of the American Forest and Paper Association—see *Regulating from the Inside*, 4.

[36] Coglianese and Nash, *Regulating from the Inside*, ch. 1.

rules and processes, it is also claimed, can be more precise than industry-wide rules, which tend to be highly complex or else vague because they attempt to deal with a problem in all its possible contexts.[37] The introduction of new rules is also easier with firm-specific rules, since it is not necessary to await industry-wide agreement. Managers are, moreover, said to be more likely to innovate and to improve controls than under a standard-setting instrument and regulatees are more likely to attune their own standards of behaviour to the expectations of society when they are given the responsibility to govern their own behaviour, rather than being dictated to with a rule. Managers who espouse the relevant objectives may perform to a level that they would not achieve under regulation and a meta-regulatory regime may improve the overall system of management with the result that 'win-win' solutions are achieved—value for shareholders is increased at the same time as the regulated mischief is controlled.[38] It is also said that the general cultures of corporations and industrial sectors can be changed as firms are asked to think for themselves about the challenges of controlling, say, pollution and levels of consciousness about responsibilities can, as a result, be raised.[39]

Most states, moreover, possess very limited enforcement resources and, as a result, inspection coverage tends to be thin. Meta-regulation can expand coverage dramatically, ease pressure on the public purse, and lead to businesses bearing the costs of their own regulation. Meta-regulation can additionally increase the quality, frequency, and rigour of inspections for rule infringements.[40] Proponents of meta-regulation will also suggest that corporate compliance staff are likely to have superior specialized knowledge and better awareness of 'where the bodies are buried' than external inspectors, and that such compliance staff may possess more extensive powers with which to detect infringements than are available to public officials.

Offenders would also be more effectively disciplined than under governmental regulation because firms can be rewarded for rigorous systems of risk management and discipline. This contrasts with the incentive to conceal infringements under government regulation. Finally, burdens of proof may be lower under meta-regulation and more violations will be dealt with by disciplinary steps than would be the case with prosecutions. The more precise

---

[37] On the complexity of across-the-board rules see R. Baldwin, *Rules and Government* (Oxford, 1995), 162.

[38] M. Porter and C. van der Linde, 'Green and Competitive' (1995) 73 *Harvard Business Review* 120–34.

[39] See N. Gunningham and J. Rees, 'Industry Self-Regulation: An Institutional Perspective' (1997) 19 *Law and Policy* 363–414; P. DiMaggio and W. Powell (eds), *The New Institutionalism in Organizational Analysis* (Chicago, 1991).

[40] On self-monitoring and constitutional issues, see W. Howarth, 'Self-monitoring, Self-policing, Self-incrimination and Pollution Law' (1997) 60 *MLR* 200.

and less complex rules that are associated with meta-regulation may, again, encourage effective enforcement.

Advocates of meta-regulation tend to place a good deal of emphasis on the need for law, legal institutions, and regulators to link the internal capacity for corporate self-regulation with the internal resolve to self-regulate. The aim is to build up companies' commitments to, as well as their capacities for, self-regulation. This can be done 'by motivating and facilitating moral or socially responsible reasoning within organizations by inducing corporate crises of conscience through regulatory enforcement action, legal liability and public access to information about corporate social and legal responsibility'.[41] Legal liabilities, moreover, must be 'tied to incentives for, and guidance on, standards for self-regulation processes through restorative justice'.[42]

A second requirement, for some commentators, is that law and regulation should hold corporate self-regulation accountable 'by connecting the private justice of internal management systems to the public justice of legal accountability, regulatory coordination and action, public debate and dialogue'.[43] This can be achieved: 'by providing self-regulation standards against which the law can judge responsibility, companies can report and stakeholders can debate. This allows private management issues to become matters of public judgement.'[44]

Christine Parker suggests that there are two main ways to use liability to increase a company's commitment to self-regulation. First, liabilities can be adjusted by reference to the company's self-regulation programme.[45] This might involve making liability (and the quantum of sanctions) depend on the existence or otherwise of an effective self-regulation system[46] (as operates with due diligence defences for strict liability offences, or could operate by linking liability to non-adherence to governmental guidelines on compliance programmes). A second strategy is an accountability approach which uses the coercive powers of courts or regulators to require or encourage a company to implement a self-regulatory system when a breach has been alleged or has

---

[41] Parker, *The Open Corporation*, 246. On the development of 'organizational virtue', see F. Haines, *Corporate Regulation: Beyond 'Punish or Persuade'* (Oxford, 1997), chs. 2 and 7–10.

[42] Parker, *The Open Corporation*, 246. 'Restorative Justice' here involves a corporation in putting right what has gone wrong (e.g. compensating an injured worker), but also in identifying errors and putting in place systems and safeguards to prevent, detect, and correct wrongdoing in the future (e.g. redesigning a manufacturing process to eliminate pollution) see Parker, *The Open Corporation*, 253–4 and generally Braithwaite, 'Meta Risk Management'.

[43] Parker, *The Open Corporation*.

[44] Ibid.

[45] Ibid., 256. See also W. Laufer, 'Corporate Liability, Risk Shifting and the Paradox of Compliance' (1992) 52 *Vanderbilt Law Review* 1343, 1382–92; J. Gobert and M. Punch, *Rethinking Corporate Crime* (London, 2003), 334–5.

[46] See *In Re Caremark International Inc Derivative Litigation* 1996 WL 549894 (Del Ch Sept 25 1996) discussed in Parker, *The Open Corporation*, 257–78.

occurred. Here, a company would be placed on 'probation' until it institutes such a regime.[47]

Regulators and governments, moreover, can encourage compliance by further strategies such as using rewards and incentives to encourage corporations to develop new regulatory and compliance approaches. In the field of pollution, for instance, tax breaks can be used to lower the costs of abatement and both practical guidance and technical assistance can be given.[48] State authorities can, in addition, encourage good risk management systems by granting public recognition to high-performing corporations (e.g. through certification processes or publications of best practice or league tables). Regulators may grant areas of freedom from inspection and detailed regulatory oversight to trusted companies or they may allow certain management teams the flexibility to devise their own methods of compliance.[49] In the alternative, certain processes or technologies can be mandated by regulators, and commitments to self-regulation can be stimulated by enforcement actions or negative publicity.[50]

Systems of meta-regulation are not, however, problem-free and, as is clear from the work of Ayres and Braithwaite and others,[51] a series of difficulties can be anticipated. Ill-intentioned, ill-informed, or inefficient firms may fail to devise appropriate rules. Experience with self-assessment procedures in the British food-safety and the health and safety sectors suggests that such firms, and most small and medium enterprises (SMEs), are very likely to do nothing about designing control systems or compliance procedures until they are

---

[47] On corporate probation see J. Coffee, R. Grunen, and C. Stone, 'Standards for Organisational Probation' (1988) 10 *Whittaker Law Review* 77; B. Fisse and J. Braithwaite, *Corporations, Crime and Accountability* (Cambridge, 1993), 147–53; F. Warwin and J. Schwartz, 'Corporate Compliance Programs as a Component of Plea Arrangements and Civil Administrative Settlements' [1998] *J of Corporation Law* 71–87. On varieties of strategy to encourage responsibility, see Gunningham and Grabosky, *Smart Regulation*. The *US Sentencing Guidelines for Organisational Sanctions, Guidelines Manual* (Washington, DC, 1991) provide for an organization's culpability scores to be reduced if they have a reasonable compliance programme, and lack of such a programme may (in larger companies) trigger a probation order—see S. Simpson, *Corporate Crime, Law and Social Control* (Cambridge, 2002), 101–2.

[48] Coglianese and Nash, *Regulating from the Inside*, ch. 8.

[49] See the discussion of the tiers of regulation operated by the Oregon Environmental Quality Commission in Coglianese and Nash, *Regulating from the Inside*, ch. 8.

[50] Parker, *The Open Corporation*, 267–70. Ancillary tools for encouragement of self-regulation may involve, e.g., licence condition concessions; exemptions from normal regulation; allowing companies the flexibility to account for outcomes, rather than detailed processes; and allowing companies immunities for self-disclosure and self-correction: F. Warwin and J. Schwartz, 'Corporate Compliance Programs as a Component of Plea Agreements and Civil Administrative Settlements' (1998) *J of Corporation Law* 71–87. On varieties of strategy to encourage responsibility, see Gunningham and Grabosky, *Smart Regulation*.

[51] Ayres and Braithwaite, *Responsive Regulation*, 120–8; R. Fairman and C. Yapp, 'Enforced Self-Regulation, Prescription and Conceptions of Compliance within Small Businesses' (2005) 27 *Law and Policy* 491–519; J. Black, 'Talking About Regulation' (1998) *Public Law* 77.

galvanized by the government regulator.[52] They are essentially reactive. This point applies to the monitoring and enforcement, as well as to the drafting of rules. In the case of SMEs, Fairman and Yapp make the point that the managers of these enterprises are likely to see compliance not as an ongoing obligation but as a periodic negotiation with an inspector.[53] They will, accordingly, tend to think of themselves as compliant until they are told otherwise by an official. SMEs, moreover, will tend to dislike a meta-regulatory system more than a prescriptive regime, since the former will have: 'all the features of a regulatory approach that SMEs will find difficult to comply with. It is complex, systems-based, not linked to harm, process-oriented, difficult to judge compliance, and difficult to implement.'[54] They will, understandably, be less compliant under a meta-regulatory regime than under a prescriptive 'command' regime or one involving an interventionist 'educative' approach.[55]

Where the firms regulated are small in size and numerous, it may thus be more effective to rely on government officials to enforce rules than to rely on firms to mobilize independent inspectoral expertise. Similarly, there may be advantages in centralized regulation where the accumulation of expertise in a government body is likely to lead to more rigorous innovation than would be the case with firm-specific controls. Firm-specific drafting of rules may, also, lead to higher levels of industry capture, and worse protections for consumers and the public, than would be the case with government regulation. Firms might be expected to expend large sums on devising rules to suit their interests and to circumvent the spirit of government requirements. The state would have to spend similarly large sums to avoid such departures from public interest objectives. (Whether this is the case or not may depend *inter alia* on the distribution of interests, resources, costs, and benefits in a sector.) Ensuring adequate access to rule-making processes for consumers and affected interests would also prove extremely difficult if firm-specific drafting was adopted.

Inconsistencies of standards might result from the rule approvals process—because, for instance, concessions might be made to economically weak firms (to protect employment) or, in contrast, made to economically powerful firms in reflection of their political influence or organizational muscle. In such scenarios, absolute standards are replaced with a 'moral relativism'[56] and middle-range firms would be prejudiced. Some firms, indeed, might be severely damaged by the costs that enforced self-regulation would impose on them. In some areas, the expenses of drafting rules might be bearable,

---

[52] Baldwin, *Rules and Government*, 162–4.
[53] Fairman and Yapp, 'Enforced Self-Regulation', 512–14.
[54] Ibid., 512.   [55] Ibid.
[56] Ayres and Braithwaite, *Responsive Regulation*, 123.

in others they might put the survival of weaker firms at risk. Rule-making and rule-approval costs, moreover, would be large, since the government regulator would have to scrutinize a large number of particular rules (often devised with low levels of commitment and competence) instead of devising a single set of general rules.[57]

The confidence that can be placed in meta-regulatory regimes thus turns in no small part on the faith that is placed in the capacity and commitment of the corporation to self-regulate in the public interest. The sanguine view is, perhaps, represented by Parker, who puts forward an ideal type of 'permeable' self-regulation in which corporate management is open to a broad range of stakeholder deliberations about values and legal regulation facilitates and enforces this permeation:

> In the open corporation management self critically reflects on past and future actions in the light of legal responsibilities and impacts on shareholders. They go on to institutionalize operating procedures, habits and cultures that constantly seek to do better at ensuring that the whole company complies with legal responsibilities, accomplishes the underlying goals and values of regulation and does justice in its impact on shareholders (even when no law has yet defined what that involves).[58]

The ideals of meta-regulation, as presented by Parker, may be easy to sympathize with, but such an approach presents a number of serious challenges.[59] A first is the difficulty of persuading corporate managers to see the world in anything like the same way that regulators view it. Commentators from a systems theory perspective, such as Luhmann and Teubner, have long pointed out how social sub-systems (such as economy, law, politics, etc.) are wedded to their own self-referential ways of understanding the world so that they fail to communicate unproblematically.[60] In the light of such analyses, a fear is that the views that business managers take of regulatory responsibilities differ

---

[57] Black, 'Talking about Regulation', 98–100, notes the contention of Ayres and Braithwaite, *Responsive Regulation*, 121, that approval costs can be reduced by routinizing the approvals process. She objects, however, that failing to deal with rules individually undermines the whole enforced self-regulation enterprise. The Office of Fair Trading (OFT, *Raising Standards of Consumer Care*, 13) has, moreover, cited the heavy resource demands involved in negotiating, monitoring, and revising voluntary codes of practice and has suggested moving towards introducing core standards to replace codes.

[58] Parker, *The Open Corporation*, 292–3.

[59] On the particular challenges of applying proactive strategies to smaller companies, which are not dealt with here, see N. Gunningham and R. Johnstone, *Regulating Workplace Safety* (Oxford, 1999), 92–4.

[60] See, e.g., N. Luhmann, 'The Self-Reproduction of Law and Its Limits' in G. Teubner (ed.), *Dilemmas of Law in the Welfare State* (Berlin, 1985); N. Luhmann, *Social Systems* (Stanford, 1995); G. Teubner (ed.), op. cit.; G. Teubner, *Law as an Autopoietic System* (Oxford, 1993).

in kind from the visions of regulators and do so to a degree that rules out effective dialogue.[61]

Field research, moreover, suggests that such fears are not ill-founded.[62] When senior corporate managers talk of their punitive regulatory liabilities, the picture is not of a single set of regulatory liabilities (e.g. regarding pollution) to be dealt with rationally, but of a host of widely differing regulatory risks that are complex, incompletely known, or assessed and dealt with in an often unprioritized and highly reactive manner. More strikingly, when managers do act in an informed manner, they may not see compliance in the same way as regulators. The regulator may see non-compliance as 'misbehaviour' and the trigger of a sanction such as a fine, but a business manager in a larger firm may see non-compliance as a mixture of business opportunities and risks.[63] Managers may see regulatory liabilities as risks to be managed, not as ethically reinforced prescriptions. Compliance provides one way of managing such risks, but another potential response is to side-step liability—notably by: 'shifting the more dangerous and criminogenic aspects of their operations to subsidiaries located in the third world or developing countries'.[64] Risk-shifting by domestic outsourcing is a potential risk management strategy closer to home, as is taking such steps as: organizing the business so that operations or production processes are not dramatically affected by the imposition of a regulatory sanction; developing public relations systems that can limit any reputational losses caused by regulatory sanctioning; developing contingency plans to reduce the market or competition effects of a sanction; working on staffing arrangements to limit the human resource impact of sanctions; designing customer and supplier relationships that are resilient in the face of regulatory sanctions; increasing insurance arrangements to cushion liability; and restricting activities that are liable to give rise to regulatory sanctions (e.g. by silencing whistleblowers).[65]

A danger with meta-regulation is, thus, that, as sanctions become tougher, corporations see 'resilience management' as the way forward, rather than compliance. In so far as this proves to be the case, this may impose limits on the state's capacity to induce even larger companies to self-regulate in

---

[61] See also J. Black, 'Proceduralising Regulation Part II' (2001) 54 *Current Legal Problems* 103 on hermeneutic accounts of differences and incompatibilities in language, understandings, schemes of perception, or cognition.

[62] See R. Baldwin, 'The New Punitive Regulation' (2004) 67 *Modern Law Review* 351–83.

[63] See W. Laufer, 'Corporate Risk Shifting and the Paradox of Compliance' (1992) 52 *Vanderbilt L R* 1343, at 1402–4; S. Simpson, *Corporate Crime, Law and Social Control* (Cambridge, 2002), 52. As noted, in an SME the manager may well be unaware of non-compliance.

[64] J. Gobert, 'Corporate Killing at Home and Abroad' (2002) 118 *Law Quarterly Review* 72, 72–3.

[65] See J. Black, 'Using Rules Effectively' in C. McCrudden (ed.), *Regulation and Deregulation* (Oxford, 1999); see also Parker, *The Open Corporation*, 252 for acknowledgement of these dangers.

pursuit of compliance. To take an example, a strategy of varying the sanction imposed on a company in accordance with the quality of its compliance regime will be the weaker insofar as the company outsources relevant regulatory risks or insofar as the formal sanction fails to trigger ancillary impacts on the company because these are managed competently (e.g. reputational effects are limited by astute public relations).

Pessimism about the possible alignment of corporate and regulatory objectives can be reduced, say some commentators, by fostering the integrity of individuals within corporations so that they can act to bring social and business values into alignment. Top managers and self-regulation professionals can, on this view, play an important role in producing such alignment and can be encouraged to do so where private managers are 'connected to public justice' within corporations that are 'permeable' in the sense that they engage in a constant deliberative dialogue with their various stakeholders and regulators.[66]

This leads to a second major challenge faced by proponents of 'meta-regulation' on the Parker model. This is to develop meta-regulation and to stimulate corporate self-regulation in a manner that produces coherence and harmony between corporate and social ends, rather than confusion and conflict. In Parker's permeable corporation (which is conceded by Parker to be an ideal) it is advocated that corporate management should be open to a broad range of stakeholder deliberations about values and that managers should reflect on their actions in the light of their legal responsibilities, potential impacts on stakeholders and inputs from regulators: ('The open corporation is the good corporate citizen in deliberative democracy.')[67]

Deliberative regulatory procedures are challenging at the best of times[68] but the strategy of stimulating corporate deliberations on self-regulatory activity is one that has to confront a particularly daunting array of difficulties. Hugely divergent interests are affected by the corporate activities to be self-regulated. These interests may range from those of managers and shareholders to regulators and interest groups, from employees to consumers, and from small business partners or suppliers to large conglomerates. These divergencies may be reinforced by differences in legal obligations and statutory objectives and duties. Where, accordingly, a corporation is encouraged to be highly deliberative regarding its potential actions, it may be difficult to be confident that such deliberations will produce agreements rather than dissent, or that they will lead to action rather than deadlocks and stultification. Parker's hope is that more, and earlier deliberation, will allow

---

[66] See Parker, *The Open Corporation*, 294.
[67] Ibid., 293.
[68] See generally, J. Black, 'Proceduralising Regulation Part II' (2001) 54 *Current Legal Problems* 103.

open corporations to 'reap the reputational rewards of leadership and innovation'.[69] Others may fear that permeability and deliberation will, at least in some circumstances, lead to regimes of high-cost, high-friction management that are characterized by delays, obfuscations, fudges, indecisiveness, confusion, and inaction.[70] Whether a given company has the resources and staff expertise to commit to such deliberation is an additional issue.[71] A further question is whether a company will see itself as a 'deliberative organization' at all. Many companies will see themselves in quite different terms—as organizations that sell products and services so as to make a return for shareholders within a framework of discipline by the market. Deliberation, they may think, is not what they are about, and they will be ill-inclined to commit to it.

A different fear is that corporate managers may often see deliberations as matters to be managed and upon which leadership is appropriately exercised. (This, they may estimate, is the only way to reconcile deliberation with the commercial need for fast, decisive action.) They may, as a result, see the way forward as 'selling' certain policies and persuading affected parties that their way of self-regulating is appropriate.[72] If such an approach flows from their self-conception, they are liable to develop 'deliberative' procedures that are manipulated and controlled, rather than genuinely participatory, and which are distorted in favour of private corporate ends, rather than the pursuit of legitimate regulatory objectives. It might be argued that such fears can be overstated and that the professionalism of key actors such as compliance professionals will reduce tendencies to manipulate self-regulation in pursuit of profits.[73] Such reassurance, however, might be more readily gleaned in businesses where the compliance professionals are necessarily close to the core of management—in, say, the pharmaceutical industry, where risks are technical and highly focused, rather than in businesses where activities are highly disparate and risk portfolios are very extensive. In a general manufacturing and distributional enterprise with a variety of products, a host of risk areas will be involved and compliance professionals may be comparatively ill-positioned to influence general managerial culture.

[69] Parker, *The Open Corporation*, 299.

[70] On the dangers of assuming that intra-firm regulation will be possible without recreating the familiar problems of external regulation, see J. Black, 'Decentering Regulation' (2001) 54 *Current Legal Problems* 103, 123–4.

[71] See Gunningham and Johnstone, *Regulating Workplace Safety*, ch. 3 on systems-based regulation and smaller companies.

[72] On techniques of political management, see M. Moore, *Creating Public Value* (Harvard, 1995). On the problems regulators may have in monitoring 'management-based regulation', see C. Coglianese and D. Lazer, 'Management-Based Regulatory Strategies' in J. Donhue and J. Nye (eds), *Market-Based Governance* (New York, 2002), 208–11.

[73] See Ayres and Braithwaite, *Responsive Regulation*, 125–6; J. Braithwaite, *Corporate Crime in the Pharmaceutical Industry* (London, 1984); Parker, *The Open Corporation*, 294–5.

A further problem is that extremely divergent ways of seeing the world will often be involved in the above deliberations. (Systems theory, as noted, points to the difficulties posed when communications are sought between the worlds of business persons, regulators, politicians, interest groups, lawyers, risk professionals, and so on.) When corporations deliberate on compliance matters, experts in an array of fields may be called upon to speak to parties who are 'lay' in various respects. One possible way out of these difficulties is through 'thick proceduralization'—processes in which 'mediators' can play an enabling role by 'translating' the messages and logics of various systems or groups so that others can understand and so that communications can be facilitated across different systems and groups.[74] In such processes, the hope is that parties with very different perspectives can engage in effective deliberation.

The challenge of making such deliberation work effectively and fairly, however, is not inconsiderable. A first question is who is to take the lead in mediating and translating—the corporation, the regulator, a pressure group or another private or public body? Mediation contests, confusions, and fragmentations, may, on a pessimistic view, substitute for first-order discussions. Even if responsibility for mediation is clearly and uncontentiously allocated, serious issues of democratic legitimacy and accountability may arise.[75] Nor can it be taken for granted that the regulators or corporations fulfilling the mediation role can do so with the disinterestedness and expertise that is required if processes are to work to the general advantage.[76] The mediators will have their own worldviews, rationalities, areas of expertise, and technical limitations. Carrying out the translator role demands receptiveness to the worldviews, logics, and value systems of other actors and unrealistic demands may be made of translators' commitments to open disclosure. The dangers are that the mediator/translator will lack the application and expertise to be able to unpack and translate the arguments of the various interests into forms that others can understand; that they fail to manage mediation in a way that is fair to all parties and avoids manipulation by the

---

[74] See Black, 'Proceduralising Regulation Part II', 599.

[75] Control over decision- and policymaking may be thought to be too distanced from elective institutions (see J. Black, 'Proceduralising Regulation Part II') and openness in corporate deliberations may be thought to fall short of full democratic accountability, not least because managers owe duties principally to their shareholders—though see Parker, *The Open Corporation*, esp. 227–33 on Corporate Justice Plans that would give 'permeability to shareholder contestation' through enforcement of stakeholders' legal rights. On the costs and challenges of monitoring the performance of self-regulatory and systems-based regimes, see Gunningham and Johnstone, *Regulating Workplace Safety*, ch 5. State monitoring may prove hugely expensive; 'paper-audits' may leave accountability weak and auditing by third-party organizations may be objected to as undemocratic, lacking independence, and unacceptably expensive for smaller companies.

[76] See Black, 'Proceduralising Regulation Part II' (on regulators as translators); K.Yeung, *Securing Compliance* (Oxford, 2004), ch. 6.

powerful; and that they fail to provide the focus that is needed if there is to be efficient production of policies, decisions, or actions.

Where, then, does this leave the argument? Scepticism about the potential of command, punitive, and rational deterrence routes to regulatory compliance might favour greater reliance on meta-regulatory strategies that involve more proactive stimulation of the self-regulatory capacities of companies. There are, however, dangers in trusting too much to the capacities of regulators, companies, and others to align the way that corporate managers and state officials will see the world, deliberative processes, or regulatory requirements and objectives. The dangers that flow from excessive trust on this front are that the integrity of compliance professionals and senior managers will not lead corporations to act in a wholly public-spirited manner, that corporations which are trusted to be open and permeable will be inefficient as organizers of deliberation (not to say as managers generally) or, worse, highly manipulative. The fear is that regulatory processes, as a result, will lack legitimacy and prove unfair, exclusive, and inefficient.

Regulatory Mixes and Networks

The best regulatory outcomes will usually involve mixtures of institutions and instruments.[77] It is no easy matter, however, to design the optimal mixes or to state in advance which institutions and instruments will work together harmoniously. The proponents of 'smart regulation'—Neil Gunningham, Peter Grabosky, and Darren Sinclair—do, however, emphasize the importance of this issue.[78] They seek to identify mixes that are: inherently complementary; inherently incompatible; complementary if sequenced; and complementary or otherwise, depending on the specific context. They suggest, for example, that information-generating instruments tend to be complementary to most other instruments (e.g. to commands, self-regulatory controls, and economic incentives). In contrast, the prescriptiveness of command instruments will often clash with the flexibility that an incentive-based measure such as a tax rule offers to the regulatee.[79] In the case of multiple, as opposed to bipartite, mixes, greater emphasis has to be placed on the particular context and the risk being controlled. Gunningham and Grabosky, however, suggest that one way to deal with the complexities of mixing instruments is to use a

---

[77] See the discussion of hybridity between different 'modalities of regulation' in A. Murray and C. Scott, 'Controlling the New Media: Hybrid Responses to New Forms of Power' (2002) 65 *Modern Law Review* 491–516.

[78] N. Gunningham and P. Grabosky, *Smart Regulation* (Oxford, 1998) pp. 422–53.

[79] Gunningham and Grabosky, *Smart Regulation*, 438.

strategy of 'sequencing'. The idea here is that: 'certain instruments would be held in reserve, only to be applied as and when other instruments demonstrably fail to meet pre-determined performance benchmarks'.[80] In the alternative, new instruments would be tried where others have failed, and the broad hope is that the overall dependability of the policy mix can be improved.

Such an incremental or trial-and-error approach, however, has two sides. On the one hand, it appears sensible to seek to improve regulatory regimes by amending strategies and mixes of instruments in the light of experience. On the other, there are dangers to be avoided. A policy of 'chance it, review, and adjust' runs the risk of doing damage through the use of ill-considered regulatory designs. An excessive propensity to adjust regulatory methods will, moreover, create uncertainty and is liable to be met with an outcry from regulated corporations.

An alternative design strategy is that offered by Malcolm Sparrow's 'regulatory craft' approach.[81] This places one version of risk-based regulation—namely problem-solving—at the centre of regulatory policymaking. It separates out the 'stages of problem-solving'[82] and stresses the need to define problems precisely, to monitor and measure performance, and to adjust strategy on the basis of performance assessments. It also accepts the 'dynamic nature of the risk control game'.[83] Sparrow tells us to target key problems and solve these by developing solutions or interventions and 'implementing the plan'.

The difficulties of the 'regulatory craft' analysis are discussed in more detail in Chapter 12 below, but it suffices to note here that focusing on a mischief by defining it as 'the problem' may only offer modest help in seeking to devise strategies for responding to it. What may be more useful is to identify the challenges that have to be faced, the available options (in terms of tools and strategies), and the kind of process that will foster working towards an optimal application of tools and strategies over time.

An approach to regulatory design that is perhaps broader than 'smart regulation' is the 'really responsive' viewpoint.[84] This will be discussed in more detail in Chapter 12 below, but its essentials should be noted here. The 'really responsive' approach has two main messages. First, that, in designing and developing regulatory systems (and especially complex, multi-actor regimes) attention has to be paid to five main matters: the *behaviour, attitudes and cultures* of regulatory actors (including associated regulators as well as regulatees); the *institutional settings* of the different regulators; the *different*

---

[80] Gunningham and Grabosky, *Smart Regulation*, 444.
[81] See M. Sparrow, *The Regulatory Craft* (Washington, DC, 2003).
[82] Ibid., ch. 10.
[83] Ibid., 274.
[84] See R. Baldwin and J. Black, 'Really Responsive Regulation' (2008) 71 *Modern Law Review* 59–94.

logics of regulatory tools and strategies (and how these interact); the *regime's own performance* over time; and finally, *changes* in each of these elements. The second message is that regulatory designs and developments should take on board the way that regulatory challenges vary across the main tasks that regulators have to carry out—namely: *detecting* undesirable or non-compliant behaviour, developing tools and strategies for *responding* to that behaviour, *enforcing* those tools and strategies on the ground, *assessing* their success or failure, and *modifying* them accordingly.[85]

What the 'really responsive' framework sets out to offer is a framework for considering how, in any given context, the main challenges of design can be addressed and how issues of regulatory mix can be analysed. It takes on board not only the issues of instutitional and instrumental variety, but also the significance of variations in regulatees and regulators, as well as the difficulties of effecting performance assessments. In addition, it addresses the needs to cope with changes in challenges and objectives, and to come to grips with all of these issues across the variety of tasks that regulators have to perform. The possible downside of really responsive regulation is that it poses a daunting set of questions for regulators and involves a high level of analysis. The upside is that it organizes strategic thinking in a way that identifies the main regulatory challenges that have to be faced if objectives are to be realized.

NETWORKS AND COORDINATION

When an activity is regulated by a network or assemblage of regulators, the arrangements may be complex. In the same field, there may be trans-national regulators setting 'soft law' standards, state regulators or departments implementing supra-national legal requirements, national regulatory agencies applying a variety of regulatory instruments, and sub-national non-state regulators such as standard-setting authorities, professional self-regulators, and industry-based certification bodies. In addition, regulation may encompass a diverse array of voluntary bodies, regulated firms, and other organizations. Many of these regulatory actors may, moreover, apply the norms of both state-based regulators and trans-national or sub-national non-state regulators, and they may be both advised by an array of consultants and have to conform to conditions imposed by other bodies such as insurance companies.[86]

---

[85] For a more detailed discussion of the 'DREAM' framework see chapter 11 below and see R. Baldwin and J. Black, *A Review of Enforcement Measures* (London, 2005).

[86] See J. Black, 'Decentring Regulation: The Role of Regulation and Self-Regulation in a "Post-Regulatory World"' (2001) *Current Legal Problems* 103–46; R. Baldwin and J. Black, 'Understanding Regulatory Cohabitation' (forthcoming).

In such networks,[87] considerable coordination challenges arise.[88] It cannot, for instance, be assumed that all of the involved regulators will have the same substantive objectives or normative conceptions of the 'good'. Their capacities, skills, and resources are also liable to vary, and this is likely to affect not only their preferred approaches to regulation but their responsiveness. Thus, some regulators within a network will possess the ability to modify their operations in order to cope with changes and others will not. There are also liable to be variations in regulatory cultures—the assumptions, conventions, and values that underpin, and are reflected in, regulatory interventions. Finally, it will often be the case that different regulators will occupy different positions within broader political and legal infrastructures so that they are answerable to, and controlled by, other governmental institutions in different ways.

Responses to these challenges tend to come in the form of different modes of coordination, and distinctions can be drawn between five different such modes.[89] One familiar approach to coordination within government networks is by means of *hierarchy*.[90] This involves a top-down arrangement in which a central control body lays down rules and policies that provide direction to inferior institutions within the network. Hierarchies are often established by legal frameworks. A second mode is *community*. Coordination of a network by community occurs when a stable group of peers engages in mutual recognition of membership and where there is a sharing of a common set of interests. A typical example is professional or industry-based self-regulation.

A third approach to coordination is *network management*—which is commonly marked by a lead party taking positive steps to facilitate concerted network actions. This type of coordination is often achieved by the 'manager' body developing or steering processes that either encourage negotiations and interactions or foster the conditions for collective behaviour by building levels

---

[87] 'Network' here refers to the situation in which numbers of regulators exert control or influence over a domain, topic, or risk—and do so concurrently. On the narrower sense of 'network'—which refers to a particular mode of non-hierarchical social organization—see G. Thompson, *Between Hierarchies and Markets: The Logics and Limits of Network Forms of Organization* (Oxford, 2003), 6; L. Martinez-Diaz and N. Woods, *Networks of Influence?* (Oxford, 2009).

[88] J. Black, 'Constructing and Contesting Legitimacy and Accountability in Polycentric Regulatory Regimes' (2008) 2 *Regulation and Governance* 137–64; E. Bardach, *Getting Agencies to Work Together* (Washington, DC, 1998); M. Sparrow, *The Regulatory Craft* (Washington, DC, 2000); on transnational coordination issues, see K. Abbott and D. Snidal, 'Strengthening International Regulation through Transnational New Governance' (2009) *Vanderbilt Journal of Transnational Law*.

[89] See W. Kickert, E.-H. Klijn and J. Koppenjan (eds), *Managing Complex Networks* (London, 1997); H. Sullivan and C. Skelcher, *Working Across Boundaries* (Basingstoke, 2002); S. Goldsmith and W. D. Eggers, *Governing By Network* (Washington, DC, 2004), ch. 2.; D. Chisholm, *Co-ordination Without Hierarchy* (Berkeley, 1989).

[90] D. Marsh and R. Rhodes, *Policy Networks in British Government* (Oxford, 1992).

of consensus to points that allow for action on a given issue.[91] Quite distinct, however, is a fourth approach—one based on *rituals*. Rituals are structured processes that serve to organize not only the actions taken by network members but the meanings that participant individuals or organizations give to events or decisions. They may be adopted voluntarily or imposed by statutes, managers, or other methods, but the essence of ritualistic network coordination is that embedded processes drive forward the collaborations that are found within the network.[92] Finally, coordination can be left to *markets*. In collaboration through markets, the idea is that coordination is achieved 'through the "invisible hand" of the self interest of participants' who are willing to exchange resources and conclude agreements in order to attain mutually beneficial solutions and higher levels of collective welfare.[93]

The significance of the particular mode of coordination that is encountered in an area may be considerable. It has been contended that when different strategies of regime or network coordination are put into effect, those different strategies may produce intra-network relationships and exchanges— 'regulatory cohabitations'—that are quite distinct in nature.[94] Thus, it can be expected that in 'hierarchical' cohabitations, there will be a very different set of relationships, negotiations, and communications from those encountered in cohabitations that might be described as 'community', 'managed', 'ritualistic', or 'market-organized'. For those regulators who would aim to justify their activities to other co-regulators and for those who would criticize other regulators within their networks, there are challenges that are quite differently conceived within the different cohabitations. Within a regime based on hierarchies, for instance, relationships will be based on lines of authority and attitudes will be shaped with reference to the requirements of authorities and rules. A key motivation will be the accepted need to comply with the requirements of those bodies that are superior within the hierarchy and with the rules that are laid down to govern behaviour. Within community-organized networks, attitudes relate to perceptions of the common interest—or the commonly accepted policies that serve as a focus for the community. A central motivation is the sustaining of continuing acceptance within the community.

---

[91] R. Agranoff, *Intergovernmental Management* (Albany, NY, 1986); W. Kickert, and J. Koppenjan, 'Public Management and Network Mangement: An Overview' in Kickert, Klijn, and Koppenjan, *Managing Complex Networks*; R. Gage and M. Mandell, *Strategies for Managing Intergovernmental Policies and Networks* (New York, 1990).

[92] See N. Machado and T. Burns, 'Complex Social Organization: Multiple Organizing Modes, Structural Incongruence and Mechanisms of Integration (1998) 76 *Public Administration* 355.

[93] See B.G. Peters, 'Managing Horizontal Government: The Politics of Co-ordination' (1998) 76 *Public Administration* 295, 298; B. Marin, 'Generalised Political Exchange' in B. Marin (ed.), *Generalised Political Exchange* (Frankfurt, 1990).

[94] See Baldwin and Black, 'Understanding Regulatory Co-habitation'.

In managed networks, attitudes and motivations will not be left to the individual regulatory organization, but will be steered and influenced by the managing agency—which will seek to manipulate these in a manner that contributes to the managerially constructed set of network objectives. It can, in turn, be expected that interrelationships and accountability issues will be set within a context of managerial/functional interactions, rather than hierarchical, rule-structured, or community-established ones.

Where rituals hold sway, the central motivation of many regulators will be to use ritualistic processes in a manner that serves their own organizational interests. Their broad attitude will be that interactions with other agencies can best be seen in terms of their impacts on achieving success in rituals. Claims and responses will be processed through embedded procedures and will be structured accordingly. As for market-based regimes, attitudes and motivations can be seen in traditional market terms—and regulatory bodies can be expected to deal and negotiate as selfish and rational maximizers of their own agency interests. In market-based cohabitations, claims and responses will bear the character of exchanges that are engaged in by different parties who aim to negotiate and advance self-serving outcomes. Messages will be designed not to achieve compliance with rules, or common positions, or understandings, but will have the character of offers to buy or sell in order to self-maximize.

'Cohabitation' theory also suggests that the production of regulatory outcomes is also liable to vary according to cohabitation style. *Hierarchical cohabitation* brings the potential to establish common goals, but the considerable risk is that in complex regimes that cross different levels of government, and which involve various types of public and private body, the available authority will not suffice to eliminate non-hierarchical relationships. The existence of such counter-regimes and cultures will, in turn impede both the establishing of common goals and delivery with respect to such goals. Adaptability to change may also be sub-optimal in hierarchical cohabitations if there is not leadership from the top and if upward communications are poor. As for accountability and other representative values, one special problem within hierarchical cohabitations is that assumptions of responsibility will tend to vary dramatically across the network and that those lower down the hierarchy will tend to shift responsibility to 'higher authorities'.

In *community cohabitations*, the establishing of common goals is again possible, but this is liable to be impeded where interests diverge. A special danger is that confusions of messaging will tend to undermine both delivery on objectives and the serving of representative values of accountability and openness. The strength of *network management* is that this can be used to broker agreements, to develop common responses to problems, and to steer attitudes and motivations in a productive direction. Managers, in addition, can often work with and around the divergent capacities and limitations that co-regulators experience. Managerial strategies can, moreover, facilitate the network's capacity to adapt to changed circumstances. In relation to representative values, the strength of managerial cohabitation is that common communications systems, claiming processes, and responding approaches can be fostered and efforts can be made to develop common understandings on such matters as modes of rendering account. Modes of evaluating performance can, accordingly, be shaped by the managers.

In *ritualistic cohabitations*, processes can be used to allocate institutional roles and to encourage the development of common aims and approaches by ordering experiences, creating shared meanings, building feelings of community, and encouraging trust. They may be used to facilitate the development of discourses that generate bodies of common knowledge, generalized ways of seeing challenges and problems, and authoritative versions of situations and values.[95] The difficulty, however, is that, in the absence of authority, rituals may not suffice to reconcile all interests and perceptions and this may impede the establishing of objectives and an organized regime for delivering on these. Rituals, moreover, can lead to stultification if they are followed unthinkingly.

In the case of *market-based cohabitations*, there may be significant difficulties in agreeing objectives in the absence of hierarchical or managerial pressures and in cases where regulatory actors are reluctant to collaborate. Outcome deliveries are likely to be prejudiced where the pursuit of self-interests will produce cohabitations that are ill-organized and which tend to be associated with frequent efforts to shift blame. Adaptability to change may also be limited in so far as self-interested regulators will seek to address new challenges through collaborations only in order to further their own agency interests. This produces the further danger that collaborative action will be undermined, as changes are seen by some regulators as opportunities to gain competitive advantages over their co-networked regulators.

Such 'pure forms' of cohabitation are unlikely to be encountered in practice and 'complex cohabitations' are liable to be widespread.[96] The value of the cohabitation analysis is, however, that it draws the connection between three elements: the mode of network coordination essayed in an area, the type of cohabitation arrangement that networked regulators inhabit, and the delivery of substantive and procedural regulatory outcomes.

---

[95] On rituals and discourses in medicine, see N. Machado, *Using the Bodies of the Dead* (Aldershot, 1998).
[96] See Baldwin and Black, 'Understanding Regulatory Cohabitation'.

Conclusions

As with many other regulatory distinctions, the contrast between regulation and self-regulation can be portrayed in ways that are too stark.[97] Nearly all regulatory mechanisms incorporate some elements of self-regulation—whether this involves an input into the drafting of rules or a firm's monitoring its own compliance. Nearly all self-regulatory mechanisms of governmental significance are subject to some degree of external state influence—even if this is merely the 'shadow' of potential governmental regulation. The trick, as was shown in discussing enforced self-regulation, is to make use of that mix of regulation and self-regulation that best serves legitimate governmental purposes and so merits the strongest claims to support. Analysis of particular regulatory tasks and contexts is essential in bringing about that deployment, as is an awareness of the potential of different varieties of regulation and self-regulation.

Self-regulatory and meta-regulatory approaches have an important role in regulation, but enough has been said above to suggest that they offer 'solutions' that are often no less contentious than those provided by command and control instruments. As for mixes of regulatory methods, these are likely to provide the only realistic responses to challenges in many regulatory contexts. The central issues in relation to mixes are how to design and identify optimal mixes and how to do so in a manner that satisfies the criteria of legitimacy that were reviewed in Chapter 3. Part of that legitimation process relates to the production of appropriate regulatory outcomes and, as the discussion of regulatory networks indicated, much here will turn on the mode of network coordination that is adopted and the kind of regulatory cohabitation that results.

---

[97] See D. Swann, 'The Regulatory Scene', in K. Button and D. Swann, *The Age of Regulatory Reform* (Oxford, 1989), 4.

9 Franchising

The importance of franchising as a policy option demands that its virtues and vices be understood. This chapter looks at different types of franchising arrangement, the key difficulties encountered in franchising, and the potential of franchising as a tool of government.

Commercial Franchising

The essence of franchising is the allocation (subject to conditions) of a protected or exclusive right to exploit or carry out an activity.[1] In the commercial world, franchising is known as a form of marketing or distribution in which one party, the franchiser, allows another, the franchisee, to exploit a trade name, trademark, process, or other resource in return for a fee.[2] The franchise agreement typically allows this exploitation to be carried out in a prescribed manner, over a certain period of time, and within a specified location. The objective of both parties to a commercial or 'private' franchise is likely to be the maximizing of profits. Within the United Kingdom public sector, the closest approach to commercial franchising to be found is the Post Office, where Post Office Counters franchises certain stores to provide retail post office services to the public.

Governmental Franchising

Governmental franchising may resemble commercial franchising closely but can be distinguished by its 'public' purpose. The aim of the franchiser is not to

[1] See H. Demsetz, 'Why Regulate Utilities?' (1968) 11 *Journal of Law and Economics* 55; S. Domberger, 'Regulation through Franchise Contracts', in J. Kay, C. Mayer, and D. Thompson (eds), *Privatisation and Regulation: The UK Experience* (Oxford, 1986); O. Williamson, *The Economic Institutions of Capitalism* (New York, 1985), ch. 13; A. Ogus, *Regulation: Legal Form and Economic Theory* (Oxford, 1994), ch. 15.

[2] J. Adams and K.V. Prichard Jones, *Franchising* (London, 1987); C.L. Vaughan, *Franchising* (Lexington, MA, 1989); C. Joerges (ed), *Franchising and the Law* (Baden-Baden, 1991); A. W. Dnes, *Franchising: A Case Study Approach* (Aldershot, 1992).

maximize profits but to deliver to consumers or the public an advantage—for example, an efficiently produced and competitively priced utility service.

As a tool of government influence, franchising is seen by proponents as particularly useful in a number of respects. It is said to avoid the restrictiveness associated with classical command and control regulation while, nevertheless, allowing some degree of control to be retained. It provides a means of using competition *for* a market as a substitute for competition *within* the market (where this is not possible), and, thereby, of inducing monopolists to behave as if subject to competitive pressures. (Such competition is generally achieved by allocating franchises according to a bidding mechanism.) It respects managerial freedoms and allows managers rather than bureaucrats to devise responses to preferences within markets. It increases market contestability by allowing firms to bid for rights to supply before they have committed resources to the enterprise. It provides the franchiser with information about the competitiveness of potential suppliers and the costs of servicing the market. It offers an effective sanction for poor performance, namely the threat of franchise termination, suspension, or non-renewal, and it reduces the dangers of regulatory capture by minimizing agency discretions.

In Britain, franchising has been most notably employed in the broadcasting sector, but the privatization process has created extensive new areas of private service provision within which franchising may have or has been given a role. One such important area is railway passenger services, where a franchising regime was established under the Railways Act 1993.[3]

Systems of franchising may combine and overlap with other modes of government or service provision, notably with licensing, competitive tendering/contracting out, and contracts for exploitation or concessions. Model forms of the different devices can be contrasted thus:

Franchising—the offer to provide a service is tendered by the franchisee in a competitive context. The regime is based on market incentives, with the franchisee bearing at least some of the revenue risk.[4] (The extent of revenue risk a franchise bears may vary widely and as it decreases the franchise resembles a normal commercial contract.) The franchiser and franchisee have a continuing relationship with the franchiser monitoring performance quality. (The prospect of renewal or non-renewal of the franchise operates as a control.)

Licensing—operators are free to compete in the market provided that they have obtained permission to do so. Permission is granted on the satisfaction of certain requirements and may be subject to conditions.

---

[3] See Comptroller and Auditor-General, *Office of Passenger Rail Franchising (OPRAF): The Award of the First Three Passenger Rail Franchises* (HC 701, 1995/6) (London, 1996).
[4] That is, the franchisee's returns vary according to the revenue yielded from sales, rather than being set at a fixed sum.

Competitive tendering/contracting out—the service is rendered by the provider to the contracting body, not directly to the public as in franchising. Revenue risks are borne by the contracting body, not the service provider and, because one of the contracting parties also consumes the services, the issue of service variation is often less acute than in franchising, and performance monitoring tends to be less problematic than with franchising.

Contracts for exploitation—the state allows a private operator to exploit a public good in return for making a capital investment and paying taxes on profits. A high degree of security is offered by a contract with a period of duration so long that the prospect of renewal or non-renewal does not operate as a control.

Modes of Franchise Allocation

All franchising allocation processes involve comparisons of bids. These may be single or multi-dimensional processes.

BIDDING ON PRICE PER UNIT

One option is to introduce bidding on price per unit so that the franchise is awarded to the competitor willing to supply the service to the public at the lowest prices. This is the scheme recommended by Demsetz.[5] Under the assumptions that the auction is vigorously contested, there is a single output, and information asymmetries play no part in determining the spread of bids; bidders will bid their average costs at each stipulated output level. With these assumptions, price-per-unit auctions identify the firm with the lowest average cost.

The advantages of this type of auction are that the process extinguishes monopoly rents; it identifies the most efficient producer (assuming bidders are not asymmetric); where the output is a clearly identifiable single product it makes for easy identification of the franchise winner. On the debit side, however, it has been argued that a price equal to average cost does not result in a welfare-optimizing level of pricing or output.[6] Where, moreover, a variety

---

[5] See Demsetz, 'Why Regulate Utilities?', and A. W. Dnes, 'Bidding for Commercial Broadcasting: An Analysis of UK Experience' (1993) 40 *Scottish Journal of Political Economics* 104.

[6] See L.G. Telser, 'On the Regulation of Industry: A Note' (1969) 77 *Journal of Political Economics* 937. The game theoretic literature on regulation suggests that the auction winner should then be paid a subsidy in exchange for price and quantity levels indicated by P_3 and Q_f (see, for example, D. Baron and R. Myerson, 'Regulating a Monopolist with Unknown Costs' (1982) *Econometrician* 911). This, however, requires that the authorities know the firm's marginal cost.

of services or products is to be provided, it becomes much more difficult to judge which bidder is offering the best deal. The price rigidity implied by a price-per-unit franchise may also become inefficient as demands and technologies change over time.

Bids can be for an average price or a weighted index of temporally viable tariffs, such as exist in the RPI–X price control baskets used to regulate many privatized UK utilities. The advantage of controlling a weighted index instead of actual prices is that it enables more price flexibility and thereby addresses one of the key criticisms of the price-per-unit form of franchise bidding. However, such bidding may make unrealistic assumptions about potential franchisees' understandings of demand conditions.

BIDDING BY LUMP SUM PAYMENT

In an industry where scale economies are such that least cost production is by a single firm, awarding a franchise to the firm that bids the highest sum will not correct for the inefficiencies of monopoly pricing and output decisions and so consumers will suffer from higher prices and lower outputs than is optimal. Without additional controls on prices, this form of franchise bidding has only a distributional effect, as the expected stream of monopoly rents would be capitalized and paid to the franchiser.

As a rule, bidding in the form of lump sum payments should be based on known regulated prices. However, this form of franchising suffers from price inflexibility just as bidding on price per unit does. Bidders would want to know the regulated prices before they determined their lump sum bids. If regulated prices were uncertain, bids would be discounted accordingly. Moreover, if prices are to be specified prior to the auction, the franchiser will have to do this without the very bidding information that would provide a basis for assessing the likely winner's production costs.

BIDDING FOR THE LOWEST LUMP SUM SUBSIDY

If, before franchising, the market has already been supplied by a public enterprise, the regulator/franchiser may decide that those prices must be maintained. The initial controls on price can, however, be eased in return for improvements in service quality. Bids can be accepted or rejected according to the quality of their business plans, as well as levels of subsidies demanded. If potential franchisees know they will be taking over existing pricing structures, they can plan more securely on the revenue side. Franchising may, indeed, be conducted by requiring the winner to begin operating as close to existing publicly operated arrangements as is possible. In this case, lump sum subsidy bidding is probably preferable to price-per-unit bidding.

Price changes can then be left to unfold according to market pressures and stated regulatory strategy.

MARGINAL RETURN BIDDING

This form of franchise is only suitable where franchisees have to erect their own infrastructures, such as might occur for new rail or underground links. Given that the franchiser has an approximate knowledge of the cost of the project, a rate-of-return schedule is constructed for capital invested, which will eventually fall short of the cost of capital to the franchisee.

It is the marginal return schedule for a given investment for which franchisees bid. With incomplete contracts, which is always the case in utility franchising, the successful franchisee will almost always have room to manœuvre within the original franchise contract. Particularly in government procurement contracts, there is a history of cost overruns arising once contracts are under way. Marginal return bidding discourages operators from inflating these costs. In cases where potential franchisees are bidding to take over the operation of existing state-subsidized services (and possibly assets), the bidding could involve a marginal annual subsidy schedule.

MENU AUCTIONS

The franchiser may choose to allow competitors to specify their bids in terms of more than one dimension—typically in terms of price and quality of service.[7] The franchiser then makes a choice from among the combinations on offer, and the quality and price conditions embodied in the franchise contract.

Allowing multiple bidding on a mix of quality of service and price/lump sum variables can provide useful information to the franchiser/regulator, which can be used if renegotiation becomes necessary once the franchisee begins operations. The main drawback of this type of franchise is that it proves more difficult for the franchiser to identify the winning bid than in other auctions. As a result, the auctioning process may lack transparency. This has been a problem with bus franchising in London and, unless carefully managed, menu bidding may provide greater gaming opportunities to bidders. Auction theory suggests, however, that where relevant information is

---

[7] The term 'menu auction' for such procedures was introduced by Bernheim and Whinston—see B. Bernheim and M. Whinston, 'Menu Auctions, Resource Allocation and Economic Influence' (1986) *Quarterly Journal of Economics* 1.

dispersed amongst bidders, introducing multiple factors as variables in an open auction reduces uncertainty, as private information is made public.[8]

CONDUCT OF THE AUCTION

Auctions can be carried out by a number of methods. These include 'public' or 'oral' auctions, in which the auctioneer successively announces prices until a buyer is found, and 'sealed bid' tenders. Public auctions may be either English—in which prices are successively raised until only one bidder remains—or Dutch—in which the price is successively lowered until the object is bought by the first bidder. Sealed bid tenders award the object to the highest bidder either at the price offered by that bidder (a first-price tender) or—more rarely—at the price offered by the second-highest bidder (a second-price tender).

In deciding how to auction a franchise, the regulator will normally seek to devise a procedure which maximizes revenue, subject to any constraints on quality. One of the major findings of auction theory is that, in the private values case (where the object of the bid is valued differently by bidders), all four models yield the same price on average (assuming risk-neutrality) and hence the method of auctioning makes no difference. (It may seem paradoxical that the first- and second-price auctions produce the same result on average, but clearly bidders' behaviour will be different in each case.) In addition, the more bidders there are, the higher the expected revenue, as bidders are led by the pressure of competition to bid right up to their own true valuation of the object on sale. With few bidders, by contrast, each company will bid the least it feels it can win with.

As we have seen, however, franchises are not usually examples of the private values case. Bids are not determined exclusively by their private tastes, but depend upon (possibly different) judgements about potential revenues and costs. This may lead to the phenomenon known as the 'winner's curse' whereby the highest bidder realizes as soon as he or she wins that he or she has placed a higher value on the franchise than anyone else, and may thus have overestimated its value. A sophisticated bidder would, however, anticipate this danger and bid less aggressively, though, as before, and for the same reasons, the more bidders there are, the higher the expected price will be. The franchiser can reduce anxieties about the winner's curse by publicizing any

---

[8] The franchiser's revenue may, as a result, rise—see P. Milgrom and R. Weber, 'A Theory of Auctions and Competitive Bidding' (1982) 50 *Econometrica* 1089; R. McAfee and J. McMillan, 'Auctions and Bidding' (1987) 25 *Journal of Economic Literature* 699. On varying the sequence of bidding and making information available to bidders, see M.L. Cripps and N. Ireland, 'The Design of Auctions and Tenders with Quality Thresholds: The Symmetric Case' (1994) 104 *Economic Journal* 316.

information available about the franchise. This reduces bidders' uncertainty and encourages them to bid closer to their true expected value than would be the case if they had poorer information and were more anxious about overbidding.

The key result from the common value model, provided the bidders are risk-neutral, is that the various forms of auction produce different average levels of revenue, because they yield different information to each bidder about other bidders' valuations. The English auction yields the most information, and hence the highest expected revenue, because any bidder can observe all other bidders' behaviour. Next is the second-price tender, which exploits the valuation of at least one other bidder. Finally, the first-price tender and Dutch auction furnish no information, and thus leave bidders most fearful of the winner's curse. When bidders are risk-averse, however, the ranking is less clear cut. The English auction can still be expected to yield more revenue than a second-price tender, and the equivalence of Dutch and first-price tenders is preserved. The first-price tender may, however, now yield higher revenue than an English auction.[9]

INTEGRATION VERSUS SEPARATION

Franchises may be used to divide industries vertically so that separate operations are made of, for example, infrastructure establishment, maintenance, operation, marketing, etc. Alternatively, franchising may involve high levels of integration.[10]

Franchises may also achieve horizontal separation, with each franchisee serving a particular area. The combination of these two forms of separation is particularly appropriate where the franchiser undertakes an activity characterized by economies of scale, while franchisees carry out locally based activities at a different cost-minimizing scale. Much commercial franchising exploits this distinction, with the franchiser providing the brand name and franchisees operating local outlets. The system of rail regulation operating in the UK is of the same kind, with track separated from train operation—although in this case franchising is undertaken by a third party.

---

[9] See S. Matthews, 'Comparing Auctions for Risk Averse Buyers: A Buyer's Point of View' (1987) *Econometrica* 633.

[10] Thus in the French water industry, two types of franchise contract are distinguished—the 'concession de service public', in which the franchisee finances initial establishment of the infrastructure, and the 'affermage contract', in which a public authority finances the initial establishment.

OPERATING FRANCHISES

With an operating franchise the responsibility for maintenance and investment in infrastructure remains with the franchiser, or perhaps some other
appointed government body, and the franchisee bears the operating-cost risk
and all, or a proportion of, the revenue risk.

Operating contracts can prove useful when it is appropriate for the franchiser to carry the investment risk, or when the economies associated with the
infrastructure diverge from those associated with its operation. This is frequently the case with utility networks, where the natural monopoly component is the infrastructure (and possibly also its operation) while downstream
operations (running rolling stock), involve fewer scale economies. In such
cases, the 'efficient' split is not to divide the utility into several vertically
integrated companies, but to maintain the network infrastructure in larger
blocks than the operational aspects—as in the case of the railways.[11]

Where the expected future investment and maintenance cost of infrastructure are very uncertain, it is usually desirable for the franchiser to bear a
significant portion of the associated risk. This is especially so in long-term
franchising, where the rules for valuing assets at the end of the franchise
period are open to doubt. Some form of operating franchise may also be
preferable when the sheer size of the infrastructure and expected investment
are so large that few, if any, qualified bidders will be attracted to the auction.

Operating franchises enable the scale of each franchise to be smaller, thus
increasing the number of franchises. This can facilitate 'yardstick competition'. It also increases the likelihood that an operating firm will have more
than one franchise. This brings into play a 'reputational' effect. Parties
holding numbers of franchises are, it is suggested, likely to behave more
responsibly than holders of single franchises because poor performance on
one franchise may have undesirable consequences in relation to renewals
of other franchises.[12]

INVESTMENT FRANCHISES

The investment franchise assigns a higher level of 'ownership' of the facilities
to the operator than does the operating franchise. Problems arise, however,
because 'ownership' of the facilities only lasts as long as the franchise contract.
As the end of the contract period approaches, the franchisee's incentive to

[11] Similarly, it has been suggested that divergent economies of scale exist between sewerage and
water delivery and that this provides a basis for the franchising of water delivery—see J.W. Sawkins,
Water and Sewage in Scotland: A Response, University of Aberdeen Discussion Papers (1993).
[12] See M.A. Zupan, 'Cable Franchise Renewals: Do Incumbent Firms Behave Opportunistically?'
(1989) 20 *Rand Journal of Economics* 473.

invest declines. Investment in infrastructure is, therefore, likely to be cyclical, rising during the early years of a franchise, and declining as the contract period comes closer to its end.

Several strategies can be employed to limit the variation in the cycle. Punishment clauses for declines in quality of service can have this effect. The problem is also mitigated if franchisees believe that the franchiser is committed to valuing the franchised facilities 'fairly'.[13]

PROGRESSIVE VERSUS 'BIG BANG' FRANCHISING

Industries may be moved from public to private sector by means of incremental franchising, or the whole sector may be put out to tender at the one time. The arguments mostly favour progressive franchising. Present British experience (for example, in London Bus operations) suggests that one advantage of the incremental approach lies in the increasing ease with which over-bidding can be identified as franchising progresses. The franchiser, rather than having to cope with a flood of applications on the basis of little experience, has the opportunity to deal with smaller numbers of tenders and to do so while developing a feel for the credible set of proposals and promises. Renewals are, moreover, staggered (if franchises are of standard duration) and incrementalism thus eases administration and makes for continuity.

Progressive franchising also offers a response to problems of uncertainty. At the time that a franchise system is introduced, there are likely to be few, if any, firms which have had direct experience of operating a complete utility or network of the type being put to tender. The sheer financial size of the individual franchises will tend to restrict the number of serious bidders. There is uncertainty about demand and cost factors and also about regulatory and governmental commitments.

Such factors are likely to lead to a restricted number of franchise bidders. A key task of the franchiser is, therefore, to reduce the level of uncertainty amongst potential bidders. Letting franchise contracts out gradually can greatly reduce bidder uncertainty. The first franchises let will almost certainly be heavily discounted. Once operations begin, uncertainty declines. An operator starts to gain a better understanding of cost and demand conditions, and of the mind of the regulator, and it becomes apparent to the market that the franchisee has obtained a good deal. Bidders for subsequent franchises will suffer less uncertainty, and—other things being equal—the bidders will be larger in number and their bids significantly less cautious. Where at least one of the bidders already operates an existing franchise it will bring valuable and

---

[13] See D. Baron and D. Besanko, 'Commitment and Fairness in a Dynamic Regulatory Relationship' (1987) 54 *Review of Economic Studies* 413.

private information to the auction. An open auction can provide useful information to the other bidders, with the outcome that the auction is more competitive and on average bids are higher. Even *post hoc* disclosure of bids will have a similar educational effect.

A contrary argument applies, however, where there are significant complementarities and/or economies of scale or scope between franchised operations, with the result that allocating one franchise at a time may prove to be inefficient. To allow bidders to gain bundles of franchises in order to capture these scale advantages, franchises should be auctioned together.[14]

Franchising: Problems to be Overcome

The literature on franchising indicates that success on four key fronts is essential if franchisers are to achieve designated objectives in an acceptable manner.[15] These fronts concern:

- specification of the franchised service;
- allocating franchises competitively;
- enforcement of franchise terms;
- terminating contracts and refranchising.

SERVICE SPECIFICATION

Adequate service specification is important in franchising, first, as a basis for competition in the bidding process and, second, to set down benchmarks for evaluating bids. If the franchiser fails to specify the subject-matter of the bid with precision, then uncertainties will result, costs of bidding will be increased, and applicants will be discouraged. Similar problems will arise if the franchiser defers specification until after the franchise is awarded or retains discretion to alter the specification post the award.

Problems of specification diminish in so far as variations in the quality of service are absent or are deemed to be immaterial and are accordingly discounted. Where, on the other hand, service variation is extreme and

---

[14] On allowing flexibility in 'bundling' franchises, see J. McMillan, 'Selling Spectrum Rights' (1994) 8 *Journal of Economic Perspectives* 145; P.C. Crampton, 'Money out of Thin Air: The Nationwide Narrow Bend PCS Auction' (1995) *Journal of Economics and Management Strategy*.

[15] See, e.g., O. Williamson, 'Franchise Bidding for National Monopolies: In General and with respect to CATV' (1976) 7 *Bell Journal of Economics* 73; Domberger, 'Regulation through Franchise Contracts'.

extends across a wide range of aspects of the service, difficulties might be expected to be the greater.

Practical experience of service specification suggests that in some sectors this has proved less of an issue than others. Until 2003, the Radio Authority (RA) franchised Independent Local Radio (ILR) services under the Broadcasting Act 1990, but it operated without a detailed specification of quality of service.[16] The RA advertised locally, asking for tenders to provide ILR services for a particular area with a designated coverage and characteristically for an eight-year period. Allocations were not uncompetitive, however. The Radio Authority looked for the applicant best able to satisfy the criteria set out in Section 105 of the Broadcasting Act 1990. Attention was thus paid to: the ability of the applicant to maintain the service for the period of the licence; the satisfaction of local tastes and interests; the meeting of interests uncatered for by existing services; and local support for the application. Successful applicants subsequently set down a 'promise of performance' stipulating the programming profile to be offered during the franchise. Such promises were often very short and some examples occupied half an A4 page.

London Transport bus service tendering under the London Regional Transport Act 1984 also involved relatively unproblematic service specification. (Tendering, as already indicated, differs from franchising, but transfer of the revenue risk to the service provider—as was practised on some LT services—does establish a franchising system and the specification functions are similar.) Those agreeing to offer a service to London Regional Transport under the 1984 Act were offered a contract with schedules on service and vehicle specification. These schedules were fairly simple, laying down, for example, requirements on frequencies of service, running times, vehicle types to be used, and displays of route numbers.

Franchising in transport sectors might generally be expected to involve comparatively few specification difficulties because such services are not highly dimensional. The Secretary of State's 1994 guidance to the Director of Passenger Rail Franchising (the Franchising Director) indicated that service levels specified in franchises should look to: frequency and capacity; service availability (throughout the seven-day week); provision of through services by fast trains; intermediate stations served; and journey time. Some complications may be anticipated, however, in sectors such as rail, where separation of the industry is pronounced and high levels of coordination between different participants in providing the service have to be provided for in specifications.

---

[16] Ofcom took over the Radio Authority's functions in December 2003.

Similarly, the degree of competition a franchisee faces may affect the precision appropriate in the service definition. As the Secretary of State's 1994 Guidance to the Franchising Director put it:

Service quality for railway passenger services and station services operated by franchisees should be specified in a degree of detail that is appropriate for the particular franchise. For some franchises, particularly those conferring monopoly power, you should ensure that the franchise agreement provides an effective substitute for market pressures. For other franchises, where market pressures are present to a greater extent, you should impose such service quality requirements as are necessary to ensure that the taxpayer obtains good value for money.[17]

Experience in television franchising has offered a contrast with the above areas and has demonstrated that, even where allocation is by highest cash bid, specification is problematic if there is a minimum quality of service to be stipulated. The Independent Television Commission (ITC) franchised regional Channel 3 licences under the Broadcasting Act 1990 until its functions were taken over by Ofcom and, in its Invitation to Apply for Regional Channel 3 Licences, the ITC's description of the quality of service threshold ran to 63 paragraphs. These paragraphs, moreover, involved the making of a number of potentially contentious judgements on programming issues and, accordingly, specification was far from cut and dried.[18]

Where service specification involves the making of judgements, the advantages of franchising may be called into question. A supposed strength of franchising lies, as noted, in its allowing private sector providers, rather than regulating bureaucrats, to be the judges of consumer and market preferences. In so far as service specification involves the making of judgements by franchise authorities, and in so far as the franchise authority selects the best menu of services for the consumer, this advantage of franchising diminishes and franchising approximates to a system of classical-style regulation.

SPECIFICATION, FLEXIBILITY, AND CHANGE

A general difficulty in service specification arises from tensions that exist between the need to lay down a precise description of the service to be provided by the successful bidder and the need to allow for flexibility and scope for innovation and responsiveness to consumer demands after the award of the franchise.

Where, in a sector, there is the prospect of a technical innovation that will demand, within the franchise period, substantial adaptations by franchisees,

---

[17] Secretary of State for Transport, *Guidance to the Franchising Director* (London, 1994).
[18] Ofcom took over the ITC's functions in December 2003.

this may call for a service specification that allows for such flexibility.[19] (Thus difficulties for the franchiser arose in the ILR sector with the prospect of Digital Audio Broadcasting (DAB), which became an issue when planned for adoption by the BBC in 1995/6 in order to offer a higher quality of service). In such circumstances, a series of uncertainties can arise in relation to costs and transmission arrangements and pressure to adjust franchise specifications and periods is to be expected.

As Armstrong, Cowan, and Vickers argue, franchising works best for straightforward products that involve low sunk costs, such as supplying licence plates for taxis, but in sectors such as the utilities, conditions are very different:

A complete contract would be immensely complex and extremely difficult to write, monitor and enforce.... Indeed it would be very hard for the government to commit not to vary some contract terms as events unfold. Much more likely, then, is some kind of incomplete contract that leaves a number of aspects to be resolved.... But this is effectively just what regulation involves—a continuing task of contract monitoring, enforcement and renegotiation. Thus in circumstances of any complexity, franchising does not do away with the need for regulation.[20]

SPECIFYING THE REGULATORY REGIME

Uncertainties in specifying regulatory regimes will affect franchise allocation processes since applicants will look for predictability of regulation. Problems may arise, therefore, where regulators retain large discretions regarding the quality of service to be provided; where changes in regulatory policy may be made, and where regulatory authority is diffused or uncertain. Particular difficulties are to be expected in a sector, such as rail, where a number of agencies and operators are interdependent and will, in addition, be perceived to be subject to political pressures.

RISK ALLOCATION

Risk allocation is a difficulty of specification that increases with the separation of an industry. Thus, problems have been encountered in the rail industry. It was clear from the Rail Regulator's July 1994 Consultation Document,

---

[19] See J. Dallas, 'Effective Franchising: A Legal Perspective', in CRI, *Franchising Network Services: Regulation in Post, Rail and Water* (London, 1993). The arrival of Digital Audio Broadcasting (DAB) thus gave rise to a series of uncertainties in independent local radio franchising in the mid-1990s and indicated that in periods of rapid technological change the role of the franchiser may also have to change—from acting in a hands-off role, it may have to become an instigator, organizer of change, and regulator.
[20] M. Armstrong, S. Cowan, and J. Vickers, *Regulatory Reform: Economic Analysis and British Experience* (London, 1994), 126.

Framework for the Approval of Railtrack's Track Access Charges for Franchised Passenger Services, that, in the period leading up to the first round of franchise allocations, a host of uncertainties remained on such matters as the extent of industry risk to be borne by Railtrack, the appropriate rate of return for Railtrack, and even whether private sector rate-of-return criteria should be applied to an assessment of Railtrack's charges. The privatizations of Railtrack, the Rolling Stock Leasing Companies (ROSCOs), and the Infrastructure Services Companies have also created uncertainties of risk allocation. The Rail Regulator acknowledged, in the above consultation paper, that 'Railtrack's longer term revenue requirements will remain subject to continuing uncertainties' (para. 1.31). A system of periodic review of charges (as familiar in other utilities) has been instituted in rail, but, as the Rail Regulator conceded, such a system may involve 'some uncertainty over the future levels of costs for franchisees' (para. 1.34).

The designers of franchising regimes have to seek to allocate risks fairly and in a manner optimizing incentives, but also in a way that allows the locus of risk-taking to be identified and the risks made capable of estimating. If franchisees are fearful of risks, their bids will reflect this, and consumers or taxpayers will suffer, since higher prices or subsidies will result.

A further consideration in allocating risks is the degree of control over costs that a franchisee enjoys. Franchisees may be wary if asked, as in rail, to bear revenue risks (with regulatory constraints) yet have high proportions of their costs fixed by mechanisms beyond their control. In terms of incentives (to bid and operate), it may be appropriate to allocate risks with an eye to those who are able to affect the relevant costs and risks.

INTEGRATION AND SEPARATION

As noted, problems of specification increase in so far as an operation is vertically separated. Within an integrated system, problems of coordination are dealt with through a central command structure. Where there is vertical separation, a complex network of contracts substitutes for the command structure. Such contracts, in an efficient system, have to force providers to internalize the costs of their own sub-optimal performance. This can be done by providing, for example in a rail context, that the infrastructure company will compensate the train-operating franchisee for track failures according to a pre-specified scale that is based on service disruption and losses of revenue. The terms of such contracts can, in theory, provide full compensation and create optimal incentives throughout the system. In practice, there may be high costs involved in writing, monitoring, and enforcing contracts that cover all contingencies (and if these cannot be anticipated, added uncertainties will affect the system). Where such contracts are used, providers, moreover, may adopt rigid, rule-bound, practices that lead to inefficiencies.

Again, bidders who anticipate such problems might be expected to reduce their bids accordingly. The costs to consumers or the public purse (depending on the mode of franchise allocation) will be greater in a system of franchising that is based on vertical separation than one in which an integrated operation is franchised. The case for franchising a vertically integrated system may also be strong where there is a need to encourage a franchisee to make complementary investments in infrastructure and operating equipment.

Vertical separation, nevertheless, has been employed in complex utilities, for example, in the Swedish railway industry, and is said to bring a number of advantages. First, it allows identification of those parts of an operation that can be made the subject of effective franchising regimes. Second, it paves the way for developing a stable of potentially competing operators and, third, it reduces the difficulties faced by potential competitors to a vertically integrated incumbent where the latter controls access to (and the quality of) the infrastructure or network.

In the final analysis, the competitive advantages of vertical separation have to be balanced against the superior coordination and incentives to invest that are associated with integrated systems. In effecting this balance, the costs of the uncertainties and contractual controls encountered in vertical separation should not be underestimated—particularly in a complex sector such as rail. Vertical separation also brings potential problems of network coordination. Thus, a criticism of rail franchising in Britain has been that operators have been slow to provide route or ticketing information concerning the services of other operators.[21]

PRICE CONTROLS AND COMPETITION

Specifying the regime of price control may be approached in a number of ways. Pricing freedom may be allowed in a competitive market (for example, Channel 3 TV franchisees may charge for advertising as the market will bear). Prices may be fixed by the franchiser, or pricing limits may be imposed. Where, as in rail, different regulators control access charges and fares structures, a level of regulatory coordination is required.

Much depends here on the franchising philosophy adopted and the priority given to encouraging competition. The following broad approaches to franchising can be contrasted:

Competition for the market—consumer benefits are gained by offering an exclusive market and by using a system of competitive bids to serve this.

---

[21] For critical comment, see C. Woolmar, *The Great British Railway Disaster* (London, 1996). The Rail Regulator responded to such tardiness—*inter alia* by imposing fines on train operators for failing to meet targets on answering calls to the National Rail Enquiry Service promptly.

Promises made in bidding are then enforced and detailed service specifications used to protect consumers.

Competition for and within the market—competitive bids to serve are employed and promises of service are enforced, but the service may be defined flexibly and the right to serve the market is not exclusive. Guarantees concerning protection from competition are limited or absent. An incremental approach to competition may be adopted.

Examples of the first approach have been seen in the UK water industry and of the second approach in independent local radio (ILR) and rail. In ILR franchising no guarantees are offered on freedom from competition within a geographic area. The railways regime seeks also to combine franchising with competition, but the Secretary of State for Transport may give exclusive use of the infrastructure to a franchisee if he judges this to be necessary for expeditious franchising of the service.[22]

In the early years of passenger rail franchising, the general problem of uncertain specification of potential exposure to competition was summarized by the Rail Regulator:

At the time at which they make bids, franchisees are unlikely to have reliable information about the extent of the competition they might face and the impact of competition on the finances of their franchise. In such circumstances, they are likely to err on the side of caution, discount the risk excessively and thus reflect less than the full value of the franchise in their bids.[23]

THE FRANCHISE TERM

The duration of a franchise affects, amongst other things, the incentive to bid for the franchise, the continuity and quality of the service offered, infrastructure investment, and the effectiveness with which the franchiser holds the franchisee to promises given during the competition for the franchise.[24] In specifying the franchise, term: two main issues arise, first, the extent of the term itself and,

---

[22] See the Railways Act 1993 as amended by the Transport Act 2000 and the Railways Act 2005. In 2006, the Secretary of State for Transport took over the franchising functions of the Strategic Rail Authority, which took over those of the Director of Passenger Rail Franchising in 2001.

[23] Rail Regulator, *Competition for Railway Passenger Services* (London, 1994), 12; also D. Kennedy, *Competition in the British Rail Industry* (London, 1996). Such uncertainties can cost taxpayers huge sums. In March 1998, the National Audit Office (NAO) reported on the Conservative government's sell-off of the British Rail leasing companies. The NAO concluded that the companies had been worth £2.9 billion but had been sold for £1.8 billion (within two years, indeed, the initial buyers had sold at a profit of £850 million), and that uncertainties about the privatization and regulatory processes for rail had reduced numbers of bidders for the companies and the prices they were prepared to offer (see *Financial Times*, 5 Mar. 1988).

[24] See Williamson, 'Franchise Bidding for National Monopolies'; Domberger, 'Regulation through Franchise Contracts'; Kennedy, *Competition in the British Rail Industry*.

second, whether there should be provision made for adjusting or 'rolling' the franchise term.

On the term itself, it is usual to effect a trade-off between factors such as saleability, continuity, and investment-enhancing, on the one hand, and quality of service enforcement on the other. Where large sunk investments are involved in an operation, a long-term franchise may be necessary to combat incentives to under-investment.[25] Under-investment in infrastructure would not be a problem if a displaced incumbent could be accurately compensated for investments made during the franchise term (for example, by providing that the franchiser will repurchase assets at fair market value). Some investment activities, however, are not readily measurable. Accounting choices (for example, asset depreciation rates) are contentious and there may be considerable sunk costs involved in planning and implementing large-scale investment projects. This suggests that where franchise terms are short (in comparison with the lives of relevant assets), these will prove expensive in terms of subsidy, even if there is competition in the bidding process. The disadvantage of long-term contracts (as indicated in the French water industry) is that incumbents become difficult to remove, new entrants are discouraged, and franchising turns into a scheme of regulation. Against this, the long-term contract may encourage service innovation by offering a longer period in which to recoup the costs of innovation.

London Bus contracts normally last three years; in ILR franchising, as noted, the usual term is eight years; Ofcom's Channel 3 franchises run for ten years; and rail operator franchises are likely to be offered for seven years or a little longer. In the rail industry around the world, franchise terms vary from one year up to thirty years.

Experience to date indicates that franchisers in some sectors put a high premium on continuity and are happy to roll franchise contracts. Foster has argued that franchise renewal has tended to become automatic, as was generally the case with public utility franchises throughout most of the nineteenth century, and as has been the case with cable television franchises in the United States.[26]

The Channel 3 franchising system, for instance, gives considerable security to franchise holders. Although a franchisee receives a ten-year contract, one or more applications for a ten-year renewal period may be made during the last four years of the contract and may only be refused when Ofcom is not satisfied that the licensee would provide a service in compliance with the

---

[25] In April 2009, the Competition Commission recommended that UK Train franchises should be of 12 to 15 years' duration, double the then normal period, to give operators more incentive to purchase new carriages and negotiate better terms with leasing companies—Competition Commission, *Rolling Stock Leasing Market Investigation* (7 April 2009), para. 59.

[26] See C.D. Foster, *Privatisation, Public Ownership and the Regulation of Natural Monopoly* (Oxford, 1992), 202; J. Vickers and G. Yarrow, *Privatisation: An Economic Analysis* (1988), 110–15; M.A. Zupan, 'The Efficiency of Franchise Bidding Schemes in the Case of Cable Television' (1989) 32 *Journal of Law and Economics* 401.

conditions in the existing licence or with legislative requirements on types of programme to be offered; or where Ofcom intends to grant a new licence on the basis of a different regional map or division of the broadcasting clock; or where it appears to Ofcom that the franchisee's sources of funds are such that renewal would not be in the public interest. Ofcom may, however, fix new financial terms where it grants a renewal—it may thus determine a sum that it considers would have been payable in a cash bid had it been granting a fresh licence under competitive tendering conditions.

In Channel 3 franchising, the original idea was to use ten-year contracts and then have new competitions. The decision to move to rolling contracts (taken at Cabinet level) was based partially on the view that controls through the market for corporate control were more appropriate in this sector than controls imposed by the franchiser. However, such a strategy places a low priority on enforcement of promises made in franchise applications, on controlling quality of service, and on competition for the market as a provider of incentives to efficiency.

TRANSFERS OF THE FRANCHISE

Two major problems may arise under this heading: first, the franchise may be assigned to another party, second, the ownership of the franchise may change in a substantial manner.[27] On the first issue, transfers are usually not allowed without permission. Thus it is a condition of Regional Channel 3 licences that the licence should not be transferred except with the prior consent in writing of Ofcom. Transport for London imposes a similar condition upon successful tenderers as does Ofcom in relation to ILR franchising. As for changes in the composition of the franchisee, Ofcom not only reserves the right to revoke ILR licences on changes occurring which 'affect the nature and characteristics' of the licensee, but it also requires prompt notification to the authority of any change in ownership of shares carrying 30 per cent or more of voting rights.

COMPETITION FOR FRANCHISES

Franchise bidders will only undertake to behave in the manner that they would adopt in a competitive market if there is effective competition in the process of allocating franchises. Such competition calls for sufficient numbers of adequately informed parties who are keen to obtain franchises and who are

---

[27] Windfall gains may give rise to controversy on changes in ownership. In March 1998, the Deputy Prime Minister, John Prescott, criticized the 'excessive profits' made by directors of privatized rail companies and hinted that he was considering ways to curb these. During that month the directors of Great Western Holdings (a franchised operator) were considering selling their business, and multi-million pound personal profits for directors were being discussed—see *Financial Times*, 4 Mar. 1998.

not deterred by undue costs or uncertainties. A good deal has been said above on the uncertainties that flow from problems of specification or from regulatory, governmental, or operational and technical unknowns. A further factor that may affect numbers of competitors in a franchising round is the imposition of a pre-qualification requirement—one that restricts entry into the franchise competition to 'approved' categories.

Pre-assessment may reduce bidding numbers, but it can be seen as a means of achieving greater precision in the franchise allocation criteria in so far as all bidders will have passed a worthiness hurdle. Such a process is used to establish bidders' credentials. Only those that can show sound financial backing and an array of skills which appear likely to enable the firm to operate the franchise within the contract specification will be permitted to bid.

A particular worry in utility franchising is that bidding numbers may be so small that real competition is not possible. In London bus franchising, for example, it has been quite common for there to be only two or three interested bidders.[28] The National Audit Office has, however, noted that a good level of competition was achieved for the first three passenger rail franchises.[29]

In general terms, the best way to encourage bidders is to reduce the associated uncertainties. The greater the uncertainties felt by potential bidders, the smaller the expected number of bidders will be, the lower the final contract price will be, and the more likely it will be that post-contract renegotiation problems will arise. Another key variable determining the number of bidders, as indicated, is the cost of bidding. Typically, bidders will bear their own costs. The more complex the franchising process, the fewer the number of bidders in equilibrium.[30] Actual reckonings of bidding costs are hard to come by, but estimates range from between US $5 and US $15 (1984 prices) per home served to obtain a cable television franchise.[31] Some Channel 3 television licence bids in the UK in 1991 are said to have cost £1 million.

ENFORCEMENT

Holding franchisees to their promises is essential if franchise allocations are to be seen as fair and if the virtues of competing for the market are to be reaped.

---

[28] See S. Glaister and M. Beesley, *Bidding for Tendered Bus Routes in London* (London, 1990). In the case of CATV in the United States, the average number of bidders per franchise was four or five (Zupan, 'The Efficiency of Franchise Bidding Schemes'). The 1991 Channel 3 television allocation round has been said to have involved aggressive rivalry, with collusion not a problem, but some incumbents were unopposed and some successful bids were notably small, for example, in the case of television areas Central Scotland, and Border: A. W. Dnes, 'Bidding for Commercial Broadcasting' (1993) 40 *Scottish Journal of Political Economics* 104.

[29] See Comptroller and Auditor-General, *Office of Passenger Rail Franchising*.

[30] See M. Canoy and M. Waterson, *Tendering, Auctions and Preparation Costs*, Discussion Paper No. 31, University of Reading (1991).

[31] M.A. Zupan, 'Non-price Concessions and the Effect of Franchise Bidding Schemes on Cable Company Costs' (1989) 21 *Applied Economics* 305.

However, since franchise specifications may incorporate flexibility and may grant franchisers a degree of discretion in the enforcement function, franchisers will commonly fulfil regulatory as well as purely enforcement roles. (It was, for example, upon the ITC's insistence in 1993 that the idea of moving News at Ten to 6.30 or 7.00 p.m. was dropped.)

INFORMATION

A first aspect of enforcement is the collection of information by the franchiser. Present franchise contracts in the UK radio, television, and transport industries routinely impose conditions concerning the supply of data on issues that are relevant in evaluating the quality of the service delivered and the extent to which promises of performance are being fulfilled.

MONITORING

Franchisers routinely monitor service quality rather than simply trust the data supplied by the franchisee. Thus, Transport for London engages in comprehensive revenue collection and control monitoring (involving uniformed and plain clothes staff). On-vehicle spot checks are conducted and service performance reporting is continuously carried out. Qualitative appraisals and specific complaints investigations are also conducted, and standardized reporting on, for example, accidents and health and safety issues occurs.

In transport franchising, the monitoring of quality might be expected to be less problematic than in some sectors, since performance and service quality is to a significant extent measurable in terms of quantitative data (on, for example, volumes, revenues, services not operated, punctuality, lost mileage, and reliability). Some problems have, nevertheless, been encountered. Thus, in February 1988, the National Audit Office (NAO) called on the rail Franchising Director, John O'Brien, to tighten procedures for verifying the train performance information provided by operators. The system under review involved Railtrack collecting much of the relevant data, but the NAO stated that the Franchising Director ought to obtain independent auditing and verification of the systems and data involved.[32] Where service quality assessments are more complex and involve the judgements of the franchiser—as in Channel 3 television franchising by Ofcom—then in addition to the information-collecting and monitoring techniques already described, franchisers may find it useful to carry out more formal periodic reviews.

---

[32] See *Financial Times*, 6 Feb. 1988.

SANCTIONS

Presently established franchising schemes give franchisers a number of sanctions for potential use. The following are common:

- powers to give directions;
- notices of non-compliance and warnings;[33]
- regulatory powers;
- fines;[34]
- reductions in the franchise term;
- suspensions;[35]
- revocation.

Franchisers are sometimes alleged by commentators to be in a weak position to sanction franchisees because there is a danger of lack of continuity of service (the 'blank screens' problem).[36] Experience in the broadcasting field indicates that where substitutability is high, this problem can be exaggerated. Thus, there would be little danger of blank screens on Channel 3 following a franchise revocation, since present technology would allow programmes from other franchisees to be transferred across to fill gaps. In some sectors, potential entrants to the market may be waiting in the wings, eager to show their mettle.

CROSS-SUBSIDIZATION

In the absence of problems of overbidding, most franchisers do not worry unduly concerning the extent to which a franchisee is fulfilling service

---

[33] The rail Franchising Director employs a system of warnings. The first stage involves a franchisee being 'called-in' to the Director's office to explain a service failure. Three call-ins within a three-year period, or a single more serious failure, will trigger a 'breach' in the regulations, which is then made public and can lead to a penalty being levied. Very serious failures to meet performance targets, known as 'defaults', can lead to the loss of a franchise. In the ten months to February 1998, eleven operators were called-in a total of 20 times to explain service failures (compared to five operators being called-in 8 times in the previous year). After three call-ins the Director usually negotiates packages of improvements, rather than imposes fines. National Express agreed in January 1998 to provide an extra £500,000 of passenger benefits as compensation for missing its deadline on introducing new trains to the Gatwick Express franchise. In March 1997, the Franchising Director threatened to fine South West Trains £1m if the company failed to satisfy him that the previously encountered level of train cancellations would not recur.

[34] In 1994, Granada Television was fined £500,000 by the ITC. The Rail Regulator has imposed fines on licence holders and employed a 'sliding scale' to punish very poor performance more heavily than performance that has just missed the target—see his Submission to the Department of Trade's 1997 *Review of Utility Regulation*, 4. In the autumn of 1997, the Rail Regulator imposed fines totalling £350,000 on train operators for failing to meet the target for promptly answering calls to the National Rail Enquiry Service. The Rail Regulator has, however, noted that fines, unlike compulsory rebates, do not compensate consumers for poor service delivery.

[35] See Broadcasting Act 1990 S. 110 (1) (c).

[36] See Foster, *Privatisation*, 202.

promises by effecting cross-subsidies from non-franchised to franchised operations. Franchisers tend to take the view that the relevant markets will regulate the extent of such cross-subsidies quite effectively.

NON-RENEWAL AS A CONTROL

As noted above, franchisers, when setting the term of the franchise, effect a balance between creating incentives to invest and increasing the enforceability of contracts. The shorter the term, the greater the enforcement leverage becomes (providing that a pool of potential competitors exists and incumbent advantages do not insulate the present franchisee). A cited danger of franchising is a form of capture in which renewals of franchises become automatic (cable television franchises in the USA are cited as an example).[37] Designers of franchising systems might, accordingly, be advised to instruct franchisers to make explicit any undertakings concerning continuity that are relied upon.

ENFORCEMENT, REGULATION, AND CHANGE

As indicated, bodies such as Ofcom have had to engage in extensive negotiations with franchisees concerning not merely the specification of contractual conditions but also the adaptation of those conditions to changed circumstances. Changes may even necessitate regulatory responses from the franchisers and occur under a number of headings:

The market. This may provide varying degrees of competition for the franchisee and, in turn, the appropriate levels of franchise specification and regulation may change.

Access. If the conditions and prices of access to networks vary over time, then the franchiser may have to act to control such variations (if this is possible) or may have to make allowances in holding the franchisee to promises made in a different context.

Regulatory/governmental changes. Enforcement has to adjust to both changes in demands made of franchisees by regulators and variations in governmental constraints.

Technological changes. These, as noted above, may demand a change of role in the franchiser from enforcer to organizer/regulator in so far as new advances change the nature of operations and have to be responded to in a coordinated fashion.

Legal innovations. New statutes or judicial rulings may alter market and regulatory conditions. Enforcement activity, again, may have to adjust.

---

[37] See Foster, *Privatisation*, 202.

Franchisees will often seek to renegotiate contractual terms, fees paid, or subsidies given—because they have overbid, made erroneous calculations, or suffered genuine changes in their costs. In a sector such as rail, where the costs of franchisees are to a large degree a product of regulatory decisions, the case for renegotiating may be strong and relatively easily evaluated. Where costs are market-determined, the franchiser may refuse to make concessions on the grounds that franchisees must bear the risks of miscalculation rather than shift these to taxpayers or consumers.

INTERDEPENDENCY

Enforcing franchisee promises becomes more difficult in so far as the franchisee is not responsible for all aspects of service provision, or where service deficiencies flow from the actions of others. Thus, if several franchisees were to run trains on the same track, the trains of efficient operator A might be delayed by the breakdowns of inefficient operator B's trains on the track ahead. (If one franchisee operates all the trains, the costs and revenue effects of such breakdowns fall fully on that provider.) Similar problems arise when there is separation of train operation, track, signalling, etc. Franchise contracts, in such situations, have to provide a complex network of compensatory provisions if all parties in separated operations are to bear the costs of their own failings. The administrative costs associated with such compensation schemes may be considerable.

ENFORCEMENT AND INCENTIVES TO EFFICIENCY

Franchisers who possess discretion, for example to control price boundaries, may wish to impose incentives to efficiency on franchisees. Thus, a system of RPI–X price controls might be adopted, with X growing incrementally. This would inject a strong regulatory dimension into franchising and, as noted, would affect bidding. The negative effects of such a pursuit of incentives may, however, be reduced in so far as the limits of such devices are set out clearly in advance (for example, by stipulating a ceiling for X or a maximum increase within a specified period). Franchisees are discouraged not so much by rigour in controls as by uncertainty.

As for incentives to invest, these will be greatest where the incumbent enjoys a high level of security in the franchise. If enforcement considerations demand a lack of security because there exist, for example, important variations in service quality, the appropriate response may lie in the approach to separation of the industry that is taken. The solution may be to retain infrastructure provision in one set of hands, organized according to certain timescales, and to franchise out operational matters according to a shorter time frame. This is the strategy seen in rail franchising at present.

TERMINATION AND REFRANCHISING

A claimed strength of franchising is that repeating tendering processes can reduce dangers of malperformance.[38] Williamson, however, has argued that the incumbent advantages at refranchising are so considerable that no real competition can take place; that, since both the incumbent and franchiser understand these advantages, the incumbent is afforded a good deal of leeway before the franchiser will terminate the contract for malperformance.[39]

Williamson identified two aspects of termination costs which, he predicted, would lead to contract performance problems: first, psychological costs on the part of publicly accountable officials—who would not want to attract attention to performance problems and so cast doubts on their own roles. Second, he pointed to the costs of gathering and interpreting information, including auditing costs, together with the expenses of the quasi-judicial hearings and appeals that would need to take place prior to termination. These would provide a disincentive on the part of officials to represent consumers' interests vigorously.

It can be responded, however, that franchisees do bear some potential costs of malperformance. Most utility franchising will involve the franchisee making highly specific investments for which there is a wholly inadequate second-hand market. These investments may be partially stranded by disciplinary actions on the part of the franchiser.

Franchisees do nevertheless enjoy certain incumbency advantages. Thus, on-the-job experience provides the franchisee with information not available to other (new) bidders. This informational asymmetry also applies between incumbent and franchiser.

In long-term utility franchise contracts, the incumbent operator is usually expected to undertake a programme of investment to maintain the long-term viability of the utility. Depreciation methods designed to yield valuations at the end of a franchise period are notoriously difficult to define with exactitude, especially in industries characterized by changing technology, and maintenance expenditure undertaken during contract fulfilment is unobservable and open to manipulation.[40]

Such incumbent advantages obtain both during the term of the franchise and when it comes to franchise renewal. In expectation of these advantages, bidders will enhance their bids in anticipation of being able to renegotiate the contract once operations are underway. However, as noted above, where a franchisee has more than one franchise, or is interested in acquiring other

[38] R. Posner, 'The Appropriate Scope of Regulation in the Cable Television Industry' (1972) 3 *Bell Journal of Economics* 98.
[39] Williamson, 'Franchise Bidding for National Monopolies'.
[40] Zupan, 'Non-price Concessions'.

franchises, it will have horizontal reputational concerns. In industries with a large number of franchises, the evidence suggests that track records are important to franchisers when assessing bids.

At the stage of contract renewal, the incumbent advantage centres on the superior information held by the incumbent and the real advantages associated with learning by doing. The result may be that the level of competition is limited. Where investment is fully transferable, any cost savings resulting from investment by the incumbent are transferred to the replacement operator, which leaves the incumbent with insufficient incentive to invest. It then becomes optimal for franchisers to favour incumbents at refranchising so as to improve their incentives to invest.

Some regulatory regimes have tried to find a middle way at franchise renewal. The 1990 UK Broadcasting Act introduced a procedure for firms to compete for certain regional broadcasting licences, based upon competitive bidding.[41] The regulator could renew the licence if the incumbent offered an amount which, in the regulator's opinion, would be payable to them if the regulator re-offered the licence. Under the 2003 Communications Act, the wording was changed to require the regulator to determine the amount which, in its opinion, would have been the cash bid of the licence holder in a competitive tender were the licence being granted afresh.

The procedure was designed to permit continuity if the licensee offered a competitive price. It left open, however, the issue of how exactly the 'competitive price' would be calculated. One approach is to calculate a price which leaves the licensee, on an expectations basis, with no abnormal profit. It was pointed out, however, that bidders in most auction processes do not simply bid an amount equal to their whole profit. Instead, they bid what they think is necessary to beat the next highest bid. In any event, the existing licensees had their licences renewed.

The broadcasters in question possessed comparatively few assets which were specific to the activity in question. In the case of a capital-intensive utility with substantial specific assets, in addition to the normal requirements for the regulation of a utility, asset valuations must be determined whenever refranchising occurs. Asset valuation problems derive from the inadequacy of formal accounting to provide values that will be accepted by all sides. The root cause of the problem is that information is imperfect and asymmetric, and thus affords the players room to influence the version of 'accounting' reality adopted. Investment in infrastructure and maintenance is not perfectly observable or verifiable and companies' accounts are not designed with franchising and regulation in mind.

---

[41] See K. Binmore, D. Harbord, and A. Hernando, 'Reviewing the Financial Terms of Channel 3 Licences: Estimating Incumbents' Bids', ITV mimeo (London, 2004).

Conclusions: Circumstances Favourable to Franchising

We have defined franchising as an arrangement whereby a course of operation is tendered by a franchisee in a competitive context and in which the franchisee bears at least some of both cost and revenue risks. Moreover, the franchiser and franchisee have a continuing relationship, with the former monitoring the latter in respect of quality of performance. The prospect of renewal also acts as a form of control. As a consequence, the franchisee must operate for a finite period—not so long that the present value of any activities after its termination is negligible.

What characteristics of an activity suggest that franchising will produce desired objectives effectively? The above discussion points to the following factors:

Openness to competition for the market. The service in question must be such that a number of firms are available to supply it and thus constitute potential franchisees. Without this characteristic, there will be no prospect of competition for the market. Franchising, accordingly, would not be an option where a proprietary technology necessary to operate the franchise is exclusively available to one firm.

Restrictions on competition in the market. If a franchise is to have any value, it must be possible to impose a limitation on entry by unfranchised rivals.

Duration. The activity must be such that a franchise contract can be formulated for a period of time which allows further competitions for new franchises.

Specification of the service. The activity to be undertaken by the franchisee has to be capable of specification in advance if it is to form the basis of a competitive franchising process. Similarly, the uncertainties attaching to the activity have to be acceptable to those competing for the franchises and must not result in excessive costs to the public purse or excessive prices to consumers. Major uncertainties are likely to relate to markets, access prices, regulatory constraints, and governmental influences. However, the activity need not be fully specified *ex ante*. If the allocation process is to be a multidimensional one, then other aspects, apart from price, need not be fully specified.

Allocation of risks. The contract must allocate cost and revenue risks explicitly between franchisee and franchiser.

Observability. It must be possible for the franchiser, at reasonable cost, to monitor adherence to the franchise agreements in respect of those attributes which are recorded in the contract.

Enforceability. The franchiser must be able to hold franchisees to their promises. This demands that alternative providers be available and can be substituted without unacceptable service interruption or transaction costs.

Transferability of assets. It must be possible for the franchiser to transfer, or to arrange the transfer of, relevant assets to each successive franchisee.

Valuation. In cases where payments are made in respect of the franchise, it must be feasible to establish its value. However, monetary transfers may be in either direction and accordingly franchising is quite practicable for loss-making operations, as well as for extracting positive rents.

Market failure. In some areas, unconstrained competition may lead to market failure. Franchising may overcome this by appropriate specification of the service.

The case for franchising weakens, and arguments for regulating strengthen, when these preconditions for effective franchising are so poorly established that the benefits of a competition for the market cannot be achieved. In such circumstances, the franchiser is likely, in any event, to be forced to adopt strong regulatory methods to achieve its designated objectives.

Combining franchising and regulation, it should be borne in mind, may produce the worst of both worlds. Competing for the market may be pointless where uncertainties exceed a certain level. The effect will be to regulate after selecting the regulatee in a highly inefficient manner. Thus, the unknowns attaching to anticipated regulatory actions may combine with other uncertainties and may distort bids in a way that imposes unacceptably high costs on the public or consumers of services. Under conditions of high uncertainty, the regulation of service providers who are selected by a method other than by competitive bidding may prove more appropriate than franchising.

When should franchising be seen as the first-choice mode of governmental influence? The case for franchising is at its strongest when limitations on market entry are justified and when the above preconditions for successful franchising are encountered (see Table 9.1). As for types of franchise, the key considerations relevant to the choice of owning versus operating franchises are the following. In favour of an operating franchise it can be noted that the short franchise duration implies frequent rounds of competition and that there should be few problems with asset transfer. Against this, however, operating franchises may involve weak incentives both to look after assets and to choose cost minimizing input combinations.

Factors in favour of ownership franchises are their tendency to promote efficient choices of technique and avoid inefficient modes of production. Counting against ownership franchises are, however, the excessive incumbent advantages that may be found at renewal, the relative infrequency of renewals, and the difficulties of asset valuation. These considerations suggest that, broadly speaking, an operating franchise is likely to be more appropriate when: limited technical choices are available; the franchisee's use of the assets can be monitored, and negligence penalized; idiosyncrasy of assets makes valuation difficult; and the activity is relatively unintensive in the use of capital. An ownership franchise, by contrast, is likely to be more desirable when the industry is capital intensive; substantial variation in choice of techniques makes efficient, well-informed investment decisions crucial; and when assets are general-purpose, facilitating valuation at franchise termination.

In the right circumstances, franchising is capable both of extracting monopoly profits, otherwise seen in the form of excess returns or inefficiency, and of encouraging the efficient use, and in some cases the efficient development, of infrastructure.

One of the great merits of franchising is its flexibility, in particular the ability to match the form and duration of the franchise contract to the particular conditions in operation. As more experience of franchising is accumulated, and as its effects come to be analysed, it should become easier to match the form of franchising with the particular circumstances encountered. Whether franchising is appropriate in any particular set of circumstances will depend on whether the preconditions set out above can be satisfied. It should be emphasized, however, that franchising does not solve, at a stroke, the difficulties that are commonly associated with traditional command and control styles of regulation (for example, setting appropriate standards, overcoming legal complexities, informational and enforcement issues) (see Table 9.2). In so far as the preconditions for effective franchising do not obtain, any franchising regime employed may rapidly come to manifest the characteristics of less successful versions of command and control regulation.

Turning from the efficient pursuit of legitimate objectives to considerations of accountability, due process, and expertise, it should be noted that franchising regimes are to be judged on these criteria as much as command and control or other regulatory mechanisms. Thus, franchising authorities should be expected to be as accountable as any other regulatory bodies (or Directors General) and the processes whereby the terms of franchises are set and enforced should be designed to be as transparent, accessible, and fair as other regulatory mechanisms. This demands, for instance, adequate disclosures and consultations on draft franchise contracts. (Proper scope for the exercise of expert judgements by franchisers should, however, be allowed within such regimes.) Franchising normally operates as a competition to offer a defined service, but resort to a competitive allocative process should not be seen as a substitute for accountability and openness concerning the nature of the service to be offered or the steps taken to ensure delivery.

Table 9.1. Allocating franchises

Modes of franchise allocation	Advantages	Problems
Bidding on price per unit	Identifies most efficient producer.	Limited usefulness when variety of products is to be provided. Price rigidity may restrict responsiveness to demand and technological change.
Bidding by lump sum	Raises funds for Treasury.	Consumers suffer from inefficiencies of monopolistic pricing and output levels. Monopoly rents remain. If prices specified in advance, responsiveness will be low.
Bidding for lowest lump sum subsidy	Reduces costs to public purse.	Price specification produces rigidity difficulties. Initial controls on price may have to be relaxed in return for higher service quality.
Marginal return bidding	Useful when franchisee erects infrastructure. Limits cost inflation problems in procurement contracting.	Franchisee may enjoy considerable room for manœuvre within the franchise contract.
Menu auctions	Bids can be made on a mix of quality and price. Renders a stock of private information available for franchiser's use and this reduces uncertainties.	Identifying winning bid raises contentious issues. Less transparency than in, e.g., price-per-unit bidding.

Table 9.2. Franchising problems

General problem	Particular difficulties
Service specification	Poor specification produces uncertainties which raise costs to consumers.
	Wide service variation makes specification especially difficult.
	If judgements are involved, bureaucrats become judges of market preferences.
	Tension between specification for bidding purposes and catering for flexibility to respond to market demands and changes or technological advances.
	Specifying regulatory regimes and price restrictions for extended periods.
	Stating how risks are allocated.
	Indicating potential exposure to competition.
	Vertical separation increases specification problems.
	Fixing a franchise term that facilitates enforcement but encourages bidding and investment.
Allocating franchises competitively	Is there a pool of potential bidders?
	Will uncertainties deter bidders?
	Collusion and secrecy of bidding.
	Costs of bidding.
	Overbidding to discourage competitors.
	Incumbency advantages.
Enforcement of franchise terms	Information on performance.
	Need to monitor and collect information directly.
	Can sanctions be exercized?
	Tension with need to encourage bidding by giving security and long terms in franchises.
	Distinguishing 'genuine' renegotiations (due to changes in the market) from manipulative franchisee behaviour.
	Where difficult to locate cause of poor performance (e.g. because of interdependency of operations).
Termination and refranchising	Incumbent advantages (e.g. information asymmetry).
	Valuation of assets.
	Creating incentives to invest and maintain long-term viability.

10 Emissions Trading

As indicated in Chapter 7, an alternative to the application of controls through 'command' instruments is the use of tradable permit regimes in which a public agency issues a given number of permits to engage in a specified course of behaviour (e.g. discharging a pollutant up to a fixed amount). Following the initial allocation, permits may be traded and this encourages permit holders to reduce emissions and to sell their excess allowances to other firms. The initial distribution of permits may be carried out by auction or according to public interest criteria and the incentives within such systems are provided by the market in permits, rather than by any regulatory body.

This chapter considers the use of such tradable permits in the context of polluting emissions. It examines the points of contention raised by emissions trading and it looks to identify the conditions for successfully using the device. What is clear from the start is that this is a control strategy of huge importance both within jurisdictions and on the world stage. The Kyoto Protocol[1] of 1997 established emissions trading as a key instrument in the control of global greenhouse gases and, in 2006, the Stern Review advocated the broad use of trading mechanisms to combat climate change.[2] Following Stern, the UK and the EU have led the way in promoting emissions trading worldwide as a main response to climate change.[3]

The Development of Emissions Trading

The first large-scale, long-term US environmental programme to rely on trading emissions permits was the 1990s US Acid Rain Programme.[4] By

[1] Kyoto Protocol to the UN Framework Convention on Climate Change (FCCC) 1997.

[2] N. Stern, *The Economics of Climate Change* (London, 2006) (hereafter 'Stern Review'); see also the comment in J. Freeman and C. Kolstad (eds), *Moving to Markets in Environmental Regulation* (Oxford, 2006), 4: 'Over the past two decades the superiority of market-based instruments has developed into a virtual orthodoxy.' See also D. Driesen, 'Alternatives to Regulation? Market Mechanisms and the Environment' in R. Baldwin, M. Cave, and M. Lodge (eds), *The Oxford Handbook of Regulation* (Oxford, 2010).

[3] See S.-J. Clifton, *A Dangerous Obsession* (London, 2009).

[4] See D. Ellerman, R. Schmalensee, E. Bailey, P. Joskow, and J.-P. Montero, *Markets for Clean Air: The US Acid Rain Program* (Cambridge, 2000); OECD, *Implementing Domestic Tradable Permits* (Paris,

January 2005 the EU Emissions Trading Scheme had been launched[5] in an effort to control greenhouse gas emissions from specific heavy industries in the EU[6] and, since that date, emissions trading markets have emerged around the world as the method of choice to price carbon.[7] In 2009, national carbon trading schemes were established or planned in 35 countries worldwide and figures for 2008 put the value of the global carbon market at US $126 billion.

Emissions trading mechanisms have numerous dimensions and there are many varieties of such systems. A basic distinction lies between 'cap and trade' and 'baseline and credit' approaches.[8] Under the former, a fixed number of permits are created and each allows the emission of a stipulated amount of pollutant. These permits are allocated or auctioned to firms, who are then free to trade them on the open market.[9] In a baseline and credit regime, companies are given performance targets or 'baselines'—often set with reference to business as usual projections—and they can generate credits by beating their emissions targets. Such credits may then be traded on the open market. With cap and trade, there is a fixed supply of permits for trading, whereas in baseline and credit the supply of credits for trading depends on the performance of permit holders in generating credits by reducing emissions below baselines.[10]

2002); and generally OECD, *Lessons from Existing Trading Systems for International Greenhouse Gas Emission Trading* (Paris, 1998); *Greenhouse Gas Emissions Trading and Project-Based Mechanism* (Paris, 2004); Environmental Protection Agency (EPA), *The United States Experience with Economic Incentives for Protecting the Environment* (EPA 2001: EPA-240-R-01-001).

[5] See Directive 2003/87/EC of the European Parliament and of the Council of 13 October 2003 establishing a scheme for greenhouse gas emission allowance trading within the Community and amending Council Directive 96/61/EC. The ETS covers the energy sector; iron and steel production and processing; the mineral, the wood pulp, and the paper and card industries. The system provides for: National Allocation Plans; a system of individual permits; a mechanism to monitor compliance and impose penalties; and a market for emissions trading between the participating parties. See European Environment Agency, 'Using the Market for Cost-Effective Environment Policy' (Copenhagen, 2006); M. Faure and M. Peeters (eds), *Climate Change and European Emissions Trading* (Cheltenham, 2008); J. Skjaerseth and J. Wettestad, *EU Emissions Trading: Initiation, Decision-Making and Implementation* (Aldershot, 2008); D. Ellerman, F. Convery, and C. de Perthuis (eds), *Pricing Carbon: The European Union Emissions Trading Scheme* (Cambridge, 2010); D. Ellerman, B. Buchner, and C. Carraro (eds), *Allocation in the European Emissions Trading Scheme: Rights, Rents and Fairness* (Cambridge, 2011).

[6] In its first phase, in 2005–7, the EU ETS regulated CO_2 emissions from installations representing around 40 per cent of EU emissions—see World Bank, *The State and Trends of the Carbon Market 2007* (Washington, DC, 2007).

[7] See R. Baldwin, 'Regulation Lite: The Rise of Emissions Trading' (2008) 2 *Regulation and Governance* 193.

[8] See OECD, *Implementing Domestic Tradable Permits* (OECD, 2002).

[9] There are four main ways to allocate permits: random access (lotteries); first come, first served; administrative rules based on eligibility criteria; and auctions—see T. Tietenberg, 'Tradable Permits in Principle and Practice' in J. Freeman and C. Kolstad (eds), *Moving to Markets in Environmental Regulation* (Oxford, 2006), 80.

[10] In a baseline and credit system aggregate emissions are not fixed in cases where they operate on emission rates (per tonne of output) from individual sources. When targets are based on emission

As for ways to classify trading mechanisms, an authoritative system is that proposed by the US Environmental Protection Agency in 2001.[11] This refers to eight basic characteristics (such as mode of allocating permits or type of limit on emissions)[12] and emissions trading mechanisms vary considerably across such properties. Different characteristics bring different strengths and weaknesses.[13] Cap and trade systems, for example, are able to fix overall levels of emissions more reliably than baseline and credit approaches. Systems that distribute permits by means of auctions may produce more benefits per unit of emission than processes that 'grandfather'[14] permits to established operators. Regimes that 'retire' percentages of allowances whenever there is trading will produce environmental benefits in a way that non-retirement approaches do not; and different allocations of liability for compliance will affect regulators' capacities to monitor and enforce compliance. Generalizations concerning emissions trading must, accordingly, be treated with care, and it is important to distinguish between the *inherent* strengths or weaknesses of emissions trading (which are due to the trading process itself) and those *contingent* matters of performance which flow not from the trading mechanism but from matters such as: the particular design or characteristics of the scheme;[15] its fit with the context of application;[16] or the intensity of the policy

rates, polluters may earn credits by improving emissions rates—even if the total mass of emissions does not drop.

[11] See EPA, *The United States Experience with Economic Incentives for Protecting the Environment* (EPA—240-R-01-001). This schema was adopted by the OECD in *Implementing Domestic Tradable Permits*, 34.

[12] *Scope* concerns the nature of restrictions on trading. *Cap* relates to the method of limiting emissions, and a key issue is whether the system is cap and trade or baseline and credit. *The Commodity Traded* refers to the precision with which the traded commodity is defined. The *Distribution of Permits* issues are whether permits are auctioned or allocated administratively. *Trading Ratio* considers whether instances of trading involve reductions in allowed emissions so that permit values lessen over time. *Banking* relates to the permissibility of storing permits in excess of current requirements. *Monitoring* is about methods for recording and monitoring holdings and trades of permits and, finally, the *Environmental Benefit* issue is whether the scheme 'designs in' benefits for the environment (e.g. through 'retirement' of a proportion of the allowance on trading).

[13] For a review of design issues, see, e.g., OECD, *Domestic Transferable Permits for Environmental Management: Design and Implementation* (OECD, 2001); S. Butzengeiger, R. Betz, and S. Bode, *Making GHG Emissions Trading Work*, HWA Discussion Paper 154 (Hamburg, 2001).

[14] Grandfathering is the admission to a scheme—usually on favourable terms—of established operators. It is a common practice within emissions trading systems—see C. Boemare and P. Quirion, 'Implementing Greenhouse Gas Trading in Europe' (2002) 43 *Ecological Economics* 213–30, 221; N. Keohane, R. Revesz, and R. Stavins, 'The Positive Political Economics of Instrument Choice in Environmental Policy' in P. Portney and R. Schwab (eds), *Environmental Economics and Public Policy* (London, 1998).

[15] See Tietenberg, 'Tradable Permits'. On key lessons in the design of emissions trading systems, see A.D. Ellerman, 'US Experience with Emissions Trading' and R. Morgenstern, 'Design Issues of a Domestic Emissions Trading Scheme in the USA' both in Hansjurgens, *Emissions Trading*. More generally on design see Freeman and Kolstad, *Moving to Markets*.

[16] That context includes the other control mechanisms being used in harness with emissions trading and which may control some of the difficulties associated with the device. A further problem

being furthered—for instance, the stringency of the pollution abatement target that has been set.[17]

Why Choose Emissions Trading?

Advocates of emissions trading mechanisms tend to claim that a number of virtues attach to the device.[18] A first of these is *efficiency*. When the trading of permits to pollute is provided for, this means that the cumulative burden of reaching a given level of pollution is minimized. Low-cost abaters will be incentivized to reduce pollution levels and sell permits to higher-cost abaters with the effect that the set level of emissions is achieved by lowest-cost methods. In addition, market mechanisms differ from flat-rate command regimes in so far as they tailor abatements to the levels that are efficient in each firm or process plant. Overall then, compliance with a limit is liable to cost less than in a command and control regime.[19] If worldwide trading is allowed, moreover, this ensures that emissions are controlled in the most cost-effective global locations.[20] Trading also produces rational controls by

in generalizing about emissions trading is that most observable regimes comprise mixes of 'command' and 'incentive' approaches—see W. Harrington, R.D. Morgenstern, and T. Sterner, *Choosing Environmental Policy* (Washington, DC, 2004), 240–1, 249.

[17] See C. Kolstad, 'Climate Change Policy Viewed from the USA and the Role of Intensity Targets' in Hansjurgens, *Emissions Trading*; D. Driesen, 'Design, Trading and Innovation' in Freeman and Kolstad, *Moving to Markets*, 437.

[18] See generally: B. Ackerman and R. Stewart, 'Reforming Environmental Law' (1985) 37 *Stanford Law Review* 1333–65; 'Reforming Environmental Law: The Democratic Case for Market Incentives' (1987) 13 *Columbia Journal of Environmental Law* 171; R. Stavins, 'Policy Instruments for Climate Change' (1997) *University of Chicago Legal Forum* 293; N. Keohane, R. Revesz, and R. Stavins, 'The Choice of Regulatory Instruments in Environmental Policy' (1998) 22 *Harvard Environmental Law Review* 313; L. Goulder, I. Parry, and R. Williams, 'The Cost Effectiveness of Alternative Instruments for Environmental Protection in a Second-Best Setting' (1999) 72 *Journal of Public Economics* 329; N. Keohane, 'Cost Savings from Allowance Trading in the 1990 Clean Air Act' in Freeman and Kolstad, *Moving to Markets*; Stern Review, esp. ch. 15.

[19] See Ellerman et al., *Markets for Clean Air*; T. Tietenberg, *Environmental and Natural Resource Economics* (3rd edn. New York, 1996); 'Tradable Permits in Principle and Practice' in Freeman and Kolstad, *Moving to Markets*, 74–6; R.N. Stavins, 'Experience With Market-Based Environmental Policy Instruments' in K.-G. Maler and J. Vincent, *Handbook of Environmental Economics* (Amsterdam, 2002); D. Burtraw, 'Cost Savings Sans Allowances' (Resources for the Future, Washington DC, 1996). Predicted cost savings have ranged from slight (5–10 per cent) to dramatic (95 per cent)—see A.D. Ellerman, 'US Experience with Emissions Trading' in Hansjurgens, *Emissions Trading*, 79. For a comparison of trading and command systems that looks at case studies, see: W. Harrington and R. Morgenstern, 'International Experience with Competing Approaches to Environmental Policy: Six Paired Cases' in Freeman and Kolstad, *Moving to Markets*; N. Keohane, R. Revesz, and R. Stavins, 'The Choice of Regulatory Instruments in Environmental Policy' (1998) 22 *Harvard Environmental Law Review* 313–67.

[20] Stern Review, 321.

generating an international price regarding, for example, carbon emissions.[21] Regulatory costs are also said to be low because it is claimed that, once established, the trading system runs on its own accord.

A second claimed strength of trading is *flexibility*. Trading gives managers and enterprises the freedom to choose how to deal with their polluting activities. Managers are less restricted than in command regimes because they are at liberty to decide not only how to reduce emissions in order to reduce permit costs but also the extent of reductions that is efficient for their operations (they are not restricted by across-the-board emissions standards or sets of commands that stipulate particular operational designs).

Trading is also said to reduce the dangers of *capture* by limiting regulatory discretions and by not involving close relations between regulators and firms.[22] It is said to do so because, within trading regimes, it is the market, rather than any bureaucrat, that exerts the relevant restraint on behaviour. A further posited strength of trading is *predictability of outcome*. A system established on cap and trade lines is said to offer far more predictable results than, say, a taxation regime. Overall levels of emissions are fixed in a cap and trade regime but, in a taxation system, they are contingent on individual firms' cumulative responses to incentives. This predictability of cap and trade is of value in restraining pollution levels below important threshold points (e.g. levels at which wildlife will be killed) and in calculating such matters as compliance with international treaty obligations.[23]

An emissions trading regime is also said to have the potential to deal with *distributional issues*, since it can control the assignment of emissions through the choice of initial allocation method for permits.[24] It is further claimed that emissions trading stimulates *innovation* in the techniques and technologies of emissions control.[25] It does so since a firm that finds a way to reduce its costs of abating can then generate allowances to sell on the market. Such firms, accordingly, will look to the producers of new technologies and operating systems to provide them with novel ways to abate. Those producers will, in turn, be incentivized to invest in the appropriate programmes of research and development regarding abatement strategies.

Competition and coordination issues are said to be handled well by emissions trading mechanisms. On the international stage, for instance, emissions trading schemes can produce a common price across countries (e.g. for emitting a tonne of carbon) and they can do so more easily than processes

---

[21] Stern Review, 327.

[22] See S. Breyer, *Regulation and Its Reform* (Cambridge, MA, 1982).

[23] See M. Faure, J. Gupta, and A. Nentjes, *Climate Change and the Kyoto Protocol* (Cheltenham, 2003).

[24] See OECD, *Implementing Domestic Tradable Permits*, 72.

[25] See the references at note 18 above.

involving the harmonizing of taxes. Trading schemes can thus, it is said, introduce carbon pricing without prompting issues of unfair competition between participating countries.[26] They are thus 'very powerful tools in the framework for addressing climate change at an international level'.[27]

Finally, emissions trading is claimed to produce *political advantages*. The trading mechanism can be said to possess four attributes that make it a specially attractive proposition when there is an urgent need to secure political support for regulatory action—as regarding, for instance, greenhouse gases. First, it holds out the prospect of a precise goal (the overall emissions cap) combined with a procedural framework, and, as such, it provides an identifiable aim that different parties or countries can negotiate and agree on. Second, it allows a nettle to be grasped now, while deferring the resolution of difficult issues such as distributional questions.

Third, emissions trading tends both to appease powerful players (by accepting their incumbent positions as givens) and to offer short-term compensation to less well-placed parties. (In 2004, Friends of the Earth dubbed the EU ETS 'a potentially huge step forward in the race to tackle climate change'.[28]) Fourth, trading has been held up as offering considerable potential to deliver the finance that can support emissions reductions by less affluent actors or developing nations.[29] All of these properties have been picked out by proponents of emissions trading but, on the global stage, it is the assumed implementability of the device that is its core strength.[30]

Advocates of emissions trading also argue that the device enhances the democratic quality of the policymaking process.[31] It does so, they say, because it focuses discussions clearly on the key issue of the overall level of pollution that should be established—which contrasts with the opacity of command and control systems that centre debates around arcane questions of best available technology versus other formulations of standards.[32]

---

[26] See Stern Review, 327.

[27] See Stern Review, 327.

[28] Friends of the Earth, 'Carbon Emissions Trading Scheme Starts Without UK on Board', 24 Dec. 2004. By 2009, however, Friends of the Earth was arguing that carbon trading was not delivering globally necessary carbon reductions and should be replaced by policies centring on taxation, regulation, and direct public investment—see Clifton, *A Dangerous Obsession*.

[29] EU states have expressed a willingness to use funds from auction revenues to support mitigation in developing countries—see Note of Council of EU, Brussels (17215/08) Clause 8, 12.12.2008 (cited: Clifton, *A Dangerous Obsession*, 19).

[30] Stern Review, p. xviii and ch. 22.

[31] See Ackerman and Stewart, 'Reforming Environmental Law' (1985); 'Reforming Environmental Law' (1987).

[32] See Ackerman and Stewart, 'Reforming Environmental Law' (1985), 1353. Hansjurgens describes the EU ETS as: 'an open, flexible and simple solution—see 'Concluding Observations' in Hansjurgens, *Emissions Trading*.

Areas of Contention

Emissions trading mechanisms raise a series of contentious issues, and a brief review of these may be useful. A preliminary caveat should, however, be entered: as already noted, emissions trading regimes come in widely differing forms and are applied in divergent contexts, and this makes generalizing a fraught process. In reviewing potential areas of contention, it should be emphasized both that some trading systems—for instance, the US Acid Rain Programme—have been heralded as considerable successes,[33] and that other policy instruments such as command regimes are by no means problem-free.[34]

DO EMISSIONS TRADING SYSTEMS TARGET AND SECURE THE RIGHT OBJECTIVES?

A first issue with emissions trading concerns the objectives to be pursued. A trading process, in itself, offers no benefit to, say, the environment. It does not reduce greenhouse gas emissions. What it does do is provide a way for a given target to be achieved at lowest cost. In a cap and trade system it is the setting of the cap that provides the opportunity for imposing limits on, say, environmental pollution. Within a baseline and credit regime, it is the setting of the baselines. Proponents of emissions trading would, however, argue, that emissions trading systems offer highly implementable ways of reaching whatever targets are decided upon and that they lend themselves to strategies for tightening controls as trading takes place.[35] (This can be provided for by requirements that a given percentage of an allowance is 'retired' each time the allowance is traded.)

In meeting targets with a trading device, much depends on the mode of defining emissions and distributing allowances. If emissions are defined absolutely (i.e. an absolute limit to discharges is set), this targets environmental objectives directly. If, however, emissions are defined relatively (as limits

---

[33] See Ellerman et al., *Markets for Clean Air*, and especially pp. 321–2, stating that one should 'extrapolate with care' from the US Acid Rain Program since it was applied in notably favourable circumstances involving accurate emissions monitoring, strong penalties for violations, a small number of relatively large sources of emissions, and a focus on specifying emissions limits once and for all. Some, more over, contest the 'success' of the US Acid Rain Program, arguing that the emissions reductions cited in its favour were caused by factors beyond the trading scheme—such as command rules and price changes within the transport and energy markets—see Clifton, *A Dangerous Obsession*, 21.

[34] For comparison of policy instruments see Harrington et al., *Choosing Environmental Policy*.

[35] See Stern Review, ch. 15; and C. Backes, K. Deketalaere, and M. Poeters. 'The Underestimated Possibility of *ex post* Adjustments' in Faure and Peeters, *Climate Change and European Emissions Trading*—both of which texts note the constraint imposed by the need for predictability of policy.

per unit of production), increases in levels of productivity may generate overall increases in emissions, even where there is full compliance.[36]

Are emissions trading systems amenable to the institution of environment-enhancing targets? Experience with the European Union Emission Trading System (EU ETS) points to a set of serious challenges to be faced—and, notably, to the difficulties that are experienced when allocating not through auctions but by means of freely allocated ('grandfathered') and governmentally quantified entitlements.[37] Crucial in the EU ETS were the initial allocations or 'allowances' for Phase I of the regime in 2005–7. Incumbent enterprises were extremely concerned to generate generous allowances that would minimize any potential costs and the emissions trading directive left it to individual member states to establish allocation plans.[38] As a result, intense lobbying ensued across the EU so that:

In most cases, these efforts resulted in lax emissions targets, complex special allocations to powerful interest groups and, in some cases, even in an over allocation compared to actual emissions.[39]

Implementation timescales were, in addition, tight in the EU ETS, and a complex set of allocation rules had to be worked to. This meant that most member state regulators had little time in which to process and verify large volumes of representations and pleadings from industry.[40] As a result, it can be argued, the trading scheme proved not to be an effective, low-capture, low-cost regime. Powerful interests were able to exploit their informational

---

[36] As would also be the case in a command regime that mandates the use of a particular process or best available technology.

[37] For Phase II of the EU ETS (2008–12), the European Directive imposes a 10 per cent limit on allocating allowances by methods other than for free—see Skjaerseth and Wettestad, *EU Emissions Trading*, 194; Faure and Peeters, *Climate Change and European Emissions Trading*. By 2008–9, the Commission was consulting on proposals that auctioning would cover over half of allocations in Phase III (2013–20)—see COM (2008) 16 final of 23.01.2008 and: http://europa.eu/rapid/pressReleasesAction.do?reference=IP/09/874&ampformat=HTML.

[38] See E. Woerdman, S. Clo, and A. Arcuri, 'European Emissions Trading and the Polluter Pays Principle: Assessing Grandfathering and Over-Allocation' in Faure and Peeters, *Climate Change and European Emissions Trading*.

[39] In 2005, total allowances exceeded emissions by 4 per cent—see Skjaerseth and Wettestad, *EU Emissions Trading*, 188. See also: S. Butzengeiger and A. Michaelowa, 'The EU Emissions Trading Scheme—Issues and Challenges' (2004) May/June *Intereconomics* 116–18, 118; G. Svendsen, 'Lobbying and CO$_2$ Trade in the EU' in Hansjurgens, *Emissions Trading*; Open Europe, *The High Price of Hot Air: Why the EU Emissions Trading Scheme is an Environmental and Economic Failure* (London, July 2006). In 2006, carbon emissions grew by 1.25 per cent on 2005, rising to their highest point since Labour came to power—see *Financial Times*, 'Carbon Emissions Rise', 30 March 2007. Over-allocation of allowances has occurred in other regimes—see the discussion of the Los Angeles Regional Clean Air Incentives Market (RECLAIM) in T. Tietenberg, *Emissions Trading* (2nd edn, Washington, DC, 2006), 12–13, 129–30.

[40] See Skjaerseth and Wettestad, *EU Emissions Trading*, 171–2, who also state that: 'the logic of the process resembled a "race to the bottom" where competitiveness concerns led member states incentives to over-allocate permits'.

advantages and to keep the constraining effects of the ETS at bay.[41] Over-allocation of allowances in Phase I meant that the prices for emissions were too low to incentivize anything like optimal investments in abatement efforts.[42] Environmental pressure groups were thus prompted to protest that the EU ETS had done little to further environmental objectives. (During Phase I of the EU ETS, emissions rose by about 1 per cent per year.)[43] As Greenpeace wrote of the EU ETS allocation, 'Governments massively over-allocated CO_2 permits as the market crash in the carbon price has shown ... [the price fell by more than 60%] ... it was because the system relies on future emissions projections as a method to set a cap and then gives out permits for free. Industry simply inflates its own emissions projections in order to ensure it maximizes the number of free permits that it gets—permits that, once allocated, have a significant market value.'[44]

The pressure group dubbed this: 'a licence for polluters to print money', and the German Environment Minister reported that the EU's four largest power producers had profiteered from the ETS at the expense of consumers[45]—and had stoked their earnings by between 6 and 8 billion Euros. In the UK, the Department of Trade and Industry published a report by consultants IPA, which suggested that UK electricity producers had reaped around £800 million in windfall profits from the ETS.[46]

Phase II of the EU ETS runs from 2008 to 2012 and it has been estimated by some interest groups that as much as 700 million tonnes worth of surplus permits could be available in this phase—and able to be rolled-over into Phase III. These excesses have been dubbed 'hot air', since firms can buy and use them without making any effort to reduce their emissions.[47] As for Phase

---

[41] For doubts about the success of the EU ETS in reducing emissions, see House of Commons Environmental Audit Committee, *The EU Emissions Trading Scheme: Lessons for the Future*, HC 70 (Second Report of Session 2006–7). (Para. 4: 'It appears to us that Phase I will have very little impact on carbon emissions across the EU. Allocations of allowances to emit carbon were too generous, and the market price of them consequently too low, to drive a transformation in business strategies and technical processes. Overall, the emissions projections appear to have been inaccurate and inflated, and the national caps derived from them too unambitious.')

[42] Skjaerseth and Wettestad, *EU Emissions Trading*, 187.

[43] Clifton, *A Dangerous Obsession*, 20.

[44] See R. Oakley, 'Greenpeace on the Fiasco of the CO_2 ETS', www.energyfuture.org.uk/index.php?option=com_content&task=view&id=149&It. See also Greenpeace, 'Increasing the Ambition of EU Emissions Trading www.Greenpeace.org/international/press/reports/increase-the-ambition-of-eu.

[45] Consumers pay in so far as the recipients of free permits are able to sell these to other firms who will pass through the costs to their customers. See Carbon Trust, *The European Emissions Trading Scheme: Implications for Industrial Competitiveness* (London, 2004), Annex p. 31.

[46] See IPA Consulting, *Implications of the EU Emissions Trading Scheme for the UK Power Generation Sector* (11 Nov. 2005), http://www.dti.gov.uk/files/file33199.pdf. See also Open Europe, *The High Price of Hot Air*.

[47] See Sandbag, *ETS SOS: Why The Flagship EU Emissions Trading Policy Needs Rescuing* (London, July 2009).

II windfall profits to investors and other holders of permits under the EU ETS, these have been estimated at between 23 and 63 billion Euros.[48]

The experience described raises doubts regarding the effectiveness of emissions trading systems and their amenability to the progressive adjustment of targets in order to improve environmental protections. Command systems have been criticized on this front,[49] but it can be argued that emissions trading regimes are similarly beset by difficulties of complexity, uncertainty, and delay when approaching the revision of standards and limits.[50] As in command mechanisms, there will also be difficulties of lobbying and pressures from potential litigants, and these are likely to prove to be at least as severe as those encountered in traditional command regimes.

The message to be drawn from the EU ETS is that if allowances are distributed at no cost, there are serious incentives to distort emissions projections so as to create windfalls. One answer to this problem is to allocate allowances by means of auctions.[51] If these are competitive, polluting enterprises will calculate their abatement costs as accurately as they can and then (a) take steps to abate where this is cheaper than purchasing permits; and (b) purchase permits to cover production up to the point of non-profitability.[52] Many 'grandfathered' firms will, of course, object to having to pay for emissions that previously had been discharged at no cost.[53] Auctioning, however, can be defended on the grounds not only that it addresses dangers of manipulation, but that polluters and the consumers of polluting products should have to pay for the harms that they inflict on the environment.

---

[48] Point Carbon Advisory Services, *EU ETS Phase II: The Potential and Scale of Windfall Profits in the Power Sector* (London, 2008), 20.

[49] See Ackerman and Stewart, 'Reforming Environmental Law' (1987), 174.

[50] See D.M. Driesen, 'Does Emissions Trading Encourage Innovation?' (2003) 33 *Environmental Law Reporter* 10094 at 10100. For arguments favouring abandoning the dichotomy between command and control and economic incentive systems, see D. Driesen, 'Is Emissions Trading an Economic Incentive Programme? Replacing the Command and Control/Economic Incentives Dichotomy' (1998) 55 *Washington and Lee Law Review* 289—where it is argued that both regimes involve establishing commands, the creation of incentives, the setting of limits, and the monitoring and enforcement of controls.

[51] On the allocative efficiency of auctions, see P. Cramton and S. Kerr, 'Tradable Carbon Permit Auctions: How and Why to Auction not Grandfather' (2002) 30 *Energy Policy* 333–45. On auctions more generally, see S. Weishaar, 'The EU ETS: Auctions and their Challenges' in Faure and Peeters, *Climate Change and European Emissions Trading*.

[52] That is: the point where the permit and other costs of producing an extra widget exceed the revenue earned from sale of that widget.

[53] Objections to auctioning may, of course, be less forthcoming from suppliers whose market positions allow them to pass on to consumers the costs of purchasing allowances. Centrica, owners of British Gas, have been reported as backing the idea of auctions for allowances in the EU ETS—see D. Gow, 'Power Tool', *Guardian Unlimited*, 17 May 2006.

INNOVATION AND TECHNOLOGY FORCING

Proponents of emissions trading schemes claim, as noted, that such mechanisms can usefully drive forward the search for more efficient abatement technologies as traders seek to lower costs.[54] Emissions traders, it is contended, will look to purchase abatement technologies when the costs of abatement per unit are rendered less than the costs of permits. Sceptics, however, argue that such incentives have limitations and that there are 'solid reasons to suspect that an emissions trading program does a poorer job of stimulating innovation than a comparably designed traditional regulation'.[55] A central argument is that in, for example, a cap and trade regime, the cap sets a limit to emissions and the effect of trading is to concentrate emissions-reducing efforts on those facilities that have the lowest abatement costs—which will tend to be the operators with low-tech systems. Emissions trading, it is said, compares poorly with traditional regulation regarding high-end innovation. This is because trading reduces the incentives for high-cost facilities to innovate in order to save costs.[56] As one critic has contended: 'Why bother making expensive long-term structural changes if you can meet your pollution rights from operators that can cut their carbon cheaply?'[57] In short, high-end buyers of credits will tend not to innovate, but low-end sellers will seek to release credits—not by engaging in the cutting-edge development of productive innovations, but by implementing low-tech changes.[58] This

---

[54] See e.g. Ackerman and Stewart, 'Reforming Environmental Law' (1985); 'Reforming Environmental Law' (1987); Stavins, 'Policy Instruments for Climate Change'; Keohane, 'Cost Savings'. Ellerman et al., *Markets for Clean Air* (p. 316) conclude that the US Acid Rain Program did stimulate progress in abatement technology.

[55] See D. Driesen, 'Design, Trading and Innovation' in Freeman and Kolstad, *Moving to Markets*, at p. 437; 'Does Emissions Trading Encourage Innovation?' and also 'Is Emissions Trading an Economic Incentive Programme?', where Driesen also argues (p. 325) that the incentive for a firm continuously to reduce emissions and sell off permits only operates to the point at which an equilibrium level is established by a programme. Fischer also notes that, where numbers of permits are fixed, reductions in abatement costs cause permit prices to fall, and this progressively reduces incentives to innovate—see C. Fischer, 'Technical Innovation and Design Choices for Emissions Trading and Other Climate Policies' in Hansjurgens, *Emissions Trading*. Fischer also makes the point that command and control regimes that apply performance standards will (like taxes per unit of pollution) incentivize innovation, but commands that call for the use of particular technologies or operational designs will not incentivize innovation beyond satisfaction of the prescribed design.

[56] D. Malueg, 'Emissions Credit Trading and the Incentive to Adopt New Pollution Abatement Technology' (1987) 16 *Journal of Environmental Economics and Management* 52. For a comparison of incentive and command instruments as drivers of innovation, see Harrington et al., *Choosing Environmental Policy*, 252–4.

[57] L. Lohmann, 'Carry On Polluting' *New Scientist*, 2 Dec. 2006.

[58] The disincentive to innovate has also been said to be exacerbated by the process of offsetting. This allows emitters to buy emissions credits from outside the trading scheme in order to comply with their targets. Most offset credits in the EU ETS come from the Clean Development Mechanism (CDM) which, under the Kyoto Protocol, allows the purchase of credits from developing countries that are implementing emissions reducing projects. Developed countries with binding emissions reduction

tendency is exacerbated in regimes where emissions are under-priced because of over-allocations. Thus, the International Energy Agency warned in late 2009 that the price of carbon credits in the EU ETS would have to more than double from the then trading level of $21 per tonne if high-tech solutions to climate change, such as carbon capture, were to become economically attractive.[59]

It might be responded that it is efficient to abate via cheap, low-tech means, rather than through expensive research and development. Such a response, however, is no answer to the concern that the effect of emissions trading may be to postpone or reduce the chances of discovering newly efficient abatement systems.[60] Nor does it take on board the syndrome of falling abatement costs—the propensity of initially expensive innovations to develop in the longer term (notably through economies of scale) into cheap, efficient abatement mechanisms.

Short-term efficiency gains may tend to be purchased in emissions trading regimes at the cost of the development, in the longer term, of new technologies that may revolutionize environmental performance. To give an example: within an emissions trading scheme the fossil-fuel burning electricity utility in the developed country may claim credits for activities undertaken abroad as a substitute for reducing greenhouse gases at home. Had the utility been faced with a command requirement, it might have been stimulated to take more radical and urgent steps such as changing fuels, or employing alternative technologies such as innovative fuel cells or solar energy solutions.[61]

Will emissions trading systems encourage the closure of old polluting premises and the building of innovative, high-tech, and low polluting establishments? If a company is considering renewing its plant, the opportunity to sell off its released allowances will create an incentive to innovate. If, however, governments seek to tighten overall caps by withdrawing allocations when installations are closed, this creates perverse incentives to keep old, inefficient units operating in order to preserve the value of those allocations. Similarly, if governments attempt to encourage new enterprises by giving free allowances to new entrants, this creates perverse incentives to maximize such allowances by building highly polluting systems. As the Carbon Trust has said of the European regime, 'The EU ETS can even act to subsidize the construction of new carbon-intensive coal plants that would not have been built without it, because they receive the revenues of higher electricity prices without paying

---

targets can offset these with Certified Emissions Reductions gained under the CDM. See Clifton, *A Dangerous Obsession*, 25.

[59] International Energy Agency, *World Energy Outlook 2009* (IEA, 2009).

[60] Driesen, 'Does Emissions Trading Encourage Innovation?', 10097; Commission on Sustainable Development, Report to the Secretary General, UN Doc. E/CN. 17/2001.PC/20 (2000); OECD, *Implementing Domestic Tradable Permits*, 20.

[61] Driesen, 'Does Emissions Trading Encourage Innovation?', 10098.

the cost of their carbon.'[62] When grandfathering is used to allocate permits at the inception of a trading regime, this also may reduce incentives to innovate.[63] This occurs because such innovations will reduce the value of permits and, accordingly, the wealth of permit holders.

UNCERTAINTY

A further difficulty with emissions trading systems is uncertainty.[64] In the first place, if firms are used to command regimes and are not certain about the longevity of an emissions trading scheme, they will not be inclined to make the strategic decisions that may be necessary in order to reduce emissions significantly.[65] Experience with the EU ETS shows how, in a baseline and credit system, excessively generous initial allocations of allowances can produce volatilities in the price of emissions.[66] Parties considering investing in research and development into abatement technologies may be disincentivized by such volatility and the uncertainties of any potential returns on their investment.[67] In 2009, more than four years after the inception of the EU ETS, the Energy Editor of the *Financial Times* was reporting: 'The volatility of the price of carbon emissions, which reached 29 euros per tonne last year and fell to 8 euros in February, before recovering to the present 14 euros, is seen by many companies as a deterrent to investment in technologies that cut emissions because it creates huge uncertainties over revenues.'[68]

The attitude of many corporate managers, when faced with such unknowns, may be one of 'wait and see'.[69] Or, alternatively, managers may use other coping strategies. Thus, in 2006, the Energy Director of Ernst and Young argued that movements in carbon prices in the EU ETS had discouraged meaningful investment in carbon-reducing technologies and had, instead,

---

[62] See Carbon Trust, *Allocation and Competitiveness in the EU ETS* (London, June 2006), 8.

[63] See Boemare and Quirion, 'Implementing Greenhouse Gas Trading?'; S. Milliman and R. Prince, 'Firm Incentives to Promote Technological Change in Pollution Control' (1989) 17 *Journal of Environmental Economics and Management* 247–65.

[64] See Stern Review, ch. 15 on the need for predictability in carbon policy.

[65] See R. Stavins, 'Implications of the US Experience' in Hansjurgens, *Emissions Trading*, at 67–8.

[66] On continuing volatilities in the EU ETS, see World Bank, *The State and Trends of the Carbon Market 2007*, 12–13. The US Acid Rain Program has avoided huge volatilities but allowance prices, nevertheless, fell from $154 to $64 from 1994 to 1996 and leaped to $200 in March 1999—see Ellerman et al., *Markets for Clean Air*, ch. 11.

[67] See Carbon Trust, *Allocation and Competitiveness*, 8.

[68] E. Crooks, 'Tories Plan Extra Help on Low-Carbon Electricity', *Financial Times*, 4 Nov. 2009. See also the UK Climate Committee's similarly reasoned conclusion that it cannot be confident that the EU ETS will deliver the low-carbon investments required to meet international obligations—Committee on Climate Change, *Meeting Carbon Budgets* (London, October 2009).

[69] S. Ben-David, D. Brookshire, S. Burness, and M. Mckee. 'Attitudes Towards Risk and Compliance in Emission Permit Markets' (2000)76 *Land Economics* 590; Stern Review, 370; W. Blyth and R. Sullivan, 'Climate Change Policy Uncertainties and the Electricity Industry', Energy, Environment and Development Programme Briefing Paper 06/02 (London, 2006).

encouraged the short-term trading of positions in order to optimize returns and limit risks.[70]

In any regime where there is a cap on permits in supply, small changes in demand can lead to large changes in prices. Where, moreover, there is the trading of emissions permits as financial assets and speculative instruments (as in the global carbon markets[71]) this will tend to generate high price volatility.[72] This situation is particularly damaging in industries such as electricity generation, where managers who make investment decisions work to long horizons and planners are highly dependent on knowing the price for carbon emissions over time.[73] When cutbacks in emissions caps are set with reference to Business As Usual (BAU) projections, this process involves particularly high levels of uncertainty, since the cutbacks are made 'from moving targets'.[74] This is because a rise in BAU projections will automatically drag up the cap and the number of emissions allowances. Command regimes will involve uncertainties regarding the stringencies of the governmentally imposed requirements of the future, but emissions trading systems can create uncertainties in relation to both the limits that governments or regulators set on caps (or baselines) and the emissions prices that are established in the marketplace.[75]

THE HEALTH OF MARKETS

Another major issue in emissions trading is the state of the market. If there is no vigour in the trading of permits (or confidence in the structural stability of the market) there cannot be a strong set of incentives that will influence abatement behaviour. The parties within the system have to be both disposed to trade and able to do so if emissions trading is to operate as an effective control mechanism. Some emissions trading systems involve healthy markets,[76] but in others, trading activities have been far lower than expected—and have sometimes been zero.[77]

---

[70] Tony Ward, *Daily Telegraph*, 16 May 2006, quoted in Open Europe, *The High Price of Hot Air*.
[71] Financial Services Authority, *Risks and Challenges* (London, 2008), 14.
[72] See United Nations, *World Economic and Social Survey* (New York, 2009), 161.
[73] M. Lockwood, *A Rough Guide to Carbon Trading* (London, 2007), 5—who notes that in the US sulphur dioxide scheme, prices have had a monthly volatility of 10 per cent.
[74] See House of Commons Environmental Audit Committee, 'The EU Emissions Trading Scheme: Lessons for the Future', HC 70 (Second Report of Session 2006–7), p. 7.
[75] See Driesen, 'Does Emissions Trading Encourage Innovation?'; J. Dennis, 'Smoke for Sale' (1993) 40 *UCLA Law Review* 1101.
[76] See Ellerman et al., *Markets for Clean Air*, ch. 7 (on the US Acid Rain Program).
[77] See OECD, *Implementing Domestic Tradable Permits*, 20; R. Kraemer and K. Banholzer, *Tradable Permits and Water Resources Protection and Management* (Paris, 1998), ch. 7; B. Swift, 'The Acid Rain Test' (1997) 14 *Environmental Forum* 17 at 21 (estimating that in the mid-nineties US Acid Rain Program, only around 1 to 3.5 per cent of allowances were involved in trading).

Experience, says the OECD, demonstrates that emissions trading programmes can take a long time to develop because constraints of acceptability and a lack of familiarity with the instruments can mean that firms do not make use of trading opportunities.[78] A problem with the first phase of the EU ETS was that, by failing to create a genuine market, it did not encourage investments in renewables and other low carbon technologies.[79] A related difficulty is that if initial allocations of permits are defective and there is governmental correction *ex post*, this may create further uncertainties in the system as the rules change.[80]

In the post-credit crisis era, moreover, there is not the same faith in the stability and efficiency of markets as there was previously.[81] A special concern about some emissions trading markets is that they may be prone to some of the fragilities that were seen in the 2007–9 sub-prime mortgage crisis.[82] Thus, it has been argued that modern global carbon trading involves increasingly complex bundles of credit instruments, an underlying basis of weak data (on such matters as offset verifications) and a high level of speculation in carbon markets by financial traders, rather that carbon emitters.[83] The alleged risk is that the world may grow increasingly reliant on carbon trading to deliver emissions reductions but that the carbon markets will mirror previous credit markets and grow more volatile and prone to crashes.[84]

TRANSACTION COSTS

Some emissions trading schemes have gained reputations for low administrative costs,[85] but others are complex and, particularly when targeted 'downstream' (i.e. towards consumers in the supply chain) will tend to raise difficult issues regarding administrative and transaction costs.[86] Thus, when the OECD considered controlling pollution by using tradable permits to ration mobility in the transport sector, it concluded that fuel taxes would be a

[78] See OECD, *Implementing Domestic Tradable Permits*, and R. Stavins, 'Implications of the US Experience' in Hansjurgens, *Emissions Trading*, at 67–8.

[79] D. Gow, 'Power Tool', *Guardian Unlimited*, 17 May 2006.

[80] See Carbon Trust, *Allocation and Competitiveness*, 8.

[81] See David Wighton, 'Efficient Market Hypothesis is Dead—For Now', *The Times on Line* 29 Jan. 09: 'I have to report the sad passing of the efficient market hypothesis. The theory was officially declared dead yesterday at the World Economic Forum in Davos. There were no mourners.'

[82] See T. Macalister, 'Carbon Trading May be the New Sub-prime says Energy Boss', *The Guardian*, 30 Jan. 09.

[83] Friends of the Earth, *A Dangerous Distraction* (Washington, DC, 2009).

[84] Clifton, *A Dangerous Obsession*, 33.

[85] See Ellerman et al., *Markets for Clean Air*, 257 (on the US Acid Rain Program). On design factors affecting transaction costs, see Tietenberg, *Emissions Trading*, 70–1.

[86] See R.N. Stavins, 'Transaction Costs and Tradable Permits' (1995) 29 *Journal of Environmental Economics and Management* 133–48; T. Sterner and H. Hammar, 'Designing Instruments for Climate Policy' in Hansjurgens, *Emissions Trading*.

cheaper solution. The foremost problems with trading were the administrative costs of targeting a large number of mobile sources and the high transaction costs involved in making permits transferable.[87] The OECD stressed that analyses of the transaction costs of trading systems were the key to measuring the value added by such systems and that they should be a focus of *ex post* evaluation studies of controls. Transaction costs have also been identified as a key issue in the Clean Development Mechanism (CDM) provided for under the Kyoto Protocol. The CDM device allows rich countries to use credits from investments in emissions reductions in developing countries to offset against their own emissions reduction commitments. The Stern Review noted that the CDM was having only a small impact because of the high transaction costs involved in demonstrating that the projects at issue offered a net gain on the default position.[88] The EU ETS has been dubbed 'an administrative nightmare' whose complexities impose huge burdens of an estimated £62 million on firms and public sector bodies.[89] These are said to be felt especially by small production plants, who are covered by the scheme but contribute little to emissions.[90]

INFORMATION

An efficient trading system will be one that is based on reliable data and within which there are good information flows.[91] An issue with such systems, however, and notably with baseline and credit approaches,[92] can be their vulnerability to data manipulation and, when allowances are issued at no cost, the incentivizing of such manipulation.[93] The EU ETS, again, has exemplified these difficulties—which include not merely the distortion of information but the emission of supra-normal quantities of pollutants so as to earn higher allowances.[94] A familiar criticism of traditional 'command' regulation is that regulated firms are able to exploit the information asymmetry between regulator and regulated. It is arguable, though, that trading mechanisms do not necessarily overcome this difficulty. In some respects, the incentive to manipulate may be worse in an emissions trading mechanism. It is, for

---

[87] OECD, *Implementing Domestic Tradable Permits*, 148.

[88] Stern Review, 505.

[89] Open Europe, *The High Price of Hot Air*.

[90] Ibid., 4.

[91] See Ellerman et al., *Markets for Clean Air*, ch. 7 (on the development of the market in the US Acid Rain Program).

[92] For contrast, in this respect, with 'cap and trade' systems, see Ellerman et al., *Markets for Clean Air*, 318.

[93] Open Europe, *The High Price of Hot Air*.

[94] On incentives to inflate historic use in order to gain larger allocations, see H. Berland, D. Clark, and P. Pederson, 'Rent Seeking and the Regulation of a Natural Resource' (2001) 16 *Marine Resource Economics* 219–33.

instance, linked to the producing of a firm-specific gain—one that can be expected to bring competitive advantages—rather than to an impact on the stringency of a command standard that applies across the board to all relevant firms.[95]

ENFORCEMENT

It should be emphasized that emissions trading markets will generally need regulatory encouragement if they are to develop.[96] This requires that the rules of trading are enforced and monitored, since non-observance of allowances will undermine the value of trading.[97] As the Stern Review pointed out, 'A transparent and well-enforced system of measuring and reporting emissions is crucial for securing the environmental credibility of a scheme as well as free trade across plants.'[98] Ceilings on emissions will be valueless if caps and credit regimes are not enforced, and enterprises will be reluctant to comply with the terms of trading systems if, due to non-enforcement, they feel that they are competitively disadvantaged. On the international front, confidence in trading systems thus demands not merely that compliance systems are strong across participating nations, but that there is agreement on standards for monitoring, reporting, and verification of emissions.

Emissions trading schemes, accordingly, do not escape the enforcement challenges that are familiar in command regimes.[99] Under some conditions, trading schemes have proved conducive to high levels of compliance.[100] Under other conditions, however, it is arguable that emissions trading systems may render enforcement particularly difficult. Within an international greenhouse gas trading regime, for instance, an enterprise within a developed country will look to buy allocations as cheaply as possible. The lowest prices are likely to be those offered by firms in developing countries and the very

---

[95] This is not to deny that in other circumstances the trading process can help to flush out information—as when the grandfathering of permits incentivizes rent-seeking incumbents to declare their emissions (which helps the regulator to inventorize emissions and sources); see J.M. Sanchez and R. Katz, 'A Market-Based Environmental Policy Experiment in Chile' (2002) 45 *JLE* 267–87; see also S. Penderson, 'Experience Gained with CO_2 Cap and Trade in Denmark', OECD Workshop on Ex Post Evaluation of Tradable Permits (Paris, January 2003).

[96] On the routine mixing of incentive and command instruments, see Harrington et al., *Choosing Environmental Policy*, ch. 12.

[97] See Tietenberg, 'Tradable Permits', 71.

[98] Stern Review p. 336.

[99] See R. Greenspan Bell, 'Choosing Environmental Policy Institutions in the Real World' and J. Kruger, K. Grover, and J. Schreifels, 'Building Institutions to Address Air Pollution in Developing Countries: The Cap and Trade Approach' both in OECD, *Emissions Trading and Project-based Mechanisms* (OECD, 2002).

[100] See Ellerman et al., *Markets for Clean Air*, ch. 5 on the 'exemplary compliance' in the US Acid Rain Program and Harrington et al., *Choosing Environmental Policy*, 259 on the US leaded gasoline regime.

lowest may be those available from firms in developing countries whose governments are poorest at monitoring and enforcing.[101] This will be the case because the selling firms will anticipate that, thanks to poor enforcement, they can sell their allowances but still carry on emitting at the usual levels.

Emissions trading systems, indeed, may incentivize lack of enforcement and corruption, since unethical members of governments will often be able to both reap personal gains and, at the same time, offer home enterprises competitive advantages. They will do so by allowing permits to be sold, emissions levels to be misrepresented, and by taking rewards for this. Emissions trading can be said to place heavy stress on enforcement but to involve enforcement under extremely difficult conditions. Offsetting mechanisms, such as those established by the Clean Development Mechanism, have been said to exacerbate enforcement issues—notably, in the CDM's case, because of the difficulties that arise when national governments are entrusted to verify whether reductions in emissions are additional to those that would have happened anyway.[102] The Green lobby's special concern is that emissions trading mechanisms involve huge verification challenges and they create the dangerous illusion that production patterns in the North can be maintained without harming the climate.[103]

IS EMISSIONS TRADING FAIR?

A fundamental problem with market-based systems of distribution is that spending power holds sway. Such systems have an inherent bias in favour of those parties who possess wealth and they possess a tendency to remove power from those who lack resources.[104] The results of trading may be claimed to be efficient, but this does not ensure fairness: 'Trades of rights in the marketplace may lead to a concentration of property and market power, denying small businesses and poor people access rights to necessary resources (e.g. water).'[105]

A first difficulty with trading systems is that, if they are to overcome the political hurdles of inception, they tend to have to 'grandfather' existing

---

[101] On the particular difficulties of enforcing emissions trading systems in developing countries, see E. Richman, 'Emissions Trading and the Development Critique: Exposing the Threat to Developing Countries (2003) 36 *International Law and Politics* 133.

[102] See Clifton, *A Dangerous Obsession*, 28–30.

[103] See the Durban Declaration on Climate Trading—www.sinkswatch.org.

[104] See Derek Walls's comment on the Stern Review that: 'Sir Nicholas and his team have reached for their micro-economics textbooks in the way that a Mid-west preacher reaches for his bible'— D. Walls, *Costing the Earth* (www.redpepper.org.uk/Dec2006/dec-06–stern.htm).

[105] OECD, *Implementing Domestic Tradable Permits*, 20. Direct action group, Rising Tide describes carbon trading as 'privatization of the climate'—see *Weekly SchNews*, 29 June 2001.

operators into the system.[106] If, however, permits to pollute are allocated on the basis of historical or current emission levels, polluters will not 'pay'—they will be *rewarded* for their records of pollution.[107] They will, moreover, be placed in positions that allow them to maximize their potential rewards by exploiting their informational advantages and their abilities to manipulate data to their advantage.

Free allocations, moreover, may result in windfall profits and, as Stern commented, 'Not surprisingly, free permits are generally favoured by existing players in industry.'[108] It is noteworthy here that the history of the UK Emissions Trading Scheme reveals it to have been very much the darling of industry. That scheme emerged from very close collaboration between the government and major UK companies, with an expressed aim of gaining early experience and first-mover advantages in international greenhouse gas emissions trading.[109]

Fairness, Stern added, demands that historical polluters are not simply rewarded: 'Given the ability to bear costs and historical responsibility for the stock of greenhouse gases, equity requires that rich countries pay a greater share of the costs.'[110] It is arguable, moreover, that the same argument holds in considering domestic trading schemes and that richer polluting concerns should pay a greater share of (capital and ongoing) costs than smaller firms,

---

[106] See L. Raymond, *Private Rights in Public Resources* (Washington, DC, 2003). OECD, *Lessons from Existing Trading Systems*, 39, reports that in New Zealand, the political feasibility of introducing Individual Tradable Quotas in fisheries was 'greatly enhanced' by initial allocations based on incumbents' catch histories and 'support from key industry players' plus compensation for any 'incumbents' losses.

[107] See Stern Review, 333; K. Neuhoff and K. Martinez 'Allocations, Incentives and Distortions' (2006) 6 *Climate Policy* 71–89; P. Baer, J. Harte, B. Haya, A. Herzog, and J. Holdren 'Equity and Greenhouse Gas Responsibility' (2000) 289 *Science* 2287. A criticism of the EU ETS has been that some member states of the EU have given their firms emissions targets based on past records, whereas others have allocated targets on the basis of forecasts—with the effect of unfairness to firms in the former group, who have to purchase permits from firms in the latter group—see Open Europe, *The High Price of Hot Air*.

[108] Stern Review, 333. DTI consultants estimated that the first round of allowances in the EU ETS has produced £800 million in windfalls and Commission consultants have estimated that airlines could make 4 billion euros in windfalls if aviation is added to the EU ETS—see Lockwood, *A Rough Guide to Carbon Trading*, 6. See also Congressional Budget Office, 'Who Gains and Who Pays Under Carbon-Allowance Trading?' (June 2000).

[109] The idea of greenhouse gas emissions trading entered the British policy agenda after heavy promotion by BP and British Airways, who suggested that a business-led institution be established in order to design a trading system for greenhouse gas emissions in the UK. See F. von Malmborg and P. Strachan, 'Climate Policy, Ecological Modernism and the UK Emissions Trading Scheme' (2005) 15 *European Environment* 143–60, 154; K. Makuch and Z. Makuch, 'Domestic Initiatives in the UK' in Faure and Peeters, *Climate Change and European Emissions Trading*.

[110] Stern Review, 472. (Stern also notes that the correlation between income or wealth and current or past emissions 'is not exact; but it is strong'—474.) See also Gordon Brown's speech to the Labour Party conference reported in *Guardian Unlimited*, Monday, 25 Sept. 2006: 'And I make this promise: tackling climate change must not be the excuse for rich countries to impose a new environmental colonialism: sheltering an unstainable prosperity at the expense of the development of the poor.'

lesser polluters, or new industry entrants.[111] The difficulty with this argument is that such redistributive approaches always tend to be countered by the regressive effects of trading systems. As for comparisons with other regulatory methods, such as command and control, it has been argued that most empirical studies find that, across a range of policy instruments, the costs of control tend to be borne disproportionately by poorer groups—but this is especially the case with grandfathered emissions permits.[112]

Nor do fairness issues disappear if permits are allocated by auctioning, rather than by free allocation. Auctioning systems tend to distribute permits at far lower administrative cost to both firms and governments than free allocation methods. Auctioning, however, is, again, a mechanism that favours those incumbents who have the existing resources to make successful bids. The principled objection here is that it is unfair that incumbent polluters— who are the parties who have accumulated wealth at the cost of the environment—should be better positioned than non-polluters or new entrants to the field.

Such unfairness can result in distortions of competition—as where incumbents buy up allocations in order to create barriers to market entry.[113] Small and medium enterprises may also complain that they suffer competitively because they are far less able than large companies to deal with the extensive administrative and informational burdens that are involved in negotiating allowances or organizing bids for permits.[114] On the international stage, it has similarly been argued, 'Only big firms can afford to hire carbon accountants, liaise with officials and pay the costs of getting projects registered with the UN. Yet these are often the companies that local people battle hardest against in defence of their livelihoods and health.'[115]

Post Kyoto, a key issue is the development effect of trading systems.[116] Internationally, emissions trading solutions have been said to involve a double injustice. The effects of existing emissions are felt disproportionately by the less developed nations and they restrict development over coming years.

---

[111] An arguable fairer alternative to historically based allowances is a benchmarking approach in which permits are issued in a manner that rewards users of clean technologies and penalizes dirty systems. Such benchmarking can be based on standardized rates of emissions for particular fuels, technologies, or plant sizes. The informational and analytic burdens of establishing such benchmarks are, however, considerable, given the complex mixes of fuels and processes to be encountered in industry, and such regulatory systems would be highly interventionist in nature.

[112] See I. Parry, 'Are Emissions Permits Regressive?' (2004) 47 *Journal of Environmental Economics and Management* 364–87; I. Parry, H. Sigman, M. Walls, and R.C. Williams, 'The Incidence of Pollution Control Policies' (Washington, DC, 2005).

[113] On market power and trading schemes, see R. Hahn, 'Market Power and Transferable Property rights' (1984) *Quarterly Journal of Economics* 753–63.

[114] See S. Butzengeiger and A. Michaelowa, 'The EU ETS—Issues and Challenges' (2004) *Intereconomics* 116, 118.

[115] Lohmann, 'Carry on Polluting'.

[116] See Richman, 'Emissions Trading'.

Trading has been called 'colonialism with a modern face' in so far as it is a device that perpetuates and deepens inequalities of access to and control of resources... 'It creates the illusion that southern countries are benefiting while masking the fact that it is [the developed] countries and companies which are profiting from access to emissions permits and control of new southern markets.'[117] Critics of trading protest that it offers a means for wealthy countries and companies to escape their historical responsibilities for greenhouse gases, to avoid making emissions reductions in their own operations, and to 'defraud developing countries of their rights to use of the global atmosphere'.[118]

The charge, then, is that if allocations are set on an historical basis, this both allows currently high emitters to impose environmental damage on other countries and it has the effect of locking the less developed nations into lower levels of development. The Clean Development Mechanism (CDM) that, post Kyoto, is linked to emissions trading has also been accused of prejudicing development. The CDM, as noted, allows governments or firms to invest in emissions reducing projects in developing countries. The reductions achieved will be counted as reductions for the purposes of the investors' own emissions targets. The sceptics' argument is that, in the early years of trading, the mechanism allows existing industrialized users to meet their targets at lowest cost and to avoid making reductions in home emissions. When, however, developing countries become faced with emissions targets themselves, the cheapest forms of emissions abatement will have been exhausted and only more expensive, high-tech forms will be left—at which time industrialized countries will be unwilling to invest abroad. In short, industrialized countries will have gained preferential use of lowest cost abatement methods and reaped a competitive advantage while suppressing development.[119] Supporters of emissions trading might argue that such considerations can be taken into account when allocations are negotiated, but this response makes assumptions about the bargaining power and positions of developing countries (or the altruism of developed countries) that may be unrealistic—a matter to be returned to below.

Firms in less developed countries may, directly or indirectly, be paid to desist from productive enterprise. This may or may not prove politically acceptable. Some commentators argue that developing countries cannot reasonably be expected to restrict their future emissions without being assured of a fair allocation scheme that will not impair their ability to

---

[117] See Rising Tide, 'The Rising Tide Coalition for Climate Justice Political Statement (http://risingtide.org.uk/about/political).

[118] See Christian Aid, *Global Warming Policy Position Paper*, Nov. 2000.

[119] See Christian Aid, *Global Warming*, 7; Richman, 'Emissions Trading'; Driesen, 'Does Emissions Trading Encourage Innovation?'

develop.[120] This demands, they say, not historically based or auction-based distributions but allocations based on equal rights to the atmospheric commons for every individual. Developing countries, they add, are unlikely to accept permanent restrictions on *per capita* emissions levels lower than those of industrialized nations.

There is, however, a further argument that suggests that, from a development point of view, it is not enough to allocate emissions rights on a *per capita* equal rights basis. The effect of this would be to allow existing wealthy polluters to purchase, from poor permit holders, sufficient allocations to allow them to continue to trade at profit maximizing levels. There would be a one-off transfer of wealth to poorer firms, but these less wealthy players would be paying a price for that transfer—in the form of forfeited opportunities to develop their wealth creative capacity by exploiting those allowances.[121] They would be giving up not merely present entitlements but also future expectations.

Proponents of emissions trading might defend their position by alleging that transfers of wealth remove any unfairness and actually encourage development. This defence, however, depends on emphasizing short-term gains to less well off parties and underplaying the longer-term losses that trading will impose on those same actors.[122] It is a defence exemplified in the *Guardian* writer Polly Toynbee's analysis of proposals for personal carbon allowances. Toynbee argues: 'Here is where social justice meets green politics for the first time.... Drive a gas-guzzling 4x4 and you will have to buy a quota from the third of the population with no access to a car. Who could complain about such transparent fairness? ... it in effect redistributes money from the rich to the poor.'[123]

Respondents to such an approach would, however, object that such plans offer not 'transparent fairness' but a means of magnifying wealth differentiations and of pricing poorer citizens out of their enjoyment of life's benefits. Such critics might observe that when Robin Hood took from the rich and gave to the poor he did not, in return, limit the poor's entitlements to exploit the resources of Sherwood Forest. To the counter-argument that the poor

---

[120] Baer et al., 'Equity and Greenhouse Gas Responsibility'; A. Agarwal and S. Narain, 'Global Warming in an Unequal World: A Case of Environmental Colonialism' (New Delhi, 1991).

[121] On the 'development critique' see Richman, 'Emissions Trading', 149–54; O. Mehmet, *Westernising the Third World* (2nd edn., London, 1999).

[122] See S. Dresner and P Ekins, 'The Distributional Impacts of Economic Instruments to Limit Greenhouse Gas Emissions from Transport', PSI Research Discussion Paper 19 (PSI, London, 2004)—and the discussion of Domestic Tradable Quotas (at Section 8), which assesses winners and losers on the basis of the costs of quotas for households but leaves the opportunity costs of selling allowances out of account. See also the claims that individual carbon trading can be "moderately progressive" in S. Roberts and J. Thumim, A Rough Guide to Individual Carbon Trading (Defra, London, 2006) p. 5.

[123] Polly Toynbee, 'This Electric Radicalism Marries Green Politics With Social Justice', *The Guardian*, 15 Dec. 2006.

could always use their new wealth to reinvest in rights to use the resource at issue, the critics may to argue that such a reinvestment capacity is liable to decline from day one as the exploitation of the resource by the wealthy purchasers of rights drives the price of entitlements beyond the pockets of the initial sellers.

Informational asymmetries would be likely to exaggerate this effect.[124] To take an example, let us suppose that it is decided internationally to cap pollution from air travel and to do so by establishing a trading scheme in which all companies are allocated x hours of flights per year (size of allocations to reflect numbers of employees). Wealthy Company A, from a developed country, would, say, purchase the emissions allowances of less developed companies B, C, and D. Would the price paid reflect the true wealth, generating potential of those allowances? It is unlikely to do so because, not only has Company A a greater capacity to develop that potential (which is what makes the system efficient), but it has superior information about that potential. After all, that greater potential lies within Company A's own operations. The overall effect of allocations trading on Companies B, C, and D is that they receive a one-off payment and, being excluded from air travel, they will have a restricted development potential and are likely to be left ever further behind in the marketplace by Company A. The propensity of companies B, C, and D to opt for the short-term profit at the expense of the longer-term gain is, furthermore, consistent with the message from the risk literature that actors tend to discount the future effects of their actions.[125]

Such informational disadvantages can also be said to be compounded by inequalities of bargaining position and capacity. In the example given, Companies B, C, and D are likely, if sited in a developing country, to be competing, as sellers of allocations, with firms who are less well-informed, less rational, and more desperate to sell than themselves—this will only weaken their capacity to strike a fairly priced deal with Company A. At the state level, Mumma has argued that many developing countries lack the financial, technical, and human resources necessary to allow them to negotiate equally with developed nations on emissions trading issues or to evaluate emissions trading programmes thoroughly enough to judge where their longer-term interests lie.[126]

---

[124] See J. Gupta, *The Climate Change Convention and Developing Countries: From Conflict to Consensus?* (Dordrecht, 1997), 122–3; Richman, 'Emissions Trading', 155.

[125] See, for example, J. Graham and J. Weiner (eds), *Risk v. Risk* (Harvard, 1997); M. Cropper and P. Portney, 'Discounting and the Evaluation of Lifesaving Programs' (1990) 3 *Journal of Risk and Uncertainty* 369–79; W.K. Viscusi, *Fatal Tradeoffs* (New York, 1992). We are grateful to Julia Black for making this point.

[126] A. Mumma, 'The Poverty of Africa's Position at the Climate Change Convention Negotiations' (2000/1) 19 *UCLA Journal of Envirnmental Law and Policy* 181; see also Gupta, *Climate Change Convention* and Richman, 'Emissions Trading'. Mumma notes (202–3) that at the Buenos Aires

According to Stern, one of the major advantages of emissions trading systems is that they allow efficiency and equity to be considered separately.[127] The UN Framework Convention on Climate Change (UNFCCC) approaches this issue and argues that developed countries should show leadership in tackling emissions, transferring technology, supporting capacity building, and financing the incremental costs of emissions reductions. It should do so, says UNFCCC, since equity calls for: the support of poorer countries by wealthier ones on grounds of ability to pay; respect for the principle that the polluter should pay when looking at historical responsibility for pollution; and allowing a rise in emissions in poorer countries in reflection of their relative per capita emissions levels and aspirations for growth and poverty reduction.[128]

These may be sentiments worthy of support, but we should be clear about the degree to which emissions trading and reallocative policies pull in opposing directions.[129] Such a tension may be so severe as to lead efficiency concerns to swamp those of equity—which negates Stern's argument that emissions trading conveniently allows equity and efficiency issues to be considered separately. Thus, on the post-Rio notion that developed countries would—for reasons of fairness—show leadership on climate change, Richman has commented, 'Emissions trading may conflict with the developed country leadership principle in several ways. Most obviously, it allows developed countries to avoid making the early and deep cuts that they committed to at Rio. Though they committed to make the first sacrifices in pollution, and thus production, developed nations can claim that they are meeting their reductions obligations through trading … emissions trading enables developed nations to "double count" trades as both domestic reductions and assistance to developing countries.'[130] This double-counting may mean that, *contra* Stern, emissions trading may actually stand in the way of decisions to redistribute resources in favour of the developing world.

Emissions trading exaggerates the effects of inequalities in wealth distribution and offers up wealth-creating opportunities to the currently wealthy (and often polluting). Reallocative policies, when linked to emissions trading, may look transparent and worthwhile but three points are worth stressing. First, any reallocative virtues will be due to distributional decisions and restrictions

---

Conference on Climate Change the US contingent numbered 83 persons, that of the EU 45, and the typical African country sent two to four persons. Developed nations' positions were based on arrays of prior publications and large numbers of prior events, whereas African positions often had to be devised on the spot.

[127] Stern Review, 473; A. Rose and B. Stevens, 'A Dynamic Analysis of Fairness in Global Warming Policy' (1988) 1 *Journal of Applied Economics* 329–62, 336.

[128] Stern Review, 473.

[129] See Richman, 'Emissions Trading'.

[130] See Richman, 'Emissions Trading', 170; Clifton, *A Dangerous Obsession*, 35–7.

that are placed on the trading mechanism—not to the trading mechanism itself—which can be said to deploy the equal trading rationale to legitimize the unfairness that is produced by inequalities of bargaining positions. Second, any protections for the less well-off, less powerful, less-developed, and less well-informed will be operating within a system that is intrinsically skewed in favour of wealth holders. Finally, it can be argued that, as far as fairness is concerned, there are grounds for doubting whether emissions trading systems match up to the performance of command or taxation regimes. The latter, after all, offer across the board approaches, are more easily enforced from the centre, and are not so vulnerable to distortion in favour of the well-resourced.

IS EMISSIONS TRADING ACCOUNTABLE AND TRANSPARENT?

It has been argued, as noted, that emissions trading combines democratic accountability with a market mechanism and that trading focuses public attention on decisions about aggregate emissions reductions.[131] In this regard, it is claimed that emissions trading can offer more democratic accountability than the rulemaking processes of traditional command regulation. Doubters, however, argue that trading systems have a special complexity that does not facilitate access. Such systems, it is complained, overlay market processes on top of the standard-setting procedures usual to command regimes. This duality, it is said, makes citizen participation in emissions trading programmes more difficult than in traditional regulation.[132] Thus, it has been protested that, 'The hope is that emissions can be cut cheaply by large corporations with the public virtually unaware that this is going on. But this lack of public awareness is the very thing that makes schemes vulnerable to industry lobbying, resulting in schemes that are ineffective and unfair.'[133]

Special criticisms may apply to systems, such as the EU ETS, in which caps are set in relation to Business As Usual projections. As noted above, such approaches mean that the caps imposed on emissions are liable to change as firms change their forecasts of emissions—a process that the House of Commons Environmental Audit Committee has criticized as creating an

---

[131] Ackerman and Stewart, 'Reforming Environmental Law' (1987). For a critique, see M. Peeters, 'Legislative Choices and Legal values' in Faure and Peeters, *Climate Change and European Emissions Trading*, 38–51.

[132] See D. Driesen, 'Free Lunch or Cheap Fix? The Emissions Trading Idea and the Climate Change Convention' (1998) 26 *British Columbia Environmental Affairs Law Review* 1.

[133] Lockwood, *A Rough Guide to Carbon Trading*, 7. As the *Financial Times* Editorial of 26 Apr. 2007 put it: 'most of the political appeal of markets is that they hide the true costs to consumers. That is why carbon markets exist in the first place.'

obvious lack of transparency.[134] There is a need, said the Committee, to set reductions from absolute levels of emissions, rather than from baselines of BAU projections which may vary significantly according to the differing assumptions that are fed into them.

In the case of emissions trading, however, such difficulties are raised to a new level by three significant factors. First, the assumptions that underpin some accountability relationships within trading are inconsistent with other modes of control. Thus, the assumption that emissions trading processes involve no losers is compatible with an efficiency-based reliance on market controls but it does not sit easily with the notion that less affluent citizens need democratically based protections from the distributional consequences of market transactions.

Second, within emissions trading there are control systems that operate with inconsistent core tenets. Thus, the idea that the market will allocate emissions abatements in an uncontentious manner is at odds with the belief that the starting points of markets call for adjustments to be made on the basis of some model of social justice. The view that distributional decisions can be overlaid on market mechanisms in a transparent way is liable to be heavily disputed by those who think that such efforts will, at best, involve tinkering in the face of the overwhelming need to preserve the workings of the market.

Third, there are incompatibilities within the system regarding the very needs for legitimacy and accountability. Emissions trading is not a system in which 'market' and 'democratic' checks and balances can be brought into line with any harmony. Normally an observer might view a 'market' mechanism as bringing accountability to consumers, shareholders, and other stakeholders and might see 'democratic' mechanisms as ensuring accountability to citizens and participants. In emissions trading, however, the 'market' is self-regarding and 'closed' in nature so that there is not even an effective regime of control by consumers, shareholders, or others. Governments who institute emissions trading systems allocate permits for trading between polluters, not between polluters and consumers. Such governments, accordingly, are involved in a process that relinquishes their own roles as holders to account and only reasserts this when they reset the emissions caps or baselines. They do not give up this control in favour of control by consumers but set the market free—often on the grounds that this is justifiable because the need for some action to combat emissions trumps any needs for legitimation beyond the group of potential compliers. Trading systems, accordingly, constitute 'accountability black holes' and, as such, cannot be harnessed alongside other accountability mechanisms in a coherent legitimizing mesh. Regarding legitimation, there might be said to be mush, not mesh.

---

[134] See House of Commons Environmental Audit Committee, 'The EU Emissions Trading Scheme: Lessons for the Future' HC 70 (Second Report of Session 2006–7), paras. 19 and 68.

The optimistic view of redundancy stresses the potential of harmony and coherence in concurrent accountability mechanisms.[135] The pessimistic vision suggests that redundancy theory may offer a valuable perspective on control regimes but that there are good reasons for thinking that mixtures of accountability systems will sometimes produce confusions, uncertainties, injustices, and democratic deficits. This is liable to occur when there are inconsistencies in the assumptions that form the basis for controls, when there are incompatibilities of relevant values, discourses and visions of accountability, and when there are variations in the accountability objectives of different systems.[136] The challenge for public lawyers and the designers of regulatory systems may be to make appropriate interventions in order to make complex networks of accountability work.[137] The emissions trading experience, however, suggests that such a challenge may be Herculean when the above three factors are encountered.

Accountability to *whom* is, of course, also a key issue, and one of the recurring criticisms of carbon trading post Kyoto is that it makes policy-makers responsive to multinational corporations, not local populations. Thus, campaigners have argued: 'The problems with carbon trading are compounded when carbon credits are used to fund destructive projects like large dams and industrial tree plantations...This never benefits the local populations who become displaced.'[138]

The emissions trading device, moreover, involves a lack of accountability by public officials for the distributional decisions of the market in allocations—for instance, regarding the location of the steps that are taken to abate emissions or the competition consequences of allocations. The emissions trading process, as a result, helps such officials to avoid specificity about the policies being furthered through the trading mechanism and the distributions of costs and benefits, winners and losers.[139] If, moreover, trading is allowed across jurisdictions, there may be additional problems of perverse incentives. Thus, the purchasers of permits may be induced, by emissions trading, to purchase credits from countries who monitor credit-generating activity poorly. Countries involved in selling permits, moreover, will have, as noted, a related incentive not to monitor emissions effectively-since such laxity will

---

[135] C. Scott, 'Accountability in the Regulatory State' (2000) 27 *Journal of Law and Society* 38–60; L. Stirton and M. Lodge, 'Transparency Mechanisms: Building Publicness into Public Services' (2001) 28 *Journal of Law and Society* 471–89.

[136] See J. Black, 'Constructing and Contesting Legitimacy and Accountability in Polycentric Regulatory Regimes' (2008) 2 *Regulation and Governance* 137–64.

[137] Scott, 'Accountability in the Regulatory State', 57.

[138] C. Guerro, quoted in D. Walls, *Costing the Earth* (www.redpepper.org.uk/Dec2006/dec-06-stern.htm).

[139] On the complexity of the UK ETS and the resultant lack of transparency, see von Malmborg and Strachan, 'Climate Policy', 153.

generate incoming purchases of credits. Monitoring in such countries will tend to be particularly weak if the pollution at issue is not inflicted on that country specifically but is spread across nations as a 'common bad'—as with greenhouse gases.[140] Such weak monitoring systems will undermine accountability and transparency will be poor.

How then does emissions trading score on general transparency? One way to summarize on this issue is to evaluate emissions trading processes with reference to Stirton and Lodge's four key transparency mechanisms (*information, choice, representation*, and *voice*).[141] *Information* allows informed choices by consumers and others but, as noted, emissions trading supplies little information to the consumers of products regarding the emissions abating efforts of suppliers and manufacturers or the locations at which any abatement efforts are being made. *Choice* allows consumers to choose the nature of products and goods—but, again, the lack of information provided to consumers in emissions trading systems means that purchasers of products are ill-placed to choose between polluting and non-polluting products. *Representation* ensures transparency by allowing access into policy processes to user and interest groups. With emissions trading mechanisms, however, such access is conferred predominantly on those suppliers who buy and sell permits—other groupings are kept at a distance by their non-inclusion in the market.[142] *Voice* allows user participation and redress. Unfortunately, however, the consumer user of goods has no access to the trading market, and the processes used to set caps and baselines tend to be dominated by conversations between supply firms and governments. Overall, then, serious doubts arise concerning the general transparency of emissions trading processes.

Conclusions

The strength of emissions trading flows from its attractiveness to different interests—it does not frighten the economically powerful and it appears to compensate those less well-placed parties who sell allowances. It is true that

---

[140] See N. Mabey, *Argument in the Greenhouse: The International Economics of Controlling Global Warming* (London, 1997), 25; Driesen, 'Is Emissions Trading an Economic Incentive Programme?', 15.

[141] L. Stirton and M. Lodge, 'Transparency Mechanisms: Building Publicness into Public Services' (2001) 28 *Journal of Law and Society* 471–89.

[142] A residual issue, as noted, is the extent to which the deficiencies of emissions trading regimes can be remedied—as where a certification or labelling scheme might address problems of transparency or consumer information—space here does not permit exploration of the potential for different combinations of regulatory and market mechanism.

emissions trading does give rise to contention regarding such matters as its efficiency, transparency, and fairness, but it might be asked whether the available alternative modes of controlling pollution—such as commands or taxes—are any less fraught with dangers regarding, for example, manipulation by powerful interests.[143] Emissions trading, it could be said, at least offers cost-effectiveness and ease of implementation.

Those suspicious of emissions trading might, however, respond to this optimism with two points. First, there are reasons, as indicated, to think that emissions trading, at least in certain circumstances, aggravates some of the problems commonly associated with traditional forms of command regulation. For instance, it can involve particular incentives to manipulate, special incumbent advantages, pronounced opportunities for windfalls,[144] and notable difficulties of enforceability, accountability, and transparency. In addition, it forgoes across-the-board standards in favour of less fair mechanisms that tend to reward past polluters. Second, it might be replied that if we are to choose emissions trading, we should not do so because 'all controls are fraught' or because it involves 'no losers' but because we place primacy on its capacity for overcoming the opposition of the economically powerful.

It has to be repeated that sweeping conclusions regarding emissions trading should be offered and treated with caution. Trading regimes display very different potential—both absolute and in comparison with other regulatory instruments—in divergent contexts. Thus, with small numbers of well-resourced emitters and continuous emissions monitoring devices—as in the US Acid Rain regime—the problems faced do not occupy the same scale as those encountered in an international greenhouse gas system with large numbers of varyingly resourced emitters and daunting challenges regarding monitoring and enforcement. It is often difficult, moreover, to pinpoint the extent to which observed difficulties are inherent in the trading device or can be explained as teething troubles (as perhaps with the EU ETS) or as implementation failures that might or might not be experienced with other regulatory instruments. Some problems (for example, of accountability and transparency) may, furthermore, be pointed out in trading regimes but may be readily addressable through supplementary controls. That said, it is to be expected that the difficulties associated with emissions trading regimes will tend to be the greater when they involve such factors as: high numbers of regulated organizations or regulators; cross-jurisdictional applications; and

---

[143] For discussions of alternatives to emissions trading in the climate change context, see G. Prins et al., *How to Get Climate Policy Back on Course*, University of Oxford, Institute for Science, Innovation and Society, and London School of Economics, Mackinder Programme (2009); Clifton, *A Dangerous Obsession*, 54–8.

[144] See, e.g., D. Helm, 'EU Climate Change Policy—A Critique' (2009): http://www.dieterhelm. co.uk/publications/SS_EU_CC_Critique.pdf.

high variations in resources and competencies across regulated enterprises or regulators. Further, such factors include: complexities in the allowances traded; inequalities of wealth or pollution records that raise contentious redistributive questions; serious enforcement and monitoring issues; and high levels of incumbency power.

In the light of the above caveat and the prior discussion, how is the global rise of emissions trading to be responded to? There are, perhaps, two ways forward. One is to accept that 'anything goes'—that when faced with catastrophic global risks, it is churlish to complain about legitimacy, accountability, or inherent biases in markets. The other way is to reassert democratic values and to work towards ways of controlling the negative aspects of trading mechanisms (such as their opacity) while holding that it is *especially* when faced with potential catastrophes—and when the most dramatic decisions are taken—that we have to place the highest premium on devising acceptable regimes of control and legitimation.

Part III
Rules and Enforcement

11 Enforcing Regulation

Applying regulatory controls on the ground involves the carrying out of a number of tasks. Even if it is assumed that regulatory objectives have been established with clarity, there is still much work to do. Information on risks, harms, and mischief creators has to be gathered, rules and other responses have to be devised, and the behaviour of regulatees has to be modified. An astute regulator, moreover, will also set about assessing whether current efforts are achieving the right results and whether there is a need to change strategy in order to improve performance. It is accordingly useful to think of enforcement, in its narrow 'behaviour modification' sense, as just one part of the broader regulatory process—a process that involves five core tasks.[1] These tasks can be set out as in the DREAM framework of Figure 11.1.

This chapter uses the DREAM framework to organize a discussion of the main challenges that regulators encounter in seeking to apply enforcement on the ground.

1.	DETECTING	The gaining of information on undesirable and non-compliant behaviour.
2.	RESPONDING	The developing of policies, rules, and tools to deal with the problems discovered.
3.	ENFORCING	The application of policies, rules, and tools on the ground.
4.	ASSESSING	The measuring of success or failure in enforcement activities.
5.	MODIFYING	Adjusting tools and strategies in order to improve compliance and address problematic behaviour.

Figure 11.1. Regulatory tasks: the DREAM framework

---

[1] See R. Baldwin and J. Black, *Defra: A Review of Enforcement Measures and an Assessment of their Effectiveness in Terms of Risk and Outcome* (London, 2005).

Detecting: Identifying Non-compliant and Undesirable Behaviour

Uncovering undesirable behaviour through detection is a first step in regulatory enforcement. Detection challenges are, however, often severe. Enforcers frequently face extreme difficulties in detecting errant behaviour when the regulated community is extensive (as where certain environmental controls cover the whole population) and where breaching rules is cheap and easily carried out in a clandestine manner. Resourcing realities often mean that enforcers have to rely on tip-offs from the public or hotlines and whistleblowing processes. As a result, the regulators will receive a good deal of unreliable information and will commonly be ill-placed to calculate the real level of 'off-the-screen' activity that detracts from the achievement of objectives.

In some areas it is, therefore, extremely difficult to state what 'compliance' involves and the problem of constructing an agreed understanding can be bedevilled by legal uncertainties. The latter sometimes stem from drafting weakness, but divergences of understanding between the judiciary and the regulators can also prove a problem—notably regarding the purposes and objectives of the regulation at issue. In cases where there are unresolved disagreements on the meaning of compliance, this renders detection activity extremely fraught.

Resourcing constitutes a perennial constraint on detection. In many controlled areas the calculation of levels of compliance and the incidence of 'off-the-screen' activity would demand the operation of registration schemes or the carrying out of surveys, but funds may not permit such activities. In other domains, such surveys are conducted and, in many sectors, programmes of random inspection are used to obtain relevant data. In yet other areas, detection can only be carried out after the event, and this impedes precautionary intervention.

In responding to these challenges, regulators must first develop clear conceptions of their aims and an appropriate disaggregation of those objectives into subsidiary aims so that achievable targets can be set and problems identified in a manageable way.[2] If this is not done, the regulators will not know what sort of errant behaviour they need to detect. Regulatory objectives, moreover, may change over time and, in addition, the threats to achieving objectives may shift continuously. A regulator of, say, fisheries will thus have to deal with changes in priorities regarding the protection of different species of fish (or regarding protecting fish versus protecting employment); it will also face emergent risks from innovative fishing technologies and new fishing enterprises.

---

[2] M. Sparrow, *The Regulatory Craft* (Washington, DC, 2000), 146–9.

Second, in such a state of flux it is essential to be able to identify levels and patterns of compliance, but change poses challenges. New methods of avoiding the rules or concealing non-compliance may be devised constantly. Enterprises may be creatively complying with, or breaking, the rules in innovative ways. A given set of rules or a licensing regime may be impacting on enterprises less than it did formerly. A regulator, accordingly, needs to be able to detect not merely the levels of any non-compliance with requirements but also the extent of any 'off-the-screen' or 'invisible' black market activity that affects the achieving of the agency's legitimate objectives. Third, regulators have to assess the extent to which compliance with the relevant legal requirements will not be enough to achieve agency objectives. In a world of change, with new problems and strategies for escaping the rules, it is essential to know, in a continuing manner, the gap between rules and objectives. How these challenges can be met will be returned to in the next chapter.

Responding: Developing Rules and Tools

A second core task of regulatory enforcement is the development of those rules and tools that are fit for purpose both in detecting non-compliance or undesirable behaviour and in producing compliance with relevant requirements. Although the potential list of enforcement tools is long,[3] not every regulator has the full complement, or indeed anything approaching it. This is no peripheral matter. The absence of a relevant tool—such as a power to take samples or to fine on the spot—may be seen by enforcers as a significant impediment to effective control.[4]

Enforcers are, however, often constrained in their development of new tools by a number of factors—including institutional environments. Legislation may often be needed in order to introduce new powers, and it is common for officials to consider that new legislation (even secondary legislation) is an unrealistic political prospect. Existing bodies of legislation (particularly European Directives) are often seen as constraints on the use of new tools and uncertainties in legislative requirements tend to blight creative approaches to new tools. Government policies and institutional factors are also often seen as

---

[3] In Defra alone over 40 different powers are deployed. Main types of enforcement tool are: tools relating to the *continuation of business/operations* (e.g. licence revocation powers); *monetary or financial tools* (e.g. fines); *restorative tools* (remediation orders; restorative conferences); *undertaking and compliance management tools* (e.g. voluntary or enforceable undertakings); *performance disclosure instruments* (e.g. league tables). These are in addition to pre-enforcement tools such as warnings, notices, etc.—see Baldwin and Black, *Defra: A Review of Enforcement Measures*.

[4] See, e.g., Defra, *Fly-Tipping Strategy* (London, 2004).

an impediment to new tool use—especially when these involve dispersions of regulatory responsibility across numbers of bodies or where attention is directed at enforcing existing tools to the detriment of forward looks at new powers. Resource constraints, as ever, constitute a hurdle—especially where these stand in the way of the surveying or inspection exercises that are needed in order to reveal the true incidence of non-compliance or unwanted activity and hence the need for new tools and strategies.

RULES AND ENFORCEMENT

In developing regulatory rules, it should be borne in mind that the type of rule adopted may impact on enforceability and the achieving of objectives. Not all kinds of rule can be enforced with the same degree of success.[5] Rules may fail for a number of reasons, for example, because they are too vague or too long and complex to understand readily or to enforce; or because they prohibit desirable behaviour or they do not cover certain undesirable conduct. Different regulatory contexts, furthermore, may demand rules with different qualities or dimensions.

Rules may vary according, *inter alia*, to: degree of specificity or precision; extent, coverage, or inclusiveness; accessibility and intelligibility; legal status and force; and the prescriptions or sanctions they incorporate.[6] Rules, moreover, have to be employed by enforcers in conjunction with different compliance-seeking strategies—be these prosecutions, administrative sanctions, or processes of persuasion, negotiation, advice, education, or promotion.

Different enforcement strategies may thus call for different kinds of rule. If prosecutions are the main mode of enforcement, this may call for precise rules so that guilt or innocence can be established easily. (As a result, these rules may be long and complex.) If broad promotion of good practice is to be used (e.g. in leaflets or guidance), then less precise but more accessible rules may be more effective.

As to the selection of enforcement strategies (and, accordingly, accompanying rule types) it has been argued that this requires an analysis of the kinds of regulatee being dealt with.[7] If the regulatee is well-intentioned (i.e. wishes to comply) and is ill-informed (about legal requirements or how to meet these),

---

[5] See generally, R. Baldwin, *Rules and Government* (Oxford, 1995); id., 'Why Rules Don't Work' (1990) 53 *MLR* 321; J. Black, *Rules and Regulators* (Oxford, 1997); id., 'Using Rules Effectively', in C. McCrudden (ed.), *Regulation and Deregulation* (Oxford, 1999); C. Hood, *Administrative Analysis: An Introduction to Rules, Enforcement and Organisations* (Brighton, 1986); C.S. Diver, 'The Optimal Precision of Administrative Rules' (1983) 93 *Yale LJ* 65.

[6] For other approaches to the dimensions of rules, see Black, *Rules and Regulators*, 21 and Diver, 'Optimal Precision'.

[7] See Baldwin, *Rules and Government*, ch. 6; I. Ayres and J. Braithwaite, *Responsive Regulation* (Oxford, 1992), ch. 2.

prosecution may be a lower priority than educating and promoting—since information rather than a big stick is required. Accessible rules will, accordingly, be useful. The well-intentioned, well-informed regulatee will be able to cope with more detailed rules. The ill-intentioned, ill-informed category may demand a higher level of prosecution and, accordingly, precise rules will be in order. Finally, the ill-intentioned, well-informed regulatee will demand strategies, rules, and sanctions that can cope with deliberate rule avoidance, and mixtures of general and specific rules may be appropriate.[8]

Effective enforcement thus calls for judgements to be made concerning blends of enforcement strategies and the rule types that will best produce compliance. This suggests that informers and rule-makers should ask the following questions:[9]

- What is the undesirable behaviour, or mischief at issue?
- Who is responsible for the mischief?
- Which enforcement strategies will best lead the mischief creators to comply?
- Which types of rules best complement those strategies?

Such an approach presupposes that types of regulatee can be identified in the various sectors regulated. This will allow strategies and rules to be designed accordingly. If this is not possible or sectors have numbers of different kinds of regulatee, it may be necessary for agencies to equip their enforcers with an array of rules and strategies to cope with all eventualities. This is very costly in rule-making resources. It can similarly be cautioned that pyramidic approaches to enforcement involve progressing through various strategies in a serial fashion and this may also make large demands on rule-making resources, since those different strategies should ideally be matched with different types of rule. When types of regulatee can be identified, a specific and a targeted, rather than a pyramidic, enforcement strategy may constitute a more effective use of resources.[10]

[8] See the discussion of creative compliance below and R. Kagan and J. Scholz, 'The Criminology of the Corporation and Regulatory Enforcement Strategies', in K. Hawkins and J. Thomas (eds), *Enforcing Regulation* (Boston, 1984)—who distinguish between corporations who are 'amoral calculators', 'political citizens', and 'organizationally incompetent'.

[9] See Baldwin, *Rules and Government*, ch. 6; id., 'Why Rules Don't Work'; and id., 'Governing with Rules', in G. Richardson and H. Genn (eds), *Administrative Law and Government Action* (Oxford, 1994) for a discussion of these questions and reasons why rule-makers may fail to adopt such an approach to rule-making. (They tend to assume enforcement is unproblematic and do not seek information on enforcement; they tend to underestimate the political problems involved in making rules; and they are subject to disruptive political pressures from within and beyond the organization.)

[10] See Baldwin, *Rules and Government*, 158 n. 25 and Ayres and Braithwaite, *Responsive Regulation*, ch. 2. On pyramidic approaches, See Chapter 12 below.

CREATIVE COMPLIANCE

Even if compliance with rules is achieved by enforcers, this is not the end of the story. Desired objectives may not be achieved for two main further reasons. The first of these is what has been termed 'creative compliance'.[11] This is the process whereby those regulated avoid having to break the rules and do so by circumventing the scope of a rule while still breaching the spirit of the rule. Let us suppose that, in order to protect small shops, a government legislates to prohibit retail premises with over 10,000 square metres of floor space from opening on Sunday afternoons. A retail firm might creatively comply with such a rule by dividing its 12,000 square metre operation into two linked operations of 6,000 square metres. It complies with the law but avoids the thrust of the legislation.

In some fields (e.g. taxation), whole industries are devoted to creative compliance and the challenge for regulatory rule-makers and enforcers is to devise ways to keep the problem under control. This may be difficult for a number of reasons. As McBarnet and Whelan note, regulated industries may apply political pressure to regulators and demand detailed rules so that the rule of law and principles of certainty are served, but such types of rules may in reality be the very formulations that are most easily side-stepped by creative compliers. One response is to reinforce detailed rules with open-textured and general rules that are more difficult to circumvent.[12]

INCLUSIVENESS

A second reason why successfully achieving compliance may still fail to produce desired results is that ill-formulated rules may prove over- or under-inclusive.[13] They may discourage desirable behaviour or fail to prevent undesirable behaviour. Bardach and Kagan[14] suggest that regulators tend to over-regulate with over-inclusive rules for a number of reasons. Amongst these are, first, the costs of gaining the information necessary for targeting rules perfectly. These costs can be very high, and rule-makers tend to solve the problem by writing over-inclusive rules and relying on selective enforcement. (This conveniently shifts costs from rule-makers to enforcers.) Second,

---

[11] See D. McBarnet and C. Whelan, 'The Elusive Spirit of the Law: Formalism and the Struggle for Legal Control' (1991) 54 *MLR* 848; id., 'Challenging the Regulators: Strategies for Resisting Control', in C. McCrudden (ed.), *Regulation and Deregulation*; D. McBarnet, 'Law, Policy and Legal Avoidance' (1988) *Journal of Law and Society* 113.

[12] See pp. 305–6 below, and, for example, the general duties for employers set out in sections 2–9 of the Health and Safety at Work Act 1984, which may catch employers who creatively comply around more precisely formulated regulations on workplace health and safety.

[13] See Black, *Rules and Regulators*, 7–10.

[14] E. Bardach and R. Kagan, *Going by the Book* (Philadelphia, 1982), 66–77.

rule-makers tend to opt for broad-brush solutions to problems. Third, pressure to avoid regulatory discretions and produce equal treatment under law tends to trade off efficiency for more rules. Finally, working on a problem while the political iron is hot tends to be necessary for rule-makers and the resultant tight deadlines rule out the precise targeting of rules.

Under-inclusiveness, on the other hand, may also result from informational problems. Thus, a rule may fail to come to grips with certain hazards because the regulator has not been able to develop the information necessary to identify the cause of the hazard.

Moreover, rules that deal with problems of inclusiveness, or coverage, may give rise to other problems. Colin Diver explains this well by supposing the need for a rule to stop airline pilots from flying when the social cost of allowing them to continue flying exceeds the social benefits of not having to replace them.[15] He suggests three formulations for such a rule.

Model I No person may pilot a commercial aircraft after their sixtieth birthday.

Model II No person may pilot a commercial aircraft if they pose an unreasonable risk of an accident.

Model III No person may pilot a commercial aircraft if they fall within one of the following categories. (There follow tables giving combinations of values for numerous variables including years, levels of experience, age, height, weight, blood pressure, heart-rate, eyesight, and a host of other medical factors affecting pilot performance.)

Model I is the most transparent and accessible rule. It is easily understood and easy to enforce, but gives rise to problems of inclusivity. Some pilots aged over 60 may present lower risks to passengers than some (unhealthy) pilots aged under 60. Model II offers a response to inclusivity (it states the rule's purpose) but, though accessible on its face, is vague, lacks clarity, and, for this reason, is difficult to enforce because it needs to be fleshed out and made precise. This is liable to prove an expensive and legally fraught process. Model III scores well on inclusivity and it precisely identifies hazard-causing factors (provided that it is constantly revised and supported by research on health risks). It is likely, however, to be very lengthy, technically complex, and difficult to apply without expert training or the hiring of specialized consultants.[16] It will also be extremely expensive for rule-makers to write, to keep up to date, and to locate within the necessary agreements on an exhaustive list of hazard-creating medical conditions. Model III is also likely to give rise to greater problems of creative compliance than Models I and II.[17]

---

[15] See Diver, 'Optimal Precision'.

[16] Model III may also give rise to issues of rule-choice. Which is the relevant rule to apply may become an issue in complex regimes.

[17] Thus a pilot suffering from a medical condition on the prohibited list might take a drug to remove that condition, but the drug might create another dangerous—but unlisted—condition.

Problems of over- and under-inclusiveness can also be approached by considering when it is better, in the face of uncertainty, to err on the side of over- or under-inclusiveness in regulating. Shrader-Frechette examines this issue in asking whether it is better to err by prohibiting the use of a technology that is falsely seen as dangerous but is really acceptable and safe (a 'Type I' error) or by allowing the use of a technology that is falsely seen as safe but which is really unsafe (a 'Type II' error).[18]

Type I errors are sometimes referred to as 'producer risks'[19] and Type II as 'consumer risks'. In practice, Shrader-Frechette contends, risk assessors tend to err on the side of avoiding Type I errors for a number of reasons: because pure science researchers prefer to suppose that no connection exists than to posit an effect (e.g. that a substance causes cancer);[20] because producers are seen as enjoying something analogous to a 'presumption of innocence' that places the burden on those asserting a harmful effect; and because many risk assessments are conducted by persons closely associated with, and sympathetic to, the product or technology at issue.[21]

Shrader-Frechette's argument, however, is that it is better, when uncertain, to err on the side of avoiding Type II errors—better to protect consumers rather than defend the producer's rights to sell products—because the burden of proof regarding risk acceptability should be placed on the person wishing to reduce producer rather than consumer risks.[22] She puts forward a number of reasons for this suggested approach:

---

[18] See K.S. Shrader-Frechette, *Risk and Rationality* (Berkeley, 1991). Such issues arise in making decisions on whether to regulate an area at all, as well as when deciding whether to draft an anticipated rule to cover a particular activity.

[19] Ibid., 132.

[20] See C.F. Cranor, *Regulating Toxic Substances* (New York, 1993), ch. 4. It has been argued elsewhere that less rigorous standards of proof are typically required to prevent the possibility of a Type II error than a Type I error—see G. Brennan, 'Civil Disaster Management: An Economist's View' (1991) 64 *Canberra Bulletin of Public Administration* 30–3. Stephen Tindale argues that the precautionary principle ('giving the environment the benefit of any reasonable doubt') has been seen in operation in some areas (e.g. new medicines or substances liable to enter the human food chain such as drinking water or meat containing growth hormones), but the Panglossian principle (optimism in the face of worrying evidence and the placing of the burden on those seeking to demonstrate that a risk arises) has also been encountered, notably in the environmental area (e.g. global warming, dog faeces, leukemia clusters around Sellafield, pesticides, and lead pollution). The prevalence of the Panglossian approach, Tindale says, leads to the undermining of respect for politics and those in authority—see S. Tindale, 'Procrastination and the Global Gamble', in J. Franklin (ed.), *The Politics of Risk Society* (Cambridge, 1998), and also A. Jordan and T. O'Riordan, 'The Precautionary Principle in UK Environmental Law and Policy', in T. Gray (ed.), *UK Environmental Policy in the 1990s* (Basingstoke, 1995).

[21] Beck argues that in 'risk society' in general, technological advances create new risks far more rapidly than conventional democratic mechanisms can devise responses—this would imply a tendency to under-regulate and to regulate in an under-inclusive manner (see U. Beck, 'The Politics of Risk Society', in Franklin, *Politics of Risk Society*).

[22] Beck also argues that the burden of proof should rest on risk creators to prove safety—'The Politics of Risk Society', 21.

- It is more important to protect from harm than to enhance welfare.
- Producers reap most of the benefits of a new technology; they should accordingly bear most of the risks and costs.
- Consumers merit greater protection than industry, since they have less information and fewer resources with which to deal with hazards.
- Lay persons should be accorded legal rights to bodily security—to minimize industry risk on efficiency grounds offends notions of such security and would be morally offensive.
- Producers may not always be able to compensate persons harmed by their products; it is better, accordingly, to err on the side of eliminating harms at source.
- If there is uncertainty about the level of harm, it is difficult to justify imposing a risk on consumers.
- On democratic grounds there ought to be no imposition of risks without the informed consent of those who are to bear the risks.
- If consumers have not given informed consent, industry ought to bear the burden of proving that imposing a consumer risk is justified.
- Minimizing consumer risk is less likely to threaten social and political stability than minimizing producer risk.

Contrary to the above approach, it can be contended that even if one accepts the value of consumer protection, there are a number of reasons why one might, on occasions, want to favour producer rather than consumer protection and accordingly err on the under-inclusive side when imposing restrictions on industry. First, if one accepts that rule-makers tend to write over-inclusive rules for a number of reasons (as discussed above), there may be a case for countering this tendency by consciously erring towards under-inclusiveness in particular cases of uncertainty.[23] Second, one might put a value on economic liberty as a good in itself or favour under-inclusiveness where compliance costs are liable to be extremely high and the benefits of a rule are low (a regulation might be proposed in such circumstances for reasons of social justice rather than on efficiency grounds). Third, if the rule at issue exerts control at the stage of preventing a dangerous action occurring (e.g. by licensing an activity) rather than at the stage where the dangerous action has occurred or the harm has been caused,[24] there may be a case for erring on the side of under-inclusion if the costs of prevention are liable to be very high and if any problems of under-inclusiveness can be countered by controls at the act or harm stage.

To summarize, rule-making does affect both the way that enforcement is carried out and the effectiveness of enforcement activity. It can be seen also that rule-making involves complex trade-offs between, amongst other things,

---

[23] See Brennan, 'Civil Disaster Management', 33.
[24] On stages of intervention, see the following section of this chapter.

attempts to solve problems of inclusivity; efforts to contain creative compliers; and endeavours to produce rules that can be enforced effectively in the field.[25]

PREDICTING COMPLIANCE: THE TABLE OF ELEVEN

In considering the design of rule systems, it is worth noting a framework that has been developed by the Dutch Ministry of Justice as an aid to estimating the levels of compliance that will be associated with a given law.[26] The 'Table of Eleven' (opposite) seeks to identify the factors that impact on compliance and is highly influential in some jurisdictions as a way not merely to judge future compliance but to evaluate the enforcement efforts of a regulator and to improve the design of rules. The Table of Eleven involves reference to eleven 'causes and motives' relevant to compliance with legislation. These are divided into two groups: factors related to spontaneous compliance, and those motivations that flow from external regulatory enforcement.

The 'Table of Eleven' does not constitute a single, complete, theory of compliance—or a theory of enforcement strategy—but it does usefully draw on several bodies of theory in order to point to causes of compliance. It also offers policymakers a framework that will expose areas requiring attention together with a checklist of relevant questions. Regarding the first of the above compliance factors—'Knowledge of rules'—for instance, the checklist prompts the following queries:

a. Familiarity
• Does the target group know the rules?
• Do they only need to make limited efforts to find out about the rules?
• Is the legislation not too elaborate?

b. Clarity
• Are the rules formulated in such a way that the target group can understand them easily?
• Is the target group actually capable of understanding the rules?
• Is it sufficiently clear to the target group what the rules apply to?
• Is it clear to the target group what rule applies?

Such checklisting usefully helps to locate potential areas of weakness in a law's formulation and potential responses to flaws in strategy. The 'Table of Eleven' framework also emphasizes that it is not enough to ensure optimality of the objective risks that flow from non-compliance—what count are the target groups' subjective judgements regarding such risks.

---

[25] On trading-off problems of inclusiveness against other factors such as costs of enforcement, see Diver, 'Optimal Precision', 74–8, and Baldwin, *Rules and Government*, 180–5.
[26] See Dutch Ministry of Justice, *The 'Table of Eleven': A Versatile Tool* (The Hague, 2004).

THE TABLE OF ELEVEN

The spontaneous compliance dimensions

1. Knowledge of rules

    a. Familiarity with rules
    b. Clarity of rules

Explanation: This factor concerns the familiarity with and clarity of legislation among the target group. (Unfamiliarity with the rules may result in unintentional violations, as may lack of clarity or complexity of legislation.)

2. Costs/benefits

    a. Financial/economic costs and benefits
    b. Intangible costs and benefits

Explanation: This concerns all financial/economic and intangible advantages and disadvantages of compliance or non-compliance with the rule(s), expressed in time, money, and effort.

3. Extent of acceptance

    a. Acceptance of the policy objective
    b. Acceptance of the effects of a policy

Explanation: The extent to which the policy and legislation is considered acceptable by the target group.

4. The target group's respect for authority

    a. Official authority
    b. Competing authority

Explanation: The extent to which the target group respects the government's authority and the extent of respect for their *own* standards and values, which may be in conflict with the government's intentions.

5. Non-official control (social control)

    a. Social control
    b. Horizontal supervision

Explanation: The risk, as estimated by the target group, of positive or negative sanctions on their behaviour other than by the authorities: either through informal social controls or by 'horizontal supervision'—influences exerted by the target group or professional group on their own members.

Enforcement dimensions

6. Risk of being reported

Explanation: The risk, as estimated by the target group, of a violation being detected by others than the authorities and being reported to a government body (by tip-off or complaint, for instance).

7. Risk of inspection

   a. Records inspection
   b. Physical inspection

Explanation: The risk, as estimated by the target group, of an inspection into compliance by the authorities (either an inspection of records or a physical inspection).

8. Risk of detection

   a. Detection in a records inspection
   b. Detection in a physical inspection

Explanation: The risk, as estimated by the target group, of a violation being detected in an inspection carried out by the authorities.

9. Selectivity

Explanation: The perceived risk that a violation will be detected from within a given body of inspected businesses, persons, actions, or areas (the anticipated 'hit-rate' of inspections).

10. Risk of sanction

Explanation: The risk, as estimated by the target group, of a sanction being imposed if an inspection reveals that a rule has been broken.

11. Severity of sanction

Explanation: The severity and nature of the sanction associated with the violation and any additional disadvantages of being sanctioned (e.g. losses of respect or reputation; legal costs, etc.).

Enforcement: Strategies for Applying Tools

STYLES OF ENFORCEMENT

Regulatory officials seek to gain compliance with the law not merely by resort to formal enforcement and prosecution but by using a host of informal techniques including education, advice, persuasion, and negotiation.[27] Reiss

---

[27] See K. Hawkins, *Environment and Enforcement* (Oxford, 1984); B.M. Hutter, *Compliance: Regulation and Environment* (Oxford, 1997); G. Richardson, A. Ogus, and P. Burrows, *Policing Pollution* (Oxford, 1988); W.G. Carson, 'Some Sociological Aspects of Strict Liability and the Enforcement of Factory Legislation' (1970) 33 *MLR* 396; R. Cranston, *Regulating Business* (London, 1979); A. Reiss, 'Selecting Strategies of Social Control over Organisational Life', in Hawkins and Thomas, *Enforcing Regulation*; N. Gunningham, 'Enforcement and Compliance Strategies' in R. Baldwin, M. Cave, and M. Lodge (eds), *The Oxford Handbook of Regulation* (Oxford, 2010); B. Morgan and K. Yeung, *An Introduction to Law and Regulation* (Cambridge, 2007), ch. 4.

has thus drawn an important distinction between 'compliance'[28] approaches to enforcement, which emphasize the use of measures falling short of prosecution in order to seek compliance with laws, and 'deterrence'[29] approaches, which are penal and use prosecutions in order to deter future infractions.

Compliance approaches can be seen as holding conformity to the law as a more central objective than deterrence approaches, which may also involve a stronger retributive dimension.[30] Within the compliance strategy, Hutter has distinguished two sub-strategies that she terms the *persuasive* and the *insistent* approaches. Both aim to secure compliance, but the persuasive approach is more accommodating. Officials educate and coax offenders into complying with the law, they explain rationales for laws and possible means of compliance, and do so in a patient, open-ended way.[31] The insistent strategy is less flexible and there are defined limits to the tolerance of officials who will increase pressures when compliance is not forthcoming within a limited period. Cultural differences may also be seen as producing differences in enforcement styles. It has been said that the American system of enforcement tends to be more adversarial, litigious, and deterrence-based than the more compliance-orientated British approach[32] but caution should be exercised in viewing national approaches as homogeneous—variations of styles may be encountered even within single agencies (on which, more below).[33]

On the relative effectiveness and desirability of compliance and deterrence approaches to enforcement, there are a number of conflicting arguments.[34] Proponents of deterrence tend to argue that compliance approaches are indicative of capture, lack of enforcement resources, and of regulator and regulatee having sufficient identification with each other (through shared experience, contacts, staff exchanges, or familiarity) as to make routine prosecution unthinkable.[35] In favour of compliance, however, it is often

---

[28] See Reiss, 'Selecting Strategies'. Richardson et al., *Policing Pollution*, use the term 'accommodative' for this style.

[29] Hawkins uses the term 'sanctioning' for this approach.

[30] See Hutter, *Compliance*, 15. For a study of the conformity of enforcement approaches to constitutional values, see K. Yeung, *Securing Compliance: A Principled Approach* (Oxford, 2004).

[31] This strategy is said to approximate to Braithwaite, Walker, and Grabosky's notion of the Diagnostic Inspectorate in their article 'An Enforcement Taxonomy of Regulatory Agencies' (1987) 9 *Law and Policy* 321.

[32] See, e.g., D. Vogel, *National Styles of Regulation* (Ithaca, NY, 1988) and for a USA/Sweden comparison, see S. Kelman, *Regulating America, Regulating Sweden* (Cambridge, MA, 1981).

[33] On variations within the Health and Safety Executive's inspectorates, see Baldwin, *Rules and Government*, 143, and C.D. Drake and F.B. Wright, *Law of Health and Safety* (London, 1983), 24.

[34] For a head-to-head confrontation, see the exchange between F. Pearce and S. Tombs, 'Ideology, Hegemony and Empiricism' (1990) 30 *British Journal of Criminology* 424, and also K. Hawkins, 'Compliance Strategy, Prosecution Policy and Aunt Sally' (1990) 30 *British Journal of Criminology* 144, and 'Enforcing Regulation: More of the Same from Pearce and Tombs' (1991) 31 *British Journal of Criminology* 427. See also Ayres and Braithwaite, *Responsive Regulation*, 20–35.

[35] See R. Brown, 'Theory and Practice of Regulatory Enforcement: Occupational Health and Safety Regulation in British Columbia' (1994) 16(1) *Law and Policy* 63.

argued that this approach offers an efficient, cost-conscious use of resources and can be justified as economically rational, rather than indicative of capture.[36] Prosecutions are so costly in time and money that selective use of less formal mechanisms may produce higher levels of compliance for a given level of state expenditure than is possible with routine prosecution.[37] Compliance approaches, it is further said, are better than deterrence strategy in fostering valuable information flows between regulators and regulated; in educating regulatees so that they think constructively about modes of compliance; and in encouraging firms to perform to higher standards than the law calls for.[38]

The case for deterrence approaches is, in contrast, based on claims that they can prove highly effective in changing corporate cultures and stimulating management systems that reduce the risks of infringement.[39] Deterrence approaches treat infractions seriously by stamping errant conduct as unacceptable—they accordingly reinforce, and give effect to, social sentiments of disapproval, and this enhances social pressures to comply. Such approaches, it is urged moreover, can induce political shifts so that firmer approaches to regulation can be taken.[40] Tough approaches to enforcement, say deterrence advocates, make it rational for firms to give a high priority to compliance.

There are, however, a number of reasons to question the effectiveness of deterrence approaches in controlling corporations. Deterrence strategy demands that sanctions are sufficiently severe to incentivize compliance beyond the immediate case. In many instances, however, the courts do not impose fines of sufficient gravity to produce this result.[41] This may happen for a number of reasons—a large fine may be seen as threatening an errant company's solvency and employees' livelihoods, for instance, or it may be viewed as depriving the rule breaker of the liquidity that is needed to remedy the mischief at issue. Whatever the cause, the frequent effect is under-inducement to comply.[42]

The assumptions of rationality that underpin deterrence theory are also questioned by numbers of critics. As with individuals, instances of non-compliance within companies may be the result of 'irrationalities' that flow

---

[36] See P. Fenn and C. Veljanovski, 'A Positive Economic Theory of Regulatory Enforcement' (1988) 98 *Economic Journal* 1055; C.G. Veljanovski, 'Regulatory Enforcement: An Economic Study of the British Factory Inspectorate' (1983) 5 *Law and Policy Quarterly* 75; Hawkins, *Environment and Enforcement*, 198–202.

[37] See Baldwin, *Rules and Government*, ch. 6.

[38] Hawkins, *Environment and Enforcement*.

[39] See Bardach and Kagan, *Going by the Book*, 93–5.

[40] See Pearce and Tombs, 'Ideology, Hegemony and Empiricism', 434.

[41] See R. Macrory, *Regulatory Justice: Sanctioning in a Post-Hampton World* (Cabinet Office, May 2006).

[42] For doubts whether increased fines necessarily increase compliance incentives, see S. Kadambe and K. Segerson, 'On the Role of Fines as an Environmental Enforcement Tool' (1998) 41 *Journal of Environmental Planning and Management* 217–26.

from such sources as poor training and ill-organization. Responding to such problems with the tool of rational deterrence may, accordingly, involve a mismatch of response and mischief.[43] For such and other reasons, it is not always certain whether punitive sanctions will work to stimulate internal controls.[44] It is worth emphasizing that corporations will often be confused and irrational about their risks of being punished for non-compliance (their 'punitive risks'); their staff may conflate individual and corporate liabilities; they may be poorly organized to deal with, anticipate, or react to punitive risks and the effects of sanctions; their Boards may under-perform in supervising or providing leadership on punitive risk-management, and they may be poorly placed to assess how they and their staff are performing as risk managers.[45] Many small and medium companies, indeed, will not know what it would cost to comply with the rules, and they may tend to assume that they are compliant until they are told otherwise.[46] They may, moreover, see compliance not as observing the rules but as behaving in accord with the last negotiation that they had with an inspector.[47] In the face of such propensities, it is difficult to see deterrent forces as bearing materially on regulated concerns.

Even if it is assumed that some companies do act along rational lines, it cannot be taken for granted that, when they do react to possible punitive liabilities, this will lead them to respond with compliance. Even on rational deterrence assumptions, they may see compliance as just one way to reduce the probability of suffering a sanction for breaching the rules. Other ways to reduce that probability might include creative compliance, bringing pressure to bear on the regulator (to discourage prosecution); shifting risk or blame on to the shoulders of individuals or outsourced business partners; or evasion, non-cooperation with regulators, and concealment.[48]

---

[43] Ibid. and see S. Stafford, 'The Effect of Punishment on Firm Compliance with Hazardous Waste Regulations' (2002) 44 *Journal of Environmental Economics and Management* 290–308.

[44] See B. Fisse and J. Braithwaite, *Corporations, Crime and Accountability* (Cambridge, 1993); C. Parker, *The Open Corporation* (Cambridge, 2002); N. Gunningham and R. Johnstone, *Regulating Workplace Safety* (Oxford, 1999), 217–25; C.D. Stone, *Where the Law Ends: The Social Control of Corporate Behaviour* (New York, 1975); J. Braithwaite and T. Makkai, 'Testing an Expected Utility Model of Corporate Deviance' (1991) 25 *Law and Society Review* 7; R. Brown, 'Administrative and Criminal Penalties in the Enforcement of the Occupational Health and Safety Legislation' (1992) 30(3) *Osgoode Hall Law Journal* 691. On deterrence in the environmental sector, see D. Chappell and J. Norberry, 'Deterring Polluters: The Search for Effective Strategies' (1990) 13 *University of New South Wales Law Journal* 97.

[45] R. Baldwin, 'The New Punitive Regulation' (2004) 67 *Modern Law Review* 351–83.

[46] J. Braithwaite and T. Makkai, 'Testing an Expected Utility Model of Corporate Deterrence' (1991) 25 *Law and Society Review* 7–39; H. Genn, 'Business Responses to the Regulation of Health and Safety in England' (1993) 15 *Law and Policy* 219–33.

[47] See R. Fairman and C. Yapp, 'Enforced Self-Regulation, Prescription and Conceptions of Compliance within Small Businesses' (2005) 27 *Law and Policy* 491–519.

[48] On the management of liability risks, see W. S. Laufer, 'Corporate Liability Risk Shifting and the Paradox of Compliance' (1999) 52 *Vanderbilt Law Review* 1343, 1410–11; J. Black, 'Using Rules

The prospect of possible sanctions may also induce companies to respond by reducing the impact of any sanction. They may thus take out insurance, share risks, or act to increase corporate resilience. On rational deterrence assumptions, companies will balance the costs and benefits of compliance with the expected costs and benefits of non-compliance, and will choose the combinations of risk-reducing responses that maximize benefits over costs.[49]

The predominant position is, however, that many companies operate largely unaware of their exposure to punitive regulatory risks, and the overall evidence is not highly consistent with effective and rational regimes in which anticipated penalties stimulate compliance. It is, however, in tune with the findings of those researchers who argue that: 'The bounded rationality of organizations and top management means that many do not make rational cost-benefit calculations about compliance until something happens to bring the risks of non-compliance to their attention. Economic costs which do not draw attention to themselves by generating some kind of crisis are often overlooked by busy management.'[50]

Other posited difficulties with deterrence approaches are that they can often prove inflexible; they may fail to identify the best ways to improve performance; and they may cause resentment, hostility, and lack of cooperation in those regulated. Where such resistance is forthcoming from regulated parties, this, in turn, is likely to reduce the effectiveness of enforcement, as well as increase overall costs.[51] A further criticism of deterrence-based enforcement is that it may produce undesired side-effects. Thus, as noted, it may drive certain firms out of business and cause unemployment, with the result that the public is alienated and, in turn, there is a reduction in regulatory effectiveness. Compliance strategies, on the other hand, can provide responses to risks (as opposed to harms actually inflicted) and can do so more effectively than deterrence approaches. They can thus prevent more harms from occurring.[52] They are consistent with making exceptions where there is a

Effectively' in C. McCrudden (ed.), *Regulation and Deregulation* (Oxford: 1999) 118–19; R. Kraakman, 'Gatekeepers: The Anatomy of a Third-Party Enforcement Strategy' (1986) 2 *Journal of Law, Economics and Organization* 53; and S. S. Simpson, *Corporate Crime, Law and Social Control* (Cambridge, 2002), 51–2. On creative compliance, see D. McBarnet and C. Whelan, 'The Elusive Spirit of the Law: Formalism and the Struggle for Legal Control' (1991) 54 *Modern Law Review* 848. For a discussion of risk-shifting by moving business activity to less rigorous legal environments, see C.E. Moore, 'Taming the Giant Corporation' (1987) 33 *Crime and Delinquency* 388, 390–4.

[49] A further barrier to compliance is noted by Diane Vaughan. In processes of 'deviance normalization' corporate decisions, practices, and cultures may stretch the boundaries of acceptable behaviour beyond the legal so that non-compliance is routinized—see D. Vaughan, *The Challenger Launch Decision: Risky Technology, Culture and Deviance at NASA* (Chicago, 1996).

[50] Parker, *The Open Corporation*, 69–70.

[51] See R. Kagan and J. Scholz, 'The Criminology of the Corporation and Regulatory Enforcement Strategies', in Hawkins and Thomas, *Enforcing Regulation*.

[52] See, e.g., R. Brown and M. Rankin, 'Persuasion, Penalties and Prosecution', in M.L. Friedland (ed.), *Securing Compliance* (Toronto, 1990).

case for them—rather than imposing uniform requirements where this makes no sense.[53]

Instead of drawing a stark contrast between compliance and deterrence approaches to enforcement it is possible, however, to see enforcement as involving a progression through different compliance-seeking strategies and sanctions. Ian Ayres and John Braithwaite comment: 'To reject punitive regulation is naive; to be totally committed to it is to lead a charge of the light brigade. The trick of successful regulation is to establish a synergy between punishment and persuasion.'[54]

These two authors popularized the concept of enforcement pyramids. One of these pyramids involves a hierarchy of sanctions, the second, a hierarchy of regulatory strategies. In this model of 'responsive regulation', those regulated are subjected to increasingly interventionist regulatory responses as they continue to infringe, and to less interventionist actions as they come to comply. The 'responsive regulation' approach is considered in the following chapter, as are a number of other enforcement theories that constitute alternatives to the traditional choice between deterrence and compliance.

WHEN TO INTERVENE

Regulators can intervene in economic or social activity not merely by different methods but at different stages in the processes that lead to harms. Thus, action can be taken to *prevent* a dangerous act or situation arising (e.g. hotels can be inspected and licensed before opening to guests in order to ensure that fire hazards do not arise); action can be taken in response to the *act* of creating a dangerous situation (e.g. operating a hotel without fire doors or sprinklers); or action can be prompted by the realization of a *harm* (e.g. injuring a hotel guest in a hotel fire). Similarly, the kinds of standards incorporated in regulatory rules may be directed towards different stages of the processes leading to harms. Thus, applying *specification* (or *design*) standards (e.g. demanding a certain type of machine be used for a procedure) has the effect of controlling the circumstances leading to dangerous acts (which will not occur if a safe design of machine is used). Applying *performance* (or *output*) standards looks to the seriousness of the dangerous acts that are involved in a procedure, and *target* standards focus on the harms that result (e.g. the amount of pollution damage to the river).[55]

---

[53] See Bardach and Kagan, *Going by the Book*, 58.
[54] Ayres and Braithwaite, *Responsive Regulation*, 25; see also J. Braithwaite, *To Punish or Persuade* (Albany, NY, 1985).
[55] For further discussion of standard-setting, see Chapter 14.

Shavell has distinguished three stages of intervention, in which actions are respectively preventative, act-based, and harm-based, and has considered the circumstances that favour particular stages of regulatory intervention.[56]

PREVENTATIVE ACTIONS

One circumstance in which preventive action is called for is where the costs of rectifying a dangerous state of affairs may be high. It may thus be better to prevent a dangerous design of steel foundry from being built than to try and change matters post-construction. Another reason for acting preventively is that a potentially catastrophic danger may otherwise arise. For both of these reasons, nuclear reactor designs are approved and licensed before the reactor is built. To allow a reactor to be constructed and then to demand changes to improve safety would be hugely expensive and to intervene only when a reactor was being run dangerously would be to run an unacceptably high risk of a catastrophe occurring. Conversely, where the potential harm is relatively small, there may be a stronger case for intervening at the harm stage, since failures to deter through punishing harm-causers will not prove catastrophic.

A further reason for preventative action is that in some circumstances, preventative steps can be successfully employed without the use of a heavy regulatory hand. Thus, a television advertisement on public safety (for example on dipping car headlights properly when night driving) may prevent a large number of dangerous acts and serious harms from arising, but it neither interferes greatly with drivers nor involves strong sanctions or expensive enforcement activity. By comparison, intervening at the act stage—by stopping drivers and bringing legal proceedings for failing to use lights properly—involves a good deal of driver inconvenience and state enforcement expense. It may also fail to prevent a large number of harms from ensuing. Waiting until the harms occur (the injuries and deaths) will demand expensive prosecutions and severe sanctions and such actions may (for reasons discussed below) also fail efficiently to prevent future harms from occurring.

The potential of preventative strategies is often restricted by informational difficulties. It may not be easy to predict when certain dangerous situations or harms may occur. To prevent dangerous driving manœuvres would thus be difficult and costly. Even if all drivers had an inspector sitting in their vehicle it would be difficult for the inspector to anticipate when a dangerous turn or stop was about to happen.[57] It may, accordingly, be more efficient to exert

---

[56] See S. Shavell, 'The Optimal Structure of Law Enforcement' (1993) *Journal of Law and Economics* 255.

[57] See Shavell, 'The Optimal Structure of Law Enforcement', 272. The licensing and testing of drivers does, however, constitute prevention at the most general level.

control at the act or harm stage by imposing sanctions for the act of dangerous driving or for causing an accident. It may, similarly, be difficult for regulators to anticipate all potential sources of harm (e.g. of damaging levels of noise in industrial processes). Preventing dangerous activity in such circumstances may, accordingly, make very severe informational demands and prove very expensive. In terms of administrative costs it will often be cheapest of all for the state to wait until the stage when harms have been caused, since only a small proportion of dangerous acts will result in actual harms and so a smaller enforcement case load will be involved.

ACT-BASED INTERVENTIONS

Intervening at the act stage may be more useful than at the preventative stage when prevention would be expensive to accomplish. Thus it might be costly and intrusive to demand prior approval for all operations on a construction site. Resources are more effectively deployed in inspecting such sites and sanctioning dangerous actions—for example, using insecure scaffolding.

Act-stage intervention may be preferable to harm-stage control where it is difficult to hold firms or individuals to account for causing harms. This may well be the case where a harm may arise from a number of concurrent sources. Thus, if it is known that ingesting certain particles may cause cancer but it is also known that the disease can be caused by a number of other common hazards (e.g. smoking), it may be preferable to regulate, say, the act of causing workers to ingest the particles than to look at the harm and attempt to establish that a particular cancer has been caused by the particles rather than some other agent.

Where the dangerous act can be identified far more easily than the resultant harm, there is, again, a case for act-based intervention. The harms caused by some acts may be cumulatively very serious but highly diffused (e.g. in the pollution field), and it will be more effective to enforce at the act level then to deal with huge numbers of individually small claims.

Intervening at the act stage may also be preferable to harm-based sanctioning where the latter will under-deter the causing of further harms. Act-based sanctions can be smaller and more frequently applied than harm-based ones because no injury has yet occurred and the instances of infraction are greater in number (since not all dangerous acts lead to harms). In order to obtain the same levels of deterrence from harm-based sanctions, the fines involved may have to be extremely high since a hazard creator may estimate the chance of actually producing a harm as extremely small and of being fined as even smaller. If the firms causing harms are unlikely to be able to pay such fines, they will be under-deterred. In some sectors there will be a correlation between poor resourcing and the causing of harms and, accordingly, there will tend to be particular problems of under-deterrence through harm-based intervention. Where potential harms may vastly exceed the resources of the causers of harm (e.g. where ill-resourced firms may injure or kill large numbers of persons) there is liable to be under-deterrence and unacceptably low incentives to take appropriate care.

HARM-BASED INTERVENTIONS

Enforcement costs may sometimes militate in favour of intervening at the stage of harm, rather than of dangerous act. It may be cheaper for the state to punish the causers of the relatively small number of instances of harm than to pursue the much larger number of persons who perform dangerous acts that are liable to cause harms in some instances. It follows from what has been said above that a policy of severely sanctioning harms will only deter adequately if detection is sufficiently effective and if potential offenders are likely to be able to pay the large fines involved (or serve the prison terms).

It cannot, however, be assumed that in all cases it is easier to apply sanctions to harms than to acts. If a construction firm erects cheap but unsafe scaffolding and makes it difficult for a regulator to detect harms—for example, by rewarding injury-free teams of workers with bonuses and thereby generating peer group pressures on workers not to report injuries—it may be easier for a regulator to penalize the (highly visible) act of using dangerous scaffolding than to punish the firm for occasioning harm to the worker.

Enforcement is a matter of deploying a strategy or mixture of targeted strategies for securing desired results on the ground.[58] The NAO found that Defra fisheries regulators prioritized inspections according to broad-based risk analyses which tended to target particular fisheries and types of activity, rather than individual vessels.[59] Thus, surveillance operations and inspections tended to focus on areas of high risk where quotas were most restrictive, stocks were of high value, fishing activity was intense, fish were known to be collecting, or fisheries were seasonal. Inspections also tended to be concentrated on points where the regulatory returns to interventions would have been the greatest—for example on those ports where landings were, given the circumstances, most likely. Major difficulties encountered in using such risk-based approaches lay in coming to terms with new risk creators and new risks

[58] See generally, Hutter, *Compliance*, ch. 1; id., *The Reasonable Arm of the Law?* (Oxford, 1988); Hawkins, *Environment and Enforcement*. On private enforcement, see J. Braithwaite, 'Enforced Self-Regulation' (1982) 80 *Michigan Law Review* 1461; Ayres and Braithwaite, *Responsive Regulation*, ch. 4; C.D. Shearing and P.D. Stenning (eds), *Private Policing* (Beverly Hills, 1986); W. Landes and R. Posner, 'The Private Enforcement of Law' (1975) 4 *Journal of Legal Studies* 1.

[59] See National Audit Office (NAO), *Fisheries Enforcement in England*, HC 563 Session 2002–3 (April 2003) (hereafter 'NAO, *Fisheries Enforcement*'), 20. On risk-based regulation, see chapter 13 below.

to fish stocks. The extent of 'off screen' activities also tended to undermine the reliability of the data underpinning the risk analyses.

HOW MUCH TO ENFORCE

It is not sensible for regulators to aim for perfect compliance or the complete elimination of a risk. This is because enforcement costs tend to escalate as targeted levels of compliance are raised, and a point will arrive where the costs of further enforcement are not justified by the gains. Breyer refers to this as the problem of the last 10 per cent[60] and quotes Sheldon Meyers: 'it frequently is relatively cheap to reduce risks from 0 to 90 per cent, more expensive to go from 90 per cent to 99 per cent and more expensive to go from 99 per cent to 99.9 per cent'.[61]

In economic terms, the socially optimal level of enforcement occurs at the point where the extra costs of enforcement exceed the resulting additional benefits to society.[62] Included within the costs of enforcement are the following:

- the costs of agency monitoring;
- the expenses of processing and prosecuting cases;
- the defence costs (of innocent and guilty parties);
- the costs of misapplications of law, convicting the innocent, and deterring desirable behaviour.

The gains from enforcement lie principally in reductions of harmful behaviour—be this from preventing the particular offender from causing harm or from deterring others. A further gain, however, flows from reductions in private enforcement costs. Thus, when public enforcement agencies forestall a harm, this saves private individuals or firms from having to spend money on protecting their entitlements.

In calculating the deterrent effects of enforcement activity, the economic approach assumes *inter alia* that potential offenders are actors who seek to maximize their own welfare in an informed, rational manner. For each potential offender deterrence flows from the expected punishment, which is

---

[60] S. Breyer, *Breaking the Vicious Circle* (Cambridge, MA, 1993), 10–13.

[61] S. Meyers, 'Applications of *De Minimis*', in C. Whipple (ed.), *De Minimis Risk* (New York, 1987), 102.

[62] See generally, G. Becker, 'Crime and Punishment: An Economic Approach' (1968) 76 *Journal of Political Economics* 161; I. Ehrlich, 'The Economic Approach to Crime—a Preliminary Assessment', in S. Messinger and E. Bittner, *Criminology Yearbook* (London, 1979); Ogus, *Regulation*, 90–4; Shavell, 'The Optimal Structure of Law Enforcement'; G.J. Stigler, 'The Optimum Enforcement of Laws' (1970) 78 *Journal of Political Economics* 526; T. Gibbons, 'The Utility of Economic Analysis of Crime' (1982) 2 *International Review of Law and Economics* 173.

the probability of punishment times the magnitude of the punishment (e.g. the quantum of the fine).

From the regulator's point of view, a key calculation is how much the group of potential offenders will be deterred by the regulator's current or prospective approach to enforcement.[63] Factors to be taken on board include not merely the level of fines or other sanctions liable to be applied and the probability of inflicting these on offenders, but also the private benefit likely to be derived from offending and the social cost of the offence. The overall wealth of the offender has also to be considered. If an offending firm cannot pay a large fine (because, say, this would drive the enterprise into insolvency and cause unemployment), a combination of small fines and high probability of application would be more appropriate than using large penalties infrequently. Similarly, if severe sanctions are unlikely to be applied for reasons of social justice (the courts may consider the offence minor) a high probability of application will have to be used, especially if the gains from offending are high.

Where, on the other hand, enforcement resources are limited and the probability of bringing sanctions to bear is, as a result, low, it may be rational for the regulator to press the appropriate authorities for penalties great enough to compensate for this improbability.[64] In response to arguments that fairness imposes limitations on the quantum of a punishment for a given offence, the regulator may reply that what matters in real life is the *expected* punishment—that if governments want low-resource regulation, they have to be prepared to impose high penalties.

To balance such talk of economic rationality, it should first be noted that policy and equitable considerations may often govern enforcement decisions. Thus, as a matter of policy, society may want to deter certain activities very strongly and not rely on an efficiency-based balancing of expected gains and penalties. Second, the assumptions of economically rational man may be questioned. In the real world, most harms are not the result of rational calculations concerning costs and benefits—they are the products *inter alia* of human failings, poor information and training, tiredness, short cuts, and accidents.[65] In so far as the model of rational man fails accurately to describe those persons or firms that are regulated, the regulator may feel (and be)

---

[63] On the imperfections of the expected cost approach to deterrence, see T. Makkai and J. Braithwaite, 'The Limits of the Economic Analysis of Regulation: An Empirical Case and a Case for Empiricism' (1993) 15(4) *Law and Policy* 271.

[64] In September 1997, the Chief Executive of the Environment Agency made a strong public attack on the current level of fines for environmental offences. During the same month, Michael Meacher, the Environment Minister, announced that the Government was drawing up plans for large increases in fines for persistent corporate polluters; *Financial Times*, 17 Sept. 1997.

[65] Makkai and Braithwaite, 'The Limits of the Economic Analysis of Regulation'.

justified in placing less emphasis on deterrence and more on active inspection and intervention in the regulated activity.

CONTROLLING CORPORATIONS

Much of regulation concerns the control of corporations, and it is worth noting here the particular difficulties that are likely to be encountered in seeking to control errant companies. Key issues concern the sanctions that can be used to influence such firms; the extent of corporate criminal fault; and the difficulties of proving liability.[66]

SANCTIONS

Regulators can resort to administrative or criminal sanctions in dealing with corporations and, as noted, a wide variety of instruments can be applied. Administrative measures operate without recourse to the courts and can be provided for either in statutes or in contracts (e.g. within the terms of franchises). Examples of statutory administrative sanctions include improvement and prohibition notices, which respectively require remedial actions to be taken within a fixed period or which order the discontinuance of a hazardous activity (e.g. the stopping of a dangerous production line).[67] Contractually based measures may include licence revocations, curtailments, or suspensions.

Criminal sanctions normally involve fines since imprisoning firms is not feasible—though directors may be found criminally liable as individuals, for example, where their personal gross negligence has resulted in a death.[68] To impose fines on firms that, say, pollute waterways or impose health risks on employees, can, however, give rise to difficulties. The firm may engage in activities liable to cause harms that have a value that exceeds any fine they are

---

[66] On criminalizing corporations, see generally: C. Wells, *Corporations and Criminal Responsibility* (Oxford, 1993); L.H. Leigh, *The Criminal Liability of Corporations in English Law* (London, 1969); id., 'The Criminal Liability of Corporations and Other Groups: A Comparative View' (1982) 80 *Michigan Law Review*; J.C. Coffee, 'No Soul to Damn, No Body to Kick' (1981) 79 *Michigan Law Review* 386; C. Clarkson, 'Kicking Corporate Bodies and Damning their Souls' (1996) 59 *MLR* 557; B. Fisse and J. Braithwaite, 'The Allocation of Responsibility for Corporate Crime' (1988) 11 *Sydney Law Review* 468; C. Stone, 'The Place of Enterprise Liability in the Control of Corporate Conduct' (1980) 90 *Yale LJ* 1; R.A. Kagan and J.T. Scholz, 'The Criminology of the Corporation and Regulatory Enforcement Strategies', in Hawkins and Thomas, *Enforcing Regulation*; T. Kaye, 'Corporate Manslaughter: Who Pays the Ferryman?', in D. Feldman and F. Meisel (eds), *Corporate Commercial Law: Modern Developments* (London, 1996).

[67] See Health and Safety at Work etc. Act 1984, ss. 21, 22.

[68] Following the Lyme Bay canoeing tragedy in which four teenagers were drowned, both the managing director of the company that owned the responsible outdoor activity centre and the company itself were found guilty of manslaughter; see Kite and Others, in *The Independent*, 9 Dec. 1994.

able to pay. Any potential fine will accordingly under-deter.[69] Firms, more-over, may treat fines as a normal business expense and may be able to pass the cost of fines through to consumers or even employees.[70] Large fines may prejudice the firm's survival, and insolvency may punish innocent parties such as employees or customers.

Fines remove ready cash from the company which might have been spent on measures to limit the harms at issue (e.g. on new filtration systems to reduce pollution). Fines that do come to bear on the corporation may, however, not deter or influence the actual decision-maker within the management structure,[71] and fines do not ensure that the problem at issue will be remedied or that the causes of failure within the corporation will be identified.

Alternative ways of sanctioning corporations have been suggested in an attempt to improve on the deficiencies of fines. A first of these is the equity fine.[72] Under an equity fine system, the convicted corporation is required to issue a given number of shares to the state's victim compensation fund. The shares would have a value equivalent to the cash fine necessary to deter the illegal activity. This strategy has the supposed advantages that it reduces the negative effect of corporate penalties on workers and consumers since the costs of deterrence are concentrated on the shareholders (whose shares lose value as a result of the mandated issue). These shareholders will accordingly have an incentive to discipline managers. The threat of insolvency and harm to employees and the community is removed. High penalties can be imposed because the market valuation of the typical corporation vastly exceeds the cash resources available to it (cash that would be the target of any fines imposed). Cash is not removed from the corporation, and so spending on harm avoidance is not prejudiced. Managers' interests are aligned with those of the corporation in so far as stock options will lose value on a mandated issue. Mandated issues will produce managerial fears of takeovers, and this will provide an incentive to good behaviour on the part of managers and, finally, shareholders will demand internal controls to reduce dangers of stock dilution through mandated issues. These controls will help avoid regulatory infringements.

Equity fines are thus superior to fines in a number of respects, but they may not prove popular with governments that are opposed to state equity holdings and they share, with fines, the weakness that their deterrent value depends on

---

[69] See Coffee, 'No Soul to Damn, No Body to Kick', 389–93.

[70] In response, it can be argued that consumers should pay a price for goods that reflects the costs of production (which should include any social costs imposed e.g. by pollution); see B. Fisse, 'Sentencing Options against Corporations' (1990) *Criminal Law Forum* 211; C. Stone, 'Controlling Corporate Misconduct' (1977) *Public Interest* 55; Coffee, 'No Soul to Damn, No Body to Kick'.

[71] See Fisse and Braithwaite, 'Allocation of Responsibility'.

[72] See Coffee, 'No Soul to Damn, No Body to Kick', 413–15.

the probability of apprehension and punishment. They furthermore make little contribution to the reform of the corporation's internal procedures and do not ensure that guilty managerial parties will be disciplined.[73]

Another, often-proposed, alternative to the fine is the punitive injunction.[74] Courts could use punitive injunctions to require corporations to remedy their internal controls and to introduce (perhaps at punitive expense) preventative equipment or procedures. Further devices are corporate probation orders[75] and enforced accountability regimes.[76] Judges who are empowered to institute such orders and regimes are able to monitor the activities of a convicted organization and to insist on reporting, record-keeping, and auditing mechanisms that are designed to remedy identified failings and to hold individuals to account. Corporations can be ordered to undertake enquiries, apply discipline, and report on steps taken, and senior managers can be threatened with personal criminal liability if they fail to take such steps to the satisfaction of the court. As with punitive injunctions, particular errant managers or sections of management can be identified and their deficiencies addressed.

Courts can also be given powers to make community service and compensation orders. These can compel corporations to provide certain services for the community or to compensate individuals or groups in an attempt both to make good harms done and to signify the need for corporate rehabilitation. Adverse publicity orders can, in addition, be deployed to instruct corporations to place notices in the media informing the public of their failings and of remedial measures taken.

All such devices have their strengths, weaknesses, and areas of most useful application. It is perhaps appropriate, therefore, for regulators and courts to approach corporate failure with the full array of such sanctions within their contemplation and to apply them bearing in mind not merely the need to punish and rehabilitate corporations but also the interests of the public in compensation, where appropriate, and in more effective compliance.

THE EXTENT OF CORPORATE FAULT AND PROVING LIABILITY

For many years, the regulators of corporations faced a significant legal challenge in Britain. It was difficult to attribute criminal responsibility to corporations because the criminal law had developed with an eye to individual fault, and for liability to apply to a corporation, it was necessary to identify an

---

[73] See Wells, *Corporations*, 35.

[74] See Fisse and Braithwaite, 'Allocation of Responsibility', 500.

[75] See Coffee, 'No Soul to Damn, No Body to Kick', 448–57; Stone, 'Controlling Corporate Misconduct'; Wells, *Corporations*, 36–7.

[76] See Fisse and Braithwaite, 'Allocation of Responsibility'.

individual managerial representative of the company who had been blameworthy: who had carried out the prohibited act (*actus reus*) with the guilty mind (*mens rea*) that the relevant offence required.[77] The deficiencies of this 'identification' approach were exposed following the P&O case of 1990,[78] which arose from the deaths of 187 people in the capsize of the *Herald of Free Enterprise* after it set sail with open doors at Zeebrugge in 1987. Acquittals were directed in the case of the P&O company and its five most senior employees, since it could not be proved that the risks of open-door sailings were obvious to any of the senior managers. As a result, no *mens rea* could be attributed to the company.[79]

In the mid-nineties, however, a less restrictive view of corporate criminal liability was taken in the courts. The Privy Council, in the *Meridian* case,[80] rejected exclusive reliance on the identification test and indicated that acts and knowledge can be attributed to a company by courts considering whose acts, knowledge, or state of mind was *for the purpose* of a particular law to count as belonging to the company. Thus, instead of applying a simple identification test, the judges would, in such an approach, consider the language of a rule, its content and policy, and construe corporate liability accordingly. The functions actually performed by individuals in the company become relevant, rather than their status in the company hierarchy—a mode of reasoning liable to lead to corporate responsibility for the acts of those at lower levels than would be the case under exclusive reliance on the identification principle.

The restrictiveness of the *Tesco* identification doctrine was also circumvented by a different route—that of vicarious liability.[81] Thus in *National Rivers Authority* v. *Alfred McAlpine Homes East* [1994] CLR 760, two employees were responsible for allowing wet cement to pollute a controlled water, but, at trial, their employing company was acquitted of the statutory pollution offence under the identification doctrine of *Tesco* v. *Nattrass*. On appeal, however, the Divisional Court applied the doctrine of vicarious liability. The court looked at the purpose of the pollution legislation, bore in mind that the

---

[77] See *Tesco Supermarkets Ltd* v. *Nattrass* [1972] AC 153; *H.L. Bolton (Engineering) Co. Ltd* v. *T.J. Graham and Sons Ltd* [1957] 1 QB 159. See generally C. Wells and O. Quick, *Lacey, Wells and Quick: Reconstructing Criminal Law* (4th edn. Cambridge, 2010).

[78] *R* v. *Alcindor and others* (Central Criminal Court, 19 Oct. 1990); *R* v. *P&O European Ferries (Dover) Ltd* (1980) 83 GAPP. R. 72; *P&O European Ferries Ltd* (1991) 93 Crim. App. R. 72; *R* v. *Coroner for East Kent ex. p. Spooner* (1989) 88 Crim. App. R. 10.

[79] Clarkson, 'Kicking Corporate Bodies', 561. Inquiries found companies to be seriously at fault, but no successful prosecutions for manslaughter were brought, following the 1987 King's Cross fire (in which 31 died); the 1988 Clapham rail crash (in which 35 died); and the 1988 Piper Alpha oil platform disaster (in which 167 died).

[80] *Meridian Global Funds Management Asia Ltd* v. *The Securities Commission* [1995] 3 WLR 413; also R. Grantham, 'Corporate Knowledge: Identification or Attribution?' (1996) 59 *MLR* 732.

[81] See Clarkson, 'Kicking Corporate Bodies', 563–6.

offence was one of strict liability (that is, it did not require proof of a guilty mind, only that the accused caused the prohibited action), and held that the nature of the offence demanded that vicarious liability be imposed on the company for the acts of employees (whether they represented the directing mind and will of the company or not). This approach has been followed in the Court of Appeal[82] and in cases where proof of negligence has been required,[83] though the House of Lords has cautioned that (at least under the Merchant Shipping Act 1988) a company could not be held liable for each and every wrongful act committed by any employee.[84]

The problems left unsolved by the *Meridian* approach were, first, that it was not wholly clear when the action of a person who did not represent the directing mind and will of the company would be attributed to the company.[85] Second, it was still necessary to find some person within the company who had perpetrated the criminal acts yet, in real life, regulatory failings may (as in the P&O case) stem from general managerial slackness and failures to allocate responsibilities rather than from the identifiable actions of particular individuals.

With respect to manslaughter by corporations, a long period of campaigning, reviews, and debates on law reform finally led to the eclipsing of the *Tesco* doctrine by the passing of the Corporate Manslaughter and Corporate Homicide Act 2007.[86] That legislation stipulated that a corporation will be liable for the offence of corporate manslaughter if the way in which its activities are managed or organized: (a) causes a person's death; and (b) amounts to a gross breach of a relevant duty of care owed by the organization to the deceased.[87] Liability only occurs, however, if the way in which its activities are managed or organized by senior management is a substantial element in the breach of the duty of care[88] and a breach is only 'gross' if the relevant conduct

---

[82] See *R v. British Steel Plc* [1995] 586.

[83] *Tesco Stores Ltd v. Brent LBC* [1993] 2 All ER 718; *Re: Supply of Ready Mixed Concrete* (No. 2.) [1995] 1 All 135.

[84] *Seabound Offshore Ltd v. Secretary of State for Transport* [1994] 2 All ER 99.

[85] See Clarkson, 'Kicking Corporate Bodies', 566.

[86] See, for example: Law. Com. No. 237, *Legislating the Criminal Code: Involuntary Manslaughter* (1996), paras 8.1–8.77 and Draft Involuntary Manslaughter Bill s. 4 (1). In October 1997, Home Secretary Jack Straw argued in favour of a 'corporate killing' offence at the Labour Party Conference. See also TUC, *Paying the Price for Deaths at Work* (London, 1994); Wells, *Corporations*, 144–5.

[87] Corporate Manslaughter and Corporate Homicide Act 2007 s.1. Under section 2 of the Act, a duty of care is owed for the purposes of the 2007 Act if, *inter alia*, a duty is owed to employees under the law of negligence or a duty is owed as occupier of premises, supplier of goods and services, or the carrying on of any construction, maintenance, or other commercial activity. On the Act, see J. Gobert, 'The Corporate Manslaughter and Corporate Homicide Act 2007' (2008) 71 *MLR* 413 and D. Ormerod and R. Taylor, 'The Corporate Manslaughter and Corporate Homicide Act 2007' (2008) *Criminal Law Review* 589.

[88] Corporate Manslaughter and Corporate Homicide Act 2007 s.1(3).

falls 'far below what can reasonably be expected of the organization in the circumstances'.[89]

Regulatory enforcement officials, as can be seen, face not inconsiderable legal difficulties in attempting to hold corporations to account by means of the criminal law. It might, moreover, be asked: 'Why, in any event, punish corporations criminally?'[90]

A first reason is that community disapproval calls, in some instances, for the stamp of criminalization to be imposed. A second is that use of the criminal law provides a set of useful incentives that are of value even when there is no great need to stigmatize conduct as particularly heinous. A third is that corporations, just like individuals, can make decisions and have the capacity to change their policies and procedures and accordingly do meet the conditions of blameworthiness and responsibility.[91] They can, moreover, be deterred by threats of punishment. Finally, the corporation may be better placed than the state to put right its internal failings, and so it may be sensible to use the criminal law to give the firm an incentive to do this. The corporation, moreover, is more likely (for informational and evidential reasons) to apply sanctions to an errant manager than is the state, and the ensuing higher 'expected punishment cost' that flows from internal controls means that higher levels of deterrence may be attained by punishing the corporation, and leaving it to take further action, than are secured by focusing the criminal law directly on the errant employee.

Assessment

A fourth task within regulatory enforcement is the development of performance sensitivity through processes that not only evaluate how well the current system is being enforced, but also calculate how much undesirable activity is escaping the impact of the current regime of controls. This task involves assessing the strength of the case for developing new tools, or adopting new enforcement strategies, or moving towards a new design of regulatory regime. Performance assessment is thus centrally important for the progressive development of regulatory policies and is integral to good regulatory management—especially across complex networks of state and other controls. It is also essential to accountability and transparency insofar as assessments provide measures of progress in meeting objectives and their

---

[89] Corporate Manslaughter and Corporate Homicide Act 2007 s.1(4)(b).
[90] See Leigh, *Criminal Liability*; Coffee, 'No Soul to Damn, No Body to Kick', part II.
[91] Fisse and Braithwaite, 'Allocation of Responsibility'.

publication enhances openness. In assessing enforcement effectiveness, four main approaches can be used. These focus on: inputs; processes; outputs; and outcomes (See pages 35–6 above).

The practical challenges are significant, however. A study of Defra enforcement highlights a number of points.[92] First, accurate assessments of overall effectiveness in achieving outcomes cannot be made (even within a single-operator, single-tool regime) unless the regulator is able to calculate not only levels of non-compliance but levels of 'off-screen' non-compliance—errant behaviour which is beyond the reach of the regulatory regime, yet is relevant to the achievement of objectives. Second, clarity of legal and policy objectives is a precondition of effective assessment. Third, risk-based systems can provide a ready means of effecting year on year comparisons of performance—risk scores can be compared quite easily. Such systems, however, will not measure the effects of regulation on parties outside the system, and are quite easily manipulated by officials. Fourth, the natural inclination to focus on enforcement inputs (which offer cheaper, quicker, and more reliable statistics to be gathered) has to be balanced with efforts to measure outcomes on the ground. Fifth, in some regulated areas it is possible to identify 'short cut' or proxy measures of effectiveness—thus in relation to pesticides it may be feasible to analyse residues in water and use this as an indicator. Finally, where responsibilities for enforcement are unclear, or spread across numbers of institutions, this may impede the accurate assessment of effectiveness—because of coordination difficulties, institutional politics or divergencies in data collection and processing methods. Rationalization of regulatory responsibilities may accordingly offer ways to improve assessments, but only where, as noted, old coordination problems are not simply contained in a new organizational wrapper,[93] or rationalization does not produce its own.

Fisheries is an area that further illustrates the challenges of assessment. In fisheries regulation a key outcome measure is state of stocks, but this is affected by many factors other than enforcement.[94] Levels of compliance are also difficult to measure. As indicated, a considerable amount of non-compliant activity goes on beyond the inspection regime and the NAO reported in 2002–3 that it was impossible, in the then current system, to determine the number of undetected infringements.[95] These infringements related to compliance both with technical regulations and with the recording of landings. It was not physically possible to inspect enough vessels to ensure that landings were

---

[92] See R. Baldwin and J. Black, *Defra: A Review of Enforcement Measures and an Assessment of their Effectiveness in Terms of Risk and Outcome* (London, 2005).

[93] See, e.g., J. Black, 'Managing Regulatory Risks and Defining the Parameters of Blame: The Case of the Australian Prudential Regulation Authority' (2006) *Law and Policy* 1.

[94] e.g. global environmental changes—see Defra, *Review of Marine Fisheries*, 113.

[95] See NAO, *Fisheries Enforcement*, 2, 15–18.

accurately recorded.[96] Such difficulties drove the regulators towards secondary measures of effectiveness (e.g. probabilities of inspection)[97] and to data on processes and outputs (such as sea inspections, port visits, and prosecutions). As a result, Defra was ill-placed to measure the effectiveness of its detection system, its enforcement system, or its processes of assessment. Nor was it able accurately to judge the need to develop and apply new tools for detection, enforcement, or assessment.[98]

The lack of clear outcome objectives and benchmarks further undermined the assessment process in this area,[99] and a separate difficulty reported by the NAO was that EU Member States placed different interpretations on what constituted a serious infringement.[100] Even within English enforcement, infringements in different inspection districts were not recorded in a consistent manner. The NAO concluded that Defra was not able to monitor whether each district was dealing with infringements appropriately or to construct a picture of the nature or frequency of infringements so as to inform enforcement activity.[101]

Modification: The Adjustment of Tools and Strategies

The fifth core task within regulatory enforcement is, again, ongoing and involves modifying the regulatory approach in a manner that is informed by prior assessments of performance. Modification takes on board the adjustments of responses—the tools and rules that are used for both detection and compliance-seeking purposes and it also encompasses the modification of enforcement strategies themselves. As already suggested, modification also demands a willingness to think 'outside the envelope' and to consider whether, instead of adjusting the tools and enforcement strategies within the current regulatory strategy, it is necessary to effect a 'third order' or 'paradigm-shifting' change[102] by adopting a new regulatory (as opposed to enforcement)

---

[96] See NAO, *Fisheries Enforcement*, 3.

[97] Said by Defra to be 'probably the best readily obtainable measure of effectiveness'—*Review of Marine Fisheries*, 113.

[98] See R. Baldwin and J. Black, 'Defra: A Review of Enforcement Measures and an Assessment of their Effectiveness in Terms of Risk and Outcome' (London, 2005).

[99] See NAO, *Fisheries Enforcement*, 16; Prime Minister's Strategy Unit, *Net Benefits* (London, March 2004), 11.

[100] See NAO, *Fisheries Enforcement*, 16.

[101] See NAO, *Fisheries Enforcement*, 24.

[102] On the distinction between 'first-order changes' of regulation (e.g. tunings in the given regulatory control as exemplified by a change in the X in a price control formula) versus 'second-order changes' such as switches of instrument (e.g. from RPI-X to rate quantum price controls) versus 'third-order changes' or 'paradigm shifts' (e.g. abandoning command and control standards in favour

strategy (or mix of strategies)—for example, by moving from a state-imposed command and control centred regime to a completely different regulatory style such as one giving centrality to a scheme of industry-administered guidance and training.

Modification is an essential task, since there is only limited value in assessing performance if the regime is not to be adjusted so as to improve performance. Moreover, as the NAO report into fisheries also found, weaknesses in assessment systems can undermine capacities to modify processes.[103] In that sector, Defra was found by the NAO to operate inflexibly in its deployment of resources and people, which reduced its capacity to adjust its inspection strategies.[104] A special problem was lack of staff mobility which reduced operational responsiveness.[105] What was clear to the NAO was that a large number of strategic options were open to Defra but that these had not been fully assessed, explored, or put into effect.[106]

Conclusions

Enforcement tools are important, but the DREAM framework makes it clear that there are dangers in attempting to achieve better enforcement through a predominant emphasis on increasing the effectiveness of certain tools (e.g. criminal penalties). In many situations, the better way forward may be to improve detection techniques, response strategies (including approaches to selecting tools), performance assessment processes, and modification capacities. In the case of certain regimes, the most positive route to improved performance may involve thinking beyond enforcement of the current regime to broader issues of regulatory technique and institutional design.

Enforcement, can influence regulatory success or failure not merely by affecting the achievement of the right objectives. It can also impinge on the quality of regulatory processes. There is, however, as much art as science in enforcement since trade-offs have to be made on a number of fronts—between, for example, punishing infringers and maximizing compliance levels or between preventing creative compliance and producing rules that are easily enforced. In making these trade-offs, issues of accountability, due process,

---

of emissions trading) see J. Black, 'What is Regulatory Innovation?' in J. Black, M. Lodge, and M. Thatcher, *Regulatory Innovation* (Cheltenham, 2005).

[103] For discussion of changes post the NAO Report see Defra, *Review of Marine Fisheries*.

[104] See NAO, *Fisheries Enforcement*, 4.

[105] See NAO, *Fisheries Enforcement*, 35.

[106] But for subsequent action see Defra, *Review of Marine Fisheries*; Prime Minister's Strategy Unit, *Net Benefits*, and also Defra, *Securing the Benefits* (London, 2005).

and expertise arise. It may, for example, be necessary to use high levels of discretion in a regime of flexible and targeted enforcement if the 'right' results are to be produced, but questions of accountability and fairness are involved and it is proper that trade-offs with legitimate outcome gains should be argued out by regulators. Not only does enforcement demand that highly complex trade-offs and balances be carried out, it also demands that these be justified. The need for regulatory legitimacy, it should be emphasized, runs through the entire regulatory process.

12 Responsive Regulation

In their 1992 book *Responsive Regulation*, Ian Ayres and John Braithwaite moved the regulatory enforcement debate away from a stale disputation between the proponents of 'deterrence' and 'compliance' models of enforcement. Both strategies had a place within regulation, said the two authors: 'To reject punitive regulation is naive, to be totally committed to it is to lead a charge of the light brigade. The trick of successful regulation is to establish a synergy between punishment and persuasion.'[1]

Thus the model of 'responsive regulation' was introduced, together with the concept of enforcement pyramids. This chapter examines the contribution of 'responsive regulation' theory and considers the critiques of this strategy. It then looks at three theories that set out to build on responsive regulation or to offer a broader approach—these are labelled 'smart regulation', 'problem-centred regulation', and 'really responsive regulation'.

Responsive Regulation

A central tenet of 'responsive regulation' as expounded by Ayres and Braithwaite was that compliance is more likely when a regulatory agency operates an explicit enforcement pyramid—a range of enforcement sanctions extending from persuasion, at its base, through warning and civil penalties up to criminal penalties, licence suspensions, and then licence revocations (Figure 12.1).[2] There would be a presumption that regulation should always start at the base of the pyramid. Regulatory interventions would thus commence with non-penal actions and escalate with more punitive responses where prior control efforts had failed to secure compliance.

The pyramid of sanctions is aimed at the single regulated firm, but Ayres and Braithwaite also apply a parallel approach to entire industries. Thus they propose a 'pyramid of regulatory strategies'[3] for industrial application (Figure 12.2). The idea here is that governments should seek, and offer, self-regulatory solutions to industries in the first instance but that, if appropriate goals are

---

[1] I. Ayres and J. Braithwaite, *Responsive Regulation* (Oxford, 1992), 25; see also J. Braithwaite, *To Punish or Persuade* (Albany, NY, 1985).

[2] Ayres and Braithwaite, *Responsive Regulation*, 35.

[3] Ibid., 38–9.

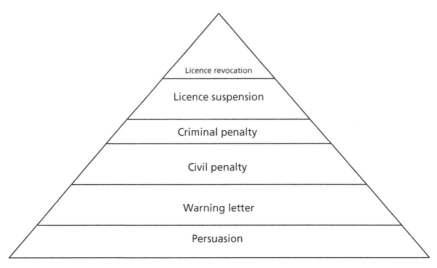

Figure 12.1. The enforcement pyramid

not met, the state should escalate its approach and move on through enforced self-regulation to command regulation with discretionary punishment and finally to command regulation with non-discretionary punishment.

Responsive regulation remains hugely influential worldwide and is applied by a host of governments and regulators. It has been further elaborated both by John Braithwaite and by the recent empirical work on the Australian Tax Office's Compliance Model led by Valerie Braithwaite.[4] The pyramidic regulatory strategy of enforcement, has, however, been the subject of a number of criticisms or reservations.[5]

The first criticism of the pyramidic approach is that, in some circumstances, step-by-step escalation up the pyramid may not be appropriate.[6] For example,

---

[4] J. Braithwaite, *Responsive Regulation and Restorative Justice* (Oxford, 2002); V. Braithwaite (ed.), Special Issue on Responsive Regulation and Taxation (2007) 29(1) *Law and Policy*. As elaborated, responsive regulation has three critical elements to its implementation: first, a systematic, fairly directed, and fully explained disapproval combined with, second, a respect for regulatees, and, third, an escalation of intensity of regulatory response in the absence of a genuine effort by the regulatee to meet the required standards.

[5] For critiques, see: R. Johnstone, 'Putting the Regulated Back into Regulation' (1999) 26 *Journal of Law and Society* 378–90; and the book reviews of *Responsive Regulation* at: (1993) 106 *Harvard Law Review* 1685–90 (Editorial); (1993) 98 *American Journal of Sociology* 1187–9 (Anne Khademian); (1993) 87 *American Political Science Review* 782–3 (John Scholz); (1993) 22 *Contemporary Sociology* 338–9 (Joel Rogers). On responsive regulation, see, e.g., N. Gunningham and P. Grabosky, *Smart Regulation* (Oxford, 1998); J. Mendeloff, 'Overcoming Barriers to Better Regulation' (1993) 18 *Law and Social Inquiry*; R. Baldwin and J. Black, 'Really Responsive Regulation' (2008) 71 *Modern Law Review* 59–94.

[6] The critique here draws on Baldwin and Black, 'Really Responsive Regulation'.

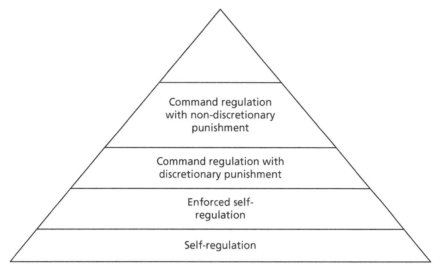

Figure 12.2. The enforcement strategies pyramid

where potentially catastrophic risks are being controlled it may not be acceptable to enforce by escalating up the layers of the pyramid.[7] In the case of non-compliance regarding high-risk activities, the appropriate reaction may be immediate resort to the higher levels of the pyramid.

Second, in some contexts it may be necessary, post-escalation, to move the regulatory response down the pyramid and to decrease the punitiveness of the approach—as where the regulatee has become more inclined to offer greater levels of compliance than formerly. Moving down the pyramid, though, may not always be easy, as Ayres and Braithwaite recognize, because use of more punitive sanctions may prejudice the relationships between regulators and regulatees that are the foundations for the less punitive strategies.[8]

Third, it may be wasteful to operate an escalating tit-for-tat strategy across the board. Responsive regulation presupposes that regulatees do, in fact, respond to the pressures imposed by regulators through the sanctioning pyramid. Corporate behaviour, however, is often driven not by regulatory pressure but by the culture prevailing in the sector or by the far more pressing forces of competition. Some authors, indeed, have distinguished between the

---

[7] Though see the argument that, where possible, persuasion should be the strategy of first choice because preserving the perception of fairness is important to nurturing voluntary compliance—discussed by K. Murphy, 'Moving Towards a More Effective Model of Regulatory Enforcement in the Australian Tax Office' (2004) *British Tax Review* 603–19.

[8] See Ayres and Braithwaite, *Responsive Regulation*, ch. 2; F. Haines, *Corporate Regulation: Beyond Punish or Persuade* (Oxford, 1997), 219; Johnstone, 'Putting the Regulated Back into Regulation'.

various motivations or characters of non-compliers.[9] These 'target-analytic' approaches suggest that in some situations it may be more efficient to analyse types of regulated firms and to tailor and target types of regulatory response accordingly. If, for example, research reveals that a particular problem is predominately being caused by firms that are ill-disposed to respond to advice, education, and persuasion, the optimal regulatory response will not be to start at the base of the enforcement pyramid—it will demand early intervention at a higher level. Whenever a group of regulatees is irrational or unresponsive to tit-for-tat approaches, the latter will tend to prove wasteful of resources. Similarly, an analysis of risk levels may militate in favour of early resort to higher levels of intervention (even where risks are non-catastrophic). The thrust of this argument is that, at least where the costs of analysis are low, it will be more efficient to 'target' responses than to proceed generally on a responsive regulation basis. (This is not, however, to deny the force of the anticipated rejoinder that, even in the light of such target analyses, it may make sense to start enforcing at the lowest point in the pyramid consistent with such analyses).[10]

Fourth, responsive regulation approaches look most convincing when a binary regulator–regulatee relationship is assumed. Such a scenario envisages the transmission of clear messages from regulator to regulatee. As Parker has suggested, it involves the creation of 'enforcement communities' in which regulator and regulatee understand the strategy that each is adopting and can predict each other's responses.[11] Such understanding may not develop, however, even in a binary relationship. In practice, moreover, such clear-cut binary relationships may be rarer than often is imagined. Regulatory regimes can be highly complex, and inspection and enforcement activities can be spread across different regulators with respect to similar activities or regulations.[12] As a result, responsive regulation may prove weak because the messages flowing between regulators and regulatees are confused or subject to interference. This may happen because regulatees are uncertain about who is

---

[9] For example, Kagan and Scholz point to three types of firm—R. Kagan and J. Scholz, 'The Criminology of the Corporation' in K. Hawkins and J. Thomas (eds), *Enforcing Regulation* (Boston, 1984), and Baldwin has suggested attention to four types of regulatee—R. Baldwin, 'Why Rules Don't Work' (1990) 53 *MLR* 321. The UK tax regulator, HM Customs and Excise, has come up with a further classification, identifying seven types of responses on a compliance continuum, and the appropriate regulatory strategy in each case: HM Customs and Excise Annual Report 2003–4, HC 119 (London, 2003), 123.

[10] On combining targeting and responsive approaches, see Braithwaite, *Responsive Regulation and Restorative Justice*, 36–40.

[11] C. Parker, 'Compliance Professionalism and Regulatory Community: The Australian Trade Practices Regime' (1999) 26(2) *Journal of Law and Society* 215–39.

[12] See J. Black, 'Decentring Regulation: The Role of Regulation and Self-Regulation in a "Post-Regulatory World"' (2001) *Current Legal Problems* 103–46. For a discussion of regulatory complexity in Defra, see R. Baldwin and J. Black, *A Review of Enforcement Measures* (London, 2005).

demanding what or which regulator needs to be listened to regarding a particular issue. Such regulatory 'white noise' may undermine the responsive regulation strategy because lack of clear messaging will detract from the impact of any responsive approach to sanctioning.

A fifth difficulty with responsive regulation is that escalating through the layers of the pyramid may not be the chosen (or the best) course of action because enforcement is not just a two-actor game in which the only factor that shapes the enforcer's response is the degree of cooperation forthcoming from the regulatee. As Mendeloff has argued, whether a responsive approach is optimal will depend on a number of other factors such as agency resource levels, the size of the regulated population, the kinds of standards imposed (and how these are received), the observability of non-compliance, the costs of compliance, the financial assistance available for compliance, and the penalty structure.[13] Enforcers may prove excessively tied to compliance approaches for a number of reasons, including their own organizational resources, cultures, and practices, and the constraints of the broader institutional environment. The agency may lack the tools or resources to progress to more punitive strategies; it may fear the political consequences of progression and may not have the judicial,[14] public, or political support for escalation; it may be reluctant to trigger an adverse business reaction to deterrence strategies; it may find it difficult to assess the need for escalation because it lacks the necessary information on the exact nature of a regulated firm's response to existing controls; and it may be disinclined to escalate unless it has sufficient evidence to make a case for the highest level of response (e.g. to prosecute or disqualify).[15] Alternatively, those at the top of the regulatory organization may have made a strategic decision to 'come down hard' on particular types of offence or offender for a range of reasons—media or political pressure, for example, or as a more general shift to a more 'deterrence' or punitive style across the board or with respect to particular regulatees,[16] or to compensate for weaknesses in other inspection and enforcement strategies adopted by the regulator. The risk-based approaches that UK regulators are obliged by law to adopt will, moreover, target regulatees according to risk analyses, and this will

[13] See Mendeloff, 'Overcoming Barriers', 717.

[14] On under-deterrence from low fines, see e.g. the complaints of the Environment Agency in *Annual Report* 2004, and the comments in the Hampton and Macrory Reports: P. Hampton, *Reducing Administrative Burdens* (London, 2005) (hereafter Hampton Report); and R. Macrory, *Regulatory Justice: Sanctioning in a post-Hampton World* (Cabinet Office, May 2006) (hereafter Macrory Report); and NAO, *Fisheries Enforcement*, paras. 2.34–2.36.

[15] NAO, *Fisheries Enforcement*, para. 2.27 stated that fisheries infringements would be dealt with by means of written warnings in some cases, but only if 'the same evidence would be likely to stand scrutiny successfully if it were presented to a court'.

[16] e.g. J. Black, 'Managing Regulatory Risks and Defining the Parameters of Blame: The Case of the Australian Prudential Regulation Authority' (2006) *Law and Policy* 1; R. Baldwin, 'The New Punitive Regulation' (2004) 67 *Modern Law Review* 351–83.

cut across the use of more general 'responsive' strategies.[17] In this situation, regulatory policy overrides the individual nature of the regulator–regulatee relationship. It doesn't matter how cooperative the regulatee is, the regulatory official is liable to adopt a particular stance in order to pursue wider organizational objectives.

There may also be legal problems in applying a responsive approach.[18] In some areas, legislatures may have decreed that defaulters shall be met with, say, deterrence strategies, and this may tie the hands of the enforcing agency.[19] Responsive regulation calls for the availability of a wide range of credible sanctions, but, in some areas, legislators may have failed to provide regulators with the sanctions and investigative tools that allow a progression up the pyramid. The UK's 2006 Macrory review of penalties, for example, highlighted many sectors where regulators possessed no big stick that allowed them to 'speak softly'.[20] Although regulators commonly have prosecution powers, the fines imposed by the courts are frequently too low to provide a deterrent to the more calculating offenders, particularly small, itinerant operators who have few reputational concerns.[21] Alternatively, the stick may be so big (e.g. licence revocation of a major utility, or de-recognition of a political party) that it simply can never be used.

A further concern relates to the fairness and democratic accountability of responsive regulatory strategies. A danger inherent in a system that tailors regulatory responses to the compliance practices of individual firms is that it involves high levels of discretion and may tend to operate in a non-transparent manner. It may also raise issues of consistency of treatment across different regulatees. Such issues can be addressed by the generation of rules and guidelines to confine, structure, and check responsive strategies, but there are dangers that such structuring may straitjacket responsive regulation within costly bureaucratic controls and that the structuring guidelines used may give effect to important policies that are likely to be under-exposed to democratic scrutiny. It is, moreover, sometimes argued that a discretionary regime that is characterized by close relationships between regulator and regulatee is prone to 'regulatory capture'. Ayres and Braithwaite's answer here is to advocate a system of tripartism—in which Public Interest Groups (PIGs) are legally empowered parties within the regulatory process that can act as informed

---

[17] Statutory Code of Practice for Regulators 2007: section 4.

[18] On responsive regulation and legality, see J. Freigang, 'Is Responsive Regulation Compatible With the Rule of Law?' (2002) 8 *European Public Law* 463–72.

[19] For example, the US Federal Deposit Insurance Corporation Improvement Act contains a provision for prompt corrective action. This stipulates the different types of action the Federal Deposit Insurance Corporation should take when capital levels in a deposit taking institution reach particular levels.

[20] See Ayres and Braithwaite, *Responsive Regulation*, ch. 2.

[21] Macrory Report; see also Hampton Report.

representatives of regulatory beneficiaries and operate as counterbalances to industrial and agency pressures.[22] Critics have, however, questioned how such a system can be made to work within responsive regulation and have cautioned: that empowered PIGs may become 'shadow regulators';[23] that disputes about the representativeness of empowered PIGs can be expected; that grid-locks may result; and that regulatory processes will not be constructively underpinned by trust and cooperation where there is (as in the USA) a backdrop of adversarial legalism.[24]

Finally, as Gunningham, Grabosky, and Sinclair noted in their 'smart' regulatory pyramid,[25] there may be arguments for not confining the regulatory response to escalating punitive responses but for thinking laterally and breaking away from the punitive pyramid. This might, for instance, involve placing more emphasis on designing out potential mischiefs or relying on *ex ante* controls, such as screening, in order to manage a problem. Alternatively, emphasis could be placed on: avoiding undesirable consequences by restructuring the relevant industry; or relying on non-state controls rather than state sanctioning; or looking beyond individual non-compliers to systemic difficulties in the sector.[26] Put more broadly, it can be contended that responsive regulation does not provide a complete answer to the problems of designing tools for regulation—or of applying tools in different combinations. The solution, in many contexts, may not be to think of escalating up the punitive pyramid but to reconsider the enforcement toolkit and the general regulatory strategy being applied. Even, indeed, if an escalatory strategy makes sense, it may be necessary to go beyond responsive regulation for guidance on choices between the different possible routes upwards.

Smart Regulation

Smart regulation builds on 'responsive regulation', but considers a broader range of regulatory actors than its predecessor theory. The proponents of smart regulation, Neil Gunningham, Peter Grabosky, and Darren Sinclair,[27] argue that the Ayres and Braithwaite pyramid is concerned only with the interaction between two parties: state and business. Smart regulation,

---

[22] See Ayres and Braithwaite, *Responsive Regulation*, ch. 3.
[23] See Mendeloff, 'Overcoming Barriers', 719.
[24] See Scholz, Review of Ayres and Braithwaite, *Responsive Regulation*, 783; Mendeloff, 'Overcoming Barriers', 720, 729.
[25] See Gunningham and Grabosky, *Smart Regulation*, ch. 6.
[26] See Johnstone, 'Putting the Regulated Back into Regulation', 383.
[27] See Gunningham and Grabosky, *Smart Regulation*, 399–400.

GOVERNMENT AS REGULATOR	BUSINESS AS SELF-REGULATOR	THIRD PARTIES (PUBLIC INTEREST GROUPS, ETC.)
DISQUALIFICATIONS	DISQUALIFICATION	DISMISSAL
PENAL SANCTIONS	SANCTIONS	DISCIPLINE
NOTICES	WARNINGS	PROMOTIONS
WARNINGS	GUIDANCE	REVIEWS
PERSUASION	EDUCATION	INCENTIVES
EDUCATION	ADVICE	TRAINING SUPERVISION
ADVICE	–	ADVICE

Figure 12.3. The three aspects of smart regulation

however, holds that regulation can be carried out not merely by the state, but by businesses themselves and by quasi-regulators such as public interest groups, professional bodies, and industry associations. The pyramid of smart regulation is, accordingly, three-sided, and considers the possibility of regulation using a number of different instruments implemented by a number of parties (Figure 12.3). It 'conceives of escalation to higher levels of coerciveness not only within a single instrument but also across several instruments'.[28]

The three-sided pyramid envisages a coordinated approach to regulation in which it is possible to escalate responses to non-compliance by moving not only up a single face of the pyramid but also from one face of the pyramid to another (e.g. from a state control to a corporate control or industry association instrument). This gives flexibility of response and allows sanctioning gaps to be filled—so that if escalation up the state system is not possible (e.g. because a legal penalty is not provided or is inadequate) resort can be made to another form of influence.[29] Seeing regulation in terms of these three dimensions allows the adoption of creative mixes, or networks, of regulatory enforcement instruments and of influencing actors or institutions. It also encompasses the use of control instruments that, in certain contexts, may be easier to apply, less costly, and more influential than state controls.

Smart regulation is, accordingly, more broadly based than responsive regulation in its classic form.[30] It, nevertheless, involves an escalation process

---

[28] See Gunningham and Grabosky, *Smart Regulation*, 399–400.
[29] Ibid., 403.
[30] The architects of responsive regulation might argue, however, that there is no inconsistency between the responsive and the smart approaches. John Braithwaite, indeed (in 'Responsive

and, as a result, runs up against many of the general difficulties that responsive regulation encounters and which were noted above. In addition, of course, the creation of regulatory networks and the processes of coordinating responses across three different systems, or faces of the pyramid, involves its own challenges.[31] As the advocates of this approach acknowledge,[32] such coordination is not always easy, and gives rise to special difficulties of information management, clarity of messaging to regulatees, resource and time constraints, and political differences between different institutional actors. Evaluating the case for an escalatory response presents challenges within the responsive regulation pyramid, but such evaluations will be all the more difficult when complex mixes of strategy and institutions are involved. Concerns about consistency, fairness, and accountability may, moreover, be even more acute than was the case with responsive regulation.[33]

Problem-centered Regulation

In both 'responsive' and 'smart' regulation, there is an emphasis on the processes, instruments, and institutions that can be used in order to further regulatory objectives. A broader focus, however, is offered by Malcolm Sparrow's 'regulatory craft' approach. In a version of risk-based regulation, this places problem-solving at the centre of regulatory strategy. It separates out the 'stages of problem-solving'[34] and stresses the need to nominate problems for attention; define problems precisely; determine how to measure impact; develop solutions or interventions; implement the plan; and monitor, review, and adjust the plan. It also accepts the 'dynamic nature of the risk control game'.[35] Central to Sparrow's approach is the need to pick the most important tasks and then decide on the important tools, rather than 'decide on the important tools and pick the tasks to fit'.[36]

Regulation and Developing Economies' (2006) 34 *World Development* 884, 888) has emphasized that responsive regulation conceives of NGOs and businesses as important regulators in their own right so that 'the weaknesses of a state regulator may be compensated by the strengths of NGOs or business regulators' (892).

[31] An important contribution of 'smart regulation' is its discussion of inherent complementarities and incompatibilities between different regulatory instruments. Gunningham and Grabosky, *Smart Regulation*, ch. 6 (by Gunningham and Sinclair).

[32] Gunningham and Grabosky, *Smart Regulation*, 402–4.

[33] See Braithwaite, *Responsive Regulation and Restorative Justice*.

[34] M. Sparrow, *The Regulatory Craft* (Washington, DC, 2000), ch. 10.

[35] Ibid., 274.

[36] Ibid., 131.

The 'craft'approach does regulatory theory a great service in, *inter alia*, drawing attention to the different tasks that regulators have to come to terms with, in emphasizing the importance of coming to grips with performance evaluation and shifting challenges, and in focusing on desired outcomes rather that mere compliance with the current rules.

The problem-centred analysis, however, is not without difficulties. What it does not do is paint a picture of the strategic choices that confront regulators in attempting to carry out different tasks or 'stages' of the problem-solving process. Sparrow tells us to target key problems and solve these by developing solutions or interventions and by 'implementing the plan'. He offers less help, however, to regulators who have to decide whether the solution to a given problem lies through the application of a 'responsive', 'deterrent', or some other approach.[37] We have no menu of options, nor are we offered an explanation of the potential interactions between different regulatory instruments and different strategies for coming to grips with the stages of the problem-solving process—matters that are more fully dealt with by proponents of smart regulation.

The 'problem-centred' approach, moreover, assumes, perhaps too readily, that regulation can be parcelled into problems and projects to be addressed by project teams.[38] This may well be the case in some scenarios—where, for instance, a particular pollution problem occurs for a narrow and identifiable set of reasons. In other situations, however, regulators may be faced with a host of different kinds of errant behaviour that cumulatively cause a set of related mischiefs. To focus on a mischief and define it as 'the problem' may not, accordingly, move regulators very far forward in their efforts to devise strategies for responding to it. As we will see in the next chapter, it is rarely the case that risk-based regulators can identify the target risk unproblematically. They usually have to make difficult decisions about the types of risks that they will target and how these are to be constructed—whether, for instance, they are risks attached to the operations of single firms or whether they are better viewed systemically, or whether problems are individual or cumulative in nature. What is important, in such scenarios, it could be argued, is the development of an acceptable scheme for detecting and identifying key risks to the achieving of regulatory objectives—and for pinpointing key risk-creators. This, it could be contended, has to be seen as logically prior to 'picking the important problems and fixing them'.[39]

---

[37] See Gunningham and Grabosky, *Smart Regulation*, ch. 6.

[38] Sparrow, *Regulatory Craft* (232) concedes that the problem-solving approach 'is predicated on the hypothesis that a significant proportion of day-to-day accidents, incidents, violations and crimes fall into patterns that can be discerned'.

[39] Sparrow, *Regulatory Craft*, 133.

Really Responsive Regulation

The theory of 'really responsive regulation', like that of 'smart regulation', seeks to take 'responsive regulation' forward. It does so by offering a more general framework for approaching regulation responsively and by addressing a number of issues that responsive regulation does not focus directly upon. 'Really responsive' regulation has two main messages. The first of these is that in designing, applying, and developing regulatory systems, regulators need to adapt their strategies to more than the behaviour of regulatees.[40] They need to be attentive and responsive to five key factors: the *behaviour, attitudes, and cultures* of regulatory actors; the *institutional setting* of the regulatory regime; the interactions between the *different logics of regulatory tools and strategies*; the *regime's own performance* over time; and, finally, *changes* in each of these elements.

WHY RESPOND TO THE ABOVE FACTORS?

It might be asked why the theory of 'really responsive regulation' should demand responsiveness to the above five factors, rather than to another group of considerations. Advocates of the theory argue that these five factors are appropriate because they encapsulate the central challenges that regulators face and which must be risen to if they are to achieve their objectives over time.

Taking on board the *behaviour, attitudes, and cultures* of regulatory actors (hereafter 'attitudes') involves taking on board a number of factors that shape the regulated firm's disposition and reaction to regulation. These will include its general attitude towards regulation and compliance; its reputation and position in the market; its internal cognitive and normative operating frameworks; and its particular power structures.[41] Further matters of relevance are how the firm's managers interact on a personal level with the regulators, whether relationships are cooperative or antagonistic, the fit between external regulatory demands and internal goals, and the way that managers perceive the fairness of the regulatory regime.[42] These are considerations that 'really

---

[40] See Baldwin and Black, 'Really Responsive Regulation', on which this section draws.

[41] As Braithwaite has pointed out, this may involve officials in escalating an issue up the organization until the regulator finds someone who will respond; more broadly, it means analysing the firm's compliance culture, organizational practices, and the ways in which it responds to its environment, including its market position: J. Braithwaite, *To Punish or Persuade: Enforcement of Coal Mine Safety* (Albany, NY, 1985).

[42] For a summary from an institutionalist perspective, see C. Oliver, 'Strategic Responses to Institutional Processes' (1991) 16(1) *Academy of Management Review* 145. See also C. Parker, *The Open Corporation* (Cambridge, 2002). On the importance of perceptions of fairness regarding the regulatory regime for compliance, see L. Feld and B. Frey, 'Tax Compliance as the Result of a Psychological Tax Contract: The Role of Incentives and Responsive Regulation' (2007) 29(1) *Law and Policy* 102; E. Ahmed and V. Braithwaite, 'Higher Education Loans and Tax Evasion: A Response to Perceived Unfairness' (2007) 29(1) *Law and Policy* 121; V. Braithwaite, K. Murphy, and M. Reinhart,

responsive' theory says have to be responded to because the motivational postures, conceptions of interests, and cognitive frameworks of regulated firms (and regulators) vitally affect the regulatory relationship and the regulator's capacity to influence regulatee behaviour.[43]

The *institutional setting* of the regulatory regime refers to the organizational normative, cognitive, and resource-distribution structures in which the regulator is situated.[44] This includes: the patterns of formal and informal control over the regulator; its position in the infrastructure of a broader regulatory regime (e.g. a transnational or EU regime); and the distribution of resources, including strategic resources, within that regime. Such matters have to be taken on board by 'really responsive' regulators because regulation, and its potential, is vitally affected by the position that each organization (regulator or regulated concern) occupies with regard to other institutions. The actions of a regulatory agency, for instance, are strongly shaped by the distribution of resources, powers, and responsibilities between that body and other organizations—notably its overseeing government department.

The interactions of different *regulatory tools and strategies* have also to be responded to, says the 'really responsive' approach, because they impact pivotally on regulatory performance. Most regulators use a wide variety of control tools and strategies, but these often have divergent logics—they embody different regulator to regulatee relationships and assume different ways of interacting.[45] Thus, command-and-sanction-based instruments operate on understandings that are very different from those that underpin educative or economic incentive systems of control. There may be harmony or dissonance between these tools and strategies—so that, for instance, applying sanctions on a deterrent basis may undermine a concurrent strategy of 'educate and persuade' by killing regulator to regulatee communications. Communications problems are also caused when different logics are based on different assumptions, value systems, cultures, and founding ideas, so that messaging across logics involves distortions and failures of contact. It is, accordingly, essential for the 'really responsive' regulator to manage tool and strategy interactions and to avoid undesirable confusions of logic.[46]

'Taxation Threat, Motivational Postures, and Responsive Regulation' (2007) 29(1) *Law and Policy* 137; T. Tyler, *Why People Obey the Law: Procedural Justice, Legitimacy and Compliance* (New Haven, 1990).

[43] Oliver, 'Strategic Responses to Institutional Processes'.

[44] W.R. Scott, *Institutions and Organization* (Thousand Oaks, CA, 1995); W.W. Powell and P.J. DiMaggio (eds), *The New Institutionalism in Organizational Analysis* (Chicago, 1991).

[45] Black, 'Decentring Regulation'.

[46] See Gunningham and Grabosky *Smart Regulation*; J. Black, *Rules and Regulators* (Oxford, 1997). Waller also refers to this, describing it as 'institutional integrity': V. Waller, 'The Challenge of Institutional Integrity in Responsive Regulation: Field Inspections by the Australian Tax Office' (2007) 1 *Law and Policy* 67.

Being sensitive and responsive to the regime's *performance* requires that the regulator is capable of measuring whether the tools and strategies in current use are proving successful in achieving desired objectives. It will demand not merely an assessment of secured compliance with the rules of the existing regime but also a quantification of performance in achieving agency objectives.[47] A really responsive regulation approach would, moreover, link assessments to appropriate modifications of tools and strategies for detection, response development, enforcement, assessment, and modification.

A really responsive approach holds such sensitivity and responsivenes to be of crucial importance, since regulators who cannot assess the performance of their regimes cannot know whether their efforts (and budgets) are having any positive effect in furthering their objectives. Nor can they either judge whether changes in tools or strategies are called for or justify their operations to the outside world. If they cannot modify and adapt their operations and strategies in the light of performance assessments, they will be saddled with poor delivery and will be incapable of dealing with the new challenges that all regulators are confronted with.

Finally, sensitivity to *change* can also be said to lie at the heart of acceptable regulatory performance. In virtually all sectors, regulatory challenges are in a state of constant shift. Thus, for instance, new risks and risk creators come on the scene, technologies and markets change, institutional structures are re-formed, political and legal obligations alter, and public expectations and preferences mutate. If regulators cannot adapt to change, they will apply yesterday's controls to today's problems and, again, under-performance will be inevitable.

As for the exhaustiveness of the above five key factors, the 'really responsive' approach holds that regulators who attend to the above matters will have cause to come to grips with all of the main challenges that are identified by the prevailing regulatory theories. Regulators are thus called on to take on board: the importance of divergent interests (be these public, private/economic, or group); the significance of variations in cultures, values, ideas, communications regimes, and control systems; and the impact of intra- and inter-institutional forces.[48]

RESPONSIVENESS ACROSS TASKS

The second message of 'really responsive regulation' is that regulatory designs, developments, and operations should take on board the way that regulatory challenges vary across the core tasks that regulators have to carry out, both

---

[47] See Sparrow, *Regulatory Craft*, 192, 272–3.
[48] See Chapter 4 above and B. Morgan and K. Yeung, *An Introduction to Law and Regulation* (Cambridge, 2007).

with respect to individual firms and in developing strategies more generally—namely: *detecting* undesirable or non-compliant behaviour, *responding* to that behaviour by developing tools and strategies, *enforcing* those tools and strategies on the ground, *assessing* their success or failure, and *modifying* them accordingly. The case for looking 'across tasks' is that there is good evidence that the work to be done to achieve real responsiveness will vary significantly from task to task and that it would be a mistake to think that a strategy that works in relation to, say, the detection of non-compliers will prove as effective in relation to the securing of compliance or the assessing of performance. Really responsive regulation, moreover, seeks to identify how adopting particular approaches to certain tasks will impact on the execution of other tasks by means of other strategies—how, for instance, enforcing punitively will affect cooperative modes of detection.

How a really responsive approach would operate with respect to the five core tasks of regulation is thus worth noting.

DETECTION: THE IDENTIFICATION OF NON-COMPLIANT AND UNDESIRABLE BEHAVIOUR

These are issues that are often left out of account in approaches to enforcement. A focus on the Ayres and Braithwaite pyramid, for instance, tends to draw attention to the need to ensure compliance, rather than to develop intelligence on the extent to which compliance falls short of objectives.[49] Risk-based systems look more directly towards objectives but tend to look towards a given set of risks and a given approach to these—they tend to underemphasize the need to detect new and 'off-the-screen' activities of a non-compliant or undesirable nature.[50]

In contrast, the really responsive regulatory body would seek to detect such matters and develop ways to assess how reliable its detection processes are. It is, after all, only through performance sensitivity—by knowing the reliability of its detection (and, indeed, other procedures)—that it can form a view on such matters as levels of compliance and the balance between activities that are covered by regulation and those that escape the system. Such detection and assessment processes are essential, moreover, if the regulatory regime is to be adjusted so as to extend its coverage to previously uncontrolled behaviour.

Dealing with change is thus a key issue for the really responsive regulator. In a fluid world, it is necessary not only to develop but to adjust detection

---

[49] But see smart regulation's taking on board the need to go 'beyond compliance' in Gunningham and Grabosky, *Smart Regulation*, 153 and N. Gunningham, 'Beyond Compliance' in B. Boer, R. Fowler, and N. Gunningham (eds), *Environmental Outlook: Law and Policy* (Sydney, 1994).

[50] See Sparrow, *Regulatory Craft*, 273–5.

techniques to meet new challenges. Enforcement, moreover, is not a mechanical process in which the fact of compliance is a given, easily identifiable matter. As many have observed, compliance is often 'constructed' through processes of negotiations between different actors in the regulatory arena.[51] Detection strategies, accordingly, have to respond to shifts in concepts and constructions of compliance and have to relate such shifts to the achieving of regulatory objectives, changes in the construction of objectives, and changes in the translation of objectives into targets and problems. Adjustments of regulatory logic, in turn, have to be made.

The really responsive regulatory body will not only lay the foundations for its detection and other work by establishing clarity on objectives, it will be clear regarding the regulatory logic that it will apply and the role of different individual logics in relation to the task of detection. The really responsive regulator will also take on board the issue of attitudes and how this affects the carrying out of detection or other tasks. Of particular concern may be instances where detection work is prejudiced by conflicts or tensions between the attitudes of the regulators and those of the regulatees.[52]

Institutional environments also have to be taken on board. In relation to many regulated activities, enforcement is carried out, as noted, by a network of different bodies—agencies, local authorities, and others. These will often enforce the same legislation in different ways and will possess different systems for gathering information on regulatory activities and compliance. Such institutional fragmentation stands in the way of the easy evaluation of detection procedures and has to be responded to with efforts to coordinate, harmonize, or rationalize.

Broader institutional settings may also impact on the effective detection of non-compliance and the estimation of 'off-the-screen' activity. In the UK, the government's general stance on reducing informational burdens on business does not encourage the surveying of industrial activity, and, in a number of important fields, the regulated industry proves highly defensive in the face of regulation. Enterprises themselves tend to be important reserves of information on compliance and, as a result, their non-cooperation is likely to impede detection work and the use of quasi-regulatory sources of data (such as trade associations).

Such difficulties of detection are considerable, but have to be faced up to if regulatory enforcement is to further the achievement of objectives. If non-

---

[51] See, e.g., K. Hawkins, *Law as Last Resort* (Oxford, 2002), ch. 8.

[52] See the NAO's review of UK marine fisheries controls and its finding that: 'Regulations may lead fishermen to act in ways which they regard as unnatural, for example, having to throw fish back into the sea to preserve their quota by only landing the best quality fish or to avoid exceeding quota.' The NAO also found that the 'unnaturalness' of throwing dead fish back into the sea was likely to undermine self-regulation through voluntary compliance and to undermine both detection of non-compliance and enforcement of quotas (NAO, *Fisheries Enforcement*, 19).

compliant and errant behaviour is not detected, it cannot be dealt with by a tit-for-tat or any other strategy. If levels of compliance and undesirable behaviour are not known, it will be impossible to work towards optimal regulation to meet changes and new challenges or to evaluate performance and estimate whether resources spent on regulation are worthwhile.

RESPONSE: DEVELOPING RULES AND TOOLS

Within the responsive regulation approach, the central focus is the use of a hierarchy of enforcement tools as applied through a process of potential escalation. What tends to be assumed within responsive regulation is that a full array of tools is available and that the given toolkit or set of rules is appropriate on a continuing basis. In practice, however, few regulators possess the luxury of a full toolkit. It is the case, indeed, that—even if state regulation is focused on, to the exclusion of quasi-regulatory or corporate controls—over forty enforcement tools are encountered.[53]

Ensuring that enforcement tools are 'really responsive' is a significant task. In the first instance, enforcers have to be performance-sensitive—they must possess systems of performance assessment that tell them whether they need to adjust or expand their toolkits—this is a matter returned to below. In addition, even those who are aware of their needs for new enforcement tools, and who are open to designing and using new tools[54] need to have the capacity to adjust tools in order to improve performance and adjust to changing circumstances and challenges.

Really responsive regulators will, in addition, examine how different attitudes and tool logics will affect both the way that particular controls operate and the manner in which tools can be combined. As was seen in discussing detection work, a tool that operates with a self-regulatory logic (such as a system of catch declaration) will tend to operate inefficiently if it is at odds with the regulatees' attitudes—as where a fish quota and catch declaration system involves the 'unnaturalness' of offloading freshly caught (and dead) fish into the sea.

ENFORCEMENT: STRATEGIES FOR APPLYING TOOLS

The logics of different regulatory tools and strategies interact and may do so positively or negatively. Where there are conflicts, these can impede the achieving of objectives.[55] On the positive front, the proponents of 'smart

---

[53] See R. Baldwin and J. Black, *A Review of Enforcement Measures* (Defra, November 2005).
[54] The evidence in Defra was that many enforcers are indeed open to designing and using new tools: see Baldwin and Black, *Reveiw of Enforcement Measures.*
[55] See Baldwin and Black, *Review of Enforcement Measures.*

regulation' suggest, with respect to *ex ante* regulatory strategies, that there may be a good deal to be achieved by combining different logics, tools, and strategies. Regulatory enforcement tools and strategies are often applied so as to achieve a number of purposes (e.g. detection and information gathering, as well as compliance seeking), and are based on different logics. Attention should, accordingly, be paid to positive interactions and combinations of tools, strategies, and logics, as these are encountered in dealing with specific regulatory tasks—how, for instance, risk-based regulation's difficulties in detecting new risks and risk-creators can be addressed by resort to a degree of random, regional, and routine enforcement.

Really responsive regulation can, similarly, suggest ways in which the messages of responsive regulation can be supplemented. Responsive regulation ranks enforcement tools in terms of punitive severity (the enforcement pyramid can, indeed, be seen as a severity pyramid). A problem in practice, however, is that tools may rank differently according to context. To some firms, naming and shaming may be seen as non-punitive, to others it may be viewed as far more punitive than a fine. In some contexts, moreover, it may be necessary to escape from the severity pyramid in favour of radically different control strategies. The 'smart regulation' approach does not overcome such difficulties by making the pyramid three-dimensional—escalation still operates on a single axis. The really responsive regulation perspective, though, does offer more assistance by dealing head-on with the issue of logics. It also takes on board the attitude of the firm. This will look to the way the firm perceives and reacts to different control tools (say, naming and shaming), and adverting to issues of attitude adds a dimension to analyses of logics and the interactions of these. Really responsive regulation thus provides a basis for assessing how best to apply a pyramidic approach to enforcement, for judging how responsive and other approaches can be combined, and for evaluating whether it is necessary to change logics—to move, for instance, from punitive to other modes of influence such as positive incentives or market-based mechanisms. Here there is a further contrast between 'responsive' and 'really responsive' regulation—the former tends to focus on the best ways to enforce a given broad strategy, whereas the latter emphasizes performance sensitivity and provides a basis for judging the case for instituting a sea-change in that strategy.

Really responsive regulation also takes on board institutional environments. Regulatory systems, as noted, more often than not involve numbers of organizations, and institutional complexities often impact on the application of different tools and strategies.[56] A really responsive approach points to

---

[56] As seen in fisheries—see NAO, *Fisheries Enforcement*, 34–5, for a discussion of confusions of institutional roles; duplications of inspections; inflexibilities in the deployment of resources across functions and institutions; and some complaints of over administration. Defra established a new

the need to analyse how variations in institutional characteristics and institutional interactivities affect, in quite particular ways, the carrying out of the various tasks that make up the process of regulation.

ASSESSMENT

A really responsive regulation approach helps to identify those key issues that have to be addressed if assessment processes are to prove valuable. Attitudes have to be considered—as has been noted, if regulatees' mind-sets are at tension with recording systems (e.g. for fish landings) the assessment procedure will be undermined. Institutional environments have to be taken on board so that there is coordination of data collection systems across different fisheries regulators and regulatees with their various budgetary and governance frameworks. The logics of different tools and strategies will also have to be considered, since these impact on assessment processes. Where, for instance, command and control methods are mixed with self-regulatory or advisory systems, there may be tensions that, as noted, will prejudice information flows and data collection schemes.[57] Performance sensitivity is, again, necessary, since assessments have to be reflexive—regulators must be able to measure their performance but also be able to evaluate the strengths or weaknesses of their measuring systems.

As for taking on board changes in objectives, industry conditions, or other matters, this usually demands that adjusting reforms are given consideration. A really responsive regulation approach would assess proposals for reforms of regulatory tools or strategies by looking at their 'logics effects' while taking into account issues of attitudes, institutional environment, needs for performance sensitivity, and adaptability to change. To take an example: one proposal might be to protect fish stocks by awarding Individual Transferable Quotas to fishermen (which, in effect, give individuals tradable property rights to sell specific quantities of fish).[58] The really responsive regulation framework would emphasize that such a system would change the regulatory roles of fishermen and state officials—with the market in quotas operating alongside the 'command' regime and taking over some of the functions of the regulator (e.g. allocating catch allowances). This would involve new mixes of attitudes, institutional responsibilities, and roles.

Marine Fisheries Agency in October 2005 to separate policy development from the delivery of enforcement, and it also set up a new Marine Fisheries Directorate. In 2006, a Regional Fisheries Manager for SW England was created as a pilot for further coordinating reforms. On the drive for such changes see, e.g., Prime Minister's Strategy Unit, *Net Benefits* (March 2004) ; Defra, *Securing the Benefits* (July 2005); *Securing the Benefits—A Stocktake* (July 2006).

[57] R. Baldwin, 'Is Better Regulation Smarter Regulation?' (2005) *Public Law* 485.

[58] A system found in New Zealand and Iceland—see NAO Report, p. 22.

MODIFICATION

In many regulatory enforcement regimes, policymaking cultures may contribute to excessive conservatism in regulation insofar as they look to address new policy challenges, rather than to assess and modify existing regimes. In contrast, however, field inspectors and their managers often possess a considerable (but unsatisfied) appetite for revising and rethinking their enforcement approaches.

What the really responsive regulatory body will be able to do is to assess the need for a given change, to see the implications across the five regulatory enforcement tasks, and to modify the regime in order to implement needed changes.[59] To take a specific example, the really responsive regulator of marine fisheries would deal with fluctuations in fish stocks by producing answers to such questions as: 'Do existing detection systems pinpoint the issues of compliance that relate to the threatened fish stocks?' 'Are new tools needed to detect and enforce in relation to threatened stocks?'[60] (Are new policies regarding such stocks required?) 'Does the present set of enforcement strategies need to be adjusted in order to prioritize currently threatened stocks?', 'Does the assessment system indicate how well the detection, response development, enforcement, assessment, and modification systems are coping with this newly defined risk to stocks?', and 'Can the regime be adjusted?'

THE CHALLENGES OF 'REALLY RESPONSIVE' REGULATION

The 'really responsive' approach makes considerable informational and analytical demands and it might be asked whether it is a strategy that can be operationalized. Taking account of cultures, institutions, logics, performance, and changes is by no means easy, and certain difficulties can be anticipated. Analysing and responding to varying cultures, for instance, demands both the collection of a considerable amount of information and the exercise of a substantial degree of judgement. If resources are limited, there may be problems in collecting the information necessary for 'real' responsiveness. The exercise of judgement also raises issues concerning the competence and consistency with which different regulatory staff make such judgements and the feasibility and cost of ensuring that there is such competence and consistency. One danger is that the processes for controlling such discretions—

---

[59] For Defra efforts to analyse needs for change following the NAO review, see Defra, *Review of Marine Fisheries* (London, 2004).

[60] The NAO noted the view of fishing concerns that Defra's data on fish stocks were generally a year out of date and adrift of fishing experience at sea—NAO, *Fisheries Enforcement*, 19.

through rules, guidelines, and review processes—can render the regulatory process unresponsive and poorly placed to react to new challenges.

A yet additional complication is that cultures and attitudes may vary within firms and across tasks. A firm, for example, may prove to be highly resistant and uncooperative in relation to the regulator's detection work, but it may be very compliant once its behaviour is placed at issue—as where it is secretive and defiant on disclosure but 'comes quietly' when its errant ways are discovered. The challenge here is to develop regulatory analyses that are sufficiently fine-grained to accommodate such variations, rather than to settle for using a crude across-the-board mode of evaluation.

Moving to the need to be responsive to the institutional and political contexts of regulation, difficulties may be that these are intrinsically hard for regulators to evaluate because they change and vary across tasks. Adapting to such evaluations may, also, prove very difficult, since the regulator may be saddled with a particular remit or set of limited powers—as was the experience of the UK's financial services regulatory regime in the period up to the 2007–9 credit crisis. This can be a special problem in relation to some regulatory tasks—as was seen in the wake of the credit crisis—when the devising of new powers and control tools for financial regulators was constrained by governmental concerns to limit regulation in order to preserve the UK's regulatory competitiveness and its position in league tables of good places to do business.[61]

Regulating really responsively can prove particularly difficult when powers are fragmented or shared. It is often the case, as noted, that risks and social or economic problems are controlled by networks of regulators, rather than bodies enjoying the luxury of a regulatory monopoly—networks in which regulation is 'decentred' rather than simple and focused.[62] In these circumstances, taking on board institutional environments may involve resource intensive investigations and analysis. It may be necessary, for example, to assess the possibilities of coping with such matters as: divergence between the various networked regulators' aims, objectives, and institutional environments; variations in regulatory cultures; differencies in capacities, skills, and resources; and varying capacities to modify their operations.[63] If, furthermore, we look across the different tasks of regulation, we can see that institutional environments arguably impact on the discharging of all of these—and not necessarily in the same ways. This is a further analytical challenge for aspirant 'really responsive' regulators.

---

[61] See, e.g., G. Tett, *Fools Gold* (London, 2009).

[62] Black, 'Decentring Regulation'.

[63] See, e.g., pp. 157–63 above and W. Kickert, E.-H. Klijn, and J. Koppenjan (eds), *Managing Complex Networks* (London, 1997); H. Sullivan and C. Skelcher, *Working Across Boundaries* (Basingstoke, 2002).

In paying attention to compatibilities of powers and tools there are also numerous challenges. Most notably, a significant amount of information is likely to be required—especially since different strategies, powers, and tools might be used in different combinations in carrying out different tasks. Thus, a regulator might employ a combination of deterrence and educative strategies in order to encourage a firm to reduce risks, but it might apply a set of incentives together with a selection of disclosure rules in order to assess performance in risk reduction. Analysing how such combinations will play out is likely to prove demanding informationally but also analytically.

In relation to performance assessment, being 'really responsive' demands that this covers the existing regime across the five core tasks of regulation. It will also require an understanding of those activities that detract from (or potentially detract from) the achievement of objectives but which are beyond the scope of the current regulatory regime or are 'off the screen' in the sense that they are going undetected.[64] In order to set the basis for such sensitivity, the regulator must, first, be clear regarding the objectives of the regulatory regime and the degree to which the rules lack congruence with those objectives. A causal connection has also to be established between regulatory inputs and substantive outcomes, but this is often extremely difficult—it is often, for instance, hard to show that a harm's non-occurrence was the result of the regulator's actions. A further challenge to those who would seek to evaluate regulatory performance is that modern regulation involves delegation of many control functions to the firms being regulated. These processes of 'meta-regulation' make assessment of a firm's internal controls a central element of evaluation but such a layering of regulatory controls makes performance assessment particularly difficult. This is not least because there is often a divergence between the values and processes that underpin managerial and regulatory systems. The further complication to be noted by the really responsive regulator is that the degree to which, and the way in which, assessment procedures can be 'delegated down' to firms' internal control systems will vary across the tasks of regulation.

Finally, a really responsive regulator faces challenges in dealing with the need to adapt to change. Changes, such as the arrival of new risks and risk-creators, have to be adapted to, but this may be hard for a number of reasons. The regulator may have become committed to a perspective on mischiefs or risks that is technically or intellectually deficient. If this is the case, it will prevent adaptation to developing challenges through the carrying out of such tasks as developing new rules and tools that will assist in detection and the ensuring of compliance with relevant requirements. Even if the regulator has properly adjusted its perspective, it may find it difficult to respond with new

---

[64] See Baldwin and Black, 'Really Responsive Regulation', 77–80.

rules and tools because of institutional constraints—the regulator may not have rule-making powers and may have to rely on an unresponsive legislature—or, indeed, legislatures at different governmental levels.

To summarize on the challenges to be faced by regulators who would be 'really responsive' it can be said that these are multiple and of different kinds. The approach makes severe informational, analytical, and resource demands. It also may be difficult to apply because externally imposed constraints may hamstring the regulator—notably governmental positions on such matters as resourcing, regulatory style, institutional structures, or business conditions. The proponents of 'really responsive' regulation would argue, however, that there are always limits to analysis and adaptability and that the contribution of their theory is to provide a framework for addressing regulatory issues. Limited resourcing is no reason, they would say, to eschew the use of a broadly based analytical framework.

Conclusions

The 'responsive regulation' debate that Ayres and Braithwaite brought to the attention of regulators and scholars has come to settle on the construction of the regulatory agenda—on identifying and addressing the array of issues with which regulators have to come to grips if they are to achieve their objectives in an acceptable manner. The concept of 'responsive regulation' moved the regulation debate forward from prior disputations and, similarly, the other approaches discussed here have sought to build on that contribution to come to grips with the growing challenges that are presented by ever more complex combinations of regulatory institutions and instruments. It is clear from the above discussion that, for most theories of regulatory strategy, there are two central questions regarding the approaches that they offer: Are they conceptually satisfactory? Are they capable of implementation in real-life circumstances?

13 Risk-based Regulation

The essence of risk-based regulation, as commonly understood, is the prioritizing of regulatory actions in accordance with an assessment of the risks that parties will present to the regulatory body's achieving its objectives.[1] This is an approach that has exploded in popularity in a host of sectors across the world and which covers both state and non-state bodies.[2] In the UK, the risk-based approach was institutionally endorsed most emphatically in 2005 when the Hampton Review recommended that all UK regulators should operate a risk-based system.[3] It is, nevertheless, a regulatory strategy that poses a number of practical and conceptual challenges for those who would apply it, and these will be the focus of attention in this chapter.

The Elements of Risk-based Regulation

Risk-based frameworks look principally to control relevant risks, not to secure compliance with sets of rules. They establish priorities in a manner that makes selective decisions clear and they aim to provide a logical structure within which decisions can be understood and explained. Generally, such frameworks have a number of central elements.[4] In the first instance, they demand that the regulator should clearly identify its objectives and the risks that the regulated organizations may present to the achieving of those

---

[1] See generally: J. Black, 'The Emergence of Risk-based Regulation and the New Public Risk Management in the United Kingdom' (2005) *Public Law* 512; *Risk-based Regulation: Choices, Practices and Lessons Being Learned* (Paris, 2008); 'The Role of Risk in Regulatory Processes' in R. Baldwin, M. Cave, and M. Lodge, *The Oxford Handbook of Regulation* (Oxford, 2010). We are grateful to Julia Black for allowing us to draw on her sole and co-authored works in composing some parts of this chapter and for her comments.

[2] See Black, *Risk-Based Regulation*, for a review of the development of risk-based regulation and its varieties.

[3] P. Hampton, *Reduction in Administrative Burdens: Effective Inspection and Enforcement* (London, 2005). Since 1999–2000 the National Audit Office has urged regulatory bodies to develop 'risk-based' approaches to regulation and inspection—see NAO, *The Gaming Board: Better Regulation* (1999–2000 HC 537). See also Sir Peter Gershon CBE, *Releasing Resources to the Front Line: An Independent Review of Public Sector Efficiency* (London, July 2004), para. 2.22; Gus O'Donnell, *Financing Britain's Future: Review of the Revenue Departments*, Cmnd 6163 (London, 2004), para. 3.80; all available from www.hm-treasury.gov.uk/.

[4] See J. Black and R. Baldwin, 'Really Responsive Risk-Based Regulation' (2010) 32 *Law and Policy* 181–213.

objectives. Second, the regulator will develop a system for assessing such risks and scoring these. Such mechanisms conventionally treat the quantum of a risk as the product of the gravity of a potential harm or impact and the probability of its occurrence. An important distinction is often drawn here between 'inherent' and 'management and control' risks. The former concept looks to the intrinsic dangerousness of the site or activity. This would take on board such matters as the substances and operations involved and the proximity to a vulnerable resource. (Are the chemicals very dangerous and is the factory near a watercourse?) *Management and control risks* relate to the propensity of an organization's internal controls to mitigate or exacerbate the risk by affecting the probability of a harm's occurrence. Both of these aspects of risk will be considered, together with other factors, in the typical risk-scoring system.

There is, however, considerable variation across regimes and jurisdictions in the approaches that are taken to risk scoring. Some systems are highly quantitative and some are heavily qualitative.[5] The risk scores of regulated concerns, nevertheless, will usually be arrived at by referring to the basket of evaluations that relate to issues of quantum and probability. (Where numerical scores are used, these will often operate as shorthand for more complex underlying judgements.) These scores may rank firms or activities according to broad categories—such as 'traffic light' regimes that divide into 'high', 'medium', or 'low' risks—or they may use more fine-grained divisions.[6] An important qualitative element is often the field inspector's estimation of a regulated firm's management and its capacity and commitment to control the given risk.

A further element in many risk-based regimes is a linkage between the scoring mechanism, or risk evaluation, and the allocation of resources. It is usual for the scoring system to guide the regulator in prioritizing regulatees for attention. High-risk firms will thus be generally accorded some priority for intervention. It is less usual for there to be a direct linkage between the risk score given to a firm and the nature of the intervention tool that is deployed with respect to that firm (whether, for instance, the regulator will use an educative, persuasive, or sanctioning tool to influence the firm). This may be changing, however, since regulators around the world are increasingly using risk-based frameworks to assist them in decisions on intervention method.[7]

Risk-based regulation was originally used as a way to justify regulatory efforts with reference to a rational calculus.[8] Regulation could thus be limited to the justifiable and could be supported on the basis of a systematic and transparent analysis. Experience, however, has revealed that risk-based frameworks are not

---

[5] See Black, *Risk-Based Regulation*.
[6] The UK Financial Services Authority has fifteen different categories, for example—see Black and Baldwin, 'Really Responsive Risk-based Regulation'.
[7] See Black, *Risk-based Regulation*.
[8] See Black, 'Emergence of Risk-based Regulation'.

neutral, technical instruments. Each aspect of a risk-based framework involves a complex set of choices and evaluations on such matters as the risks to be focused on and how such risks are to be defined. Risk-based regimes also demand that the regulator takes decisions on the risks that it will not prioritize. Its risk tolerance is thus exposed to public glare, and this can lead to difficult political challenges—not least when an accident or harm occurs at a site that the regulator had not prioritized. The result is that, in practice, a regulator's risk tolerance is often ultimately driven by political considerations and that using the risk-based framework becomes more of a political art than a technical application. The nature of that art becomes more clear as we now consider in more detail the main challenges to be faced by risk-based regulators.

The Challenges of Risk-based Regulation

IDENTIFYING AND EVALUATING RISKS

The first challenge for any risk-based regulator is, as noted, to identify the risks to its achieving its objectives. These are the risks that it will evaluate and seek to control. To this end, it will normally translate its statutory objectives into key risks and use the resultant breakdown to organize the evaluation of more particular risks. This process is, however, not mechanical, since it demands that judgements be made on a number of matters, most notably on how risks are to be defined and 'bundled'. A central question here is whether the 'risk' at issue is the danger presented by: a particular site (e.g. farm 'X'); a particular operation at that farm (e.g. sheep-dipping); or a given general activity (e.g. sheep-dipping by the 300,000 or so active farms in the UK). In most regulated areas it is difficult to find technically 'correct' answers to such questions, and regulators will have to make judgements—which will often be open to question. Indeed, a general concern on this front is that risk-based regulation tends to be operated in a manner that places too much emphasis on individual sites (or 'silos' of risk) and that, as a result, this approach is slow to come to terms with systemic and cumulating risks.[9] This was a point that many commentators thrust home with some force after the credit crisis took hold in 2008.[10]

---

[9] For a discussion of FSA strategies for dealing with systemic risks, see Black, 'Emergence of Risk-based Regulation', 535–6.

[10] On risk-based regulators' failures to address the systemic risks associated with the sale of complex securitized products before the credit crisis, see G. Tett, *Fools Gold* (New York, 2009); US Government Accountability Office, *Financial Crisis: Recent Crisis Reaffirms the Need to Overhaul the US Regulatory System*, GAO-09–1049T (Washington, DC, 2009); E. Gerding, 'The Subprime Crisis and

Another danger with risk-based regulation is that if regulators pay the closest attention to those firms that present the greatest risks, this inevitably means that some firms will 'fly under the radar' to a lesser or greater degree because they do not meet the risk threshold for such priority of attention. The potential problem then becomes that the 'forgotten' regulatees become slack managers of their own risks because they are not contacted by the regulator with any frequency or because they know or suspect that they are 'immune' from regulation because of the modesty of their risk scores. As a result, such firms may become higher risk-creators who are liable to escape regulatory attention unless the regulator operates review mechanisms that will pick up such changes.

One more area of contention relates to the assumption that it is efficient to prioritize for attention those sites or activities that present the greatest risks to the regulator's objectives. The difficulty here is that the costs of influencing regulatees may vary according, *inter alia* to the regulatees' dispositions, cultures, and capacities. The regulator may, as a result, have to spend far more resource to induce a given change of behaviour at one site than at another. It follows that, if it is the case that, for the same resource expenditure, much greater gains in, let us say, reducing polluting discharges, can be achieved at site X rather than site Y (which presents a larger pollution risk than site X) it may be efficient to prioritize site X for attention. Taking action at the lower risk site X will produce the greatest reduction in pollution but this is not a strategy of targeting the greatest risk creator. Whenever there is the possibility of such scenarios, and it is feasible to calculate these effects,[11] regulators will have to decide whether to take on board the 'amenability'[12] of the regulatee in the risk-scoring mechanism that drives their priorities. This, moreover, is liable to be no easy and uncontentious decision. If risk scores are raised when regulatees are amenable to regulatory direction, the effect is to reward those businesses who are low in amenability (the ill-disposed and recalcitrant businesses) by reducing their exposure to regulatory intervention. If firms with higher amenability are, in contrast, rewarded with lower risk scores, this involves an inefficiency since the regulatory resource will be directed away from the location where it would produce the greatest positive effect. There is liable to be no easy answer to this dilemma, and the

the Outsourcing of Financial Regulation to Financial Institution Risk Models: Code, Crash and Open Source' (2008), available at SSRN: http://ssrn.com/abstract=1273467.

[11] It is not always simple for a regulator to calculate with accuracy the amount of risk reduction that an intervention strategy will produce in a regulatee. Such estimations are unlikely to be possible where the risk is one that is low in frequency and idiosyncratic and where contacts with the regulatee are infrequent.

[12] Where 'amenability' is the regulatee's propensity to come into line with the regulator's directions at low cost—see Black and Baldwin, 'Really Responsive Risk-based Regulation'.

risk-based regime fails to operate mechanically to produce an unproblematic steer.[13]

A second major challenge for risk-based regulators is to take on board the extent to which managerial attitudes will affect the level of risk presented by a firm.[14] The quality and character of management and their risk controls will affect the probability of a harm's occurrence and, as noted, many risk-scoring systems will seek to incorporate evaluations of managers for this reason.[15] (Management and control assessments, for instance, have a significant impact in the risk-scoring systems of many financial regulators, since these can lower or raise the 'net risk' of the firm.) Whatever weighting is given to 'management and control' within a given regime, however, the general practice is to lower the risk score overall where the regulator has confidence in the management team's ability to control relevant risks. This is no simple task, however, since risk-based assessments attempt to evaluate the risks that will be presented by a firm in the future. Different types of risk-based systems are better equipped to do this than others. Mere references to past compliance records tend to lack responsiveness and dynamism and yet prospective judgements can present difficulties. Individual field officers' judgements about managers may have to be incorporated within a risk regime in a manner that ensures that similar approaches are adopted across evaluators and regulatory managers may find it hard to balance their needs to foster both discretion and consistency. The related danger is that the processes of overseeing discretionary decision-making can prove excessively costly in staff time and resources and that centrally administered controls, checks, and structuring procedures can render the agency slow to respond to changes in the regulatory challenges that they face.[16]

IMPLEMENTATION

A first challenge in seeking to give effect to a risk-based system is to be clear about the degree to which risk evaluations will be used as drivers of regulatory actions. The challenge arises because risk evaluations may prove far more helpful in relation to some regulatory tasks than others. Thus, risk scoring

---

[13] Some regulators do seek to take amenability characteristics on board in their risk scoring: the Portuguese environmental regulator, IGOAT, for example, includes, in its assessment of management and control an evaluation of the firms' interaction with the regulators and uses this as an indicator for the firm's amenability to intervention (Black, *Risk-based Regulation*).

[14] See Black and Baldwin, 'Really Responsive Risk-based Regulation'.

[15] The weight that is attached to such managerial assessments does vary: the England and Wales Environment Agency gives such assessments relatively little weight, but the Portuguese environmental regulator's scheme applies a multiplier of three to the 'management and control' score as it wants to incentivize firms to improve their risk-management systems and thus lower their risk scores—see Black, *Risk-based Regulation*.

[16] Ibid.

may provide a very ready basis for detecting high-risk sites, activities, and actors, but it may offer far less assistance in identifying the modes of intervention that will best reduce risks—whether the best way to reduce the risks posed by the firm is to use a 'zero-tolerance' command and control regime or whether an educative, disclosure, or other strategy would prove more effective. The *kind* of intervention required may, at best, be loosely linked to the level of risk that the firm presents.

The major determinant of the optimal style of intervention is liable to be revealed by an analysis of the likely responsiveness of the firm to different stimuli—and this may involve a departure from an overly rigid risk-based system and a drawing on other theories, such as 'compliance', 'deterrence', responsive regulation, problem-centred, and other approaches to fit the context.[17] Two firms with similarly high-risk scores may, for instance, vary in their informational positions and dispositions to comply with regulatory demands. One may respond well to an educative programme and the other may not. One may not need to be met with a punitive threat, the other may have to be. How best to deal with these two firms is not readily identified by reference to a risk assessment system. Even when a risk-scoring system evaluates a firm's risk management performance, this will not assist greatly in determining the best intervention style. The fact that a risk management team may operate with a certain level of competence does not, for instance, mean that it will respond to one kind of intervention tool rather than another.

A second implementation challenge is to put a risk-based system into effect within the organizational setting in which it is sited. As noted, risk assessment demands that regulatory officials make discretionary judgements when they assess such matters as managerial quality. A central organizational difficulty, as suggested above, is for the regulator to control these discretionary judgements and make them consistent but to avoid instituting processes that render the regime expensive and unresponsive. Cultural changes may also have to be made within regulatory bodies so that a focus on rules and compliance-seeking gives way to a concern with risks and their assessment: 'regulators have to lose the "tick the box" mentality and get used to assessing risk'.[18] If this cultural change is not pushed through the organization, the danger is that regulatory officials 'reverse engineer' the system by scoring risks in a manner that is dictated by their traditional methods of appraising firms.[19]

A further organizational challenge may stem from the broader institutional and political contexts that regulators occupy. These are often critical to the

---

[17] See Chapters 11 and 12 above.

[18] Black, 'Emergence of Risk-based Regulation', 539; C. Briault, *The Rationale for a Single National Financial Services Regulator*, FSA Occasional Paper No. 2 (London, 1999).

[19] Black, 'Emergence of Risk-based Regulation', 539; and FSA, *Practitioner Panel Annual Report 2003–4*, 7–8.

performance of a risk-based regime and certain regulators may experience special difficulties in dealing with these settings.[20] Thus, it could be argued that at least some of the failures of the UK's financial services regulatory regime in the period up to the credit crisis can be put down to key aspects of the institutional environment within which the regulators worked: notably the way that the UK government's 'light-touch' regulatory philosophy shaped regulatory interactions and understandings about the appropriateness of regulatory demands;[21] the degree to which domestic regulators placed faith in controls by other national regulators to control globally interconnected markets; and the extent to which domestic regulators considered themselves constrained by regulatory competition within the international institutional environment.[22]

Another organizational difficulty for risk-based regulators may arise when their powers are shared with other bodies.[23] Thus, the effectiveness of the UK's regulation in the lead up to the credit crisis was arguably weakened by the way in which regulatory powers were distributed between the Treasury, the Bank of England, and the Financial Services Authority. It may be especially difficult for regulators to adhere to the logics of risk-based systems when they are faced with divergence between the various networked regulators' aims, objectives, and institutional environments; variations in regulatory cultures; differences in capacities, skills, and resources; and varying capacities to modify their operations.[24]

Risk-based regulators may be especially vulnerable to their political contexts. All regulators need political support if they are to act robustly against

[20] Black and Baldwin, 'Really Responsive Risk-based Regulation'.

[21] In 2009, the chairman of the FSA and the Governor of the Bank of England both emphasized to the Treasury Select Committee that they would have faced considerable political and market hostility if they had sought to 'stop the party' and required banks to rein in their activities (Lord Turner's evidence in response to Q 2145 HC Treasury Select Committee 25 Feb. 2009; Mervyn King's evidence in response to Q 2354 HC Treasury Select Committee 26 Feb. 2009).

[22] Ibid., and see HM Treasury, *Reforming Financial Markets* (London, 2009); G. Tett, *Fools Gold* (New York, 2009); A. Turner, *A Regulatory Response to the Global Banking Crisis* (London, 2009). It is widely accepted by the G20 governments, including the UK Treasury, that a key contributing cause of the credit crisis of 2007–9 was the failure of national regulators to respond, in coordination with other national regulators and supra-national regulators, not only to the excessive risks being taken by some individual firms, but to the problems of global system-wide risk—see HM Treasury, *Reforming Financial Markets*, para. 3.1; G20, *Declaration—Summit on the Financial Markets and World Economy, November 2009* (Washington, DC, 2009).

[23] On networks in which regulation is 'decentred' rather than simple and focused, see J. Black, 'Decentring Regulation: The Role of Regulation and Self-Regulation in a "Post-Regulatory World"' (2001) *Current Legal Problems* 103–46, and on the challenges of network coordination, see E. Bardach, *Getting Agencies to Work Together* (Washington, DC, 1998); W. Kickert, E.-H. Klijn, and J. Koppenjan (eds.), *Managing Complex Networks* (London, 1997); H. Sullivan and C. Skelcher, *Working Across Boundaries* (Basingstoke, 2002).

[24] J. Black, *Managing the Financial Crisis: The Constitutional Dimension*, LSE Law, Society and Economy Working Papers 12/2010 (London, 2010).

firms, but risk-based regulation may tend to prejudice that support in so far as it involves the regulator in making transparent decisions about intervention priorities and the actions that it will *not* take. When such prioritizations clash with political and public expectations of protection, the regulator may encounter political troubles. In times of crisis (as with the credit crunch) such difficulties may be acute.[25]

A third implementation challenge for risk-based regulators is to ensure that the various strategies that they deploy do not undercut each other or the logic of risk-based regulation itself. Thus, one issue might be whether applying a deterrence-based enforcement strategy will impact adversely on the detection and information collection functions that are central to the logic of the risk-based regime. Such an impact would pose significant practical difficulties for risk-based regulators, but the regulator's choices may be limited. They may have to use formal enforcement actions, such as fines, to change the behaviour of many firms. In such circumstances, responding to non-compliance with a deterrence approach may cut across the ability to detect that non-compliance in the first place. Firms know that any information they give to the regulator may potentially be used against them in an enforcement action and this can have a chilling effect on their cooperation with that regulator.[26]

COPING WITH CHANGE

A special danger in a risk-based regime is that the regulators become 'locked-in' to an established method of identifying key risks and of dealing with these. One reason why this problem may arise is that risk-based regimes are often 'sold' to politicians, to agency staff, and to the public, as a rational guide that justifies intervention and can be used to ward off criticism.[27] This can mean that following the given framework becomes the institutionalized process so that regulators become slow to explore the risk model's inherent weaknesses. They also become unresponsive to changing circumstances so that they fail to detect and deal with new risks and changes in risk profiles (notably increases in risks). The danger is that the framework is historically rooted in a way that does not enable the regulator to react sensitively to an unpredicted, and sometimes unpredictable, future. The Hampton Review, indeed, was well aware of the danger that risk frameworks can prove too static. Hampton argued that regulation 'should always include a small element of random inspection' in order to check on the validity of the risk assessment system.[28] A value of random inspection, on this view, is that it holds out the prospect of

---

[25] Ibid. See also J. Black and R. Baldwin, 'Risk-based Regulation: How Low Can You Go?' (forthcoming).

[26] See Black, *Risk-based Regulation*.

[27] See Black, 'Emergence of Risk-based Regulation'.

[28] Hampton Report, para 2.38; Statutory Code of Practice for Regulators 2007, para. 6.2.

uncovering new risks and risk-creators in a way that is unlikely to flow from an inspection programme that is based on analyses of previously identified risks.

Random inspections only, however, serve to combat model myopia if they break away from the normal risk assessment framework and if regulatory supervisors feel able to communicate new or emerging risks to those in the policy or risk division in the course of their day-to-day monitoring and assessment activities. At best, there should be an institutionalization of a dynamic process for identifying new or emerging risks.[29]

Coping with change demands, at its core, that the regulator can be performance-sensitive—that it can measure whether its current approaches are proving successful in achieving desired objectives; that it can justify the strategies adopted; and that it can adjust these when needed. Risk-based regulators, however, may find such performance sensitivity difficult. In the first instance, there is the counterfactual issue. Risk-based regulation is, in essence, directed towards future events that may or may not happen. If a harm does not ensue from a risk, it can be difficult, if not impossible, to show that this outcome was the result of the regulator's actions. Performance assessment will tend to be the easier when the regulated area involves the control of numerous incidents of a similar nature and where data is routinely and easily collected.[30] Matters are far more difficult where the regulated domain provides no set of data on past incidences from which probabilities can be derived or against which regulatory strategies can be correlated.

A further difficulty may confront risk-based regulators when they strive for performance sensitivity. This stems from the risk-based approach's commonly substantial delegation of control functions down to the risk management systems of the firms being regulated. It is a regulatory method that focuses attention on the quality of a firm's internal controls. As Black has said: 'meta-regulation is inevitable: regulators simply do not have the resources to do anything else. Reliance is a fact of life. What the risk-based frameworks are intended to do is to help the regulator identify where it is well placed, where it is not, and how it can be made so.'[31] In such 'meta-regulation' regimes, however, this reliance on delegated regulatory controls makes performance assessment especially difficult. A particular challenge arises because different actors—be they corporations, regulators, credit ratings agencies, or other bodies—may use different models or 'codes' to evaluate risks and they may operate with different cultures. Regulators may think of risk control objectives

---

[29] See, for example, the Canadian Office for the Supervision of Financial Institutions (OSFI) and its 'emerging risks committee' procedure.

[30] In the area of health and safety, there are particular types of recurrent injuries at work, such as 'slips and trips'—see Black, 'Emergence of Risk-based Regulation'.

[31] Black, 'Emergence of Risk-based Regulation', 544.

with reference to statutory purposes, whereas firms may see internal risk management as properly directed at profits and market share. The risks that the regulator is concerned with will, indeed, not always be the same as the risks that the firms are focused on.[32]

This means that, in so far as regulators enrol regulatees or other actors in the regulatory regime, this involves a substituting of the latter's codes for the judgements and decisions of the regulators—and it does so in a manner that renders risk evaluations all the more opaque to regulators, as well as to the broader community.[33] When layers of such codes are involved in the provision and evaluation of services—as when corporations, credit ratings agencies, financial institutions, and regulators are involved with a securitized product—there can be a worrying lack of connection between the regulator and the risk evaluation.[34]

An additional problem that risk-based regulators may experience in seeking to cope with change relates to the manner in which regulatory performance is assessed. On this point, it might be thought that risk-based regulation offers a ready means of judging performance. The risk scores of regulated firms and individuals can be compared year on year (or month on month) and this will reveal whether overall levels of risk are increasing or decreasing. This approach, however, tends to focus on a given set of historically established risks and, if this is so, they will reveal little about the regulator's success or failure in coming to grips with new risks and new risk-creators. Using a given framework for risk analysis presupposes, furthermore, that there is a perfect fit between the risk framework and the regulator's objectives—and it will, accordingly, give no indication of the extent to which undesirable risk creation is escaping the regulatory net. There is liable to be no measure, for instance, of the prevalence of creative compliance or new types of risk creation or risk-creators that are not covered by the current rules. As a result, analyses of relative risk scores will not indicate whether the regulatory regime is addressing a major portion of threats to regulatory objectives or only a small percentage of these.

A further problem that risk-based systems may encounter in dealing with change is that it may be difficult for regulators to adapt to shifts in preferences

---

[32] One of the difficulties the FSA has faced in implementing ARROW is communicating to firms that the risks that the FSA is concerned with are not always the same as the risks the firms are concerned with—see Briault, *Rationale for a Single National Financial Services Regulator*, and Black, 'Emergence of Risk-based Regulation'.

[33] On enrolment, see J. Black, 'Enrolling Actors in Regulatory Processes: Examples from UK Financial Services Regulation' (2003) *Public Law* 62–90.

[34] E. Gerding, 'The Subprime Crisis and the Outsourcing of Financial Regulation to Financial Institution Risk Models: Code, Crash and Open Source' (2008), available at SSRN: http://ssrn.com/abstract=1273467; J. Gray, 'Is it Time to Highlight the Limits of Risk Based Financial Regulation?' (2009) 4(1) *Capital Markets Law Journal* 50–62.

and objectives. Risk-based regimes always have to contend with possible disjunctures between the regulator's perceptions of risk and those of the public (or certain groups of interests), but the additional problem is that those disjunctures are not static. Preferences concerning regulation often change—as seen in the post-credit crisis period in the UK when sections of the public, the government, the regulators, and the media lost a good deal of faith in 'light-touch' regulation. The public may want different things of regulators at different times, and so may governments, legislators, extra-jurisdictional bodies, and particular groups of interests. The problem is that if regulators are committed to the given framework, they may be slow to respond to changes—especially when the processes of constructing and developing that framework are positioned deep within the bureaucratic process and are, as a result, insulated from the public pressures that might be expected to galvanize change.

One more problem is that if risk-based regulation involves a misalignment between the institutional risks of the regulator (i.e. the risks to the regulator's reputation and objectives) and risks to society (e.g. of harms such as injuries or deaths), this may make the regulator unresponsive to changes in risks to society's interests. Thus, to cite Rothstein et al.'s example of rail safety, a rail regulator may tend to focus on risks of multiple fatality accidents to a degree that is not commensurate with the attention it devotes to the control of common minor accidents that cumulatively cause as many or more fatalities.[35] It may do so because it is aware that multiple fatality accidents may detract from the regulator's reputation in an especially negative and disproportionate manner. In these circumstances, the focus on risks to the regulator renders the regulator less responsive to changes in risks to society (e.g. new kinds of minor but frequently ocurring accident) than it might otherwise be.

Finally, note should be taken of the special difficulties of contemplating radical changes in regulatory strategy from 'within' a risk-based regulatory regime. The problem here is that a mindset that centres on analysing and reacting to risks will not be readily attuned to the consideration of ways in which risks can be 'designed out' of economic or social processes by moving towards pre-emptive managerial strategies. Such shifts of approach may demand a breadth of analysis that the 'process myopia' of the risk-based system does not encourage. The message of the 'really responsive' approach here is that the risk-based regulator should always be aware of the possible need to move beyond the merely responsive.[36]

---

[35] H. Rothstein, P. Irving, T. Walden, and R. Yearsley 'The Risks of Risk-based Regulation: Insights From the Environmental Policy Domain' (2006) 32 *Environment International* 1056–65.
[36] See Black and Baldwin, 'Really Responsive Risk-based Regulation'.

JUSTIFYING RISK-BASED REGULATION

Regulatory decisions that are based on risk appraisals will often prove to be more difficult to justify than involved parties have initially anticipated. The reason is that this is an approach that makes considerable promises— notably that the challenges and complexities of regulation can be rationalized, managed, and controlled. As has been said of risk-based regulation: 'it suggests that the notoriously complex task of regulating can be rendered manageable, and that the contingencies of unpredictable events can be made controllable... hesitancies are lost in the confident exposition of risk identification, assessment and validation'.[37] Risk-based regulation is thus commonly seen as not only more rational, cost-effective, and controllable than other systems but more transparent and more easily justified.[38] At the political level, risk-based regulation was, indeed, welcomed in the UK as a way to curb what was seen as the insatiable appetite of politicians and the wider public for regulation.[39]

Delivery on these undertakings is extremely difficult, not least because there is often considerable dissonance between the regulator's understanding of risk priorities and those of the firms, or indeed the wider public. Choosing which risks to focus on is, as noted above, a political, not a technical issue, and judgements have to be made on such matters as: whether to target the largest risks or the places where the largest risk reductions can be effected for a given level of resource input; whether to focus on individual risk-creators or specific types of risk; the right balance between acting on systemic risks and controlling individual risks; and ultimately what is an acceptable level of risk. A further issue of difficulty is whether to err on the side of over-intervention (assuming that certain firms pose risks when they do not) or of under-intervention (assuming that they do not pose risks when they do). Each position on these issues brings contention and problems.[40]

Nor, to repeat, does transparency always assist in legitimation. Regulating according to a risk-based framework exposes the reality that there will be a limit on the resources that can be spent on controlling certain types of risk creators (e.g. low-impact firms), or certain types of risk (for example, those with medium/high impact but low probability). Such a framework also exposes

---

[37] Black, 'Emergence of Risk-based Regulation'.

[38] Better Regulation Taskforce, *Enforcement* (London, 1999); *Higher Education: Easing the Burden* (London, 2002); *Bridging the Gap: Participation in Social Care Regulation* (London, 2004); *Avoiding Regulatory Creep* (London, 2004); Hampton Report; Gershon, *Releasing Resources to the Front Line*, para. 2.22; O'Donnell, *Financing Britain's Future*, para. 3.80 (available from www.hm-treasury.gov.uk/).

[39] Black, 'Emergence of Risk-based Regulation'.

[40] Black, 'Emergence of Risk-based Regulation', notes 141–51. (London, 2004).

the balance between individual and systemic risk controls. This means that officials are required to leave certain risks or types of risk uncontrolled or subject to limited supervision. This can be difficult for regulatory managers to justify to the public and to regulatees.[41] After a harmful event has occurred at a firm it may, for example, be difficult to explain to the media that firms of that class are not regulated as a priority because they have risk scores that are too low. Similarly, it may be difficult, after a systemic catastrophe such as the credit crisis, to explain why systemic issues had not been given a higher priority.

Some regulators manage these challenges by incorporating public perceptions explicitly into their risk-based frameworks. For the UK Pensions Regulator, for example, a key criterion for assessing risk is whether a failure in a particular area would lead to a loss of public confidence in the regulator and in the pensions system. Other regulators seek to deal with public attitudes reactively, but a general difficulty in taking public attitudes on board is that a regime of risk-based regulation that is too responsive to the public will lose much of its identity as a systematized and rational way for regulators to manage their resources.

Risk-based systems may also be difficult to justify to staff who have to reconcile the advertised technical neatness of those systems with the political messiness of the world that they seek to control. An irony here is that, in its early years, risk-based regulation was promoted within some regulatory bodies as a defence mechanism—on the basis that if one followed the book, one would be immune from criticism.[42] The bureaucratic reality, however, has been that if senior management fail fully to articulate the extent to which they will 'buy in' to the risk-based process so that they accept that mistakes will be made and that things will be left undone, this will reduce the confidence of staff in the system and lead to the taking of self-protective steps such as operating on the basis of factors other than risk analyses (such as perceptions of political risks to themselves). This is liable to hamper the implementation of the risk-based regime and reduce the rationality that lies at the heart of its justificatory claims.

A special justificatory challenge for risk-based regulation is that of satisfying expectations regarding openness, transparency, and accountability. Here again there are paradoxical elements. On the one hand, risk-based regulation holds out the prospect of transparency through the exposure of its numerical/analytic basis. On the other, a closer look at the operation of such systems reveals that they are built on high levels of discretion and politically contentious judgements and that the important policies and decisions tend to be hidden away behind the

---

[41] The FSA has discussed the gap between public expectations of what regulators should or should not be able to achieve, and what 'reasonable' expectations should be—see FSA, *Reasonable Expectations: Regulation in a Non Zero-Failure World* (London, 2003); see also Black, 'Emergence of Risk-based Regulation', 541–2. On approaches to low risks, see Black and Baldwin, 'Risk-based Regulation: How Low Can You Go?' (forthcoming).

[42] Black, 'Emergence of Risk-based Regulation', notes 172–3.

apparently neutral language of the risk assessment model.[43] This point applies especially to the definitions of thresholds for intervention, the risk assessments themselves, and the subsequent categorizations and scoring of firms.

All regulators have to prioritize the use of resources, but it is best to understand the implications of doing this through risk-based processes. What can be seen is that framing the regulatory task in terms of risk involves buying into particular conceptions of the problem at hand. It leads to the framing of a solution in a particular way, and produces special challenges of justification and legitimation. In adopting risk-based frameworks, regulators attempt to define the acceptable limits of their responsibility and hence accountability. In such processes, risk-based regulation implicitly or explicitly defines what risks the regulator should be expected to prevent, and those which it should not—those it should be blamed for not preventing and those which it should not be blamed for not preventing. As Power has argued, attempting to manage risk requires a new 'politics of uncertainty', involving not only assessments of who should be responsible for dealing with its consequences but an appreciation that no-one is to blame for true uncertainty.[44] Risk-based regulation, argues Black, also requires a new and related politics of accountability and a quite distinct mode of legitimation.[45] That politics involves new debates on who should be making decisions on the risks that are important and those that are not.

Such issues of justification and legitimation, moreover, can be expected to vary across the various core tasks of regulation. The above discussion of risk-scoring, for instance, relates to the task of discovery—of identifying targets for intervention. Quite different, but nevertheless risk-based-specific sets of issues will arise when looking at the processes of enforcement and compliance-seeking on the ground, or the processes of assessing performance by means of risk analyses, or those of modifying regulatory strategy. The need to come to grips with all of these issues is the important message of what has been called the 'really responsive' approach.[46]

Conclusions

Risk-based regulation has achieved broad acceptance within many governments and regulatory organizations, but it is an approach that has to overcome many hurdles if it is to succeed on the ground. Risk-based regulation is

---

[43] Black, 'Emergence of Risk-based Regulation'.
[44] Power, *The Risk Management of Everything*.
[45] See Black, 'Emergence of Risk-based Regulation'.
[46] See Black and Baldwin, 'Really Responsive Risk-based Regulation'.

perhaps best seen not as a free-standing and technical guide to regulatory intervention but as a particular way to construct the regulatory agenda and as a control strategy that has to be combined with other control strategies in different (and often contentious) ways across different contexts and regulatory tasks. Coming to grips with the challenges of risk-based regulation might appear to be daunting and difficult to operationalize. Those difficulties are, however, vastly outweighed by the costs of regulatory failure. If there is one message to take from the credit crisis, it is that there is a colossal price to pay if regulators do not deal adequately with the challenges discussed here—notably, in the case of banking, those produced by changes in the nature of risks or risk-creators and by the constraints that flow from the institutional environments in which the regulators and regulated firms work.

14 Standards and Principles

Regulatory rules often link a regulatory response (e.g. a fine, tax, or administrative order) to a standard of performance. Use of standards is not exclusive to command and control regimes and standard-setting issues may arise as commonly when incentives, rather than sanctions, underpin regulation.[1] Regulators are faced with two core questions when standards are incorporated into rules: 'Which types of standards should be used?', 'What level of performance should be demanded?' This chapter examines how those questions can be answered and reviews the general problems of standard-setting.[2] It then considers the case for regulating in furtherance of broad principles, rather than precise rules.

Which Types of Standards?

Standards vary across a number of dimensions. As was seen in Chapter 11, a key issue in enforcement is the timing or stage of process at which the regulator wishes to intervene. A standard may look to behaviour at the *prevention* stage, it can focus on the *act* that gives rise to a harmful result, or it can look to the *harmful result* itself. Thus a rule might apply a standard to the safety policies that a firm is called upon to develop in order to *prevent* injuries; an alternative (or additional) rule might attach a sanction to dangerous *acts* and apply a standard to the use of equipment (e.g. scaffolding) that is dangerous if employed improperly; and a further rule might apply a standard to define the *harmful result* of an activity and to impose sanctions accordingly.

Standards can thus be divided into three categories in correspondence with these three stages of intervention.

---

[1] On standard-setting generally, see A. Ogus, *Regulation: Legal Form and Economic Theory* (Oxford, 1994), chs. 8, 9; S. Breyer, *Regulation and Its Reform* (Cambridge, MA, 1982), ch. 5; G. Richardson et al., *Policing Pollution* (Oxford, 1983), 35–8; C. Scott, 'Standard-Setting in Regulatory Regimes' in R. Baldwin, M. Cave, and M. Lodge (eds.), *The Oxford Handbook of Regulation* (Oxford, 2010); J. Black, 'Which Arrow? Rule Type and Regulatory Policy' (1995) *Public Law* 94–117. For a detailed study of standard-setting in the health and safety sector see HM Treasury, *The Setting of Safety Standards* (London, 1996).

[2] This chapter does not deal with the scope (or inclusiveness) of standards or rules, on which see Chapter 11, above.

SPECIFICATION (OR DESIGN) STANDARDS

Specification standards focus on prevention by controlling the processes that give rise to dangerous situations—by demanding, for example, that industrial activities conform to specification on plant construction, equipment to be used, or modes of operation. Such standards can be relatively inexpensive to enforce (since monitoring compliance with a given specification is a fairly simple operation), and a further advantage is that compliance costs may be readily calculated. (If use of a particular design of machinery is required, then this can be costed quite easily.) Such standards are, however, highly intrusive in so far as the regulator is strongly involved in structuring, say, the manufacturing process. The technique may also inhibit innovation and the development of new, perhaps safer and more efficient, designs of equipment or operation. The regulated firm is called upon to install the specified design and has no incentive to innovate—indeed, it is the regulator who has to lead the way technically. This may be desirable in certain sectors where the regulator possesses expertise and information unavailable to private producers, but in other sectors it may be preferable to allow private designers and researchers to generate technological advances, not least for reasons of international competitiveness.

A further problem with specification standards is the difficulty of predicting the total harm that will result from the anticipated use of the specified equipment or method. Suppose a process is specified on the basis that it will produce each hour only a given level of pollution in a river. This will not guarantee the survival of life in the river unless the number of hours of use is stipulated and enforced. If the river's capacity to absorb pollution varies (according to flow and temperature levels) it will be particularly difficult to achieve desired ends by using specification standards.

PERFORMANCE (OR OUTPUT) STANDARDS

Performance standards demand a given level of delivery at the act stage but do not specify how that delivery is to be arrived at. In the pollution field an emission standard comes within this category and may govern the concentration of a pollutant that may be discharged from a given point. The focus is on the level of risks that a process creates, rather than the actual harms done.

Such standards are less technologically restrictive than specification standards—they offer, and give, firms an incentive to design processes with superior performance levels—but it is still difficult to relate different levels of performance to regulatory goals, for example to calculate the cumulative consequences of discharges for the watercourse.[3] Enforcement costs are also liable to be higher with performance than with specification standards, since it will be more difficult to check ongoing levels of pollution throughout the day and night than to see if the specified filtration system is in use.

TARGET (OR OUTCOME) STANDARDS

Target standards seek to overcome the problems of linking standards to regulatory goals by stating those goals or outcomes directly. These standards prescribe no particular type of process or level of risk creation, but call for the avoidance of certain harmful consequences (e.g. removing the water's capacity to support fish life). The advantage of such standards is that firms are left free to decide how best (and most cheaply) to achieve the set targets. It is the firms, moreover, rather than the state regulators, that have to bear the costs of calculating how to achieve stipulated targets. Where, however, the harms at issue are caused by firms who are insufficiently resourced or coordinated to calculate the best means of achieving targets, it may be socially efficient to collect information centrally in the regulatory agency and to employ specification (or design) standards.

What Level of Performance Should be Demanded?

If the regulators of an activity were to call for the total eradication of risks, this would generally mean that the activity could not be carried out. Reducing harms or risks of harm becomes more and more expensive as reductions advance and so the question arises: 'How can regulators, in controlling harms or risks, fix standards at the right levels?'

One response is to seek to set optimal levels on efficiency grounds by a process in which the costs of harm avoidance are balanced against the benefits. There are, however, objections to making regulatory decisions turn purely on considerations of efficiency—these were discussed in Chapter 3. For instance, society might want to place an absolute ban on the use of some items of dangerous equipment (e.g. unguarded saws[4]) and might want to do so to

---

[3] 'Ambient' standards do, however, look to the maximum pollution concentration permitted in the environment at a given place and 'receptor' standards look to the perceptible harm that a discharger causes to the environment. These can be seen as bridges between performance and target standards. On specification and performance standards, see J. Braithwaite, 'The Limits of Economism in Controlling Harmful Corporate Conduct' (1982) 16 *Law and Society Review* 481 and Richardson et al., *Policing Pollution*, 37–40.

[4] See the Factories Act 1961, section 14, which requires every dangerous part of any machinery to be securely fenced—it is not permissible to argue that this is impractical or expensive.

protect certain rights rather, than to reflect a balancing of costs and benefits. This is not to say, however, that decisions primarily concerned with the distribution of rights should pay no heed to the costs and benefits involved. Judgements as to the optimal level of harm abatement demanded by a regulatory standard may quite properly be informed by economists' approaches, even if they are not driven by these.[5]

Standards, and the ways in which these are stated, may in practice be influenced *inter alia* by lay, historical, political, commercial, and other factors.[6] Thus, if safety standards are taken as an example, it is possible to distinguish between four different approaches.[7]

TRADITIONAL FORMULATIONS

These may demand that potentially dangerous activities be made wholly safe or *as safe as possible*, or they may adopt a *rule of thumb*. The latter approach demands that dangers should not be allowed to increase, even if the balance of costs and benefits changes. Examples would be stipulations that the annual number of fatal commercial air crashes or cumulative atmospheric pollution levels should not be allowed to increase above current figures.

WORKING LIMITS AND TARGETS

Working limits are used to define, in flexible terms, the maximum levels of risks, emissions, or harms allowed within good practice. Targets are aspirational and give policies presentational focus—thus published targets for road accident deaths might be used to set goals for promoting safety.

COST-BENEFIT TRADE-OFFS

Some standards may explicitly allow the costs of avoiding dangers to be weighed (in varying degrees) against the benefits of greater safety. In the health and safety field a series of formulations allow the balancing, and these are covered by acronyms such as ALARP, ALARA, SFAIRP, and BATNEEC.[8]

---

[5] See HM Treasury, *Setting of Safety Standards*.

[6] For other influences, see the different explanations of regulatory developments that are reviewed in Chapter 4.

[7] See HM Treasury, *Setting of Safety Standards*, 6–9, on which this section builds.

[8] Standing for: As Low as Reasonably Practicable; As Low As Reasonably Achievable; So Far As Is Reasonably Practicable; and Best Available Technology Not Entailing Excessive Costs. On cost-benefit analysis and regulation see Chapter 15, below.

TOLERABILITY APPROACHES

If it is accepted that standards ought to look to individuals' rights and distributional questions but should also take on board considerations of costs and benefits, a combined approach can be adopted. An example is the Tolerability of Risks (TOR) framework developed by the Health and Safety Executive (HSE) in the 1980s. This framework applies a cost-benefit approach to standards but imposes absolute maximum levels of risk, set on the basis of equity. It is accepted that risks of harm beyond certain levels shall not be imposed even in exchange for very high gains. It is also accepted, however, that below such levels, a cost-benefit approach can be explicitly employed.

EFFICIENT STANDARD-SETTING: THE PROBLEMS

An efficiency-based strategy would aim to set standards so as to achieve optimal loss abatement—that is, to fix standards at levels where total benefits would exceed total costs by the greatest amount.[9] Even leaving aside distributional and perceptual issues,[10] a series of problems faces those who seek to apply such a strategy.[11] Thus, suppose an agency responsible for a single district sets out to fix a standard for the maximum number of potentially harmful dust particles per cubic metre of air that it will allow in its factories. The following difficulties are likely to be encountered. The first concerns information. It is generally difficult and expensive for agencies to acquire unbiased data for use in standard-setting.[12] Those industries that are subject to regulation will possess most of the relevant raw data, but they will tend to distort this information when passing it to the controlling agency (e.g. exaggerating anticipated compliance costs) and firms may use the possession of information as a lever with which to exert influence over the agency. Independent data may be very expensive to generate in-house and resort to experts in the field may produce findings that are tainted by the industry's influence over the experts they frequently employ as consultants. Pressure groups and other branches of government may be in no better position to generate data than the regulator.

---

[9] See Ogus, *Regulation*, 153–4 and T. Makkai and J. Braithwaite, 'The Limits of the Economic Analysis of Regulation: An Empirical Case and a Case for Empiricism' (1993) 15 *Law and Policy* 271. ('The trouble is that the optimum level of stringency in a regulatory standard identified by an economic analysis is always false' (272).)

[10] On the problems that different perceptions of dangers and risks present for 'rational' regulators, see Chapter 6 above.

[11] On the difficulties of applying cost-benefit approaches to regulation generally, see Chapter 15 below.

[12] See Breyer, *Regulation*, 109–12.

A second problem is that assessing the costs of imposing a standard is an enormously complex matter, even assuming away the general informational problems just noted. An initial calculation concerns the expenses of rule-making, administration, monitoring compliance-seeking, and enforcement. A further, more difficult matter, relates to compliance costs—the expenses of bringing equipment up to standard and any losses that may be incurred, for example, through diminutions in the efficiency of the manufacturing process (e.g. a slowing down of the production line due to the operation of safety guards). If each factory in a district is operating different dust-emitting and controlling processes, calculations will have to relate to each and every set of premises. The side-effects of regulation also have to be anticipated. Thus, increasing the rigour of a standard may change enforcement strategies or policies and also make enforcement more difficult (changing even the equipment demanded for measuring compliance). Patterns of compliance, furthermore, may not be constant, but may be dynamic. Factory owners may, for example, give up on complying with standards if they see them as unreasonable or draconian[13] and the relationship between degrees of regulatory rigour and levels of compliance may be indirect and uncertain.[14]

Other unintended effects of fixing standards at particular levels may have to be assessed and these can include: displacement from one mode of production to another that is less regulated and (perversely) more harm-causing;[15] creative compliance and the avoidance of regulatory purposes by shifts in production methods;[16] and the over-deterrence of desirable activity by frightening manufacturers into withdrawals from the field.[17] Increased rigour in standards may also create barriers to entry that prevent competition from developing in a sector—it may, additionally, distort existing competition within the sector. Putting figures on such indirect costs may be extremely difficult because the effects at issue are often diffused and difficult to track and data is not readily available.

A third difficulty that standard-setters are likely to encounter is that of calculating benefits. Cost and benefit calculations are affected by a number of common difficulties (e.g. assumptions concerning displacement and enforcement effects) but benefit assessments may be particularly fraught because regulatory benefits tend to be more diffused (temporally and spatially) and less easily located than costs.[18] (One factory may bear the costs but a host of workers and passers-by may benefit from harm reductions.) Causal

---

[13] See Makkai and Braithwaite, 'The Limits of the Economic Analysis of Regulation'.
[14] Ibid.
[15] See P. Grabosky, 'Counterproductive Regulation' (1995) 23 *International Journal of Sociology of Law* 347; J. Graham and J. Baert Weiner, *Risk vs Risk* (Cambridge, MA, 1995).
[16] See p. 232.
[17] On over- and under-inclusiveness see Chapter 11 above, pp. 232–6.
[18] Ogus, *Regulation*, 156.

connections between benefits and the imposition of a standard may be difficult to establish, never mind quantify, and figures cannot be placed on non-market benefits, especially if these stand to be enjoyed over an extended period of time.[19]

Principles-based Regulation

Regulatory authorites can demand that regulatees comply with precise rules but, in the alternative, they can call on them to act to further certain principles.[20] In principles-based regulation (PBR), principles are used to outline regulatory objectives and values, and regulatees are left free to devise their own systems for serving such principles.[21] This has proven to be a popular regulatory strategy over the past two decades but, following the credit crisis of 2007–9, the reputations of both principles-based regulation and its UK regulatory counterpart, risk-based regulation, have fallen. PBR has been criticized for allowing firms to escape from rigorous control and for providing inadequate protection to consumers and others. It has been seen as the soft epitomization of 'light-touch' regulation and as sufficiently discredited to demand a new change of regulatory tack.[22]

However, the deficiencies of PBR may have been exaggerated. PBR is arguably a regulatory tool that can be used astutely or crudely and, as with all tools, its utility turns on its manner of application—on how it is implemented and on such matters as the institutional context which surrounds it. Before we can explore the challenges associated with PBR, we need to be clear what we mean by this approach to regulation.

THE NATURE OF PBR

PBR can play different roles in the regulatory process. Principles can thus be incorporated in the regulatory norms (the written rules) or they can come

---

[19] Ibid., 156–9.
[20] 'Rules prescribe relatively specific acts; principles prescribe highly unspecific actions'—see J. Raz, 'Legal Principles and the Limits of Law' (1972) 81 *Yale Law Journal* 823–54, at 823.
[21] See generally, J. Black, 'Forms and Paradoxes of Principles-based Regulation' (2008) 3(4) *Capital Markets Law Journal* 425–58; 'The Rise, Fall and Fate of Principles Based Regulation', LSE Law Working Paper Series 2011; J. Black, M. Hopper and C. Band, 'Making a Success of Principles Based Regulation' (2007) 1 (3) *Law and Financial Markets Review* 191–206. See also J. Braithwaite, 'Rules and Principles: A Theory of Legal Certainty' (2002) 27 *Australian Journal of Legal Philosophy* 47–82 (ejournal); C. Ford, 'New Governance, Compliance and Principles-based Securities Regulation' (2008) 45(1) *American Business Law Journal*, 1–60.
[22] See B. Masters, 'Spurred Into Action', *Financial Times*, 26 Oct. 09.

into play when regulatory requirements are applied on the ground. When principles operate at both of these levels, this might be termed *full PBR*.[23] The regulatees are not instructed in detail, as in traditional 'command' approaches, and the regulator, in turn, depends on firms to devise methods of controlling risks. PBR is thus consistent with the delegation of controls that is a central part of 'meta-regulation'. Regulators concentrate, not on compliance with the precise rules, but on the firms' finding ways to manage the relevant risks so as to serve the principles that govern the system.[24]

Black points out that PBR thus both relies on and reinforces the image of the self-observing, responsible organization.[25] It also involves a continuing 'regulatory conversation' between regulators and regulatees regarding the meaning and application of the rules.[26] Central to the success of PBR is, accordingly, trust in the competence and responsibility of the regulatees. According to the PBR optimists, this is a method of encouraging regulatees to think for themselves and assume responsible approaches. It fosters a move beyond mere box-ticking approaches to compliance towards higher levels of performance. It helps to avoid the practice of creatively complying around detailed rules and adapts to changing circumstances better than prescriptive rules.[27] To pessimists, PBR is a soft approach to regulation that allows the regulated actors to do what they want without fear of breaching strict rules.

THE CHALLENGES OF PBR

Principles-based regulation can be placed under closer scrutiny by examining its capacity to discharge the main challenges of regulation: to establish clear objectives and then to carry out the tasks of detection, response development, enforcement, performance assessment, and modification of approach.[28]

For PBR, establishing objectives is a special challenge. In a hierarchical, rule-based regime, the process of defining objectives commonly involves fleshing out a statutory statement of aims with agency or governmentally issued statements and rules so as to provide an implementable and coherent statement of the mandate that the regulatory body intends to further. Within a PBR system, the challenge is to provide such a statement by focusing on indications of general principles and values, rather than specific rules and requirements. This approach possesses the virtue of establishing broadly stated aims and values in a manner that can be sustained in the face of

---

[23] See Black, 'Forms and Paradoxes', 435.
[24] Ibid., 432.
[25] Ibid.
[26] Ibid., 439.
[27] See Ibid., 432 on the FSA's reasons for endorsing PBR.
[28] See R. Baldwin and J. Black, 'Really Responsive Regulation' (2008) 71(1) *Modern Law Review* 59–74.

small-scale changes in the risks and processes that are regulated. Minor variations of approach will not impact on the overarching principles, and the constant shifts of regulatory agendas that are usual in most regimes will not prove destabilizing.

The difficulty of establishing objectives within a PBR approach, however, is that translating principles into substantive objectives on the ground requires the exercise of a good deal of judgement, and the various actors involved in the regime may have quite distinctive and divergent approaches to making such judgements. Even if there is general agreement on the governing principles for a regime, the relevant group of regulatory actors may treat those principles not as a statement of objectives but as starting points for debates on substantive aims—debates that they engage in with different conceptions of the game being participated in and different understandings regarding key aspects of that game (such as what constitutes 'compliance' or a 'reasonable practice'). Nor is it possible for one regulator to lay down a definitive and precise ruling on objectives from on high—that would be the hallmark of rule-based regulation. PBR, after all, is, at its heart, about keeping centralized and definitive statements to the highest levels of generality and sharing out the responsibility for rendering these specific.

In relation to matters of detection, response development, and enforcement, the central challenge for PBR stems from the delegation of these tasks to the regulated firms' managers. For any PBR regulator, accordingly, a first factor that has to be considered is the nature of the parties and organizations that are to be regulated. Effective PBR demands that there be close engagement between regulator and regulatee and that this is based on mutual trust. Firms need to be concerned to go beyond minimal compliance with the regulatory requirements, outcomes and goals have to be clearly communicated and understood, and the enforcement regime has to be one that can be justified to both regulatees and outside observers. It is the case, however, that, across the body of regulatees, attitudes and dispositions to comply may vary, but so may capacities to comply. As a result, regulators may have to apply PBR to regulated concerns that differ in their compliance stances. Some may be well-disposed to comply and highly capable of doing so. Others may be well-disposed and of low capacity, and there may also be those who are ill-disposed and of low capacity and those who are ill-disposed and highly capable.[29]

For the principles-based regulator, a preliminary challenge is to gain information on, and to assess, the characteristics of, the firms within its remit. That

---

[29] See R. Baldwin, 'Why Rules Don't Work' (1990) 53 *Modern Law Review* 321 and Chapter 11 above. See also R. Kagan and J. Scholz, 'The Criminology of the Corporation and Regulatory Enforcement Strategies', in K. Hawkins and J.M. Thomas, *Enforcing Regulation* (Boston, 1984)— who distinguish between corporations who are 'amoral calculators', those who are 'political citizens', and those who can be labelled as 'organizationally incompetent'.

regulator will want to know not only the natures of the individual firms that it deals with but the distribution of the firms across the four types discussed. The ensuing task will be to devise strategies for dealing with the very different challenges that the respective regulatee types pose. Firms who are well-disposed and highly capable will possess the inclination and ability to respond well to PBR that is applied within a regime of information supply and gentle encouragement. Those who are well-disposed and of low capacity will present greater problems. As noted, PBR, like risk-based regulation, involves the delegation of a host of regulatory functions down to the firms' own risk management regimes. It follows that the risk management capacity of such regimes is of central importance to regulatory success or failure. Research in some sectors—and notably in financial services—suggests, however, that compliance systems are the least developed aspect of many regulated organizations' internal control mechanisms, that they are often overloaded by regulators' expectations, and that they are not necessarily in a position to carry out the roles that PBR gives to them.[30] A familiar criticism of PBR is that it is inappropriate as a control over companies who lack the expertise, scale, or resources to develop interpretations of principles and strategies for complying with their obligations.[31]

The population of ill-disposed and low-capacity firms will prove even more difficult to control through PBR. They will neither be inclined to devise ways of implementing the relevant principles nor have the information or organizational skills necessary for such implementation. Trust lies at the heart of PBR, but it will be extremely difficult for the regulator to create relationships of trust with these firms because they are essentially untrustworthy and because the application of the kind of sanctions that will be needed to produce compliance will not foster trust. Such firms may have to be controlled by the rigorous application of command-based rules.

As for the ill-disposed and highly capable firms—the 'amoral calculators' and 'creative compliers'—these are organizations who are predisposed to circumvent the relevant principles whenever this is to their advantage. They will not respond to principles with the 'good faith' that would be desired by the regulators, but their excesses may be held in check by the use of principles, since they will find it more difficult to creatively comply around these than they would in the case of more precise rules.[32] Such regulatees may need to be

---

[30] See Black, 'Forms and Paradoxes', 453.

[31] See Black, Hopper, and Band, 'Making a Success of Principles-Based Regulation', 191, 200. On the preference of small firms for regulator-produced rules and guidance, see R. Baldwin, *Rules and Government* (Oxford, 1995). Regulators' own capabilities are also relevant. The skillset required of regulators for PBR is quite different from under traditional command and control regulation. This means that the staffs of regulatory bodies (and of firms) have to be capable of conducting detailed and sophisticated negotiations on the modes of compliance that are appropriate to specific settings.

[32] See D. McBarnet and C. Whelan, 'The Elusive Spirit of the Law' (1991) 54 *Modern Law Review* 848.

dealt with by deploying combinations of precise rules, more general rules (e.g. outcome-related rules), and 'back-up' principles.[33]

Overall then, the diversity of regulated concerns means that PBR will have to respond in customized ways, and in different combinations, with other regulatory styles, according to the types of regulated firms that it has to control. This presents both informational and tactical challenges.

A second problem faced by PBR is that, the strategy may be confronted by significant interpretive challenges and cultural variations.[34] A danger is that managers, with their specific ideas and cultures, will not only tend to enforce in a manner that the regulator sees as sub-optimal, but they may also differ from the regulators in their interpretations of the demands made by the principles and in their working definitions of compliance.[35] Firms and regulators are liable to interpret regulatory requirements in divergent ways because they see the world differently—even if the regulatees are well-disposed and highly capable. This is a core difficulty with the meta-regulatory aspect of PBR. The regulated firms' own processes will be geared towards the firms' own ends, notably the production of shareholder returns, and these will not be the regulators' objectives. The firms that are made the primary managers of risks may, moreover, come to see the consequences of non-compliance as merely another risk to be managed. As Black puts it: 'non-compliance becomes an option'.[36]

Black's review of the 'paradoxes' of PBR reveals a number of further implementation challenges.[37] Even if statements of principles help some firms to interpret the relevant regulatory responsibilities in a way that is acceptable to the regulators, the same principles may fail to produce consistent interpretations from other actors. Such divergencies may arise because of differences in intention and information, as discussed, but also because of variations in values and aims and even because of particularities in disciplinary or professional structures. Lawyers, for instance, may not understand the

---

[33] For arguments favouring the use of general anti-avoidance rules (GAAR) in combination with more precise rules in the taxation field, see J. Braithwaite, *Making Tax Law More Certain: A Theory*, ANU/Aus Tax Office Working Paper No. 44 (2002): http://dspace.anu.edu.au/bitstream/1885/42640/1/44.pdf (visited 7 Dec. 2010); 'Rules and Principles: A Theory of Legal Certainty' (2002) 27 *Australian Journal of Legal Philosophy* 47–82; J. Freedman, 'GAAR: Challenging Assumptions', www.taxjournal.com, 27 Sept. 2010, p. 12.

[34] Analysing a firm's attitude and culture will involve an examination of not only the organization's past behaviour but also its values, aims, modes of operation, and animating ideas.

[35] A posited strength of PBR is that it allows firms a degree of freedom in deciding how to comply with regulatory requirements. As Black points out, however: 'in practice a lack of certainty as to what enforcers will accept as compliance can lead firms to adopt quite conservative behaviour'. The result may be that the firms act as if they were bound by detailed rules—see Black, 'Forms and Paradoxes', 427.

[36] See Black, 'Forms and Paradoxes', 454.

[37] Ibid.

principles in the same way as the regulators, since they approach the task of interpretation from different sets of framing assumptions.[38]

A further challenge—the 'communicative challenge'—may also be expected to arise when PBR involves numbers of culturally divergent actors.[39] Principles can facilitate communication by expressing the purpose of the rule, but they can also hinder communication for a number of reasons. They can, for instance, operate as pegs upon which various parties can hang arguments that are presented from very different perspectives. The result may be that different actors adopt entrenched positions and regulation operates in a disjointed and high-friction manner. Principles can, in the alternative, lead to explanatory statements that hinder communications in practice—as where the inputs of different parties are swamped by proliferations of guidance that emerge from particular sources. This syndrome has a tendency to occur when regulators are undisciplined in their provision of guidance.

A further difficulty for PBR may stem from tensions between the 'logics' of different control systems and tools.[40] Different regulatory strategies can operate with different logics (e.g. of punishment or restoration or rehabilitation or 'professional' or 'commercial' logics). Particular logics involve distinctive relationships and modes of conversing with regulated parties—a punitive message, for instance, will be framed and received differently from a rehabilitative message. They are based on different assumptions, value systems, cultures, and founding ideas so that messaging across logics tends to involve distortions and failures of contact.

A substantial difficulty for PBR is that principles rarely operate in a freestanding manner. They are usually supplemented by explanatory guidance notes, policy statements, court decisions, and so on.[41] PBR, though, possesses a logic that differs from that of detailed rules.[42] Instead of taking actions to secure compliance with precise requirements, PBR involves the developing of trust and the cooperative identification of ways to meet the goals enshrined in principles. The difficulty is that the logic of rules will often undermine the force of principles. Firms respond to the threat of sanctions for non-compliance by increasingly seeking guidance on the meaning of the principles, and the regulators will tend to provide this with detailed prescriptions. The more severe the sanctioning approach, the harder it is for PBR to withstand the pressure to supply rules. As this contest between rules and principles plays out, there is a similar tension between the regulator's efforts to build trust and their concerns to enforce the rules. Where, for instance, court actions are

---

[38] Ibid., 447.

[39] See Ibid., 447–8.

[40] See Baldwin and Black, 'Really Responsive Regulation', 59–74.

[41] See Black, 'Forms and Paradoxes', 429–30 and Black, Hopper, and Band, 'Making a Success of Principles-Based Regulation', 191, 201; Braithwaite, *Making Tax Law More Certain*.

[42] See Black, 'Forms and Paradoxes', 453.

pursued in enforcement of the rules, the effect is to remove trust and to chill the communications that are central to PBR.

When, moreover, PBR is combined with risk-based regulation, there is a further clash of logics. PBR, as noted, is centrally about delegating to regulated firms the tasks of designing and applying compliance-seeking strategies. Risk-based regulation also involves the delegation of functions to regulated concerns but it does so by means of controls that work with a different logic—it translates compliance issues into risk-management challenges in a more formal way than PBR sets out to do. As a result, the two regimes will operate with different modes of oversight and communication—they involve different discourses and different ways of conceiving of compliance. The ways in which PBR and risk-based systems may clash is seen in the following account:

The FSA needs to be prepared to offer predictability in the [supervisory] process by committing to judgements on the appropriateness or inappropriateness of firms' interpretations of the Principles in particular purposes. This has particular implications for those firms who are ranked as low priorities in the FSA's risk-based supervisory regime (Arrow II). These firms do not have individual supervisors assigned to them but are referred to a call centre. Developing the appropriate dialogues and relationships of trust in this context will be particularly challenging.[43]

For those concerned with democratic accountability, an additional worry about the logic of PBR is that it does not offer the accessibility and transparency that would be normal in the case of rules. Thus, it has been argued that agencies such as the FSA can change their principles in a manner that bypasses the statutory requirements that would apply to the promulgation of rules and guidance (which require public consultation and subjection to cost-benefit evaluation).[44] Here we see that where regulatory strategies with different logics are combined, the tensions between these make it difficult to ensure that desired outcomes and process values are furthered unless careful analysis and regulatory designs are put in place. This point applies with even greater force when PBR is combined with risk-based regulation, since the logic of the latter gives rise to another set of acute issues concerning accountability—which, notably, arise through the tendency of risk-based regulation to bury important policy decisions deep within the weave of the risk-scoring mechanism that is the foundation of the regime.[45] In the case of risk-based regulation, it has been said that this requires a 'new politics of accountability'[46] but that

---

[43] See Black, Hopper, and Band, 'Making a Success of Principles-based Regulation', 202.

[44] Ibid., 199, 203.

[45] See J. Black, ' The Emergence of Risk-Based Regulation and the New Public Risk Management in the UK' (2005) *Public Law* 512–49.

[46] See J. Black and R. Baldwin, 'Really Responsive Risk-based Regulation' (2010) 32 *Law and Policy* 181–213; M. Power, *The Audit Society* (Oxford, 1995).

politics is all the more challenging when a tense hybrid of PBR and risk-based regulation is being applied

Turning to the assessment and modification tasks, clarity of objectives is, as discussed above, a central underpinning of performance evaluation and, to this end, some comfort might be found in substantive PBR's focus on regulatory outcomes. The complication is that these outcomes tend to be defined in qualitative and/or behavioural terms. Regulatees, for example, may be called upon to act 'with integrity', 'fairly', or 'in the best interests of the client'.[47] As Julia Black points out, these kinds of purposive provisions are hard to game, but their exact meaning can be difficult to pinpoint.[48] The product of such uncertainty is that it becomes extremely difficult to assess performance because any assessments are redolent with contested qualitative judgements. Steps, such as the issuing of guidance, can be taken to give more precise content to principles, but this may involve quite intensive action by the regulator.[49]

The broader danger with PBR is that, in the face of the above challenges of performance assessment—and because PBR involves management-based controls, the evaluation system degenerates into a mechanism that focuses on compliance with processes rather than outcomes, which are far harder to assess. This sets up an undesirable tension between management-based controls and outcome-based regulation and the use of principles.[50]

A further assessment challenge is that, as noted, performance measurement is extremely difficult under a PBR regime in which attitudinal and cultural divergencies mean that there may be little agreement on whether any given behaviour constitutes compliance or a furthering of the relevant principles. If, moreover, the regulator is applying a risk-based approach in harness with a PBR strategy, there is the potential for two parallel assessment regimes to operate in ways that may differ markedly in the criteria applied and the conclusions that are reached. As for modifying the regulatory regime in response to existing or new challenges, the main hurdle to be overcome by a PBR regime is that modification requires that the regulator is in possession of evidence regarding the deficiencies of the existing regime and that it has the potential to remedy these by instituting changes. As just said, though, the challenges of performance assessment are severe in most PBR regimes and if these are not risen to, there is not likely to be a body of evidence that could serve as a basis for modification.

[47] Black, 'Forms and Paradoxes', 442.

[48] Ibid.

[49] See Black's discussion of the FSA's Treating Customers Fairly (TCF) initiative at Black, 'Forms and Paradoxes', 442–3.

[50] See Black, Hopper, and Band, 'Making a Success of Principles-based Regulation', 191, 200.

Performance measurement may also prove difficult within a PBR regime where regulators, firms, and other bodies share the control functions but differ in their capacities, governance frameworks, resources, and processes for assessment. When, moreover, the regulator is applying a risk-based approach in harness with a PBR strategy, divergencies of capacity, process, and institutional setting may differ in nature between the PBR and the risk-based systems—which is likely to increase frictions and uncertainties within the regulatory system as a whole.

The capacity to modify the PBR regime to respond to new challenges or to improve performance is an important feature of good PBR regulation. For PBR, however, such responsiveness involves quite particular challenges. Being responsive to change requires that the regulator possesses solid evidence regarding the performance of the existing regime. It is clear, as noted however, that performance assessment is extremely difficult within a PBR mechanism and all the more so in a hybrid PBR/risk-based system. A second challenge arises because a PBR regime generally involves a number of regulatory actors and a high level of regulatory delegation and task-sharing. This means that achieving the level of coordination that is necessary to institute adaptive changes will tend to prove no easy matter—and will be far more difficult than in a traditional command regime. Different regulatory actors, moreover, may have very different capacities and inclinations to adapt their systems and this may further undermine responsiveness—even if it assumed that they are collectively able to produce the performance assessments that would indicate the need to modify the regulatory system.

Conclusions

Regulatory standard-setting cannot be reduced to a mechanical process in which the regulator calculates an optimal strategy and level of rigour in an uncontentious manner. As a consequence, standard-setting procedures tend, in the real world, to involve lengthy rounds of negotiation and revision, compromise and accommodation.[51] These procedures may be influenced by the internal politics of the regulatory institution as much as the external political environment within which regulation takes place.[52] It is because standard-setting is a non-mechanical matter, involving politically contentious judgements, that its legitimacy cannot be established readily by appeals to the expertise of the regulator. It is not surprising, accordingly, that the fairness

---

[51] On the 'Problem of Process' and rule-making, see Baldwin, *Rules and Government*, 167–9.
[52] Ibid., 169–74.

and transparency of standard-setting processes, as well as the accountability of the standard-setters, are factors that tend to loom large when such legitimation is under discussion.

As for the value of principles-based regulation, it has been seen above that PBR faces a daunting number of challenges when seeking to discharge the key tasks of regulation. This is a set of challenges, moreover, that is joined by an array of further difficulties when PBR is sought to be implemented through a risk-based regime. The interface between these systems clearly affects the discharge of all of the core regulatory tasks but that interface—and the clashes of logics involved—is one that few regulators have to date come to grips with.

Part IV
Quality and Evaluation

15 Cost-Benefit Analysis and Regulatory Impact Assessment

This chapter considers the role of regulatory impact analyses and other forms of economic appraisal as means of evaluating and influencing regulatory policy.[1] It outlines the growing importance of such analyses within government before examining the general challenges of using cost-benefit analysis (CBA) to evaluate regulatory proposals and actions. The focus then turns to the difficulties of incorporating economic impact analyses within policymaking and legislative processes. Finally it is asked whether the use of impact analysis is likely to lead to 'better' regulation.

The Governmental Use of Regulatory Impact Assessments

The central idea of regulatory impact assessment is that, in evaluating regulatory policy proposals, regimes, or rules, attention should be paid to an analysis of the anticipated costs and benefits associated with the relevant controls.[2] The governmental use of CBA as a tool for evaluating regulation was pioneered by the Reagan administration in the United States of America. In 1981, Executive Order 12291 was issued and required all executive agencies

---

[1] See generally, T.O. McGarity, *Reinventing Rationality: The Role of Regulatory Analysis in the Federal Bureaucracy* (Cambridge, 1991); R. Baldwin, *Rules and Government* (Oxford, 1995), ch. 7; G. Bryner, *Bureaucratic Discretion* (New York, 1987) and on economic appraisal of regulation in Britain see G.R. Baldwin and C.G. Veljanovski, 'Regulation by Cost-Benefit Analysis' (1984) 62 *Public Administration* 51; J. Froud, R. Boden, A. Ogus, and P. Stubbs, 'Toeing the Line: Compliance Cost Assessment in Britain' (1994) 24 *Policy and Politics* 4; J. Froud and A. Ogus, '"Rational" Social Regulation and Compliance Cost Assessment' (1996) 74 *Public Administration* 221; A. Ogus, 'Risk Management and Rational Social Regulation' in R. Baldwin (ed.), *Law and Uncertainty* (London, 1996); A. Ogus, *Regulation: Legal Form and Economic Theory* (Oxford, 1994), 153–65; R.H. Pildes and C.R. Sunstein, 'Reinventing the Regulatory State' (1995) 62 *University of Chicago Law Review* 1.

[2] On theories of regulatory impact assessment, see C. Radaelli and F. De Francesco, 'Regulatory Impact Assessment' in R. Baldwin, M. Cave, and M. Lodge (eds), *The Oxford Handbook of Regulation* (Oxford, 2010).

in the United States to submit all major regulations to CBA and only to put forward for presidential approval those regulations predicted to produce a surplus of benefits. The burden of proof rested on the agencies putting forward the regulation—they had to be able to demonstrate cost-effectiveness.

The stated objectives of Order 12291 were to reduce the burden of regulation, to increase agency accountability, to provide for more effective presidential oversight of the regulatory process, and to ensure better-reasoned justifications for regulating. Commentators have concluded that, although Office of Management and Budget (OMB) review has produced withdrawal or rejection of proposed regulations in a fairly small percentage of cases, the impact of CBA scrutiny has been very significant in US regulation.[3] In the USA, the broad system continues to this day under the Obama administration.[4]

In Britain, the origins of economic appraisal are to be found in the mid-1980s in the work of the Enterprise Unit of the Cabinet Office and in concerns, particularly within the Conservative government, to reduce regulatory burdens on business.[5] After various moves between departments, the current UK appraisal system is now run centrally by the Better Regulation Executive (BRE), which is part of the Department for Business, Innovation and Skills (BIS). In the UK, any proposal that imposes or reduces costs on businesses or the third sector requires an Impact Assessment[6] and any proposal similarly affecting costs in the public sector also requires an Impact Assessment, unless the costs fall beneath a pre-agreed threshold (generally £5m).[7] Impact Assessments are applicable to all government interventions affecting the private sector, the third sector, and public services, regardless of source: domestic or international.

The UK's Impact Assessment (IA) procedure is supposed to be a continuous element within the policy process and comes into effect from the earliest stages of identifying a policy challenge and developing policy options. It continues through public consultations and the production of legislative drafts to the implementation of legislation and the review of the measure's performance. The process is, moreover, supposed to restart when new policy challenges and new bodies of evidence emerge.[8]

---

[3] See, e.g., McGarity, *Reinventing Rationality,* 22; see also R. Hahn and R. Litan, 'Counting Regulatory Benefits and Costs' (2005) 8 *Journal of International Economic Law* 473–508; C. Sunstein, *The Cost-Benefit State* (Chicago, 2002).

[4] See http://www.whitehouse.gov/omb/inforeg_regmatters/#gi.

[5] See, e.g., DTI, *Burdens on Business* (London, 1985); White Papers: *Lifting the Burden,* Cmnd 9571 (London, 1985); *Building Business, Not Barriers,* Cmnd 9794 (London, 1986); *Releasing Enterprise,* Cmnd 512 (London, 1988).

[6] See BRE, *Impact Assessment Guidance* (2009).

[7] In 2008–9 (April to March) 196 IAs were carried out—see BRE, *The Total Benefit/Cost Ratio of New Regulations 2008–9* (BRE, London, 2009). In 2006 and 2007 between 300 and 400 IAs were produced—see NAO, *Evaluation of Regulatory Impact Assessments 2006–07,* HC 606 Session 2006–2007, p. 5.

[8] See BRE, *Impact Assessment Guidance.*

There are, in addition, stated to be certain points when the IA should be published or republished—notably when a policy proposal is taken out to public consultation; when a Bill is introduced into either House of Parliament; and when a draft Statutory Instrument is laid in Parliament. Publication should also occur immediately prior to the implementation of an Act or Statutory Instrument or other regulatory measure and on post-implementation reviews of regulatory measures.

According to BRE guidance, Impact Assessment documents should contain summaries of such matters as: the problem under consideration and the rationales for government intervention; the policy objectives and the intended effects of the policy; the policy options that have been considered, and the justifications for the preferred option.[9] They should also indicate the date at which a review would be undertaken to establish the actual costs and benefits of the policy and to see whether it has achieved, or is achieving, the desired effects. The summary must take account of the full range of costs and benefits: economic, social, and environmental, and these should be monetized as far as possible. As for the enforcement of a proposed regulation, the IA should indicate the organization that will enforce and the total annual cost of enforcement. Any significant impacts on competition also have to be described, as do the anticipated effects on the UK government's Administrative Burdens Baseline.

IAs are presented to Ministers, who are required to sign them off at early and late points in the policymaking process. At the consultation stage, they would sign a declaration that, on the basis of the available evidence, the Impact Assessment represents a reasonable view of the likely costs, benefits, and impact of the leading options and, at the final proposal/implementation stage, they would sign a declaration that indicated that they were satisfied that it represented a fair and reasonable view of the expected costs, benefits, and impact of the policy; and that the benefits justify the costs.

The modern importance of the IA flows from its position as a central tool within the 'better regulation' programmes of the UK, EU, OECD, and other jurisdictions. In the UK, the search for 'better' (as opposed to less) regulation can be traced to the Blair government in 1997. By 2006, the Better Regulation Executive had been established in the Cabinet Office with the tasks of reducing regulation and promoting the better regulation agenda in Europe. When the BRE published its consultation on *The Tools to Deliver Better Regulation* in July 2006, the only such tool to be discussed was the IA—which was described by the Minister for the Cabinet as 'the cornerstone of our approach to better regulation'.[10]

---

[9] See BRE, *Impact Assessment Guidance*, and for more details: BRE, *Impact Assessment Toolkit* (2009).

[10] See Hilary Armstrong, *The Tools to Deliver Better Regulation* (Better Regulation Executive, 2006), 4.

Within the EU itself, the European Commission's White Paper on *European Governance*[11] provided the foundations for the Commission's 2002 Action Plan for Better Regulation.[12] Key elements of this included the introduction of a two-stage impact assessment process.[13] The Commission committed itself gradually to carry out impact assessments for all major legislative and policy initiatives.[14]

On the broader international stage, the OECD has been the major proponent of impact assessment as a central element in the pursuit of better regulation. Over the past 20 years its concerns have moved focus away from deregulation, regulatory reform, and 'regulatory management' towards 'better regulation' through 'regulatory policy'—government-wide policy that aims continuously to improve the quality of the regulatory environment.[15] In 1995, the OECD set out the first internationally accepted set of principles on ensuring regulatory quality, which included a ten-point OECD Reference Checklist for Regulatory Decision-Making.[16] Since that time, the OECD has sought to promote better regulation in member countries by devoting attention to regulatory policies, institutions, and tools.[17] *Regulatory policies* involve the systematic development and implementations of government-wide policies on how governments use their regulatory powers.[18] *Regulatory institutions* are bodies that take forward regulatory policy and *regulatory tools* are devices aimed at improving regulatory design and implementation. Within the vocabulary of the OECD there are seven main regulatory improvement tools:

---

[11] COM (2001) 428 final.

[12] European Commission, *Action Plan on Simplifying and Improving the Regulatory Environment*, CDM (2002) 278 final. A protocol attached to the Treaty of Amsterdam (1995) had set out the principles of good regulation to be respected at the European level. Further coordinated action was stimulated when the 2000 Lisbon Council of Europe emphasized the need to develop better regulation as a part of making the EU the most competitive and dynamic knowledge-based economy in the world. See also the *Mandelkern Report on Better Regulation*, Final Report (Brussels, 13 November 2002).

[13] See generally A. Meuwese, *Impact Assessment in EU Lawmaking* (Leiden, 2008).

[14] Communication on Impact Assessment COM (2002) 276.

[15] See OECD, *Regulating Policies in OECD Countries* (Paris, 2002); OECD, *Report on Regulatory Reform* (Paris, 1997).

[16] OECD, *Improving the Quality of Government Regulation*, OECD/GD (95) 95 (Paris, 1995).

[17] The OECD has produced, since 1997, a series of leading-edge publications on strategies for improving regulatory policies, tools, and institutions. Reports have, for instance, dealt with the following: *Choices of Policy Instruments* (1997); *Regulatory Reform* (1995, 1997); *Regulatory Impact Analyses: Best Practices in OECD Countries* (1997); *Voluntary Approaches for Environmental Protection* (1998, 1999); *Information, Consultation and Public Participation* (2000); *Regulatory Compliance* (2000); *Business Views on Red Tape* (2001); *Administrative Simplification in OECD Countries* (2003); *Regulatory Reform in the UK* (2002). Numbers of national reviews of regulatory reform have also been conducted—the UK Review was carried out in 2001–2: see OECD, *United Kingdom: Challenges at the Cutting Edge* (Paris, 2002).

[18] See OECD, *United Kingdom*, 29 and OECD, *Regulatory Reform* (Paris, 1997). By late 2000, 24 out of 30 OECD countries had adopted government-wide regulatory policies; the UK did so in 1985 (OECD, *United Kingdom*, 40).

- Regulatory Impact Assessments (RIAs);
- Consultations and Transparency;
- Reducing Burdens and Red Tape: Administrative and Regulatory Simplification;
- Enforcement Guidelines;
- Alternatives to Traditional Regulation;
- Sunset Provisions;
- Regulatory Policies and Reviews.

It is, however, the RIA that is seen as the centrally important tool of regulatory improvement in the OECD.[19] Whether this is a tool that can easily be incorporated within the policy process, and whether it will lead to better regulation will be returned to after considering the more general challenges of carrying out economic appraisals.

Appraising Economic Appraisals

Advocates of economic appraisal mechanisms make a number of claims that can be seen as addressing the five benchmarks for regulation that were discussed in Chapter 3.[20]

The legislative mandate—appraisals are said to improve the pursuit of mandated policy goals by measuring regulatory alternatives against such goals.

Accountability—appraisals subject rule-makers to an objective eye; they reveal costs borne by society; they expose policy judgements; and avoid the pursuit of hidden agendas within bureaucracies.

Due process—appraisals keep rule-making procedures open and encourage access to those who argue for alternative options; they avoid moving towards premature solutions and guide towards rational decision-making.

Expertise—appraisals encourage experts to clarify their justifications for regulating in a particular way; they highlight the need to review goals; and draw attention to gaps in information and to research needs.[21]

---

[19] For OECD endorsement of the RIA see, e.g., OECD, *Report on Regulatory Reform* (Paris, 1997); *Regulatory Policies in OECD Countries* (Paris, 2002). See also the European Commission, *Communication on Impact Assessment* (5 June 2002). On practice in the EU, see 'A Comparative Analysis of Regulatory Impact Assessment in Ten EU Countries'—a report prepared for the EU Directors Better Regulation Group (Dublin, May 2004).

[20] For a general defence of CBA, see M. Adler and E. Posner, *New Foundations of Cost-Benefit Analysis* (Harvard, 2006) and for a critique of this book, see A. Sinden, D. Kysar, and D. Driesen, 'Cost-Benefit Analysis: New Foundations on Shifting Sand' (2009) *Regulation and Governance* 48–71.

[21] See Sunstein's argument that: 'cost-benefit analysis is best defended as a means of overcoming predictable problems in individual and social cognition. Most of these problems might be collected under the general heading of selective attention. Cost-benefit analysis should be understood as a

Efficiency—appraisals conduce to more efficient regulation by insisting on strategies that minimize costs for given benefits; they encourage the systematic use of information on the advantages and disadvantages of policies; and they identify 'correct' decisions on an efficiency basis.

When, however, we consider how appraisals are affected by the variety of legal, political, and practical constraints that impinge on regulatory or governmental actions, the above claims may, in many respects, seem overstated.

Thus, with regard to claims under the legislative mandate heading, a problem arises if efficiency tests are sought to be satisfied in the face of statutory objectives that are not stated in efficiency terms. The tension between statutory objectives and a CBA will be greatest where the statute is strongly redistributive or promotes ends other than efficiency.[22] Economic appraisers' actions might thus be vulnerable to judicial review if attempts are made to overrule mandates in favour of efficiency-related ends that are not sanctioned by the relevant legislation.[23]

As for accountability and due process, a problem with CBA testing may be that the process of analysis may mask policymaking and come between regulatory rule-makers and those being consulted. It may, accordingly, reduce accountability and participatory access. This may occur if the analysis stresses quantifiable factors to the detriment of 'softer' components or if policy issues are buried in a mass of economic technicalities and arcane language.[24] Nor can it be assumed that economic appraisal is a neutral exercise. Analysts conducting such appraisals may operate on the basis of certain value-infused premises, for instance biases against regulation or favouring the satisfaction of private preferences, rather than values associated with procedural rights or collective or public goals—and CBAs may be prone to manipulation by prejudiced parties.[25]

Accountability may also become fragmented by the process of appraisal. Thus, such oversight in the US has been said to obscure responsibilities and

method for putting "on screen" important social facts that might otherwise escape private and public attention.'—C. Sunstein, 'Cognition and Cost-Benefit Analysis', University of Chicago Law School, J.M. Olin Law and Economics Working Paper 25 (2nd Series) (1999), at http://www.law.uchicago.edu/Publications/Working/index.html and SSRN Collection at http://papers.ssrn.com/paper.taf?abstract_id=186669

[22] See C.R. Sunstein, 'Cost Benefit Analysis and the Separation of Powers' (1981) 23 *Arizona Law Review* 1267.

[23] See, e.g., the test in *Wednesbury* [1948] 1KB 223. The European Court of Justice has also ruled that economic factors may not be superimposed on a directive—see C-44/95 *R* v. *Secretary of State for the Environment ex p. Royal Society for the Protection of Birds*, ECJ, FC, 11 July 1996 (reported *Financial Times*, 8 Oct. 1996).

[24] See P. Self, *Administrative Theories and Politics* (2nd edn, London, 1978), 212.

[25] See P. Self, *Econocrats and the Policy Process: The Politics and Philosophy of Cost Benefit Analysis* (Basingstoke, 1975).

reduce democratic accountability so that it becomes unclear who bears final responsibility for regulatory decisions—the agency, the OMB, federal judges, or elected individuals.[26]

Further concerns under the due process heading are that participatory rights may be devalued in so far as economic analysis may, in practice, offer certain groupings unfairly preferential access to the policymaking and regulatory processes and that it may allow well-organized private groups and regulated industries to dictate national policy. The OMB has been criticized on this front[27] and, in Britain, the DTI made it clear during the Conservative years of the 1980s and 1990s that its appraisal procedures were designed specifically to offer privileged business access to regulatory rule-making processes.[28]

As for the exercise of regulatory expertise, economic analysis may operate, again, in a prejudicial manner. OMB review in the USA has been said to work not so much as a means of imposing objective, rational scrutiny on regulators but as a means of exerting control over the substantive policies of regulators— as a way to give preference to undisclosed goals.[29] This may devalue regulatory expertise (not to say accountability and the satisfaction of the mandate) in so far as regulators may be slow to develop balanced regulatory rules if they anticipate reorientation of those rules through the analysis process. Regulatory authority, moreover, may be shifted from specialist agencies to less expert regulatory review staff who not only lack in-depth knowledge in relevant areas but do not have the time or resources to conduct properly expert assessments.

Finally, in relation to efficiency claims, it might be contended that CBA testing militates in favour of policies that maximize net social benefits, but CBAs do not hold out the prospect of clear-cut answers to regulatory problems and a number of technical difficulties afflict the appraisals process. Sceptics might also urge that the process tends to produce not better regulation but burdens and delays for regulators—that it does not lead towards the right kind or level of regulation but to the reduction of regulation even where it is beneficial.[30]

---

[26] See S. Breyer, *Regulation and Its Reform* (Cambridge, MA, 1982).

[27] Ibid., 285–6; E.D. Olson, 'The Quiet Shift of Power: OMB Supervision of Environmental Protection Agency Rulemaking under Executive Order 12291' (1984) 4 *Virginia Journal of Natural Resources* 31; noted Pildes and Sunstein, 'Reinventing the Regulatory State', 5.

[28] See the White Paper, *Building Business, Not Barriers*, Cmnd 9794 (London, 1986).

[29] See Bryner, *Bureaucratic Discretion*, 285–6; Pildes and Sunstein, 'Reinventing the Regulatory State', 4.

[30] See R.V. Percival, 'Checks Without Balance: Executive Office Oversight of the Environment Protection Agency' (1991) *54 Law and Cont. Prob.* 127. In March 1998, the US Senate considered the Regulatory Improvement Bill—proposed legislation to increase the complexity of the economic analyses to be conducted by would-be rule-makers. Opponents of the Bill characterized it as an attempt to paralyse efforts to protect the public interest—see *Financial Times*, 10 Mar. 1998.

DISTRIBUTIONAL ISSUES

CBA testing may apply efficiency yardsticks but distributional concerns may be the primary rationales for regulatory programmes. On these questions CBAs will offer little help. They tend to assume, for instance, that the present distribution of wealth is acceptable, that this does not skew the analysis, and that regulation or deregulation has an insignificant distributional effect. In reality, though, the way that people attribute value is a product, at least in part, of their wealth and this biases the valuations that are the components of CBAs in favour of those who are economically well-placed.[31] If, moreover, the existence of a regulatory regime implies that the given distribution of wealth is undesirable (for example, because polluters are externalizing some of the costs of production and are accordingly enjoying too much wealth) it may be a mistake to presuppose, for the sake of a CBA test, that the present distribution is satisfactory. The legislature's choice of regulation for either explicit or implicit redistributive purposes may be inconsistent with the use of CBA as a benchmark for regulatory rules.

DATA CONSTRAINTS AND MEASUREMENT

Technical difficulties beset most economic appraisals. Assessing the impact of an item of regulation may, for instance, be difficult because adaptive responses are involved.[32] (Regulations requiring the wearing of hard hats on construction sites may reduce skull fractures but workers wearing hats may behave generally more dangerously because they feel protected. As a result, leg and arm injuries may increase.) Quantification of such displacement effects may be very difficult to build into a CBA.

The costs and benefits associated with a regulation will also depend on how it is enforced and the pattern, not merely the level, of compliance that results. A particular difficulty may be that the highest levels of compliance with a new law are likely to be achieved in the ranks of those actors who already comply voluntarily—and the mischiefs that are sought to be controlled may predominantly be caused by those who are least likely to be brought to compliance. If this is the case, it will be very easy to overstate the value of regulating by a number of factors unless a good deal of analysis is carried out into expected distributions of compliance.[33] This

---

[31] See H. Otway, 'Public Wisdom, Expert Fallibility: Towards a Contextual Theory of Risk', in S. Krimsky and D. Golding (eds), *Social Theories of Risk* (Westport, CT, 1992).

[32] See S. Peltzman, 'The Effects of Automobile Regulation' (1975) 83 *Journal of Political Economics* 677; W. K. Viscusi, 'The Impact of Occupational Safety and Health Regulation' (1979) 10 *Bell Journal of Economics* 117.

[33] The National Audit Office has stressed the need for a stronger emphasis on compliance and enforcement issues, including the distribution of compliance, within UK Impact Analyses—see NAO, *Evaluation of Regulatory Impact Assessments 2006–07* HC 606 Session 2006–2007, p. 7.

may give rise to serious quantification difficulties. The effects of regulation on industry, moreover, may involve 'hidden' costs such as reductions in productivity, a dulling of incentives, expenditure on responding to regulation, and distortions on investment and production—these factors further aggravate quantification problems. Regulatory analysts will often lack the time, resources, and data to explore such factors in detail.[34] Any information available 'off the shelf' is, in addition, liable to come from industry and be subject to bias. The interests of, and costs borne by, large numbers of unorganized or ill-represented individuals may in such a process be inadequately considered and the public interest insufficiently attended to in the CBA.

Benefit measurement is likely to be at least as difficult as quantifying costs because there is liable to be an absence of relevant data (for example, on the value of cleaner rivers) and economists may differ by several orders of magnitude when valuing such benefits as human life or good health.[35] Many intangibles will defy pricing and CBA testing procedures usually recognize this by requiring non-quantifiable benefits to be described. The danger of the CBA process is, however, that 'hard' figures take precedence over those 'soft' factors that are less susceptible to quantification in numerical terms. Regulation tends to occur where markets have, for various reasons, failed, and, accordingly, there tends to be an absence of good market-based data in exactly those circumstances where there is a case for regulating. This suggests that CBAs will be at their least persuasive or reliable where the need for rational and effective regulation is greatest.[36]

CBAs may also beg questions about the valuation of different risks. Thus, Pildes and Sunstein argue that experts and lay persons may value, say, the avoidance of certain hazards, quite differently. Lay persons may, for instance, value reductions in the risks of certain modes of death more highly than others because some deaths are particularly dreaded.[37] CBAs based on expert valuations may, accordingly, fail to take on board competing approaches to evaluation. CBAs may, moreover, deal with aggregations of costs and benefits, whereas the public may be concerned to know how distributions of costs and benefits will be produced—to know who wins and who loses from a regulatory action.

---

[34] See McGarity, *Reinventing Rationality*, 126–32.

[35] US studies have used valuations of life ranging from $300,000 to $3.5m—see McGarity, *Reinventing Rationality*, 275; C. Noble, *Liberalism at Work* (Philadelphia, 1986), 112–15.

[36] Baldwin and Veljanovski, 'Regulation by Cost-Benefit Analysis', 56.

[37] Pildes and Sunstein, 'Reinventing the Regulatory State', 50–2; see more generally, Chapter 6 above; S. Hill, *Democratic Values and Technological Choices* (Stanford, CA, 1992), 55–89; P. Slovic, 'Perception of Risk', in S. Krimsky and D. Golding (eds), *Social Theories of Risk* (Westport, CT, 1992). See also C. Sunstein, *Risk and Reason* (Cambridge, 2002).

BUREAUCRATIC PROBLEMS

If appraisal mechanisms are to be applied to regulators, then a bureaucratic mechanism will be required in order to carry these out. One immediate danger is of duplication and adding to the cost and weight of governmental bureaucracy. (In the USA, the average cost of an analysis was put at $100,000 over two-and-a-half decades ago.[38]) If extra resources are not allocated to regulators, a straight diversion of money from regulation to analysis is effected. This leads to the criticism that analysis is best seen as a way of slowing down regulatory activity, rather than as a means of improving regulation.[39] A balanced view is perhaps that economic scrutiny can be expected to deter the making of extravagantly inefficient rules but can also be expected to increase the resource requirements for making a desirable regulatory rule.

The constraints that attend the implementation of appraisals may also cast further doubts on the notion that CBAs encourage the consideration by policymakers of a wide variety of regulatory options. Included amongst those constraints are: limitations on information; the costs of analysis; the need to select and analyse facts with a policy end in sight; the need to meet political or policymaking deadlines; the attachment of policymakers to certain types of solution or modes of analysis; and the limited ability of top policymakers to consider widely ranging options.[40] In real life, economic appraisers may be tied to appraising options that have already been identified by policymakers.

Delay is a particular problem occasioned by CBA testing. Some regulatory actions may have to be taken rapidly to respond to crises, and satisfactory CBAs, accordingly, may not be feasible in the timescales presented. Other deadlines, as noted, may restrict the level of analysis that can be achieved.

The most serious impediment to the effective use of CBA within regulation has been said to be the bureaucratic resistance encountered.[41] This may be due to a variety of causes. Regulatory officials may, for instance, distrust economic analysis and its techniques, they may be wedded to established responses to problems, or they may think that economic analysis impedes the compromises and bargains that have to be struck in regulatory and political life. (British Civil Service traditions, in particular, may encourage a rejection of CBA styles of policy discussion.) Regulators, moreover, may have their own

---

[38] US General Accounting Office, *Improved Quality, Adequate Resources and Consistent Oversight Needed if Regulatory Analysis is to Help Control Costs of Regulations* (Washington, DC, 1982).

[39] See Bryner, *Bureaucratic Discretion*, 83–4; A. B. Morrison, 'OMB Interference with Agency Rule-making: The Wrong Way to Write a Regulation' (1986) 99 *Harvard Law Review* 1059; C. De Muth and D. Ginsberg, 'White House Review of Agency Rule-making' (1986) 99 *Harvard Law Review* 1075.

[40] McGarity, *Reinventing Rationality*, 160.

[41] See D. Braybrooke and C.E. Lindblom, *A Strategy of Decision* (New York, 1963) on the limitations of a comprehensive approach to planning.

interests and policy objectives which they do not see in pure efficiency-seeking terms. These may be the results of, for example, statutory requirements, organizational traditions, personal and bureaucratic objectives, or managerial interests. Forces within the regulatory and governmental processes may, accordingly, thwart the CBA testing process.

Impact Assessments and the Legislative Process

Proponents of impact assessments must confront a number of challenges if they are to use these procedures as valuable means of influencing policies and regulatory lawmaking.[42] In the first instance, they must be able to carry out IAs to an acceptable technical standard. On this point, the UK holds itself out to be a world leader in carrying out IAs, but it appears that the current fit between the IA and policy processes does not conduce to the production of high-quality IAs. A succession of reports from the National Audit Office (NAO) and the British Chambers of Commerce (BCC) has revealed a number of weaknesses. In an early study, the National Audit Office (NAO) looked at 23 'test case' IAs in 2001[43] and reported on ten further sample IAs in 2004.[44] The NAO revealed in 2004 that only half the IAs examined included 'a reasonably clear statement of objectives' and seven out of ten did not consider any option for regulation other than the one preferred by the department. None of the ten IAs considered what would happen in the absence of the regulation, and most did not offer a quantified comparison of expected costs and benefits. As for considering the likely effects of regulations on the ground, only half of the sample IAs considered enforcement and sanctioning effects. The NAO's 2005–6 evaluation of IAs[45] stated that only two out of twelve IAs analysed levels of compliance well, and the same report produced the finding that: 'The purpose of IAs is not always understood; there is a lack of clarity in the presentation of the analysis; and persistent weaknesses in the assessments.'[46] By 2006–7 things were not much better, with 14 out of 19 IAs showing major defects or room for improvement on assessing costs and benefits. Only one-quarter of RIAs considered compliance and enforcement issues fully, and under half contained sufficient details of how the new

---

[42] For a set of useful discussions, see C. Kirkpatrick and D. Parker (eds), *Regulatory Impact Assessment: Towards Better Regulation* (Cheltenham, 2007).

[43] NAO, *Better Regulation: Making Good Use of Regulatory Impact Assessment*, HC 329 2001–2 (London, 2001).

[44] NAO, *Evaluation of Regulatory Impact Assessments Compendium Report 2003–4*, 2003–4 HC 358 (London, 2004).

[45] NAO, *Evaluation of Regulatory Impact Assessments 2005–6*, 2005–6 HC 1305 (June 2006).

[46] Ibid., p. 2.

legislation would be monitored and evaluated. The NAO also stated that, in the sample studied, there was insufficient consideration of the impact of regulations following implementation.[47]

The NAO's findings were broadly in line with, though perhaps less critical than, the British Chambers of Commerce (BCC) studies of 2003 and 2004, which looked respectively at 499 and 167 IAs produced by government in the two periods studied (1998–2002 and 2002–3).[48] The BCC studies noted a series of problems with IAs and concluded that ministerial statements that benefits justified costs were not in general supported by the evidence in the IAs. Some departments, indeed, were under-resourced or badly managed for conducting IAs. On choice of regulatory strategy, the BCC found that the option of not regulating was considered in only a minority of cases (11% in 1998–2002 and 23% in 2002–3) and less than half of IAs quantified all the options considered. IAs are supposed to pay acute attention to business (and especially SME) compliance costs but (in 2004) the BCC reported that costs for business were not quantified in 23% of IAs, and 93% of IAs did not consider additional costs for SMEs at all. A substantial minority of IAs contained little factual data about consequential costs and benefits and 'scant attention' was given to 'sunset' clauses or to subsequent monitoring or evaluation. Nor was the BCC impressed by new efforts to improve IAs—it found that the IA process showed little recent evidence of improvement.[49]

Such criticisms suggest *prima facie* that the way that IA processes are accommodated within policymaking procedures is not conducing to technically impressive assessments. Clearly, there is room to improve the technical quality of IAs and such improvements may be necessary if IAs are to conduce to better regulation. It would be a mistake, however, to assume that technical improvements in IAs will be sufficient to improve regulation. Those IAs would still have to be located within legislative and regulatory policymaking processes in a manner that allows them to influence emergent laws and

---

[47] NAO, *Evaluation of Regulatory Impact Assessments 2006–07*, HC 606 Session 2006–2007, p. 6.

[48] See T. Ambler, F. Chittenden, and M. Shamutkova, *Do Regulators Play by the Rules?* (London, 2003) and T. Ambler, F. Chittenden, and M. Obodovski, *Are Regulators Raising Their Game?* (London, 2004).

[49] Ambler et al. *Are Regulators Raising Their Game?*, pp. 3–4. The European Commission has, for its part, carried out impact assessments (in qualified form) since the Business Impact Assessment system was introduced in 1986. European impact assessments have, however, possessed many shortcomings. These were analysed between 2000 and 2002 and a new Impact Assessment system was outlined by the *Communication on Impact Assessment of* 5 June 2002. This formed part of the Better Regulation Action Plan and aimed to analyse the effects of European regulatory proposals on business in order to conduce to competitiveness, innovation, and growth. The first year for carrying the new Impact Assessment process was 2003. See generally Meuwese, *Impact Assessment in EU Lawmaking*.

policies. There are, however, a number of reasons why IAs tend to prove less influential than might at first be supposed.[50]

Timing is often a difficulty. In 2007, the NAO concluded that IAs were often not commissioned or used early enough in policy formation to really challenge the need for new regulations.[51] Government commitments may also prove a problem. Ministers may be wedded to certain regulatory steps and strategies for ideological reasons, or because of manifesto commitments, or because a political settlement has been made with various interests. They will, accordingly, not be minded to pay too much attention to IAs that send contradictory signals. Ministers, moreover, tend to be predisposed towards legislative solutions and, if they have promised to legislate in order to address a problem, they will not respond enthusiastically to IAs that propose non-legislative solutions. The costs and benefits of regulation, moreover, tend, as noted, to be difficult to quantify[52] and the perceived 'softness' of IAs may reduce their impact on the policy or legislative process. This is liable to be the case especially where costs and benefits can only be calculated on the basis of guesses about the use that various regulatory actors will make of their powers or about the strategies that will be deployed to apply regulatory rules. In 2007, the NAO stated that RIAs were only occasionally used by Parliamentary Committees and to inform Parliamentary debate: 'A lack of awareness and Committee clerks' perceptions of weaknesses in the quality of analysis prevented RIAs from playing a greater role in informing the Parliamentary process.'[53]

It is also frequently the case that the full nature of the regulatory proposal is unclear from a given item of primary legislation because this merely establishes a broad framework for control and leaves matters of real regulatory substance to be spelled out in secondary legislation. The effect will be that regulation escapes a good deal of parliamentary and IA scrutiny. It might be responded that the relevant secondary legislation will be IA-tested in its own right at a later date, but this may be no complete answer to the point. The framework regulatory strategy within which that secondary legislation is to operate will often have been established by the primary legislation that has 'escaped' IA influence. Many key regulatory issues will already have been decided by the time the 'secondary' IA is carried out.

Another concern is that even when the secondary legislation is IA-tested, it may be extremely difficult to assess the substance of a regulatory proposal because the nature of outcomes will depend on the use that will be made of the

---

[50] On the role of IAs in the policy process, see NAO, *Evaluation of Regulatory Impact Assessments 2006–07*, HC 606 Session 2006–2007, pp. 17–24.

[51] Ibid., p. 6.

[52] The RIA relating to the Employment Act 2002, for instance, noted that 'a great many assumptions' had to be made in its execution.

[53] NAO, *Evaluation of Regulatory Impact Assessments 2006–07*, HC 606 Session 2006–2007, p. 6. See also NAO, *Evaluation of Regulatory Impact Assessments 2005–6*, HC 1305 Session 2005–6, June 2006, p. 2 ('IAs are only occasionally used to challenge the need for regulation and influence policy decisions').

delegated powers involved. Additionally, of course, secondary legislation will not be debated in Parliament in the way that primary legislation is[54] and any IA-based messages are, accordingly, the less likely to influence decisions in the legislature.

A further problem that arises in the legislative process is that amendments of laws and rules may be introduced at a late stage in the progression of legislation and the proposals involved may, for that reason alone, escape IA attention. The BRE *Guidance* (para. 9) does state that the IA process is continuous and ongoing, but there is a limit to the responsiveness that can be achieved in the face of material amendments.

The culture of governmental policymaking may, moreover, prove resistant to the influential use of IAs. This has been a special concern to the NAO, which found in 2006 that IAs were often seen by officials as a bureaucratic task, rather than being integral to the process of policymaking. The NAO, accordingly, recommended that the importance of the IA should be re-emphasized to policymakers; that policymakers should start impact assessments early and that they should use the IA to project manage the decision-making process. The NAO also suggested the greater and earlier use of departmental expertise and, as far as possible, embedding expertise into policy teams.

Cultural changes, however, are easier pleaded for than achieved. The recommendation that IAs should be used earlier in the policy process than presently may, for instance, prove more difficult to implement than might be assumed.[55] A real problem in some areas may arise from tension between the politics of a process and the IA principles. Within the IA procedure, policy-makers are supposed to consider and compare the array of regulatory routes to a policy objective[56] but, in the real world, a proposal may be the product of a process of political negotiation. The policy becomes 'live' when compromises and concessions have been made between different interests and, as such, it may be the only feasible option politically. To compare this proposal with an array of alternatives via the IA procedure may be to compare a living horse with a number of dead non-runners. (Such a comparison is also likely to be seen by relevant policymakers as an exercise too far.) This is not to say that IAs have no value—it is, however, to point out that there may be strict limits to the extent to which IA processes can be fully 'embedded' within policy processes so that they can influence political decision-making.

---

[54] See generally Baldwin, *Rules and Government*, ch. 4.

[55] As noted, the NAO still found in 2007 that IAs were often not being used early enough in policy processes to challenge the supposed need to regulate—NAO, *Evaluation of Regulatory Impact Assessments 2006–07*, HC 606 Session 2006–2007, p. 6.

[56] The BRE's *Impact Assessment Toolkit* (2009) demands that Ministers sign-off, at the consultation stage of an IA, to certify that it presents a reasonable view of the likely costs, benefits, and impact of the leading options.

Impact Assessments and Better Regulation

A further concern regarding the IA process is whether it is liable to conduce to optimal regulation—even assuming that it impacts significantly on legislative and rule-making processes. A worry may be that IA processes are not wholly compatible with the requirements of 'better' regulation—if better regulation is seen in terms of a preference for lighter-touch controls as per the language of 'smarter' regulation.[57]

Here it is necessary to pause in order to recap on the requirements of 'smart' regulation. Proponents of 'smart' regulation have argued convincingly that designing good regulatory systems demands a central focus on how best to combine different institutions and techniques.[58] Smart regulation thus moves beyond state controls and looks to mixes of control methods as applied not merely by public bodies but by other institutions and actors including trade associations, pressure groups, corporations, and even individuals. It advocates deploying those combinations of instruments that will be most appropriate in a given setting and designing strategies that mix instruments and institutional actors to optimal effect.[59]

The messages of 'better' and 'smart' regulation appear at first glance to be consistent. If, however, we investigate the capacity of the current better regulation movement to deliver smart regulation on the ground, we see that the route to delivery is not unproblematic. Here it is useful to measure the better regulation movement against the five core principles for smart regu-latory design.[60] These principles can be summarized as follows:

1. Prefer policy mixes incorporating a broader range of instruments and institutions.
2. Prefer less interventionist measures.

---

[57] This section draws on R. Baldwin, 'Is Better Regulation Smarter Regulation?' (2005) *Public Law* 485–511; see also R. Baldwin, 'Better Regulation: The Search and the Struggle' in R. Baldwin, M. Cave, and M. Lodge (eds.), *The Oxford Handbook of Regulation* (Oxford, 2010); Kirkpatrick and Parker, *Regulatory Impact Assessment.*

[58] On 'smart' regulation, see N. Gunningham and P. Grabosky, *Smart Regulation* (Oxford, 1998). For other discussions of mixed public and private, or 'combined' regimes of regulation see, e.g., D. Osborne and T. Gaebler, *Reinventing Government* (Boston, 1992); I. Ayres and J. Braithwaite, *Responsive Regulation* (Oxford, 1992); C. Sunstein, 'Paradoxes of the Regulatory State' (1990) 57 *University of Chicago Law Review* 407; C. Sunstein, *After the Rights Revolution* (Cambridge, MA, 1990); C. Parker, *The Open Corporation* (Cambridge, 2002); G. Burchell, C. Gordon, and P. Miller (eds.), *The Foucault Effect: Studies in Governmentality* (Chicago, 1991); J. Black, 'Dencentring Regulation: The Role of Regulation in a Post-Regulatory World' (2001) *Current Legal Problems* 103; 'Enrolling Actors in Regulatory Processes' (2003) *Public Law* 62; M. Sparrow, *The Regulatory Craft* (Washington, DC, 2000). On the British regulatory state as a 'smart state', see M. Moran, *The British Regulatory State* (Oxford, 2003) 21–6.

[59] Gunningham and Grabosky, *Smart Regulation*, 91.

[60] Ibid., 387–422.

3. Ascend a dynamic instrument pyramid to the extent necessary to achieve policy goals.[61]
4. Empower participants who are in the best position to act as surrogate regulators.
5. Maximize opportunities for win-win outcomes.[62]

Regarding the first principle, the better regulation movement might be expected to perform well, since it repeatedly emphasizes the need to consider alternative, more imaginative, ways of regulating.[63] In practice, however, a number of factors may militate against its delivery of imaginative regulation. First, the IA occupies a central place in 'better regulation', but the evidence is that IA processes are not highly effective in leading policymakers to consider alternative ways of regulating. IA processes, moreover, are more attuned to measuring the effects of traditional 'command' systems of control than 'alternative' methods and this may positively discourage the canvassing of more imaginative regulatory strategies—especially those 'softer' strategies involving voluntary and incentive-driven controls where predicting effects (and hence calculating costs and benefits) is extremely difficult.

Second, smart regulation is about cumulative regulatory effects and the coordination of regulatory systems with widely varying natures. IA processes, however, are best suited to looking at the costs and benefits associated with a single, given, regulatory proposal, rather than combinations of approach. They are most attuned to the 'single strategy'.[64] Those officials who are charged to carry out IAs would find it very difficult to calculate the costs and benefits of a simultaneously acting combination of very different regulatory strategies and institutions. It would, for instance, be extremely hard for proponents of a combination of, say, state, corporate, and trade association laws, codes, and guidelines to predict how all the relevant actors will draft, design, and apply their different control strategies. This would make calculations of costs and benefits a matter of heroic guesswork and the ensuing uncertainties would

---

[61] The idea here is that regulation should be 'responsive' and escalate in severity as necessary to achieve compliance. Ayres and Braithwaite (in *Responsive Regulation*) are concerned with state and business relationships but Gunningham and Grabosky argue for escalating approaches on three planes—not merely one based on state controls, but also one founded on commercial and non-commercial quasi-regulation and another on corporate self-regulation. These planes make up the three sides of their pyramid—see Gunningham and Grabosky, *Smart Regulation*, 397–9.

[62] A win-win outcome is where higher levels of socially desirable behaviour produce higher profits—see N. Gunningham 'Beyond Compliance: Management of Environmental Risk' in B. Boer, R. Fowler, and N. Gunningham (eds), *Environmental Outlook* (Sydney, 1994); M.E. Porter and C. Van der Linde, 'Green and Competitive' (1995) *Harvard Business Review* 120–34; J.C. Robinson, 'The Impact of Environmental and Occupational Health Regulation on Productivity Growth in U.S Manufacturing' (1995) 12 *Yale Journal of Regulation* 388.

[63] See e.g. the BRTF's *Imaginative Thinking for Better Regulation* (London, 2003); *Alternatives to State Regulation* (London, 2000); OECD, *Regulatory Policies in OECD Countries* (Paris, 2002), pp. 51–7.

[64] See Gunningham and Grabosky, *Smart Regulation*, 388.

undermine the essential value of the IA. Smart regulation involves too many variables, estimates, and judgements to lend itself to the IA process.

Bureaucratic incentives should also be borne in mind. An official who is contemplating regulating—and knows that the IA process has to be undertaken—will experience little impetus to propose complex combinations of regulatory institutions and strategies with all the attendant predictive and calculative difficulties. Rather than aim for a 'smart' form of regulation, he or she will incline towards a simpler regime that can be predicted to pass an IA. Such bureaucratic incentives may, moreover, militate against the application of a high level of 'regulatory craft' as advocated by Malcolm Sparrow.[65] Such craft calls for the placing of problem-solving at the centre of regulatory design.[66] Problems, when identified, are on this view to be responded to with a variety of strategies in a manner consistent with smart regulation.[67] For an official who faces a potential IA, however, the incentive to adopt a problem-centred approach may be weak, not merely because this would require the evaluation of costs and benefits regarding a variety of institutions and strategies, but also because it may demand an unpacking of the way that a host of existing regulatory regimes impinge on a problem, and an examination, within the IA process, of potential ways to reshape and re-deploy those regimes in combination with any new regulations.[68] The political and bureaucratic implications would be daunting—the proponent of the IA would often be questioning the way that numbers of established regulators go about their jobs in order to evaluate his or her proposed regulation. A far more attractive proposition will be to take any existing controls as givens and consider whether the addition of a new regulation will pass a cost-benefit test.[69] The consideration of alternatives is liable, accordingly, to be strait-jacketed by existing regulatory frameworks. Overall, then, if IA processes are retained at the centre of better regulation, they may not conduce to smarter regulation as encapsulated by its first principle.

The second principle of smart regulation holds that less interventionist measures should be preferred. Again, it might be anticipated that the 'better regulation' approaches will encourage less prescriptive, less coercive modes of influence. IA procedures, as noted, however, are not well attuned to

---

[65] See Sparrow, *Regulatory Craft*.

[66] Ibid., ch. 9. Similar comments could be made regarding compatibility with the 'really responsive regulation' approach—R. Baldwin and J. Black, 'Really Responsive Regulation' (2008) 71 *Modern Law Review* 59–94.

[67] See Gunningham and Grabosky, *Smart Regulation* and also Black, 'Enrolling Actors in Regulatory Processes' on enrolling a variety of regulatory actors.

[68] See Sparrow, *Regulatory Craft*, 310.

[69] The Cabinet Office guide, *Better Policy Making: A Guide to Regulatory Impact Analysis* (London, 2003), ch. 2, focuses on the effects of the new regulation at issue and takes existing regulations as givens.

either the measurement, or the consideration, of alternative, less interventionist, softer controls. Smart regulation, moreover, demands that attention is paid to enforcement strategy, not merely the formal design of regulatory laws.[70] It is, after all, how a regulatory power is used on the ground that tends to determine its essential character. Here again, though, the IA process draws attention away from how regulations are applied in practice. First, it is the case (as was noted above) that very many IAs do not attend to implementation and enforcement issues at all well.[71] There are, furthermore, structural reasons why IAs cannot be expected to come to grips with enforcement strategy in a routinely well-informed manner—IAs tend to focus *ex ante* on the general design of regulation, and it may be impossible to predict how any regulator or set of regulatory bodies will go about deploying the powers that they are to be given in a proposed regulation.

Smart regulation's third principle urges that 'responsive' strategies of regulation should be adopted and should be employed across mixes of regulatory strategies—as applied by numbers of different institutions and instruments. Smart regulation thus holds out the possibility of escalating degrees of coercion through the interaction of different but complementary instruments and parties.[72] It is difficult, however, to argue that 'better regulation' approaches sit easily alongside this principle. The IA process, as noted, encounters difficulties in dealing either with questions of enforcement or with 'combined' strategies of regulation. These difficulties are likely to be compounded by attempts to evaluate incremental and coordinated escalations up the three sides of a strategic pyramid that reflect the combined use of quasi-regulatory and corporate self-regulatory as well as state controls.[73]

Fourth, smart regulation, advocates the empowerment of those participants who are in the best position to act as surrogate regulators. This, accordingly, favours using the influence of quasi-regulators, such as public interest groups, where appropriate. Here again, the better regulation toolkit might be expected to prompt consideration of alternative regulatory methods but it may fail, for reasons discussed above, to come to grips with 'combined' regulation where quasi-regulatory functions have to be evaluated alongside other regimes.

Yet another reason why an IA process may be slow to make best use of surrogate regulators and mixtures of controls is because empowering quasi-regulators or

---

[70] On the centrality of enforcement and the 'practice of regulation' See Sparrow, *Regulatory Craft*, 3–7.

[71] See NAO, *Evaluation of Regulatory Impact Assessments 2005–6*, HC 1305 Session 2005–6, June 2006, p. 4.

[72] See Gunningham and Grabosky, *Smart Regulation*, 400.

[73] On the need to integrate different levels of action from different sides of the pyramid (e.g. non-punitive state controls with more severe quasi-regulatory and self-regulatory controls), see Gunningham and Grabosky, *Smart Regulation*, 398–401.

corporate self-regulatory controls within combined regimes of control may require an incremental approach to regulatory design in which key actors negotiate and adjust the roles of different controlling institutions and influences over behaviour. This kind of regulation—as is envisaged by smart regulatory theory—involves a reflexive, adaptive approach in which regulatory strategies are constantly revised and 'tuned' to changes in circumstances, preferences, and so on. It is difficult, however, to see how ongoing regulatory coordination, with all its dynamics, can be assessed and designed in advance through an IA process as if it is a static system that can be captured in a single snapshot.

The final principle of smart regulation suggests that opportunities for win-win outcomes should be maximized—so that, for instance, corporations can behave more responsibly and maximize profits at the same time.[74] Win-win outcomes, however, may not always be possible and, in certain circumstances, there are tensions between corporate profit-seeking and some regulatory objectives.[75] In practice, therefore, regulators will need to identify areas and issues that will lend themselves to win-win outcomes if certain stimuli are applied. The targeting of regulatory approaches will, accordingly, be central to success. Regulators of a variety of kinds will have to deploy a wide range of strategies and aim these at different kinds and sizes of enterprise, as well as activities, in order to maximize win-win outcomes. This, again, is exactly the sort of flexible and adaptive regulatory strategy that is extremely difficult to set out and evaluate in advance according to the IA-centred better regulation toolkit as now encountered.

For the above reasons, it can be contended that IA processes are at tension with the prescriptions of smarter regulation. There is, moreover, a further question to ask when discussing whether IA processes conduce to 'better' regulation. This is the query: 'Better for whom?'. It is clear from field research that 'better 'regulation is conceived of differently by different interests—such as by small and by large businesses.[76] The former, for instance, put an especially high premium on regulatory systems that pay attention to their special sensitivities to certain regulatory effects.[77] Potential dangers of IA processes are that, as with all cost-benefit analyses, they skew calculations in favour of those parties who benefit from the existing distribution of wealth[78] and that they place emphasis on overall costs and benefits, rather than

---

[74] On win-win, see M.E. Porter and C. Van Der Linde, 'Towards a New Conception of the Environment–Competitiveness Relationships' (1995) 9 *Journal of Economic Perspectives* 97–118; J. Gobert and M. Punch, *Rethinking Corporate Crime* (London, 2003), 342–5. It is arguable that the main advance on this front is to be made by providing information to firms on how to achieve such outcomes—see Gunningham and Grabosky, *Smart Regulation*, 416–18.

[75] See R. Baldwin, 'The New Punitive Regulation' (2004) 67 *MLR* 351.

[76] See R. Baldwin (for the Federation of Small Businesses), *Better Regulation: Is It Better for Business?* (London, 2004); see also the discussion of 'good' regulation in Chapter 3 above.

[77] Thus small businesses find that regulation diverts managerial resources away from wealth creation in a far more acute manner than is the case with large enterprises—see ibid.

[78] See Baldwin and Veljanovski, 'Regulation by Cost-Benefit Analysis'.

distributional issues—notably who bears the costs and who enjoys the benefits. What may be better regulation for large enterprises may not be better regulation for small businesses or consumers, and the IA process may unduly favour the beneficiaries of historic under-regulation.

Conclusions

Economic appraisal techniques present significant problems under all the five criteria for good regulation that were set out in Chapter 3. This is not, however, to argue that such appraisals have no place in evaluating regulation. There is a role for the appraisal of costs and benefits in regulation but it is a constrained one because of imperfections in appraisal systems and the need to satisfy non-efficiency values such as are involved under the mandate, accountability, due process, and expertise headings. To make regulation, and questions as to its extent, *turn* on CBA testing would be to give efficiency too central a place in regulatory affairs. What can be done is to use economic appraisals not to impede regulation (as an end in itself), or in order to give business a preferential say in regulatory policymaking, but as a supplement to the policymaking process. This might be achieved by adopting the following approach.[79]

Appraisals should focus on questions set by policymakers, not by the appraisers themselves, and should look to the costs and benefits of 'live' proposals for rules. They should briefly note alternative methods of achieving set objectives but should not purport to offer a comprehensive review of options with a 'correct' solution. They should avoid spurious elaboration and levels of technicality that impede policy discussions, and values that the appraisal cannot take into account should be explicitly identified and addressed.

Assumptions on imponderables should be spelled out, as should those on enforcement and adaptive responses, and particular groups or individuals should not be given preferential access to appraisal processes.

Appraisals, and the information upon which they are based, should be openly disclosed as a part of the rule-making process. Such documents should be available to the public and to the scrutinizing agents and committees of Parliament. The limitations of appraisals, in general, and of the particular appraisal, should be openly disclosed. Participatory mechanisms should be incorporated into the appraisals process in order to allow citizens to express their judgements about different risks in different contexts;[80] and, finally, the courts should continue to ensure that appraisals do not loom so large in the

---

[79] See Baldwin, *Rules and Government*, 215.
[80] A proposal of Pildes and Sunstein, 'Reinventing the Regulatory State', 75.

rule-making process as to constitute a resort to irrelevant considerations, or indeed do not themselves take into account irrelevant considerations.

Such a way of dealing with economic appraisals pays heed to those commentators who argue that economic approaches to risk-benefit analysis should be guided by democratic processes and ethical principles, should allow participation by affected parties, and should be exposed to alternative assessment techniques.[81]

Finally, it bears stressing that the most fundamental objection to a purely economic approach—one tailoring regulation to economically efficient ends—is an ethical one. To aim for efficient solutions is, as indicated in Chapter 3, no morally justifiable answer to questions regarding the distribution of rights and issues of justice, since wealth maximization provides no convincing normative basis for action.[82]

As far as the impact of IAs on legislative processes and the pursuit of better regulation is concerned, the above discussion raises some worrying points. It suggests that IA may impact on policy and legislative processes far less than many of its proponents might imagine and that IAs may not produce 'smarter' regulation or conduce to lighter-touch regimes of control.

The way forward is not to focus simply on carrying out IAs in a technically superior manner. Nor is it to settle for embedding the IA within the policy-making process more fully. Such steps would not ensure that IAs would impact on legislative processes in a satisfactory manner or that they would lead to smarter regulation.[83] It is arguable that what needs to be done is to rethink the better regulation philosophy as a whole. At present, the centrality of the IA means that better regulation is pursued by making predictions about the future effects of regulatory regimes, attaching costs and benefits to these, and attempting to convince policymakers and legislators that they should give weight to what they will often see as a good deal of guesswork. The key change has to

---

[81] See K.S. Shrader-Frechette, *Risk and Rationality* (Berkeley, CA, 1991). Note Pildes and Sunstein's criticism of the proposal in S. Breyer, *Breaking the Vicious Circle* (Cambridge, MA, 1993), 59–63, that an expert elite should advise on the rationalization of regulatory priorities. They urge that this places too much emphasis on the technical as opposed to the democratic side of regulation—Pildes and Sunstein, 'Reinventing the Regulatory State', 86–7.

[82] For criticism of cost-benefit analysis as efficiency-based, see D. Kennedy, 'Cost-Benefit Analysis of Entitlement Problems: A Critique' (1981) 3 *Stanford Law Review* 387; R.S. Markovits, 'Duncan's Do Nots: Cost-Benefit Analysis and the Determination of Legal Entitlements' (1984) 36 *Stanford Law Review* 1169; M.S. Baram, 'Cost-Benefit Analysis: An Inadequate Basis for Health, Safety and Environmental Regulatory Decisionmaking' (1980) 8 *Ecology LQ*; M. Sagoff, 'At the Shrine of our Lady of Fatima or Why Political Questions are Not All Economic' (1981) 23 *Arizona Law Review* 1283; C.R. Sunstein, 'Cost-Benefit Analysis and the Separation of Powers' (1981) 23 *Arizona Law Review* 1267.

[83] The Better Regulation Executive's report, *The Tools to Deliver Better Regulation* (London, 2006) can thus be seen as excessively narrow in its approach to improving IAs and their impact. The report's 'key' recommendations are staggeringly modest in highlighting the needs to: take steps to make IAs more transparent; shorten the IA guidance; and have IAs signed off by Chief Economists as well as Ministers.

involve a shift away from the predictive approach to policy assessment and towards one that gives centrality of place to review—a process that involves both evaluation and modification. Assumptions of comprehensive rationality have to give way to incrementalist strategies[84] so that it is accepted that regulatory systems cannot be designed *ex ante* (on the basis of ever more sophisticated analyses) and left alone. A shift to incrementalism demands, first, that, once regulatory regimes are established in the form that seems most promising, steps are taken to measure whether regulatory systems are working as well as they can (and better than alternatives) and, second, to bring about changes in regulatory strategy in order to effect improvements. It might be argued from within the BRE and OECD that a movement 'from design to review' has already been instituted. It is true that the UK government, like the OECD, has expressed a commitment to '*ex post*' regulatory reviews.[85] There is limited evidence, however, of delivery on regulatory reviews,[86] and the ongoing challenge is to give new emphasis to that review and adjustment process so that, within government, it is seen as more important than design by IA. Embedding a review philosophy also means that regulatory policymakers will have to come to grips with the difficulties of post-implementation evaluation and adjustment.

These problems should not be understated. A first difficulty is that reviews and changes may create regulatory uncertainties and trigger adaptation costs. Some regulatory systems may be adjustable at low cost, but others may be difficult to change because high uncertainty and high adjustment costs are involved. In the case of the latter, any adjustments will be likely to prompt political attacks on the regulator and claims that the regulatory goalposts are being moved unfairly and to the detriment of business interests. All regulators will, accordingly, have to make context-specific judgements about the trade-off between improvements in regulation and the uncertainty (and political) costs involved in regime adjustments.

A second problem is that evaluating regulatory performance is extremely difficult technically, not least because formulations of objectives will be

---

[84] On comprehensive rationality versus incrementalism, see e.g. Y. Dror, 'Muddling Through: Science or Inertia' (1964) 24 *Public Administration Review* 153; D. Braybrooke and C. Lindblom, *A Strategy of Decision* (New York, 1963).

[85] Government policy since June 2001 has required departments to review the impact of major pieces of regulation within three years of implementation (OECD, *United Kingdom*, 34). The BRTF recommended post-implementation review in April 2000 (*Helping Small Firms Cope with Regulation*) and the BRE's 2009 *Impact Assessment Guidance* (para. 13) provides that after the intervention or regulation has been implemented it should be reviewed to establish what are its actual costs and benefits and whether it is achieving its desired effects. On the OECD view that *ex post* evaluation of regulatory policies, tools, and institutions is of value see OECD, *United Kingdom*, 115–16. On the case for revisiting regulatory systems, see G. Mather and F. Vibert, *Reducing the Regulatory Burden* (London, 2004).

[86] In 2007, the NAO reported: 'There continues to be an unstructured and ad hoc approach to post-implementation review across all departments.... Our census of departments highlighted resource constraints and time pressure as the main reasons why reviews were not more widespread.'— NAO, *Evaluation of Regulatory Impact Assessments 2006–07*, HC 606 Session 2006–2007, p. 6.

contentious, appropriate benchmarks will be difficult to identify, and regulatory objectives are liable to change over time. Regulatory statutes tend to allocate large discretions and mandates that are unclear—this means that little legislative guidance on yardsticks can be assumed.

Nor, third, will a move from design to review escape the difficulties of assessing the 'regulatory mixes' that were discussed above in looking at 'smart' regulation. In multi-actor, multi-strategy regimes, attributions of responsibility will be far more difficult to make than in simpler regimes. Other evaluative problems will be severe when mixes are involved. The application of performance measures always produces a danger of counter-productive effects[87] but, in mixed regulatory regimes, such effects may be particularly difficult to assess because they will be experienced by a variety of actors in quite different ways. Similarly, the complexity of smart regimes makes it difficult both to evaluate the case for alternative mixes of controls and to bring about adjustments in numbers of institutions and rule systems. What can be said, however, is that evaluations of and adjustments to regulatory mixes, though never simple, will be far more easy to carry out in an *ex post* incremental manner, rather than through an *ex ante* design approach as seen in the IA process.

With these caveats in mind, it can be reasserted that a movement from a philosophy of design to one of regulatory review can be expected to hold out a far more realistic prospect of better regulation than current approaches that give centrality of place to the predictive IA. Review processes make advancements towards smarter methods of control more realistic. They give greater emphasis to the measurement of results—and improve accountability and transparency. They offer superior ways to evaluate the quality and reliability of regulatory data and they allow policymaking cultures to be reshaped over time, rather than presuppose that they can be overridden in a single operation.

At the level of UK regulation, the case for the suggested change in better regulation philosophy seems strong. It should not involve an abandoning of the IA process or an ending of attempts to improve IAs and embed them within policymaking practices. A review philosophy would retain such efforts but would not put all eggs in the IA, or design, basket. The IA would be seen as the start of the regulatory assessment process rather than the end, and the real locus for shaping regulation would become the review stage.

---

[87] On perverse effects, see e.g. NAO, *Good Practice in Performance Reporting in Executive Agencies and Non-Departmental Public Bodies* (London, 2000), para. 11; HM Treasury, *Executive Agencies: A Guide to Setting Targets and Measuring Performance* (London, 1992); J. Sandbach, 'Performance Indicators Could Damage Universities' Health' (1987) *Public Finance and Accountancy* 19; G. Bouckaert, 'Improving Performance Measurement' in A. Halachmi and G. Bouckaert (eds), *The Enduring Challenges of Public Management* (San Francisco, 1995); C. Pollitt, 'Performance Indicators: Root and Branch' in M. Cave, M. Kogan, and R. Smith (eds), *Output and Performance Measurement in Government* (London, 1990).

16 Accountability, Procedures, and Fairness

Questions about explaining and justifying conduct have long been at the forefront of regulation debates. What constitutes an acceptable level, or mechanism, of accountability has remained a matter of controversy. Familiar questions abound: 'What should be the level of public engagement in the setting of standards?', 'To what degree should enforcement actions be open to outside input and scrutiny?', 'To what extent should holdings to account occur after the event or in 'real time' (at the time when processes occur)?', 'Who should be held to account when things go wrong?'[1]

Traditionally, debates regarding accountability have centred on the political and legal ways in which public power is checked—and how the exercise of public power is legitimized (see Chapter 3 on what is 'good' regulation).[2] Such discussions have, however, been given a new urgency in contemporary times. The age of the regulatory state has brought an increased use of institutions that lie outside the direct influence of electoral politics, and this development has added a new dimension to accountability debates. In addition, regulatory regimes are said to have become more polycentric, fragmented, and 'decentred' as responsibilities have been spread vertically and horizontally across governmental systems.[3] Such changes bring new challenges to traditional understandings of accountability. They suggest that conventional assumptions and doctrines are at least challengeable and that

---

[1] Discussions of different accountability regimes have produced various classifications and categorizations: see R. Mulgan, *Holding Power to Account* (Basingstoke, 2004); M. Lodge and L. Stirton, 'Accountability in the Regulatory State' in R. Baldwin, M. Cave, and M. Lodge (eds), *Handbook of Regulation* (Oxford, 2010); R. Mulgan, 'Accountability: An Ever-Expanding Concept?' (2000) 78(3) *Public Administration* 555–73; C. Pollitt, *The Essential Public Manager* (Buckingham, 2003); J. Mashaw, 'Accountability and Institutional Design: Some Thoughts on the Grammar of Governance' in M. Dowdle (ed.), *Public Accountability* (Cambridge, 2006); M. Bovens, 'Public Accountability' in E. Ferlie, L. Lynn, and C. Pollitt (eds), *Oxford Handbook of Public Management* (Oxford, 2007); M. Lodge, 'Accountability and Transparency in Regulation: Critiques, Doctrines and Instruments' in J. Jacint and D. Levi-Faur (eds), *The Politics of Regulation* (Cheltenham, 2004).

[2] For a detailed study of the mechanisms of accountability in ten major UK regulatory agencies, see T. Prosser, *The Regulatory Enterprise: Government Regulation and Legitimacy* (Oxford, 2010). Prosser (pp. 4–6) distinguishes betweeen regulation as infringement of private autonomy (which correlates to accountability through legal rules) and regulation as collaborative governmental enterprise (which correlates to accountability through representative and participatory processes).

[3] See J. Black, 'Critical Reflections on Regulation', *CARR Discussion Paper, Number 4* (London, 2002).

more nuanced concerns about complex trade-offs between different institutional choices should move to the forefront of debates. Elsewhere, too, the discussion on increased participation has moved beyond traditional desires that regulators render account through parliamentary or political channels. Indeed, one of the key debates in recent years has been how 'targeted transparency' can be used to influence (or 'nudge') consumer behaviour in order to rectify the limitations of more conventional and political-bureaucratic understandings of accountability.[4]

As the debate on regulatory accountability has come to grips with the above issues it has moved towards a better understanding of the trade-offs and potential conflicts that are involved in the pursuit of different objectives such as participation and accountability on the one hand, and expert and efficient decision-making on the other. It has done so through a more comprehensive understanding of numerous accountability architectures and their implications.[5]

This chapter begins by outlining the conventional debate about accountability and procedural appropriateness. This places the regulator, usually in the form of the 'regulatory agency', at the heart of discussions. The chapter then notes how polycentric and 'decentred' understandings of regulatory regimes expose the inherent limitations of such narrow debates. Finally, we consider different accountability regimes and their inherent trade-offs.

Traditional Concerns: Accountability and Procedures

The term 'accountability' originates from the Old French 'aconter', which applied to the official registration of property. This emphasis on the duty of private parties to account to public authority has given way to an understanding of accountability that stresses the obligation of officials to account for their behaviour.[6] The ensuing focus, in the field of regulation, has come to rest on the discretionary use of delegated powers by regulatory agencies, bodies that are not directly elected and, therefore, are unaccountable for their actions through the ballot-box. For this reason, the 1937 Brownlow Commission in the US warned about regulatory commissions being an unaccountable 'fourth' branch of government.[7]

---

[4] A. Fung, M. Graham, and D. Weil, *Full Disclosure* (Cambridge, 2007); D. Weil, A. Fung, M. Graham, and E. Fagotto, 'The Effectiveness of Regulatory Disclosure Policies' (2006) 25(1) *Journal of Policy Analysis and Management* 155–81. On 'nudge' strategy see Chapter 7 above.

[5] M. Power, *The Audit Society* (Oxford, 1997).

[6] M. Bovens, 'Analysing and Assessing Accountability: A Conceptual Framework' (2007) 13(4) *European Law Journal* 447–68.

[7] A. Roberts, 'Why the Brownlow Committee Failed: Neutrality and Partisanship in the Early Years of Public Administration' (1996) 28(1) *Administration and Society* 3–38.

As a result, one recurrring preoccupation has been the design of procedures that render activities accountable, especially when outputs and outcomes are difficult to observe or measure. Procedural fairness is said to be an important aspect of any regulator's legitimacy. The contemporary interest in 'deck-stacking' in the institutional design literature reflects this interest in steering behaviour through procedural means (see Chapter 4).[8] As a result, the wider literature has noted a number of key mechanisms for controlling and constraining discretionary decision-making.[9] Examples include, in the first instance, *reason-giving*. Demanding extensive 'reason-giving' places emphasis on requirements that regulators publish their decision-criteria, the options under consideration, and their respective anticipated consequences, together with relevant data and evidence. Such requirements are often already part of the consultative programme of regulators, but the further these instructions go, and the more legally binding they become, the more they are likely to add to decision-making time. Increasing procedural stringency is also likely to incentivize the regulator to avoid the sorts of regulatory actions that will call for resort to such processes.

A second procedural requirement of note is that of *information disclosure*. One of the key ideas regarding transparency is that the more light that is shone on particular aspects of decision-making, the less space there will be for corruption (as noted by former Supreme Court Justice Louis Brandeis: 'Sunlight is the best disinfectant'). Related to this notion is the idea of demanding enhanced information disclosure, especially regarding comparative information. Similarly, 'freedom of information' provisions that force openness about 'reason-giving' are said to offer an important *ex post* 'fire alarm' mechanism: decision-makers will be influenced by the possibility that their rejection of particular options might be made public at a later stage. Extending these disclosure rules has been a key policy trend over the past two decades or so. Experiences with information disclosure suggest, however, that there are limits to information disclosure requirements.[10] One is that there is a continuing conflict about methods of handling 'commercially confidential information' and the exact boundaries of confidentiality. A further potentially limiting factor is the impact of disclosure rules on decision-making. It is said, for example, that critical and controversial decisions or options are no longer put in writing in order to avoid later discovery. In addition, the comparative

---

[8] M. McCubbins, R. Noll, and B.Weingast, 'Structure and Process, Politics and Policy: Administrative Arrangements and Political Control' (1989) 75 *Virginia Law Review* 431–82; M. McCubbins, R. Noll, and B.Weingast, 'Administrative Procedures as Instruments of Political Control' (1987) 3(2) *Journal of Law, Economics and Organisation* 243–86.

[9] These can be both substantive and procedural and have been associated with the possibility of offering participatory devices along the model of a 'regulatory democracy'—see M.-F. Cuéllar, 'Rethinking Regulatory Democracy' (2005) 57 *Administrative Law Review* 411–99.

[10] A. Roberts, 'Spin Control and Freedom of Information' (2005) 83(1) *Public Administration* 1–23.

experience with disclosure rules points to a 'life cycle' in so far as the reach of disclosure regimes is usually reduced over time as access becomes more costly and more restrictive.[11] Finally, it is also questionable how individuals respond to disclosed information, in particular whether it changes their habits and whether it is too costly to become informed.

A third key process that is incorporated in many regulatory systems is the *hearing*. One of the key differences that is often drawn between the North American tradition of regulatory commissions and the initial UK model of utility regulation that emerged throughout the 1980s was a different emphasis on hearings. Advocates of hearings suggest that such events maximize participation and increase information and interest in regulatory decisions. One response to the poor reputation of food regulation in the UK, for example, was that all board meetings of the Food Standards Authority were made publicly accessible.[12] Similarly, the UK Civil Aviation Authority has exemplified a more long-standing tradition of trial-type hearings, where it has been said to offer enhanced openness.[13] Those who are more critical of hearings point to the experience of the more 'trial-based' variant of hearings in the US. These critics argue that hearings offer an inappropriate forum for dealing with multifaceted, polycentric issues. It is further argued that independence of decision-making, which is necessary for trials, is difficult to reconcile with the governmental interests that are inherently at the heart of most regulatory activity. Sceptics suggest, furthermore, that systems of precedent tend to offer an unwelcome hindrance to adjusting regulatory activity in the light of environmental change, that trials are slow and cumbersome, and that they encourage challenges regarding access. A further concern is that the infrequency of decisions and the randomness with which issues appear on the agenda of hearings means that no general rules can be applied or continuous policies can be developed.

Rules on rules constitute a fourth means of regularizing procedures. These provisions are often noted (in the legal literature especially) as an alternative to inquiry-type or trial-type processes as discussed above. In particular, the so-called notice and comment provisions as included in the 1946 US Administrative Procedure Act are said to hardwire regulatory decision-making (and thereby to stack the deck in particular ways). The 'notice and comment' procedures include requirements to publish proposed rules in a national register, and these allow interested parties to comment in writing, to issue a statement setting out the basis and purpose of rules, and to provide a period

---

[11] Ibid.

[12] H. Rothstein, 'Precautionary Bans or Sacrificial Lambs? Participative Regulation and the Reform of the UK Food Safety Regime' (2004) 82(4) *Public Administration* 857–81.

[13] T. Prosser, *Law and the Regulators* (Oxford, 1997), ch. 8 and ch. 10; R. Baldwin, *Regulating the Airlines* (Oxford, 1985).

of post-promulgation delay before rules come into effect. Similar consultation requirements apply to regulators in other jurisdictions and, as with reason-giving, the more legally required they become, the more they can be used as a tool of contestation. The flipside of avoiding 'juridification' is that any mere 'vocal' commitment towards 'rules on rules' is likely to be open to creative interpretation by regulators.

Another device that is commonly used to 'guide' decision-making by regulators is *structural hardwiring*. Amongst the various devices discussed as structural 'hardwiring' is agency leadership. Here, the central debate has been between those who advocate collegiate decision-making and those who support 'presidential' leadership structures. The latter position follows the well-established idea that accountability and responsibility should be placed in one single person. This, its proponents contend, reduces the possibility of 'hiding' from responsibility and also enhances the visibility of the office. In addition, 'presidential'-style regulators are said to offer more flexibility and speed in decision-making. The opposing argument suggests that such personalized regulation concentrates too much authority in one person, which can lead to either extreme risk aversion (because of the fear to be seen to take 'extreme' actions) or to over-personalized regulatory styles that over time produce an inconsistent approach towards regulation. Regulating through a collegiate structure is therefore said to offer more consistency, more collective 'protec-tion' against outside opposition, and the possibility of greater expertise and 'specialization' on particular aspects of the leadership structure. These argu-ments were used by the then UK Labour government post-1997 when shifting most utility regulators towards 'commission'-type structures.

Yet another procedural device is that of *objectives and guidance*. Regulators are usually required to follow objectives that are set out in legislation. In addition, ministers are often empowered to issue binding guidance for regulatory deci-sion-making. The problem with legislative objectives is that they seldom provide the kind of guidance that will allow for straightforward decisions: social, envi-ronmental, and economic efficiency objectives as enshrined in legislation do not offer a consistent and clear-cut direction. The difficulty with ministerial direc-tives is that they tend to outdate rapidly, that they involve a bifurcation of policymaking (between minister and agency) and that, as a result, they increase uncertainties concerning the direction of regulatory strategy. They can, more-over, give rise to legal uncertainties in so far as they create pegs upon which challenges to the regulator's actions can be hung.[14]

A final means of rationalizing regulatory processes is the imposition of particular *methodologies*. As noted in Chapter 15, Regulatory Impact

---

[14] See, e.g., *Laker Airways v. Secretary of State for Trade and Industry* [1977] QB 643; *R v. Director of Passenger Rail Franchising ex p. Save Our Railways*, *Independent*, 20 Dec. 1995, *The Times*, 18 Dec. 1995.

Assessment serves not merely to structure the informational basis for regulatory decisions, it also acts (say its advocates) to render decision-making more accountable by encouraging greater consistency in regulatory decision-making processes (through the application of a common methodology). Standardized processes thus function as means of control'[15] not just as mechanisms to ensure procedural safeguards or to facilitate participation. Indeed, it could be argued that the complexity of procedural methodologies places too heavy a burden on the poorly organized parts of society and that this thereby leads to further exclusion.[16]

These seven procedural ways to ensure fairness and participation lead directly to wider debates about accountability. This discussion has focused on the questions of *who is accountable, for what, and to whom*. Answers to these questions have considered accountability relations in different areas, namely the political domain, the professional domain, and the legal domain (i.e. courts). We consider each in turn, assuming that 'regulators' are central to the question of accountability.

Accounting for regulatory actions *to the political domain* includes two separate aspects. One is accountability to legislative bodies, the other is accountability to the 'elected' part of executive government. Accountability to legislative bodies is often regarded as one of the key 'problems' of the regulatory state. It is argued that, in the age of public ownership, ministers had direct responsibility for particular industries and therefore were, to an extent, answerable for each one's performance in Parliament. In an age of private-service providers and free-standing, autonomous regulators, ministerial answerability and responsibility are restricted and not 'compensated for' by equivalent regulators' obligations to be responsive to parliamentary forms of accountability. While, however, there is no direct answerability in the parliamentary chamber, regulators do usually have an obligation to appear in front of select committees and to contribute to committee investigations. The 'fear' of receiving a grilling in front of a parliamentary committee might be regarded as a key means through which to keep regulators 'on their toes'. The concomitant danger is that risk-averse regulators will tend to act excessively conservatively in order to protect themselves against such political oversight.

Accountability to the elected arm of the executive is limited in the case of supposedly autonomous or independent regulators. To some extent, this is a matter of intentional design: if politicians enjoy direct involvement in a regulator's decision-making, there is little point in having a formal separation between policymaking and regulatory activities. This arrangement does not mean, however, that accountability is absent. One way to effect this is to issue

[15] S. Rose-Ackermann, 'Law and Regulation' in K.E. Whittington, R.D. Kelemen and G.A. Caldeira (eds), *Oxford Handbook of Law and Politics* (Oxford, 2008).

[16] P. Self, *Administrative Theories and Politics* (London, 1972).

guidance (usually of a 'general' rather than a specific nature) on key government priorities that regulators are to take account of in their decisions (and to account for).[17] Another way to provide for accountability to the political domain is through reporting and monitoring, for example, through national audit offices that conduct not just reviews of expenditure, but also wider evaluative analyses. The potential for audit offices to act as 'meta-regulators' is one key idea that has been influential in recent years. This is regarded as a device that is designed to facilitate greater consistency in regulatory decision-making across domains, but it is also seen as one way to ensure that regulators are accountable for their actions to some kind of review body.

A related idea is that specific monitoring, review, or 'meta-regulatory' bodies should exist to oversee decision-making across regulators in different domains (in particular, by monitoring compliance with procedural devices rather than outputs or outcomes). Such bodies might also function as appeal mechanisms, as exist, for example, in the case of UK competition law (that also applies to utility regulators) where an appeal to the Competition Commission against regulatory decisions is possible (under the 1998 Competition Act) and a further appeal to the Competition Appeal Tribunal is also possible. In other jurisdictions (such as Germany), appeals are made to an administrative court. Such appeal opportunities are regarded as an essential safeguard. However, they come at the price of delays and potential obstructive practices by those interests seeking to postpone decisions.

The idea of accountability *to the profession* relates to arguments that favour self-regulation. Instead of formal reporting to outside bodies, accountability is directed towards one profession (however formally organized). Such 'internal' accountability is said to encourage informed conversations within a profession and to facilitate openness, as those 'account-givers' are not required to face adversarial interrogation by outside interests. Giving account therefore is also associated with the possibility to learn through updating on knowledge. The argument against too much openness is that the more afraid individuals or organizations are about the consequences of giving account, the less open they will be in their answerability (and the less they will be able to enjoy the advantages of learning lessons). However, the extent to which these professional regimes are indeed functioning as methods to make individuals and organizations accountable has come under greater scrutiny in various sectors, most of all in the area of medical self-regulation.[18] Indeed, it could be argued that a move towards more formal and external accountability

---

[17] Ministerial guidance may be binding legally within the terms of a statute, but a further way by which elected politicians can put pressure on regulators is through informal means, such as disputing a regulator's jurisdiction on a particular matter, informal briefings to the media, or explicit withdrawals of support. On guidance systems, see R. Baldwin, *Rules and Government* (Oxford, 1995).

[18] M. Davies, *Medical Self-Regulation: Crisis and Change* (Aldershot, 2007); M. Moran, *The British Regulatory State* (Oxford, 2003), 82–3.

relationships reflects a wider societal demand for self-regulation to be accountable beyond the confines of any one profession.[19]

Accountability *to the legal system* varies according to the given jurisdiction's specific tradition. The basic idea—that courts should be used to check on agency disrespect for the limitations of legal powers and procedural due process—is long established, and chapters on 'judicial review' across different administrative law traditions testify to that effect.[20] In general terms, regulators will not be allowed by reviewing courts to act illegally (by going beyond the limits of their powers); irrationally (by basing a decision on irrelevant considerations, failing to take relevant matters on board, or making a wholly unreasonable decision or policy); or procedurally improperly (by, for example, failing to follow a statutory procedure).[21] Such review power comes at a price, however: it raises the possibility of judges being actively involved in developing regulatory decisions and policy. It raises the question whether courts should defer to regulators' decisions and expertise in case of ambiguity or whether courts should be actively engaged in scrutinizing decisions to the degree that they engage in fresh examinations of the merits of decisions. The modern stance of the UK courts is generally to defer to regulators' judgements where Parliament has established the regulator as the authority in an area[22] or where the regulator possesses a special expertise that the courts lack.[23] The courts will, however, interfere with regulators more readily on more particular issues of legality—to ensure, for instance, that different parties are treated fairly by the regulator or to demand that binding guidelines have been followed properly.[24]

In the case of the British utilities, one explicit intention of post-1980s reforms was to keep the judges outside regulation. In other jurisdictions,

---

[19] See the discussion of self-regulation in Chapter 8.

[20] See, for example, K.F. Warren, *Administrative Law in the Political System* (4th edn, Boulder, 2004); R. Baldwin and C. McCrudden, *Regulation and Public Law* (London, 1987); S. Breyer and R. Stewart, *Administrative Law and Regulatory Policy* (Boston, 1992); P. Craig, *Administrative Law* (6th edn, London, 2008).

[21] See *Associated Provincial Picture Houses* v. *Wednesbury* Corporation [1948] 1 KB 223; *Council of Civil Service Unions* v. *Minister for the Civil Service* [1985] AC 374.

[22] *R* v. *Secretary of State for Trade and Industry ex p. Lonrho* [1989] 1 WLR 525—where Lord Justice Watkins recognized the danger of the court substituting its view for that of the body designated by Parliament as having authority in an area. See also *Ex p. Centro* v. *Secretary of State for Transport* [2007] EWHC 2729; *Hutchinson 3G UK Ltd* v. *Ofcom* [2009] EWCA Civ 683.

[23] *R* v. *Independent Television Commission, ex p. TSW Broadcasting Ltd*, *Independent*, 27 Mar. 1992; *R* v. *Director General of Telecommunications ex p. Let's Talk (UK) Ltd*, QBD 6 Apr. 1992; *R* v. *Independent Television Commission ex p. TSW Broadcasting Ltd Independent* [1996] EMLR 291; *R* v. *Independent Television Commission ex p. Virgin Television Ltd* [1996] EMLR 318; *R* v. *DG Telecoms ex p. Cellcom* [1999] COD 105 para. 26.

[24] *Mercury Communications Ltd* v. *Director-General of Telecommunications and Others*, *Financial Times*, 10 Feb. 1995; *R* v. *Director of Passenger Rail Franchising ex p. Save Our Railways*, *Independent*, 20 Dec. 1995, *The Times*, 18 Dec. 1995; *R* v. *National Lottery Commission ex p. Camelot* [2001]; *R* v. *DGES, ex p. Scottish Power*, Lexis, 3 Feb. 1997.

such as Germany or Brazil, judges play an important role through appeals procedures and even 'development' (in the case of Brazil, an important role in environmental enforcement is played by public prosecutors).[25] Regardless of intention, it is difficult to deny that the emergence of the 'regulatory state' has brought about increased legal formalization and therefore an increased tendency to resolve conflicts through legal means.

The importance of judicial oversight has been particularly prominent in the United States. During the period of social regulation in particular, the so-called 'hard look' judicial review was supposed to check administrative (regulatory) discretion.[26] For some, this generated a judicialization of agency decision-making that turned agency hearings into something more trial-like.[27] This trend was to some extent reversed by the *Chevron* ruling.[28] This suggested that courts should recognize administrative decisions as acceptable as long as the decision was reasonable and followed the meaning of the statute.[29] The *Chevron* decision has been said to restore an emphasis on professional expertise of regulators, as it requires a court to defer to the agency's interpretation of its legislative mandate, thereby restricting a lower court's authority in reviewing agency decisions. This doctrine has been widely interpreted as emphasizing the importance of agency accountability to the President, as the agencies are part of the wider executive.[30]

Much has been said about the contribution (positive and otherwise) of courts to regulation. The powers of courts to restrict discretionary decision-making is one aspect of these discussions. Critics point to a series of issues. For example, trial-like proceedings are said to be inappropriate for dealing with polycentric issues.[31] They are costly, are unlikely to provide the kind of conditions conducive to a gradual development of regulatory principles, and induce a bias towards less reviewable modes of operation. The extent to

---

[25] L. McAllister, 'Dimensions of Enforcement Style' (2010) 32 *Law and Policy* 61–78.

[26] D. Rodriguez, 'Administrative Law' in K.E. Whittington, R.D. Kelemen, and G.A. Caldeira (eds), *Oxford Handbook of Law and Politics* (Oxford, 2008).

[27] D.L. Horowitz, 'The Courts as Guardians of the Public Interest', (1997) 37(2) *Public Administration Review* 148–54, esp. 150.

[28] *Chevron* v. *Natural Resource Defense Council*, 464 US 837, 3.

[29] C. Sunstein, 'Law and Administration after Chevron' (1990) 90(8) *Columbia Law Review* 2071–120; C.H. Koch Jr, 'Judicial Review of Administrative Policymaking' (2002) 44 *William and Mary Law Review* 375–404; M. Seidenfeld, 'Cognitive Loafing, Social Conformity and Judicial Review of Agency Rulemaking' (2002) 87 *Cornell Law Review* 486–548.

[30] The scope of *Chevron*, often criticized for its 'extreme deference' stance towards agency discretion, has arguably been reduced since *United States* v. *Mead Corp.*, 533 US 218 (2001). More generally, there have been opposite empirical findings as to whether courts have taken uniform notice of the *Chevron* doctrine (see W.T. Merrill, 'Judicial Deference to Executive Precedent' (1992) 101(5) *Yale Law Journal* 969–1041; M. Hertz, 'Deference Running Riot' (1992) 6(2) *Administrative Law Journal* 187–234).

[31] L.L. Fuller, 'The Forms and Limits of Adjudication' (1978) 92 *Harvard Law Review* 353–409; B.B. Boyer, 'Alternatives to Trial-Type Hearings for Resolving Complex Scientific, Economic and Social Issues' (1972) 71(1) *Michigan Law Review* 111–70.

which judicial review actually matters in terms of overall regulatory decision-making is also open to question. Judicial review focuses on formal decisions, and arguably many important regulatory decisions (and therefore also potential injustices) occur in areas of informal discretionary judgements. It therefore offers only very weak protection against abuses of informal regulatory power.[32]

To summarize, this section has provided a brief discussion of some of the traditional debates regarding accountability. It has centred on the relationship between the regulator or regulatory agency and the wider political and legal system. In this area, a central concern has been to devise checks on discretionary decision-making. There is, however, a clear tension between the principles of accountability and autonomy. Furthermore, the legitimacy of those holding to account may also be considered as problematic. Finally, focusing on the regulatory agency itself is an inherently narrow viewpoint to adopt in an era of increasingly polycentric or 'decentred' regulatory regimes.

The Changed Context: More or Less Accountability?

Three particular changes have challenged traditional approaches to understanding regulatory accountability. These changes also call for wider reflections on whether regulatory reform (and wider public sector reform) has led to a decline in accountability or not. These debates are ultimately unresolvable, but they pitch those who prioritize certain types of accountability mechanisms against those who highlight the many and varied ways through which regulatory regimes can be held accountable. Whether one type of accountability mechanism can be easily used as a substitute for another mechanism is, however, highly controversial in itself. This section covers those changes that are said to have challenged the traditional debates regarding accountability (as outlined above), and it considers whether it is possible to suggest that these changes have increased or decreased accountability.[33] The final section of the chapter will then deal with different approaches to understanding accountability.

The first change that has challenged the framing of the traditional accountability debate has been the increasing 'hollowing out' of the state that has taken place in the contemporary era of regulatory reform and privatization. The period since the 1980s has witnessed widespread privatization and marketization of public services. It is unlikely that this trend will be reversed to any great extent, in spite of the growth in government control that has been

---

[32] Warren, *Administrative Law in the Political System*, 443.
[33] Lodge and Stirton, 'Accountability in the Regulatory State'.

seen in the 'post-credit crisis' banking sectors of many developed-world countries.[34] The idea of privatized public services has been seen as a direct challenge to the social citizenship rights that emerged as part of the evolving welfare state. The addition of regulatory agencies to the administrative landscape (outside North America in particular) proved problematic for traditional legal understandings of administrative structures, and this confusion was further complicated by novel legal constructs. It raised accountability issues that have been discussed in the section above, and these concerns offered a direct parallel to the earlier preoccupations that had dominated the North American literature. An emphasis on marketization also went hand in hand with a different emphasis in terms of accountability: administrative actions were supposed to be justified and legitimized through output and outcome controls, rather than through inputs or procedures; through markets and consumer responses, rather than representative mechanisms.[35]

A second (related) change that has led to greater fragmentation of government, as well as to a more complex setting for accountability discussions, has been a diversification of regulatory actors. This has involved a greater reliance on self-regulatory bodies and international standards and regulatory bodies of varying kinds (see Chapter 18). This decentred, complex, world of regulation has been described thus:

Control over an economic or social issue in any regulatory regime will often involve a network or assemblage of regulators and these can include trans-national regulators setting 'soft law' standards, state based regulators or departments legislating in accordance with supra-national legal requirements, a number of regulatory agencies in the same jurisdiction applying a variety of regulatory instruments, and sub-national non-state regulators such as standard-setting authorities, professional self-regulators and industry-based certification bodies. In addition, regulation may encompass a diverse array of voluntary bodies, regulated firms and other organizations. Many of these regulatory actors may, moreover, apply the norms of both state based regulators and trans-national or sub-national non-state regulators and they may be both advised by an array of consultants and have to conform to conditions imposed by other bodies such as insurance companies.[36]

Such diversification and fragmentation makes the search for any one source or mode of accountability highly challenging.[37] Indeed, holding to account at

---

[34] Indeed, the taking into public ownership of the large parts of the banking sector as well as other administrative constructions to rescue the banking sectors (such as Ireland's National Asset Management Agency) raise considerable 'old-fashioned accountability' debates, namely those that point to problems how bodies can be accountable in the face of potentially contradictory objectives.

[35] G. Majone, 'Regulatory Legitimacy' in G. Majone (ed.), *Regulating Europe* (London, 1996).

[36] R. Baldwin and J. Black, 'Understanding Regulatory Cohabitation' (forthcoming). See also J. Black, 'Decentring Regulation: The Role of Regulation and Self Regulation in a "Post-Regulatory World"' (2001) *Current Legal Problems* 103–46.

[37] J. Black, 'Constructing and Contesting Legitimacy and Accountability in Polycentric Regulatory Regimes' (2008) 2(2) *Regulation and Governance* 137–64.

the national level became yet more highly problematic as production mobility increased in the international business environment. Accountability of the regulator not only lost focus amidst this fragmentation, but it gave way at least in part to accountability of the corporation, and any seeking to hold a regulated organization to account involved potential resistance. The holders to account were often faced by superior corporate resources and counter-learning, but also international mobility. As a result, imposing greater transparency requirements on corporations, for instance, might have the effect not of 'whipping companies into line' but of encouraging them to exercise an exit option.[38]

The third change that reframed accountability issues involved wider societal changes and the demand for more accountability. Social value change—towards more individualist and egalitarian positions—is said to have increased opposition and distrust of authority and official discretion and to have led to demands for explicit verification. According to Michael Power, the tragic consequence of this shift is that those instruments (in particular 'audit') that are supposed to address societal distrust are not merely questionable technologies for verifying anything, but they are also likely to jeopardize existing accountability mechanisms, and to fail to advance the overall quality of the given regulatory regime.[39]

These three trends are widely said to have led to a decline in overall accountability.[40] Regulators are not directly accountable to Parliament, private providers are, at best, accountable to markets, and the tools to ensure some degree of accountability are ritualistic and doubtful in their capacity to ensure 'account-giving'. Some commentators, however, have been more sanguine and have suggested that the diversification and fragmentation of the regulatory state across levels of government, and between private and public spheres, are developments that have not necessarily reduced accountability. Instead, arguably, these changes have shifted emphasis from one set of tools to another, and this has produced an increased diversity of channels in which systems are kept accountable.[41] On this view, for example, marketization can be seen as enhancing the accountability of service providers by reducing the ability of monopolies to abuse their information asymmetry. Marketization therefore provides enhanced accountability to the market (as customers might wish to exercise choice) and to regulators (as regulators can benchmark information).[42] Others have noted that the formalization of

[38] B. Cook, *Democracy and Administration* (Baltimore, 2007), 96.
[39] M. Power, *Organized Uncertainty* (Oxford, 2007); M. Power, *The Audit Society* (Oxford, 1997).
[40] Lodge and Stirton, 'Accountability in the Regulatory State', 354–7.
[41] C. Scott, 'Accountability in the Regulatory State' (2000) 27(1) *Journal of Law and Society* 38–60.
[42] G.-Z. Jun and P. Leslie, 'The Effect of Information on Product Quality: Evidence from Restaurant Hygiene Grade Cards' (2003) 118(2) *Quarterly Journal of Economics* 409–51.

relationships between regulated entities and regulators has increased commitments towards consultation.[43]

One issue here concerns choices of accountability mechanism. The question whether accountability has declined or not is likely to be affected by the position that is adopted on the relative normative importance of different accountability mechanisms. A second issue, however, is whether divergent accountability mechanisms are viewed as essentially harmonious or potentially conflicting. On this point, the sanguine position can be associated with the 'redundancy' model of accountability. This model suggests that, in complex systems of modern government, conflicts and tensions exist within the complex accountability webs that apply within a regulated domain, but that: 'the objective should not be to iron out conflict, but to exploit it to hold regimes in appropriate tension'.[44] The approach is optimistic in so far as it stresses that the various accountability systems that operate concurrently in an area 'have the character of a complex system of checks and balances' which have the potential for harnessing into an effective accountability system 'even as public power continues to be exercised in more fragmented ways'.[45]

The more pessimistic view suggests that, in decentred regulatory systems, the mechanisms and processes of holding to account involve not merely variations in institutions, procedures, discourses, systems, and expectations across actors or constituencies, but also the potential for destructive, rather than harmonious, interactions between mechanisms. Such difficulties arise, for instance, when certain types of accountability relationships are constructed between parties in ways that are at tension with other relationships. This can occur because different processes are used, but also where there are inconsistencies in the assumptions that form the basis for controls, when there are incompatibilities of relevant values, discourses, and visions of accountability, and when there are variations in the accountability objectives of different systems. It has been argued, in looking at emissions trading, for instance, that the market-based controls that are established by trading mechanisms conflict with notions that less affluent citizens need democratically based protections from the distributional consequences of market transactions.[46] The pessimistic vision suggests that redundancy theory may offer a valuable perspective on control regimes, but that there are good reasons for thinking that mixtures of accountability systems are likely to produce confusions, uncertainties, injustices, and democratic deficits.

---

[43] M. Thatcher, 'Institutions, Regulation and Change' (1998) 21(1) *West European Politics* 120–47.

[44] Scott, 'Accountability in the Regulatory State', esp. 57.

[45] Ibid., 55; also, L. Stirton and M. Lodge, 'Transparency Mechanisms: Building Publicness into Public Services' (2001) 28(4) *Journal of Law and Society* 471–89.

[46] See R. Baldwin, 'Regulation Lite' 2(2) *Regulation and Governance* 193–215.

Competing Views on Accountability

If discussions of accountability focus on regulatory regimes, rather than on regulatory agencies alone, it is possible to move beyond the traditional administrative law concern that decision-making should be visible, reasonable, and justifiable. For instance, it takes on board the growing attention that is paid to instruments widely associated with 'targeted transparency', namely those regulatory requirements that are supposed to shape the behaviour of consumers or organizations through their naming and shaming consequences.[47]

To take a more extensive perspective on accountability, it is necessary to undertake two steps. First, it is necessary to explore how a regulatory regime perspective points to the various regulated activities that need to be held accountable. Second, it requires an ordered approach in examining the diversity of ideas and doctrines that address the issue of accountability.

Taking the regulatory regime perspective (i.e. standard-setting, information-gathering, and behaviour-modification) means that any thinking about holding activities to account needs to consider the following five aspects:[48]

- the decision-making process that leads to the creation of a regulatory standard in the first place;
- the existence of a regulatory standard for affected participants within the regulated policy domain;
- the process through which information about the regulated activities is gathered and how this information is 'fed back' into standard-setting and behaviour-modification;
- the process through which regulatory standards are being enforced;
- the activities of the regulated parties themselves.

These five dimensions may apply to different levels of government and different organizations, suggesting that what is required is a view of the overall accountability of a regulatory regime's elements, rather than a narrow focus on a given regulator's decision-making. The idea here is that regulatory regimes constitute a problem of 'many hands': given the complexity of processes and different aspects of regulatory regimes, it is difficult to identify any single one 'accounter'. Instead, we are faced with the need to consider contending demands as to 'whom' to hold accountable for what and in what manner.

As a consequence, debates are increasingly moving towards distinguishing between different 'grammars' and values that underpin the instrumental value of the regulated service itself. Four different perspectives on accountability can be distinguished. These different perspectives can be distinguished by

---

[47] Fung, Graham, and Weil, *Full Disclosure*.
[48] Lodge and Stirton, 'Accountability in the Regulatory State'.

their view as to why things go wrong and how, their view of the capability of any one individual to exercise choice and process information, and their view as to why authority should be checked. They are also divided as to the kind of mechanisms they advocate to make regulatory regimes accountable.

A fiduciary trusteeship perspective is often associated with authors who are troubled by the kind of regulatory reforms applying to public services in recent decades. Emphasis is placed on those devices that make public officials' decision-making accountable. Experts are 'trusted' in the sense that they are regarded as most competent to make decisions, but they are required to 'give reasons' and their decision-making has to stand up to some degree of scrutiny, by *ex post* control devices (i.e. oversight), as well as through procedural means (as outlined above).

The consumer sovereignty perspective, in contrast, holds that the citizen-consumer knows best, or, rather, should be placed in a position to exercise informed choice. This view shares some ground with those who have diagnosed a shift towards 'targeted transparency' in so far as it suggests that particular information devices can be utilized to change behaviour, by allowing consumers to exercise 'choice'. Such choice can be fostered, for example, by requirements that consumers be supplied with efficiency-rating information, or information regarding food hygiene (on restaurant windows). In similar vein, medical doctors can be required to disclose to potential patients how many patients have died in their care.[49] This information can be provided by regulators or by the regulated organizations themselves.

The citizen empowerment perspective suggests that all authority is to be distrusted and that what proper accountability requires is not some trust in experts or market-type processes (as advocated by the consumer sovereignty perspective). Rather, what is demanded is direct accountability through participation. Accountability is therefore about reducing 'relational distance' (thus placing an emphasis on a degree of self-regulation). In a more extensive interpretation, accountability, according to this perspective, is about greater citizen involvement. This is a perspective that is inspired by the well-established 'town hall' view, namely that those with power should account directly to those affected.

Finally, according to the distrust and surprise perspective, there is very little point in trusting any method to ensure accountability. Any institutionalized and stable system of holding someone to account is limited. Individuals are not necessarily competent to undertake informed choices (especially as information may not be valuable), social participatory processes are likely to be dominated by those with the time and resources to mobilize, while formal oversight is likely to be open to capture and information asymmetries. As a

---

[49] C. Hood, *Administrative Analysis* (Hemel Hempstead, 1986), 178–9.

Table 16.1. Regulatory regimes and perspectives on accountability

	Fiduciary trusteeship	Consumer sovereignty	Citizen empowerment	Surprise and distrust
Decision-making regarding rule (standard)-setting	Professional and authoritative decision.	Competition between different standards.	Participative deliberation.	Ad hoc adaptation.
Standard	Authoritative statement.	Allows for information to advance individual choice.	Available for public understanding.	Fixed, but uncertainty regarding enforcement.
Information-gathering and feedback mechanisms	Review by experts.	Market selection process.	Participation.	Ad hoc and contrived randomness.
Behaviour-modification	Procedural application of sanctions.	Via market selection mechanism.	Persuasion.	Unannounced inspections.
Disclosure of activities of regulated parties	Formal disclosure requirements.	Disclosure requirements.	Maximum exposure to population.	Formal standards but unpredictable requirements.

Source: Lodge and Stirton, 'Accountability in the Regulatory State', 363.

result, the most likely way to achieve an accountable system of regulation is through unpredictability. Instead of having 'the lights constantly on', this strategy relies on uncertainty as to when and where there will be illumination. This latter view may be seen as offensive to some: after all, a core legitimating characteristic of the liberal state is that it exercises its power in a rule-orientated and predictable way. Nevertheless, holding organizations with considerable discretionary power to account through means of unpredictability has been a long-standing instrument in the regulation of government by itself.[50]

Taking the dimensions from a regulatory regime perspective and looking across the four perspectives on accountability points to a diversity of potential instruments. Table 16.1 offers such a summary.

Each of these different perspectives, of course, has its specific pitfalls. A reliance on information requires that the information provided is of a nature that allows meaningful choice. Either some information is not useful in offering guidance as to the quality of the whole product, or the information provided is (at best) 'gamed' or is too complex for any competent individual to make sense of. Similarly, a reliance on participation and involvement might be seen as advancing the status of citizenship, but it could be argued that certain regulatory actions involve such high expertise that such devices might

---

[50] See M. Lodge and C. Hood, 'Regulating Inside Government', in R. Baldwin, M. Cave, and M. Lodge (eds), *Oxford Handbook of Regulation* (Oxford, 2010).

be inherently limited. Equally, a sole reliance on unpredictability is problematic in that it undermines any form of trust and, arguably, the prerequisites that make the in-depth holding of account possible in highly complex contexts. According to this argument, we are only willing to account for our actions if we have a sense of trust in the understanding nature of those that hold us to account.

Finally, traditional 'fiduciary trusteeship' views are often seen as limited, as they underestimate the possibilities of citizen-customers to undertake informed choice and overestimate the 'neutrality' of expertise. In short, every set of accountability instruments is faced with some limitations. If it is also noted that accountability issues are likely to be dealt with against a background of competing understandings regarding legitimacy, the search for accountability becomes yet more complex. Nor are matters simplified by noting that each of the different models of accountability will build on basic institutional prerequisites (so that transnational private regulation is unlikely to be held to account through a 'fiduciary trusteeship' model). Indeed, where the 'starting point' of any particular accountability perspective should be is a matter of ideational preference. Should we, for instance, assume that citizen-consumers are inherently able to choose and that alternative accountability approaches should only be used where choice appears to be limited? Or should we assume that expertise and authority are important and should only be 'relaxed' when proven?

In sum may, this section has suggested that the more traditional accountability debates are limited, not just in underplaying the decentred and polycentric nature of regulatory regimes, but also because they do not take into account the possibilities of applying other perspectives and related mechanisms.

Conclusions

Accountability is one of the key concepts in the study of regulation. In regulatory practice, the 'accountability' word has been widely used, especially in the context of demands for 'more accountability'. The problem, however, is that there has been excessive focus on the traditional administrative law/ public law concerns regarding the formal checking of delegated discretionary power. Such a narrow view is highly problematic when looking at complex regulatory regimes that involve diverse organizations that are sited at different levels of government. What is needed is to move beyond a concentration on regulatory agencies alone. The traditional position is also problematic in overlooking the variety of ways in which accountability is considered. This chapter does not intend to suggest that the traditional accountability debates—those focusing on regulators' obligations to give account for their actions—are meaningless, but they need to be considered in the light of competing doctrines.

How we decide to think about accountability arrangements depends on fundamental views: about the capacity of individuals to make informed choices; about the complexity of particular regulatory activities; and about the effectiveness of particular accountability strategies in specific settings. Addressing these issues and considering different options is more likely to produce informed discussions on accountability than is the devotion of more attention to institutional arrangements concerning the accountability of particular regulators. Talking about 'more accountability' therefore is simply not enough; such calls need to be transparent about which aspect of the regulatory regime they are focusing on, they need to be transparent about the set of doctrines and justifications they employ, and they also need to account for the potential side-effects that any system of accountability is likely to incur. In short, debates regarding accountability need to be accountable in their assumptions, their targets, and their likely side-effects.

17 Regulatory Competition and Coordination

Regulatory competition involves the competitive adjustment of regulatory regimes in order to secure some advantage.[1] Regulators, indeed, can be seen as potential competitors in offering (or 'selling') a product, namely a regulatory regime involving standards, information-gathering, and enforcement activities. Competitions, moreover, can operate on a number of fronts. Regulators can lower standards, for example, so as to make compliance relatively easy and cheap for industry. Equally, they can court potential regulatees by offering more attractive styles of regulation than competitors (e.g. incentive- rather than command-based systems) or they can offer more assistance and advice than their competitors. They can operate procedures that are more amenable to regulatees and allow greater accessibility, transparency, or fairness. Alternatively, they might seek to persuade regulatees that their regimes will be more certain than the available alternatives (because they eschew goalpost moving) or that they have greater expertise than competing regulators and will be able to offer superior leadership and organizing capacity when changes have to be adapted to.

Regulatory competition, however, is associated with certain concerns. The idea that regulators and jurisdictions compete on the basis of regulatory standards or matters of broader 'regulatory environment', such as corporate governance requirements, tax levels, and environmental standards, is often used to highlight the dangers of a lack of national or international coordination. It is often suggested that processes of competition will lead to an inevitable race to (undesirably) low levels of regulation that undermine social or environmental standards. One specific accusation has been that in an age of mobile production systems, firms will exploit loose regulatory frameworks and move to those jurisdictions that offer them the least burdensome regulation. It is thus

---

[1] See generally: J.-M. Sun and J. Pelkmans 'Regulatory Competition in the Single Market (1995) 33 *Journal of Common Market Studies* 67–89; C. Radaelli, 'The Puzzle of Regulatory Competition' (2004) 24(1) *Journal of Public Policy* 1–23; J. Braithwaite and P. Drahos, *Global Business Regulation* (Oxford, 2000), chs 21, 24; W. Kerber and R. Van den Bergh, 'Mutual Recognition Revisited: Misunderstandings, Inconsistencies, and a Suggested Reinterpretation' (2008) 61 *Kyklos* 447–65; J. Pelkmans, 'Mutual Recognition in Goods: On Promises and Disillusions' (2007) 14(5) *Journal of European Public Policy* 699–716; F. Scharpf, 'Negative and Positive Integration in the Political Economy of European Welfare States' in G. Marks et al., *Governance in the European Union* (London, 1996), 15–39; S. Vogel, 'International Games with National Rules: How Regulation Shapes Competition in "Global Markets"' (1997) 17 *Journal of Public Policy* 169–93.

suggested that firms can often threaten to exit from regulatory regimes and can thereby persuade governments either to regulate lightly or to offer other kinds of side-payments in order to avoid negative outcomes and, in particular, any associated job losses. A particularly prominent charge has been that regulatory competition contributed to the financial crisis of the late 2000s. US banks, for example, were accused of 'venue-shopping' between different regulators who sought to please their regulatees in order to maintain their regulatory 'businesses'.[2] Similarly, the German banks that required financial bailouts in the late 2000s were said to have been largely driven into their financial distress by the 'off-balance sheet' operations of subsidiaries, many of whom were operating in 'light-touch' regulatory environments such as Ireland.[3] The collapse of the former insurance giant AIG was at least partly triggered by that firm's dealings at its London office—which enjoyed lighter oversight than it experienced in the US.[4] It can also be noted that changing EU regulations led Ireland to relax its local rules on hedge funds in order to battle Luxembourg for the position as 'location of choice' for onshore hedge funds in 2010.[5]

These are a few examples of negative developments that can be associated with regulatory competition. Whether such worries about regulatory competition are well-founded is one issue to be dealt with in this chapter. It commences by outlining the emergence of the term 'regulatory competition' and noting arguments in its favour. The discussion then moves to a wider argument, namely whether there is evidence of a 'race' between jurisdictions and, if so, whether such races tend to take a particular direction.

Regulatory Competition—and its Prerequisites

The origins of the regulatory competition debate are usually associated with the so-called 'Delaware effect'. This phenomenon was associated with competition among US states regarding company law (US states are legally required to recognize other states' charters). The state of Delaware put into effect particularly modernized incorporation statutes that consequently led a considerable number of New York listed firms to move to incorporation in Delaware—a shift that drove mirroring statute changes in a series of other

---

[2] C. Provost, 'Another Race to the Bottom? Venue Shopping for Regulators in the American Financial System', paper presented at the 3rd Biennial Conference of the Standing Group on Regulatory Governance, Dublin, 17–19 June 2010.

[3] 'Hypo-Retting könnte Steuerzahler über 50 Milliarden Euro kosten', *Spiegel Online*, 5 Oct. 2008 (http://www.spiegel.de/wirtschaft/0,1518,582251,00.html, last accessed 8 Dec. 2010).

[4] 'AIG Trail Leads to London "Casino"', *Daily Telegraph*, 18 Oct. 2008.

[5] 'Dublin Entices Funds with Softer Regulation', *Financial Times*, 6 Sept. 2010.

states.[6] The so-called Delaware effect is thus associated with an uncoordinated adjustment or 'race' across states that involved a 'downward' adjustment in regulatory standards (in this case, making chartering requirements particularly attractive to management).[7]

The debate concerning regulatory competition, especially its normative justification, is linked to Charles Tiebout's contribution on the appropriate size of municipal governments.[8] In opposition to those who argued in favour of large municipal areas, Tiebout offered a model of (small-scale) municipal government that suggested that city managers should attract 'consumer-voters' with particular local expenditure patterns that would please different sets of preferences. This was a theoretical argument that suggested that voters would vote with their feet in the way that consumers might choose the market stall for their daily vegetable shop. Consumer-voters (his term) would favour jurisdictions that best reflected their preferences: some would opt for low tax/low public service destinations, others would pay more for lifeguards on beaches, whilst others would prefer the provision of good schools. Municipalities offer so-called club goods (or 'toll goods'); they are 'public goods' until the time when crowding occurs and individuals can be excluded from their consumption. As a result, every jurisdiction is said to have an optimal size, and communities will seek to attract new residents up to the optimal point to reduce the average cost of providing services.

There are five prerequisites for the 'voting with your feet' effect. These are: that (1) consumer-voters are fully mobile; (2) consumer-voters are fully aware of the different 'bundles' on offer; (3) there is a large number of communities to choose from; (4) there are no restrictions on employment; and (5) there are no externalities.[9] It is clear from these five prerequisites that this is largely a model of heuristic value that informs wider debates about the benefits or otherwise of relying on decentralized governance structures.[10] In particular,

---

[6] J.A. McCahery and E.P.M. Vermeulen, 'Does the European Company Prevent the "Delaware-effect?"', TILEC Discussion Paper No. 2005–010 (2005) (available at SSRN: http://ssrn.com/abstract= 693421 or doi:10.2139/ssrn.693421), esp. pp. 8–10.

[7] Some, however, argue that regulatory competition can in fact lead to a 'race to the top' in some areas of corporate law. L. Bebchuk, A. Cohen, and A. Ferrell, 'Does the Evidence Favor State Competition in Corporate Law?' (2002) 90 *California Law Review* 1775–821.

[8] C. Tiebout, 'A Pure Theory of Local Expenditures' (1956) 64 *Journal of Political Economy* 416–24. Also (for a critical comment) W. Bratton and J. McCahery, 'The New Economics of Jurisdictional Competition' (1997) 86 *Georgetown Law Journal* 201–78; J.P. Trachtman, 'Regulatory Competition and Regulatory Jurisdiction' (2000) 3(2) *Journal of International Economic Law* 331–48; W.E. Oates, 'Fiscal and Regulatory Competition' (2002) 3(4) *Perspektiven der Wirtschaftspolitik* 377–90.

[9] Tiebout, C. 'A Pure Theory of Local Expenditures', 419.

[10] Tiebout noted the limitations of the argument and noted that where 'external economies and diseconomies are of sufficient importance, some form of integration may be indicated' (Tiebout, 'A Pure Theory of Local Expenditures', 423; see also R. Imman and D. Rubinfeld, 'The Political Economy of Federalism' in D. Mueller (ed.), *Perspectives on Public Choice* (Cambridge, 1997). See also the discussion of 'polycentricity' in Chapter 18. Generally, Tiebout, together with Vincent Ostrom

transaction costs of moving are never zero, and the assumption that customer-voters live on 'dividend income' instead of having a job is arguably heroic. The important idea, however, is that consumer-voters choose which governments satisfy their set of preferences best.

In relation to regulatory competition, the key prerequisites remain the same; it is still assumed that there is an optimal size of jurisdictions, that the supply of jurisdictions is perfectly elastic, that mobility is costless, that households and firms are fully informed (about standards and enforcement), and that there are no inter-jurisdictional externalities.

Advocates of regulatory competition therefore suggest that 'exit' should be facilitated to restrict the potential power of government, and competition would be facilitated by allowing for a choice of legal rule.[11] Challenges to the assumptions underlying this particular view of regulatory competition are numerous. One relates to the idea of costless freedom of movement, especially across jurisdictions. Indeed, it is likely that only some actors are able to move freely—for example, mobile capital faces fewer difficulties in moving than labour, leading to inherent power asymmetries. Second, there is the criticism that rationality is inherently bounded and that information will never be 'complete'—which places constraints on both regulator and regulatee decision-making. Third, there are evident limits to the argument about 'optimal size' of jurisdictions that relates to externalities: some issues clearly call for a cross-border inter-jurisdictional regulatory approach (for example, pollution, where 'scale' matters); regulatory approaches in one jurisdiction are likely to impact on other jurisdictions, and what exactly constitutes a significant externality (i.e. one that is regarded as deserving political attention) is mostly a matter of political and societal preferences, rather than a clear-cut economic calculus. Fourth, there is only modest evidence that there is a 'perfectly elastic supply of jurisdictions'. Overall, it can be said that limits on the extent to which it is possibly to realize a 'pure' Tiebout world mean that the degree to which Tiebout-type regulatory competition can lead to superior efficiency can be questioned.[12]

---

and Robert Warren, pointed to the potential superiority of polycentric over centralized decision-making, especially for public services. Small and medium-sized municipalities were more effective than large cities in monitoring performance and cost, citizens were able to 'exit' if they were dissatisfied and 'vote with their feet', and and there was greater autonomy of local decision-makers in decentralized systems (see also V. Ostrom, C. Tiebout, and R. Warren, 'The Organization of Government in Metropolitan Areas: A Theoretical Inquiry' (1961) 55 *American Political Science Review* 831–42.

[11] A. Hirschman, *Exit, Voice and Loyalty: Responses to Decline in Firms, Organisations and States* (Cambridge, MA, 1970).

[12] Trachtman, 'Regulatory Competition and Regulatory Jurisdiction', 338; W. Kerber and R. Van den Bergh, 'Mutual Recognition Revisited: Misunderstandings, Inconsistencies, and a Suggested Reinterpretation' (2008) 61 *Kyklos* 447–65.

The Effects of Regulatory Competition

As noted, the Tiebout-informed view of regulatory competition is one that advocates decentralized decision-making. It therefore argues that there are significant advantages in taking regulatory decisions at the lowest level possible. Regulators will seek to attract the 'optimal' number of regulatees and will be responsive to their demands because they fear 'exit' or a 'voting with their feet' response. Regulators, accordingly, are forced into a responsive 'race to the top', involving regulatory rules, processes, and enforcement practices that are responsive to citizen-consumers and regulatees.[13] In addition, advocates of regulatory competition stress a number of its advantages. The first of these is *responsiveness*. Regulators will seek to respond to changing environments and demands in order to prevent 'exit'. They are also less likely to be captured by particular interests, as the result of capture may be an exit by affected constituencies. Regulatory competition therefore puts constraints on the Leviathan-character of regulators and governments. Furthermore, responsiveness is also likely to reduce regulatory complexity created by centralized and harmonized regulation. A second posited advantage of regulatory competition is *diversity and choice*. Consumers and regulatees will be able to choose between different 'bundles' of regulation. Regulation therefore is 'tailored' to the needs of specific economies, constituencies, and sectors of demand. A further positive aspect of competition is *innovation*. Decentralized systems that are in competition with each other are said to encourage market-driven innovation and discovery processes. Finally, competitions between regulators are said to encourage *responsiveness* to local needs and concerns rather than to produce the 'lowest common denominator' of different regulatory interests and challenges.

Against these supposed advantages of regulatory competition can be placed a number of concerns. In the first instance, the Tiebout-informed world of regulatory competition assumes, as noted, costless mobility, adequate information regarding regulation, and that enforcement is predictable. Exit (and voice) need to be available to all parties so that regulatory regimes can be responsive. A more critical look at these assumptions, however, raises considerable problems, and suggests that the overall effects of regulatory competition are likely to be negative. One (already mentioned) point is that some actors are more likely to be able to move freely than others.[14] This means that the

---

[13] See also R. Romana, 'Is Regulatory Competition a Problem or Irrelevant for Corporate Governance' (2005) 21 *Oxford Review of Economic Policy* 212–31.

[14] On this basis, Streeck and Schmitter have made an argument about the power of internationally moving capital over nationally fixed labour markets, suggesting that in a world in which states have lost boundary-control over their national economies, states are required to be responsive to business but not labour, therefore challenging welfare states (W. Streeck and P. Schmitter, 'From National Corporatism to Transnational Pluralism' (1991) 19 *Politics and Society* 133–64.

threat of moving will often be sufficient to persuade regulators (and governments) to grant 'benevolent' regulatory treatment to these highly mobile actors, rather than to those that are unlikely to move or incapable of moving. Thus, local governments or regulators will listen more readily to highly mobile large firms than to residents who are unlikely (unable) to move. In the wider context, it has often been suggested that 'voting with your feet' will mostly benefit the mobile and wealthy and that 'voting with your feet' is likely to compound socio-economic inequality. Rich consumer-voters will move to and congregate in low-tax, well-serviced areas, and poorer individuals will be left to inhabit jurisdictions that are too hard-pressed to provide high levels of service.[15] A related fear is that governmental policies are skewed by decisions to compete on certain fronts rather than others. Thus, one of the key worries about structures, such as the EU Single Market and its mutual recognition principle, is that it encourages an emphasis on regulatory competition in favor of economic over social and/or environmental interests.[16]

A further concern relates to the issue of externalities and the problem of overlapping and unpredictable application of regulatory approaches. Voters in jurisdiction A may have 'voted with their feet' for high regulatory environmental standards, but jurisdiction B may offer 'low' environmental standards, and the pollution allowed in jurisdiction B may cross the border and afflict jurisdiction A. The result is that jurisdiction A will still suffer from high pollution as a result of the choices made in jurisdiction B. Where regulation in one area is poorly organized or slack, moreover, it might have wider systemic effects. A banking crisis in one particular jurisdiction, for instance, may still cause a run on banks in another, even if the latter jurisdiction's regime is said to be stable and functioning. Finally, this is a world where material self-interest through the 'exit' option and not through political processes decides on regulatory standards. This may offend some observers who believe in ideas of liberal-democratic accountability.

The Tiebout-world also gives rise to the more general worry that it can produce inherent instability, with regulatory regimes constantly adjusting to mimic and outdo each other. This leads to the suggestion that such instabilities will require 'centralized' regulation or the application of other means to achieve coordination.[17] This instability is said to encourage particular 'races' between jurisdiction (a topic we will consider in the next section) and, even if races do not occur, the fear is that regulators will not be able to offer 'stable' packages of regulatory regimes. Rather, what would emerge is a

---

[15] See P. Self, *Government by the Market?* (Basingstoke, 1993).

[16] For a discussion of the pros and cons of mutual recognition in EU goods markets, see J. Pelkmans, 'Mutual Recognition in Goods: On Promises and Disillusions' (2007) 14 *Journal of European Public Policy* 699–716.

[17] Trachtman, 'Regulatory Competition and Regulatory Jurisdiction', 339; Bratton and McCahery, 'New Economics'.

broadly directionless regulatory regime that would be forced to adjust to outside pressures.

The main attraction of the Tiebout model has been its heuristic value. The wider literature on 'polycentricity' has highlighted the varied nature of ways in which social systems can achieve desired outcomes and has highlighted the varied ways in which governance systems that go beyond states and markets (i.e. including regulatory regimes) can be set up. In the end, there may be no simple and universal conclusion on the advantages or disadvantages of encouraging regulatory competition; the calculations will rather depend on particular constellations. Indeed, the debate about regulatory competition is arguably leading to a much wider debate about the appropriate level of jurisdiction; we return to this discussion in Chapter 20.[18]

Races to the Bottom and to the Top

Regulatory competition is widely associated with two key ideas. The first is the notion of the 'race to the bottom', in which jurisdictions are in a 'prisoner dilemma'-type constellation that drives them to adopt ever-decreasing regulatory standards to attract mobile factors of production. In this world, regulators compete by relaxing regulation and indulging in such practices as reducing social or environmental standards, applying loose enforcement practices, or implementing other steps to offer a 'light-touch' environment. In this context, having stricter social and environmental standards becomes a source of cost and competitive disadvantage. Labour costs rise if social obligations are imposed, and measures to reduce emissions are similarly seen as merely raising the costs of production.

The opposite race—'to the top'—is said to exist where jurisdictions move to higher standards that they would not have adopted if it had not been for the presence of rival jurisdictions.[19] This process has also been termed the 'California effect' by the political scientist David Vogel.[20] According to Vogel, competing regulatory standards can lead in some cases to a 'race to the top', as in the case of environmental emission standards for cars in the US. He observed that California's adoption of tight environmental standards for cars was quickly followed by other US states, and led to a harmonization at

---

[18] See Trachtman, 'Regulatory Competition and Regulatory Jurisdiction', 333.

[19] We ignore here the kind of regulatory 'race to the top' that emerges in the context of moral panics and media-feeding frenzies. In these situations, politicians, on heat to regulate in response to public pressure, demand the 'toughest law'.

[20] D. Vogel, *Trading Up: Consumer and Environmental Regulation in a Global Economy* (Cambridge, MA, 1997).

a higher level that formed the basis for the next round of minimum federal requirements.[21] The underlying dynamic here is that producers, when faced with segmented markets, will demand the adoption of common standards to reduce production costs. Thus, stricter regulation represents a source of competitive advantage for domestic producers, while richer countries, more likely to have higher environmental standards, are likely to force importers to adjust to these standards to guarantee continued market access. In addition, international agreements allow richer countries to facilitate access to rich markets *in exchange* for agreement on stricter standards.[22] The California effect, therefore, suggests that domestic producers do not have a narrow interest in 'loose' regulation; rather, they will demand a 'level playing field' in terms of similarly strict regulatory standards elsewhere. Should they be successful, they face no adjustment costs, whereas their competitors in other jurisdictions will be required to alter their products, thereby incurring considerable compliance costs. Vogel also notes why, therefore, EU environment standards have been higher rather than lower: the higher standards reflected the interests and the domestic rules facing German producers. The self-interest of industry therefore coincides with environmentalist or 'green' interests, leading to the emergence of so-called 'baptist–bootlegger' coalitions.[23]

A 'race to the top' may drive regulatory standards and rigour to higher levels, but this does not necessarily mean that the race will be to the 'optimal' regulatory regime—where the optimal comprises the level of standards and enforcement rigour that coincides with the preferences of an informed body of consumers or an informed electorate. If information is imperfect, or influences over regulators are weak, the 'race to the top' may lead to supra-optimal regulation where, for instance, the standards applied are higher than are justified (as where airline security controls are too risk-averse) and the consumers of services will be ill-placed to evaluate the costs and benefits of regulatory measures or to bring excessive levels of control down to acceptable positions.

---

[21] Ibid., 259.

[22] Ibid., 259–60.

[23] The term 'Baptist–bootlegger coalition' emerged in the context of demands for prohibitions on alcohol sales on Sundays. Baptists demanded the prohibition of the selling and drinking of alcohol on Sundays on moral grounds. Bootleggers wished alcohol sales to be illegal so that they could maintain their business (i.e. they demanded sales restrictions, not a prohibition on drinking alcohol). Politicians advocating sales restrictions were therefore in the enviable position of being able to endorse moral arguments while pocketing contributions from the bootleggers. Conveniently, the Baptists acted as 'information gatherers' to monitor compliance of the restrictions that are advantageous to bootleggers. Overall, as noted in Chapter 4, the 'Baptist–bootlegger' theory of regulation represents a contribution to interest group accounts on the lines of George Stigler and Sam Peltzman. It suggests that for regulatory advocacy to be successful, it requires concentrated industry interest and successful 'moral' rhetoric (the 'locus classicus' for the 'Baptist–bootlegger coalition' term is B. Yandle, 'Bootleggers and Baptists: The Education of a Regulatory Economist' (1983) 7 *Regulation* 12–16.

The broad distinction between 'races to the top' and 'races to the bottom' has given rise to further discussions of the areas of regulation that are likely to experience particular types of races. Jurisdictions can be engaged in different regulatory races at the same time. One key distinction here lies between product- and process-type regulation.[24] *Product standards* are those that change the qualities of a product. They provide, for example, for more energy-efficient freezers or less polluting cars. Diverse product standards, furthermore, also segment markets. It is, therefore, these kinds of regulatory standards that are more likely to witness a 'race to the top'. Consumers in rich countries are willing to pay 'extra' to feel good about purchasing a 'better' product. They will thereby place pressure on producers to deliver these higher standard products.

Product standards have two effects that encourage harmonization at a higher level: they have a certification effect (in that consumers receive a visible sign that they are consuming a superior good) and, more importantly, they are 'market-making' and 'market-enabling' in that they reduce production costs between segmented markets. Industries in 'low-regulation' jurisdictions with interests in accessing 'high-regulation' markets, therefore, have self-interests that are served by producing to the higher standard.[25] The interest in homogeneous standards, of course, has its limits when it comes to those standards associated with high fixed asset and switching costs (such as electronic sockets).

None of these self-reinforcing mechanisms exists in the case of *process standards*. These standards merely enhance the costs of production without altering the quality of the product as such. A process standard, therefore, is neither market-making nor has it an inherent certification effect. Male truckers, for example, are not rendered more competitive as a result of higher fuel taxes or provisions that reduce working hours or establish more extensive paternity leave rights than in neighbouring jurisdictions with lower standards. The same logic, however, does not necessarily apply to service industries. In this case, the services rendered (i.e. the processes of providing particular services) constitute the products, and these, therefore, can in some way be regarded as 'certifiable'.[26] It is therefore possible that process standards in particular industries can be linked to the possibility of a 'certification effect'. It might be possible to observe 'races to the top' in some cases.

In general, though, process standards are more likely to experience a 'race to the bottom' due to their 'market-correcting' nature. Producers have the

---

[24] Scharpf, 'Negative and Positive Integration', 15–39; C. Radaelli, 'The Puzzle of Regulatory Competition' (2004) 24 *Journal of Public Policy* 1–23.

[25] Ogus therefore talks of 'facilitative' regulation that is market-making, A. Ogus, 'Competition between National Legal Systems: New Insights for Comparative Law?' (1999) 48 *International and Comparative Law Quarterly* 1–14.

[26] Similarly, higher safety rules may, in some cases, be regarded as having a 'certification effect'.

incentive to move to the jurisdiction that offers the lowest process standards, thereby putting pressure on other jurisdictions to adjust their social and environmental process standards downwards. As a result, federal states usually have national rules that apply to process- or market-correcting regulation. Such structures do not exist in the European or international economy. This leads to the fear that the internationalization of economies (and the enhanced mobility of particular factors of production which combine to reduce the national 'boundary control' over economic regulation) will lead to a 'race to the bottom' in the case of process standards.[27] While producers in 'high-regulation' jurisdictions might have an interest in exporting their high process standards to low-cost jurisdictions, there are no incentives for the low-cost producers to accommodate these demands.

When comparing the empirical results, it is very difficult to establish conclusive evidence that regulatory jurisdictions are engaged in extensive races. There are some signs, as illustrated above, that environmental standards have witnessed something of a 'race to the top', following the logic of 'market-making/enabling regulation'. There has, however, been little sign of an explicit race to the bottom. Instead, racing has been prevented by the introduction of process regulation (or market-correcting regulation). These measures were usually effected on the basis of lowest common denominator bargaining, taking the form of minimum standards. They usually also involve side-payments from 'high-regulation' to 'low-regulation' countries (as 'high-regulation' jurisdictions also face political opposition against any potential lowering of standards). The same pattern emerges from extensive studies of 'mutual recognition' in the context of the European Union. The broad idea—that goods being sold according to the regulations of any member state can be marketed in principle in all other member states[28]—seems to endorse notions of regulatory competition and has led to fears about 'races to the bottom'. Studies, however, suggest the limits of the mutual recognition principle—so-called 'equivalence' must be observed and member states have defined objectives and prescribed minimum standards. Indeed, the European world of mutual recognition has so far been one of 'mediation'.[29] Similarly, studies of US regulatory enforcement in environmental regulation have not found a clear-cut 'race to the bottom' trajectory, although regulators are said to

---

[27] F. Scharpf, 'Balancing Positive and Negative Integration', *MPIfG Working Paper* 97/8 (Cologne, 1997) (http://www.mpifg.de/pu/workpap/wp97-8/wp97-8.html); F. Scharpf, 'What Have We Learned? Problem Solving Capacity of the Multi-level Polity', *MPIfG Working Paper*, 01/4 (Cologne, 2001) (http://www.mpifg.de/pu/workpap/wp01-4/wp01-4.html)

[28] S. Schmidt, 'Mutual Recognition as a New Mode of Governance' (2007) 14 *Journal of European Public Policy*, 667–81, esp. 667.

[29] Ibid., 677; also J. Pelkmans, 'Mutual Recognition in Goods: On Promises and Disillusions' (2007) 14 *Journal of European Public Policy* 699–716; and A. Heritier, 'Mutual Recognition: Comparing Policy Areas' (2007) 14 *Journal of European Public Policy* 800–13.

interact strategically with each other. They do, however, respond in their enforcement practices to perceived disadvantages that arise from the enforcement practices of their competitor jurisdictions. Equally, however, and supporting a 'race to the top' argument, regulators seem to be adjusting their enforcement 'upwards' in interaction with their competitors.[30]

This discussion suggests that the 'racing' analogy has important implications for the study of regulation.[31] The indications, however, are that it is far less prevalent than many observers have suggested. Of course, the potential of 'exit' and regulatory competition means that regulators may anticipate exit and therefore adjust their regulatory standards, processes, and enforcement practices. It is difficult, though, to estimate how extensive this process of adjustment is. Instead, 'races' are inherently limited because of the stickiness of national politics. Taking steps to reduce regulatory standards in social protection, for instance, is unlikely to be electorally popular (although reducing environmental regulatory compliance cost to attract major investment and employment opportunities could be attractive to voters) and key 'protective' interests have arguably some degree of 'veto power' in national legislative processes. Indeed, states may not wish to attract polluting industries; instead, they may wish to encourage particular industries by signalling their commitment towards a 'clean' environment through tough environmental regulation. This suggests that 'races' are hardly straightforward and that regulators and jurisdictions have to weigh competing interests. Indeed, it is not always clear what exactly constitutes 'top'- or 'bottom'-level regulation. Commentators on regulatory races often assume that there is a normative position about what 'optimal' means. What 'optimal'-level regulation looks like in a given context, however, is inherently contested.[32]

Regulatory Coordination

The threat of a 'race to the bottom' as well as the realization that some problems require cross-jurisdictional approaches has prompted considerable

---

[30] D. Konisky, 'Regulatory Competition and Environmental Enforcement: Is There a Race to the Bottom?' (2007) 51 *American Journal of Political Science* 853–72. Also N.D. Woods, 'Interstate Competition and Environmental Regulation' (2006) 86 *Social Science Quarterly* 792–811; A. Prakash and M. Potoski, 'Racing to the Bottom? Trade, Environmental Governance, and ISO 14001' (2006) 50 *American Journal of Political Science* 350–64.

[31] J. Braithwaite and P. Drahos, *Global Business Regulation* (Oxford, 2000), chs. 21, 24.

[32] C. Radaelli, 'The Puzzle of Regulatory Competition' (2004) 24 *Journal of Public Policy* 1–23. When considering investment decisions and the business friendliness of different jurisdictions, it should be noted that the costs of regulatory compliance may only be a limited factor in decisions about investment locations—see Vogel, *Trading Up*, 142.

debates regarding the possibilities and potential of regulatory coordination. Coordination, 'joined-up regulation', or other terms are used to advocate greater harmonization of approaches. At the same time, coordination is also about controlling processes (to make them more harmonious)—and therefore inherently about political strategies. Calls for coordination are, in practice therefore, usually associated with the political desire to eliminate the perceived advantages of competing jurisdictions.[33]

Coordination can occur horizontally and vertically. Different forms of coordination can be imagined, ranging from loose interaction, an emphasis on joint professional norms among regulators, the adoption of common methodologies, to the outright formal merger of regulatory regimes. We address this particular debate in Chapters 8 and 18 in looking at regulatory mixes and multi-level governance, respectively. In such discussions, central issues are how regulatory networks can be coordinated and how different coordinating approaches can impact on outcomes. For present purposes it suffices to set out two key arguments in favour of coordination.

The first argument stresses the importance of cross-sectoral or cross-jurisdictional overlap. For example, some 'bads' or regulatory concerns are of a trans-boundary or cross-sectoral nature and require a regulatory approach that addresses the cross-boundary aspect of this particular problem. For example, pollution often calls for cross-jurisdictional regulation, since it can be externalized across boundaries (as when one country's poorly regulated factory pollutes the air that drifts into another country). Similarly, industries sometimes demand reduced compliance costs through a harmonized regulatory approach when operating in a different or even the same market. For example, if industries are increasingly operating both in electricity and gas retail markets and when there is a degree of substitution between these two goods, an argument can be made that regulators should take a unified approach to these goods as they are competing in the same market. A similar argument has been made in the context of converging communications regulators. Here the argument has been that as telecommunications, broadcasting, and other forms of communications can no longer be seen as separate industries, this requires a regulatory merger to reflect a converging market. Cross-sectoral approaches to regulation through the merger of separate regulators can also be advocated in terms of organizational cost and resources. Especially in those contexts where regulatory staff resources are thinly spread, it makes sense to concentrate resources in one regulatory body, thereby concentrating expertise and encouraging consistency of regulatory approach at the same time.

---

[33] S. Gadinis, 'The Politics of Competition in International FInancial Regulation' (2008) 49 *Harvard International Law Journal* 447–508.

The second argument in favour of coordination points to the potential costs of a lack of coordination. Most of these suggested costs relate to the debate on regulatory competition and the possibility of a 'race to the bottom' and its impact on fairness. As noted in the context of the EU, member states have been careful to protect themselves against 'racing' by agreeing on minimal standards, even though, at times, these take on the character of lowest-common-denominator bargaining. Similarly, coordination is advocated in the face of explicit industry gaming, such as when industries strategically exploit regulatory and other (such as tax) loopholes by shifting particular activities across different jurisdictions.

Whatever the potential advantages of regulatory coordination, any attempt to achieve regulatory coordination is neither problem-free nor cost-free. Regulatory bureaucracies, like all bureaucracies, are keen to protect their own turf. Different professions have different views on what is important and how to deal with particular problems. Industry too may resist coordination if this decreases their opportunities to exploit fragmented regulatory regimes. Indeed, how many resources should be placed into achieving coordination depends on fundamental questions regarding the extent of coordination sought to be achieved. The less tolerant we are of diversity, the more resources will have to be spent on information-gathering and behaviour-modification. Indeed, considerable effort and cost will have to go into agreeing the detailed standards supposedly guiding the regulatee's behaviour. Compromise, especially when conducted between jurisdictions, is more likely to lead to somewhat looser agreements, unless powerful interests offer considerable side-payments.

Conclusion

Regulation is a key part of any country's or region's competitiveness. How regulators go about their business, what kind of standards they set, and how they interact with regulatees matters fundamentally. The idea of regulatory competition is, therefore, powerful and relevant. Pressures to compete and to coordinate approaches are imposed on regulators at the sectoral, domestic, and international levels. The extent to which regulatory competition in the form of Tiebout-type processes is feasible, and to what extent it is desirable, depends on a number of factors. Coordination similarly can be both of a beneficial and of a detrimental nature. In this chapter we have emphasized the importance of understanding the heuristic value of the Tiebout-model for encouraging debates about regulatory competition and its desirability. We have also sought to highlight the limited extent to which regulatory competition has led to straightforward empirical trends. More fundamentally, the extent to which regulatory competition is regarded as a potentially benevolent or, more likely, malevolent force depends on whether we regard markets as inherently problem-solving. The above discussion of process and product standards suggests that we should be observing different kinds of effects across different regulatory standards and regimes.

Part V
Regulation at Different Levels of Government

18 Multi-level Regulation

A claim that has dominated institutional debates over the past decades has been the assertion that we are living in an age of the regulatory state.[1] The rise of this regulatory state is said to have taken place amidst an internationalization of markets and problems, an increased complexity of technical knowledge, and a supposed globalization of communications and social action.[2] All of these factors put pressures on states to respond, and one of these responses has been to question the level of government that offers the best location for regulation. This chapter, together with the following five chapters, is concerned with different aspects of this internationalization of regulation and markets.[3]

Attempts at international regulation can be seen, in many instances, as efforts to contain the effects of a 'deterritorialized' economy in which internationalized markets challenge domestic governments' abilities to impose certain standards. The resulting internationalization of regulation frequently produces a plurality of regulatory regimes, often based on different norms, with the potential option of actors being able to 'regime-shop' and where contestation extends to conflicts over what norms are applicable in any particular context.

Debates about the appropriate governmental level of regulation also relate to discussions of regulatory style. Thus, when regulatory authority is dispersed across different actors and levels of government, hierarchical types of regulation are said to face inherent limitations, leading to a greater emphasis on modes of regulation that stress bargaining and deliberation. This raises the issue of regulatory 'networks'—regimes that involve numbers of regulators who impact concurrently on an issue or domain. These regulators may be spread both horizontally and vertically across jurisdictions and they may (or may not) seek to coordinate their efforts in different ways. The practice of

---

[1] G. Majone, 'The Rise of the Regulatory State in Europe' (1994) 14(3) *West European Politics* 77–101; G. Majone, 'From the Positive to the Regulatory State' (1997) 17 *Journal of Public Policy* 139–67.

[2] L. Hooghe and G. Marks, 'Unraveling the Central State, But How?' (2003) 97(2) *American Political Science Review* 233–43.

[3] This chapter therefore does not consider wider debates, such as the nature of the state and regulation in changing contexts of the international economy, such as those interested in 'regulatory capitalism' (J. Braithwaite, *Regulatory Capitalism* (Cheltenham, 2008); D. Levi-Faur, 'Varieties of Regulatory Capitalism' (2006) 19(3) *Governance* 497–525) or those interested in the 'competition state' (P. Cerny, 'Paradoxes of the Competition State' (1997) 32(2) *Government and Opposition* 251–74). Ideas regarding the rise of the 'competition state' and the 'regulatory state' emerged in parallel in the 1990s, the former emphasizing more the ways in which politics supported particular industrial or financial domains as part of neo-liberal economic reforms.

regulating through networks raises a host of issues, and these are returned to in the next chapter.

This chapter focuses on three concerns and also introduces key themes that shape the chapters that follow. The first concern relates to the contextual conditions that are said to have given rise to the regulatory state at various levels of government, and particularly within the European Union. The second centres on debates about the levels of government at which it is best to regulate and on questions of institutional design. The third and final part of this chapter contrasts different accounts of the ways in which regulatory ideas are adopted within a multi-level governance setting.

The Rise of the Regulatory State

The claim that the past three decades have witnessed a rise of the regulatory state was initially formulated in the context of the European Union.[4] Since then, the debate has been extended to encompass other jurisdictions and levels, such as the national and the global levels of regulation, more generally.[5] The posited rise of the regulatory state is associated with an emphasis on three developments. The first concerns institutional characteristics. Here, broad consensus exists that the regulatory state combines three key elements: a split between provision and production (with production often being privatized), a reliance on non-majoritarian regulatory bodies, and a formalization of relationships across actors in the regulated domain.[6]

Moving beyond an interest in institutional rearrangements is the second development: the assertion of a shift in the wider objectives of the state. The notion here is that, following an exhaustion of resources for achieving equity through redistribution and the direct production of economic and social services, there has been a move towards emphasizing the importance of efficiency and the control of the service-providing activities of third parties.

A third related development sees the rise of the regulatory state as a by-product of the growing Europeanization, if not the internationalization of markets.[7] The dynamic of this 'rise' of the regulatory state at the European

---

[4] Majone, 'The Rise of the Regulatory State in Europe'.

[5] Ibid.

[6] Ibid.; M. Loughlin and C. Scott, 'The Regulatory State' in P. Dunleavy, A. Gamble, I. Holliday, and G. Peele (eds.), *Developments in British Politics 5* (Basingstoke, 1997). Lodge and Stirton suggest that the regulatory state label hides significant difference, see M. Lodge and L. Stirton, 'Withering in the Heat? In Search of the Regulatory State in the Commonwealth Caribbean' (2006) 19(3) *Governance* 465–95.

[7] The regulatory state in the context of the European Union is explored in more detail in the following two chapters.

level follows a 'demand' and 'supply' logic. On the demand side, national states respond to the increasing internationalization of markets and to uncertainty about technical and scientific knowledge, by demanding rules that regulate market exchange across boundaries.[8] They, therefore, push for cross-border rules that govern transactions. National states are thus said to have reacted to an exhaustion in their capacity to steer national economies through ownership and redistribution. They have therefore, to a considerable extent, lost boundary control over their own national markets in the wake of international and European-wide markets and agreements. In particular, as will be noted in Chapter 21, the idea of mutual recognition is said to have reduced the ability of national states to control their own economic markets significantly.[9] On the supply side, there are international actors, such as the European Commission, that 'supply' regulatory solutions to the problems of transacting across boundaries. In addition, international actors (and regimes) provide for supposedly neutral refereeing roles in case of conflict.

The rise of regulatory regimes at the supranational level and beyond the level of the national or the intergovernmental can thus be seen as rooted in the need of national states to deal with the complexities of integrating market economies. In addition, in a world in which public services and critical infrastructures are privatized, the regulation of international providers of public services has become a growing international concern, and international providers have pressed for the harmonization of regulatory approaches in order to reduce their compliance costs. These pressures have further raised demands for 'transnational' solutions for international economies—at the same time, the activities of these transnational providers of public services has become part of the regulatory expertise that is shaping the evolution of multi-level regulatory states itself.

Equally, the search for international regulation not only reflects the perceived powerlessness of national regulatory approaches to shape market behaviour, but also the practice of attempting to 'export' regulatory approaches and make them binding on other jurisdictions—a step that is calculated to produce a competitive advantage.

At the national level, the response to these pressures of internationalization has been a shift towards governing through the regulation of private providers and an emphasis on efficiency. Relying on regulating private providers makes the penalty of regulating 'badly' more stark: private investors will invest in response to assumptions about the stability and predictability of regulatory

---

[8] N. Fligstein and A. Sweet Stone, 'Constructing Markets and Politics' (2002) 107 *American Journal of Sociology* 1206–43.

[9] F.W. Scharpf, 'Negative and Positive Integration in the Political Economy of European Welfare States' in G. Marks et al. (eds), *Governance in the European Union* (London, 1996); S. Schmidt, *Liberalisierung in Europe* (Frankfurt, 1998).

regimes. As has been explored when looking at theories of regulation in Chapter 4, ideas focusing on 'credible commitment'—the assurance by a state that regulatory goalposts will not be moved—have become particularly prominent in the contemporary context of regulation.[10] If national governments require international private parties to invest into their infrastructures, then regulation becomes the frontier not just of conflicts over approaches and instruments, but also over power relationships. As Levy and Spiller have noted, credible commitment is essential to attract investor confidence: investment levels, and as a result development, depend on 'regulatory risk', and this 'regulatory risk' (i.e. the availability of discretion to regulators) can be, to some extent, dealt with through institutional design.[11]

If, therefore, credible commitment has become a critical issue for national states, this also has implications for regulatory design—both at the national and other levels. At the national level, one response to demands for 'credible commitment' has been the creation of 'non-majoritarian regulatory institutions'— bodies that are outside the electoral politics of liberal democracy and that are supposedly 'depoliticized', because their decision-making supposedly does not follow immediate electoral considerations.[12] In addition, free-standing and 'focused' bodies provide for expertise and specialization in contrast to previous ages that were supposedly characterized by oversight through ministerial bureaucracies.

In short, the rise of bodies that are solely concerned with 'regulation', and supposedly taken out of the processes of explicitly political decision-making, is one institutional manifestation of this rise of the regulatory state. This is a development that has been witnessed across various levels of government.

The fragmentation of regulatory authority carries, in addition, implications for styles of decision-making. Growing institutional fragmentation has put a premium on formalized and explicit rules that govern decision-making, and this trend has been encouraged by a growing social heterogenization and internationalization of economic actors, along with a broader reliance on formal contracts to structure relationships between actors.[13] Moran has drawn on wider ideas regarding 'relational distance' to argue that, as national economic and political elites have become increasingly heterogenous, because of population mobility and internationalized economies, systems that previously relied on

---

[10] B. Levy and B. Spiller, 'The Institutional Foundations of Regulatory Commitment' (1994) 10 *Journal of Law, Economics and Organisation* 201–4; A. Estache and L. Wren-Lewis, 'On the Theory and Evidence on Regulation of Network Industries in Development Countries' in R. Baldwin, M. Cave, and M. Lodge (eds), *Oxford Handbook of Regulation* (Oxford, 2010).

[11] Levy and Spiller, 'Institutional Foundations'.

[12] M. Thatcher and A. Sweet Stone, 'Theory and Practice of Delegation to Non-Majoritarian Institutions' (2002) 25(1) *West European Politics* 1–22.

[13] The idea of formalized (i.e. contractualized) relationships applies in particular to the relationship between freestanding regulatory bodies overseeing privately provided public services.

control by informal relations were required increasingly to 'write things down' and to formalize rules.[14]

As with all contracts, however, attempts at formalizing regulatory relationships tend to be afflicted with the problem of 'incomplete contracts'. Any formal relationship requires informal understandings in order to deal with under- and overlaps as well as 'surprises'. As a result, the multi-level character of the regulatory state has gone hand-in-hand with both a greater emphasis on formalized relationships *and* an emphasis on fora for deliberation, but these fora for informal deliberation and emerging understandings are framed through the language and priorities of the instruments and values of the regulatory state.

The rise of the regulatory state is therefore not just about changing national policy preferences and institutional rearrangements. It also involves the seeking of regulatory solutions in a market and political context that places a greater premium on getting regulation 'right'. This supposed age of the regulatory state is characterized by fragmentation not just within national states and across sectoral regimes, but also 'upwards' at the regional and international level. A fragmentation of regulatory authority, apart from raising issues regarding the politics of 'who regulates what', also points to the diverse legitimacy concerns that have been discussed in Chapter 16. Understanding the rise of the regulatory state as a phenomenon that occurs across different levels of government raises issues regarding the level of government at which it is appropriate to place a given scheme of regulation. We now focus on this particular discussion.

Choosing Levels of Government

Identifying the level of government at which it is appropriate to locate regulatory authority is an issue that has been shaped by considerations drawing on a range of literatures that explore the appropriate territorial composition of states and issues of fiscal federalism.[15] Those literatures can be separated into different strands. One discussion centres on issues of market failure, another on concerns about the effects of regulatory competition

---

[14] M. Moran, *The Regulatory State in Britain* (Oxford, 2003); D. Black, *The Behavior of Law* (New York, 1976); D. Black, 'Compensation and the Social Structure of Misfortune' (1987) 21(4) *Law and Society Review* 563–84.

[15] W.E. Oates, 'An Essay on Fiscal Federalism' (1999) 37 *Journal of Economic Literature* 1120–49; W.E. Oates, *Fiscal Federalism* (New York, 1972); R.M. Musgrave, *The Theory of Public Finance* (New York, 1959); G. Brennan and J. Buchanan, *The Power to Tax* (Cambridge, 1980); A. Schakel, 'Explaining Regional and Local Government' (2010) 23(2) *Governance* 331–55.

(explored in Chapter 17) and another involves wider debates on the appropriate design of political systems. This section explores these literatures in turn.

Arguments that focus on questions of market failure consider how the negative and positive externalities of any activity should be regulated at a level where they can most effectively be dealt with. It can be contended, for example, that actions to combat air pollution need to be sited at a different level of government than hunting laws because the negative externalities caused by hunting do not extend beyond the immediate vicinity of a particular hunt. Equally, the allegedly positive externalities of hunting (such as the fostering of dog-breeding skills) are limited to particular areas. In contrast, the problems of air pollution (such as that of 'acid rain') or climate change are clearly transboundary in nature[16] and require some degree of intergovernmental, if not international cooperation. Equally, regulatory function may be allocated according to *scale* required.

Such an account's stressing of functional optimalities may have some prescriptive mileage but it has descriptive limitations. One potential difficulty is empirical. Numerous examples exist where the same problem is regulated at different governmental levels in different contexts. For instance, the regulatory definition of a 'dangerous' dog is formulated at the national level in the UK and France, at the *Land* (state) level in Germany and (mostly) at the county level in the United States. This suggests that functional responses to 'externalities' have only a limited mileage in explaining the governmental levels at which regulatory activities are placed.[17] More explanatory force is often to be found by looking at the relevant constitutional-institutional framework (i.e. the decision-rule system) that defines political decision-making. As has been noted in other contexts, decision-making rules matter: if we rely on extra-large majorities to agree on changing jurisdictional competency for regulatory authority, this will not just reduce the possibility of agreement in the first place, but it will also make any reversal of an initial decision more difficult (and more costly).[18]

A further point to make in describing why regulation is placed at a certain governmental level is that any decision-making process may be shaped by the

---

[16] A. Boin, 'The New World of Crises and Crisis Management' (2009) 26(4) *Review of Policy Research* 367–77.

[17] Of course, the counter-argument to this objection would be that externalities differ across context, i.e. the appropriate level of government should vary across states, taking into account issues of population density and, more importantly, size.

[18] Fritz Scharpf has described how the 'joint decision trap' led to inefficiencies in the European Union's Common Agricultural Policy; similar in the context of German federalism, the idea of *Politikverflechtungsfalle* (Scharpf's older German term for joint-decision trap) suggests the inherent problems of achieving reform in a system characterized by negotiation, bargaining, and veto-powers. See F.W. Scharpf, 'The Joint-Decision Trap: Lessons from German Federalism and European Integration' (1988) 66(3) *Public Administration* 239–78.

default position: whether, for example, the 'normal' level of regulatory activity is seen to be the local or the national level. Such choices matter, since they define issues of control and delegation: whether the 'national' level is 'delegating' authority for regulation to the local/sub-national level, or whether sub-national entities are delegating regulatory authority 'upwards'.[19] Finally, decisions as to where regulatory functions are allocated are also said to reflect societal consensus over particular issues; in other words, the more heterogeneous a population, the more decentralized regulatory functions should be to be responsive to diverse demands.

Related debates suggest that multi-level regulation can be understood as a response to the dynamics of regulatory competition. As noted in Chapter 17, the idea of 'regulatory competition' has been shaped by ideas concerning 'voting with one's feet'—notably the suggestion that regulatory competition allows economic actors to move to those locations that offer the 'right' combination of economic benefits and regulatory 'burdens'.[20] Multi-level regulation may, therefore, be regarded as a response to the fear of a 'race to the bottom': if jurisdictions are able to compete on regulatory regime characteristics, then governments may anticipate that economic actors will move to those 'low-regulation' jurisdictions, and they may fear that this will create widespread pressures for competing jurisdictions to lower their regulatory standards. Multi-level regulation can therefore be seen as an attempt to prescribe similar regulatory standards in order to prevent such a 'race to the bottom' from occurring.[21]

Debates about multi-level regulation do not, however, focus exclusively on the challenges of establishing the appropriate level at which regulatory functions should be carried out. A far more basic concern in the literature is that regulatory activity may be inherently multi-level.[22] Far from being concentrated within one agency, many regulatory regimes, especially in the environmental area, are spread across governmental levels with standard-setting occurring at the international or supranational level, behaviour-modification occurring at the local level, and information-gathering at the national or

---

[19] An associated normative issue—and one that relates to debates raised earlier in this volume—is more a matter of participation than level of government as such: to what extent should international regulatory regimes be negotiated and operated between governments, to what extent should they be exposed to external scrutiny (and by whom), and/or to what extent can such regimes rely on private parties.

[20] See the 'voting with your feet' account by Tiebout, as noted in Chapter 17. As noted there, in the original formulation this process was defined as a 'bundle' of taxes and services in which local governments were defined as 'club goods'.

[21] As noted in Chapter 17, regulatory competition may also be characterized by 'races to the top', especially if large economic markets are able to set the agenda for higher regulatory standards. As noted too, such debates reflect broader debates as to whether markets operate as 'prisons' in which mobile production factors dominate processes of regulatory standard-setting or whether the encouragement of markets reduces the likelihood of 'government failure', namely the incurrence of high opportunity costs through regulatory activity that outweighs intended benefits.

[22] R. Rodrigo, L. Allio, and P. Andres-Amo, 'Multi-level Regulatory Governance' (2009) 13 *OECD Working Papers on Public Governance*.

regional level.[23] Discussions of multi-level regulation are thus concerned not merely to locate any particular domain at any particular plane of government, but to understanding the way that a given domain's regulatory regime is being shaped by multi-level dynamics themselves.

A particular issue arises where there is significant reliance on local regulatory enforcement. Different countries face considerable difficulties in enforcing a harmonized regulatory approach from the centre, given different constitutional contexts. A key question here is how ideas regarding so-called High Quality Regulation can be advanced downwards, upwards, and sideways.[24]

The fragmentation of regulatory activities across different levels may raise further questions for explanation: 'Can the shifting of regulatory authority upwards (for standard-setting) and downwards (for behaviour modification) be accounted for by functional, market-failure arguments, or by political (notably blame avoidance) motives?'[25] More broadly, the nature of regulatory competition is said to be shaped by differences between process- and product-regulation.[26] All of these aspects are relevant to debates about the appropriate levels of regulation, as well as regarding the type of regime we might be able to expect. For example, if regulatory competition is said to lead to an undesirable 'race to the bottom' that undermines welfare standards, then regulatory standards need to be set in a manner that undercuts the possibilities for various jurisdictions to engage in such competitive behaviour. Whether such a race can be prevented, however, depends on power-relations and decision-making rules between the different affected jurisdictions, as well as the ability to compensate potential losers from prescribing regulatory regimes.

Debates that point to the importance of market failures and regulatory competition in determining the optimal allocation of regulatory authority across levels of government ultimately involve competing views on the 'appropriate' state of the world. It is, therefore, unlikely that there will ever be agreement on the level of government at which any particular regulatory activity should be located. Rather, we should expect that multi-level regulation is inherently as contested as other areas of regulation discussed in this volume. Without claiming an exhaustive or mutually exclusive set of approaches, we

---

[23] C. Hood, H. Rothstein, and R. Baldwin, *The Government of Risk* (Oxford, 2001); C. Scott, 'Standard-Setting in Regulatory Regimes', in R. Baldwin, M. Cave, and M. Lodge (eds), *Oxford Handbook of Regulation* (Oxford, 2010); M. Atlas, 'Enforcement Principles and Environmental Agencies' (2007) 41(4) *Law and Society Review* 939–80; D.L. Weimer, 'The Puzzle of Private Rulemaking' (2006) 66(4) *Public Administration Review* 569–82; M. Lodge and K. Wegrich, 'Governing Multi-level Governance: Comparing Domain Dynamics in German Land–Local Relationships and Prisons' (2005) 83(2) *Public Administration* 417–42.

[24] Rodrigo, Allio, and Andres-Amo, 'Multi-level Regulatory Governance'; M. Lodge and K. Wegrich, 'High Quality Regulation: Its Popularity, its Tools and its Future' (2009) 29(3) *Public Money and Management* 145–52.

[25] C. Hood, 'The Risk Game and the Blame Game' (2002) 37(1) *Government and Opposition* 15–37.

[26] Scharpf, 'Negative and Positive Integration'.

AD HOC	QUASI-FEDERAL
Multi-level regulation as a process shaped by ad hoc responses. No overall consistency.	Multi-level regulation as a (quasi-) federal order.
POLYCENTRIC	DELIBERATIVE
Multi-level regulation as polycentricity: allows for discovery processes.	Multi-level regulation as a process encouraging deliberation and participation.

Figure 18.1. Four views on multi-level regulation

can distinguish between four different views of 'multi-level regulation'. Figure 18.1 provides an overview of these approaches.

The 'quasi-federal' perspective would suggest that regulation should be allocated across levels of government according to particular decision-rules, with supranational/international problems being dealt with at the international level. The problem here, of course, is that of establishing a consensus on the level of regulation that is appropriate and any account must explore the importance of the dynamics within the differentiated federal order. Accordingly, this perspective on the 'regulatory location' debate would tend to favour a stable distribution of regulatory authority and hierarchy that involves a strong role for international regimes in addressing trans-boundary problems and in making regulatory allocations to national and sub-national regimes. Such a position would, therefore, take seriously the dangers of regulatory standards being undermined through processes of regulatory competition and it would address these potential threats through the reallocation of regulatory authorities across levels of government.

From the 'polycentricity' perspective, decentralization is inherently more desirable than 'large-scale organization'. This perspective emphasizes the benefits of market-type processes that are created through regulatory competition.[27] Regulatory authority, on this view, should remain at the lowest level of authority possible, and the overall picture of regulatory activity would be one of diversity: with different types of regimes and types of coordination devices operating side-by-side. Centrally prescribed modes of regulation would be resisted as liable to reduce both the possibilities of discovery and the potential to learn across different regulatory approaches. Different strands

---

[27] V. Ostrom, 'Polycentricity I', in M.D. McGinnis (ed.), *Polycentricity and Local Public Economies* (Ann Arbor, 1999).

of the polycentricity argument exist, though. One such strand emphasizes the importance of decentralized discovery and market-type processes. Polycentricity, therefore, is about enabling decentralized regulatory responses and adaptation, to encourage discovery processes, and about reducing the potential of market distortions. Another, very different, line of thought emphasizes the importance of *subsidiarity*. The subsidiarity principle, historically used by the Roman Catholic Church to suggest that welfare provision should start with the family before states (or other institutions) should become involved, advocates that the default position for locating regulatory functions is the lowest level possible, and higher levels of intervention should be regarded with scepticism. Finally, the contemporary literature on meta-regulation also reflects this view of polycentricity by allowing companies to regulate themselves in the light of particular principles. Advocates of meta-regulation would thus cite the beneficial prospect that its version of polycentricity would produce more flexible and better-informed compliance with particular standards than would be possible with regulation from on high.[28]

The 'deliberative' perspective stresses the capacity of multi-level regulation to deliver opportunities for increased deliberation and bargaining among actors—and to do so where participation cuts across institutional boundaries. Fragmentation relies not so much on chains of hierarchy (i.e. standards backed by sanctions), but rather on deliberation and negotiation. Deliberation and negotiation are the natural outcome of a process that relies on international standard-setting, private actor compliance and local and/or national information-gathering and behaviour modification. This approach is consistent with wider accounts that note the importance of local knowledge and responses when it comes to regulatory enforcement in particular. The implication of this viewpoint is that questions about the appropriate levels at which to regulate are of little relevance: the reality of dispersed regulatory authority transforms regulation into a process characterized by 'decentredness', namely bargaining and deliberation.[29] The key challenge therefore is to

---

[28] C. Parker, *The Open Corporation* (Cambridge, 2001); J. Braithwaite, 'Meta Risk Management and Responsive Regulation for Tax System Integrity' (2003) 25(1) *Law and Policy* 1–16; P. May, 'Performance-based Regulation and Regulatory Regimes: The Saga of Leaky Buildings' (2003) 25(4) *Law and Policy* 381–401; C. Parker, 'Regulator-Required Corporate Compliance Program Audits' (2003) 25(3) *Law and Policy* 221–44; S. Courville, 'Social Accountability Audits: Challenging or Defending Democratic Governance?' (2003) 25(3) *Law and Policy* 269–297; N. Gunningham, 'Corporate Environmental Responsibility, Law and the Limits of Voluntarism' in D. McBarnett, A.Voicelescu, and T. Campbell (eds), *The New Corporate Accountability: Corporate Social Responsibility and the Law* (Cambridge, 2007); M. Bloor, R. Datta, Y. Gilinsky, and T. Horlick-Jones, 'Unicorn among the Cedars: On the Possibility of Effective "Smart Regulation" of the globalized Shipping Industry' (2006) 15(4) *Social and Legal Studies* 534–51.

[29] In the domestic setting, the concept of regulatory space suggests that regulatory regimes have historically been fragmented, allowing for a blurring of regulatory authority between public and private actors. See L. Hancher and M. Moran, 'Organizing Regulatory Space' in L. Hancher and M. Moran (eds), *Capitalism, Culture and Economic Regulation* (Oxford, 1989).

open regulatory processes to inputs and engagement (often involving new social movements), rather than to establish new boundaries.[30]

The fourth, 'ad hoc', view of multi-level regulation regards all such debates with a degree of scepticism. Instead, it contends that multi-level regulation is characterized by ad hoc responses to particular problems and that there is not much consistency across different regimes. Instead, multi-level regulation is largely seen as a response to political demands for action (especially in times of political heat) or as a response to powerful economic or geopolitical interests. As a result, according to this view, the emerging 'order' of multi-level regulation conforms neither to the world of well-ordered federalism, nor to the world of competing decentralized regimes, nor to the world of deliberating and participatory regulatory regimes.

These four perspectives point not merely to different understandings of multi-level governance and its constitutive elements. They also offer inherently competing views as to the kind of relationships that characterize (and should characterize) relationships across different levels of government. These four perspectives therefore constitute competing logics of action: it is unlikely that deliberation can easily sit side-by-side with a logic of action that emphasizes polycentricity through market-type mechanisms.

In summary, what therefore might appear as a simple question regarding the appropriate allocation of regulatory authority turns out to be highly problematic. Analysing the degree of market failure and then allocating it to the appropriate level of government is hardly straightforward. Even if such an analysis of market failures could be conducted, it would lead to a blurred world of overlapping circles of authority with considerable overlap and complexity, rather than some well-ordered world of clearly defined constitutional spheres of regulatory authority. The world of multi-level regulation therefore easily fits into wider discussions of 'compound political orders'.[31] Such orders are characterized by competing, overlapping, and inconsistent logics of governing, and what holds for wider systems of executive government should therefore also be expected to exist for regulatory regimes.[32]

The problem of 'who regulates' becomes even more complex in the light of contests about definitions and diagnoses of market failure—which raise further issues regarding the extent of negative and positive externalities. Indeed, debates on 'who regulates' also feed into wider discussions on the most desirable ways of ordering political affairs. As the following chapters suggest, the world of multi-level regulation is not a world of straightforward choices

---

[30] J. Braithwaite and P. Drahos, *Global Business Regulation* (Cambridge, 2000).

[31] J.P. Olsen, *Europe in Search of Political Order* (Oxford, 2007).

[32] K. Orren and S. Skowronek, *The Search for American Political Development* (Cambridge, 2004); S. Skowronek, *Building a New American State* (Cambridge, 1982); M. Lodge and K. Wegrich, 'Governance as Contested Logics of Control' (2011) *Journal of European Public Policy* (18)1 90–105.

where an ideal order of 'regulatory federalism' can easily be established; instead, the dynamics of multi-level regulation are inherently contested.

Diffusion of Institutional Design and Regulatory Instruments

As noted, it has been widely suggested that we are living in an age of the regulatory state, with its emphasis on questions of efficiency and institutional design. But which factors and processes are shaping this world of multi-level regulation? Again, we can distinguish between different strands within the literature.[33]

One such approach emphasizes the importance of 'prototyping' by powerful national and international actors. In a multi-level regulation world, particular institutional devices are chosen because of their links to material and immaterial benefits. Particular institutional devices may, for example, be linked to development funds or increases in reputations that encourage outside investments. According to this view, the design of regulatory institutions and instruments is shaped by ideas of 'credible commitment' and the extent to which particular institutions are regarded as 'credible' depends on reputation and external recognition. In short, this is a world of what Paul DiMaggio and Walter Powell have called 'coercive isomorphism': national regulatory institutions increasingly resemble other regulatory institutions elsewhere by a process of resource dependency.[34] Templates emerge from a 'single source of broadcasting' and, in this process of hegemonic templates, there is little scope for deliberation, exchange, or extensive evaluation. In other words, countries will adopt particular templates (say, a regulatory agency) not because of any extensive evaluation whether such an agency is likely to cause the desired effects, but because of the demands of external actors.

In contrast to the 'prototyping' account, other approaches note the roles of deliberations and negotiations in bringing about important changes. In an age of high uncertainty, national states are said to search for 'solutions' either bilaterally or through international fora. Karen Sahlin-Andersson, for example,

---

[33] One further strain would suggest that multi-level regulation increases the competitive pressures on regulatory regimes to adjust. Given factor mobility and visibility of regulatory approaches, knowledge diffuses rapidly and leads to adjustment. As we explored in Chapter 17 (Regulatory Competition), the assumptions of such a model are highly restrictive and the implications for the world of regulation at best limited. We therefore concentrate on three strains emphasized in the institutionalist literature.

[34] P. DiMaggio and W. Powell, 'The "Iron Cage Revisited": Institutional Isomorphism and Collective Rationality in Organizational Fields' in P. DiMaggio and W. Powell (eds), *The New Institutionalism in Organizational Analysis* (Chicago, 1991).

has noted how such processes of institutional diffusion progress through a process of selective editing.[35] First, 'lessons' from particular contexts are edited by those who have gone through the particular exercise, in order to provide for generalized knowledge. Such generalized knowledge about any particular 'lesson' may of course already suppress important contextual or other information critical for the success (or failure) of any particular intervention. In a second stage, these 'lessons' are edited by those who seek to 'import' templates into their own context. Again, such processes are defined by selective and deliberate editing, taking note not just of the power-relationships within the important jurisdiction, but also seeking to address particular local issues. This is a process of mimicry, in which lessons are drawn from cases that *appear* legitimate and successful and it is characterized by considerable selectivity. Given limited resources for extensive searches, select experiences are being sought, and these experiences do not just arrive in an edited version, but they are further edited in their application. In other words, multi-level regulation is about the transfer of ideas regarding regulation and its design, and it is a process that is marked by significant filtering, distortion, and bias.[36]

A third noted mechanism of communication within this world of multi-level regulation is seen to be constituted by professional communities, or what are often called 'epistemic communities'. Multi-level regulation, on this view, is shaped by professional conversations, often at the international level, and between 'experts'. These settings are not just about exchanging knowledge, they are about rules of inclusion and exclusion. Indeed, it is likely that such fora develop their own specific understandings about 'cause and effect' and about the right way to deal with regulatory problems. For example, it is often said that the various groups working as part of OECD review processes constitute 'communities' with particular views about the 'right' way of regulating (or budgeting, for that matter). These communities do not just build on their supposed legitimacy as 'professional experts', they are also crucial in using international benchmarking exercises for legitimizing national reforms and in putting forward their favourite solutions. In short, professional networks shape reforms at multiple levels of regulation as the same actors appear in different settings and advocate particular reform proposals.

This suggests that multi-level regulation is not a process that is 'open' in the sense that it allows for exchanges of competing ideas regarding regulation and the adoption of some of these in a process of contestation. Rather, this is a process in which dominant networks of actors, in different degrees of resource

---

[35] K. Sahlin-Andersson, 'National, International, and Transnational Constructions of New Public Management', in T. Christensen and P. Lægreid (eds), *New Public Management: The Transformation of Ideas and Practice* (Aldershot, 2002).

[36] R. Laughlin, 'Environmental Disturbance and Organizational Transitions and Transformations: Some Alternative Models' (1991) 12(2) *Organizational Studies* 209–32.

dependency to each other, communicate. Such networks are held together by resource dependency *and* by shared beliefs and knowledge.[37] According to this mode of analysis, validity of knowledge is found to be in tension with reliability of knowledge. This means that contradictory evidence will be excluded to sustain the view that preferred options are indeed superior. The spread and diffusion of regulation institutions and instruments in the context of multi-level regulation does not, accordingly, approximate to a market-type competitive process in which the 'fittest survive'; it is about processing and communicating information selectively and it is about different power relationships.

Conclusion

Empirically one does not have to look far for examples of multi-level regulation. Most domestic regulatory regimes rely on different levels of government for standard-setting, behaviour-modification, and information-gathering. To state that regulation is multi-level is, therefore, hardly novel or exciting. However, what is new and somewhat exciting nowadays is the placing of regulatory activities at increasingly numerous layers of government. Such shifting of levels, upwards (to the supranational and international), downwards (to the regional and local) and sideways (to specialized agencies and away from ministerial departments) is at the heart of debates regarding 'who regulates' and how.

This chapter has dealt with three concerns that also inform the chapters that follow. First, it has considered the developments that are said to have led to the 'regulatory state'. Ideas of the regulatory state are said to have become prominent across levels of government as there has been a shift in government preferences (from equity to efficiency). Part of this development has been a fragmentation of government activities, upwards, downwards, as well as sideways. Second, we have argued that debates on multi-level regulation have, at their heart, competing ideas regarding the 'best order' for the solution of particular problems. Third, the above discussion has pointed to the mechanisms that are said to have caused and characterize the world of multi-level regulation.

The following chapters go into greater depth on various aspects of these issues. It is, however, important to summarize the context in which contemporary multi-level regulation is encountered. It takes place in a world that is more complex and internationalized than ever before. This implies that

---

[37] J.S. March, L.S. Sproull, and M. Tamuz, 'Learning from Samples of One or Fewer' (1991) 2(1) *Organizational Science* 1–13.

markets are international, technologies are complex, government budgets are generally depleted (and therefore reliant on private investment), and national governments are faced with the considerable power of few select international commercial interests. It also means that regulatory activities in one jurisdiction are likely to have an impact on others. Complexity tends to require specialization in regulatory activities, and this, therefore, encourages the rise of free-standing bodies tasked with 'regulation'. Furthermore, in a world of international and mobile private investment, the quality of domestic regulation is said to have become increasingly important for attracting investment and therefore economic growth and development.

The issues raised by the growth of multi-level regulation, as a result, are integral to debates regarding the regulatory state, and the ways in which different aspects of this multi-level system communicate. As noted, there are considerable differences in the characterizations and definitions of these communication patterns, and different domains and jurisdictions are likely to display differentiated patterns. Furthermore, debates about multi-level regulation and 'who regulates' point to more far-reaching conversations about regulatory jurisdiction, they go to the heart of statehood and what we regard as 'natural order' for regulating economic and social affairs. Indeed, these discussions also raise the wider question whether we should expect converged, divergent, or 'mixed' patterns in the trajectories of regulatory reform across states and domains. The debate about multi-level regulation thus offers further reinforcement to the argument that regulation, far from offering a world of depoliticized 'regularization', continues to be at the heart of politics.

19 Regulation and the European Union

The Rise of the Regulatory State in Europe

It is difficult to overstate the importance of the EU to the regulatory dynamics of its member states.[1] Few domestic regulatory regimes have remained unaffected by developments at the European level, although the extent to which national regulation is dominated by EU provisions has remained a matter of debate. What has emerged at the European level is a specific kind of 'regulatory state' that is marked by variations in the dynamics of different regulatory processes, an increasing resort to networks, and an intermeshing of EU and national considerations. The combination of two trends has accentuated fragmentation and encouraged the development of coordinating devices that are designed to engage national regulatory authorities. The first of these trends is a growing EU-level involvement in regulatory activities. The other trend, at the national level, has been towards separating regulatory activities from other executive functions. The European Union has also developed an extensive interest in the use of policies, institutions, and tools to encourage 'better regulation'.[2] The latter include the use of impact assessments and administrative simplification measures.

Even for those not specifically interested in EU-developments, the European Union regulatory state offers an example of key questions that are at the heart of any debate regarding multi-level regulation. These questions include how 'racing' between different jurisdictions can be avoided, how regulation provides for a coordinating function, how different understandings regarding regulatory approaches travel across national jurisdictions that have lost their boundary control when it comes to their economic sovereignty, and how activities can be legitimated in a process marked by efficiency-related

---

[1] This chapter concentrates on some key regulatory debates that involve the European Union and which offer insight into mechanisms and effects of regulation in a multi-level system. It cannot cover the immense literature that has evolved on the European Union's political and legal system, especially debates more normally reserved for EU administrative law discussions. See instead: D. Chalmers et al., *European Union Law* (2nd edn, Cambridge, 2010).

[2] See generally S. Weatherill (ed.), *Better Regulation* (Oxford, 2007); R. Baldwin, 'Better Regulation: The Search and the Struggle', in R. Baldwin, M. Cave, and M. Lodge (eds), *The Oxford Handbook on Regulation* (Oxford, 2010).

argumentation and an emphasis on procedural as well as output-based forms of accountability.

As noted, it has been suggested that the past three decades have witnessed a rise of a regulatory state at the level of the European Union. According to Majone, this process was driven by the demands of member states and transnational firms to establish common rules of exchange and by the supply of regulatory proposals from the European Commission.[3] This largely functional account suggests that changing markets force states to adjust their regulatory structures. At the same time, it is in the self-interest of the European Commission to rely on regulation to maximize its influence over policy content, given the absence of other means of turf expansion (i.e. the use of budgets). Alternative accounts regarding the emergence of the European regulatory state place their emphasis on the supranational forces that drive European integration—and therefore growing regulatory activity. In contrast is the emergence of European regulatory activity seen as part of an intergovernmental bargaining game. According to that perspective, the degree and extent of regulatory jurisdiction is a matter not just of the formal powers of supranational institutions, such as the European Commission in conjunction with the European Parliament and the European Court of Justice. Instead, the degree to which European government develops an extensive reach into national regulatory policies also depends on the degree of political 'acceptance' by member states and the degree to which regulatory proposals at the EU level meet relatively similar national regulatory structures. It follows that the more diverse national regulatory regimes are, the less likely it is that we will observe uniform and extensive EU regulatory provisions.

Much has also been said about the traditional 'Community' method by which the European Commission has legislated as part of its role in the 'EU regulatory state'. This 'Community method' has been defined by key characteristics: exclusive competence for making policy and proposing legislation lies with the Commission; these proposals are filtered and adopted by the legislative machinery of the Council of Ministers and the European Parliament (using different legislative processes depending on the legal basis), while the European Court of Justice monitors the respect of the rule of law; the European Commission monitors member state compliance and can use administrative and judicial infringement proceedings where transposition

---

[3] G. Majone, 'The Rise of the Regulatory State in Europe' (1994) 14(3) *West European Politics* 77–101; M. Lodge, 'Regulation, the Regulatory State and European Politics' (2008) 31(1/2) *West European Politics* 280–301; K. Armstrong and S. Bulmer, *Governance of the Single Market* (Manchester, 1998); M. Egan, *Constructing a European Market* (Oxford, 2001); H. Majone, *Dilemmas of European Integration* (Oxford, 2005); N. Jabko, *Playing the Market* (Ithaka, 2006); N. Fligstein, *Euro-Clash* (Oxford, 2008); N. Fligstein and I. Mara-Drita, 'How to Make a Market: Reflections on the Attempt to Create a Single Market in the European Union' (1996) 102(1) *American Journal of Sociology* 1–33; F.W. Scharpf, 'The European Social Model' (2002) 40(4) *Journal of Common Market Studies* 645–70.

and implementation fall short. Since the late 1990s, the centrality of the 'Community method' has become increasingly overshadowed by the concerns with 'governance' and the use of 'soft law' to deal with its increasingly perceived limitations.

This chapter considers the specific regulatory characteristics of the European Union regulatory state, in particular as it applies to key aspects of the internal market.[4] It starts with an account of the different techniques or modes of regulating, and then moves to the infrastructure of the European regulatory state, namely the emergence of agencies and their interaction with national agencies. Finally, it discusses the differential effect of the European Union on member-state regulation.

Modes of Regulating

At its most basic (and formal), EU legislation distinguishes between different types of requirement[5] (focusing here on those measures that constitute a legal obligation):

- Regulations[6] are the most centralizing of all instruments and are utilized to ensure uniformity; they therefore have general application and direct applicability. They enter into force after a specified date (as stated or 20 days following publication in the Official Journal[7]), and are therefore automatically incorporated into the domestic legal order of member states. No transposition is necessary (although in some cases national implementing measures will be required).
- Directives are binding as to the results to be achieved. They leave, however, member states some discretion as to the form and methods used to transpose its obligations (within set deadlines for transposition).
- Decisions are binding upon those to whom they are addressed and require the addressee to be notified of any decision. These Decisions are usually addressed to member states, rather than private parties, apart from the area of competition law. Decisions also exist that have no direct addressee—and in these cases too, the intention is that they should be binding on the Union as an entity (and therefore also on its member states).

---

[4] Single Market measures have to facilitate the functioning of the internal market itself (by facilitating trade or reducing internal barriers). They cannot be used to regulate all aspects of economic life (see 'Tobacco Advertising' case, *Germany* v. *Parliament and Council* [2000] ECR I-8419.

[5] Art. 288, 2008/C 115/01.

[6] In this chapter, 'Regulation' is used to signify this particular EU legal instrument, whereas 'regulation' is used in the wider sense as applied throughout this volume.

[7] Art. 297.

In addition, so-called Framework Decisions are binding on member states as to the results to be achieved, but providing them with discretion as to the form and methods of implementation.[8] The diversity of legal instruments is further confused by the absence of any clear order or structure; one instrument does not appear superior to the other. Instead, Regulations can be found that appear similar to Directives, and equally, Directives exist that have all the characteristics of Regulations in that they considerably constrain member state discretion. Indeed, Decisions are encountered with no addressee and, therefore, display the same characteristics as Directives.[9]

The 2000s, it has been argued, evidence a growing emergence of 'soft law', in particular through use of the so-called 'open method of coordination' (OMC).[10] Starting in the late 1990s with employment policy (an OMC *avant la lettre*), OMC-type processes were initially used in both social and economic areas and then deployed in an ever-increasing number of domains (and sub-domains) that were outside the core legal competencies of the European Union. The 'open method' was a response to frustration with the legislative process (especially its duration), scepticism about the effectiveness of traditional regulatory (legislative) approaches, and an understanding that varieties of national institutional frameworks reduced the feasibility of EU-wide approaches having an impact, together with a belief in the power of benchmarking exercises. Although the OMC's effectiveness has been questioned, its processes are nevertheless of continuing relevance.[11] They require:

- a joint definition by member states and the development of objectives, indicators, and (possibly) guidelines;

---

[8] The legal difference from a Directive is that Framework Decisions cannot be invoked directly in national courts, although national measures are to be interpreted in the light of these Framework Decisions. See Chalmers et al., *European Union Law*.

[9] Chalmers et al., *European Union Law*, 98.

[10] Other examples include 'declarations' setting out particular kinds of commitments or the issuing of 'Action Plans'.

[11] There is a considerable literature on the OMC, the amount of which is disproportionate to the significance of this policy trend in terms of impact. See D. Chalmers and M. Lodge, 'The Open Method of Co-ordination and the European Welfare State', *ESRC Centre for Analysis of Risk and Regulation, Discussion Paper 11* (London, 2003); M. Lodge, 'Comparing New Modes of Governance in Action' (2007) 45(2) *Journal of Common Market Studies* 343–65; J. Zeitlin, 'Introduction: The Open Method of Co-ordination in Question' in J. Zeitlin, P. Pichot with L. Magnusson (eds), *The Open Method of Co-ordination in Action: The European Employment and Social Inclusion Strategies* (Brussels, 2005); J. Zeitlin, 'Conclusion: The Open Method of Co-ordination in Action: Theoretical Promise, Empirical Realities, Reform Strategies', in J. Zeitlin, P. Pichot with L. Magnusson (eds), *The Open Method of Co-ordination in Action: The European Employment and Social Inclusion Strategies* (Brussels, 2005); D. Hodson and I. Maher, 'The Open Method as a New Mode of Governance: The Case of Soft Economic Policy Co-ordination' (2001) 39(4) *Journal of Common Market Studies* 719–46; C. Meyer, 'The Europeanization of Media Discourse: A Study of Quality Press Coverage of Economic Policy Co-ordination since Amsterdam' (2005) 43(1) *Journal of Common Market Studies* 121–48; N. McGuinness and C. O'Carroll, 'Benchmarking Europe's Lab Benches: How Successful has the OMC been in Research Policy' (2010) 48(2) *Journal of Common Market Studies* 293–318.

- national action plans that monitor performance in the light of the indicators and propose reforms;
- peer review among member state officials to allow exchanges regarding 'good practice' and the development of recommendations; and
- re-evaluation of national policy experiences.

These areas of 'soft law' were designed to develop a 'learning' process in which national regulatory (and policy) systems would seek to formulate their well-considered responses in the light of common benchmarks and peer-pressure. After ten years of this experience (and some reform in 2005), it is fair to say that the OMC has failed to achieve its policy objectives, although some may argue that its effects have been positive but not measurable (notably a fostering of greater participation). Critics have pointed to the lack of member-state interest in changing their behaviours in the light of peer-review pressure, and have also faulted the legal ambiguity of these measures for a lack of clarity and reliability. It could be argued that OMCs not only failed in terms of meaningful indicators, but also lacked information-gathering and behaviour-modification tools.[12] Member states reported selectively and it was difficult to trace change in policy style or substance that could be linked to peer-review processes. Enthusiasts, however, noted that in the light of the weaknesses of 'hard law' and its tendency towards uniformity, a more flexible approach that reflected national diversity (and subsidiarity) as well as uncertainty about the effectiveness of particular policy strategies held more promise in terms of achieving desired policy outcomes.

Nearly two decades earlier, the limitations of a harmonizing EU regulatory approach had also been stressed in the argument that the internal market project required a move from the 'old' to the 'new approach' to the standardization of goods or services to be traded across EU member states. The 'old approach' sought to replace diverse national laws with one single European-wide piece of legislation, thereby requiring the use of Community legislation that harmonized national provisions, the use of mutual recognition in terms of inspections, and a procedural provision that would update the legislation in question in the light of technical progress. This 'old approach' has been widely criticized on a number of accounts. It was considered time-consuming, given member-state sensitivities and decision-making rules that allowed for blockages, and it involved such a time-lag that by the time rules were adopted, they were already technically out of date. Other difficulties were that the regulations were too entrenched once passed, there was a degree of uniformity that reduced consumer choices and innovation, and the process made insufficient use of technical standardization and industrial norms—which led to duplications, delays, and inconsistencies.

---

[12] Lodge, 'Comparing New Modes of Governance in Action'.

The 'old approach', nevertheless, remains attractive to industry, as it holds out the prospect of legal certainty and strong guarantees on market access.[13] Indeed, others argue that the criticisms of the 'old approach' fail to acknowledge the inherent flexibilities built into this approach that allow for updating through so-called 'comitology': Commission proposals will be approved by a regulatory committee constituted by representatives from member states.[14]

Regardless of the above attractions, the arrival of the 1980s brought suggestions that the 'old approach' would potentially frustrate the ambitions of the Single Market project. The Commission, as a result, proposed a so-called 'new approach'. This was also prompted by the changing environment associated with the European Court of Justice's *Cassis de Dijon* case.[15] The Court ruled that goods that had been legally marketed in one member state should not be prevented from entering another in the absence of compelling national policy sensitivities or concerns. This gave rise to the principle of 'mutual recognition', and the European Commission put forward the 'new approach'.[16] As noted earlier (Chapter 17), the evidence that mutual recognition would become a widespread mechanism has been limited and may be explained as the result of different member states' distrust of each others' respective regulatory regimes.

The key characteristics of this 'new approach' are:[17]

- mandatory essential requirements: these are to ensure a high level of protection and are to be uniformly enforceable to evaluate compliance;
- manufacturers are free to choose their own technical solution that meets the essential requirements—harmonized standards are to be provided by technical standardization bodies;[18]
- the definition of procedures for conformity assessment;

---

[13] Chalmers et al., *European Union Law*, 683. Indeed, one can suggest that the 'old approach' recognized political legitimacy in terms of decision-making and provided national regulators with a veto over supposedly 'unsafe goods' entering their national markets. Elsewhere, since 2002 there has also been a move towards 'co-regulation' in social and environmental regulation as part of the 'better regulation' programme. Here, formal 'framework' legislation is 'filled in' by quasi-private or self-regulatory agreements; see P. Verbruggen, 'Does Co-regulation Strengthen EU Legitimacy?' (2009) 15 (4) *European Law Journal* 425–41.

[14] Chalmers et al., *European Union Law*, 696.

[15] *Rewe-Zentrale* v. *Bundesmonopolverwaltung für Branntwein* [1979] ECR 64. See also J. Pelkmans, 'The New Approach to Technical Harmonization and Standardization' (1987) 25 *Journal of Common Market Studies* 251–69.

[16] OJ 1985 C136/1.

[17] The formal new term for the 'new approach' is the 'New Legislative Framework', which placed a strengthened emphasis on market surveillance, rules applying to the notification of conformity assessment bodies as well as accreditation, and clarifying the definition of CE marking. Regulation (EC) 764/2008, Regulation (EC) 765/2008, Decision 768/2008/EC.

[18] These standardization bodies are the 'European Committee for Standardization' (CEN), the 'European Committee for Electrotechnical Standardization' (CENELEC), and the 'European Telecommunications Standards Institute' (ETSI). They apply to EU and EFTA member states.

- the introduction of CE marking as a tool for verification that a product conforms to all harmonization provisions and has been subject to the applicable conformity assessment procedures;
- the obligation on member states to take enforcement measures and conduct market surveillance.

The 'new approach' has proved to be less extensive in its application than initially expected, and this has led to its ongoing adjustment. In particular, it was seen to be failing to provide sufficient confidence in the marketplace, triggering uneven national regulatory oversight activities, as well as a 'flexible' use of safeguard mechanisms among member states. To respond to these limitations, a 'New Legislative Framework' was put forward to provide greater consistency in the whole regulatory framework. This Framework was to apply to both 'new' (voluntarily backed by minimum legislative standards) and 'old' (legislatively specified standards) approaches by enhancing market surveillance and strengthening accreditation provisions.

In the regulatory context, the biggest innovation of the 'new approach' was the reliance on three standardization bodies to provide harmonized standards, CEN, CENELEC and ETSI (see footnote 18). These bodies are inherently interlinked in international standardization processes, and the overall bias is towards global rather than European standards. Responsibility for the development of standards is placed on a so-called technical committee, consisting of experts from member countries, industry, and other societal representatives. Drafts decisions are then voted on, not just by the technical committees themselves, but also by the national standardization bodies (apart from ETSI), although unanimity is preferred.[19] The standardization process has not escaped criticism either. It has been accused of taking too long and being likely to be of poor quality given competition among producers to 'fight' for 'their' national standards, thus leading to attempts to impose 'hegemonic' (and inevitably outdated) rather than functionally superior standards. Furthermore, the overall process has been criticized for lacking openness to outside interests apart from well-organized industry groups. It finally also raises issues about liability: it has been suggested that compliance with a standard provides an appropriate level of protection, thereby disallowing challenges against the appropriateness of the standard itself.

The final key instrument of the European regulatory state is mutual recognition.[20] As noted already, the EU might be a standard-setter, but apart from rare exceptions (such as food inspections, where the overall

---

[19] Chalmers et al., *European Union Law,* 697–8.
[20] S. Schmidt, 'Mutual Recognition as a New Mode of Governance' (2007) 14(5) *Journal of European Public Policy* 667–81.

approach has moved towards checking the robustness of national systems of food regulation), it does not check compliance at the local level. The administration of most EU activities is in the hands of national and regional civil services, who act within the substantive legal obligations placed upon them through supranational law. The principle of mutual recognition expresses most extensively this reliance on national administrations: officials should generally allow products that have been lawfully traded in one member state to be sold in their own jurisdiction (as justified in the famous *Cassis de Dijon* case).[21]

A reliance on mutual recognition also imposes certain obligations. These include *ex ante* measures, such as the need to notify the Commission of planned technical regulations,[22] as well as *ex post* measures, namely the need of member states to notify each other about restrictions on trade[23] and the need to communicate any obstacle to free trade to the Commission.[24] Finally, it also places an obligation on member states to ensure that all products sold in their own jurisdiction are safe. Member states are to notify the Commission about the imposition and lifting of safety-related restrictions,[25] as well as the duty to use the so-called RAPEX procedure, by which the Commission, and thus other member states, are informed about the occurrence of a serious risk.[26] In 2005, the Danish food regulator was widely criticized for not having initiated these procedures when faced with a *Norovirus* outbreak following the import of contaminated raspberries. More generally, mutual recognition has failed to have extensive application—it largely operates in those areas that are heavily regulated by EC laws and/or international standards. In other policy fields, producers have tended to show an unwillingness to bear the regulatory risk of mutual recognition when exporting their products to other member state markets and have tended to resort to the standards of the 'destination' jurisdiction.

The Infrastructure of European Regulation

As noted earlier, EU regulation is inherently about coordination between and across different levels of government and it routinely involves the transfer and sharing of expertise across networks of regulators. It therefore extends beyond the vision of the European Commission as the regulator and monitor of

---

[21] See Chalmers et al., *European Union Law*, 497–504.   [22] Directive 83/189/EEC.
[23] Decision 3052/95/EC.   [24] Regulation 2679/98/EC.
[25] Directive 2001/95/EEC.   [26] Directive 2001/95/EC.

national transposition (backed by the possibility of legal infringement proceedings). The centrality of coordination issues arises from the separation involved in locating standard-setting at the EU level (for matters relating to the Internal or Single Market in particular) and the placing of information-gathering and behaviour-modification functions at the national and subnational levels among member states. Regulation plays a central part in this constellation as it is the most prominent policy instrument in the EU's toolbox, as noted. The notion of a regulatory state may provoke images of a synoptic, calculating, and predictable machinery of government reliant on law, but the EU regulatory state is fundamentally about the need to coordinate within and across levels of government, the accommodation of contestation and demands to combine both a toleration of national (administrative) diversity, and the need for somewhat consistent application. These needs became particularly prominent in the wake of increasing demands that were placed on member states to deal with processes of market liberalization. Coordination pressures lie at the heart of the dynamics that have underpinned the EU regulatory state over the past decade in particular and will be considered in this section.[27]

The three dynamics to be explored here are: the rise of EU agencies; the evolving character of regulatory decision-making in the cases of competition law and the 'Lamfalussy process'; and the conflicts between expertise and politics. This section cannot provide an exhaustive account, but seeks to illuminate some key aspects of these developments.

Turning first to agencies, the idea of 'agencification' has become increasingly prominent in the EU regulatory landscape since the 1990s.[28] This has

---

[27] Thatcher and Coen distinguish between various potential institutional arrangements in the 'European regulatory space': EU supervision, 'forum governance', informal networks across national regulators, formalized European networks of regulators, a 'European regulatory agency' (in different institutional shapes ranging from national regulators acting together, a mix of Commission and national regulatory staff, to purely 'EU-level regulators' and the EU Commission acting as regulator). See M. Thatcher and D. Coen, 'Reshaping European Regulatory Space' *West European Politics* (2008) 806–36.

[28] In particular, the European Commission has relied on so-called comitology and working groups to involve expertise. The growing agencification can be seen as a growing formalization of (national) regulatory presence at the EU level. Outside policing and security and defence policy, there were 31 agencies at the time of writing. See: J.G. Christensen and V.L. Nielen, 'Administrative Capacity, Structural Choice and the Creation of EU Agencies' (2010) 17(2) *Journal of European Public Policy* 176–204; R. Dehousse, 'Regulation by Networks in the European Community' (1997) 4 *Journal of European Public Policy* 246–61; W. Hummer, 'From "Interinstitutional Agreements" to "Interinstitutional Agencies/Offices"' (2007) 13 *European Law Journal* 47–74; R. Kelemen, 'The Politics of "Eurocratic" Structure and the New European Agencies' (2002) 22 *West European Politics* 93–118; A. Kreher, 'Agencies in the European Commuity: A Step towards Administrative Integration in Europe' (1997) 4 *Journal of European Public Policy* 225–45; B. Eberlein and E. Grande, 'Beyond Delegation: Transnational Regimes and the EU Regulatory State' (2005) 12 *Journal of European Public Policy* 89–112; T. Gehring and S. Krapohl, 'Supranational Regulatory Agencies between Independence and Control' (2007) 14 *Journal of European Public Policy* 208–26; Thatcher and Coen, 'Reshaping European

involved the increasing intermeshing of regulatory responsibilities and the erosion of any clear vertical separation in responsibilities by the increasing reliance on national regulators in deliberating at the transnational level and in their becoming EU executive organs themselves. The agency landscape evolved over time, based on different formative decisions, either through EU legislation or through domain-specific agreements among member states.[29] Agencies became a particularly prominent feature of the 'EU governance' agenda post-2000. This was an attempt by the European Commission to respond to a wider legitimacy crisis after the resignation of all European Commissioners under the presidency of Jacques Santer following accusations of inappropriate expenditures and patronage.[30] According to an early argument made by Giandomenico Majone, the authority of these EU-level regulatory agencies is not based on formal legal sources, but on their ability to provide credible information.[31] Agencies therefore provide additional administrative capacity through their access to specialist and scientific expertise, although these networks of expertise are shaped by a strong representation of member states (and the European Commission) on their governing boards. The rise of agencies could therefore be seen as a solution to the European Commission's credible commitment problem as identified by the member states. On this account, member states have diagnosed the European Commission with a problem of overstretch as a result of the Single Market, leaving

---

Regulatory Space'; D. Coen and M. Thatcher, 'The New Governance of Markets and Non-Majoritarian Regulators' (2005) 18(3) *Governance* 329–46; A. Wonka and B. Rittberger, 'Credibility, Complexity and Uncertainty: Explaining the Institutional Independence of 29 EU Agencies' (2010) 33(4) *West European Politics* 730–52; M. Busuioc, 'Accountability, Control and Independence: The Case of European Agencies' (2009) 15(5) *European Law Journal* 599–615; J. Trondal and L. Jeppesen, 'Images of Agency Governance in the European Union' (2008) 31(3) *West European Politics* 417–41.

[29] The agencies' authority is further constrained by the legal *Meroni* doctrine that limits the delegation of executive power away from the European Commission. Organizationally, the agencies follow similar structures with an appointed agency head (an appointment based on merit) and a hierarchical structure. Decision-making can be by unanimous or majority vote.

[30] European Commission 2001; Agencies (not all with a regulatory remit) include: Office for Harmonization in the Internal Market, Community Plant Variety Office, European Aviation Safety Agency, European Food Safety Authority, Community Fisheries Control Agencies, European Medicines Agency, European Maritime Safety Agency, European Chemicals Agency, European Network and Information Security Agency, European Railway Agency, European Union Agency for Fundamental Rights, Agency for the Cooperation of Energy Regulators, Community Fisheries Control Agency, European Agency for Safety and Health at Work, European Agency for the Management of Operational Cooperation at the External Borders, European Centre for Disease Prevention and Control, European Centre for the Development of Vocational Training, European Environment Agency, European Foundation for the Improvement of Living and Working Conditions, European Institute of Gender Equality, European Monitoring Centre for Drugs and Drug Addiction, European Training Foundation, European GNSS Supervisory Authority.

[31] G. Majone, 'The New European Agencies: Regulation by Information' (1997) 4 *Journal of European Public Policy* 262–75; G. Majone, 'The Credibility Crisis of Community Regulation' (2000) 38 *Journal of Common Market Studies* 273–302; G. Majone, 'The European Commission: The Limits of Centralization and the Perils of Parliamentarization' (2002) 15 *Governance* 375–92.

the Commission with accusations of being politicized in so far as it developed tendencies both to give in to member-state interests and to be excessively swayed by its accountability to the European Parliament.[32] The way in which member states have designed their input into agency decision-making further suggests their limited interest in vesting these EU-level agencies with any considerable (formal) power, and this reluctance to transfer authority upwards was further shared by national regulators, who opposed a weakening of their position in their particular national institutional setting.

As a response to these various motivations, there has been an institutional strengthening of networks of national regulators and authorities, as well as the emergence of trans-European bodies. These bodies allow for EU Commission and national regulatory staff to interact and move beyond a reliance on purely national adaptation. Key examples of these emerging networks are the so-called 'Florence forum' (for electricity, established in 1998) and the 'Madrid forum' (for gas, established in 1999). Unsurprisingly, these networks have become increasingly formalized within the setting of EU energy regulation (the 'European Regulators Group for Electricity and Gas'[33]), and, as part of the 'third energy package', there has been a further institutionalization in that a formal 'European Regulatory Network' was formed. This network later became the 'Agency for the Cooperation of Energy Regulators' that oversaw the 'European Network of Transmission System Operators' and was to support coordination among national regulatory decision-making and to facilitate oversight over cross-border infrastructure provision.[34] The gradual formalization of this agency was one aspect of a general shift towards a greater concern with security of supply in EU energy regulation.[35] More broadly, it was also seen as an indicator of a fundamental shift in the underlying values of the tools of the European regulatory state—away from an emphasis on a reliance on liberalization and markets. A similar move occurred in the area of telecommunications with the establishment of the 'Body of European Regulators of Electronic Communications (NEREC) that replaced the 'European Regulators Group' as part of the European Electronic Communications Regulatory Framework.[36] This was supposed to facilitate cross-border integration, following dissatisfaction with national regulatory inconsistencies (for example, the debate whether Deutsche Telekom should enjoy a 'regulatory holiday' in exchange for investment into high-speed broadband networks). As noted below, similar trends have also occurred in the area of financial regulation. This formalization has taken the form of 'European regulatory

[32] Majone, 'European Commission'.
[33] Commission Decision 2003/796/EC.
[34] Regulation 713/2009.
[35] S. Haghighi, 'Energy Security and the Division of Competences between the European Community and its Member States' (2008) 14(4) *European Law Journal* 461–82.
[36] Regulation 1211/2009; Directive 2009/136/EC; Directive 2009/140/EC.

networks' to advise the Commission on proposals and to coordinate imple-mentation. The significance of these developments is not necessarily the emergence of agencies at the EU level that represent a blend of intergovern-mental/inter-regulatory and supranational elements, based on limited formal powers. Rather, it is the authority of these agencies to shape decisions which advances technocratic knowledge over 'non-scientific' knowledge in the deci-sion-making process, thereby potentially placing these agencies in a most powerful position.[37]

Moving towards a focus on the interaction between national and EU levels further accentuates the impression of a growing networkization of relation-ships in which there is a fusion of different levels of executive government, especially at the bureaucratic level. Two key examples will be explored below: the reform of competition law (as formulated in Regulation 1/2003) and the reforms widely known as the Lamfalussy process.

Turning first to competition law, it is widely said that the competition regime of the European Union was the first supranational policy.[38] The 'Europeanization' of national competition regimes has therefore been a fea-ture of competition policy since the signing of the Treaty of Rome; indeed, the period since the formulation of the European competition regime (in the Treaty of Rome and the subsequent Regulation 17/62) witnessed the rise of national administrative capacity among national competition regimes.[39] However, the expanding significance of the European competition regime also led to further calls: regarding on the one hand the limitations of the European Commission to deal with the number of notifications and cases; on the other hand, there were also criticisms concerning the supposed inconsis-tency of decisions, in particular the potential for the politicization of deci-sion-making within the college of commissioners. As a result, some argued

---

[37] This point is made by Gehring and Krapohl in their study of the authorization of pharmaceu-ticals. Below the degree of similarity, different modes of interaction across actors within the different domains have been emerging. See T. Gehring and S. Krapohl, 'Supranational Regulatory Agencies between Independence and Control' (2007) 14 *Journal of European Public Policy* 208–26.

[38] S. Wilks and L. McGowan, 'The First Supranational Policy of the European Union: Competition Policy' (1995) 28(2) *European Journal of Political Research* 141–69; M. Cini and L. McGowan, *Competition Policy in the European Union* (Basingstoke, 2009); D. Gerber, *Law and Competition in Twentieth Century Europe* (Oxford, 1998); D. Gerber, 'Modernising European Competition Law' (2001) 22(4) *European Competition Law Review* 122–30; H. Vedder, 'Spontaneous Harmonisation of National (Competition) Laws in the Wake of the Modernisation of EC Competition Law' (2004) 1(1) *Competition Law Review* 5–21; S. Wilks and L. McGowan, 'Competition Policy in the European Union: Creating a Federal Agency?', in G.B. Doern and S. Wilks (eds.), *Comparative Competition Policy* (Oxford, 1996); P. Akman and H. Kassim, 'Myths and Myth-Making in the European Union: The Institutionalization and Interpretation of EU Competition Policy' (2010) 48(1) *Journal of Common Market Studies* 111–32.

[39] S. Eyre and M. Lodge, 'National Tunes and a European Melody? Competition Law Reform in the UK and Germany' (2000) 7(1) *Journal of European Public Policy* 63–79; M. Lodge, 'Isomorphism of National Policies? The "Europeanization" of German Competition and Public Procurement Law' (2000) *West European Politics* 89–107.

the case for a 'European Cartel Office'.[40] The eventual reform of the competition regime was widely regarded as a 'revolution', with considerable consequences for the evolution of regulatory relationships.[41] It also reflected a reluctance of member states to hand over further authority to the European Commission or the EU level.

The provisions were 'revolutionary' in a number of ways. First, the reforms moved from an *ex ante* centralized notification system to an *ex post* decentralized deterrence regime. This placed responsibility on firms to formulate agreements that were in compliance with EU competition law. Second, it altered the role of the European Commission. It allowed it a more 'strategic' role in the sense that the resources thus released should be concentrated on 'hard core cartels'. Its other main role was to issue guidance to national competition authorities in order to ensure consistent application. It also allowed the European Commission to take on particular cases[42] and strengthened the role of the Commission by granting it closer oversight over national enforcement actions. In addition, the scope for the application of national competition laws was further marginalized. Third, and critically, the real work of applying and enforcing EU competition law was to be undertaken by the national competition authorities. As a consequence, these latter (and the national courts) were enrolled as executive organs of the EU as the European treaty provisions became directly applicable throughout the EU. The altered arrangements required not just provisions that guided the potential reallocation of cases (sideways and 'upwards'), but also provisions that would facilitate communication and knowledge transfer.[43] The 'European Competition Network' was created to provide a flexible mechanism for enhancing cooperation; to facilitate knowledge and staff exchanges; and to coordinate enforcement activities and allocate cases. It was also intended to coordinate investigations across borders and to ensure consistency in the application of EU competition law principles.

The risk involved in such a network approach is that the various national authorities might apply EU law in different ways. Such an outcome would not just lead to diversity, it would also require the European Commission to use its freed resources to monitor national competition authorities and to re-allocate cases. Such a network can only work within a network of authorities that is characterized by trust (in the expertise of other jurisdictions' authorities) and by a shared philosophy. Competition law and policy is arguably one domain in which core ideas regarding the role of 'competition' in

---

[40] Wilks and McGowan, 'The First Supranational Policy of the European Union'.

[41] S. Wilks, 'Agency Escape: Decentralisation or Dominance of the European Commission in the Modernization of Competition Policy' (2005) 18(3) *Governance* 431–52; Regulation 1/2003.

[42] Similarly, in telecommunications, the European Commission was granted veto powers to overrule national regulators in the definition of 'relevant markets', and 'significant market power'.

[43] D. Gerber and P. Cassinis, 'The "Modernisation" of European Community Competition Law: Achieving Consistency in Enforcement—Part 1' (2006) 27(1) *European Competition Law Review* 10–18.

economic life are shared within an epistemic community. Whether, however, such epistemic communities can ensure consistent application of competition law principles in the face of the national politics and resource constraints is another matter. Indeed, some therefore argue that the reliance on 'networks' to deal with case allocation and evolving doctrines is inherently unsatisfactory and requires more formal provisions.[44] Such formal (federal) provisions, however, fly in the face of the strategic interests of various actors on the one hand, and the possibilities of decentralized enforcement and of informal adjustments in terms of conflict and 'learning' on the other.

The second key example of an increasing fusion of European and national levels that generates networks of knowledge is the Lamfalussy process which has emerged in the context of financial market regulation since the turn of century.[45] It was argued that existing national regulatory approaches were too diverse and fragmented and that existing European ways to deal with financial regulation were insufficient in so far as they were based on mutual recognition and minimal harmonization with limited cross-national coordination. More far-reaching EU-level regulations were stifled by national reluctance, although the rise of large-scale national financial services businesses created demand for European-wide provisions. This led to the creation of a new EU policy framework in 2004, the 'Lamfalussy process' (named after the chairman of the advisory committee, Alexandre Lamfalussy). At the time of writing (summer 2010), the institutions of financial regulation at the EU level were in a state of flux (as were the wider international regulatory settings for financial regulation, such as Basel 3), but proposals suggested a dynamic of growing institutionalization of regulatory fora, on the lines noted above.

Noteworthy here are the emerging processes in financial regulation that changed rule-making procedures and intended to facilitate coordination across jurisdictions; the emphasis on decentralized implementation through processes dominated by technical-regulatory expertise also made the tracing of its key effects particularly difficult. The option of a single European regulator for the financial sector was rejected.[46] The Lamfalussy process was built on four different levels, the key motivation being to rely on a process that linked broad instruments with delegated legislation.[47] Again, the overall

---

[44] O. Budzinski and A. Christiansen, 'Competence Allocation in the EU Competition Policy System as an Interest-Driven Process' (2005) 25(3) *Journal of Public Policy* 313–37.

[45] It was introduced in February 2002 in the securities sector and in 2003 in the banking and insurance sectors. The extension further added particular committees to support Commission decisions.

[46] L. Quaglia, 'The Politics of Financial Services Regulation and Supervision Reform in the European Union' (2007) 46 *European Journal of Political Research* 269–90.

[47] A. Schaub, 'The Lamfalussy Process Four Years On' (2005) 13(2) *Journal of Financial Regulation and Compliance* 110–20; Quaglia, 'The Politics of Financial Services Regulation'; D. Josselin, 'Domestic Policy Networks and European Negotiations' (1996) 3(3) *Journal of European Public Policy* 297–317; S. Lütz, 'Convergence within National Diversity' (2004) 24(2) *Journal of Public Policy* 169–97;

trend has been one of reliance on national regulatory agencies to deal with 'implementation', while EU-level rules as well as coordination and enforcement mechanisms constrain national autonomy. The reforms partly built on existing regulatory fora as well as on new committees.

To take the field of securities as an example, the first level of regulation was constituted by 'framework' decisions following 'traditional' EU legislative (co-decision) means. At the second level, however, decisions were made on the basis of more 'technical' and implementing measures. Here, the European Commission relied not only on a committee of regulators ('European Securities Regulators Committee') to prepare proposals and provide expert advice, but also on a 'normal' comitology committee (of the regulatory type) consisting of national ministry officials ('European Securities Committee'). At a third level, greater reliance was placed on stronger coordination between national financial regulators through the 'European Securities Regulators Committee'. It is this transgovernmental committee that is said to have emerged as the key body, based on claims of its technical expertise. It was also central in ensuring consistent cross-national application by its national members. It performed this function through a process of internal peer-review. At a fourth level, the Commission was to exercise stricter enforcement should member states fail to apply EU provisions consistently. In addition, an inter-instititutional monitoring group provided for external review.

The field of securities provides a good example of cross-border services in an expanding sector where industries demand legal harmonization to reduce legal risk. At the same time, national regulators and politicians might be sensitive about a transfer of legal competencies to the EU level, but are also faced with their inability to exercise national regulatory 'boundary control'. The context of the financial crisis resulted in a further institutional strengthening of European regulatory bodies: a 'European Systemic Risk Board' (consisting of the European Central Bank, European Commission, and European regulatory authorities) was to monitor broad risks, while the existing committees were turned into 'authorities', setting standards, monitoring national enforcement actions, and able to take emergency measures, mediate in conflicts between national regulators, and oversee credit rating agencies.[48] Again, the institutional pattern points towards a growing formalization and strengthening of oversight bodies at the EU level.

M. Moran, 'The State and the Financial Services Revolution' (1994) 17(3) *West European Politics* 158–77; B. Simmons, 'The International Politics of Harmonization' (2001) 55(3) *International Organization* 589–620; Thatcher and Coen, 'Reshaping European Regulatory Space'; C. DeVisscher, O. Maiscocq, and F. Varone, 'The Lamfalussy Reform in EU Securities Markets' (2008) 28(1) *Journal of Public Policy* 19–47.

[48] The authorities are the European Banking Authority (based in London), the European Insurance and Occupational Pensions Authority (based in Frankfurt), and the European Securities Markets Authority (based in Paris).

Conflicts within such networks of regulators—and therefore also within networks of knowledge—are, however, unavoidable. The application of the so-called precautionary principle (see Chapter 6), provides a particularly pertinent insight into such conflicts and the role of expertise in decision-making more generally.[49] The rise of the agencies at the EU level (as noted earlier) can be linked to a wider aspiration to depoliticize decision-making by moving advisory functions to regulatory agencies, for example in the areas of pharmaceuticals, financial services, consumer protection, food safety, or ecological protection. The reliance on 'scientific' advice (or scientifically framed) advice raises issues that have already been considered elsewhere in this volume: what role should science play and how should decision-making processes seek to represent non-science positions in sensitive issues such as risk? Similarly, the changes to decisions regarding the marketing of genetically modified food and feedstuffs (Regulation 1829/2003) suggest a growing centralization of authority at the level of the European Food Safety Authority (EFSA) in terms of agenda-framing in particular, whilst reducing the scope of national regulators to authorize these goods or to object to the marketing of these goods.[50]

These trends place an onus on industry to show that a product is safe when applying for the approval of particular foods and feedstuffs. The important point here, however, is that this industry accountability is not to one single regulator, but to all the involved regulators. In other words, industry faces multiple accountabilities, national regulators are faced with a process of mutual justification towards each other, and the overall regime is based on the belief that regulatory expertise will develop in a process of mutual learning and exchange. One side-effect of this system has been the success of industry demands in creating stringent regulatory provisions to facilitate an international food system that requires a 'transparent' production process from 'farm to fork'. However, the problem of such a regime is that it does not account for competing logics or contestation in terms of knowledge.[51] This conflict emerges in particular with regard to the so-called precautionary principle, i.e. those cases where

---

[49] See also Art. 95(4–7) EC that sets out procedures in which member states and Commission deal with cases where member states seek to reject harmonization measures and maintain a higher level of protection. Member states are required to set out their reasoning through the formal language of risk assessment; at the same time, it requires the European Commission to question its own approach. See also M. Van Asselt and E. Vos, 'The Precautionary Principle and the Uncertainty Paradox' (2006) 9(4) *Journal of Risk Research* 313–36; G. Majone, 'What Price Safety? The Precautionary Principle and its Policy Implications' (2002) 40(1) *Journal of Common Market Studies* 89–109; G. Majone, 'Foundations of Risk Regulation: Science, Decision-Making, Policy Learning and Institutional Reform' (2010) 1(1) *European Journal of Risk Regulation* 5–19; V. Heyvaert, 'Guidance without Constraint: Assessing the Impact of the Precautionary Principle on the European Community's Chemicals Policy' (2006) 6 *Yearbook of European Environmental Law* 27–60.

[50] D. Chalmers, 'Risk, Anxiety and the European Mediation of the Politics of Life' (2005) 30(5) *European Law Review* 649–74.

[51] Ibid., 656.

issues of scientific doubt are raised. A hyper-politicized environment is not necessarily one that allows mutual learning between different member states' assessments (especially not where scientific authorities present their expertise to different bodies at the same time). Such learning is particularly problematic when even the slightest voicing of doubt will lead to a mobilization of opposition (which is not interested in the language of risk), and where the need to come to any one opinion requires the balancing of conflicting scientific findings.

The famous *Pfizer* case of 2002 further illustrated the tensions that regulatory regimes face when there is uncertainty about interpretations of the precautionary principle.[52] In this case, a ban was applied to an antibiotic (Virginiamycin) used in animal feed. This product had been legally marketed across the European Union, but the ban was instituted following the Danish regulator's conclusion that the antibiotic could lead to the emergence of resistant viruses. The European-level Standing Committee on Animal Nutrition (SCAN) suggested that the scientific evidence did not justify a ban, as it did not constitute an immediate risk to Danish public health, but the Council nevertheless decided on a ban. It did so following a Commission recommendation to do so, but after disagreement among member states in the standing committee on feedstuffs. The producer, Pfizer, challenged this ban on the basis that there was insufficient scientific evidence to justify the use of the precautionary principle. The European Court of First Instance backed the ban, but placed emphasis on the importance of there being scientific knowledge (provided by technocratic regulatory agencies) that would justify the application of the precautionary principle. The judicial requirement of *scientific* knowledge to be marshalled for the application of the precautionary principle on the one hand reduces the formal potential of pure commercial or moral objections to shape the politics of the precautionary principle. It furthers the powerful role of scientific advice-giving bodies. On the other hand, it also suggests that the attempt to regulate through 'scientific' knowledge and procedures will inherently clash with the everyday logics of politics, and it is unlikely that a mere reliance on supposedly 'detached' regulators will reassure publics about new products and technologies, especially in sensitive areas such as food, where universally agreed 'once and for all' scientific findings are unlikely to exist. Indeed, it suggests that the precautionary principle can be applied to areas of 'uncertainty' when this uncertainty is largely defined by the presence of diverging expert opinions and where the Court has to act as 'super-regulator' in assessing the validity (or otherwise) of scientific claims.

---

[52] *Pfizer Animal Health* v. *Council* [2002] ECR II-3305. See also Van Asselt and Vos, 'The Precautionary Principle and the Uncertainty Paradox'.

EU–National Dynamics

The growing institutionalization of EU agencies has combined with a growing integration of national networks of regulatory expertise to produce new issues of accountability, participation, and legitimacy. Such developments also raise fresh questions about what 'counts' as a *national* regulatory policy. As a result, much of the 'Europeanization' literature has considered how member states seek to impose their preferences on other EU members, or how they transpose Directives into their respective national systems.[53] Especially regarding the latter, a picture of diversity emerges, with member states not only displaying different response rates for transposing Directives on time and doing so correctly, but also for responding to infringement proceedings in a timely fashion. A further look at the way in which Directives have been transposed also points to diversity in content—with some member states meeting their own particular 'problems' (such as those of 'gold-plating' and 'capture'). This suggests that, in many cases, EU provisions do not necessarily determine the precise shape of national legislative and regulatory responses and that the way in which 'Europe' impacts on domestic regulation varies. A series of mechanisms have been explored as the search for a 'prototyping' EU provision that imposes particular institutional solutions on member states has been found wanting. Rather, member states adjust to EU requirements through their distinct political and administrative structures, with EU measures strengthening (or weakening) domestic coalitions demanding particular solutions.

As noted above, arguments about why some sectors have become increasingly shaped by EU actions, whereas others have witnessed more cautious patterns, are based on different academic visions. At one level, the key distinction in approaches has been between those that emphasize the importance of supranational factors and those that highlight the importance of intergovernmental bargaining. Those who take the former view point to the promotion of integrationist measures by bodies such as the European Commission (eager to maximize its influence over policy content within the given constraints on its ability to expand discretionary budgets), the European Parliament, and the European Court of Justice (or the European Central Bank, etc.), as well as the growing transnational interests of major business sectors.[54] Those who emphasize

---

[53] T. Börzel, 'Why There is No "Southern" Problem' (2000) 7(1) *Journal of European Public Policy* 141–62; G. Falkner, M. Hartlepp, and O. Treib, 'Worlds of Compliance' (2007) 46 *European Journal of Political Research* 395–416; G. Falkner, O. Treib, M. Hartlepp, and S. Leiber, *Complying with Europe* (Cambridge, 2005); C. Knill, *The Europeanisation of National Administrations* (Cambridge, 2001); A. Héritier, D. Kerwer, C. Knill, D. Lehmkuhl, M. Teutsch and A.-C. Douillet, *Differential Europe* (Lanham, MD, 2001); M. Kaeding, 'In Search of Better Quality of EU Regulations for Prompt Transposition' (2008) 14(5) *European Law Journal* 583–603.

[54] A. Moravcsik, 'Preferences and Power in the European Community' (1993) 31(4) *Journal of Common Market Studies* 473–524; A. Stone Sweet and W. Sandholtz, 'European Integration and Supranational Governance' (1997) 4(3) *Journal of European Public Policy* 297–317.

bargaining place a central focus on changing balances among the economic interests of member states where decisions to shift authority over select issues across policy domains are a result of lowest common denominator decision-making. Others point to the more incremental pattern in which policy develops, with the European Commission and member states moving through package deals towards diverse regulatory frameworks that resemble broad 'patchworks'.[55] These institutional developments then trigger demands for further institutional adjustment and 'institutionalization'.[56] A primary example of such institutional arguments is the agencification and the growing formalization of regulatory networks that was described in the previous section. Thatcher and Coen therefore argue that the 'regulatory space' in the European Union is one characterized by an evolving trajectory in which experimentation, dissatisfaction, learning, and actor self-interest produce a 'layering' of institutional arrangements and mechanisms (see Chapter 4).[57]

Apart from this trend towards the institutionalization of networks, it is difficult to point to any major regulatory dynamics which would confirm suggestions of a universal 'race to the bottom' or a 'race to the top'.[58] Within single domains, there are contrasting patterns, pointing to the importance of differences as to whether measures are market-making/creating or market-correcting. For example, standards that have facilitated information transparency about the production chain for food products are said to have been passed at a 'high' level, given industry demand for clarity on each part of the production chain. However, when it came to the 'traffic light' information system regarding the content of food products (such as salts, fats, and overall calories), industry successfully managed to persuade EU decision-makers to reject such moves. It is therefore impossible to make any general comments on whether the European Union is 'deregulatory' or 'pro-regulatory'. Rather, it is fair to suggest that the European Union has had a considerable 're-regulatory impact' on its member states, with differentiation a continuing theme.[59] The need to adjust has not merely affected the way in which the substance and procedures of regulatory provisions have changed (for example, in environmental regulation, from 'best available technology' to more discretionary 'quality' objectives). It has also affected the political and administrative infrastructure of member state transposition, with member states

---

[55] A. Héritier, 'The Accommodation of Diversity in European Policy-Making and its Outcomes' (1996) 3(2) *Journal of European Public Policy* 149–76; M. Jachtenfuchs, 'The Governance Approach to European Integration' (2001) 39(2) *Journal of Common Market Studies* 221–40.

[56] A. Héritier, *Policy-Making and Diversity* (Cambridge, 1999).

[57] Thatcher and Coen, 'Reshaping European Regulatory Space'.

[58] See also Chalmers et al., *European Union Law*, 705–10.

[59] D. Howarth and T. Sadeh, 'The Ever Incomplete Single Market: Differentiation and the Evolving Frontier of Integration' (2010) 17(7) *Journal of European Public Policy* 922–35.

responding in different ways to the need to monitor national transposition in order to accommodate deadlines and the avoidance of fines.

Conclusion

To understand the European Union it is necessary to appreciate that regulation lies at the heart of its endeavours. In its overall reliance on authority, the European Union represents the key example of a regulatory state that operates across multiple levels of government—with standard-setting, behaviour-modification, and information-gathering separated between different organizations at different levels of government. The EU regulatory state has displayed considerable problem-solving capacity (see the liberalization of telecommunications and energy markets, the adoption of environmental and social regulatory standards, amongst others), and it has also been proven to have avoided any form of 'racing', especially 'races to the bottom'.[60]

At the same time, the past two decades have shown considerable limitations to this regulatory state. Finite capacities have triggered the growing institutionalization of EU-level agencies and regulatory networks that support the coordination of national regulatory agencies and shape EU-level decision-making. The EU regulatory state is characterized by a blurring and inter-meshing of different levels of government. This intermeshing and 'networking' stands parallel to institutional separation, such as in that between 'risk assessment' and 'risk management'. A further limitation has been the increasing recognition of the tensions in accommodating national diversity with demands for consistency across borders, especially in industries that have witnessed growing cross-border ownership. This tension has added further complexity to the interactions between European Commission and EU member states and can be seen as further support for the growth of networks at the EU level. At the same time, it has placed considerable importance on national regulatory adjustments, whether through national transposition or actual implementation 'at the coalface'. Issues of implementation raise the question as to how to evaluate different national regulatory accommodation that moves beyond a mere interest in hitting transposition deadlines.

A third limitation on the notion of the European regulatory state is the advocacy of regulation as a depoliticized tool. This view has been particularly associated with those that have argued that regulation and regulatory agencies

---

[60] There has also been considerable attention paid to 'better regulation' since the early 2000s as a further attempt to deal with the aftermath of the legitimacy crisis surrounding the resignation of the college of Commissioners under President Santer (see Chapter 13).

can support depoliticization. Indeed, for many the reliance on regulation and the achievement of policy outputs and outcomes are the key to EU legitimacy in the absence of other forms of legitimization (whether through election or 'common European identity' or *demos*).[61] EU regulation is inherently political and the conflicts over the application of the precautionary principle, for example, have further added to the tensions in regulation that have been noted throughout this volume. A reliance on 'science' and 'regulation' is supposedly adding to a rational decision-making process, but it is inherently faced by limitations in the presence of contested knowledge and sceptical publics.

In conclusion, therefore, the European regulatory state offers fascinating insights into numerous debates that have shaped the regulation literature, and its evolution is ongoing. It is impossible, given the contemporary regulatory patchwork, to make any broad-brush statements as to the direction of future travel, but the past two decades have highlighted the importance of coordination through networks and a reliance on national administrative and regulatory capacity.

[61] Majone, 'Credibility Crisis'; for a discussion of the 'demos' argument, see J.H.H. Weiler, 'Does Europe Need a Constitution? Demos, Telos and the German Maastricht Decision' (1995) 1(3) *European Law Journal* 219–58.

20 Regulation and Development

Regulation is a key means by which a state can foster an economic environment that encourages activity and growth. Less developed or industrializing countries, therefore, present a critical area for the study and practice of regulation. It is not surprising, therefore, that international donor organizations have paid considerable attention to issues of regulatory design and operation—whether through conditionality requirements regarding the creation of particular institutional devices, or through the making available of resources to allow strengthened regulatory capacity (i.e. staffing). Similarly, much attention has been paid to 'alternatives to regulation' which can come to grips with limited monitoring and enforcement capacities.[1] At the same time, the presence of international organizations and transnational operators in the context of developing industries has attracted considerable criticism and opposition. The standard worry here has been that international organizations impose their 'off-the-shelf' solutions without due regard to the specific context, while transnational operators outgun national regulators with their superior resources and expertise.

One core area in the study of the regulation of infrastructure industries has, accordingly, been the relationship between regulatory institutions and issues of economic growth and investment. This chapter is not concerned to present the results of such studies,[2] but to examine the underlying debates that shape the field of regulation and development. First, it sets out the diagnosed challenges that the development context poses for regulation. Second, it explores key lines in the literature that point to potential responses for the diagnosed problems. Third, it looks at key issues in the literature on enforcement. At the same time, it should be noted that any attempt to summarize the vast literature on regulation and development requires some brave generalizations. Immense differences of economic development and access to infrastructure services are encountered across and within countries that qualify as 'lesser developed' or 'industrializing'. In the case of countries such as China,

---

[1] World Bank, *Greening Industry: New Roles for Communities, Markets and Governments* (Oxford, 2000).
[2] A. Estache and L. Wren-Lewis, 'On the Theory and Evidence on Regulation of Network Industries in Developing Countries' in R. Baldwin, M. Cave, and M. Lodge (eds), *Oxford Handbook of Regulation* (Oxford, 2010).

India, and Brazil, growth brings with it enormous development challenges, and this raises important issues about the trade-offs between regulatory goals, such as sustainability, labour, and environmental standards, and overall policy preferences for economic growth.

Are Developing Countries 'Special'?

Issues of regulatory reform in developing countries have been much written about.[3] Regulatory reform in infrastructure industries (i.e. telecommunications, electricity, public transport and, most critically, water) is at the heart of changing doctrines of development. As noted, it is difficult to overestimate the importance of access to functioning water and sanitation networks for public health.

Development has traditionally been associated with state-driven development, and therefore public corporations and monopolies have long been seen as natural outcomes of a process of independence from former colonial 'masters' and a growing emphasis on development. Regulation, especially in the case of infrastructure activities, was largely in the hands of the publicly owned companies themselves, and this placed governments at a natural disadvantage (notably through asymmetric information) when seeking to control these providers. At the same time, companies were exposed to political pressures to keep rates low.

This belief in state-led development was replaced, by the 1980s, with a growing scepticism regarding the possibilities of achieving desirable developmental outcomes via state-driven economic policies—a scepticism that was further reinforced by reforms in the industrialized world. Greater currency was given to arguments that regarded existing regulatory controls on companies as inherently dysfunctional—arguments that were underpinned by examples of continuous political intervention in price setting and staffing (to please particular constituencies), poor management, and disappointing developmental outcomes. As a result, the argument turned into a 'pro-privatization' sentiment that, initially, placed little emphasis on the importance of regulation

---

[3] For examples, see Estache and Wren-Lewis, 'On the Theory and Evidence'; J.E. Castro, 'Neoliberal Water and Sanitation Policies as a Failed Development Strategy' (2008) 8(1) *Progress in Development Studies* 63–83; P. Cook, C. Kirkpatrick, M. Minogue, and D. Parker (eds.), *Leading Issues in Competition, Regulation and Development* (Cheltenham, 2004); M.A. Crew and D. Parker, 'Development in the Theory and Practice of Regulatory Economics' in M.A. Crew and D. Parker (eds), *International Handbook of Economic Regulation* (Cheltenham, 2006); H. Esfhani and M.T. Ramirez, 'Institutions, Infrastructure and Economic Growth' (2003) 70(2) *Journal of Development Economics* 443–77; P. Gourevitch, 'The Role of Politics in Economic Development' (2008) 11 *Annual Review of Political Science* 137–59; S. Haggard, A. MacIntyre, and L. Tiede, 'The Rule of Law and Economic Development' (2008) 11 *Annual Review of Political Science* 205–34; J.J. Laffont, 'Enforcement, Regulation and Development' (2003) 12(2) *Journal of African Economics* ii193–ii211.

and wider market institutions in shaping economic activities and promoting development and economic growth. At least since the mid-1990s, experiences in the aftermath of the collapse of the economies of the former Soviet block as well as elsewhere re-emphasized the message that 'institutions matter'. At the heart of this adjustment in development thinking was the World Bank and its sponsored work—outputs that were strongly influenced by institutional economics.[4]

The literature over the past two decades or so ranges across different perspectives, disciplinary backgrounds, and viewpoints, especially regarding the potential benevolence of privately owned regulated infrastructures. Accounts that are interested in regulation and development range from economic evaluation studies that seek to explore the impact of particular types of regulatory interventions (for example, concessions) on the development of particular sectors, to those analyses that see regulatory reform largely as a result of forms of neocolonialism, inspired by hegemonic states, ideologies and/or business interests. According to these observers, regulation is little else than the expression of the brute self-interest of dominant actors. Others laud the emergence of private investment and attempts at depoliticizing the running of infrastructure industries through regulatory devices as a core instrument to break the vicious cycle of under-development.

More generally, three key lines of argumentation exist, and each has distinct implications for analyses of regulation's role in economic (and social) development. One view points to the dominance of economic interaction and interdependence in shaping domestic regulation. According to this perspective, states suffer a loss in boundary control over rules that apply to their markets and so regulation is shaped by demands of international markets. A second position suggests that there is 'nothing new under the sun'—that, in the world of development, some states and firms are more autonomous and dominant than others and the remainder are merely at the receiving end of regulatory changes. A third view points to the transformative character of contemporary globalization and the processes whereby technological and social changes encourage complex interaction effects with the 'old' world of established economic and political power.[5] The politics of regulation is at the

---

[4] World Bank, *World Development Report* (Washington, DC, 1997); World Bank, *Greening Industry* (Oxford, 2000); P. Levy and P. Spiller, *Regulations, Institutions and Commitment* (Cambridge, 1995); J. Gómez-Ibáñez, *Regulating Infrastructure: Monopoly, Contract and Discretion* (Harvard, 2003); A. Estache and L. Wren-Lewis, 'Towards a Theory of Regulation for Developing Countries' (2009) 47(3) *Journal of Economic Literature* 729–70.

[5] M. Lodge and L. Stirton, 'Regulatory Reform in Small Developing States' (2002) 7(3) *New Political Economy* 415–33; D. Held, A. McGrew, D. Goldblatt, and J. Perraton, *Global Transformations* (Cambridge, 2000); P. Evans, 'The Eclipse of the State' (1997) 50(1) *World Politics* 62–87; P. Hirst and G. Thompson, *Globalization in Question* (Cambridge, 2000); L. Weiss, *The Myth of the Powerless State* (Cambridge, 1998). P. Drahos and J. Braithwaite, 'The Globalization of Regulation' (2001) 9(1) *Journal of Political Philosophy* 103–28; J.E. Rauch and P. Evans, 'Bureaucratic Structure and Bureaucratic

heart of all three debates, and the rest of this section explores key factors that are arguably particularly prominent when regulation is viewed in the context of development.

Turning first to those factors that shape the overall context of regulation and development, the first factor that is often cited as key is the prevalence of the *transnational company*. Privatization in particular is said to have led to the rise of companies that provide services in diverse jurisdictions. Indeed, former state-owned companies have emerged as globally trading companies. The existence of internationally trading companies is, of course, hardly new (see, for example, the East India Company). In many jurisdictions (especially those with mineral resources), government spending has been highly dependent on the willingness of a small number of companies to pay their taxes. The rise of new hegemonic transnational private actors is encouraged by such factors as depleted state budgets, extensive needs to modernize infrastructures (roads, energy networks, water pipes, and sanitation), and a growing complexity in technological and regulatory developments. These transnational service providers easily outgun domestic regulators and politicians, especially in smaller markets (and, given their resources, easily poach staff from regulators).[6]

A second key shaper of development regulation is said to be the role played by *international organizations* and the presence of hegemonic states.[7] The key aspect here is that international organizations or hegemonic states are conditional on the adoption of particular institutional blueprints in exchange for requested material resources or other support. These conditionality requirements in particular encourage the adoption of blueprints that are inappropriate or insensitive to the particularities of any political context, especially when aided by the presence of an international consultancy business seeking to sell

Performance in Less Developed Countries' (2000) 75 *Journal of Public Economics* 49–71; T. Jamasb, 'Between the State and Market: Electricity Sector Reform in Developing Countries' (2006) 14 *Utilities Policy* 14–30; L. Gutierrez, 'Regulatory Governance in the Latin American Telecommunications Sector' (2003) 11 *Utilities Policy* 225–40; D. Rodrik, 'Goodbye Washington Consensus, Hello Washington Confusion? A Review of the World Bank's Economic Growth in the 1990s: Learning from a Decade of Reform' (2006) 44 *Journal of Economic Literature* 973–87; J. Stern, 'Electricity and Telecommunications Regulatory Institutions in Small and Developing Countries' (2000) 9(3) *Utilities Policy* 131–157; F. Mairoano and J. Stern, 'Institutions and Infrastructure Investment in Low and Middle-Income Countries: The Case of Mobile Communications', *City University London Department of Economics Discussion Paper, 07/06* (2007), http://www.city.ac.uk/economics_data/assets/pdf_file/0010/89767/0706_majoranostern.pdf L. Gutierrez, 'The Effect of Endogenous Regulation on Telecommunications Expansion and Efficiency in Latin America' (2003) 23(3) *Journal of Regulatory Economics* 257–86; D. Rodrik, A. Subramanian, and F. Trebbi, 'Institutions Rule: The Primacy of Institutions over Geography and Integration in Economic Development', *NBER Working paper No. 9305*, November 2002, http://www.nber.org/papers/w9305.

[6] See P. Dunleavy, 'The Globalization of Public Services Production' (1994) 9(2) *Public Policy and Administration* 36–64.

[7] X. Yi-chong, 'Models, Templates and Currents: The World Bank and Electricity Reform' (2005) 12(4) *Review of International Political Economy* 647–73.

'off-the-shelf' advice. Similarly, it is not as if the presence of hegemonic states in contemporary politics has declined. An example of such effects is an order by the US Federal Communications Commission (FCC) on international settlement rates for telecommunications traffic in August 1997.[8] This order undermined the financial basis on which many jurisdictions had initially cross-subsidized local telecommunications services (and modernization investment), namely the ability to raise considerable funds through the charges raised by terminating incoming international calls (i.e. for 'receiving' the call and 'connecting' it to the final destination). The FCC's judgement was one of the key triggers for widespread liberalization of telecommunications markets in the Caribbean (after initial reforms had relied on exclusivity licences). The actual outcome of that liberalization policy shift was arguably positive, but nevertheless, this example reminds us of the international effects that domestic decisions in particularly powerful markets can have. A further international factor that has increasingly impacted on domestic regulation more generally has been the signing of international trade agreements, especially the GATS (General Agreement on Trade in Services) agreement that came into force in 1998 and allowed developing countries to commit themselves to broad principles of liberalization.[9]

A third major cited influence on development regulation is the presence of a 'globalization ideology' that is often casually dismissed as the 'Washington consensus'. This 'ideology' is said to be constituted by a set of doctrines that include the preference for private over public ownership, a reliance on mechanisms to ensure 'discipline' and 'control' (i.e. regulatory agencies and other commitment devices) and a resistance to demands for specific strategic or 'national' interests to be recognized in key industries (for example, through ownership requirements, 'golden shares', and the like).[10] The attraction of these ideas may have weakened considerably amidst the global meltdown of the late noughties of the twenty-first century, and some emerging economies such as China and Brazil have, indeed, openly disputed the appropriateness of the 'globalization ideology'. Nevertheless, it can be argued that industrializing and lesser developed countries are particularly exposed to the needs to follow trends and fashions when it comes to regulation, given their dependence on international investment.

Finally, a fourth factor that is said to impact on regulation is the presence of *domestic elites*. All international pressures are moderated through domestic

---

[8] FCC Docket No. 96–261, FCC report and order 97–280, http://www.fcc.gov/Bureaus/International/Orders/1997/fcc97280.html

[9] T. Cohen, 'Domestic Policy and South Africa's Commitments under the WTO's Basic Telecommunications Agreement: Explaining the Apparent Inertia' (2001) 4(4) *Journal of International Economic Law* 613–43.

[10] M. Moran, *The British Regulatory State* (Oxford, 2003); A. Roberts, *The Logic of Discipline* (Oxford, 2010).

actors. It is often argued that income inequality and the absence of contestation among the very small domestic elite prevent regulation taking into consideration the wider challenges set by development. Rather, domestic regulation reflects domestic elite interests, whether in terms of access to markets, pricing, availability of products, or in terms of enforcement—such as in environmental or land ownership conflicts.

The four just mentioned factors have been said to shape the broad context of regulation in the less developed world, but the literature, in addition, stresses four key institutional components that are regarded as particularly problematic when regulating in less developed or industrializing countries.[11] The first such component is *limited capacity*. The state structure as well as the internal resources of the state are often regarded as being too limited to stand up to well-resourced private interests. For example, the ability of regulatory offices to attract staff, to maintain a well-trained bureaucracy, and to sustain sufficient funding to be able to challenge market actors are seen as highly problematic in the context of less developed and industrializing countries. A second institutional issue is *limited commitment*. As noted earlier, any political system is vulnerable to so-called (political) time inconsistency problems. It is frequently argued that the governments of the developing and industrializing world are particularly prone to shirking on their 'promises' or commitments, whether this includes cutting the funding of regulators or forcing renegotiations of terms in the case of contracts.[12] In other words, the time inconsistency problem is said to be particularly prominent in the politics of developing countries and to place a premium on the importance of limiting discretion in regulatory and political decision-making.

A third, and often-cited, difficulty of regulation in developing countries is that of *limited accountability*. Where governments face limited demands for transparency and their decisions are relatively free from challenge, such factors increase the likelihood of capture or other forms of arbitrary or biased decision-making. A further noted regulatory challenge is said to stem from *limited fiscal efficiency*. Where this is encountered, governments tend to lack the capacity to raise sufficient tax revenues to allow the subsidizing of access to essential infrastructures. Such constraints are particularly prominent in countries (especially in Sub-Saharan Africa) where large parts of the population are unlikely to be able to afford to pay for the infrastructure services.[13]

---

[11] J.J. Laffont, *Regulation and Development* (Cambridge, 2005); Estache and Wren-Lewis, 'On the Theory and Evidence', 376–8. The classification follows Estache/Wren-Lewis.

[12] Guasch, Laffont and Straub estimated that 40 per cent of concessions were renegotiated in Latin America in the time period 1985–2000 (L.P. Guasch, J.J. Laffont, and S. Straub, 'Renegotiations of Concession Contracts: A Theoretical Approach' (2006) 29 *Review of Industrial Organization* 55–73.

[13] Estache and Wren-Lewis, 'Towards a Theory of Regulation for Developing Countries'. Indeed, one of the key aspects is how to deal with populations that are unlikely or unwilling to pay for services rendered, especially in electricity.

Taken as a whole, the above factors point to a bleak picture of regulation's potential to achieve a development that is of broader social value. Transnational companies dominate the regulatory process, international organizations produce imposed blueprints, and domestic elites shape international pressures in their own self-interests. At the same time, institutions are unlikely to possess the 'sticking power' that is needed to resist capture by industry, to withstand politically driven interference or even to provide capable regulation in the first place. The results of these institutional limitations are reduced investments, the likelihood of biased decision-making, if not capture, and thus, overall, a sub-optimal developmental outcome. The rest of this chapter considers how different literatures have sought to confront these challenges.

Building Credible Commitment through Institutional Design

One seminal response to the diagnosis of institutional weaknesses has been to focus on 'commitment'. This position is encountered especially in the work by Bruno Levy and Pablo Spiller (and the wider economic institutionalist literature).[14] According to their well-known argument, the need to attract private investment takes on a higher priority when countries lack the resources to undertake economic development projects themselves. Private investment (especially in those industries characterized by a high degree of asset specificity) will only be forthcoming if private investors do not have to fear 'administrative expropriation'. This means that investment decisions will not face legislative reversal or discretionary regulatory action that may be outside the boundaries of legitimate expectations (such as imposing additional social or environmental obligations, refusing legitimate price increase demands, and such like).

According to Levy and Spiller, three dimensions underlie any regulatory commitment: (1) substantive, written restraints on the discretionary action of the regulator; (2) restraints hindering reversal or amendment of the overall regulatory regime; and (3) institutions that safeguard these restraints. Designing regulatory institutions in these contexts is about reducing the potential unpredictable use of discretion. As noted earlier (Chapter 4), the extent to which discretion matters is a question of a country's 'institutional endowment'. This is

---

[14] B. Levy and P. Spiller, 'The Institutional Foundations of Regulatory Commitment: A Comparative Study of Telecommunications Regulation' (1994) 10(2) *Journal of Law, Economics and Organisation* 201–46; B. Levy and P. Spiller (eds), *Regulations, Institutions and Commitment: Comparative Studies in Telecommunications* (Cambridge, 1996).

defined by the country's political system (the constitutional checks and balances, the existence of coalition or single-party government, bicameral versus unicameral legislatives, the role of constitutional courts, etc.) and the inheritance of particular institutional features, such as whether the bureaucracy has a reputation for being neutral and strong-minded (ministerial departments and regulators) and what kind of legacies exist in terms of state–industry relations.

The repertoire of institutional commitment devices is extensive. First, there may be '*hardwiring*' of the regulatory bargain in precisely specified legislation. In Westminster-type democracies, however, the decisions of dominant executives are difficult to check, and such legislative devices will offer little commitment as legislative reversal is relatively easy. A second commitment device involves '*delegation*' to other parts of executive government, especially to freestanding regulatory agencies. Taking some areas of decision-making outside the scope of electorally motivated politics is seen as one key device to reduce time inconsistency and enhance expertise in decision-making. Again, such delegation is relatively vulnerable to 'cheating' over time, especially where the resources of the regulator are in the hands of elected politicians, where regulatory bodies face considerable resource constraints (in terms of staff and finance) and/or single regulated industries.[15] A third option is the use of legally binding '*licence provisions*' that set out the rights and responsibilities of service providers. These rights and responsibilities are checked by a credible and independent judiciary. Such devices naturally offer a lower level of commitment in jurisdictions where the judiciary has a more ambiguous record in upholding obligations and rights against government.

The kinds of regulatory solutions that are required to deal with the problem of 'commitment' depend on the particular institutional endowment. One single 'off-the-shelf' solution does not exist. In particular, it is also the case that regulatory agencies cannot be regarded as a universal remedy to deal with time inconsistency problems either. That is—in contexts without any institutional 'veto-points'—those political systems where governments do not face resistance from either coalition partners, regional governments, constitutional rules, or constitutional and administrative courts, any legislative enactment of regulatory rules and institutions can be reversed quickly. In those contexts, hardly any device exists to allow for credible commitment, apart from legally enforceable contracts or licences. In those contexts where governments are faced with considerable hurdles (if not gridlock), devices such as regulatory institutions do enjoy a degree of autonomy, as their legislative status is unlikely to be reversible that easily. Countries whose institutional endowment

---

[15] J. Stern, 'Effective Utility Regulation and Independent Regulation: What Makes an Independent Regulator Independent?' (1997) 8(2) *Business Strategy Review* 67–74; J. Cubbin and J. Stern, 'The Impact of Regulatory Governance and Privatization on Electricity Industry Generation Capacity in Developing Countries' (2006) 20(1) *The World Bank Economic Review* 115–41.

confers few effective commitment devices makes incentive-based regulation highly inappropriate—the discretion inherent in these sophisticated regulatory instruments is exposed to potential administrative expropriation.[16]

The idea that institutional designs can be utilized to deal with the challenges of development regulation is an attractive one and has enjoyed widespread currency, in academic and practitioner worlds. For example, it was used to explain why Jamaica enjoyed a phenomenal catch-up in terms of telecommunications network availability in the 1990s, especially in contrast to other Commonwealth Caribbean islands.[17] The argument made was that the terms of the exclusivity licences granted to Cable & Wireless in the late 1980s facilitated investment and thereby also development. The story of Jamaica, however, also points to the limitations of this particular institutional design argument. The Jamaican government did everything to undermine the terms of the initial deal: it introduced a discretionary regulatory body (of a cross-sectoral nature), it committed itself to liberalization through the signing of international trade deals, and it allowed the opening of different communications niche markets by the Jamaican competition authority. In other words, the empirical pattern suggests that the licences were unable to provide for the kind of commitment devices that the literature suggested were required to attract extensive infrastructure modernization—but Jamaica did not seem to be penalized by reductions in investment.

Institutional design accounts, moreover, run up against the problem that 'contracts' are always incomplete, since the future is inherently unpredictable and no hardwiring can foresee all changes in technological, economic, social, or international environments (such as changes in international settlement rates, as noted above). The idea that licences and contracts offer a 'discretion-free' regulatory instrument to deal with potential commitment problems is inherently limited, especially when the political climate changes (as has been witnessed internationally in numerous cases of water concessions). In other words, the initial literature may have overestimated the way in which institutional design not only can incorporate the inherent bounded rationality in all human decision-making, but also the more specific institutional weaknesses inherent in development administration, as noted above.

There has, furthermore, been a growing insight into the inherent trade-offs affecting institutional design. One is the trade-off between commitment and flexibility. If commitment devices are designed and used in order to reduce

---

[16] Levy and Spiller argue that the nature of institutional endowment might limit regulatory options to third- or fourth-best. See Levy and Spiller, *Regulations, Institutions and Commitment*.

[17] Lodge and Stirton, 'Regulatory Reform in Small Developing States'; M. Lodge and L. Stirton, 'Withering in the Heat? In Search of the Regulatory State in the Commonwealth Caribbean' (2006) 19 (3) *Governance* 465–95. Jamaica was characterized as a jurisdiction with a dominant executive, a weak bureaucracy, and few substantive informal restraints on arbitrary decision-making, although with an effective judiciary.

the problem of inconsistency over time, this creates considerable problems on those issues where flexibility might be seen as desirable or legitimate: as when it is argued that newly elected governments should be able to respond to demands expressed through electoral processes. Similarly, flexibility may also be required because of changing technological environments. This may raise the question whether commitment should ever be hardwired in terms of relying on one single technology. Such a reliance on a single technology would require the full confidence that other technologies ('killer applications') or new social uses of technologies will not emerge.

In summary, the past two decades have witnessed a growing awareness of the inherent incompleteness of contracts and this has pointed to wider debates about industry and regulatory structures. Regulatory agencies have been found to offer no clear-cut route to the achieving of good developmental outcomes, but at the same time, other models, such as 'concession'-type models, have witnessed considerable controversy and reversal. In addition, there has been a growing awareness of the inherent institutional limitations and constraints within which regulatory regimes operate and the considerable differences in capacity that exist across jurisdictions and sectors.

Building Institutional Capacity

In the field of developmental regulation, the absence of straightforward success stories has led scholars to a position of broad humility. The insight that formal institutions are only one key influence on regulation has led to renewed interests in 'discretion' and 'agents' and to a fresh concern with ideas regarding institutional capacity—a concern that is particularly related to wider debates about the importance of 'governance'.[18]

As illustrated earlier, many commentators display considerable scepticism regarding the potential for building institutional capacity in the context of development. This scepticism has been directed at the capability of any one regulatory body to deal with technical complexity, as well as the need to prevent the arbitrary exercise of discretion—and this scepticism has led to the endorsement of 'discretion-free' concession and contractual arrangements.[19] Such worries about deficiencies of capacity relate to a widely diagnosed lack of material and human resources to competently regulate highly complex industries. A further diagnosis is the absence of societal interests that offer a

---

[18] World Bank, *Governance: The World Bank's Experience* (Washington, DC, 1993); World Bank, *World Development Report* (New York, 1997).

[19] B. Levy, 'Comparative Regulation' in P. Newman (ed.), *A New Palgrave Dictionary of Economics and the Law* (Basingstoke, 1998), 355.

counterweight to potential industry capture. As a result, efforts and proposals on building institutional capacity have focused on a number of key issues.[20]

The first of these relates to *checks and balances*. One of the key debates that has surrounded the issue of regulatory jurisdiction and the relationship between different state bodies within the wider system of executive government relates to the design of regulatory jurisdictions and 'concurrency'. Two strands exist in this debate. The first strand is interested in whether regulatory regimes should encourage overlap or not. For some, overlap is a critical design component that serves to deal with the risk of capture. Should one body be seen as being too close to industry interests (or to political interests for that matter), then the risks of biased decision-making can be somewhat moderated through the presence of other bodies. Competition authorities, for example, have used their powers to deal with particular restrictions in telecommunications markets and thereby facilitated wider liberalization tendencies that arguably otherwise would not have been feasible. The alternative view suggests that overlap encourages gridlock, requires a high degree of cooperation, and constitutes a lack of straightforward accountability relationships.

The second strand in the debate on jurisdiction addresses the question whether agencies should be cross-sectoral or focused on single industries. The case for a single industry regulatory agency involves the contention that regulators need specific expertise and focus and that this focus cannot be guaranteed if resources within one organization are shifted across priorities, or where political heat demands attention on the urgent, rather than the important. The counter-argument suggests that regulators in the development context in particular are faced by particular resource constraints. One resource constraint is staff—and requiring skilled staff for a number of regulatory bodies threatens to result in an overall weakening of human capacity in any one regulatory agency. A second limitation is finance, and special issues arise where regulators rely on a private monopoly to provide for all (or most) of the financing of regulation. This practice has often proven to be problematic where it creates a degree of agency dependency on the punctual payment of industry levies. Such challenges have often led, especially in smaller size jurisdictions, to the advocacy of multi-sectoral regulatory bodies as a means of concentrating and developing overall capacity.

A second focus for capacity building efforts is related and is that of *human resources*. The central concern here is the availability of staff to conduct regulatory activities competently, in particular in the face of technical complexity. Debates concerning human resources relate not just to the presence

---

[20] M. Lodge and L. Stirton, 'Embedding Regulatory Autonomy in Caribbean Telecommunications' (2002) 73(4) *Annals of Public and Cooperative Economics* 667–93; M. Grindle, 'The Good Government Imperative: Human Resources, Organisations and Institutions' in M. Grindle (ed.), *Getting Good Government: Capacity Building in the Public Sector of Developing Countries* (Cambridge, MA, 1997).

(and supply) of professional and technical staff through active training and recruitment, but also to the need for salaries that will both attract personnel and limit the incentive for talented staff to seek work-opportunities with the better-paying regulated industries.[21] The human resource dimension also involves debates on how regulators can establish management systems to generate information flows, to effect coordination across different regulatory activities, and to retain institutional memory.

A third focus in capacity-building relates to *embeddedness*. The idea of embeddedness has witnessed considerable interest in the development literature. The initial argument highlights the importance of social ties. There will be a lack of embeddedness if either the institution is too closely linked into the politics of executive government, or it is completely decoupled ('too loose') from wider political processes.[22] Either way it is unable to capably conduct its business. Embeddedness also partly challenges those views that stress the importance of formal institutions, by stressing the importance of linkages between state and society.[23] It is therefore an approach that relates to those institutional accounts of the 'regulatory space' and 'decentred' network kind by emphasizing the importance of ongoing social relations[24] and the nature of regulation as an ongoing process of negotiation and renegotiation.[25] In the first instance, the idea of embeddedness and its emphasis on social ties between different parties engaged in a regulatory regime points to the importance of industry structure. It is not just in the world of industrializing and less developed countries that the political and economic weight of a private monopolist is said to pose considerable regulatory problems. One of the key insights of the work on embeddedness has been that industry structure is as important as regulatory structure to prevent problems of capture. Being able to rely on alternative sources for industry information does address informational asymmetry problems to some extent.

The notion of 'embeddedness' goes beyond raising industry structure as a key component in regulation. Embeddedness is not just about increasing the number of interorganizational linkages; it is also about allowing for a regulatory interaction that is characterized by mutual acceptance of actors' authority and legitimacy. One example of embeddedness is the industry's acceptance of the regulatory agency's status.

Highlighting these three dimensions of capacity suggests that credible commitment in regulation is concerned not merely with formal institutional

---

[21] Grindle, 'The Good Government Imperative'.

[22] J.S. Migdal, *Strong Societies and Weak States* (Princeton, NJ, 1998).

[23] C. Polidano, 'Don't Discard State Autonomy' (2001) 49(3) *Political Studies* 513–27; L. Hancher and M. Moran, 'Organizing Regulatory Space' in L. Hancher and M. Moran (eds), *Capitalism, Culture and Economic Regulation* (Oxford, 1989), 292.

[24] Hancher and Moran, 'Organizing Regulatory Space', 292.

[25] Evans, 'The Eclipse of the State', 12.

design, but with issues of mutual acceptance and interactions across actors in the day-to-day operation of a regulatory regime. Embeddedness also highlights the fact that institutional endowment is hardly static (although in the way it is defined by authors such as Levy and Spiller it takes on a largely static nature). Rather, institutional endowment is arguably sector-specific (rather than country-specific) and is based on communication, interaction, and, arguably, reputation, rather than mere formal institutional design. This insight is not unique to the world of development, but it is arguable that, in this particular context, one way in which one can address the problems of capture is to view regulation as taking place in an interactive space including domestic industry actors within an international environment. The challenge for regulatory capacity in the context of industrialization and development is therefore not just one of formal institutional design and the maintenance of 'intelligent' regulatory institutions, it is also about the far more difficult process of embedding relationships within a wider regulatory space in order to reduce opportunities of capture and/or of arbitrary state behaviour.

Enforcing Regulation

The above discussion has noted the importance of institutional design—and its limitations.[26] Often, however, the laws and regulations applicable to the sector are hardly the problem. One of the key areas in which regulation is particularly challenged in the context of development is enforcement. Developmental contexts are widely associated with weak enforcement capacity, widespread violations of the law, and a broader capture-prone governance context.[27] Weak enforcement capacity is related to insufficient financial resources and capable staff, but also to a lack of insulation from external influences. Indeed, the kind of resources available to any one regulator—as well as the nature of the 'delivery process' (for example, whether central government standards are being enforced by regional or local government staff) provide for particular challenges in a developing political and economic system. Apart from procedural and substantive weaknesses, achieving compliance is even more problematic. Firms, often benefitting from blurred boundaries between states and markets as well as from the dominance of informal networks over formal enforcement structures, are often seen as

---

[26] J.L. Esquirol, 'The Failed Law of Latin America' (2008) 56(1) *American Journal of Comparative Law* 75–124.

[27] L. McAllister, B. Von Rooij, and R. Kagan, 'Reorienting Regulation: Pollution Enforcement in Industrializing Countries' (2010) 32(1) *Law and Policy* 1–13; L. McAllister, 'Dimensions of Enforcement Style: Factoring In Regulatory Autonomy and Capacity' (2010) 32(1) *Law and Policy* 61–78.

unwilling to comply with regulatory requirements and, if necessary, as willing to challenge regulatory decisions through legal redress systems.[28]

This particular version of 'adversarial legalism' points to the problems of enforcement more generally, as noted earlier in this volume.[29] Enforcement strategies have increasingly been said to require a 'mixed strategy' that includes formal-punitive and informal-persuasion components. But such strategies are under considerable challenge in the context of development. For example, despite considerable inspection activity and the subsequent imposition of fines, regulators in Brazil face considerable problems in actually collecting these fines. This raises the wider concerns about how regulators can credibly enforce their decisions, given internal management problems as well as determined industry actions to prevent regulators from achieving their objectives. Thus, overly formalistic enforcement action with punitive sanctions has been linked to a lack of actual behaviour modification.

A further key question with particular relevance to development and regulation relates to the staffing of regulatory offices. One issue is the extent to which incentive structures can succeed in maintaining regulatory staff in all regions of a country or whether there is not an inevitable 'migration' of regulatory staff towards more attractive/metropolitan postings. A further matter of concern is the societal background of regulatory staff. The 'representativeness' of regulatory staff is a matter that has attracted a considerable discussion in related debates in public administration.[30] Suffice to say, regulatory enforcement, especially when involving controversial endowments such as property rights over land, is about making choices of a fundamentally political nature. It is unlikely that social ties will not matter in such decisions.

The context of development also raises issues with regard to two further key aspects of the enforcement literature. First, the literature on alternatives to traditional regulation tends to have its roots in the industrialized and developed world. As a result, these mechanisms constitute a response to perceptions of 'over-regulation' and to worries about the costs of 'command and control' techniques. In the context of development, one that is arguably characterized by overlapping and underlapping regimes as well as over- and underregulation at the same time, the so-called alternatives are often

---

[28] Of course, less merciful ways of challenging 'inconvenient' regulatory action exist, such as contract killing.

[29] R.A. Kagan and L. Axelrad (eds), *Regulatory Encounters* (Berkeley, 2000).

[30] V. Subramaniam, 'Representative Bureaucracy: A Reassessment' (1967) 61(4) *American Political Science Review*; M.J. Esman, 'Public Administration, Ethnic Conflict, and Economic Development' (1997) 57(6) *Public Administration Review* 527–33; T. Sowell, *Preferential Policies: An International Perspective* (New York, 1990); M. Weiner, 'The Pursuit of Ethnic Inequalities through Preferential Policies: A Comparative Public Policy Perspective' in R. Goldmann and A.J. Wilson (eds), *From Independence to Statehood: Managing Ethnic Conflict in Five African and Asian States* (London, 1984); M.J. Esman, 'Public Administration and Conflict Management in Plural Societies: The Case for Representative Bureaucracy' (1999) 19(4) *Public Administration and Development* 353–66.

proposed in order to offer a substitute to often non-existing or non-functioning state regulation. Empirical studies suggest, however, that these alternatives can only function within a setting that allows for systematic monitoring and sanctioning (i.e. they function under the shadow of a hierarchy).[31] A second matter relates to other enforcement mechanisms, such as civil liability mechanisms (utilized by prosecutors and courts). Problems in the developmental context are the asymmetric power relationships within society. These reduce the potential of 'fire-alarm' mechanisms that operate through alternative venues. For some, the role of public prosecutors is therefore taking on considerable importance—as Lesley McAllister noted in her seminal study on environmental law enforcement styles in two Brazilian states, Sao Paolo (rich) and Pará (poor).[32] She found that it was not merely the more orthodox dimensions of regulatory enforcement (formalism and coercion) that mattered. Even more significant were issues of autonomy (the ability to determine enforcement goals) and capacity (the proactive nature of regulators in identifying violations).

In summary, studies of regulatory enforcement give considerable reason to despair about the effectiveness of regulation in the context of industrialization and development. Weak capacity is coupled with a weak regard for self-motivated compliance with regulatory standards if they are not linked to material producer self-interest. Some commentators have noted, however, the effectiveness of some programmes, such as state-backed certification programmes or projects that involve state actors and societal participants. It is questionable, though, whether such projects can be sustained when social and environmental regulatory goals conflict with economic interests.[33]

Conclusion

The literature on regulation and development has witnessed considerable change over the past three decades.[34] The starting point was an overall

---

[31] L. McAllister, B. Von Rooij, and R. Kagan, 'Reorienting Regulation: Pollution Enforcement in Industrializing Countries' (2010) 32(1) *Law and Policy*, esp. 7–9.

[32] L. McAllister, *Making Law Matter* (Stanford, CA, 2008).

[33] A. Blackman, 'Can Voluntary Environmental Regulation Work in Developing Countries?' (2006) 36 *Policy Studies Journal* 119–41; B. Van Rooij, *Regulating Land and Pollution in China* (Leiden, 2006).

[34] World Bank, *Infrastructure at the Crossroads* (Washington, DC, 2006); E. Aurid and P. Picard, 'Infrastructure and Public Utilities Privatization in Developing Countries' (2009) 23(1) *World Bank Economic Review* 77–100; H. Jalilian, C. Kirkpatrick, and D. Parker, 'The Impact of Regulation on Economic Growth in Developing Countries' (2007) 35(1) *World Development* 87–103; A. Estache, A. Goicoechea, and L. Trujillo, 'Utilities Reforms and Corruption in Developing Countries' (2009) 17 (2) *Utilities Policy* 191–202.

pessimism regarding the potential effect of administration in achieving development. There was then a temporary optimism that the separation of production and regulation, coupled with appropriate institutional design of regulatory incentives, would lead to developmental outcomes. By the late noughties, though, such optimism had been considerably shaken, although it had not evaporated entirely. On the one hand, the story of the development of telecommunications markets suggests that technological changes and liberalizations can bring positive effects for development (and possibly regulation). Other industries have witnessed a lesser share of the 'success story' and, in particular, these include the 'stationary' infrastructure industries such as water and electricity. More specifically, the rapidly industrializing 'giants', China and Brazil, have provided examples where state interests (across all levels of government) and producer interests have been inherently interlinked, leading to considerable (and well-known) tensions between the regulatory and the ownership interests of the state, as well as the interests of these strategic industries.[35]

In conclusion, the area of development remains one of the frontier areas for the study and practice of regulation. Many of the questions and theories that have been developed in the context of the developed industrialized world can be carried across to the world of development and industrialization, even when electoral politics do not always necessarily play a key role in the thinking of political principals. At the same time, the development domain offers a key area where regulation is faced with limited capacity to affect behaviour and to gather information. This places considerable limitations on the types of standards and intervention tools that can be used to improve economic, environmental, and social well-being.

---

[35] B. Van Rooij and C.H.W. Lo, 'A Fragile Convergence: Understanding Variation in the Enforcement of China's Industrial Pollution Law' (2010) 32 *Law and Policy* 14–37.

21 Global and International Regulation

Traditionally, the notion of global regulation has been associated with international agreements between states. These agreements related to such matters as international labour, communications services, pharmaceutical or pesticide standards. They involved such international bodies as the International Labour Organization, the International Telecommunications Union, the World Health Organization, and the Food and Agriculture Organization. International regulatory schemes were often established in the wake of major disasters. The sinking of the *Titanic* in 1911, for instance, prompted numerous such agreements including the 1914 *Convention for the Safety of Life at Sea* and the 1912 London Radio Conference that sought to develop the use of bandwith for the sending of distress signals.[1] In telecommunications, international regulatory agreements governed call settlements, and standards were conducted in the intergovernmental fora of the International Telecommunications Union.[2] Private standard-setting for electrical and electronic engineering was institutionalized at the international level in 1906 with the formation of the International Electro-Technical Commission (ETC), a sister-organization of the International Organization for Standardization (ISO), which was formed in 1947.[3] Both of these were voluntary and privately funded and relied on national adaptation and enforcement.

---

[1] We ignore the long history of international regimes that go back to ancient times and concentrate largely on the period starting in the late nineteenth century. For wider literature, see: J. Braithwaite and P. Drahos, *Global Business Regulation* (Cambridge, 2000), 420; M.L. Djelic and K. Sahlin-Andersson (eds), *Transnational Governance* (Cambridge, 2006); D. Kerwer, 'Rules that Many Use: Standards and Global Regulation' (2005) 18(4) *Governance* 611–32; M. Koenig-Archibugi, 'Global Regulation' in R. Baldwin, M. Cave, and M. Lodge (eds), *Oxford Handbook of Regulation* (Oxford, 2010); K.W. Abbott and D. Snidal, 'The Governance Triangle: Regulatory Standards Institutions and the Shadow of the State' in W. Mattli and N. Woods (eds), *Politics of Global Regulation* (Princeton, NJ, 2009); W. Mattli and T. Büthe, 'Setting International Standards: Technological Rationality or Primacy of Power?' (2003) 56 *World Politics* 1–42; W. Mattli, 'The Politics and Economics of International Institutional Standards Setting: An Introduction' (2001) 8(3) *Journal of European Public Policy* 328–44; K. Holzinger, C. Knill, and T. Sommerer, 'Environmental Policy Convergence: The Impact of International Harmonization, Transnational Communication, and Regulatory Competition' (2008) 62 *International Organization* 553–87.

[2] With the ITU's members largely representing publicly owned telecommunications providers—see P. Genschel and R. Werle, 'From National Hierarchies to International Standardization: Modal Changes in the Governance of Telecommunications' (1993) 13(3) *Journal of Public Policy* 203–25.

[3] Mattli and Büthe, 'Setting International Standards', 6. ISO was in itself a merger of two bodies, the International Federation of National Standardizing Associations (ISA) and the United Nations Standards Coordinating Committee (UNSCC).

This earlier, mostly state-centred age of global regulation, came, however, to be challenged by changing industry structures as well as the internationalization of economic activities. Demands for compatibility across and between technologies and networks created growing calls for standardization at the global or international level. The International Standards Organization (ISO) (and ETC) enjoyed growing recognition, and moved beyond the earlier dominance of national standard-setting bodies such as Berlin's Deutsches Institut fur Normung (DIN). As a result of such developments, global regulation shifted from its basis in intergovernmental agreements and it came to represent an intermeshing of domestic and international, and often overlapping, regimes. As such, it came to follow the patterns associated with 'decentred regulation'. Purely intergovernmental processes became less prominent and, instead, global regulation witnessed a pluralization of engaged parties, along with a growing number of regulatory orders that were engaged in a continuous process of renegotiation.[4]

In the modern era, these global regimes tend to manifest a variety of characteristics, ranging from their key participants (governments, industry, and/or non-governmental organizations (NGOs)) to their instruments (ranging from the prescriptive to the ambiguous). This newer shaping of global regulation has implications for statehood in so far as workers and consumers are exposed to global regulation that originates outside their national governmental sphere. However, it also has implications for debates regarding 'good regulation' and raises questions whether global regulation is suffering from an 'effectiveness' deficit and whether global regulation lacks legitimacy and accountability.

This chapter starts by outlining some key variations in global regulation and then explores how the emergence and nature of these global regulatory regimes can be explained. It suggests that these debates resemble closely those primarily interested in domestic regulation. Finally, it discusses the key challenges that are presented by global regulation, namely the questions whether global regulation suffers deficits in terms of effectiveness, accountability, legitimacy, and consistency.

Variations in Global Regulation

Global—or international—regulation tends to emerge as a response to those externalities that are generated by international interdependencies and which

---

[4] N. Krisch, 'The Pluralism of Global Administrative Law' (2006) 17(1) *European Journal of International Law* 247–78; E. Meidinger, 'Beyond Westphalia: Comparative Legalization in Emerging Transnational Regulatory Systems' in C. Brütsch and D. Lehmkuhl (eds), *Law and Legalization in Transnational Relations* (Oxford, 2007).

lead states and/or firms to demand a degree of coordinated regulatory responses that goes beyond national boundaries. Here it is helpful to distinguish regimes with reference to two core dimensions. The first of these is the degree to which they are 'contested' in so far as they apply regulatory standards that are subjected to question at the state level. The other dimension considers the extent to which regulatory activities are dominantly shaped by state- or by non-state actors.

Table 21.1 can only offer a starting point since, as our following discussion shows, differences become blurred the closer we look at particular examples. Global regulation has as its 'targets' both domestic regulation as well as international private economic actors. Global regulation may be sector-specific or of a more generic nature. There are also changes over time: when looking at the regulation of human rights, one can diagnose a shift away from state to individual responsibility, with largely domestic enforcement taking place in the light of international standards (as evidenced by the rise of human rights trials).[5] In this section, we consider three examples of global regulation (Boxes A–C). Those sectors in which different national regulatory jurisdictions are in competition with each other (Box D) are treated elsewhere in this volume (see Chapter 17 on 'Regulatory Competition').

One example of privately driven and contested global regulation is forest certification (Box A).[6] The motivating concern behind the establishing of this regime was accelerating deforestation at a time when state-based attempts to deal with the problem were seen as largely ineffectual, especially following the failure of the 1992 UN Conference on Environment and Development in Rio.[7] The Forest Stewardship Council (FSC) was founded by a number of

Table 21.1. Variations in global regulation

	Non-state-dominated	State-dominated
Contested regimes	A: *Private regimes* Examples: Forestry stewardship, social corporate responsibility codes.	D: *Competition between national regulatory standards.*
Non-contested regimes	B: *Private exclusive standard setting* Example: Accounting Standards Board.	C: *Trans-governmental standard-setting* Examples: OECD, International Telecommunications Union.

---

[5] K. Sikkink, 'From State Responsibility to Individual Criminal Accountability: A New Regulatory Model for Core Human Rights Violations' in W. Mattli and N. Woods (eds), *Politics of Global Regulation* (Princeton, NJ, 2009).

[6] Further examples are provided in T.M. Smith and M. Fischlein, 'Rival Private Governance Networks: Competing to Define the Rules of Sustainability Performance' (2010) 20 *Global Environmenal Change* 511–22.

[7] Meidinger, 'Beyond Westphalia'; E. Meidinger, 'On Explaining the Development of "Emission Trading" in US Air Pollution Regulation' (1985) 7(4) *Law and Policy* 447–79; K. Brown, 'Cut and Run?

transnational environmental advocacy groups (including Greenpeace and the Worldwide Fund for Nature) in 1993. Its decision-making takes account of different interests and hemispheres. The overall regime is built on a system of certification, inspection, and enforcement, the latter function becoming more prominent in the wake of the FSC's endorsement by leading retailers. Overall, the FSC provides for a performance-based regulatory regime: assessment is conducted through an external organization and the system relies on relative uniform performance standards.[8]

The FSC's regime contrasts with rival industry-based forestry regimes that place their emphasis on management-based standards (such as the Pan-European Forest Certification Council) or with the intergovernmental Programme for the Endorsement of Forest Certification. Such competition between regimes may be seen to imply fragmentation, but observers such as Errol Meidinger suggest that in the case of forestry, competing regulatory regimes triggered interaction effects which led to an adoption of increasingly stringent and similar standards more generally. He diagnoses the emergence of interdependent and interlinked networks that import each other's instruments through a process of 'institutional isomorphism'.[9] Indeed, the emergence and prominence of these private regulatory regimes has also led to their incorporation in national state-centric regulatory activities.

An emerging similarity between different and contested codes of conduct has also been diagnosed in the area of so-called corporate social responsibility.[10] In this field, codes were initially used to respond to demands by non-governmental advocacy groups that firms should not base their conduct solely on their private business interests. These codes are supposed to impact on the behaviour of international actors (including firms, states, and non-governmental organizations), but they are widely said to suffer from weak enforcement. These codes have, in addition, emerged in more sector-specific settings. Global trade associations, for example, have sought to bind their members' conduct in the coffee and cocoa industries. A final example of contested private regulatory standards is provided by the university rankings that are generated by international publications, such as the *Financial Times*. These relate in particular to business management programmes. Such rankings, and in particular the kind of indicators

---

Evolving Institutions for Global Forest Governance' (2001) 13 *Journal of International Development* 893–905.

[8] Meidinger, 'Beyond Westphalia', 125–6.

[9] Ibid., 129–30.

[10] Apart from the guideline ISO 26000 that has no certification or other requirement, there are a number of private approaches, including Earthcheck, the Fair Labor Association, the Fair Wear Foundation, the Prince's Accounting for Sustainability Project's Connected Reporting Framework, and Social Accountability International.

chosen, are said to provide for pressures for a growing homogenization of curriculums and programmes.[11]

The accounting standards regime constitutes a relatively non-contested international private regulatory system that relies on principles-based regulation (Box B).[12] The International Accounting Standards Board (IASB) was founded in 2001 and was modelled on the US-Financial Accounting Standards Board. The IASB's standards are not legally binding, but require businesses and national accountancy practices to adopt their standards. International standards, therefore, operate through incorporation into national accountancy standards and, indeed, they have become a central feature of the private regulation of accounting practices. Traditionally, national accounting standards reflected broadly on the type of 'variety of capitalism' associated with any particular country, with clear differences diagnosed between Anglo-Saxon 'liberal' and more 'coordinated' economies, and between different legal traditions.[13] International Accounting Standards (as devised by the International Accounting Standards Board) were promulgated in order to facilitate a convergence in national and business accounting practices and to harmonize the available information on individual businesses' performance. A further aim (one driven in particular by the UK Accountancy profession) was to avoid public (especially European Community) regulation of international accounting standards.[14]

---

[11] T. Hedmo, K. Sahlin-Andersson, and L. Wedlin, 'The Emergence of a European Regulatory Field of Management Education' in M.L. Djelic and K. Sahlin-Andersson (eds), *Transnational Governance* (Cambridge, 2006).

[12] M. Barth, W. Landsman, and M. Lang, 'International Accounting Standards and Accounting Quality' (2008) 46(3) *Journal of Accounting Research* 467–98; W. Mattli and T. Büthe, 'Global Private Governance: Lessons from a National Model of Setting Standards in Accounting' (2005) 26 *Law and Contemporary Problems* 225–62; J. Perry and A. Noelke, 'International Accounting Standard Setting' (2005) 7(3) *Business and Politics*, available at: http://www.bepress.com/bap/vol7/iss3/art5 (last accessed 27 Dec. 2010); Braithwaite and Drahos, *Global Business Regulation*, 121.

[13] S. Botzem and S. Quack, 'Contested Rules and Shifting Boundaries: International Standard Setting in Accounting', *Discussion Paper SPIII 2005–201*, Wissenschaftszentrum für Sozialforschung (Berlin, 2005).

[14] Ibid.; A. Hopwood, 'Some Reflections on the Harmonization of Accounting in the EU' (1994) 3 (2) *European Accounting Review* 241–53. The aim of this 'private authority'-based regulatory regime has been to achieve broad harmonization between international practices. This also links to attempts to converge international standards with those applicable to US businesses, in particular by relying on so-called Fair Value Accounting. Since the 1980s, developments have been driven by the growth in foreign direct investment and by international equity markets, thereby leading to a growing importance attached to the US accounting standards (US GAAP). It has been noted that this is relatively non-contested (there is still contestation with US Accounting Standards). International Accounting Standards are now legally binding on all public companies in the European Union. Contestation therefore largely exists *within* rather than purely between competing standards. A related example of private uncontested global regulation is the 'Institute of International Finance'. This body represents major international banks that developed a code of conduct in response to debt-restructuring proposals. This occurred in response to potentially 'threatening' proposals developed within the International Monetary Fund.

A somewhat different (and arguably blurred) kind of dynamic is evident in the so-called Kimberley process, which applies to the mining industry, in particular to diamonds mined in civil war territories (i.e. 'blood diamonds').[15] This regime is uncontested in character and was established in the wake of public protest about the financing of civil wars through the selling of high-end jewellery and evidence that diamond-related revenues were 'informalized' by local political elites to their own monetary advantage (especially in Sierra Leone, Angola, and Congo (Zaire)). The Kimberley process emerged partly in response to initiatives in the UN Security Council that were designed to deploy economic sanctions against the trading of 'conflict diamonds'.[16] These attempts to impose diamond embargoes were largely said to have failed due to a reluctance of the UN to enforce these standards. Two NGOs (Partnership Africa Canada and Global Witness) launched a process of consumer boycotts with support from other NGOs. Faced with these pressures and fearful of wider consequences for diamond markets, South Africa initiated the Kimberley Process so as to restrict the selling of rough 'blood diamonds' while protecting the 'legitimate' selling of diamonds. The process thus represents a cooperation between advocacy groups, the dominant diamond producers (De Beers), and affected exporting and importing governments. It is a regime that is particularly dependent on the technical expertise of the dominant supplier, but it relies to some extent on external auditing of compliance, monitoring, and enforcement. Its overall effectiveness has, however, been questioned,[17] as has that of other attempts at international self-regulation such as the regime operated by the Marine Stewardship Council for the protection of sustainable fisheries.

Turning to those state-centric regimes that are not characterized by contestation (Box C), regulatory systems have been set up across a number of regimes, such as health, occupational health, agriculture, and maritime pollution, under the auspices of the United Nations or the OECD.[18] The OECD is involved in the regulation of tax, especially regarding so-called tax havens in areas such as shipping, insurance, and banking secrecy. International tax cooperation can primarily be interpreted as a response to demands by multinational enterprises. These enterprises were particularly interested in the reduction of perverse effects arising from cross-border trading and in the avoidance of 'double taxation'.[19] According to Eden and Kudrle, the OECD's

---

[15] C. Jojarth, *Crime, War, and Global Trafficking* (Cambridge, 2009).

[16] UN Resolution, S/1998/1173.

[17] 'Diamonds: Does the Kimberley Process Work?', *BBC News*, 28 June 2010, http://www.bbc.co.uk/news/10307046 (last accessed 24 Dec. 2010).

[18] For example, the International Maritime Organization passed guidance that restricted access by cruise ships to polar waters (the 'polar code').

[19] L. Eden and R.T. Kudrle, 'Tax Havens: Renegade States in the International Tax Regime?' (2005) 27(1) *Law and Policy* 100–27; OECD, *Harmful Tax Competition* (Paris, 1998); OECD, *Tax Haven Update* (Paris, 2003).

role in regulating taxation through the blacklisting of particular jurisdictions since the late 1990s emerged in the context of earlier initiatives by the US (since the 1960s) and the European Union. It also reflected a growing internationalization of business transactions that was said to have potential implications for the fiscal powers of the state.[20] The OECD approach has largely been based on the strategy of 'naming and shaming' and has led, to some extent, to an adjustment in the identified tax havens' reporting practices. In later years, the emphasis has increasingly shifted towards encouraging national tax transparency and information exchange.[21]

A different kind of regulatory instrument that is associated with the OECD is the 'peer review' process. In so-called regulatory reviews, for instance, OECD member states receive an evaluation report by the OECD that assesses the key characteristics of domestic regulatory regimes (and relevant competition policy). These reports are produced by OECD staff and fellow member state delegates and are said to provide for regulation of state regimes through processes of peer-review and evaluation. They also encourage domestic reconsideration of regulatory strategies in so far as member states have to participate within a structured process of review.[22]

A more sector-specific example of an intergovernmental, non-contested global regulator is the International Telecommunications Union, which emerged from earlier cooperation on the sending of telegraphs across borders.[23] It used to operate as the key international regulator in telecommunications, and was constituted by national governments (and their usually publicly owned national telecommunications providers). The role of the ITU as central international regulator has, however, become increasingly challenged as a result of extensive technological changes and a period of liberalization in and privatization of national telecommunications markets. The ITU's place has become contested by a multitude of standardization bodies that represent the variety of industries involved in the communications sector. This set of challenges has led, however, not to the ITU's disappearance but to a change in its role. It has moved to become a body that is increasingly attuned to networking and which recognizes the inherently decentred character of contemporary standard-setting in which private industry plays a predominant role.[24]

---

[20] See Eden and Kudrle, 'Tax Havens', 121, who further list a series of other international 'naming and shaming' regulators.

[21] OECD, *Tax Co-operation 2009: Towards a Level Playing Field* (Paris, 2009).

[22] M. Lodge, 'The Importance of Being Modern: International Benchmarking and National Regulatory Innovation' (2005) 12(4) *Journal of European Public Policy* 649–67.

[23] Braithwaite and Drahos, *Global Business Regulation*, 326.

[24] R. Werle, 'Institutional Aspects of Standardization: Jurisdictional Conflicts and the Choice of Coordination Organizations' (2001) 8(3) *Journal of European Public Policy* 392–410.

A process that mixes governmental and industry elements and which is not contested is represented by the Hazard Analysis Critical Control Point analysis (HACCP) for food safety. This approach emerged as a private regime in the 1960s and was driven by a US food processing company, Pillsbury. This company set up this type of food safety regime because it sought to develop a systems approach that resembled the one used by NASA.[25] It was endorsed by the World Health Organization in 1972, and, at the same time, it was also recommended by the US Food and Drug Administration. In 1985, it became part of the Codex Alimentarius (a subsidiary of both the World Health Organization and the UN's Food and Agriculture Organization).[26] HACCPs have also become legally binding as part of the EU's changing food regime (2003/53/EC) and, earlier, the *Agreement of Sanitary and Phytosanitary Measures* as part of the 1993 GATT Uruguay Round. The regime moved from a private to a public form of global regulation—one in which the principles-based self-regulation of private organizations is checked by public authorities.

The above discussion provides an indication of key variations across global regulatory regimes. The regime variations that are noted do blur at the edges, especially the closer we look at the way in which privately initiated regimes become powerful through incorporation into national (state-centred) regulation. Overall, however, it can be concluded that global regulation across all its variants resembles 'decentred regulation' in that these processes are hardly ever dominated by states, and they are also characterized by considerable contestation not just between regimes, but also in terms of expertise.

Explaining Variations in Global Regulation

A core variation across global regulatory regimes is the degree to which they vary in the specificity of their standards, sanctions, enforcement machineries, and information-gathering requirements. One of the key terms that the literature has used in discussing variation across global regulatory regimes is that of 'legalization'.[27] Some international regimes impose highly specific

---

[25] Pillsbury was tasked to develop flight food and nutrition for astronauts—see D. Demortain, 'Standardising through Concepts: Scientific Experts and the International Development of the HACCP Food Safety Standard', *CARR Discussion Paper 45* (London, 2007).

[26] The Codex was established in 1962 as part of an intergovernmental agreement; it is said to be the 'most important international organization in the globalization of food standards' (Braithwaite and Drahos, *Global Business Regulation*, 405). An earlier example is the Codex Alimentarius Austriacus that had governed food in the Austro-Hungarian empire since the 1890s.

[27] K.W. Abbott and D. Snidal, 'Hard and Soft Law in International Governance' (2000) 54(3) *International Organization* 421–56; P. Rosendorff and H. Milner, 'The Optimal Design of International Institutions: Uncertainty and Escape' (2001) 55(4) *International Organization* 829–57; K. Abbott,

obligations and others leave considerable delegated autonomy to the participants in the regime.[28] Why this should be so is a matter for consideration, as are the reasons why global regulatory bodies are in some cases state-centric (in that they are accountable to intergovernmental fora) and in other cases non-state-centric, in so far as they are dominated by private interest associations.

There are a number of main approaches to accounting for these differences and, in many ways, these types of explanation echo the approaches that were first discussed in relation to domestic regulation in Chapter 4.

One of the key accounts of differences in legalization has centred on ideas of institutional design. The advantages of strict 'legalization' are framed through the lens of regulatory commitment: the more things are written down, allow for limited subsequent interactions, or are shifted to a clearly defined agent with distinguished expertise, the less scope there is for regulated parties to shirk or cheat. At the same time, in areas of high uncertainty or ambiguity, highly contentious politics that make 'contracting' between states problematic or in areas of high national sensitivity, a lesser degree of legalization may be seen as advantageous to core actors, since it allows them to exercise discretion. As a result, differences in legalization can partly be explained by the underlying specifics of a domain as these relate to such matters as asset specificity, observability, and enforceability.[29] These underlying aspects therefore relate to aspects such as the number and nature of participants in the particular domain (a fragmented industry or a near-monopolistic one, for example). Furthermore, asset specificity points to the wider characteristics that are associated with the regulated target. Thus, legalization therefore also relates to the kind of 'negative externality' it poses for those participants that are in a position to initiate or even impose global regulatory regimes.[30] Such accounts also place a premium on explaining the formation of regulatory bodies by pointing to expertise requirements, with private bodies said to provide for more expertise-rich regulatory involvement (this argument is made in the case of accounting, for example).[31]

Such institutional design accounts offer a particularly valuable approach to understanding differences across regulatory regimes. Other kinds of account are more interested in the forces that drive the emergence of global regulatory regimes. According to Braithwaite and Drahos, a variety of mechanisms explain different aspects of the global regulation phenomenon, including political and economic coercion, modelling (emulation), and rewards. They

R. Keohane, A. Moravcsik, A.M. Slaughter, and D. Snidal,'The Concept of Legalization' (2000) 54(3) *International Organization* 401–19.

[28] Abbott and Snidal, 'Hard and Soft Law in International Governance'.

[29] Jojarth, *Crime, War and Global Trafficking*.

[30] Abbott and Snidal, 'Hard and Soft Law in International Governance'; Jojarth, *Crime, War and Global Trafficking*.

[31] Mattli and Büthe, 'Global Private Governance', 236.

also suggest that the dynamics of global regulation have an unsurprisingly differential impact across policy sectors. They produce a 'ratcheting up' in those areas such as environment, safety, and financial security, where economic exchanges require verification, and a 'ratcheting down' in most areas of economic regulation. For Braithwaite and Drahos, regulation is largely driven by well-resourced international actors (mostly corporations), but they also suggest that occasions have existed when powerful interests have 'lost out'.

Some commentators have shown themselves to be particularly interested in the role of coercive pressures in shaping global regulation. These accounts stress the role of hegemony (reflecting a wider literature in international relations). For Beth Simmons, financial regulation can be explained by the United States' resistance to any adverse effects that might result from other jurisdictions choosing to diverge from its preferred regulatory standards. According to Simmons, international regulation emerges where the effects (or externalities) are negative (on the US), but where there is overall uncertainty about the ways in which this externality can be produced. If the source of the negative effect is clearly identifiable, Simmons argues, the US will opt for bilateral agreements.[32] A similar argument has been made by Daniel Drezner, who also emphasizes the importance of the costs of national adjustment to international regulation. He suggests that those business interests that are most likely to benefit from continued nationally fragmented regulation can be seen as key actors in shaping the extent to which international regulatory regimes in any one sector are feasible.[33]

Such views are primarily interested in the roles of economic actors. They acknowledge that capture does not have to be universal—as analysts of domestic regulation have long found (see Chapter 4). Followers of interest group-based explanations therefore suggest that changes in global regulation can be understood with reference to changing actor constellations and shifts in the economic rents that are available to different actors. For example, in those sectors that are characterized or affected by technological change, a different and more diverse set of economic interests emerge, leading to challenges to existing regimes and power constellations. Growing formalization and demands for verification can also be explained by changing interests. In an age where international production chains are increasingly important, a growing emphasis has been placed on demanding formal verification processes at each stage of production. Insurance companies, too, have played an increasingly important role in shaping global regulation. Faced with growing bills, they are seen as one of the key drivers in demanding more stringent and

---

[32] B. Simmons, 'International Politics of Harmonization: The Case of Capital Market Regulation' (2001) 55 *International Organization* 589–620.

[33] D. Drezner, *All Politics is Global: Explaining International Regulatory Regimes* (Princeton, NJ, 2007).

explicit standards to deal with potential liability claims, for example in maritime shipping.

The existence of blatant biases or dysfunctionalities in any one regulatory regime may lead to well-mobilized opposition (as approaches building on the work by Gary Becker would suggest).[34] For example, consumer outrage over conditions in particular plants or plantations can quickly lead to boycotts and the demand of retailers and high-end brands for a tightening of international regulatory regimes. Regulatory regimes that are not responsive to demands by global or national publics might thus be expected in areas where information is particularly costly, even if information only emerges in times of major media outcry over wrong-doing. Others, however, would argue that change is not necessarily a result of a public outcry: they would highlight that the Bhopal disaster of December 1984 has led to hardly any major international regulatory response, despite considerable media pressure.[35]

In other sectors, it can be seen that industry actors have responded to public outcry over major failures. Following the Chernobyl disaster of 1986 (and the earlier Three Mile Island incident of 1979), for example, nuclear operators formed the 'World Association of Nuclear Operators' (in 1989), and developed binding performance indicators for the industry. In the aftermath of those disasters, and in particular following public outcry over the safety of nuclear energy installations, the industry defined itself as a 'community of shared fate' that facilitated the adoption of common standards. These emerging global standards largely reflected US regulatory standards.[36] In 2011, the oil industry's response to criticism of its self-regulatory role was to echo the response taken by the nuclear industry and to opt for institutional reform.[37] More broadly, such a focus on the content of regulatory regimes highlights the importance of expert communities and 'epistemic communities' in the shaping of international standards.[38]

A different line of research has focused on explaining the content of global regulatory regimes. There is considerable evidence of institutional isomorphism across global regulatory regimes, even where they are in competition with each other. Such processes of growing homogenization are partly driven by overlapping networks of standard-setters that transcend the different

---

[34] G. Becker, 'A Theory of Competition among Pressure Groups for Political Influence' (1983) 98 *Quarterly Journal of Economics* 371–400.

[35] The Bhopal disaster involved a gas leakage from a Union Carbide pesticide plant. The chemical industry developed a 'Responsible Care' voluntary code. See J. Rees, 'Development of Communitarian Regulation in the Chemical Industry' (1997) 19(4) *Law and Policy* 477–528; A. King and M. Lenox, 'Industry Self-Regulation without Sanctions' (2000) 43(4) *Academy of Management Journal* 698–716.

[36] Braithwaite and Drahos, *Global Business Regulation*, 301–3; C. Heimer, *Reactive Risk and Rational Action* (Berkeley, 1985).

[37] See, 'Oil Companies Plan New Safety Body', *Financial Times*, 30 Jan. 2011.

[38] J. Black, 'Frameworks for Understanding Regulatory Innovation' in J. Black, M. Lodge, and M. Thatcher (eds), *Regulatory Innovation* (Cheltenham, 2005), 33–7.

organizations. Homogenization is driven by the need to avoid conflict between different standard-setting organizations (both through formal and informal organizations), and it is driven by the intention to harmonize procedures and approaches.[39] Similarly, international regimes draw on each other. The so-called 1988 UN-based Vienna convention against illegal traffic in narcotic drugs and psychotropic substances, for example, builds on earlier international agreements on drug trafficking.[40] In contrast, in areas where no domain-specific approach is available, ideas from other domains may be 'copied'. Christine Jojarth suggests, for instance, that the Kimberley Process (noted above) followed the fashionable prescriptions regarding 'good governance' that flourished in the 1990s. In short, institutional isomorphism can help explain why in some cases global regulatory regimes build on domain-specific examples, and in other cases from ideas outside the policy domain.[41]

In general, much of global regulation can be interpreted as a response to societal and political pressures. One of the key features that shapes global regulation has, however, been weak enforcement—especially where political interests have declined in a field or where less well-resourced actors are unable to monitor the conduct of the well-endowed. International regulation can also be seen to be shaped by the capacities of domestic institutions, especially how national actors are able to negotiate and implement international agreements (as institutionalists would emphasize).

Global regulatory regimes can also be said to reflect the politics of interest and institutional design (the allocation of authority, the procedural and structural design)—and they can be analysed using the lenses that have been explored in more detail in previous chapters. International regulation is 'decentred' and 'fragmented', it can be assessed considering different, if not competing theoretical lenses—with authors displaying a dominant concern with interest,[42] ideas,[43] institutional,[44] and functional approaches, as in the literature on domestic regulation. Indeed, questions about the effectiveness of these different global regulatory standards are also likely to vary across observers, depending on preferences regarding the nature of self-regulation or the nature of non-governmental organizations, or the capability of hierarchical modes of oversight.

---

[39] Werle, 'Institutional Aspects of Standardization', 400–2.

[40] Jojarth, *Crime, War and Global Trafficking*, 274–5.

[41] Jojarth, *Crime, War and Global Trafficking*; M. Lodge, *On Different Tracks: Designing Railway Regulation in Britain and Germany* (Westport, 2002).

[42] Abbott and Snidal, 'Hard and Soft Law in International Governance'; D. Lazer, 'Regulatory Interdependence and International Governance' (2001) 8(3) *Journal of European Public Policy* 474–92.

[43] M. Finnemore, *The Purpose of Intervention* (Ithaca, 2003); M. Finnemore and K. Sikkink, 'International Norm Dynamics and Political Change' (1998) 52 *International Organization* 887–917.

[44] N. Brunsson and B. Jacobsson, *A World of Standards* (Oxford, 2000).

Good Global Regulation

Views about the nature of global regulation mirror those of domestic regulation. One key conclusion, on which all literatures agree, is that global regulation requires variety to deal with the diversity of problems it seeks to deal with. It is also generally agreed that global or international regulation gives rise to special challenges—notably because it tends to lack enforceable accountability or procedural requirements. Whether regulation can ever be 'good', however, depends on the particular analytical angle that observers choose. For some, global regulation is a heaven for those highly resourced, developed-world interests that are able to capture international standards.[45] In the case of non-state regimes, private interests are, furthermore, able to escape accountability requirements. Others see global regulation as a venue that has the potential to overcome poor domestic regulation.[46] These observers do not necessarily suggest that existing international regimes offer effective or adequate solutions to problems; however, they do suggest that management practices are affected, leading to improved practices and creating local regulatory networks.[47]

How, then, can it be ensured that international level regulation does not merely serve the interests of those that have the resources to effect capture at the international level? Walter Mattli and Ngaire Woods have suggested a number of recipes. These include: the provision of information about the effects of the international regime; the presence of 'entrepreneurs' that are resourceful enough to demand change (and these may include non-governmental organizations); and the presence of a broad 'policy mood' that particular regulatory interventions are required.[48] The problem that these recommendations seek to tackle is the 'regulatory life-cycle', where the demands of NGOs or outraged publics are initially recognized, only inevitably to fade away as the public concern with any one particular issue fades away or moves to another policy domain.

Such discussions link to the wider concerns about good regulation that were discussed in Chapter 3. One debate is directed at *transparency* and, in particular, how the activities of international regimes are made visible. These concerns relate to the way in which especially non-state-centred global regulatory regimes select their rules and enforce them, and how private parties supply information about their compliance. In other words, the concern is

[45] K. Stiglitz, *Making Globalization Work* (London, 2006).
[46] Braithwaite and Drahos, *Global Business Regulation*.
[47] Meidinger, 'Beyond Westphalia', 136.
[48] W. Mattli and N. Woods, 'In Whose Benefit? Explaining Regulatory Change in Global Politics' in W. Mattli and N. Woods (eds), *Politics of Global Regulation* (Princeton, NJ, 2009).

about the verifiability of the activities of global regulatory regimes such as the Kimberley Process.

A separate concern relates to *accountability*. Here two key aspects are central. The first relates to the traditional concern with all forms of international or global regulation, namely the issue of the parties or institutions to whom or which the global regulators should render account—and how they should do so. Intergovernmental processes are (supposedly) legitimized through bargaining between governments, but greater concerns emerge the more regulatory regimes rely on non-state actors. One key argument in response might be that accountability is towards each other, and therefore allows for a process of deliberative learning over time. Whether such processes actually occur, however, is somewhat difficult to assess. The second key aspect of accountability-based debates relates to participation: how can less well-resourced actors remain involved? On this point, the argument that may be made in defence of international regulation is that the contestability and openness that distinguishes global from domestic regulatory regimes creates considerable opportunities for outside actors to become involved or to take an interest.

Such questions can relate to all areas of regulatory activity, but are acute in the area of global regulation. Further pressing questions that affect global regulations are those relating to *effectiveness*. As noted, those critical of current contemporary regimes question whether all these activities provide for effective problem-solving mechanisms. Others note that the key of global regulatory regimes is the change of practices among key actors, rather than the immediate solution of particular policy problems. A further question relates to *reliability* and whether the chosen regimes offer a valid and robust regulatory response to diagnosed policy problems. Given the uncertainties that often obtain on this front, it is sometimes suggested that the presence of competing global regulatory regimes might be helpful in developing insights and learning.

A different issue is the *fairness* of global regulatory regimes and the concern that the regimes are particularly directed towards the interests of the wealthy northern hemisphere consumer and retailer. Global regulatory regimes, however, have the capacity to support market access for producers from lesser developed countries. The presence of global regulatory regimes may raise labour standards in particular jurisdictions, but it may also reduce opportunities to exercise market discrimination.

In summary, debates about what is 'good' global regulation centre on many of the same concerns that have affected wider debates regarding 'good regulation'. Global regulation, though, constitutes a special case—it raises distinct accountability and transparency issues across all the variants of global regulation that were discussed earlier. It also raises issues about how to develop procedures for regulatory regimes, and the potential distributional impacts of global regulatory regimes across hemispheres and within countries.

Conclusion

Global or international regulatory regimes provide distinct examples of multi-level regulation. At the same time, they display many of the characteristic features that are well-known to students of domestic regulation. Further, international regulation prompts a set of distinct and acute questions about its accountability and transparency—especially in those regimes that are characterized by a predominance of private interests. As can be seen from some of the examples provided in this chapter, however, what starts as a system of private regulatory arrangements can turn into a publicly endorsed regulatory regime and may often be backed by the legal force of international treaties and/or national legislation. Contestation between regulatory regimes is said to have led to considerable interactive effects, and observers are divided whether such contestation has, overall, merely contributed to fragmentation and confusion, or whether contestation has led to copying and increasingly stringent or dense provisions. A second key consideration is whether global regulatory regimes are having, by penetrating local regimes, a homogenizing effect that is increasingly intolerant of the specificities of local regimes, or whether these homogenization effects are adding to overall problem-solving capacities across countries.

Looking at global regulation forces us to come to grips with the inherently multi-level character of contemporary regulation. It emphasizes the value of thinking of regulation as 'decentred' and of bearing in mind that 'order' and 'authority' do not require a central state. The state, it can be concluded, is only one participant in the growing networks of global regulation.

Part VI

Network Issues

22 Regulating Prices in Natural Monopolies

This and the following four chapters are concerned with economic regulation of the utilities sector—including communications, energy, transport, and water. These are often described as network industries, because they rely upon some form of physical distribution network, such as gas or water pipes, electricity or telecommunications wires, train tracks or a postal delivery round.[1] This chapter focuses on the nature and implications of natural monopoly in such industries. Natural monopoly can be defined as a situation in which the market can most cheaply be supplied by a single firm. (A gas distribution network is a good example.) A natural monopolist, left to itself, would for reasons discussed below be likely to charge excessive prices, and there is accordingly a need for some form of regulation of price and quality, and scope for debate about the kind of regulation that is appropriate.

Historically, utility companies in Europe and elsewhere (excluding the United States) were typically government departments or public enterprises, undertaking all aspects of production of the service in question in a vertically integrated manner. Thus the same gas enterprise often owned the gas fields, landed the gas, piped it to homes and businesses, and retailed it to customers.

When privatization occurred, as it has in many countries, the starting point for regulatory discussion was often how to regulate a privately owned vertically integrated firm which either was a monopoly by law, because other firms were prohibited from entering the relevant market, or was a monopoly in practice because competitors were unable to establish themselves in the face of the market power wielded by the 'historic monopolist' or incumbent. In these circumstances, regulators saw their task as controlling the prices of a vertically integrated monopoly, by setting a retail price the firm could not exceed.

It has been a key insight of utility regulation in the past twenty or so years that not all of these activities undertaken by a utility are natural monopolies. Thus while the gas distribution network may be a natural monopoly, other activities in the 'value chain' such as retailing or extracting gas, need not be. Once this is recognized, decisions have to be made about the degree to which

---

[1] Networks can be defined more broadly to include virtual networks, such as the set of users of a particular computer operating system. Here we focus on physical networks.

the separate activities undertaken by utilities can be broken down or 'un-bundled', about where the market can be liberalized by allowing competitors to enter, and about the terms on which competitors are permitted to have access to the incumbent's natural monopoly assets. This may lead to a reorganization of production so that different firms or divisions are created or separated to perform different tasks.

Whether we are looking at the problem of regulation as one of controlling retail prices paid by a vertically integrated monopolist, or the prices at which competitors have access to the incumbent's facilities, there is a general problem of setting prices in a context with elements of natural monopoly. This chapter contrasts the outcome in the absence of regulation with what price regulation can achieve. It shows how closely such regulation can get to efficient pricing based on marginal costs. The next chapter deals with the use of competition in network industries. The following three chapters then deal, respectively, with issues of contestability and separation (Chapter 24), the implementation of price controls (Chapter 25), and questions of efficiency and innovation (Chapter 26).

What is a Natural Monopoly?

A natural monopoly arises when the market is served most cheaply by a single firm, rather than by a multiplicity of competing firms. In cases where the firm is producing a single product or service—for example, the distribution of gas to homes in a particular location—the situation can be represented as in Figure 22.1, which shows how average cost (AC) per unit house served falls as the number of homes served increases. The fundamental reason is that laying down the gas distribution network accounts for the majority of the costs; connecting an individual home to it involves a relatively small additional expense.

Thus the declining average cost of service derives from the fact that the marginal cost of serving a new customer is less than the average cost. This situation is shown in Figure 22.1 by the marginal cost curve (MC).

Possible sources of declining unit costs are many.[2] In the case of pipelines, the capacity of the pipe can be increased without a commensurate increase in investment cost. Firms with a larger scale of operation may also be able to reduce costs by having proportionately lower overheads or by being able to employ more specialized and efficient personnel. In the case of distribution

---

[2] See D.A. Hay and D.T. Morris, *Industrial Economics and Organisation* (2nd edn, Oxford, 1991), ch. 2.

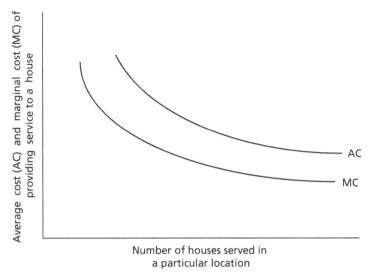

Figure 22.1. Average and marginal cost in a natural monopoly
As the number of houses served grows, there is a fall in the average cost (AC) of service—both operating costs and investment or capital costs. This implies that the cost of serving an additional customer (the marginal cost or MC) always lies below the average cost: what drags the average down is the (low) additional cost of serving a new home.

networks for electricity, gas, telecommunications, posts, and water, the reason for declining costs is what can be called an economy of density. Thus, it is cheaper on a per household basis for a single distribution company to deliver gas to all the houses in an area than to have two competing networks each serving half of them. This is because the latter arrangement requires unnecessary duplication of a major part of the distribution network.

In other areas of utilities, such as high-voltage electricity transmission, capacity can be increased without a commensurate increase in costs. Thus the same pylons can carry more or less electricity, and the costs of burying cable are insensitive to the number of kilowatts transmitted.

The degree to which an activity exhibits the characteristics of a natural monopoly depends not only on engineering factors, but also upon management processes and the operation of social and economic factors within the enterprise. It might theoretically be possible for a monopolist to serve a market at a lower unit cost than two or more competing firms can achieve. But incentives to efficiency under a monopoly may be very weak, and as a result, it may in practice be cheaper to have the market supplied by two competitors in spite of the theoretical advantage of the monopoly.

The declining unit costs associated with economies of scale of the kind described above are one aspect of natural monopolies. A second factor is economies of scope, which are encountered in many industries when it is cheaper for one firm to provide two or more related products and services together, than for each of them to be provided by a separate firm. A good example from the communications industry is provided by telecommunications and cable television networks, each of which can deliver voice calls, broadband, and video entertainment services.[3] Economies of scope, which typically arise from the use of common assets to produce separate products, are likely over time to have the effect of reducing the number of firms in an industry.

The tendency towards natural monopoly is most pronounced when economies of scale and density are combined with economies of scope. The former reduce the number of firms producing each service individually, while the latter encourage each firm in the market to produce a range of services. Acting in combination, they may generate a situation in which a significant number of markets are served by the same monopolist.

Determining whether a particular area of activity is a natural monopoly is a complex process. Natural monopolies are vulnerable to technological development. Thus, the argument that telecommunications, particularly the access network or local loop which connects households and firms to the local exchange, is a natural monopoly has been significantly weakened by the development of new technologies based on wireless distribution. These give customers access to the exchange without the necessity to construct fixed-link networks. The natural monopolies of energy and water distribution systems, however, appear to be well rooted.

Basic Concepts for Regulated Pricing

The implications for pricing of services provided by a natural monopoly can be tackled by asking two questions: what price would emerge in the absence of intervention, and what prices should regulation try to attain? The first

---

[3] Telecommunications services (at that time mainly voice calls) and cable TV services were initially provided, for technical reasons, over quite separate networks. From about 1990, technical developments permitted a single network to provide both.

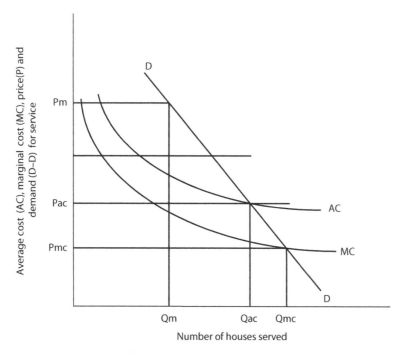

Figure 22.2. Pricing options for a natural monopolist
An unregulated monopolist would charge a high price (Pm), thus raising the price of service
to the household. The ideal price would be Pmc, where the demand curve (D–D) cuts the
marginal cost curve (MC). If this price were charged, the price to the household would be
the true marginal cost to the economy of providing the service. A household making the
decision whether to connect would thus face a price reflecting the resource cost to the
economy of making the connection. However, a price equal to Pmc would fail to cover the
firm's average cost (AC); hence the firm could not survive in the long run. The lowest price
consistent with the firm breaking even is Pac. If the regulator must ensure that the firm
breaks even—to meet the expectation of its private-sector owners—and if more sophisticated pricing strategies are not available, this is the best feasible price.

question can readily be answered in relation to Figure 22.2. This reproduces
the shape of the curves in Figure 22.1, with the addition of a demand curve
DD, which shows how demand for, say, gas distribution services varies with
the price charged.

If the price of the gas distribution is higher, the implied price of gas
delivered to consumers will be higher, and gas consumption will diminish.
As the price of gas distribution services falls, this will be reflected in lower
prices at the retail level, and demand for gas will rise.

In these circumstances, a monopolist controlling a distribution network
will maximize its profits by setting a relatively high price, Pm, which lies

above average cost and hence delivers a monopoly profit.[4] As a result, gas prices paid by consumers will be high, and those consumers will suffer, to the benefit of shareholders in the monopoly, who will enjoy excess profits.

This unsatisfactory state of affairs can clearly be mitigated by the regulation of prices, but what price for gas distribution should the regulator set? Ideally the prices of goods and services sold in the economy should be set at their marginal costs,[5] whether they apply to final demand such as gas purchased by households or to an intermediate product such as gas distribution. This is desirable because at a price (Pmc in Figure 22.2) where the demand curve cuts the marginal cost curve, output has been expanded up to the point where the buyer's willingness to pay for an additional unit of the service provided, shown by the height of the demand curve, exactly equals the marginal cost to the economy of producing that final unit of output. At a price higher than this, the buyer's willingness to pay would exceed the marginal cost of providing an extra unit. At a price lower than this, the marginal cost to the economy of providing the last unit of output is greater than the buyer's willingness to pay for it. The best price for the service is, therefore, a price equal to marginal cost.

As inspection of Figure 22.2 demonstrates, however, if the service were priced at Pmc, then the price charged would fail to cover average cost. As a result, the firm would make a loss.

If it were a public enterprise, that loss could be made up from general taxation. A privately owned single product firm which did not receive state aid or another form of subsidy would, however, go out of business. If the firm is constrained to avoid losses and break even, then the most appropriate regulated price is shown by Pac in Figure 22.2. This is more satisfactory than the monopoly price Pm, but less efficient than a price equal to marginal cost, Pmc.

The implication is that a regulator who is setting prices for a single-product firm which has to break even should seek to drive prices down to average costs.

Most regulated firms, however, produce several services, and this gives more flexibility in the pricing process. A traditional example comes from telecommunications, where end users pay a monthly rental for connection to the network and then pay additional sums for making calls. It is not possible in the case of a multi-product firm to identify individual average costs for the separate services, because those services will typically have common inputs such as switches in the local exchange, and as a result it will not be possible to attribute all costs unambiguously to individual services. It will, however, be

---

[4] For how that price is determined, see D. Begg, G. Fischer, and R. Dornbusch, *Economics* (8th edn, London, 2005), Ch. 8.

[5] See Armstrong, Cowan, and Vickers, *Regulatory Reform: Economic Analysis, and British Experience*, 14–18.

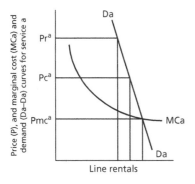
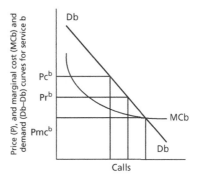

Figure 22.3. Efficient pricing for a multi-service utility
The ideal prices are where the demand curves (Da–Da and Db–Db) cut the marginal cost curves (MCa and MCb for each service). A firm charging such prices would, however, make losses, as both products are produced in conditions of economies of scale. Hence the need for a mark-up over marginal costs. One possibility would be to have an equal mark-up to cover common and fixed costs; i.e. to choose Pc^a and Pc^b. Such prices, though, have different distorting effects on demand for the two services; it falls much more for calls than it does for line rental. A preferred option is so-called Ramsey pricing, which involves a high proportionate mark-up on line rentals, where demand is unresponsive to price (Pr^a), and a low proportionate mark-up on calls, where demand is more responsive to price (Pr^b).

possible to establish the marginal cost of each service, by identifying the increase in overall costs associated with increasing the output of any service when the output of other services is held constant.

As before, the most efficient price for each service occurs where the demand curve Da Da or Db Db crosses the marginal cost curve (MCa or MCb), as illustrated by Pmc^a and Pmc^b in Figure 22.3.

We face once again, however, the problem that, if the firm sells each service at a price equal to its marginal cost, which lies below average cost (not shown), the firm will incur losses. In order to break even, it must, therefore, charge a mark-up above marginal costs.

One simple way of achieving this objective would be to fix prices that contain an equal proportionate mark-up on each service, of a size which just allows the firm to break even. These prices are shown in Figure 22.3 as Pc^a and Pc^b, respectively. This is the solution consistent with average cost pricing for the single-product firm. It is preferable in most circumstances, however, to set a proportionate mark-up over marginal cost for each service which varies from service to service in accordance with demand conditions.

These preferred prices are illustrated in Figure 22.3 by Pr^a and Pr^b; they are also known after their inventor as Ramsey prices.[6] The logic behind them is as

[6] Armstrong, Cowan, and Vickers, *Regulatory Reform: Economic Analysis, and British Experience*, 47–51; S.J. Brown and D.S. Sibley, *The Theory of Public Utility Pricing* (Cambridge, 1986), 39–44.

follows. In the case of line rentals, demand is relatively unresponsive to price, and a high mark-up can be charged without that mark-up having a major effect on consumption, compared with the case where price is equal to marginal cost. Demand for calls, by contrast, falls much more as price rises. A high mark-up on calls will lead to a major distortion of the amount consumed.

To express this principle more generally, when prices are being set for a regulated monopoly which produces a variety of services and which—because it is privately owned—is required to break even, they should embody the minimum mark-ups over marginal costs that are necessary to allow the firm to break even. Services where demand is relatively responsive to price should generally have a lower than average proportionate mark-up, while services where demand is relatively unresponsive to price should have a higher than average mark-up over their marginal costs. This enables common costs to be recovered in a way that reduces to a minimum the harmful effects of distortion in output caused by the mark-up over marginal cost.[7]

As it happens, for many decades telecommunications regulators did the opposite of what the principle set out above implied. That is, they imposed a low mark-up on line rentals, and a high mark-up on calls. Why was this? At least part of the reason was a desire to encourage the spread of telecommunications, to be achieved by making as many households subscribe as possible. This universal service objective, discussed in Chapter 24 below, in effect took priority over the requirements of economic efficiency. This is a useful reminder of the variety of goals which affect pricing by regulators.

The institutional setting for the kind of price control described is one in which the regulatory body is implicitly in centre stage. Its job is to find a set of permitted prices which balances the interest of investors in utilities and consumers of their services, and we have set out above some of the concepts which can be adopted. We return in Chapter 25 to consider how this might be done in practice, and, also to describe an alternative approach in which price setting is accomplished by a form of negotiation between suppliers and customers or their representatives.

Conclusions

This chapter has defined natural monopoly, which occurs when a market is most cheaply served by a single producer. Natural monopolies arise from

---

[7] For an implementation of Ramsey pricing to the telecommunications sector, see Brown and Sibley, *Theory of Public Utility Pricing*, ch. 7.

economies of scale, which mean that the largest firm has a cost advantage over its competitors, and is hence likely to become a monopolist. Where two or more products or services are produced more cheaply by a single firm than separately by two firms, economies of scope are in question. A combination of economies of scale and economies of scope is likely to lead to dominance of the market by a single multi-product firm.

Such a firm has the market power to charge prices which generate excessive profit. The natural regulatory response is to control prices. In the case of a single-product firm, if the firm is required to break even, the most satisfactory regulated price which can be imposed at any point in time is equal to average cost. In the case of a multi-product firm, a break-even constraint should lead to differential mark-ups on services. It has been suggested that such mark-ups should be greater where demand is relatively unresponsive to price and smaller where it is relatively responsive.

This analysis has allowed us to identify what might be efficient pricing rules for a natural monopoly. Utility regulators in practice have to undertake the prior, and crucial, process of determining whether regulation of price and other aspects is in fact necessary. Our discussion has also assumed that regulators know the costs of the firms they regulate. In practice they do not, and they need to develop incentives for firms to show how they can reduce their costs and keep them down. These issues are discussed in the following chapters.

23 Using Competition in Network Industries

Competition and its Virtues

Competition involves rivalry among firms for the customer's business across all the dimensions of the service—price, quality, and innovation. Its opposite is a situation in which a single firm can effectively act independently of its customers and competitors, and impose a chosen offering in the marketplace. Inevitably, competition is a matter of degree, rather than something which is either fully present or absent. Industries differ in their structure, ranging from the situations where there is a multiplicity of small producers, through more concentrated markets with a small number of larger producers with or without a competitive fringe, to the state of monopoly. The degree of rivalry encountered also depends upon firm behaviour, which ranges from out-and-out competition in all dimensions of the service, through more limited forms of competition in which, for example, firms compete in terms of quality but not in terms of price, to openly or tacitly collusive or parallel behaviour in all the dimensions of service provision.

As a method for getting the best deal for consumers, detailed regulation is seen by many to be inferior to systems that allow competition subject to the safeguard of general competition law. Thus Steven Littlechild, in his 1983 report for the British government on price controls for BT, wrote:

Competition is by far the most effective means of protection against monopoly. Vigilance against anti-competitive prices is also important. Profit regulation is merely a 'stop-gap' until sufficient competition develops.[1]

Hence the expression: competition is the best regulator. Underlying this proposition is the belief that firms have the strongest incentives to give customers what they want in terms of price and quality of service when they are in competition. In such circumstances, firms also have a strong incentive to gain a temporary advantage over their rivals through innovation and the development of new services. Compared with this scenario, the regulation of a monopoly that faces no competition has many disadvantages. A monopoly is under very limited pressure to produce services which meet

---

[1] S.C. Littlechild, *Regulation of British Telecommunications Profitability* (London, 1983), 1. Similar expressions of enthusiasm for the use of competition, where possible, can be found in D.M. Newbery, *Privatisation, Restructuring and Regulation of Network Industries* (Cambridge, 1999), ch. 1.

customers' needs. If the regulator controls profits, the firm has no incentive to reduce costs, or to introduce an innovation which enhances customers' willingness to pay or creates new services. If the regulator controls the price of the service, the firm producing it may retaliate by reducing quality. In order to counteract this, the regulator may then become involved in specifying an increasing number of the characteristics of the service, and runs the risk of eventually micro-managing its production and distribution.

A final argument in favour of competition is that it encourages firms to price whatever services they produce more efficiently. Chapter 22 showed how goods and services should ideally be priced in a way that takes account of marginal and incremental costs and of the demand conditions to which the firms are subject. In particular, if common or fixed costs have to be recovered, it is desirable that they be recovered disproportionately on services for which the demand is relatively unresponsive to price. Firms operating in markets subject to competitive entry are on certain conditions drawn to set prices in this fashion, because this tends to maximize their own profits.[2] An unregulated monopolist not subject to the threat of entry would set prices in similar proportions, but at much higher levels which would reduce consumers' welfare.

Competition is just a means to the end of consumer welfare, and it is necessary that it should achieve that end. Over the years, different forms of competition have been identified.[3] On the spectrum between competition which involves a large number of firms, none of which can set prices itself (perfect competition) and pure monopoly, there lies a large intermediate area of rivalry. This includes relatively good outcomes, in which competition is not perfect but 'workable',[4] as well as poor outcomes, including those where firms collude in setting prices, thus often generating the worst of both worlds—high 'fixed' prices and production at an inefficiently small scale.

In the theory and practice of regulation, the most frequently adopted description of the form of competition which is acceptable is 'effective competition'. Pinning down precisely what is meant by effective competition is, however, a difficult task, perhaps best attempted by identifying those forms of competition that are ineffective. These include particularly situations in which one firm exercises such dominance in the market that it is in practice able to act with a high degree of independence from its customers and

[2] See W. Baumol, J. Panzar, and R. Willig, *Contestable Markets and the Theory of Industry Structure* (New York, 1968), chs. 2–5, 11, 12.

[3] See J. Vickers, 'The Concept of Competition' (1995) 47 *Oxford Economic Papers* 1–23.

[4] The concept of workable competition was introduced 75 years ago by J.M. Clark, 'Toward a Concept of Workable Competition' (1940) 30(3) *American Economic Review* 149–57. It is still extensively used in New Zealand, where the Commerce Act requires the regulator to seek outcomes consistent with workable competition. See Commerce Commission, *Commerce Act Electricity Distribution Services Input Methodologies Determination* (Dec. 2010).

competitors.[5] Situations of this kind are likely to emerge particularly where, as in the case of many utilities, a market has just been opened up to competition and the historic monopolist starts with a market share of, and a knowledge of, 100 per cent of the customers, while its rivals start with zero customers and no information about them.

This notion of effective competition as the absence of dominance is best exemplified in the regulation of European telecommunications discussed in this chapter. In that sector, where competition is not effective, there must be a firm or a group of firms with 'significant market power'. In other sectors, broadly similar terms are used for market structures which can trigger regulation.[6]

Another form of ineffective competition can arise when too many firms enter an industry which, because of its cost conditions—manifested in significant economies of scale—is best served by a single firm or a small number of firms. The problem here is that excessive entry involves a needless duplication of fixed costs which are either recovered in prices, to the detriment of consumers, or which leave entrants with losses, borne by their investors. While competition of this type would also be ineffective, there are reasons to doubt that the ordinary operation of the market process would bring it into being, since potential entrants would be aware of the risks of making substantial investments which they would be unlikely to recover.[7] For this reason, the dangers of 'excess entry' in network industries are likely to be quite small, unless such inefficient investments arise as an unintended consequence of regulation.

There are thus good reasons for permitting and in some circumstances even encouraging as much competition as is possible in the utilities sector. The scope for competition, however, depends upon a variety of considerations. The chief of these is the cost conditions in the industry—a topic discussed in Chapter 22 above. The distribution networks that characterize the utilities demonstrate significant economies of scale, which give firms with large numbers of customers cost advantages over their smaller competitors. These advantages arise both from unit cost reductions that are associated with greater throughput and from economies of density. This consideration makes the local distribution network in electricity, gas, and water effectively a natural monopoly, and hampers the development of competition in the access network for telecommunications.

Several economists have pointed out that the presence of economies of scale is not sufficient by itself to eliminate the possibility of some form of

---

[5] The language used here deliberately reflects the well-known definition of dominance in European competition law: see R. Whish, *Competition Law* (6th edn, Oxford, 2009), ch. 5.4.

[6] For example, the UK government proposed a regime for regulating airports which confined certain powers to airports with substantial market power; Department for Transport, *Reforming the Framework for the Economic Regulation of Airports* (Dec. 2009).

[7] M. Armstrong, S. Cowan, and I. Vickers, *Regulatory Reform: Economic Analysis and British Experience* (London, 1994), 107–11.

competition. They argue that while head-to-head competition *in* the market may not be feasible, competition *for* the market can be achieved. This might be done by putting activities, including certain capital projects, out to tender. This is considered in Chapter 24 below, under the heading of contestability. This can also be done more comprehensively through a variant of a franchising process: essentially, competing suppliers are asked to bid a price at which they would supply a specified market. The franchisor—usually a government or regulatory body—then appoints the firm which offers the lowest price. We discuss this further in the Chapter 9 on franchising.

These technological considerations are not the only factors influencing the scope for competition. Many utilities have pricing structures that embody considerable amounts of cross-subsidy. These stem from their histories within the public sector and from the major impact which the energy, telecommunications, transport, and water industries have on economic and social development and the distribution of income. Utilities, for example, traditionally charge a uniform tariff to all customers of the same category (business or residential) in a service area, even though cost of service differs from one customer to another. BT thus offers the same menu of quarterly rental payments to residential telephone subscribers, whether they live in suburban areas, which are relatively cheap to serve, or in remote and sparsely populated parts of the country, where service is costly. There was also a tradition in the telecommunications industry in Europe and elsewhere for monthly or quarterly rental payments for access to the network to be set below cost, with the deficit being recovered by relatively high and profitable call charges.

When competition is introduced into a market involving cross-subsidies of these kinds, both across customers and across services, there is a risk that it will be distorted. Entrants will naturally seek out profitable markets, leaving the incumbent to serve the unprofitable ones. In the long run, entry of this 'cream-skimming' form may undermine the incumbent's capacity to meet its pricing and service obligations. The presence of social as well as economic considerations in the pricing of utility services adds additional complexity to the development of competition, and ways have to be—and can be—found of accommodating these constraints within a competitive framework, as discussed below.

Unbundling to Achieve Competition

Providing a utility service requires the performance of a number of separate activities, with different economies of scale and scope, different degrees of 'sunkness' of costs, and hence different prospects for the introduction of competition. In the early days of regulation, it was the practice to lump the different activities together, treat them as monopolies normally to be supplied by a single vertically integrated firm, and then to regulate the firm as a single entity on an end-to-end basis.

The modern approach to utility regulation takes a different approach. It breaks down or 'unbundles' the value chain into its separate components, and asks which are potentially competitive and which are monopolistic. Entry into the competitive activities is then liberalized. Where monopoly bottlenecks exist, especially in distribution networks, their owners are required or mandated to make the assets available to competitors. The latter, through a combination of buying services from the incumbent and making them itself, can thus retail services to customers.

Table 23.1 gives a simplified breakdown of activities involved in six industries, together with an indicative judgement of the scope for competition in each activity. In practice, the scope for competition depends crucially on local conditions. In a small market, there may not be room for more than one electricity generator. The scope for two or more fixed telecommunications networks is different in a business district than in the countryside. Postal delivery can be competitive in cities but not in sparsely populated areas.

However, the table shows two regularities: distribution networks are with few exceptions monopolistic, while retailing (i.e. marketing and billing) is always competitive.[8]

In particular, Table 23.1 shows how the potential for competition in each industry varies with each stage of the production process under consideration. One approach to regulating industries with different competitive potential at each stage is to break them up at privatization, and sell the monopolistic and competitive elements as different units. The monopolistic components can then be subject to price control, while the competitive activities can be deregulated. This approach brings the great advantage that it overcomes problems associated with vertical integration, when a monopolist in one area of activity has an opportunity to apply its market power across from that area into related competitive markets. The disadvantage of such break-ups, however, is that they prevent the realization of those economies of scope that might be available to a firm undertaking several connected activities. A single telecommunications operator running both a monopoly local and a competitive long-distance network may, for example, have lower costs than two separate firms operating the networks independently.

In the UK, the successive privatizations of the 1980s and the early '90s show how the government's views on this issue changed. British Telecom, in 1984, and British Gas, in 1986, were privatized as integrated firms. The electricity supply industry, by contrast, was privatized in 1989 in the form of three

---

[8] For a review of the situation in general, and in electricity, gas, and telecommunications, see Newbery, *Privatisation, Restructuring and Regulation of Network Industries*, chs 5–8.

Table 23.1. Competitive potential in electricity, gas, posts, railways, telecommunications, and water and sewerage

Industry	Scope for competition
Electricity:	
generation	Good
high-voltage transmission	Nil
regional distribution	Nil
retailing	Good
Gas:	
extraction	Good
national and regional distribution	Nil
retailing	Good
Posts:	
collection	Good
sorting	Good
trunking	Good
delivery	Limited
Railways:	
track, stations, and signalling	Very limited
services	Moderate
Telecommunications:	
local network	Moderate
long-distance and international network	Good
services	Good
Water and sewerage:	
abstraction of water	Good
treatment	Moderate
pipes	Nil
retailing	Good

separate activities: electricity generation, which was considered to be potentially competitive and not subject to price regulation; regional distribution and retailing, which was carried out by twelve regional electricity companies (RECs); and high-voltage transmission, carried out by the National Grid company, jointly owned by the RECs. Retailing of electricity, initially a monopoly of the RECs, was progressively opened up to competition. The National Grid Company was subsequently floated off as a separately owned entity. The privatization of electricity in Scotland, by contrast, was carried out on the basis of two vertically integrated firms.

The railways industry was also broken up at privatization. The track, stations, and signalling were sold as a single integrated firm, Railtrack. The rolling stock owned by British Rail was divided among three leasing companies, and the running of services was entrusted to twenty-five train-operating companies. In the water industry, some parts of the country are served by companies providing both water and sewerage services, but in other areas the two functions are carried out by separate firms. All the water companies are vertically integrated monopolies in their areas, responsible for abstracting water, treating it, delivering it, and retailing it to customers.

It is noteworthy that British Gas, which was privatized as a whole, decided voluntarily to break itself up into two companies through de-merger. This followed a Monopolies and Mergers Commission recommendation of compulsory break-up in 1992, which was rejected by the Secretary of State. In 1996, however, British Gas retailing activity, British Gas Trading, was de-merged as a separate company known as Centrica. The exploration and production business was subsequently separated from its pipeline business, and the latter then merged with National Grid Company's high-voltage electricity distribution business, subsequently selling off some local gas distribution businesses. The energy sector in the UK under regulation thus exhibits a very tortuous history of separation and integration, some of the logic of which is reviewed in Chapter 24.

Unbundling in the Telecommunications Sector

Telecommunication regulators, faced with the opportunities for increasing competition described above, have converged on a strategy for deregulation which seeks to limit regulation to cases where there is a significant risk of abuse of market power.[9] The most comprehensive of these is the one adopted in the European Union, which we now describe. Other countries adopt or aspire to adopt broadly the same approach, in the sense that regulation is reduced over time by making its application to any service dependent in some way on a demonstration that market power or dominance would, absent regulation, create competition problems or market failures. The main exception is the United States, which experimented with unbundling, and then rejected it.

After a tortuous and prolonged legislative process, the new European regulatory framework came into effect in July 2003, and its fundamental basis emerged unchanged from revised legislation in 2009. It is based on four Directives and an array of other supporting documentation in the form of 'soft law' legal instruments, which lend themselves to modification and revision relatively quickly in response to technological and commercial

---

[9] This section draws on P. Alexiadis and M. Cave, 'Regulation and Competition Law in Telecommunications and Other Network Industries' in R. Baldwin, M. Cave, and M. Lodge (eds), *Oxford Handbook on Regulation* (Oxford, 2010), 500–22.

innovation.[10] At one level, the new regime is a major step down the transition path between the stages of monopoly and normal competition, to be governed almost entirely by generic competition law. Its provisions are applied across the range of 'electronic communications services'. It represents an ingenious attempt to corral the regulators in the EU, the national regulatory agencies or NRAs, down the path of normalization—allowing them, however, to proceed at their own speed (but within the uniform framework necessary for the EU's common or internal market). Since the end state is supposed to be one that is governed by competition rules, the regime is designed to shift towards something that is consistent with those rules. These rules are to be applied (in certain markets) not in a responsive *ex post* fashion, but in a preemptive *ex ante* form. However, a screening mechanism is used to limit recourse to such *ex ante* regulation, insofar as it should only be applied when the so-called 'three criteria test' has been fulfilled for any particular form of market-based intervention—these criteria being (1) the presence of non-transient barriers to entry, (2) the absence of a tendency towards effective competition behind the entry barriers, and (3) the insufficiency of competition rules to be able to address the market failures identified in the market review process.

The new regime therefore relies on a special implementation of the standard competition triumvirate of: (a) *market definition*; (b) identifying *dominance*; and (c) formulating appropriate *remedies*. According to the underlying logic of this regime, a list of markets where *ex ante* regulation is permissible is first established, the markets being defined according to standard competition law principles. These markets are analysed with the aim of identifying dominance (on a forward-looking basis, and known as 'significant market power' or SMP). Where no dominance (expressed as the 'lack of effective competition') is found to exist, no remedy can be applied. Where dominance is found, the choice of an appropriate remedy can be made from a specified list of primary and secondary remedies which is derived from best practices.[11] The practical effect of this is to create a series of market-by-market 'sunset clauses' for regulation, as the scope of effective competition expands.

To get the NRAs started, the European Commission prepared a list of markets requiring automatic analysis for the presence of significant market power. These included the principal bottlenecks in the provision of fixed (wire-based, rather than mobile) voice and broadband services—notably

---

[10] Directives of the European Parliament and of the Council of 7 March 2002: 2002/21/EC; 2002/20/EC; 2002/19/EC; 2002/22/EC.

[11] Because the process is forward-looking, there is no need to prove that abusive practices are taking place, although evidence that such practices have occurred in the past provides support that *ex ante* regulatory intervention is necessary.

the local loop which connects homes and business premises to the local exchange, which is expensive to replicate and which is often a monopoly.[12]

The first such list, issued in 2003, comprised 18 products. The second, issued in 2007, cut the number to 7—allowing the European Commission to claim that the tendency towards more competitive markets was gaining ground.

A more controversial aspect of market definition is the identification of the geographic dimension of a relevant wholesale product market (namely, those product markets in relation to which various forms of *ex ante* access remedy are prescribed). The conventional wisdom has been for all geographic markets in the telecommunications sector to be identified as being national in scope, but fundamental changes over time in the competitive conditions faced by fixed incumbent operators in certain regions in the provision of broadband services have meant that the competitive environment is no longer the same across the whole country. The response of some NRAs has been to define sub-national geographic markets, in some of which regulation can be removed. Other NRAs have opted to achieve the same net result by a different means— namely, by continuing to define a wholesale market as being national in scope while at the same time targeting remedies only at those geographical regions which do not benefit from any meaningful competition. Although both approaches are designed to achieve the same result (that is, the lifting of *ex ante* regulation in response to the creation of effective competition), the former is the more 'purist' approach, insofar as it is more compatible with the European goal of achieving a more harmonized analytical approach to regulation, as opposed to merely achieving a similar end result.

Once market definitions are determined, NRAs have to determine whether significant market power is present. Since what is at stake is *ex ante* regulation (see above), they do so on a forward-looking basis—i.e. they form a view about how markets are likely to develop over a 3–4-year time horizon. Significant market power can be exercised by a single firm or by several firms likely to act in a tacitly collusive fashion. Some NRAs have found mobile operators to be collectively dominant in this way.

Under the Directives, NRAs have the power to impose obligations on firms found to enjoy significant market power in a properly defined market. In keeping with the logic of unbundling, according to which the pure retailing activity (marketing and billing) is likely to be competitive, regulatory intervention principally takes the form of requiring an incumbent exercising SMP in an input market (for example; having a monopoly of the local loop) to make it available to its competitors, enabling them to serve customers directly.

The major remedies available for firms found to exercise Significant Market Power in a particular market are set out in the Access Directive. One is a

---

[12] Except areas where there is a cable network.

requirement not to discriminate in favour of itself, or in favour of particular access seekers, in the provision of wholesale services. Others are to make its terms and conditions for granting access transparent and to provide the regulator with accounting data on the operation of its activities on a separated basis (see the next section).

However, inevitably, the major issue in unbundling concerns the terms and conditions on which the incumbent makes services such as the local loop available to its competitors. Clearly, this is key to their commercial survival, especially in early years, when they may be heavily reliant on inputs which are bought from the incumbent rather than made by the competitor.

The most important of these terms and conditions concerns the price at which access services are made available. This determines indirectly the price of service available to end users, since a lower access price will allow competitors to set a lower retail price, which is likely to have the effect of lowering the incumbent's price as well. It also determines entrants' shares of the retail market.

The second impact of access prices is on investment decisions. If access prices are low, entrants will be happy to buy wholesale services from the incumbent, and may prefer to continue to do this than to invest in competing assets. But low access prices may make the incumbent unwilling to invest further (for example, in a new fibre, based network) if it has to allow competitors access to its new facilities immediately and at a low price.[13] The decision over how to set access prices thus depends to some degree upon the type of competition the NRA wants to establish—competition in services between operators using the same basic infrastructure (service competition), or competition between competing infrastructures (infrastructure competition).[14]

The European telecommunications regulatory regime allows two options for pricing access products.[15] The first is to set the prices based on the cost of supplying the services, normally evaluated on the basis of what it would cost to build a new network to supply the service; this is known as 'cost-based pricing'. This is intended to be a solution which is neutral between incumbent and entrant, in the sense that the entrant pays the average cost of provision of the service.

---

[13] See C. Cambini and Y. Jiang, 'Broadband Investment and Regulation: A Literature Review' (2009) 33(11) *Telecommunications Policy* 559–74.

[14] The literature on access pricing in telecommunications discusses how a regulator can use access prices over time gradually to transform service into infrastructure competition. See M. Cave, 'Encouraging Infrastructure Competition via the Ladder of Investment' (2006) *Telecommunications Policy* 223–37 and M. Bourreau, P. Doğan, and M. Manant, 'A Critical Review of the "Ladder of Investment" Approach' (2010) *Telecommunications Policy* 683–96.

[15] The extensive literature on access prices in telecommunications and other regulated sectors corresponds to its importance. See J. Hauge and D. Sappington, 'Pricing in Network Industries' in R. Baldwin, M. Cave, and M. Lodge (eds), *Oxford Handbook of Regulation* (Oxford, 2010), 462–99.

The second option permits the charging of a broader category of 'reasonable' prices, which may be above cost in circumstances where an innovative asset has recently been installed or where the regulator wants to pursue an objective of 'holding up' some prices in order, on social grounds, to 'hold down' the price of others.

What has been the effect of these unbundling policies in the telecommunications sector? This remains a matter of considerable controversy, on which different authors have reached different conclusions. A study of the effect of access regulation on investment in telecommunications in Europe identified a negative effect on investment by incumbents and a broadly neutral effect on investment by entrants.[16]

A study conducted at Harvard University produced conclusions more favourable to unbundling.[17] One of the key problems is deciding the counterfactual to unbundling. It may be no regulation of any sort, on the hypothesis that losses to consumers arising from unconstrained pricing by the monopoly or dominant supplier will be counterbalanced by the benefits which subsequent infrastructure competition will bring. Or it might be a regime of regulation of an end-to-end monopolist across the whole value chain.

Unbundling of telecommunications in Europe has certainly contributed to significant competition and choice at the retail level. By 2010, the share of the historic monopolists in retail-fixed broadband markets in member states of the European Union had fallen considerably. The share of cable and other technologies such as wireless was 21%, almost all supplied by non-incumbents. Of the remaining 79% delivered using the telecommunications network, more than half was supplied by the incumbents' access-based competitors.[18]

Liberalization in Other Sectors

Other regulated sectors have experienced unbundling. Here we consider particularly electricity supply and posts. One of the features of the telecommunications example discussed above is the moving line between competitive and monopoly activities. This requires constant re-evaluation of which assets should be subject to mandatory unbundling, and which assets competitors could either supply for themselves, or acquire by entering into unregulated,

---

[16] M. Grajek and L.-H. Röller, *The Effect of Regulation on Investment in Network Industries: Evidence from the Telecommunications Industry*, ESMT Working Paper (Berlin, 2009).

[17] Berkman Center, Harvard University, *Next Generation Connectivity: A Review of Broadband Internet Transitions and Policy from around the World* (February 2010).

[18] European Commission, *Progress Report on the Single European Electronic Communications Market 2009* (15th Report), SEC(2010)630.

purely commercial, access arrangements with others. Postal services have this in common with telecommunications to some degree.

POSTS

In postal services, the key monopoly bottleneck is the local delivery network—the (usually daily) routine of postal employees delivering letters and packages to individual business premises and homes.[19] Within posts, this is the key activity characterized by the significant economies of scale.[20] Other activities involved in postal services are generally regarded as being replicable by competitors, although there may be some sparsely populated areas where collection of mail from mail boxes is difficult for competitors.

Posts have two attributes which deserve mention. First, mail volumes are widely under threat, as electronic communications replace letters. This is compensated to some degree by the greater use of electronic commerce, which requires goods to be delivered to the home. Second, historically, the obligation imposed upon the postal monopolist to provide a universal service (delivery of a letter from any collection point to any delivery point in a country) at a uniform price (often known as a 'postalized' price) is a very important element of the regulatory regime which complicates the insertion of competition, especially when declining volumes are adding to unit costs. This is considered further below.

Within the European Union, successive Directives have opened up progressively more and more categories of mail to competition.[21] The United Kingdom is one of a small but growing number of countries in which the postal service has been unbundled to permit competitors to access the delivery services of the former monopolist, the Royal Mail. The process permitted them to gain over 60% of the market for pre-sorted bulk mail by 2010, under the guidance of the regulator, the Postal Services Commission. Essentially, competitors deliver previously sorted mail to the local delivery offices of the Royal Mail, where it is integrated with Royal Mail's own collected and sorted mail into a bag which is then carried on the round by the postal delivery worker.[22]

This process is fairly straightforward and easy to monitor. But as in other contexts, the price of access to the local delivery service is key. In the terms of the discussion of access pricing in telecommunications, the regulator did not

---

[19] In 2010, 99% of UK letters were delivered by the Royal Mail, the historic postal monopolist.

[20] To see this, think of the difference in unit costs of delivering a bag of mail to 100 addresses concentrated in a single street, to the cost of delivering a bag of the same size to 100 addresses scattered over a large town.

[21] See the first (97/67/EC), the second (2002/39/EC), and the third (2008/06/EC) European Postal Directives. Postal markets in most member states were liberalized by the end of 2010.

[22] See R. Hooper, *Modernise or Decline: Policies to Maintain the Universal Postal Service in the United Kingdom*, Cmnd 7259 (December 2008).

set access prices in a cost-based fashion, but in a way which left a specified gap between the Royal Mail's price of a stamp, and the delivery charge. Suppose this gap, known as 'headroom', were 30 cents. Then if the price of a stamp for a letter were 70 cents, the delivery charge would be 40 cents. If it went up to 80 cents, the delivery charge would go up to 50 cents. If entry is to be feasible, the headroom must allow competitors to cover the costs of their own retailing, collection, sorting, and trunking (the transport of post between sorting offices). In fact, the headroom granted in the UK permitted them to gain 60% of the market for pre-sorted bulk mail within two years.

This has led to allegations that the regulatory system has favoured competitors unduly, or alternatively to the view that while such a system is appropriate at the early stage of competition, it is no longer so when competitors are established. Consideration is now being given to a new approach which will change the basis for access pricing, give Royal Mail greater freedom of retail pricing, and reduce other regulatory burdens on it.[23] This would be accompanied by a partial or total privatization.[24]

ENERGY

Within the energy sector, we shall focus upon electricity supply, though the case of gas has many similar features, while it is easier because gas, unlike electricity, is storable. In the case of electricity supply, it is possible to discern a standard model of liberalization, applied in varying degrees all over the world.[25] One version of it includes the following principal elements:[26]

- privatization of state owned monopolies;
- vertical separation (in various forms—see chapter 24) of potentially competitive from persistently monopolistic activities;
- ensuring non-discriminatory access by retailers to monopolistic, regulated transmission and distribution assets;
- restructuring of electricity generation, to permit competition;
- creation of an independent systems operator to manage the transmission network, to schedule generation capacity to meet demand, and to guide investment in transmission infrastructure;

---

[23] R. Hooper, *Saving the Royal Mail's Universal Postal Service in the Digital Age*, Cmnd 7937 (September 2010).
[24] Department for Business Innovation and Skills, *Delivering for the Future: A Universal Mail Service and Community Post Offices in the Digital Age*, Cmnd 7946 (October 2010).
[25] For good surveys, see F. Sioshansi (ed.), *Competitive Electricity Markets: Design, Implementation, Performance* (Amsterdam, 2008); F. Sioshansi (ed.), *Electricity Market Reform: An International Perspective* (Amsterdam, 2006).
[26] For a fuller account, see P. Joskow, 'Lessons Learned from Electricity Market Liberalization' (2008) *Energy Journal* 9–43.

- the creation of wholesale spot energy market institutions to balance supply and demand in real time;
- encouraging retail competition where possible.

There are undeniable problems in implementing this model, associated with the leveraging of market power in transmission and distribution into generation and retailing, organizing the spot market, and dealing with possibly harmful consequences of a retail market comprising a small number of firms integrated into generation. Nonetheless, Joskow concludes that 'significant performance improvements have been observed in some of the [liberalizing] countries as a result of these reforms. . . . Wholesale markets have stimulated improved performance from existing generators and helped to mobilize significant investments in new generating capacity in several countries.'

However, the greatest challenge to the liberalization model comes from policies to decarbonize the electricity supply industry in the light of climate change. Meeting sustainability targets in many countries requires a major reconfiguration of generating capacity away from coal and gas and towards wind and nuclear, and the redesign of electricity distribution networks to permit input of energy from more sources, including local ones (known as distributed distribution).[27] Doubts have been expressed as to whether, given the urgency of the problem and the long gestation times for the big investments required, the framework of a liberalized market will permit these tasks to be accomplished in the time available.[28]

Other regulated sectors have been subjected to the unbundling approach. In water, legislation has been passed in several states in Australia which allows competitors to set up treatment works for clean or dirty water and provide services to customers using the existing networks of pipes on an unbundled or so-called 'common carriage' basis.[29] In the UK, the water regulator OFWAT has developed proposals for extending competition, and a developed overall proposal has been put to the UK government in an independent review.[30] But Australia and the UK are exceptions. The water sector throughout the world is generally exempt from unbundling, and consists of vertically integrated monopoly firms, mostly under the control of local government.

---

[27] See C. Mitchell and B. Woodman, 'Regulation and Sustainable Energy Systems' in R. Baldwin, M. Cave, and M. Lodge (eds), *The Oxford Handbook on Regulation* (Oxford, 2010), 572–89.

[28] This is discussed in Department of Energy and Climate Change, *Electricity Market Reform Consultation Document*, Cmnd 7983 (2010).

[29] Productivity Commission, *Australia's Urban Water Sector*, Draft Report (2011).

[30] OFWAT, *Future Price Limits: Possible Sectoral Structures* (July 2010); M. Cave, *Independent Review of Competition and Innovation in Water Markets* (April 2009).

24 Separation and Contestability in Network Industries

Separation

The unbundling and liberalization described above leads directly to the issue of separation. Before the wave of privatization in Europe since 1980, utility companies were typically vertically integrated public corporations. Many remain in this form—such as the Royal Mail. Others are in partial public ownership. Privatization creates an opportunity for the government to impose a different structure, for example creating several companies for sale, broken down horizontally by service area and/or vertically by function. It is an unrepeatable opportunity, since restructuring assets in private ownership, through such measures such as compulsory divestment, is much harder to achieve.

Many privatizations retained the previous vertically integrated structure, on which the unbundling strategies described above have had to be imposed. There are exceptions. In England and Wales, the electricity supply industry was privatized in 1989 in three separate blocks: two large generating companies were sold, with a third nuclear-based one remaining in public ownership; the high-voltage transmission grid was sold as a monopoly; and 11 regional distribution companies were sold with the associated monopoly retailing functions. Since then the sector has gone through multiple transformations, leaving it in 2011 with a variety of competing generating companies, the largest six of which are vertically integrated with major retailers; a monopoly high-voltage grid company, which also owns one half of the gas distribution network; and six separate companies holding distribution licences.[1]

Much restructuring has been a response to business objectives. Thus combining generation and retailing activities in electricity supply enables a company to hedge the risks of generating too much or too little electricity. However, in some sectors, particularly energy and telecommunications, regulators have imposed separation remedies, usually to ensure fair competition in an unbundled environment.

Suppose a vertically integrated telecommunications firm has been required to make its local loop available to competitors, in the interests of permitting

---

[1] D. Newbery, *Privatisation, Restructuring and Regulation of Network Industries* (Cambridge, 1999), ch. 6.

or promoting retail competition. To retain its market share, it might first of all seek to over-charge its competitors for the local loop. This can be seen as a form of price discrimination, as its retail arm is implicitly paying less for the local loop than its competitors are being charged. The regulator's natural response to this is to set an appropriate access price.

The incumbent might then try to ensure that the competitors are unable to provide a decent quality of service to their customers, for example by refusing to repair loops serving their competitors' customers, when they break down. This is colourfully known as 'sabotage'. It would be intended to reduce the constraint competitors impose on the incumbent in the retail market and enable it to make profits at the retail level. It has been shown that this would be a profit-enhancing strategy where:[2]

- the regulator has prevented such excess returns being made on the local loop;
- the incumbent is a reasonably efficient retailer; and
- incumbent and competitors are selling essentially the same product.

The simplest solution to this problem is for the regulator to deter non-price discrimination by the threat of punishment—a behavioural remedy. But if this does not work, a more intrusive structural remedy may be required. This may involve some form of separation of the monopoly activity, which precludes its managers from discriminating in favour of the firm's retail affiliate.

The most thorough way of achieving this goal is what is called ownership or structural separation, under which one of the two activities is divested or sold off. With separate sets of shareholders now owning the two companies, neither has a motive to discriminate in favour of the other.

But this has costs as well as benefits. A recent survey of the literature on the effects of integration and separation across a range of industries, not confined to utilities, has concluded that integration does generally produce benefits. The authors write:[3]

We did not have a particular conclusion in mind when we began to collect the evidence. We are therefore somewhat surprised by what the evidence is telling us. It says that in most circumstances profit-maximising vertical integration decisions are efficient not just from the firms' but also from the consumers' point of view. The vast majority of studies support this claim,... even in industries which are highly concentrated.

---

[2] T. Beard, R. Kaserman, and J. Mayo, 'Regulation, Vertical Integration and Sabotage' (2001) 49(3) *Journal of Industrial Economics* 319–33.

[3] F. Lafontaine and M. Slade, 'Vertical Integration and Firm Boundaries' (2007) 45(3) *Journal of Economic Literature* 629–85.

Ownership separation

Functional separation

Accounting separation

Figure 24.1. Alternative forms of separation

One possible cost of separation is the harm which it may cause to investment. To take a current illustration, many telecommunications operators are installing fibre local loops in place of current copper loops, in order to increase broadband speeds. This is a very costly process. If the network were structurally separated from any retailing activity, there is a risk that it might make the investment, but the retail sector would not promote the fibre to customers. Fearing this, the network might not make the investment.

Concerns about ownership separation have led regulators to consider less radical alternatives, illustrated in Figure 24.1, which shows a hierarchy of separation.[4] The first step is accounting separation, under which a firm is required to produce separate profit-and-loss and balance sheet information (showing how much capital is employed) for components of the business (for example, the local loop or retailing) determined by the regulator. These data will expose where profits are being made, and in particular if the business is cross-subsidizing or discriminating in favour of some activities. However, this approach will not expose non-price discrimination.

The second form of separation, known as functional separation, involves redesigning the firm's business processes and managerial incentive systems to force the separated businesses to behave more independently. The redesign of business processes makes it easier to verify that competitors and the affiliated retailer are treated equally; meanwhile detaching managers' bonuses from the performance of the group as a whole should deter them from favouring affiliated business units. This approach lies between accounting separation and the ownership separation considered above.

Functional separation is now a remedy of last resort under the European regulatory regime for telecommunications discussed in Chapter 23 above.[5] It has been adopted in one form or another by several national regulators, in Italy, Sweden, and the UK. The choice of this intermediate form of separation remedy reflects both concern about retaining investment incentives, and

---

[4] M. Cave, 'Six Degrees of Separation' (2006) 64 *Communications and Strategies* 1–15.
[5] See R. Cadman, 'Means Not Ends: Deterring Discrimination through Equivalence and Functional Separation' (2010) 37(4) *Telecommunications Policy* 366–74.

recognition that the boundary between competitive and monopoly activities in telecommunications is a shifting one.

An extraneous factor has, however, given considerable impetus to separation in telecommunications. Replacing copper networks with fibre is a once-in-a-century change requiring massive investments. Governments do not want to get left behind in this process, and accordingly are prepared, at local and national level, to make significant investments, ranging from a plan in Australia effectively to renationalize the local loop, to major municipal investments. Such public investments, or public/private partnerships, usually have to be made through separate companies, to reflect their different ownership structure. The application of public funds may solve the problem of financing the investment (without necessarily leading to the right investments being made), but it may lead to a patchwork quilt of different ownership structures.[6]

Energy has also faced calls for separation driven by concerns that integration between transmission and distribution on one hand and generation and retailing on the other was distorting electricity and gas markets.[7] The European Commission conducted an energy sector inquiry, which concluded that the resulting adverse effects on the European single market warranted the separation of transmission from production and retailing.[8] In the event, substantial fines were imposed on French and German operators, and separation was achieved in a limited number of cases.

In railways, there has been an ongoing debate about the desirability of separating provision of the network of tracks and stations from running freight or passenger services. The experience of a more complex separation in the UK, where the provision of rolling stock and track maintenance were also separated functions, was not a success.[9] Nonetheless, after a careful review, the OECD concluded that separation had both costs and benefits, and that 'decisions not to separate [ownership] should only be made after careful consideration of the costs that will result in the form of the additional regulatory burden and ongoing residual discrimination'.[10] The final sentence draws attention to the fact that one of the benefits of separation is that, if the motive to discriminate goes, regulation to prevent it can be wound back.

---

[6] See the papers on public–private interplay in next-generation communications in (2010) 34(9) *Telecommunications Policy.*

[7] For a review of the arguments, see M. Pollitt, 'The Arguments For and Against Ownership Unbundling in Energy Transmission Markets' (2008) 36 *Energy Policy* 704–13.

[8] European Commission, *DG Competition Report on Energy Sector Inquiry* (2007).

[9] On separation in UK railways (and more generally), see J. Gómez Ibáñez, *Regulating Infrastructure: Monopoly, Contracts and Discretion* (Harvard, 2003), chs 11 and 13.

[10] OECD, 'Structural Reform in the Railway Industry' (2005) 46 DAF/COMP.

Making Capital Investment Contestable

When a 'natural monopoly' asset is to be installed in a utility sector, by definition there is no scope for efficient duplication.[11] The firm equipped with the asset will not be in head-to-head competition, or 'competition in the market'. However, as the chapter on franchising notes, there may be scope for 'competition for the market'—i.e. rivalry among firms for the right to install and operate the asset. This process is often called making the activity or asset contestable.

Various contestability options are available, ranging from simple outsourcing of construction to the full transfer to another party of responsibility for delivering, financing, owning, and operating the relevant assets.

The possible benefits of contestability include:

- better specification of projects and increased cost efficiency; this is a natural consequence of increasing the pool of suppliers above one;
- better alignment of investment to customer priorities, in cases where bids are allowed not only from the infrastructure monopolist, but also from service providers. For example, if a train-operating company is allowed to bid to undertake a project to improve a station, it may have a better understanding of its passengers' needs from station services than a track operator has;
- improvements to innovation and dynamic efficiency, arising from the introduction of competitive ideas;
- comparative information on the performance of different firms in the same activity, which the regulator can use to demand cost reductions.

Downsides might include:

- reduction in scale and scope economies arising from separating a previously integrated operation; the extent of these is likely to be case-specific;
- more complex and costly coordination; the issue here is that coordination of activities is required in all large organizations—the choice is between undertaking it within an organization through an administrative process and performing it contractually across a transaction boundary, where separation can also sharpen conflict;[12] the difficulty of coordination is likely to vary with the task at hand; for example, in the water sector, having separate organizations responsible for different parts of the network of pipes may pose few problems of coordination in normal times, but may severely complicate dealing with floods;
- two particular respects in which failures of coordination may manifest themselves are through delays in procurement processes arising from the organization of contests and increased risk in the execution phase;

---

[11]   This section is based on joint work by Martin Cave and Janet Wright.
[12]   These alternatives are well captured in the title of a book by Oliver Williamson—*Markets and Hierarchies* (1975).

- there may also be changes in the cost of capital—the rate at which firms can borrow in the capital markets to finance their activities; this particular element of cost can be affected by project-specific risk, the extent of which may vary with the degree of contestability of the project; systematic risk will depend on the nature of the activity, rather than the identity of the executant, but different contestants may face different borrowing constraints, which will be reflected in their marginal costs of capital.

In practice, contestability can be introduced in a wide range of formats. The key differentiator is the level at which decisions are taken. Here we identify two categories:

a. Tenders for projects are conducted by the incumbent; this might be either required or encouraged by the regulator, in preference to the incumbent undertaking the project itself. The range of outsourcing options includes any or all of design/build/operation/finance. However, the assets remain in ownership of the incumbent, or are transferred back to it at the end of the contract.
b. Tenders for projects are conducted by an external party such as the regulator, a government body, or an independent system operator.

The former and less radical form of contestability arises where the outsourcing decision is made by the incumbent, which determines the scope of the activity to be outsourced. The less the project is specified in detail by the incumbent, the greater will be the scope for innovation by the contractor. A potential downside of the more broadly specified contract is that it may introduce a greater risk of the contractor failing to deliver the outcome, because of the reduced predictability of the delivered outputs and costs.

Regulators have in the past tended to eschew mandatory outsourcing. There are a number of reasons for this:

- Most regulated sectors already demonstrate a significant degree of voluntary outsourcing, and the full range of contract types may be employed. This may be in direct response to the efficiency incentives in the price cap, discussed in the following chapter.
- Whilst a number of contract forms may be used, regulated networks, given their inherent risk aversion, may prefer outsourcing of a more tightly specified project. However, this is not necessarily undesirable, and may often fit with the incumbent's duties and incentives. Outsourcing that involves increasing execution risk (e.g. where more innovative designs may be proposed) may therefore require a reassessment of those regulatory frameworks.

- It is not clear that regulatory bodies have or could acquire the required skills and insight to be well placed to assess the efficiency of outsourcing by a regulated company. Procurement by public sector organizations in many countries has a poor record of efficiency (for instance, the Ministry of Defence). However, to address this, it may be possible for a regulator to employ an expert procurement advisory panel to undertake the evaluation. Given the competitiveness of the infrastructure design and construction sector, there is already a considerable degree of transparency regarding the development of alternative procurement models, enabling a ready spread of best practice. The additional benefit from greater regulatory intrusion in procurement is unclear.

The second form differs from the first, in that it would be a party other than the incumbent or other interested party that determines the need for the project and the specification of the outcome, and decides who delivers the project, typically through a tendering process. That third party might be the regulator or the government. The advantage of this approach would be that it would ensure consideration of options for delivery by non-incumbents (i.e. extension of compulsory outsourcing), where otherwise the incumbent, in control of the tender process, may have incentives to maintain a greater proportion of the project 'in-house'. It might also ensure that the project actually takes place, by relaxing constraints on capital availability, by enabling alternative bidders to come forward with a range of objectives, financial capacity, and financing sources.

This option allows for the bidder to own (and operate) the new infrastructure, effectively introducing an alternative network owner. And it also provides the opportunity for existing assets to be transferred as part of the 'package' to the new provider—for instance, where the investment is to enhance or add to an existing asset (again, the motivation would be greater efficiency in delivery and operation by the new party, and a spur to greater efficiency by the incumbent elsewhere in its operations).

A key question in evaluating this approach is whether the incumbent is allowed to tender itself at any stage in the process. On one hand, excluding an experienced supplier is generally harmful to a contest; on the other hand, if potential competitors assume that the incumbent has a very high probability of success, they will not bother to bid.

A problem arises with the second approach because it is not clear that regulatory bodies or governments may not have the skills required to assess competing tenders. It may be sufficient to address this problem that the regulator employ an expert procurement advisory panel to undertake the evaluation.

A number of examples provide some useful insights:

a. Argentina: electricity transmission;[13]
b. UK: offshore transmission;[14]
c. UK: rail.[15]

The key lessons from this material are summed up as follows:

• Contestability can bring in external finance (many of the examples cited have this as a key feature—the cost of doing so depends very much on the contract type and process).
• It can be used to enable customers or those closer to the end user to have a greater say in outcome (see the Argentinian example, where a 'public contest' was held for major electricity transmission asset expansions, with user groups being directly involved in proposing, tendering, approving, and paying for the delivery of projects).
• The tender process can be designed in stages to enable the incumbent to bid, in order not to exclude the incumbent if it might be the most efficient provider on account of scale/scope economies for instance, while ensuring that it is still subject to the competitive pressures of having to compete in a tender.
• A very important potential drawback from third-party tendering is that it has frequently added significantly to delays and costs; there is evidence of this both with the UK offshore transmission project and with some rail projects.
• All the examples involve large-scale schemes, usually with the creation of new and largely discrete assets.
• They are also 'separable' to a large degree from the main core of the existing network.

Summing up the lessons of this experience, the UK energy regulator OFGEM draws the conclusion that this approach is only likely to be appropriate for large and discrete projects, where significant benefits can be expected to outweigh the high costs of administering the process and where time is not of the essence.[16]

An analysis of the scope for contestability of track and station projects concluded that separable, customer-facing investments were most likely to

[13] See a series of papers by S. Littlechild and C.J. Skerk, 'Transmission Expansion in Argentina, 1–6' (1994) 30 *Energy Economics* 1367–1527.

[14] OFGEM, *Offshore Transmission: First Transitional Tender Information Memorandum* (2009), http:// www.ofgem.gov.uk/Networks/offtrans/Pages/Offshoretransmission.aspx.

[15] M. Cave and J. Wright, *Options for Increasing Competition in the Great Britain Rail Market: On Rail Competition in the Passenger Rail Market and Contestability in Rail Infrastructure Investment*, Report to ORR (2010).

[16] OFGEM, *RIIO: A New Way to Regulate Energy Networks* (October 2010).

benefit from contestability. These include the development of stations, for example by property companies, and the extensions of or enhancements to track utilized predominantly by a single train operator. Complex upgrades to track which continues to be kept in operation by its operator are less suitable for the introduction of contestability.

Liberalization and Social Objectives

Liberalization and unbundling have the normal effect of competitive measures of creating pressures for prices to come into line with costs. But this may come into conflict with the desire of many governments and regulators to maintain 'universal service' in the utilities sector, in recognition of the centrality of the services which they provide to economic, political, and social life, the significant proportion of household spending they account for, and the role of utility prices in affecting the location of industry, and hence regional development.

Universal service has two aspects: it means that the service must be made available to all households within a given area, and that it should be made available at a uniform and affordable price. The desire to maintain affordability often leads to prices of particular services which are less than cost. Uniformity of prices in the presence of cost differences imposes a problem in itself, however, because it means that servicing customers in high-cost areas may be a loss-making activity. When the sector is open to competition, competitors will have no interest in serving such customers, and the incumbent operator, which has to provide service universally, is left with them. This arrangement might at the end of the day cause the whole system of universal service to unravel, as competitors would progressively attract more customers, leaving the universal service operator with a remainder characterized by increasingly high costs; it would then be forced to progressively raise its tariffs to cover these higher costs.

When utility markets were initially opened up to competition, the power of the incumbent was such that it was able to deal with this problem fairly painlessly. However, as competitors' market shares increased, the danger grew that competition might be distorted by imposing the burden on a single operator.

One response is to leave the obligation on the incumbent, but to introduce a burden-sharing regime. This involves a complex calculation of the net costs which the 'universal service operator' incurs in serving non-commercial loss-making customers, and then dividing them among all operators above a minimum size in proportion to revenues.[17] Where the incumbent has the largest revenues, it pays the largest share of the costs. This regime has been available for voice telecommunications in Europe since 1997.[18]

In postal services, a similar regime is contemplated for the Royal Mail in the UK, subject to the proviso that it would only take effect when the Royal Mail, which is the universal service operator, had achieved efficiency—to prevent it from shifting the cost of its own failings onto its competitors.[19]

This seems a sensible and practical solution for existing universal services. But it is tested when there are new candidates for the designation. Broadband is a good example.[20] In some countries, it has now reached the 70–80 per cent penetration levels, which permit a service to be made universally available without imposing a crippling cost either on the designated provide, or on existing consumers—assuming that it will be financed by cross-subsidies within the marketplace rather than subsidies from general taxation. Note that we are not necessarily talking here about high-speed broadband of the kind supplied by fibre networks—which governments are keen to install in certain areas to improve competitiveness for industrial policy reasons—but about a more basic service made available to all. However, given the competitive structure of the broadband market in much of Europe (see above), there is no natural retail supplier on which the obligation can be placed. Moreover, in addition to the fixed suppliers of broadband discussed above, mobile broadband has become both faster and vastly more popular.

This is both a challenge and an opportunity. A government or regulator seeking to offer broadband universally can hold a technologically neutral 'reverse auction', in which competing suppliers can bid for the minimum sum of money which they would require to make broadband of a particular standard available universally in a specified geographical area.[21] Subject to the difficulty of fully specifying a 'franchise contract' of this kind, discussed in Chapter 9 on franchising above, this may prove an effective and competitive method of delivering a 'new' universal service.

---

[17] The calculation should also take account of marketing and other benefits which the universal service operator receives by virtue of its role as ubiquitous supplier.

[18] Directive 97/33/EC of the European Parliament and the Council of 30 June 1997 on interconnection in telecommunications with regard to ensuring universal service and inter-operability through application of the principles of ONP.

[19] Department for Business, Innovation and Skills, *Delivering for the Future: A Universal Mail Service and Community Post Offices in the Digital Age*, Cm. 7946 (2010), 16–17.

[20] See the 'Symposium on Broadband for All' in (2010) 80 *Communications and Strategies*.

[21] S. Wallsten, 'Reverse Auctions and Universal Telecommunications Service: Lessons from Global Experience' (2009) 61(2) *Federal Communications Law Journal*.

25 Implementing Price Controls

Even when the scope for competition is fully utilized, a significant part of the value chain of utility companies is likely to remain monopolistic, or subject to limited competition, at least for a period of transition from monopoly. In such circumstances, it is natural for the regulator to respond by introducing some form of price control.

We have argued in Chapter 22 above that, in the case of a privately owned utility, the price-control regime must strike a balance between the interests of customers—protecting them from monopolistic exploitation—and the interests of investors, who, when they have sunk considerable sums of money into irrecoverable investments, will be concerned lest the regulator should impose a level of charges that makes it impossible for them to recover their investments. Even the fear of this eventuality may be sufficient to deter them from making the investment in the first place. The twin functions of price regulation are thus to protect consumers from exploitation and to provide investors with the confidence to maintain and develop the infrastructure needed to provide service.[1] This chapter describes how this can best be accomplished.

Rate of Return Regulation

There are a number of ways in which price control can be achieved. The simplest means is to impose a regime of cost-plus pricing. Under such a regime, the regulator sets prices for the utility in such a way that they cover the utility's cost of production and include a rate of return on capital that is sufficient to maintain investors' willingness to replace or expand the company's assets. (This is why cost-plus regulation is also known as 'rate-of-return' regulation.) In some cases, the firm is required to set the price for each service equal to its costs. In others, individual services can be sold at either above or below cost, but the regulator constrains prices overall so that total regulated revenues cover costs. This regime, or a version of it, was widely practised in regulated industries in the United States until about 1990.[2]

---

[1] For a detailed analysis of solutions to this dilemma, see B. Levy and P. Spiller (eds), *Regulations, Institutions and Commitment* (Cambridge, 1996).
[2] A.E. Kahn, *The Economics of Regulation* (2nd edn Cambridge,1988), chs 2–3, 5.

Rate-of-return regulation is subject to one obvious flaw and one more subtle one. The obvious flaw is that the company in question has no incentive to operate efficiently, as it knows that it will be able to recover increasing costs with a subsequent increase in price. Provided that price reviews take place with sufficient frequency that there is no lag in recovery, the firm pays no penalty for inefficiency. The less obvious flaw is that the arrangement may give an incentive for the firm to over-invest in capital equipment. Suppose that the regulator calculates the allowable rate of return on assets at 15% per year, whereas the firm's cost of capital—the return required to keep investors replacing and expanding assets in the firm—is only 10% per year. In these conditions, the regulator's estimate allows the firm's investors to make an excess rate of return of 5% per year on whatever investment they put into the business. If this is so, they will have an incentive to inflate the asset base artificially by adopting very capital intensive techniques and by unnecessary extravagance in designing plant (sometimes known as 'gold plating'). Essentially, the more they invest the greater their excess returns. This phenomenon, known after its discoverers as the Averch-Johnson effect,[3] will skew inefficiency in the direction of excessive use of capital, and it may be difficult for the regulator to identify such extravagance by inspecting investment plans, especially if comparable firms are subject to the same incentives. This consequence is, however, secondary to the sheer lack of incentive to control costs of production that is encountered under rate-of-return regulation.

These deficiencies were recognized, and measures were taken to counteract them. For example, some regulators introduced a requirement that assets would only be remunerated if they were 'used and useful'.[4] Nonetheless, despite these improvements, rate-of-return regulation remains a 'low-powered' incentive mechanism—low-powered because the firm benefits little from any efficiency gain. This arises because if cost savings are made, they will almost at once be taken from the firm and given to consumers in the form of lower prices. This naturally raises the question of what would amount to a 'high-powered' incentive mechanism. Clearly, its distinguishing feature must be that the firm retains, at least temporarily, a significant proportion of the benefits of any greater efficiency. This can be achieved by decoupling the revenues that a firm can generate from the costs that it incurs.

---

[3] M. Averch and L. Johnson, 'Behaviour of the Firm under Regulatory Constraint' (1962) 92 *American Economic Review* 1052–69.

[4] D. Newbery, *Privatization, Restructuring, and Regulation of Network Utilities* (Cambridge, MA, 1999), 44.

Price Capping

A very high-powered incentive mechanism would operate by setting a trajectory of prices for the firm's products indefinitely into the future—requiring them, for example, to fall by 2% per year in real terms for ever. In such circumstances, a firm not subject to competition would be able to keep in perpetuity the benefits of any cost savings that it achieved. If they exceeded 2% a year, profits would rise indefinitely. If they fell short of 2%, the firm would ultimately go bankrupt. The former outcome would be politically unacceptable; the latter might interrupt service. For this reason, regulators have increasingly looked for some intermediate variant under which prices are set in advance for a period (usually 3 to 5 years), allowing the firm to benefit from any cost savings made during that period, but recalculated at regular intervals in order to bring them back into line with underlying costs. This regime is known as price capping. Although a few American precursors can be identified, it was first applied on a large scale in the United Kingdom to British Telecom in 1984, and then extended to other UK utilities as they were privatized.[5] It is now used widely throughout the world in the energy, communications, transport, and water industries, and applied both to privatized utilities and to public sector firms.

In order to take account of unpredictable rates of inflation in an economy, a price-capping regime typically allows a firm to vary its prices in any year by an amount that is linked to the overall level of inflation. A price cap usually permits a utility to increase its overall level of prices by the previous year's rate of inflation in the economy, as measured by the retail price index (RPI), which is then varied by a percentage (the value of X) that reflects the real cost reduction that the regulator expects.[6] Thus, if the firm is subject to a cap of RPI−5 and if inflation in the previous year were 3%, it would have to lower nominal prices by 2%.

THE FORM AND SCOPE OF THE PRICE CAP

As discussed in Chapter 23, initially caps were applied to retail prices and covered the whole value chain. In the simplest case, a single product was sold

---

[5] For the influential report proposing RPI-X for British Telecom, see S.C. Littlechild, *Regulation of British Telecommunications' Profitability* (London, 1983); M. Armstrong, S. Cowan, and J. Vickers, *Regulatory Reform* (London, 1994), ch. 6; M. Beesley and S. Littlechild, 'The Regulation of Privatised Monopolies in the United Kingdom' (1989) 20 *Rand Journal of Economics* 454; Newbery, *Privatization, Restructuring and Regulation*, ch. 2; D. Sappington, 'Price Regulation' in M. Cave, S. Majumdar, and I. Vogelsang, *Handbook of Telecommunications Economics* (Amsterdam, 2002), 225–93; J. Hauge and D. Sappington, 'Pricing in Network Industries' in R. Baldwin, M. Cave, and M. Lodge (eds), *Oxford Handbook of Regulation* (Oxford, 2010), 462–99.

[6] Price capping is often known as RPI-X regulation; or as CPI-X regulation when a consumer price index (CPI) is used.

at a uniform price. Thus in the energy sector the same product, a kilowatt hour of electricity or a cubic metre of gas, may be sold to all customers. The price cap regime can thus require an energy utility to reduce the average price of all the energy it sells by a pre-specified amount.[7] In telecommunications, by contrast, a variety of different final services were sold, including customers' rental of a connection to the network paid for by a monthly or quarterly rental, and local, long-distance, and international calls which are charged on a per minute basis. Broadband services may also be supplied, although these latter are not normally subject to a retail price cap. A telecommunications firm subject to a retail price cap for its voice service would thus have had to demonstrate to the regulator that its proposed price increases for individual services, when weighted by the proportion of revenue accounted for by each service, satisfied the overall price cap. This is known as the tariff basket. In order to demonstrate that the cap is satisfied, the firm will typically have to seek approval from the regulator before it introduces price changes. The calculations required are illustrated in Table 25.1.

This form of price capping gives the firm considerable flexibility in setting prices for individual services, or services sold to different classes of customer, such as domestic or industrial users. The firm can thus increase significantly the price charged for one service, provided it makes equivalent reductions for prices in other services. Such changes in the structure of prices may bear particularly hard upon particular consumers, and as a result, regulators sometimes introduced side constraints to prevent excessive changes in the balance of tariffs. For example, they might prevent the regulator raising any price in real terms.

Table 25.1. Implementing a price cap regime: an illustration

Price cap: RPI−7.5
Previous year's RPI: 2.5
Permitted weighted average change in nominal prices: 2.5−7.5 = −5%

Service	Previous year's revenues (£bn)	Previous year's revenue proportion	Proposed price change (%)
1	8	0.5	−2
2	6	0.375	−10
3	2	0.125	−2

Weighted average price change
= (0.5 × −2) + (0.375 × −10) + (0.125 × −2)
= (−1) + (−3.75) + (−0.25) = −5
Price changes compliant with price cap.

[7] In some network (not retail) caps in the energy sector, the regulator controls not the unit price of the service being controlled, but the total revenue the regulated company can charge its customers. This means that the unit price of the service falls as the volume rises. The effect is to guarantee the firm a particular level of revenue. This may be desirable when the costs of the activity are fixed and not sensitive to volumes—a gas pipeline may exhibit a structure of costs of this kind.

As discussed in Chapter 23, the focus of price control has shifted away from retail prices to wholesale or network prices—the price charged for high-voltage transmission between two points or the price charged to rent a copper loop connecting a customer to her local telecommunications exchange. The result is a heterogeneous range of services, each with its own metric. But the basic principle of price caps—creating an incentive to cut costs by fixing prices for a period ahead—works in the same way for both retail and wholesale caps.

A price cap is typically set every three to five years, and in calibrating the cap (choosing the value of X in the formula) the regulators will typically try to achieve a balance between costs and revenues over the three- or five-year period as a whole. This may seem to make it the same as rate of return regulation. But the key difference is that, while under the simplest form of rate-of-return regulation, the regulator is allowing the firm to recover whatever costs it has historically incurred, with a price cap the regulator is making a projection of costs into the future, and setting overall prices so that they will cover those expected costs. If the regulated firm is able to increase its efficiency and reduce costs further than the regulator anticipates, its profits will go up. If it is less efficient than expected, its profits will go down.

The price cap set for the next period will, however, take account of the level of profits that the firm is earning when that new cap comes into operation. If the regulator body takes the view that excess profits are being earned, it will adjust prices in the subsequent period accordingly, either by a once-and-for-all adjustment to bring prices back into line with costs (known as a 'Po adjustment'), or by a gradual process of elimination of excess profits over the next period (known as a 'glide path'). This means that the benefits that a firm reaps from cost savings in the course of a price cap will depend not only upon the number of years that pass before the cap is revised, but also upon how the regulator takes account of excess profits (or losses) at the end of a period in determining allowable prices in the next period.

Procedures for Setting Price Caps—the Building Block Approach

The rationale of price capping is essentially based on incentives to cut costs. If prices are set for a period in advance, the firm has an incentive to become more efficient, as it keeps the difference between the predetermined price and its actual costs. At first sight, that might make the choice of the level of prices irrelevant, as the incentive effect of additional profit would be the same wherever prices were set (unless they were set so low that the firm stopped producing).

There are two reasons why this might not be so. First, suppose a lax cap evokes the effort to reduce costs; it will still lead to high prices—above average cost (see Chapter 22)—which will distort consumption. Second, it may be necessary to put the firm's management under some form of pressure to make them improve efficiency. It has been said that 'the true monopoly profit is a quiet life'. Too lax a cap, and possibly too tight a one also, may discourage effort.[8]

This issue bears on the question of how much effort should be put into setting price caps. Two approaches can be identified. According to the first, a simple procedure can be employed. For example, the regulator can examine how much productivity growth the sector has exhibited in the past. Thus if total factor productivity has grown at 5% over the past 10 years, it might be reasonable to expect it to continue at that rate in the future. A combination of this number and expectations of how the wages and other factor prices will grow yields an expected fall in unit costs. This figure can then be used to calculate the trajectory of prices which forms the cap.

More sophisticated versions of this relatively simplified approach have been used in the United States.[9] But the practice in the UK and some other European countries, and in Australia and New Zealand, has been to develop a more elaborate modelling approach. It may be preceded by more simplified forms of price capping based on international benchmarks,[10] but over the longer term the so-called building blocks approach is used.

The process of setting a price cap has often embedded within it a lengthy set of consultation and appeal processes. Table 25.2 gives an example of what this may entail. The core of the process is the construction of a simplified forward-looking financial model of the regulated firm, which shows how alternative regulated price levels will affect the demand for (and production of) the regulated service, and how that level of production will determine the regulated firm's costs. Note again that the service subject to price control is now more likely to be not the retail service one purchased by end users but a wholesale or network one (for the services of a gas pipeline, for example) purchased by retailers.

---

[8] See F. Erbetta and M. Cave, 'Regulation and Efficiency Incentives: Evidence from the England and Wales Water and Sewerage Industry' (2007) 6(4) *Review of Network Economics* 425–52. This paper analysed productivity growth in the sector over the first three price control periods. It found that growth in total factor productivity over the fifteen-year period was heavily concentrated around the start of the third price cap, generally considered to have been appreciably tighter and more demanding than its two predecessors.

[9] D. Sappington, 'Price Regulation' in M. Cave, S. Majumdar, and I. Vogelsang, *Handbook of Telecommunications Economics*, vol. 1 (Amsterdam, 2002), 248–51.

[10] See Chapter 26 below.

Table 25.2. An illustrative timetable for resetting a price cap

−30 months	Regulator publishes first consultation on general issues—form of price control; coverage; conceptual basis for asset valuation; cost of capital, etc. Work on financial models begins, within the Office.
−24 months	Responses to consultation document received from price-controlled firm, competitors, consumer groups, and others; brief period for respondents to comment on or rebut other responses.
−24 to −18 months	Financial model developed and validated; data collected and analysed on comparative efficiency; demand projections prepared.
−18 months	Regulator publishes second consultation document, setting out ranges for assumptions and range of values for X.
−18 to −12 months	Assumptions underlying modelling narrowed, in light of responses and latest data; financial modelling continues.
−15 months	Responses received to second consultation document.
−12 months	Regulator publishes third consultation document, proposing value of X and other details.
−10 months	Responses received to third consultation document.
−8 months	Regulator publishes price cap proposal. Firm accepts associated licence amendment or appeals it.
−8 to 0 months	Appeals, if any, are heard.
Implementation date	Price cap comes into force.

This is illustrated by the selected list of price caps in operation in the UK in 2011, shown in Table 25.3. It is an interesting feature of the table that the price caps it lists generally imply price rises in excess of inflation, as measured by the retail price index or RPI. This is visible from the fact that the formulae allow a positive value of X, signifying that the price of the service in question can rise faster than the RPI. This is a consequence of increased demands on investment in many sectors, which outweigh efficiency gains. The UK price caps over the previous 20 years had, by contrast, generally but not invariably, imposed falling real prices, through a formula such as RPI−4.

One reason for this change is that in the earlier period, regulated firms were inefficient; as a result, they could reduce their costs and service prices too. In addition, the need for massive investment in infrastructure has recently been recognized in the UK, and this has had an upward effect on prices.[11]

The basic structure of the building blocks model is set out in Figure 25.1.[12] The goal is to construct a simplified forward-looking financial model of the

---

[11] See D. Helm, 'Infrastructure Investment, the Cost of Capital and Regulation: An Assessment' (2009) 25(3) *Oxford Review of Economic Policy* 307–26.

[12] Figure 25.1 assumes that the regulated firm is the only producer of the price-controlled service. The model can be amended to allow for smaller competitors in the market. Of course, if the market were effectively competitive, price capping would not be required.

Table 25.3. Selected price caps operating in the UK utilities

Firm	Coverage	Period	Level
Communications BT[1]	Unbundled local loops	2009–2011	RPI+5.5%
Transport Network Rail[2]	Provision of track and station services to train operators	2009–2013	not applicable
BAA[3]	Supply of airport services at Heathrow	2008–2013	RPI+7.5%
Water Water and sewerage companies in England and Wales[4]	Supply of water and sewerage services to end users	2010–2015	RPI+0.5%

1. OFCOM, *A New Pricing Framework for Openreach* (May 2009).
2. ORR, *Determination of Network Rail's Output and Funding, 2009–2014* (2008).
3. CAA, *Economic Regulation of Heathrow and Gatwick Airports, 2008–2013: CAA Decision* (2008).
4. OFWAT, *Future Water and Sewerage Charges 2010–2015: Final Determinations* (2009).

firm as it will be in the final year of the period of price control. This involves projecting the demand for the service, which will depend upon demand conditions in the economy as a whole, particular features of demand for the service in question, and, of course, the price which the regulator will set for it. The demand for a wholesale service is derived ultimately from demand for the final service it goes to make.

Producing to meet any specified level of demand will impose costs on the firm. Some of these costs will be operating expenditure—labour, energy, and material costs. Because utilities are highly capital intensive, capital costs are important too. Assets in use at the end of the price control period will be of two types—those already in existence at the start of the period, already subject to some level of depreciation, and new capital expenditure. The running total of the depreciated value of assets used by the firm and recognized by the regulator is known as the Regulatory Asset Base, or RAB. Capital costs in the final year of the period will consist of two types—an annual depreciation charge, based on the expected life of the asset, and the so-called cost of capital, or the return on capital a regulated firm must offer its investors to persuade them to maintain investment in the business. We can think of the process of setting a price control in the following way. The goal is to set a trajectory of prices which will allow the regulated firm to break even if it operates efficiently. In terms of Figure 25.1, this means choosing a value of X, the rate of change of real prices over the period, which will equate revenue and costs. Imagine that the regulator chooses a trial value of X. This will determine prices, and these prices will, in conjunction with other demand-side factors shown on the right side of the diagram, fix quantity demanded and hence, given the price, revenue. Now, turning to the right side of the figure, the regulator calculates how much it will cost in total to produce the projected output level. Note that

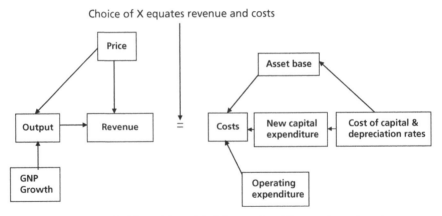

Figure 25.1. A simplified financial model of the regulated firm used to set a price cap

this includes the cost of capital or normal profit that the firm must make in order to maintain the flow of investment into the business.

Projected cost and revenues can then be compared. Suppose that revenues exceed costs. This indicates excess returns, and the regulator can alter the level of X to reduce prices. Conversely, if costs exceed revenue, the firm is projected, at the trial prices, to make a loss, implying that prices must rise on the next iteration. In this stylized account, the process finishes when a value of X is found at which costs and revenues are the same.

The key point is that the model is a forward-looking projection made by the regulator, of the position of the firm in several years' time. The outcome is a trajectory of future prices which is laid down as a challenge for the firm to beat by costs reductions. The process is thus driven by a variety of assumptions, which the regulatory body will make as best it can, on the information available to it. But subject to the points made above, the incentive effect will operate even if the regulator's combined assumptions are not exactly realized.

The key assumptions on the *demand* side (apart from the regulated price, which is used as a control variable by the regulator to equate revenues and costs) are the growth of national income, or of general economic activity over the price control period. There are other positive or negative trends as well. For example, in communications there are trend declines in demand for letters, and hence both for demand for retail postal services and for the wholesale service provided by the postal incumbent of delivering its own and competitors' letters to recipients' homes and business premises. Conversely, the vast increase in mobile calls has increased commensurately the demand for the service provided by mobile operators of terminating on their own networks calls received from other operators' networks.

On the *cost* side a key assumption is the level of operating expenditure over the price control period, which depends upon an assessment of the scope for efficiency savings considered in more detail in Chapter 26. In relation to capital costs, which may represent the bulk of costs, there are a range of difficult questions:

- how to determine whether new capital investment is necessary;
- how to value capital inherited from previous periods; this is controversial if there is a conflict between alternative forms of accounting valuation or between accounting valuations and values exhibited in the marketplace, notably at the time of privatization;
- the rate of depreciation, especially if the technology is becoming obsolete or if a natural resource (such as gas delivered by a particular pipeline) is running out;
- the cost of capital or allowed rate of return used in the building blocks calculation.[13]

The way in which regulators have faced these issues in practice can best be seen from their own price control documents, some of which are cited above.

The Performance of Price Control Mechanisms

Establishing the separate impact of price caps is made more difficult by the fact that, both in the UK and in countries other than the United States (where utilities have always been in private rather than public ownership), the change in price control mechanisms coincided with privatization and the creation of independent regulatory bodies.

The US is therefore a good place to look. Sappington's analysis of US data relating to telecommunications, across 50 states which adopted different forms of control, concluded that 'incentive regulation appears to increase the deployment of modern switching and transmission equipment, to spur an increase in total factor productivity growth, and to foster a modest reduction in certain service prices. There is little evidence, though, that incentive regulation leads to a significant reduction in operating costs. There is some evidence that earnings may be higher under price cap regulation.'[14] A later review notes the dominance of price caps in telecommunications regulation

---

[13] For documents on calculating the cost of capital, see OFCOM, *Proposals for WBA Price Control* (2011); Europe Economics, *The Weighted Average Cost of Capital for Ofgem's Future Price Control* (2010).

[14] D. Sappington, 'Price Regulation' in M. Cave, S. Majumdar, and I. Vogelsang, *Handbook of Telecommunications Economics* (Amsterdam, 2002), 285. Sappington's term 'incentive regulation'

in the USA; they were used in 33 states, while only three states relied on rate-of-return regulation.[15]

Several authors have found evidence that returns to investors from regulated utilities in the UK were excessive in the period of up to ten years following privatization and the introduction of price caps, though this may be due in part to deliberate underpricing of shares at privatization.[16] It is also relevant that it was the norm in the UK for the initial price cap to be set by the government, not by an independent regulator. In 1997, the incoming government responded to this state of affairs by imposing a windfall tax on utilities, yielding £5.2 billion. Abnormal returns have, however, generally declined over longer periods following privatization.

This evidence is consistent with a hypothesis that UK regulators initially underestimated the potential for cost savings and accordingly set caps which were too lax. As firms cut operating costs and eliminated some slack, and as regulators acquired better knowledge of their sectors, the scope for higher-than-expected profits diminished.

The control of capital costs is more problematic. As noted above, monopoly regulation rests upon an informal bargain between the regulator (acting for consumers) and the firm (acting for investors). Under the terms of the bargain, consumers are protected from excessive prices and investors are guaranteed a return over time on their efficiently made sunk investments. The bargain is codified to an important degree in the regulatory asset base or RAB, which lists the value of assets which the regulator acknowledges as warranting a return both of capital (through depreciation) and on capital (by an appropriate allowed rate of return).

It has proved difficult in some regulated sectors to ensure that capital investments are well chosen. We know that if investments are remunerated on a cost-plus basis there may be gold-plating or over-investment. Several commentators, including the regulator,[17] have discussed an alleged bias towards capital solutions in the England and Wales water industry. One possible way of dealing with this is to make the implementation of investment more contestable, as discussed in Chapter 24.

---

embraces a wider class of price control mechanisms than the price caps considered here, but price caps are the form of incentive regulation most often employed.

[15] D. Sappington and D. Weisman, 'Price Cap Regulation: What Have We Learned from 25 Years of Experience in the Telecommunications Industry?' (2010) 38 *Journal of Regulatory Economics* 232.

[16] L. Channells 'The Windfall Tax' (1997) 18 *Fiscal Studies* 281; M. Florio, *The Great Divestiture* (Cambridge, 2004), ch. 5.

[17] OFWAT, *The Form of Price Control for Monopoly Water and Sewerage Services in England and Wales* (2010), 21.

The UK energy regulator undertook a review of price capping of network activities after about 20 years of their operation in the sector.[18] To some degree the review was driven by the challenges the energy sector faces associated with sustainability and decarbonization, but other more generic issues were examined too. The starting point was a recognition that price caps had benefited consumers but that they needed adaptation.

Among the elements of adaptation most relevant to the present discussion is a greater focus of regulation on outputs, leading to a move away from the specification of inputs which leads to cost-plus regulation. *Ex ante* regulatory instruments (i.e. price caps) would be retained, incorporating a return on the regulatory asset base (RAB). The length of the price control would be extended to eight years, with provision for a mid-term review. Certain large and separable investments would be made contestable. Special measures would be taken to promote innovation, to be discussed in Chapter 26 below.

Controlling Quality of Service with Price Controls

The technological level, reliability, quality, and safety of utility services are often as important to end users as their prices. This makes it important to address the issue of how to control prices simultaneously with that of how to regulate quality of service. As a simple example, a firm regulated as to price by a price cap can cut cost simply by degrading the quality of service it provides to its customers. In fact, doing so is a means of evading the price control, as reducing quality at a given price is virtually the same in its effects on customers as increasing prices at the same quality. One simple approach to resolving this problem, considered below, is to impose a financial penalty on a firm failing to meet specified quality standards. This was introduced or strengthened in the UK in relation to airports subject to price control. If they fail to meet certain quality standards relative to such things as time spent waiting in queues for security checks, they can be fined.[19] However, other quality failings, such as a culpable inability to keep the airport open, may not be penalized.

In the UK, the various statutes governing the regulation of utilities create slightly different frameworks for the regulation of quality. Broadly, the regulator can set standards of performance, and fine or require a refund to customers if they are not met. The problem is to find a means of satisfactorily

---

[18] OFGEM, *RIIO: A New Way to Regulate Energy Networks* (October 2010); OFGEM, *Handbook for Implementing the RIIO Model* (October 2010).

[19] CAA, *Economic Regulation of Heathrow and Gatwick Airports, 2008–2013*, CAA Decision (2008), ch. 12.

capturing the dimensions of quality which customers really care about in the metrics. An example of overall service standards are those set by the regulator for UK regional distribution companies. These include a standard for the time taken to replace a distributor's fuse in the customer's premises (three hours if notified in working hours in 2008/9) and the associated charge for non-compliance (£20); or the guaranteed standard for restoring electricity supply following a fault (18 hours), with a penalty for non-compliance of £50 in the case of domestic customers.[20] In 2008/9 payments made against failure to meet the latter standard grew sharply. While the standards seem individually sensible, they are unlikely to guarantee overall customer satisfaction. The advantages of having a competitive regime which gives customers a genuine choice are very obvious.

From a theoretical point of view, a number of factors give rise to the difficulties encountered in regulating quality.[21] Consider first the case of an unregulated monopolist supplying a good of uniform quality to its captive market. In pricing output of a given quality, its route to profit maximization is clear: raise prices up to the point where any further increase will reduce demand so much as to lower profits. When quality is a choice variable, however, what are the monopolists' incentives? The answer is that the unregulated monopolist will either under-supply or over-supply quality,[22] the departures from the optimum arising because the monopolist chooses the quality level with an eye to the preference of the consumer, who, at the price charged, is just on the margin of buying or not buying the product. The opinions of all others are ignored.

Suppose now that the firm is subject to rate-of-return regulation (see the first section above). Consumers are likely to benefit chiefly because price of output of a given quality is controlled. In addition, the quality of output may rise if rate-of-return regulation encourages capital intensity; and if capital is normally required to increase service quality, the result may be excessive quality. An electricity generation network, for example, may contain far more excess capacity to deal with the risk of supply interruptions than customers would ideally like to pay for.

Now replace rate-of-return regulation with a price-cap. The situation now becomes less ambiguous, as the regulated firm with a given price cap will be able to make extra profits by degrading the quality of service. In other words, quality degradation is a means of evading the price cap.

---

[20] Consumer Focus, *2008/9 Report on the Guaranteed Standards of Performance for Electricity Distribution* (2010).

[21] See L. Rovizzi and D. Thompson, 'The Regulation of Product Quality in Public Utilities' in M. Bishop, J. Kay, and C. Mayer (eds), *The Regulatory Challenge* (London, 1995).

[22] See M. Spence, 'Monopoly Quality & Regulation' 16 (1975) *Bell Journal of Economics* 417–29.

Where quality of service can be differentiated *ex ante* or *ex post* across customers, the natural solution is to offer customers a choice of tiered levels of service, and to pay compensation for failure to deliver these as due to individual customers. Such arrangements exist in the telecommunications industry, where customers can pay a higher quarterly payment in return for a quicker guaranteed repair service.

The issues then arising are how the gradations of service or conditions of eligibility for compensation should be set and how prices for each should be determined. On compensation levels, damages should ideally equal losses borne by the representative consumer divided by the probability that compensation will be sought, as this will give firms an appropriate deterrent against breaching standards which takes account of the problem that not everyone will complain. Thus, if only half complain, the payment will have to be twice the actual damage imposed, in order to give the operator a strong incentive to maintain service standards. In practice, however, some conventional figure tends to be chosen. Tiered service charges could either be cost-based or reflect demand factors as well, as in Ramsey pricing (see Chapter 22). It is likely that service levels and prices will require regulatory scrutiny, to ensure that they match the range of consumers' preferences.

Where the quality attribute is public (such as the taste of tap water or probability of a call failure in a telecommunications network), one superficially attractive means of combining price and quality regulation is to incorporate quality measurements directly into the price cap. This could be achieved by simply appending an extra term or terms to the RPI−X formula—turning it into RPI−X+aQ (or RPI−X+a_1Q_1+a_2Q_2 if there were two quality variables of interest). Thus a regulated company that increased its quality of service (and hence raised its quality index Q) would be allowed to raise its prices faster than it could if quality levels remained constant. Equally, any decline in service quality would be accompanied by a fall in the price which could be charged. However, a formula of this type might see quality (and price) raised above what most consumers wanted, because it allowed a further price increase.

Regulators are attaching increasing importance to establishing what customers want. In the UK, price setting for water and sewerage services involved a major exercise by the regulator, by companies, and by the organization representing end users to establish consumer preferences.[23] The UK energy regulator's amendments to the regulatory regime include measures which give stakeholders greater opportunities to influence company and regulator decisions.[24] At the same time, the difficulty of achieving this in practice has given

---

[23] See OFWAT, *Involving Customers in the Price Setting Process: A Discussion Paper*, 2010.
[24] Ofgem, *RIIO: A New Way to Regulate Energy Networks*, October 2010, ch. 3.

impetus to proposals to give customers an even greater role, via direct negotiations with suppliers.

Negotiated Settlements

Over the past 50 years in North America, and with increasing momentum since 2000, recourse has been had within the utility sector to settlements negotiated between the service provider—an airport, energy company, or telecommunications operator, for example—and its customers.[25] Initially this was seen as a means of speeding up and economizing on the regulatory process. Increasingly, negotiated settlements are seen as a way of encouraging a direct dialogue between supplier and customer and reducing the role as intermediary of the regulator, which may be required to ensure the fulfilment of social and environmental obligations but which may also have its own interests to pursue, including the maintenance of the regulatory system.

If such settlements are to produce efficient outcomes, there must be some means of avoiding the standard monopoly outcome, in which the supplier uses its market power to impose an unequal outcome on its customers. This is achieved by ensuring that the bargaining takes place 'within the shadow' of a regulatory regime. This can take several forms. For example, major airports in Australia and New Zealand are not subject to price controls of the kind which apply, for example, to airports in the south-east of the UK such as Heathrow. Instead, the regime encourages them to negotiate with airlines over the provision of airport services and to publish their financial results. Present in the background is the implicit threat that an unfair outcome will lead to the imposition of price controls.

In other contexts, the role of the regulator is more developed. It may have to approve the settlement; it may make certain decisions itself and delegate others to negotiation; it may control or approve the process of choosing customer representatives to negotiate with the supplier.

The benefit claimed for the process is that it speeds up regulation, introduces innovative solutions which a more formal and bureaucratic system may not discover, introduces direct interchange between supplier and customer over complex quality dimensions, and makes regulation more light-handed.

An interesting recent example is furnished by the use of negotiated settlements or so-called 'constructive engagement' to set price controls for airports in the south-east of England over the period 2008–13. The aim was to bring

---

[25] J. Doucet and S. Littlechild, 'Negotiated Settlements: The Development of Legal and Economic Thinking' (2006) 14 *Utilities Policy* 266–77.

the owner of the airports in question, BAA, into engagement with airlines, particularly over issues of airport expansion and terminal quality. The process foundered at the airport where the operator favoured construction of a new runway, which was opposed by the airlines, which would have to pay for it through their landing charges. At two other airports, where disagreements were less fundamental, it had some benefits, though the outcome was marred by mistrust and disputes over information disclosure.[26]

The number and degree of homogeneity of customers, and their depth of sectoral knowledge, are likely to have a major effect on the process. A small number of gas suppliers may negotiate with a pipeline operator more easily than a combination of low-and high-cost airlines can negotiate with an airport operator over terminal quality. Organizing negotiations involving household customers presents challenges of ensuring fair representation of different geographical and income groups.

Despite these potential difficulties, negotiated settlements look a fruitful alternative to, or adjustment and supplement to, the traditional approach to setting price and quality controls.

---

[26] Competition Commission, *BAA Ltd (Heathrow and Gatwick Quinquennial Review, Final Report)* (October 2007), paras. 4.15–4.19.

26 Efficiency and Innovation in Network Industries

Regulation and Innovation

Network industries play a major role in economic growth and development and it is, accordingly, vital that they operate efficiently. Energy prices are fundamental to a country's competitiveness, and reducing reliance on non-renewable energy sources is essential to sustainability objectives. World Bank data also suggest that the spread of telecommunications services, especially mobile voice and broadband, gives a significant boost to GNP.[1]

The challenges created in the face of climate change increase the importance of adequate incentives for investment in regulated industries. They are often both capital- and energy-intensive. Rising energy prices or direct energy-saving measures may be brought to bear. This may necessitate solutions based on replacing capital expenditure with operating expenditure. It will probably involve more extensive use of information technology, and of metering and telemetry. The right incentives have to be brought into play to achieve these results.

The traditional organization of utilities as monolithic state-owned enterprises was generally inimical to efficiency and technical advance.[2] However, there is no guarantee that privatization would rectify the situation, as incentives towards efficiency will depend upon the structure of the industry, the degree of regulation it is subject to, and the form of regulation.

The impact of the form of regulation is illustrated by the now familiar contrast between rate-of-return or cost-plus regulation and the operation of price caps. Under rate-of-return regulation in its pure form, the regulated company receives enough revenue to cover its costs. If it gets more efficient, it has to cut its prices. It may have an incentive to install more capital equipment if its allowed rate of return on capital employed exceeds what it actually cost it to borrow on capital markets, but the decision to invest is based not on efficiency but on the desire to 'gold-plate'. Although this is an exaggeration of

---

[1] World Bank, *Information and Communications for Development: Extending Reach and Increasing Impact* (Washington, DC, 2009), 35–50.
[2] J. Netter and W. Megginson, 'From State to Market: A Survey of Empirical Studies on Privatisation' 2001 39(2) *Journal of Economic Literature* 321–89.

how rate-of-return regulation actually works, the lack of incentive for efficiency remains limited.

What about price caps? In principle, a long-term price control does give an incentive for efficiency. However, as noted in Chapter 25, price caps are based on forecasts which are subject to an increasing margin of error as they extend into the future. Concerns about excess profits being earned or losses incurred effectively limit the term of price cap. This almost inevitably introduces an element of cost-plus into the process. When a cap is reset, the regulator's starting point is almost unavoidably the existing level of costs, in the sense that the initial data-set for projecting costs forward is inevitably current observed costs. This introduces an element of cost-plus into the process.

A consequence of this is that, as shown below, the firm's returns to efficiency gains are reduced. In particular, if an efficiency gain is won near the end of the price control period, very few of the benefits go to the firm, as the resulting cost reduction is almost immediately reflected in lower prices in the next control period. Various methods have been implemented to mitigate the resulting effect on incentives to reduce cost. Essentially, they allow some kind of 'carry-over' of efficiency gains by the firm from one price control period to the next.

The problem is illustrated in Figure 26.1. Suppose a regulated company is considering two alternative means of realizing a particular outcome. For example, the options might be two alternative technologies for a water treatment plant. One (project A) uses a tried and tested technology, with

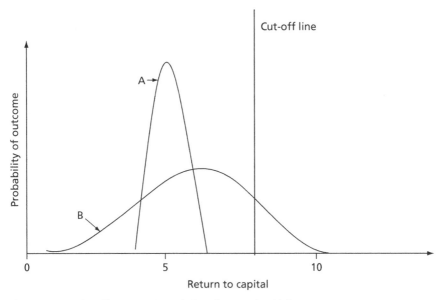

Figure 26.1. The effect on project choice of truncating high returns

nearly certain outcomes. A second innovative approach to achieving the same outcome (project B) is also available, which yields a higher average but more variable return. The expected distribution of returns for the two are shown in the figure. It is clear that B has the higher expected (average) return.

Absent regulation, the firm which was broadly neutral to risk would choose project B, on the strength of its higher expected returns. But now suppose that regulation operates in the way described above, and that rate-of-return or cost-plus elements in it bring about a situation in which, if the project earns high returns, the regulator brings prices down accordingly. This would happen if, in setting prices for a new control period, the regulator started from observed costs.

To represent this, we assume that prices are reduced if the 'cut-off line' in the figure is reached. In other words, where returns lie above that level, the distribution is 'truncated'. Eliminating this segment of the distribution brings the returns the firm gets from B to the same level as returns from A. B still has the same downside, or risk of failure. It also probably requires more managerial effort. As a result, A is likely to be chosen—not only this year but next year too.

The obvious regulatory response is to extend the degree to which the regulated firm can keep excess returns—in other words, to move the cut-off line to the right. If this is done skilfully, both investors and end users can benefit: investors because they are allowed to keep higher returns, if they eventuate, and end users because in this case the 'better' project B is chosen, and more generally, innovations are implemented. This drives costs down in the long run and may also improve quality of service.

Some regulators are fully aware of this issue.[3] But implementing it is not without difficulties. If an innovation introduced by a regulated firm turns out to be very successful in the event, end users may well forget the risks involved in implementing it, and resent the high returns the firm is making. Fear of this outcome may deter the regulator from making the reform.

Several of the revisions to the regulatory regime, under the title RIIO, made by the UK energy regulator focus on innovation.[4] Some augment the returns to successful regulation, in the manner described above. Another strand is an innovation stimulation package designed to allocate money on a competitive basis to promote sustainable energy. Amongst other things, this would allow for awards or prizes to be awarded to parties developing new commercial solutions. A similar proposal has been made in the water sector.[5] The notion

---

[3] See OFWAT, *The Role and Design of Incentives for Regulating Monopoly Water and Sewerage Services in England and Wales* (2010).

[4] OFGEM, *RIIO: A New Way to Regulate Energy Networks* (October 2010). RIIO stands for **R**evenue set to deliver strong **I**ncentives, **I**nnovation, and **O**utputs.

[5] M. Cave, *Independent Review of Competition and Innovation in the England and Wales Water Sector* (2009).

of prizes for innovation, which goes back at least as far as the Longitude Prize offered in 1714 by the British government for a device capable of establishing a ship's longitude, has made an unexpected reappearance in regulatory policy.[6]

What else can a regulator do to promote innovation, in addition to improving regulatory incentives? It is natural to look to competition as an important instrument. There is significant evidence that industries where there is more intense competition exhibit more innovation than monopolies,[7] although some argue that both monopolies and very fragmented sectors are poor at innovation, and that the best results are gained in markets with a small number of rivalrous producers.[8] This suggests that unbundling strategies described in Chapter 23 are likely to promote innovation.[9] The problem is that the reliance of all firms in the market on a common input, access to which the regulator has mandated, may limit the extent of product or service differentiation and thereby the scope for innovation. However, it is unlikely that an end-to-end monopoly with no unbundling would produce better results in terms of innovation.

Another form of competition might have an effect on efficiency and innovation in network industries. This is capital market competition, which takes the form of takeovers of underperforming assets by better managed companies which can deploy those assets more efficiently, make more profit from them, and hence bid more for the underperforming company's shares. This may be an optimistic version of how the takeover market works. For example, mergers and acquisitions may be directed at increasing market power rather than enhancing efficiency. And acquirers might be driven on by optimism and the desire to get bigger, rather than by anything else. Nonetheless, there are reasons to believe that the discipline of the capital market is more likely than not to be a stimulus to efficiency.

This generates a conflict between improving efficiency by this means, and the development and use by the regulator of a database of regulated firms' comparative performance which can be used to expose poor performers. The next section describes how this can operate.

---

[6] See L. Cabral, G. Cozzi, V. Dencolo, G. Spagnolo, and M. Zanza 'Procuring Innovation' in N. Dimitri, G. Piga, and G. Spagnolo (eds), *Handbook of Procurement* (Cambridge, 2006), 483–529.

[7] See R. Blundell, R. Griffith, and J. van Reenen, 'Market Share, Market Value and Innovation in a Panel of British Manufacturing Firms' (1999) 66 *Review of Economic Studies* 529–54; see also F. Etro, *Competition, Innovation and Anti-trust: A Theory of Market Leaders and its Policy Implications* (Berlin, 2007).

[8] P. Aghion, M. Bloom, R. Blundell, R. Griffith, and P. Howitt, 'Competition and Innovation: An Inverted-U Relationship' (2005) 120 *Quarterly Journal of Economics* 710–28.

[9] For a discussion of this complex issue, see J. Vickers, 'Competition Policy and Property Rights' (2010) 120 *Economic Journal* 375–92.

Analysis of comparative performance plays a particularly large role in the regulation of the England and Wales water and sewerage industry. At privatization in 1989, a special merger regime was set up, which now means that any merger between two water companies, where the turnover of at least one is more than £10 million, must be examined by the UK Competition Commission to establish whether the merger prejudices the regulator's ability to make comparisons between different water companies for the purpose of regulating them.[10] If the Commission makes this finding, it can prohibit the merger, require a divestment of assets, or require the companies to cut prices.

As a result of this provision, only one merger took place among the 20 or so companies between 2004 and 2010. A recent independent review of competition and innovation in the sector has proposed weakening substantially this limitation on the normal operation of the capital markets.[11]

Benchmarking

A major problem in setting forward-looking price controls is to forecast the level of efficient costs at some future date—typically the end of the price control period—which can be used to set a limit on permitted prices at that date. The trajectory of efficient cost will typically depend on:

- the rate of growth of output. The output being regulated is typically produced in conditions of natural monopoly, which normally means that there are increasing returns to scale (see Chapter 22 above). This in turn means that unit costs fall as output rises. When it rises very fast, as has been the case in the telecommunications traffic as a result of broadband, this may be a major effect. This issue can be addressed by estimating the degree of economies of scale in the sector in question, possibly on the basis of past observations of cost changes. But such observations will also be affected by the two additional factors listed below.
- the level of cost reduction of best practice producers. Costs will fall in most sectors as a result of technological progress, for example developments in the use of information technology. Sectors will vary in the rate at which such developments are attainable by firms which are 'on the frontier', or at the theoretical limit of efficiency. Technical advance has probably been faster in telecommunications, as a result of the application of digital technologies, than it has in water, where advance occurs much more slowly.

---

[10] Competition Commission, *Water Merger References* (London, 2004).
[11] M. Cave, *Independent Review of Competition and Innovation in Water Markets* (2009).

Again, analysing past experience and projecting it into the future can be helpful here, provided the impact of other factors is eliminated.

- the gap at the start of the price control period between a regulated firm's actual performance and best practice. This is likely to be large at the start of operation of incentive regulation. If price caps work as they should, it should diminish over time. Where a gap exists, the regulator has to decide how quickly it is reasonable for it to be closed. This might be in the course of the period for which the price control is being set. If the gap is large, it might be longer.

Benchmarking is applied to the last of these problems. It operates on the basis of collecting comparable data covering several firms; adjusting for differences in 'environmental factors', or factors outside the firms' control which affect their costs; and choosing a particular observation or an average of observations to act as the target to which the regulated firm should aspire.

It is immediately obvious that this procedure does not yield an estimate of theoretical best practice or of the technological frontier. If all the observations are of inefficient firms, the best that comparisons can deliver is a 'least worst' observation. If, as usually happens, the whole sample is subject to some kind of dysfunctional regulation (incorporating elements of cost-plus, for example, which may encourage inefficiency), this can be a serious problem.

We will discuss two examples of benchmarking: first an example based on international benchmarking in the telecommunications industry; then benchmarking in the water and electricity sector in the UK.

It is the practice in New Zealand, when a network input in telecommunications is mandated to be made available by the incumbent to its competitors, for the regulator to set an initial pricing principle based on benchmarking, which is then followed if appropriate by a full cost-modelling exercise. In the case to be reviewed here, in which a benchmark was sought for the price of unbundled local loops (the annual cost of providing a copper connection between end users' premises and the local telephone exchange), the regulator, the Commerce Commission, was required to undertake 'benchmarking against prices for similar services in comparable countries that use a forward looking cost-based pricing method'.[12]

The procedure involved the following steps:

(a) Identify countries in which similar services were provided.
(b) Eliminate those countries that do not use a forward-looking cost-based method.

---

[12] New Zealand Commerce Commission, *Standard Terms Determination for the Designated Service Telecom's Uunbundled Copper Local Loop Network*, Decision 609 (7 December 2007), 20–32.

(c) Select comparability criteria to identify comparable countries within the group which used a forward-looking cost-based method (and provided similar services).

(d) Apply benchmarking to that group of countries.

Application of the first two tests left 15 country observations, as well as 51 observations from the 50 states in the USA and the District of Columbia.

Statistical tests were then applied to identify which factors appeared to affect costs (or cost-based prices) in the sample. This revealed a clear and strong relationship between the unbundled copper loop prices and the proportion of urban population, and weaker relationships between the same prices and the number of lines per 100 population and population density. A search was then made of the data to identify countries or states which exhibited values of these three variables similar to those observed in New Zealand. Eleven were found.

The cost-based prices in these 11 jurisdictions are in local currencies and need to be converted into New Zealand dollars at an appropriate exchange rate. This was done at an average of the exchange rate over the past 10 years at the Purchasing Power Parity (PPP) exchange rate.[13]

In this case, the Commission adopted the median of the 11 rates (here the sixth highest or sixth lowest). In earlier exercises, it had chosen a different point in the sample; but in this case it gave reasons for choosing the median.

The second example is of the use of comparative analysis in the electricity supply and water and sewerage industries in England and Wales. The benchmarking here is done on a national basis, and is made possible because the industry is structured regionally, with each regional electricity company or water company serving a specified area.[14] This simplifies the process, amongst other things by removing the need for exchange rate conversions.

In the electricity and water industries, benchmarking has been used at the time of periodic price reviews. Essentially, the regulator has sought to identify, on the basis of comparative cost observations, and after adjustment for environmental factors, which firms are relatively efficient and which are relatively inefficient. Because the sample is small, it is not possible to eliminate divergent observations as was done in the New Zealand case above. Instead, all observations are used and attempts are made to identify and remove the effects of environmental variables.

This can be done in various ways. Figure 26.2 shows information which might be collected about the average costs of supplying water to different areas, characterized by different population densities. The minimum costs,

---

[13] A PPP exchange rate is one which makes a fixed basket of goods and services cost the same in both countries.

[14] In fact, there are ten water and sewerage companies in England and Wales, and an additional nine water-only companies.

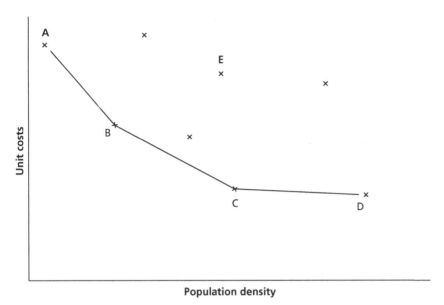

Figure 26.2. Identifying the efficiency frontier
Each × represents the population density and unit costs of an operator.

known as the efficiency frontier, are shown by the line in Figure 26.2 , which is found by connecting the lower envelope of cost observations. Other operators can then be graded on the basis of the proximity of their cost observation to the frontier. Firm E, for example, is far from the frontier, suggesting the existence of a considerable inefficiency gap, and scope for 'catch-up'. The regulator would, therefore, be justified in assigning to firm E a relatively high value of X in the RPI−X price cap formula. Operator B, by contrast, is on the frontier and might be assigned a value of X which reflected only the trend in cost reduction available to an efficient operator, ignoring 'catch-up'.

These, or similar, techniques have been employed by the UK water and energy regulators in their price control reviews for water and sewerage companies and for regional electricity companies. Inevitably, there are disputes over which relevant environmental factors should be taken into account. For statistical reasons to do with the limited number of observations available, only a relatively small number of environmental variables can be accommodated.[15] This gives firms an opportunity to promote their own favourites—those which show their performance in the best possible light. The regulator has to make its own decisions as to which approach to adopt.

---

[15] This problem can be resolved if it is possible to assemble and use a 'panel' of data for several years for each company. See S. Kumbhakar and A. Horncastle, 'Improving the Econometric Precision of Regulatory Models' (2010) 38(2) *Journal of Regulatory Economics* 144–66.

The procedures described above were used by Ofwat in setting its price controls for the period 2010–15.[16] Efficiency targets are set for both capital and operating costs. In relation to operating costs, all observations fell in the top three of bands A to E, and three-quarters of these were in bands A or B. Where firms fell short of the assumed efficiency frontier, it was assumed that they would make up 60% of the shortfall in the five-year price control period. The catch-up factors range from 0 to 2.9% a year for water and from 0 to 2.2% a year for sewerage.

The regulator found that the tendency over previous price controls for firms' efficiency levels to converge was not exhibited over the 2005–10 period, possibly because of changes in incentives which gave good performers in 2005 an enhanced incentive to improve their performance.

Yardstick Competition

Benchmarking is a tool available to the regulatory agency to assist it in setting forward-looking cost-based prices. But it can be taken further to represent a complete mechanism for setting price controls. In this form it is known as yardstick competition. This involves placing similar firms in competition with one another with respect to their cost levels, even if they are not competing in the same services market.

To explain how it works, we suppose that there are 100 identical towns served by identical water companies. Clearly, a regulator could try to establish the efficient costs of a representative company, and set prices on that basis. However, this comes up against the regulator's problem that the firms probably know more about their costs than it does—the problem of informational asymmetry. It also fails to exploit the fact that many observations are available. As an alternative, therefore, the regulator could proceed as follows:[17]

(i) Collect information on the actual cost of providing water by each of the 100 companies;
(ii) Allow each company to charge a price for water equal to the average cost of the other 99 companies.

The beauty of this arrangement is that each operator is set a price which depends not on its costs but upon the costs of the other operators. Its

---

[16] OFWAT, *Future Water and Sewerage Charges 2010–2015: Final Determinations*, 2010, pp 106–14. See also OFWAT, *Scope for Efficiency Studies*, 2009.
[17] This approach was first formalized by A. Shleifer, 'A Theory of Yardstick Competition' (1985) 16 *Rand Journal of Economics* 319–27. See also M. Armstrong, S. Cowan, and J. Vickers, *Regulating Reform: Economic Analysis and British Experience* (Cambridge, 1994), 74–7.

revenues are thus detached from its costs, in the manner of the 'high-powered' price caps discussed in Chapter 25. If the company is unusually efficient, its costs will beat (i.e. be lower than) the average of the rest, and it will make good profits. If its costs are above average, it will make a loss. Its revenues do not depend in any way upon its own costs and so it has the maximum incentive to reduce them. The process should thus drive all operators down to the most efficient costs, with prices set accordingly.

Unfortunately, a number of difficulties lie in the way of implementing this regime. The first arises because prices normally have to be set before the cost observations are made. This can be overcome by introducing a lag, so that this year's prices are based upon last year's average costs, possibly adjusted to take account of expected productivity gains.

Second, there is the risk of collusion. If the operators organize together and agree to maintain their costs at an unnecessarily high level, each will be entitled to a correspondingly higher price, and will be spared the effort of producing efficiently. If the number of firms involved is small, then this will be a serious danger, but, as in other contexts, the risk of collusion diminishes as the number of firms grows.

Third, there is the obvious problem that regulated firms typically do not provide their services in identical circumstances. The areas they serve differ in terms of topography, factors such as climate and soil, and the level and structure of demand: both the size of the population and the breakdown of demand between business and residential users of services will vary from place to place. These factors will influence unit costs in ways which should be taken into account in setting prices. It would be possible to estimate the relationship between environmental factors and costs in the manner described in the previous section, use that estimated relationship to approximate the costs of all firms in a uniform or standard environment, allow each firm to set a price equal to the average of such standardized costs, and then adjust each price back to match the specifics of each firm's own environment. But this takes us some way from the simplicity of yardstick competition.

Conclusion

Efficiency and innovation are key to a successful regulatory regime. This chapter has first discussed ways in which incentives can be designed to encourage efficiency and innovation; this basically involves moving away from cost-plus regulation. Competition of various kinds can also be deployed to encourage innovation.

We then examined how regulators can collect information which helps them set stretching but realistic efficiency targets for firms within the framework of a price cap. It is clear that benchmarking on an international basis can provide a solution. Unlike the approach of yardstick competition, it relies upon a set of judgements made by the regulator—judgements which firms are likely to contest. Nonetheless, benchmarking has been successfully applied as either a temporary or a permanent feature of price controls throughout the world. It has thus played an auxiliary role in implementing what has become a very popular form of incentive regulation.

Part VII
Conclusions

27 Conclusions

Regulation often appears to be a game in which the rules are uncertain, the method of scoring is in dispute, and the distinction between players and spectators is unclear. This is because regulators' mandates tend to be imprecise, identifying good regulation involves contention, and rights of participation are often subject to debate. Regulators, moreover, carry out a number of functions that are not always compatible. They not only exercise control—over, for example, monopoly power—but they also act to organize and enable the development of competitive markets. They seek to encourage efficiency, but often—if not always—have to take on board a variety of different objectives or values, such as fairness and resilience.[1] Regulators have constantly to balance various interests and to perform trade-offs of different values. Balances have to be made between: providers and consumers; different service providers; commercial and domestic consumers; incumbents and potential new entrants; infrastructure suppliers and operators of services; and a host of other sets of divergent interests. Such conflicts are particularly prominent regarding investments in infrastructure—this requires that choices be made on the extent of infrastructure capacity and quality, and it gives rise to questions on how to balance the inevitable costs to different parties, be they users of the services, industry providers, or taxpayers at large.

As for trading-off values, each of the benchmarks discussed in Chapter 3 may have to be weighed against the others in any given context. Should more accountability be established at a given cost in efficiency? Should greater freedom to exercise expert judgements be given in spite of the loss of accountability involved? Should more efficient regulation be sought by reducing access to the regulatory process? These and similar questions have to be faced by regulators on a daily basis.

Nor are there any easy answers. The arguments presented in this book suggest that we should be highly sceptical of regulatory solutions or designs that are couched in terms of single values—notions, for instance, that certain strategies will be efficient and therefore are justifiable and should be pursued without further debate.

---

[1] See T. Prosser, *Law and the Regulators* (Oxford, 1997), 304.

It also follows that in such an uncertain and politically contentious world, any regulator will live a precarious existence. No claim to legitimacy that a regulator makes will ever be recognized as clear-cut or beyond argument and, to render life more difficult, no set of regulatory conditions or even public expectations of regulation is liable to remain static.

The regulator's world is also, we have seen, one in which it is difficult to deal with issues in isolation—it is a domain of overlaps, interactions, and blurred boundaries. Regulation, for example, is difficult to tease apart from self-regulation; 'public' actions, decisions, policies, and rules are difficult to separate from 'private' ones; regulated spheres are not easy to distinguish from those that are unregulated; domestic systems of regulation interact with supra-national regimes; different regulatory mechanisms operate in coordination as well as in competition; and questions of enforcement cannot be completely disentangled from those concerning policies and rules. As for understanding regulatory origins and developments, we saw, in Chapter 4, that an array of different, often competing, approaches to explanation is readily uncovered in the literature.

Not only, therefore, is regulation a politically contentious activity, it is one that presents a host of technical and intellectual challenges. Does such a catalogue of difficulties, however, offer a counsel of despair? Does it imply that since any regulatory action will give rise to contention, anything goes? The answer to both questions is definitely 'no'. We have suggested that regulatory activities be judged according to the five benchmarks of Chapter 3 and we have sought to consider how various strategies tend to measure up to those different benchmarks in a variety of settings. To recognize that judgements about regulation will give rise to contention, even if it is assumed that everyone in society agrees on the five benchmarks, is not to counsel despair but to recognize that the choices made in regulation are inevitably political ones. Being clear about those benchmarks that are relevant in evaluating regulation, and discussing regulation with reference to these yardsticks, brings clarity to the regulatory debate rather than imposes any particular political vision on participants in that conversation. Not only does it help to identify certain pitfalls of regulatory analysis (such as single benchmark evaluations), but it also assists in identifying the trade-offs that have to be considered when, for example, assessing reforms.

As for the search for 'better' regulation, it has been noted in the chapters above that a number of strands of policy exist at tension and at various levels of government. Many governments desire less burdensome regulation but more evidence-based regulation; they have faith in Regulatory Impact Assessments but favour those less formal types of control that are not easily assessed quantitatively. These are not tensions that are easily resolved or legislated around. Another theme from this book suggests, indeed, that new laws in themselves can only provide part of any answer to the perceived shortcomings of regulation—even if agreement is assumed on deficiencies and political objectives. The achievement of regulatory aims does not merely depend on formal statements of ends, it turns (arguably critically) on such matters as strategic choices, tools of enforcement, and detection mechanisms. Regulatory systems should be seen in the round—as comprising not merely sets of laws and rules but also: institutional frameworks; policy and governmental settings; sets of procedures; enforcement, monitoring, and information-using strategies and approaches; clusters of ideas and assumptions about how things are to be done; configurations of regulated firms and individuals; levels of resourcing; and groups of persons with their backgrounds, preferences, cultures, disciplines, ideas, incentives, and expectations.

Viewing regulation as a whole in this way implies that changes in laws and rules, no matter how sophisticated, are unlikely to come to grips with all of the aspects of a regulatory system that are of potential concern. Reforms, for example, to increase accountability and place newly powerful enforcement powers in regulators' hands may well fail to address problems that stem from, say, the culture, personnel, accepted practices, or resourcing levels that are encountered in the regulatory system. Changes, it follows, may be required on a huge variety of fronts and may require not so much new laws as, for example, new ideas, staff, training methods, enforcement philosophies, modes of organization, informal procedures, or levels of financial support.

As for the future of regulation, what is clear is that the abiding regulatory questions are as relevant as ever in current times and are liable to remain so. Crises, such as those that have been experienced in the financial sector in recent years, have brought a new urgency to well-established regulatory challenges, rather than replaced these with fresh sets of concerns. Above all, it can perhaps be asserted that the political dimension of the regulators' work will not disappear. Not only that, it may prove increasingly to be the case that direct democratic influence will be demanded not merely with respect to the decisions, actions, and policies of regulators but also with regard to those of the 'private' firms that provide regulated or public services. It has been seen already that service-providing firms can no longer assume that they are in all respects private and, accordingly, outside the scope of such concerns. Difficult political judgements will remain and will be the proper province of democratically legitimated bodies.

The main hope for improving regulation lies not in taking such judgements away from legitimate institutions but in developing our understandings on two fronts: first, concerning the array of choices between various goals that different regulatory arrangements present us with, second, about the potential of new regulatory mechanisms to provide us with more attractive ranges of choice. It is on these fronts that we hope to make a contribution with this book.

■ SELECT BIBLIOGRAPHY

Abbott, K.W. and Snidal, D. 'The Governance Triangle: Regulatory Standards Institutions and the Shadow of the State', in Mattli, W. and Woods, N. (eds), *Politics of Global Regulation* (Princeton, NJ, 2009).

——————. 'Hard and Soft Law in International Governance' (2000) 54(3) *International Organization* 421.

——, Keohane, R., Moravcsik, A., Slaughter, A.M., and Snidal, D. 'The Concept of Legalization' (2000) 54(3) *International Organization* 401.

——————. 'Reforming Environmental Law' (1985) 37 *Stanford Law Review* 1333–65.

Ackerman, B. and Stewart, R. 'Reforming Environmental Law: The Democratic Case for Market Incentives' (1987) 13 *Columbia Journal of Environmental Law* 171.

Aghion, P. et al., 'Competition and Innovation: An Inverted-U Relationship' (2005) 120 *Quarterly Journal of Economics*.

Akman, P. and Kassim, H. 'Myths and Myth-Making in the European Union: The Institutionalization and Interpretation of EU Competition Policy' (2010) 48(1) *Journal of Common Market Studies* 111–32.

Armstrong, K. and Bulmer, S. *Governance of the Single Market* (Manchester, 1998).

Armstrong, M., Cowan, S., and Vickers, J. *Regulatory Reform: Economic Analysis and British Experience* (Cambridge, 1994).

Associated Provincial Picture Houses v. *Wednesbury Corporation* [1948] 1 KB 223; *Council of Civil Service Unions* v. *Minister for the Civil Service* [1985] AC 374.

Atlas, M. 'Enforcement Principles and Environmental Agencies' (2007) 41(4) *Law and Society Review* 939–80.

Aurid, E. and Picard, P. 'Infrastructure and Public Utilities Privatization in Developing Countries' (2009) 23(1) *World Bank Economic Review* 77.

Ayres, I. and Braithwaite, J. *Responsive Regulation* (Oxford, 1992).

Baer, P. et al., 'Equity and Greenhouse Gas Responsibility' (2000) 289 *Science* 2287.

Baggott, R. 'Regulatory Reform in Britain: The Changing Face of Self-Regulation (1989) 67 *Public Administration* 435.

Baldwin, G.R. and Veljanovski, C.G. 'Regulation by Cost-Benefit Analysis' (1984) 62 *Public Administration* 51.

Baldwin, R. *Regulating the Airlines* (Oxford, 1985).

Baldwin, R. *Regulation in the Balance* (London, 1996).

——. *Rules and Government* (Oxford, 1995).

——. 'Why Rules Don't Work' (1990) 53 *Modern Law Review* 321.

——. 'Better Regulation: The Search and the Struggle', in Baldwin, R., Cave, M., and Lodge, M. (eds), *The Oxford Handbook of Regulation* (Oxford, 2010).

Baldwin, R. and Black, J. *Defra: A Review of Enforcement Measures and an Assessment of their Effectiveness in Terms of Risk and Outcome* (London, 2005).

Baldwin, R. and Black, J. 'Really Responsive Regulation' (2008) 71 *MLR* 59–94.

—— ——. 'Understanding Regulatory Co-habitation' (forthcoming).

—— and McCrudden, C. *Regulation and Public Law* (London, 1987).

——, Scott, C., and Hood C. (eds), *A Reader on Regulation* (Oxford, 1998).

Bardach, E. *Getting Agencies to Work Together* (Washington, DC, 1998).

—— and Kagan, R. *Going by the Book: The Problem of Regulatory Unreasonableness* (Philadelphia, 1982).

Barth, M., Landsman, W., and Lang, M. 'International Accounting Standards and Accounting Quality' (2008) 46(3) *Journal of Accounting Research* 467.

Baumol, W.J. and Dates, W. 'On Taxation and the Control of Externalities' (1972) 62 *American Economic Review* 307.

Beard, T., Kaserman, R., and Mayo, J. 'Regulation, Vertical Integration and Sabotage' (2001) 49(3) *Journal of Industrial Economics* 319.

Bebchuk, L., Cohen, A., and Ferrell, A. 'Does the Evidence Favor State Competition in Corporate Law?' (2002) 90 *California Law Review* 1775–821.

——. 'The Politics of Risk Society', in J. Franklin (ed.), *The Politics of Risk Society* (Cambridge, 1998).

——. 'Living in the World Risk Society' (2006) 35(3) *Economy and Society* 329–45.

Beck, U. *The Risk Society* (London, 1992).

Becker, G. 'A Theory of Competition among Pressure Groups for Political Influence' (1983) 98 *Quarterly Journal of Economics* 371.

Begg, D., Fischer, G., and Dornbusch, R. *Economics* (9th edn, London, 2008).

Berkman Center, Harvard University, *Next Generation Connectivity: A Review of Broadband Internet Transitions and Policy from Around the World* (Harvard, February 2010).

Bernstein, M.H. *Regulating Business by Independent Commission* (New York, 1955).

Black, D. *The Behavior of Law* (New York, 1976).

——. 'Compensation and the Social Structure of Misfortune' (1987) 21(4) *Law and Society Review* 563–84.

Black, J. 'Constitutionalising Self-Regulation' (1996) 59(1) *MLR* 24–55.

——. *Rules and Regulators* (Oxford, 1997).

——. 'Talking about Regulation' (1998) *Public Law* 77.

——. 'Decentring Regulation: The Role of Regulation and Self-Regulation in a "Post-Regulatory World"' (2001) *Current Legal Problems* 103–46.

——. 'Proceduralising Regulation Part II' (2001) 54 *Current Legal Problems* 103.

——. 'Critical Reflections on Regulation' *CARR Discussion Paper, Number 4* (London, 2002).

——. 'Enrolling Actors in Regulatory Processes' (2003) *Public Law* 62.

——. 'Frameworks for Understanding Regulatory Innovation', in Black, J., Lodge, M., and Thatcher, M. (eds), *Regulatory Innovation* (Cheltenham, 2005).

——. 'The Emergence of Risk-Based Regulation and the New Public Risk Management in the United Kingdom' (2005) *Public Law* 512.

——. 'Constructing and Contesting Legitimacy and Accountability in Polycentric Regulatory Regimes' (2008) 2(2) *Regulation and Governance* 137–64.

——. 'Forms and Paradoxes of Principles-based Regulation' (2008) 3(4) *Capital Markets Law Journal* 425–58.

——. *Risk-Based Regulation: Choices, Practices and Lessons Being Learned* (Paris, 2008).

—— and Baldwin, R. 'Really Responsive Risk-based Regulation' (2010) 32 *Law and Policy* 181–213.

—— ——. 'Risk-based Regulation: How Low Can you Go? ' (forthcoming).

——, Hopper, M., and Band, C. 'Making a Success of Principles-Based Regulation' (2007) *Law and Financial Markets Review* 191.

Blackman, A. 'Can Voluntary Environmental Regulation Work in Developing Countries? (2006) 36 *Policy Studies Journal* 119.

Bloor, M., Datta, R. Gilinsky, Y., and Horlick-Jones, T. 'Unicorn Among the Cedars: On the Possibility of Effective "Smart Regulation" of the Globalised Shipping Industry' (2006) 15(4) *Social and Legal Studies* 534–51.

Blundell, R., Griffith, R., and van Reenen, J. 'Market Share, Market Value and Innovation in a Panel of British Manufacturing Firms' (1999) 66 *Review of Economic Studies* 529.

Boemare, C. and Quirion, P. 'Implementing Greenhouse Gas Trading in Europe' (2002) 43 *Ecological Economics* 213–30.

Boin, A. 'The New World of Crises and Crisis Management' (2009) 26(4) *Review of Policy Research* 367–77.

——. 'Preparing for Future Crises' in B.M. Hutter (ed.), *Anticipating Risks and Organising Risk Regulation* (Cambridge, 2010).

—— and t'Hart, P. 'Institutional Crisis and Reforms in Policy Sectors' in H. Wagenaar (ed.), *Government Institutions* (Boston, 2000).

——, McConnell, A., and t'Hart P. (eds), *Governing after Crisis* (Cambridge, 2008).

Börzel, T. 'Why There is No "Southern" Problem' (2000) 7(1) *Journal of European Public Policy* 141–62.

Botzem, S. and Quack, S. *Contested Rules and Shifting Boundaries: International Standard Setting in Accounting, Discussion Paper SPIII 2005-201* (Berlin, 2005).

Bovens, M. 'Analysing and Assessing Accountability: A Conceptual Framework' (2007) 13(4) *European Law Journal* 447–68.

——. 'Public Accountability', in Ferlie, E., Lynn, L., and Pollitt, C. (eds.), *Oxford Handbook of Public Management* (Oxford, 2007).

Braithwaite, J. 'The Limits of Economism in Controlling Harmful Corporate Conduct' (1982) 16 *Law and Society Review* 481.

——. *Making Tax Law More Certain: A Theory*, ANU/Aus Tax Office Working Paper No. 44 (2002): http://ctsi.anu.ed.au/publications/wp/44.pdf (visited 3 August 2011).

——. *Responsive Regulation and Restorative Justice* (Oxford, 2002).

——. 'Meta Risk Management and Responsive Regulation for Tax System Integrity' (2003) 25(1) *Law and Policy* 1–16.

——. *Regulatory Capitalism* (Cheltenham, 2008).

—— and Drahos, P. *Global Business Regulation* (Cambridge, 2000).

Bratton, W. and McCahery, J.A. 'The New Economics of Jurisdictional Competition' (1997) 86 *Georgetown Law Journal* 201–78.

BRE, *Impact Assessment Guidance* (2009).

Brennan, G. 'Civil Disaster Management: An Economist's View' (1991) 64 *Canberra Bulletin of Public Administration* 30–3.

Brennan, G. and Buchanan, J. *The Power to Tax* (Cambridge, 1980).

Breyer, S. *Regulation and Its Reform* (Cambridge, MA, 1982).

——. *Breaking the Vicious Circle: Toward Effective Risk Regulation* (Cambridge, MA, 1993).

—— and Stewart, R. *Administrative Law and Regulatory Policy* (Boston, 1992).

Briault, C. *The Rationale for a Single National Financial Services Regulator*, FSA Occasional Paper No. 2 (London, 1999).

Brown, G.T. and Sibley, D.S. *The Theory of Public Utility Pricing* (Cambridge, 1986).

Brown, K. 'Cut and Run? Evolving Institutions for Global Forest Governance' (2001) 13 *Journal of International Development* 893.

Brunsson, N. and Jacobsson, B. *A World of Standards* (Oxford, 2000).

Bryner, G. *Bureaucratic Discretion* (New York, 1987).

Budzinski, O. and Christiansen, A. 'Competence Allocation in the EU Competition Policy System as an Interest-Driven Process' (2005) 25(3) *Journal of Public Policy* 313–37.

Busuioc, M. 'Accountability, Control and Independence: The Case of European Agencies' (2009) 15(5) *European Law Journal* 599–615.

CAA, *Economic Regulation of Heathrow and Gatwick Airports, 2008–2013, CAA Decision* (London, 2008).

Cabral, L., 'Procuring Innovation', in Dimitri, N., Piga, G., and Spagnolo, G. (eds), *Handbook of Procurement* (Cambridge, 2006).

Cambini, C., and Jiang, Y. 'Broadband Investment and Regulation: A Literature Review' (2009) 33(11) *Telecommunications Policy* 559.

Carbon Trust, *Allocation and Competitiveness in the EU ETS* (London, June 2006).

Castro, J.E. 'Neoliberal Water and Sanitation Policies as a Failed Development Strategy' (2008) 8(1) *Progress in Development Studies* 63–83.

——. 'Encouraging Infrastructure Competition via the Ladder of Investment' (2006) *Telecommunications Policy* 223.

——. 'Six Degrees of Separation' (2006) 64 *Communications and Strategies* 1.

——. *Independent Review of Competition and Innovation in Water Markets* (2009).

—— and Wright, J. *Options for Increasing Competition in the Great Britain Rail Market: On Rail Competition in the Passenger Rail Market and Contestability in Rail Infrastructure Investment* (London, 2010).

Chalmers, D. 'Risk, Anxiety and the European Mediation of the Politics of Life' (2005) 30(5) *European Law Review* 649–74.

—— and Lodge, M. 'The Open Method of Co-ordination and the European Welfare State' *ESRC Centre for Analysis of Risk and Regulation, Discussion Paper 11* (London, 2003).

——, Davies G. and Montiø, G. *European Union Law* (2nd edn, Cambridge, 2010).

Channells, L. 'The Windfall Tax' (1997) 18 *Fiscal Studies* 281.

Chevron v. *Natural Resource Defense Council* 464, US 837, 3.

Christensen, J.G. and Nielen, V.L. 'Administrative Capacity, Structural Choice and the Creation of EU Agencies' (2010) 17(2) *Journal of European Public Policy* 176–204.

Christian Aid, *Global Warming Policy Position Paper* (Nov. 2000).

Cini, M. and McGowan, L. *Competition Policy in the European Union* (Basingstoke, 2009).

Clarkson, C. 'Kicking Corporate Bodies and Damning their Souls' (1996) 59 *MLR* 557.

Clear Communication V. *New Zealand Telecommunications Corp.* [1994] 6 TCLK 138 (1995) INZLR 385 (PC).

Clifton, S.-J. *A Dangerous Obsession* (London, 2009).

Coen, D. and Thatcher, M. 'The New Governance of Markets and Non-Majoritarian Regulators' (2005) 18(3) *Governance* 329–46.

Coffee, J.C. 'No Soul to Damn, No Body to Kick' (1981) 79 *Michigan Law Review* 386.

Cohen, T. 'Domestic Policy and South Africa's Commitments under the WTO's Basic Telecommunications Agreement: Explaining the Apparent Inertia' (2001) 4(4) *Journal of International Economic Law* 613–43.

Coglianese, C. and Nash, J. (eds), *Regulating From the Inside* (Washington, DC, 2001).

Commerce Commission. *Standard Terms Determination for the Designated Service Telecom's Unbundled Copper Local Loop Network*, Decision 609 (New Zealand, 7 December 2007).

——. *Commerce Act Electricity Distribution Services Input Methodologies Determination* (London, December 2010).

Competition Commission. *Water Merger References* (London, 2004).

——. *BAA Ltd (Heathrow and Gatwick Quinquennial Review, Final Report* (London, October 2007).

Comptroller and Auditor-General. *Office of Passenger Rail Franchising (OPRAF): The Award of the First Three Passenger Rail Franchises* (HC 701, 1995/6) (London, 1996).

Consumer Focus. *2008/9 Report on the Guaranteed Standards of Performance for Electricity Distribution* (London, 2010).

Cook, P., Kirkpatrick, C., Minogue, M., and Parker, D. (eds), *Leading Issues in Competition, Regulation and Development* (Cheltenham, 2004).

Cooter, R. and Ulen, T. *Law and Economics* (Glenview, IL, 1988).

Council of Civil Service Unions v. *Minister for the civil service* [1985] AC 374.

Courville, S. 'Social Accountability Audits: Challenging or Defending Democratic Governance?' (2003) 25(3) *Law and Policy* 269–97.

Craig, P. *Administrative Law* (3rd edn, London, 1994).

Cranor, C.F. *Regulating Toxic Substances* (New York, 1993).

Crew, M.A. and Parker, D. 'Development in the Theory and Practice of Regulatory Economics', in Crew, M.A. and Parker, D. (eds), *International Handbook of Economic Regulation* (Cheltenham, 2006).

Cubbin, J. and Stern, J. 'The Impact of Regulatory Governance and Privatization on Electricity Industry Generation Capacity in Developing Countries' (2006) 20(1) *The World Bank Economic Review* 115.

Cuéllar, M.-F. 'Rethinking Regulatory Democracy' (2005) 57 *Administrative Law Review* 411–99.

Daintith, T.C. 'The Techniques of Government' in J. Jowell and D. Oliver (eds), *The Changing Constitution* (3rd edn, Oxford, 1994).

Defra. *Review of Marine Fisheries* (London, 2004).

——. *Securing the Benefits* (London, 2005).

Dehousse, R. 'Regulation by Networks in the European Community' (1997) 4 *Journal of European Public Policy* 246–61.

Demortain, D. 'Standardising through Concepts: Scientific Experts and the International Development of the HACCP Food Safety Standard', *CARR Discussion Paper 45* (London, 2007).

Demsetz, H. 'Why Regulate Utilities?' (1968) 11 *Journal of Law and Economics* 55.

Department for Business Innovation and Skills. *Delivering for the Future: A Universal Mail Service and Community Post Offices in the Digital Age* (London, October 2010).

Department of Energy and Climate Change, Cmnd 7983 *Electricity Market Reform Consultation Document* (London, 2010).

Department for Transport. *Reforming the Framework for the Economic Regulation of Airports* (London, December 2009).

DeVisscher, C., Maiscocq, O., and Varone, F. 'The Lamfalussy Reform in EU Securities Markets' (2008) 28(1) *Journal of Public Policy* 19–47.

'Diamonds: Does the Kimberley Process Work?', *BBC News*, 28 June 2010, http://www.bbc.co.uk/news/10307046 (last accessed 24 December 2010).

Diver, C.S. 'The Optimal Precision of Administrative Rules' (1983) 93 *Yale Law Journal* 65.

Djelic, M.L. and Sahlin-Andersson, K. (eds). *Transnational Governance* (Cambridge, 2006).

Domberger, S. 'Regulation Through Franchise Contracts', in J. Kay, C. Mayer, and D. Thompson (eds), *Privatisation and Regulation: The UK Experience* (Oxford, 1986).

Doucet, J. and Littlechild, S. 'Negotiated Settlements: The Development of Legal and Economic Thinking' (2006) 14 *Utilities Policy* 266.

Douglas, M. *Risk and Blame* (London, 1992).

—— and Wildavsky A. *Risk and Culture* (Berkeley, 1982).

Drahos, P. and Braithwaite, J. 'The Globalization of Regulation' (2001) 9(1) *Journal of Political Philosophy* 103–28.

Drezner, D. *All Politics is Global: Explaining International Regulatory Regimes* (Princeton, NJ, 2007).

Driesen, D. 'Is Emissions Trading an Economic Incentive Programme? Replacing the Command and Control/Economic Incentives Dichotomy' (1998) 55 *Washington and Lee Law Review* 289.

Driesen, D.M. 'Does Emissions Trading Encourage Innovation?' (2003) 33 *Environmental Law Reporter* 10094.

Dunleavy, P. 'Policy Disasters: Explaining the UK's Record' (1995) 10 *Public Policy and Administration* 52–70.

Eberlein, B. and Grande, E. 'Beyond Delegation: Transnational Regimes and the EU Regulatory State' (2005) 12 *Journal of European Public Policy* 89–112.

Eden, L. and Kudrle, R.T. 'Tax Havens: Renegade States in the International Tax Regime?' (2005) 27(1) *Law and Policy* 100–27.

Egan, M. *Constructing a European Market* (Oxford, 2001).

Ellerman, D., Schmalensee, R., Bailey, E., Joskow, P., and Montero, J.-P. *Markets for Clean Air: The US Acid Rain Program* (Cambridge, 2000).

Erbetta, F. and Cave, M. 'Regulation and Efficiency Incentives: Evidence from the England and Wales Water and Sewerage Industry' (2007) 6(4) *Review of Network Economics* 425.

Esfhani, H. and Ramirez, M.T. 'Institutions, Infrastructure and Economic Growth' (2003) 70(2) *Journal of Development Economics* 443.

Esman, M.J. 'Public Administration, Ethnic Conflict, and Economic Development' (1997) 57(6) *Public Administration Review* 527.

——. 'Public Administration and Conflict Management in Plural Societies: The Case for Representative Bureaucracy' (1999) 19(4) *Public Administration and Development* 353–66.

Esquirol, J.L. 'The Failed Law of Latin America' (2008) 56(1) *American Journal of Comparative Law* 75.

Estache, A. and Wren-Lewis, L. 'Towards a Theory of Regulation for Developing Countries' (2009) 47(3) *Journal of Economic Literature* 729–70.

——————. 'On the Theory and Evidence on Regulation of Network Industries in Developing Countries', in Baldwin, R., Cave, M., and Lodge, M. (eds), *Oxford Handbook of Regulation* (Oxford, 2010).

Estache, A., Goicoechea, A., and Trujillo, L. 'Utilities Reforms and Corruption in Developing Countries' (2009) 17(2) *Utilities Policy* 191–202.

Etro, F. *Competition, Innovation and Anti-trust: A Theory of Market Leaders and Its Policy Implications* (Berlin, 2007).

Eurofound. *Catalogue of Economic Incentive Systems for the Improvement of the Working Environment* (Dublin, 1994).

European Commission. *DG Competition Report on Energy Sector Inquiry* (Brussels, 2007).

Evans, P. 'The Eclipse of the State' (1997) 50(1) *World Politics* 62–87.

Exp. Centro v. Secretary of State for Transport [2007] EWHC 2729.

Eyre, S. and Lodge, M. 'National Tunes and a European Melody? Competition Law Reform in the UK and Germany' (2000) 7(1) *Journal of European Public Policy* 63–79.

Fairman, R. and Yapp, C. 'Enforced Self-Regulation, Prescription and Conceptions of Compliance within Small Businesses' (2005) 27 *Law and Policy* 491–519.

Falkner, G., Treib, O., Hartlepp, M., and Leiber, S. *Complying with Europe* (Cambridge, 2005).

——, Hartlepp, M., and Treib, O. 'Worlds of Compliance' (2007) 46 *European Journal of Political Research* 395–416.

Faure, M. and Peeters, M. (eds). *Climate Change and European Emissions Trading* (Cheltenham, 2008).

Financial Times. 'Dublin Entices Funds with Softer Regulation', 6 Sept. 2010.

Finnemore, M. *The Purpose of Intervention* (Ithaca, 2003).

—— and Sikkink, K. 'International Norm Dynamics and Political Change' (1998) 52 *International Organization* 887.

Fisse, B. and Braithwaite, J. 'The Allocation of Responsibility for Corporate Crime' (1988) 11 *Sydney Law Review* 468.

Fligstein, N. *Euro-Clash* (Oxford, 2008).

—— and Mara-Drita, I. 'How to Make a Market: Reflections on the Attempt to Create a Single Market in the European Union' (1996) 102(1) *American Journal of Sociology* 1–33.

—— and Sweet Stone, A. 'Constructing Markets and Politics' (2002) 107 *American Journal of Sociology* 1206–43.

Florio, M. *The Great Divestiture* (Cambridge, 2004).

Foster, C. *Privatisation, Public Ownership and the Regulation of Natural Monopoly* (Oxford, 1992).

Francis, J.G. *The Politics of Regulation: A Comparative Perspective* (Oxford, 1993).

Franklin, J. (ed.), *The Politics of Risk Society* (Cambridge, 1998).

Freeman, J. and Kolstad, C. (eds) *Moving to Markets in Environmental Regulation* (Oxford, 2006).

Fung, A., Graham, M., and Weil, D. *Full Disclosure* (Cambridge, 2007).

Gadinis, S. 'The Politics of Competition in International Financial Regulation' (2008) 49(2) *Harvard International Law Journal* 447–508.

Gehring, T. and Krapohl, S. 'Supranational Regulatory Agencies between Independence and Control' (2007) 14 *Journal of European Public Policy* 208–26.

Gerber, D. *Law and Competition in Twentieth-Century Europe* (Oxford, 1998).

——. 'Modernising European Competition Law' (2001) 22(4) *European Competition Law Review* 122–30.

—— and Cassinis, P. 'The "Modernisation" of European Community Competition Law: Achieving Consistency in Enforcement—Part 1' (2006) 27(1) *European Competition Law Review* 10–18.

Germany v. *Parliament and Council* [2000] ECR I-8419.

Gershon, P. *Releasing Resources to the Front Line: An Independent Review of Public Sector Efficiency* (London, 2004).

Giddens, A. *Beyond Left and Right* (Cambridge, 1994).

Gómez Ibáñez, J. *Regulating Infrastructure: Monopoly, Contracts and Discretion* (Harvard, 2003).

Gourevitch, P. 'The Role of Politics in Economic Development' (2008) 11 *Annual Review of Political Science* 137.

Grabosky, P. 'Counterproductive Regulation' (1995) 23 *International Journal of the Sociology of Law* 347–69.

Graham, C. 'Self-Regulation', in G. Richardson and H. Genn (eds), *Administrative Law and Government Action* (Oxford, 1994).

Grajek, M. And Röller, L.-H. *The Effect of Regulation on Investment in Network Industries: Evidence from the Telecommunications Industry*, ESMT Working Paper (Berlin, 2009).

Grindle, M. (ed.), *Getting Good Government: Capacity Building in the Public Sector of Developing Countries* (Cambridge, MA, 1997).

——. 'The Good Government Imperative: Human Resources, Organisations and Institutions' in M. Grindle (ed.), *Getting Good Government: Capacity Building in the Public Sector of Developing Countries* (Cambridge, MA, 1997).

Guasch, L.P., Laffont, J.J, and Straub, S. (2006) 'Renegotiations of Concession Contracts: A Theoretical Approach' (2006) 29 *Review of Industrial Organization* 55.

Gunningham, N. 'Corporate Environmental Responsibility, Law and the Limits of Voluntarism', in McBarnett, D., Voicelescu, A., and Campbell, T. (eds), *The New Corporate Accountability: Corporate Social Responsibility and the Law* (Cambridge, 2007).

—— and Grabosky, P. *Smart Regulation* (Oxford, 1998).

—— and Johnstone, R. *Regulating Workplace Safety* (Oxford, 1999).

Gupta, J. *The Climate Change Convention and Developing Countries: From Conflict to Consensus?* (Dordrecht, 1997).

Gutierrez, L.'Regulatory Governance in the Latin American Telecommunications Sector' (2003) 11 *Utilities Policy* 225.

——. 'The Effect of Endogenous Regulation on Telecommunications Expansion and Efficiency in Latin America' (2003) 23(3) *Journal of Regulatory Economics* 257.

HM Treasury, *The Setting of Safety Standards* (London, 1996).

Haggard, S., MacIntyre, A., and Tiede, L. 'The Rule of Law and Economic Development' (2008) 11 *Annual Review of Political Science* 205.

Haghighi, S. 'Energy Security and the Division of Competences between the European Community and its Member States' (2008) 14(4) *European Law Journal* 461–82.

Hampton, P. *Reducing Administrative Burdens* (London, 2005). [Hampton Report]

Hancher, L. and Moran, M. 'Organizing Regulatory Space', in Hancher, L. and Moran, M. (eds), *Capitalism, Culture and Economic Regulation* (Oxford, 1989).

Hansjurgens, B. (ed.), *Emissions Trading for Climate Policy* (New York, 2005).

Harrington, W., Morgenstern, R.D., and Sterner, T. *Choosing Environmental Policy* (Washington, DC, 2004).

Harris, R.A. and Milkis, S.M. *The Politics of Regulatory Change* (2nd edn, New York, 1996).

Hauge, J. and Sappington, D. 'Pricing in Network Industries', in Baldwin, R., Cave, M., and Lodge, M. (eds), *Oxford Handbook of Regulation* (Oxford, 2010).

Hawkins, K. *Environment and Enforcement* (Oxford, 1984).

—— and Thomas, J. TM. (eds), *Enforcing Regulation* (Boston, 1984).

Hedmo, T., Sahlin-Andersson, K., and Wedlin, L. 'The Emergence of a European Regulatory Field of Management Education', in Djelic, M.L. and Sahlin-Andersson, K. (eds), *Transnational Governance* (Cambridge, 2006).

Held, D., McGrew, A., Goldblatt., D., and Perraton, J. *Global Transformations* (Cambridge, 2000).

Helm, D. 'Infrastructure Investment, the Cost of Capital and Regulation: An Assessment' (2009) 25(3) *Oxford Review of Economic Policy* 307.

Héritier, A. 'The Accommodation of Diversity in European Policy-Making and Its Outcomes' (1996) 3(2) *Journal of European Public Policy* 149–76.

——. *Policy-Making and Diversity* (Cambridge, 1999).

——. 'Mutual Recognition: Comparing Policy Areas' (2007) 14(5) *Journal of European Public Policy* 800–13.

Hirst, P. and Thompson, G. *Globalization in Question* (Cambridge, 2000).

H. L Bolton (Engineering) Co. Ltd v. *T. J. Graham and Sons Ltd* [1957]/ QB159.

——. *Reforming Financial Markets* (London, 2009).

HM Treasury. *The Setting of Safety Standards* (London, 1996).

Hodson, D. and Maher, I. 'The Open Method as a New Mode of Governance: The Case of Soft Economic Policy Co-ordination' (2001) 39(4) *Journal of Common Market Studies* 719–46.

Holzinger, K., Knill, C., and Sommerer, T. 'Environmental Policy Convergence: The Impact of International Harmonization, Transnational Communication, and Regulatory Competition' (2008) 62 *International Organization* 553.

Hood, C. *The Art of the State* (Oxford, 1998).

——. *Explaining Economic Policy Reversals* (Buckingham, 1994).

——. 'The Risk Game and the Blame Game' (2002) 37(1) *Government and Opposition* 15–37.

——, Scott, C., James, O., Jones, G., and Travers, G. *Regulation Inside Government* (Oxford, 1999).

——, Rothstein, H., and Baldwin, R. *Government of Risk* (Oxford, 2001).

Hooghe, L., and Marks, G. 'Unraveling the Central State, But How?' (2003) 97(2) *American Political Science Review* 243.

Hooper, R. et al. *Modernise or Decline: Policies to Maintain the Universal Postal Service in the United Kingdom*, Cmnd 7259 (December 2008).

Hooper, R. *Saving the Royal Mail's Universal Postal Service in the Digital Age* (London, September 2010).

Horowitz, D.L. 'The Courts as Guardians of the Public Interest' (1997) 37(2) *Public Administration Review* 148–54.

Howarth, D. and Sadeh, T. 'The Ever Incomplete Single Market: Differentiation and the Evolving Frontier of Integration' (2010) 17(7) *Journal of European Public Policy* 922–35. http://www.ofgem.gov.uk/Networks/offtrans/Pages/Offshoretransmission.aspx.

Hummer, W. 'From "Interinstitutional Agreements" to "Interinstitutional Agencies/Offices"' (2007) 13 *European Law Journal* 47–74.

Hutchinson 3G UK Ltd v. *Ofcom* [2009] EWCA Civ 683.

Hutter, B.M. *Compliance: Regulation and Environment* (Oxford, 1997).

In Re Caremark International Inc Derivative Litigation 1996 WL 549894.

Jabko, N. *Playing the Market* (Ithaka, 2006).

Jachtenfuchs, M. 'The Governance Approach to European Integration' (2001) 39(2) *Journal of Common Market Studies* 221–40.

Jalilian, H., Kirkpatrick, C., and Parker, D. 'The Impact of Regulation on Economic Growth in Developing Countries' (2007) 35(1) *World Development* 87–103.

Jamasb, T. 'Between the State and Market: Electricity Sector Reform in Developing Countries' (2006) 14 *Utilities Policy* 14.

Jojarth, C. *Crime, War, and Global Trafficking* (Cambridge, 2009).

Johnstone, R. 'Putting the Regulated Back into Regulation' (1999) 26 *Journal of Law and Society* 378–90.

Joskow, P. 'Lessons Learned from Electricity Market Liberalization' (2008) *Energy Journal* 9.

Josselin, D. 'Domestic Policy Networks and European Negotiations' (1996) 3(3) *Journal of European Public Policy* 297–317.

Kaeding, M.'In Search of Better Quality of EU Regulations for Prompt Transposition' (2008) 14 (5) *European Law Journal* 583–603.

Kagan, R.A. and Axelrad, L. (eds), *Regulatory Encounters* (Berkeley, 2000).

Keeler, T. 'Theories of Regulation and the Deregulation Movement' (1984) 44 *Public Choice* 103–45.

Kelemen, R. 'The Politics of "Eurocratic" Structure and the New European Agencies' (2002) 22 *West European Politics* 93–118.

Kennedy, D. *Competition in the British Rail Industry* (London, 1996).

Keohane, N. 'Cost Savings from Allowance Trading in the 1990 Clean Air Act' in J. Freeman and C. Kolstad (eds), *Moving to Markets in Environmental Regulation* (Oxford, 2006).

Kerber, W. and Van den Bergh, R. 'Mutual Recognition Revisited: Misunderstandings, Inconsistencies, and a Suggested Reinterpretation' (2008) 61 *Kyklos* 447–65.

Kerwer, D. 'Rules that Many Use: Standards and Global Regulation' (2005) 18(4) *Governance* 611–32.

Kickert, W., Klijn, E.-H., and Koppenjan J. (eds), *Managing Complex Networks* (London, 1997).

King, A. and Lenox, M. 'Industry Self-Regulation without Sanctions' (2000) 43(4) *Academy of Management Journal* 698.

Kirkpatrick, C. and Parker, D. (eds), *Regulatory Impact Assessment: Towards Better Regulation* (Cheltenham, 2007).

Koch Jr C.H., 'Judicial Review of Administrative Policymaking' (2002) 44 *William and Mary Law Review* 375–404.

Koenig-Archibugi, M. 'Global Regulation', in Baldwin, R., Cave, M., and Lodge, M. (eds), *Oxford Handbook of Regulation* (Oxford, 2010).

Konisky, D.M. 'Regulatory Competition and Environmental Enforcement: Is There a Race to the Bottom?' (2007) 51(4) *American Journal of Political Science* 853–72.

Kreher, A. 'Agencies in the European Commuity: A Step Towards Administrative Integration in Europe' (1997) 4 *Journal of European Public Policy* 225–45.

Krimsky, S. and Golding, D. (eds) *Social Theories of Risk* (Westport, 1992).

Krisch, N. 'The Pluralism of Global Administrative Law' (2006) 17(1) *European Journal of International Law* 247–78.

Kumbhakar, S. and Horncastle, A. 'Improving the Econometric Precision of Regulatory Models' (2010) 38(2) *Journal of Regulatory Economics* 144.

Laffont, J.J. 'Enforcement, Regulation and Development' (2003) 12(2) *Journal of African Economics* ii193–ii211.

——. *Regulation and Development* (Cambridge, 2005).

Lafontaine, F. and Slade, M. 'Vertical Integration and Firm Boundaries' (2007) 45(3) *Journal of Economic Literature* 629.

Laker Airways v. Secretary of State for Trade and Industry [1977] QB 643.

Landis, J.M. *The Administrative Process* (New Haven, 1938).

Laughlin, R. 'Environmental Disturbance and Organizational Transitions and Transformations: Some Alternative Models' (1991) 12(2) *Organizational Studies* 209–32.

Law v. National Greyhound Racing Group Club [1983] 3 All E R 300.

Lazer, D. 'Regulatory Interdependence and International Governance' (2001) 8(3) *Journal of European Public Policy* 474.

Leigh, L.H. *The Criminal Liability of Corporations in English Law* (London, 1969).

Levi-Faur, D. 'Varieties of Regulatory Capitalism' (2006) 19(3) *Governance* 497.

Levy, B. 'Comparative Regulation', in Newman, P. (ed.), *A New Palgrave Dictionary of Economics and the Law* (Basingstoke, 1998).

——. and Spiller, P. 'The Institutional Foundations of Regulatory Commitment: A Comparative Study of Telecommunications Regulation' (1994) 10(2) *Journal of Law, Economics and Organisation* 201–46.

——— —— (eds), *Regulations, Institutions and Commitment: Comparative Studies in Telecommunications* (Cambridge, 1996).

Littlechild, S., and Skerk, C.J., 'Transmission Expansion in Argentina, 1–6' (1994) 30 *Energy Economics* 1367.

Lockwood, M. *A Rough Guide to Carbon Trading* (London, 2007).

Lodge, M. 'Isomorphism of National Policies? The "Europeanisation" of German Competition and Public Procurement Law' (2000) *West European Politics* 89–107.

——. *On Different Tracks: Designing Railway Regulation in Britain and Germany* (Westport, 2002).

——. 'The Wrong Type of Regulation? Regulatory Failure and the Railways in Britain and Germany' (2002) 22 *Journal of Public Policy* 271–97.

——. 'Accountability and Transparency in Regulation: Critiques, Doctrines and Instruments', in Jacint, J. and Levi-Faur, D. (eds), *The Politics of Regulation* (Cheltenham, 2004).

Lodge, M. 'The Importance of Being Modern: International Benchmarking and National Regulatory Innovation' (2005) 12(4) *Journal of European Public Policy* 649.

——. 'Comparing New Modes of Governance in Action' (2007) 45(2) *Journal of Common Market Studies* 343–65.

——. 'Regulation, the Regulatory State and European Politics' (2008) 31(1/2) *West European Politics* 280–301.

—— ——. 'Embedding Regulatory Autonomy in Caribbean Telecommunications' (2002) 73(4) *Annals of Public and Cooperative Economics* 667–93.

—— ——. 'Regulatory Reform in Small Developing States' (2002) 7(3) *New Political Economy* 415.

—— ——. 'Withering in the Heat? In Search of the Regulatory State in the Commonwealth Caribbean' (2006) 19(3) *Governance* 465.

——. and Stirton, L. 'Accountability in the Regulatory State' in R. Baldwin, M. Cave, and M. Lodge (eds), *Handbook of Regulation* (Oxford, 2010).

——. and Wegrich, K. 'Governing Multi-level Governance: Comparing Domain Dynamics in German Land–Local Relationships and Prisons' (2005) 83(2) *Public Administration* 417–42.

—— ——. 'High Quality Regulation: Its Popularity, Its Tools and Its Future' (2009) 29(3) *Public Money and Management* 145–52.

——, Wegrich, K., and McElroy, G. 'Dodgy Kebabs Everywhere? Variety of Worldviews and Regulatory Change' (2010) 88 *Public Administration* 247–66.

Lohmann, L. 'Carry on Polluting' *New Scientist*, 2 Dec. 2006.

Loughlin, M., and Scott, C. 'The Regulatory State', in Dunleavy, P., Gamble, A., Holliday, I., and Peele, G. (eds), *Developments in British Politics 5* (Basingstoke, 1997).

Luhmann, N. 'Law as a Social System' (1989) 83 *Northwestern University Law Review*.

Lütz, S. 'Convergence within National Diversity' (2004) 24(2) *Journal of Public Policy* 169–97.

Macrory, R. *Regulatory Justice: Sanctioning in a post-Hampton World* (Cabinet Office, May 2006) [Macrory Report].

Mairoano, F., Telephony and Stern, J. 'Institutions and Infrastructure Investment in Low and Middle-Income Countries: The Case of Mobile (2007)', *City University London Department of Economics Discussion Paper 07/06*, http://ideas.repec.org/p/reg/wpaper/448.html (visited 3 August, 2011).

Majone, G. 'The Rise of the Regulatory State in Europe' (1994) 14(3) *West European Politics* 77–101.

——. 'The New European Agencies: Regulation by Information' (1997) 4 *Journal of European Public Policy* 262–75.

——. 'The Credibility Crisis of Community Regulation' (2000) 38 *Journal of Common Market Studies* 273–302.

——. 'The European Commission: The Limits of Centralization and the Perils of Parliamentarization' (2002) 15 *Governance* 375–92.

——. 'What Price Safety? The Precautionary Principle and its Policy Implications' (2002) 40(1) *Journal of Common Market Studies* 89–109.

——.'Foundations of Risk Regulation: Science, Decision-Making, Policy Learning and Institutional Reform' (2010) 1(1) *European Journal of Risk Regulation* 5–19.

Majone, G. *Dilemmas of European Integration* (Oxford, 2005).

Makkai, T. and Braithwaite, J. 'The Limits of the Economic Analysis of Regulation: An Empirical Case and a Case for Empiricism' (1993) 15(4) *Law and Policy* 271.

March, J.S., Sproull, L.S., and Tamuz, M. 'Learning from Samples of One or Fewer' (1991) 2(1) *Organizational Science* 1–13.

Markovits, R.S. 'Antitrust: Alternatives to Delegalisation' in G. Teubner (ed.), *Juridification of Social Spheres* (Berlin, 1987).

Mashaw, J. 'Accountability and Institutional Design: Some Thoughts on the Grammar of Governance', in Dowdle, M. (ed.), *Public Accountability* (Cambridge, 2006).

Mattli, W. 'The Politics and Economics of International Institutional Standards Setting: An Introduction' (2001) 8(3) *Journal of European Public Policy* 328–44.

—— and Büthe, T. 'Setting International Standards: Technological Rationality or Primacy of Power?' (2003) 56 *World Politics* 1–42.

————. 'Global Private Governance: Lessons from a National Model of Setting Standards in Accounting' (2005) 26 *Law and Contemporary Problems* 225.

—— and Woods, N. 'In Whose Benefit? Explaining Regulatory Change in Global Politics', in Mattli, W. and Woods, N. (eds), *Politics of Global Regulation* (Princeton, NJ, 2009).

May, P. 'Performance-based Regulation and Regulatory Regimes: The Saga of Leaky Buildings' (2003) 25(4) *Law and Policy* 381–401.

McAllister, L. *Making Law Matter* (Stanford, CA, 2008).

——. 'Dimensions of Enforcement Style: Factoring in Regulatory Autonomy and Capacity' (2010) 32(1) *Law and Policy* 61.

——, Von Rooij, B., and Kagan, R. 'Reorienting Regulation: Pollution Enforcement in Industrializing Countries' (2010) 32(1) *Law and Policy* 1–13.

McCahery, J.A. and Vermeulen, E.P.M. 'Does the European Company Prevent the "Delaware-effect"?' (2005) *TILEC Discussion Paper No. 2005–010*. Available at SSRN: http://ssrn.com/abstract=693421 or doi:10.2139/ssrn.693421.

McCubbins, M., Noll, R., and Weingast, B. 'Administrative Procedures as Instruments of Political Control' (1987) 3(2) *Journal of Law, Economics and Organisation* 243–86.

——————. 'Structure and Process, Politics and Policy: Administrative Arrangements and Political Control' (1989) 75 *Virginia Law Review* 431–82.

McGarity, T.O. *Reinventing Rationality: The Role of Regulatory Analysis in the Federal Bureaucracy* (Cambridge, 1991).

McGuinness, N. and O'Carroll, C. 'Benchmarking Europe's Lab Benches: How Successful has the OMC been in Research Policy?' (2010) 48(2) *Journal of Common Market Studies* 293–318.

Meidinger, E. 'Beyond Westphalia: Comparative Legalization in Emerging Transnational Regulatory Systems', in Brütsch, C. and Lehmkuhl, D. (eds), *Law and Legalization in Transnational Relations* (Oxford, 2007).

Mendeloff, J. 'Overcoming Barriers to Better Regulation' (1993) 18 *Law and Social Inquiry.*

Mercury Communications Ltd v. *Director-General of Telecommunications and Others* (1995) *Financial Times*, 10 Feb.

Meridian Global Funds Management Acla Ltd v. The Securities Commission [1995] 3 WLR 413.

Meyer, C. 'The Europeanization of Media Discourse: A Study of Quality Press Coverage of Economic Policy Co-ordination since Amsterdam' (2005) 43(1) *Journal of Common Market Studies* 121–48.

Migdal, J.S. *Strong Societies and Weak States* (Princeton, NJ, 1998).

Mitchell, C. and Woodman, B. 'Regulation and Sustainable Energy Systems', in Baldwin, R., Cave, M., and Lodge, M. (eds), *The Oxford Handbook on Regulation* (Oxford, 2010).

Mitnick, B. *The Political Economy of Regulation* (New York, 1980).

Moran, M. 'The State and the Financial Services Revolution' (1994) 17(3) *West European Politics* 158–77.

——. *The British Regulatory State* (Oxford, 2003).

Moravcsik, A. 'Preferences and Power in the European Community' (1993) 31(4) *Journal of Common Market Studies* 473–524.

Mulgan, R. 'Accountability: An Ever-Expanding Concept?' (2000) 78(3) *Public Administration* 555–73.

——. *Holding Power to Account* (Basingstoke, 2004).

Musgrave, R.M. *The Theory of Public Finance* (New York, 1959).

National Audit Office (NAO), *Fisheries Enforcement in England*, 2002–3 HC 563 (London, April 2003).

National Consumer Council, *Self-Regulation* (London, 1986).

National Rivers Authority v. *Alfred McAlpine Homes East* [1994] CLR 760.

Netter, J. and Megginson, W. 'From State to Market: A Survey of Empirical Studies on Privatisation' (2001) 39(2) *Journal of Economic Literature* 321–89.

New Zealand Commerce Commission. *Telecommunications Industry Inquiry Report* (Wellington, June 1992).

——. *Standard Terms Determination for the Designated Service Telecom's Unbundled Copper Local Loop Network, Decision 609* (New Zealand, 7 December 2007).

Newbery, D. *Privatization, Restructuring and Regulation of Network Utilities* (Cambridge, MA, 1999).

Niskanen, W.A. *Bureaucracy and Representative Government* (Chicago, 1971).

Oates, W.E. *Fiscal Federalism* (New York, 1972).

——. 'An Essay on Fiscal Federalism' (1999) 37 *Journal of Economic Literature* 1120–49.

——. 'Fiscal and Regulatory Competition' (2002) 3(4) *Perspektiven der Wirtschaftspolitik* 377–90.

O'Donnell, G. *Financing Britain's Future: Review of the Revenue Departments*, Cmnd 6163 (London, 2004).

OECD, *Harmful Tax Competition* (Paris, 1998).

——. *Lessons from Existing Trading Systems for International Greenhouse Gas Emission Trading* (Paris, 1998).

——. *Implementing Domestic Tradable Permits* (Paris, 2002).

——. *United Kingdom: Challenges at the Cutting Edge* (Paris, 2002).

——. *Tax Haven Update* (Paris, 2003).

——. *Structural Reform in the Railway Industry* (Paris, 2005).

——. *Tax Co-operation 2009: Towards a Level Playing Field* (Paris, 2009).

OECD. *Energy Supply Probe: Initial Findings Report* (London, 2008).

———. *Offshore Transmission: First Transitional Tender Information Memorandum* (London, 2009).

———. *RIIO: A New Way to Regulate Energy Networks* (London, October 2010). [RIIO stands for Revenue set to deliver strong Incentives, Innovation and Outputs.]

———. *Handbook for Implementing the RIIO Model* (London, October 2010).

OFT. *Raising Standards of Consumer Care: Progressing Beyond Codes of Practice* (London, 1998).

OFWAT. *Scope for Efficiency Studies* (London, 2009).

———. *Future Price Limits: Possible Sectoral Structures* (London, July 2010).

———. *Future Water and Sewerage Charges 2010–2015: Final Determinations* (London, 2010).

———. *Involving Customers in the Price Setting Process: A Discussion Paper* (London, 2010).

———. *The Form of Price Control for Monopoly Water and Sewerage Services in England and Wales* (London, 2010).

———. *The Role and Design of Incentives for Regulating Monopoly Water and Sewerage Services in England and Wales* (London, 2010).

Ogus, A. *Regulation: Legal Form and Economic Theory* (Oxford, 1994).

———. 'Rethinking Self-Regulation' (1995) 15 *OJLS* 97.

———. 'Corrective Taxation and Financial Impositions as Regulatory Instruments' (1998) 61 *MLR* 767–88.

———. 'Competition between National Legal Systems: New Insights for Comparative Law?' (1999) 48(2) *International and Comparative Law Quarterly* 1–14.

Oliver, C. 'Strategic Responses to Institutional Processes' (1991) 16(1) *Academy of Management Review* 145.

Olsen, J.P. *Europe in Search of Political Order* (Oxford, 2007).

Open Europe, *The High Price of Hot Air: Why the EU Emissions Trading Scheme is an Environmental and Economic Failure* (London, July 2006).

Orren, K. and Skowronek, S. *The Search for American Political Development* (Cambridge, 2004).

Osborne, D. and Gaebler, T. *Reinventing Government* (Reading, MA, 1992).

Ostrom, V. 'Polycentricity I', in McGinnis, M.D. (ed.), *Polycentricity and Local Public Economies* (Ann Arbor, 1999).

P&O European Ferries Ltd (1991) 93 Crim. App. R. 72.

Page, A. 'Self-Regulation: The Constitutional Dimension' (1986) 49 *MLR* 141.

Parker, C. *The Open Corporation* (Cambridge, 2001).

———. 'Regulator-Required Corporate Compliance Program Audits' (2003) 25(3) *Law and Policy* 221–44.

Pearce, F. and Tombs, S. 'Ideology, Hegemony and Empiricism' (1990) 30 *British Journal of Criminology* 424.

Pelkmans, J. 'Mutual Recognition in Goods: On Promises and Disillusions' (2007) 14(5) *Journal of European Public Policy* 699–716.

Peltzman, S. Levine, M. and Noll. R. 'The Economic Theory of Regulation after a Decade of Regulation' (1989) *Brookings Papers in Macroeconomics* 1–59.

Perrow, C. *Normal Accidents* (New York, 1999).

Perry, J. and Noelke, A. 'International Accounting Standard Setting' (2005) 7(3) *Business and Politics*. Available at: http://www.bepress.com/bap/vol7/iss3/art5 (last accessed 27 December 2010).

Pfizer Animal Health v. *Council* [2002] ECR II 3305.

Pildes, R.H. and Sunstein, C.R. 'Reinventing the Regulatory State' (1995) 62 *University of Chicago Law Review* 1.

Polidano, C. 'Don't Discard State Autonomy' (2001) 49(3) *Political Studies* 513–27.

Pollitt, C. *The Essential Public Manager* (Buckingham, 2003).

Pollitt, M. 'The Arguments For and Against Ownership Unbundling in Energy Transmission Markets' (2008) 36 *Energy Policy* 704.

Powell, W. and Di Maggio, P. (eds),*The New Institutionalism in Organizational Analysis* (Chicago, 1991).

Power, M. *The Audit Society* (Oxford, 1997).

———. *The Risk Management of Everything: Rethinking the Politics of Uncertainty* (London, 2004).

Prakash, A. and Potoski, M. 'Racing to the Bottom? Trade, Environmental Governance, and ISO 14001' (2006) 50(2) *American Journal of Political Science* 350–64.

Prime Minister's Strategy Unit, *Net Benefits* (London, March 2004).

Productivity Commission. *Australia's Urban Water Sector Draft Report* (Australia, 2011).

Prosser, T. *Law and the Regulators* (Oxford, 1997).

———. 'Regulation and Social Solidarity' (2006) 33 *Journal of Law and Society* 364–87.

———. *The Regulatory Enterprise: Government Regulation and Legitimacy* (Oxford, 2010).

Quaglia, L. 'The Politics of Financial Services Regulation and Supervision Reform in the European Union' (2007) 46 *European Journal of Political Research* 269–90.

R v. *DG Telecoms ex p. Cellcom* [1999] COD 105.

R v. *Director General of Telecommunications ex p. Let's Talk (UK) Ltd* [1992] QBD, 6 Apr.

R v. *Director of Passenger Rail Franchising ex p. Save Our Railways* (1995) *Independent*, 20 Dec.; *The Times*, 18 Dec.

R v. *Independent Television Commission ex p. TSW Broadcasting Ltd* (1992) *Independent*, 27 Mar.; [1996] EMLR 291.

R v. *Independent Television Commission ex p. Virgin Television Ltd* [1996] EMLR 318.

R v. *Secretary of State for Trade and Industry ex p. Lonrho* [1989] 1 WLR 525.

Radaelli, C. 'The Puzzle of Regulatory Competition' (2004) 24(1) *Journal of Public Policy* 1–23.

—— and De Francesco, F. *Regulatory Quality in Europe* (Manchester, 2007).

Rauch, J.E. and Evans, P., 'Bureaucratic Structure and Bureaucratic Performance in Less Developed Countries' (2000) 75 *Journal of Public Economics* 49.

Rees, J. 'Development of Communitarian Regulation in the Chemical Industry' (1997) 19(4) *Law and Policy* 477.

Reiss, A. 'Selecting Strategies of Social Control over Organisational Life' in K. Hawkins and J. Thomas (eds), *Enforcing Regulation* (Boston, 1984).

Renn, O. 'Concepts of Risk: A Classification', in Krimsky and Golding, *Social Theories of Risk.*

———. *Risk Governance* (London, 2008).

Richardson, G., Ogus, A., and Burrows, P. *Policing Pollution* (Oxford, 1988).

Richman, E.'Emissions Trading and the Development Critique: Exposing the Threat to Developing Countries' (2003) 36 *International Law and Politics* 133.

Roberts, A. 'Why the Brownlow Committee Failed: Neutrality and Partisanship in the Early Years of Public Administration' (1996) 28(1) *Administration and Society* 3–38.

——. 'Spin Control and Freedom of Information' (2005) 83(1) *Public Administration* 1–23.

——. *The Logic of Discipline* (Oxford, 2010).

Rodrigo, R., Allio, L., and Andres-Amo, P. 'Multi-level Regulatory Governance' (2009) 13 *OECD Working Papers on Public Governance* 1–48.

Rodriguez, D. 'Administrative Law', in Whittington, K.E., Kelemen, R.D., and Caldeira, G.A. (eds) *Oxford Handbook of Law and Politics* (Oxford, 2008).

Rodrik, D. 'Goodbye Washington Consensus, Hello Washington Confusion? A Review of the World Bank's Economic Growth in the 1990s: Learning from a Decade of Reform' (2006) 44 *Journal of Economic Literature* 973.

——, Subramanian, A., and Trebbi, F. 'Institutions Rule: The Primacy of Institutions over Geography and Integration in Economic Development', *John F Kennedy School of Government Working Paper* (Harvard, 2002) http://ideas.repec.org/nbr/nberwo/9305.html/ (visited 3 August 2011).

Romana, R. 'Is Regulatory Competition a Problem or Irrelevant for Corporate Governance?' (2005) 21(2) *Oxford Review of Economic Policy* 12–31.

Rose-Ackermann, S. 'Law and Regulation', in Whittington, K.E., Kelemen, R.D., and Caldeira, G.A. (eds), *Oxford Handbook of Law and Politics* (Oxford, 2008).

Rosendorff, P. and Milner, H. 'The Optimal Design of International Institutions: Uncertainty and Escape' (2001) 55(4) *International Organization* 829.

Rothstein, H. 'Precautionary Bans or Sacrificial Lambs? Participative Regulation and the Reform of the UK Food Safety Regime' (2004) 82(4) *Public Administration* 857–81.

Rovizzi, L. and Thompson, D. 'The Regulation of Product Quality in Public Utilities', in Bishop, M., Kay, J., and Mayer, C. (eds), *The Regulatory Challenge* (London, 1995).

Royal Society, *Risk: Analysis, Perception, Management* (London, 1992).

Sahlin-Andersson, K. 'National, International, and Transnational Constructions of New Public Management', in Christensen, T. and Lægreid, P. (eds), *New Public Management: The Transformation of Ideas and Practice* (Aldershot, 2002).

Sappington, D. 'Price Regulation', in Cave, M., Majumdar, S., and Vogelsang, I. (eds), *Handbook of Telecommunications* (Elsevier, 2002).

—— and Weisman, D. 'Price Cap Regulation: What Have We Learned from 25 Years of Experience in the Telecommunications Industry?' (2010) 38 *Journal of Regulatory Economics* 232.

Schakel, A. 'Explaining Regional and Local Government' (2010) 23(2) *Governance* 331–55.

Scharpf, F.W. 'Negative and Positive Integration in the Political Economy of European Welfare States', in Marks, G. , Scharpf, F., Schmitter, P., and Streeck, W. (eds), *Governance in the European Union* (London, 1996).

——. 'Balancing Positive and Negative Integration', *MPIfG Working Paper*, 97/8 (Cologne, 1997). Max Planck Institute for the Study of Societies: http://www.mpifg.de/pu/workpap/wp97-8/wp97-8.html.

——. 'What Have We Learned? Problem Solving Capacity of the Multi-level Polity', *MPIfG Working Paper*, 01/4 (Cologne, 2001). Max Planck Institute for the Study of Societies http://www.mpifg.de/pu/workpap/wp01-4/wp01-4.html.

——. 'The European Social Model' (2002) 40(4) *Journal of Common Market Studies* 645–70.

Schaub, A. 'The Lamfalussy Process Four Years On' (2005) 13(2) *Journal of Financial Regulation and Compliance* 110–20.

Schmidt, S. 'Mutual Recognition as a New Mode of Governance' (2007) 14(5) *Journal of European Public Policy*, 667–81.

Scholz, J. Review of Ayres and Braithwaite, *Responsive Regulation* (1993) 87 *American Political Science Review* 782–3.

Schrader-Frechette, K.S. *Risk and Rationality* (Berkeley, 1991).

Scott, C. 'Accountability in the Regulatory State' (2000) 27 *Journal of Law and Society* 38–60.

———. 'Analysing Regulatory Space' (2001) *Public Law* 329–53.

———. and Black, J. *Cranston's Consumers and the Law* (3rd edn, Cambridge, 2000).

Seidenfeld, M. 'Cognitive Loafing, Social Conformity and Judicial Review of Agency Rulemaking' (2002) 87 *Cornell Law Review* 486–548.

Seabound Offshore Ltd v. *Secretary of State for Transport* [1994] 2 All ER 99.

Self, P. *Administrative Theories and Politics* (London, 1972).

———. *Government by the Market?* (Basingstoke, 1993).

Sharkey, W.W. *The Theory of Natural Monopoly* (Cambridge, 1982).

Shavell, S. 'The Optimal Structure of Law Enforcement' (1993) *Journal of Law and Economics* 255.

Shleifer, A. 'A Theory of Yardstick Competition' (1985) 16 *Rand Journal of Economics* 319.

Sikkink, K. 'From State Responsibility to Individual Criminal Accountability: A New Regulatory Model for Core Human Rights Violations', in Mattli, W. and Woods, N. (eds), *Politics of Global Regulation* (Princeton, NJ, 2009).

Simmons, B. 'International Politics of Harmonization: The Case of Capital Market Regulation' (2001) 55 *International Organization* 589–620.

———. 'The International Politics of Harmonization' (2001) 55(3) *International Organization* 589–620.

Sioshani, F. (ed.), *Competitive Electricity Markets: Design, Implementation, Performance* (Elsevier, 2008).

Sioshani, F. (ed.), *Electricity Market Reform: An International Perspective* (Elsevier, 2006).

Skjaerseth, J. and Wettestad, J. *EU Emissions Trading: Initiation, Decision-Making and Implementation* (Aldershot, 2008).

Skowronek, S. *Building a New American State* (Cambridge, 1982).

Smith, T.M. and Fischlein, M. 'Rival Private Governance Networks: Competing to Define the Rules of Sustainability Performance' (2010) 20 *Global Environmenal Change* 511.

Sowell, T. *Preferential Policies: An International Perspective* (New York, 1990).

Sparrow, M. *The Regulatory Craft* (Washington, DC, 2003).

Stavins, R. 'Policy Instruments for Climate Change' (1997) *University of Chicago Legal Forum* 293.

Stern, J. 'Electricity and Telecommunications Regulatory Institutions in Small and Developing Countries' (2000) 9(3) *Utilities Policy* 131.

Stern, N. *The Economics of Climate Change* (London, 2006).

Stewart, R.B. 'The Reformation of American Administrative Law' (1975) 88 *Harvard Law Review* 1667.

———. 'Regulation and the Crisis of Legalisation in the United States' in T. Daintith (ed.), *Law as an Instrument of Economic Policy* (Berlin, 1998).

Stigler, G. 'The Theory of Economic Regulation' (1971) 2 *Bell Journal of Economics*.

Stiglitz, K. *Making Globalization Work* (London, 2006).

Stone, C. 'Controlling Corporate Misconduct' (1977) *Public Interest* 55.

Stone Sweet, A. and Sandholtz, W. 'European Integration and Supranational Governance' (1997) 4(3) *Journal of European Public Policy* 297–317.

Sunstein, C. *After the Rights Revolution: Reconceiving the Regulatory State* (Cambridge, MA, 1990).

——. 'Law and Administration after Chevron' (1990) 90(8) *Columbia Law Review* 2071–120.

——. 'Paradoxes of the Regulatory State' (1990) 57 *University of Chicago Law Review* 407–41.

Tesco Stores Ltd v Brent LBC [1993] 2 All ER 718.

Tesco Supermarkets Ltd v. *Nattrass* [1972] AC 153.

Thatcher, M. and Coen, D. 'Reshaping European Regulatory Space' (2008) 31(4) *West European Politics* 806–36.

—— and Sweet Stone, A. 'Theory and Practice of Delegation to Non-Majoritarian Institutions' (2002) 25(1) *West European Politics* 1–22.

Tiebout, C. 'A Pure Theory of Local Expenditures' (1956) 64 *Journal of Political Economy* 416–24.

Tietenberg, T. *Emissions Trading* (2nd edn, Washington, DC, 2006).

——. 'Tradable Permits in Principle and Practice' in J. Freeman and C. Kolstad (eds), *Moving to Markets in Environmental Regulation* (Oxford, 2006).

Trachtman, J.P. 'Regulatory Competition and Regulatory Jurisdiction' (2000) 3(2) *Journal of International Economic Law* 331–48.

Trondal, J. and Jeppesen, L. 'Images of Agency Governance in the European Union' (2008) 31(3) *West European Politics* 417–41.

Turner, B. *Man-Made Disasters* (London, 1978).

United States v. *Mead Corp.*, 533 us 218 (2001).

Van Asselt, M. and Vos, E. 'The Precautionary Principle and the Uncertainty Paradox' (2006) 9 (4) *Journal of Risk Research* 313–36.

Van Rooij, B. *Regulating Land and Pollution in China* (Leiden, 2006).

—— and Lo, C.H.W, 'A Fragile Convergence: Understanding Variation in the Enforcement of China's Industrial Pollution Law' (2010) 32 *Law and Policy* 14–37.

Vedder, H. 'Spontaneous Harmonisation of National (Competition) Laws in the Wake of the Modernisation of EC Competition Law' (2004) 1(1) *Competition Law Review* 5–21.

Veljanovski, C. G.'Wealth Maximisation, Law and Ethics: On the Limits of Economic Efficiency' (1981) 1 *International Review of Law and Economics* 5.

Verbruggen, P. 'Does Co-regulation Strengthen EU Legitimacy?' (2009) 15(4) *European Law Journal* 425–41.

Vickers, J. 'Competition Policy and Property Rights' (2010) 120 *Economic Journal* 375–92.

Vogel, D. *Trading Up: Consumer and Environmental Regulation in a Global Economy* (Cambridge, MA, 1997).

Vogel, S. 'International Games with National Rules: How Regulation Shapes Competition in "Global Markets"' (1997) 17(2) *Journal of Public Policy* 169–93.

von Malmborg, F. and Strachan, P. 'Climate Policy, Ecological Modernism and the UK Emissions Trading Scheme' (2005) 15 *European Environment* 143–60.

Wallsten, S. 'Reverse Auctions and Universal Telecommunications Service: Lessons from Global Experience' (2009) 61(2) *Federal Communications Law Journal*.

Warren, K.F. *Administrative Law in the Political System* (4th edn, Boulder, 2004).

Weatherill, S. (ed.) *Better Regulation* (Oxford, 2007).

Wednesbury [1948] LKB 223.

Weil, D., Fung, A., Graham, M., and Fagotto, E. 'The Effectiveness of Regulatory Disclosure Policies' (2006) 25(1) *Journal of Policy Analysis and Management* 155–81.

Weimer, D.L. 'The Puzzle of Private Rulemaking' (2006) 66(4) *Public Administration Review* 569–82.

Weiner, M. 'The Pursuit of Ethnic Inequalities through Preferential Policies: A Comparative Public Policy Perspective' in Goldmann, R. and Wilson, A.J. (eds), *From Independence to Statehood: Managing Ethnic Conflict in Five African and Asian States* (London, 1984).

Weiss, L. *The Myth of the Powerless State* (Cambridge, 1998).

Wells, C. *Corporations and Criminal Responsibility* (Oxford, 1993).

Werle, R. 'Institutional Aspects of Standardization: Jurisdictional Conflicts and the Choice of Coordination Organizations' (2001) 8(3) *Journal of European Public Policy* 392.

Whish, R. *Competition Law* (6th edn, Oxford, 2009).

Wilks, S. 'Agency Escape: Decentralisation or Dominance of the European Commission in the Modernization of Competition Policy' (2005) 18(3) *Governance* 431–52.

Wilks, S. and McGowan, L. 'The First Supranational Policy of the European Union: Competition Policy' (1995) 28(2) *European Journal of Political Research* 141–69.

————. 'Competition Policy in the European Union: Creating a Federal Agency?', in Doern, G.B. and Wilks, S. (eds), *Comparative Competition Policy* (Oxford, 1996).

Williamson, O. 'Franchise Bidding for National Monopolies: In General and with Respect to CATV' (1976) 7 *Bell Journal of Economics* 73.

Wilson, J.Q. *The Politics of Regulation* (New York, 1980).

Wonka, A. and Rittberger, B. 'Credibility, Complexity and Uncertainty: Explaining the Institutional Independence of 29 EU Agencies' (2010) 33(4) *West European Politics* 730–52.

Woods, N.D. 'Interstate Competition and Environmental Regulation' (2006) 86(4) *Social Science Quarterly* 792–811.

World Bank, *Governance: The World Bank's Experience* (Washington, DC, 1993).

————. *Greening Industry: New Roles for Communities, Markets and Covernment* (Oxford, 2000).

————. *Infrastructure at the Crossroads* (World Bank, 2006).

————. *The State and Trends of the Carbon Market 2007* (Washington, DC, 2007).

————. *World Development Report* (World Bank, 1997).

————. *Information and Communications for Development: Extending Reach and Increasing Impact* (Washington, DC, 2009), pp. 35–50.

Yeung, K. 'Government by Publicity Management: Sunlight or Spin?' (2005) *Public Law* 360–83.

Yi-chong, X. 'Models, Templates and Currents: The World Bank and Electricity Reform' (2005) 12(4) *Review of International Political Economy* 647–73.

Zeitlin, J. 'Conclusion: The Open Method of Co-ordination in Action: Theoretical Promise, Empirical Realities, Reform Strategies', in Zeitlin, J., Pichot, P. with Magnusson, L. (eds), *The Open Method of Co-ordination in Action: The European Employment and Social Inclusion Strategies* (PIE, 2005).

——. 'Introduction: The Open Method of Co-ordination in Question', in Zeitlin, J., Pichot, P. with Magnusson, L. (eds), *The Open Method of Co-ordination in Action: The European Employment and Social Inclusion Strategies* (PIE, 2005).

Zupan, M.A. 'Non-price Concessions and the Effect of Franchise Bidding Schemes on Cable Company Costs' (1989) 21 *Applied Economics* 305.

——. 'The Efficiency of Franchise Bidding Schemes in the Case of Cable Television' (1989) 32 *Journal of Law and Economics* 401.

■ INDEX

Bold entries refer to tables.

Lightning Source UK Ltd.
Milton Keynes UK
UKOW07n1125021214

242514UK00001B/91/P